A Companion to Modern European History

1871–1945

Edited by
Martin Pugh

Blackwell
Publishing

© 1997 by Blackwell Publishing Ltd

350 Main Street, Malden, MA 02148-5018, USA
108 Cowley Road, Oxford OX4 1JF, UK
550 Swanston Street, Carlton South, Melbourne, Victoria 3053, Australia
Kurfürstendamm 57, 10707 Berlin, Germany

First published 1997 by Blackwell Publishing Ltd
Reprinted 1998, 2000, 2003

Library of Congress Cataloging-in-Publication Data

A companion to modern European history, 1871–1945 / edited by Martin
  Pugh.
        p. cm.
  Includes bibliographical references and index.
  ISBN 0–631–19217–4 — ISBN 0–631–19218–2 (pbk.)
    1. Europe—History—1871–1918. 2. Europe—History—1918–1945.
I. Pugh, Martin.
D395.C59 1997
940.2'8—dc21   96–48185
                                                            CIP

A catalogue record for this title is available from the British Library.

Set in 11 on 13 pt Bembo
by Graphicraft Typesetters Ltd., Hong Kong
Printed and bound in the United Kingdom
by Athenaeum Press Ltd., Gateshead, Tyne & Wear

For further information on
Blackwell Publishing, visit our website:
http://www.blackwellpublishing.com

Contents

Tables, Figures and Appendices

Maps

Contributors

Lynn Abrams lectures in modern European History at the University of Glasgow. She is the author of *Workers' Culture in Imperial Germany* (1992) and co-editor of *Gender Relations in German History* (1996). Her current research interests include the history of marriage and divorce in nineteenth-century Germany and European child welfare policy.

P. M. H. Bell is Honorary Senior Research Fellow at the University of Liverpool, where he was formerly Reader in History. He is the author of *The Origins of the Second World War in Europe* (1986), *France and Britain 1900–1940* (1996) and *France and Britain 1940–1994* (1997).

Eugenio Biagini is a Fellow of Robinson College, Cambridge, and Secretary of the M. Phil. programme in European Studies at the Faculty of History, University of Cambridge. His publications include *Liberty, Retrenchment and Reform: Popular Liberalism in the Age of Gladstone* (1992), and *Citizenship and Community: Liberals, Radicals and Collective Identities in the British Isles, 1865–1931* (1996).

Gerard J. DeGroot has taught in the Department of Modern History at the University of St Andrews since 1984. He is the author of three books, including *Douglas Haig: 1861–1928* (1988) and *Blighty: British Society in the Era of the Great War* (1996). He is currently working on a book and a television series on the US War effort in Vietnam.

Michael Drake, who is Professor Emeritus at the Open University and Visiting Professor at the University of Tromsø, is a social historian with a special interest in family and community history. His most recent publications are *Time, Family and Community* (1994) and (with Ruth Finnegan) *From Family Tree to Family History* (1994) and *Source and Methods for Family and Community Historians* (1994; 2nd edn 1997).

E. J. Feuchtwanger was born in Munich, educated at Winchester and Cambridge, and teaches at Southampton University. His specialisms are British political history in the Disraeli-Gladstone era and German history in the Weimar period. His publications include *Disraeli, Democracy and the Tory Party* (1968), *Prussia: Myth and Reality* (1970), *Gladstone* (1975; 2nd edn, 1989), *Democracy and Empire: Britain 1865–1914* (1985) and *From Weimar to Hitler: Germany 1918–33* (1993; 2nd edn, 1995).

David French was educated at the University of York and King's College, London. He is now Professor of History at University College, London. His most recent book, *The Strategy of the Lloyd George Coalition*, was published in 1995.

Rodney Lowe is Professor of Contemporary History at the University of Bristol. He is the author of *The Welfare State in Britain since 1945* (1993) and of the forthcoming *The Watershed Years: The Replanning of the Welfare State in Britain, 1957–64*, as well as many articles on twentieth-century welfare policy.

David Omissi is Senior Lecturer in History at the University of Hull. Born and raised in Jersey, he gained a First in History at Lancaster University, then took an MA and a PhD in War Studies at King's College, London. His main publications include *Air Power and Colonial Control: The Royal Air Force, 1919–39* (1990) and *The Sepoy and the Raj: The Indian Army, 1860–1940* (1994). Before moving to Hull, he was Lecturer in British Empire History at the University of Edinburgh, and Prize Research Fellow at Nuffield College, Oxford.

Sidney Pollard studied economics and economic history at the London School of Economics. Now retired, he taught at the University of Sheffield 1950–80 (professor of economic history from 1963) and at the University of Bielefeld 1980–90. He is especially interested in the modern economic history of Britain and Europe.

Martin Pugh is Professor of Modern British History at the University of Newcastle-upon-Tyne. His latest books are *Women and the Women's Movement in Britain, 1914–1959* (1992) and *State and Society: British Political and Social History, 1870–1992* (1994).

A. W. Purdue is Senior Lecturer in History at the Open University and has contributed to many OU courses including *War, Peace and Social Change: Europe 1900–1955*. He is the author with J. M. Golby of

The Civilisation of the Crowd (1984), *The Making of the Modern Christmas* (1986), and *The Monarchy and the British People* (1988).

Duncan Tanner is Head of the School of History and Welsh History, University of Wales, Bangor, where he teaches modern British history and the history of European socialism. His publications include *Political Change and the Labour Party 1900–18* (1990). He is currently working on British Labour politics between the wars, and on several pan-European investigations into aspects of inter-war political history.

Richard Thurlow is a Lecturer in the History Department of the University of Sheffield. He is the author of *Fascism in Britain: A History 1918–85* (1987) and *The Secret State* (1994). He also co-edited, with Kenneth Lunn, *British Fascism* (1979).

James D. White is Reader in Russian and Soviet History at the Institute of Russian and East European Studies, University of Glasgow. He has published extensively on Russian history (particularly on the 1917 revolution), Baltic history and Chinese history. He is author of *The Russian Revolution 1917–21: A Short History* (1994) and *Karl Marx and the Intellectual Origins of Dialectical Materialism* (1996).

Keith Wilson, educated at Keble College and Nuffield College, Oxford, has from 1969 been part of the international history section of the School of History at the University of Leeds. His most recent monograph is *Channel Tunnel Visions 1850–1945: Dreams and Nightmares* (1994). He edited and contributed to *Decisions for War, 1914* (1995) and *Forging the Collective Memory: Governments and International Historians through Two World Wars* (1996).

Introduction

A Companion to Modern European History has been designed as a tool to help students to handle a field of history characterized by an extensive and growing literature, abundant source material and lively historiographical debates. It may be used in the preparation of essays and papers, as a guide to more advanced reading and as an aid to revision. To this end the volume does not attempt to offer either a traditional chronological survey or a series of national histories. Instead it approaches European history by means of sixteen thematic chapters dealing with economic and social change, politics, and war and international diplomacy. As a result the treatment given to individual states varies considerably from one chapter to the next. In the discussion of conservatism, for example, the cases of Germany, Britain and France loom large. In the case of fascism Italy and Germany receive most discussion, followed by Spain and the less significant fascist movements of Britain and France.

The student may draw upon four resources in the book: first, he or she will focus on the most directly relevant chapter; but this should be seen simply as the centre of several overlapping circles; it leads on to a reading of a whole group of chapters which complement the original one. To take an example, a study of the evolution of social welfare in Europe might draw upon the following sections:

Socialist Parties
and Policies

Prosperity and Depression:
The International Economy

The Rise of
European Feminism

**The State and the Development
of Social Welfare**

The Dilemmas
of Liberalism

The First World War
as Total War

A project on imperialism might involve the following reading:

European Diplomacy 1871–1914	Conservatism and Nationalism

European Imperialism 1871–1945

Appeasement	The Second World War

In the case of an essay dealing with a single country the student will be able to consult the index for a comprehensive guide to all the references. The second resource is the chronological table at the end of the volume which will enable the student to place developments in one country in relation to those occurring elsewhere at the same time, and will also assist at the revision stage. The third resource is the large section of biographies of leading figures. Each entry is indicated by * in the text when the name is first mentioned in each chapter. By consulting these the student will be able to develop his or her understanding of the issues raised in the text. Finally, the reading in the chapters and biographies may be followed up by examining the detailed guide to more specialist publications in English. These list books and articles on individual countries as well as overviews of the general topic.

Part I

Society and the State

1

Population: Patterns and Processes

Michael Drake

Introduction

For Europe, demographically speaking, the years 1870–1945 were as exciting as they come. For much of the time its population continued to grow at a historically rapid rate; European populations (both within and outside the continent itself) formed a higher proportion of the world's population than at any time before or since; birth rates fell dramatically – in most countries to historically low levels; death rates, too, fell in all age groups, especially amongst children under one year of age, in spite of two world wars in which first combatants (in the First World War) and then civilians (in the Second World War) suffered unprecedented losses; migration within countries accelerated, with the growth of major concentrations of population, whilst emigration carried vast numbers overseas, especially to the USA. Some things, however, changed relatively little. Most people married at ages broadly similar to those in the years before and since, though there were considerable variations within countries and between social classes. Most children were born within marriage though, again as before and since, many firstborn children were conceived out of wedlock. Divorce was made more widely available, although relatively few marriages ended in this way, with death being the major cause of marital breakdown. The nuclear family household continued to dominate throughout Europe. The fall in the birth rate began to produce an ageing population though its impact in these years was not profound. The number of people living alone showed little increase.

That we know so much about the population of Europe in this period is due to the development of governmental statistical services. It was not that they began in this period. Scandinavian countries had begun to take national censuses in the eighteenth century. The civil registration of births, marriages and deaths was begun in England and Wales in 1837, followed by Scotland in 1856 and Ireland in 1864. The first modern census was taken throughout the British Isles in 1841 and improved somewhat in 1851. The distinguishing feature of this type of census was that, as is still the case today, information was provided on each *named* individual. What is more significant for our period is that by the 1870s, the heads of Europe's state statistical offices were not only meeting each other (the first such meeting took place in Brussels in 1853) but were agreeing on a standard format for a decadal census (at the International Statistical Congress held in St Petersburg, in 1872). The registration of births, marriages and deaths also became more standardized.

Table 1.1 shows how far the process of standardization had gone by around 1870. Not very far, it would appear, so far as the timing was concerned; even the Nordic countries (Norway, Denmark, Sweden and Finland) chose different years. There was greater uniformity as to month with almost all countries choosing December and either its first or last day being census day itself. The United Kingdom was a notable exception. Of the heads of information regarded as essential for any census by delegates to the International Statistical Congress in 1872, we see, from table 1.1, that a good number were set in train by 1880 by the majority of European countries. Individual enumeration was the essence of these censuses, with the census enumerator describing each individual by surname and first name, sex, age, relationship to the head of the family or household (wife, son, lodger, servant etc.), civil status (single, married, widowed, divorced), occupation, place of birth and (almost everywhere) religious allegiance, though not in Britain, Belgium or France. Britain's experiment with a religious census in 1851 was not to be repeated, in spite of strenuous efforts, principally by supporters of the Church of England. They wanted a census of religious persuasion unlike that of 1851 which had been one of attendance at religious services, and from which the Nonconformists had done well. This revealed how the way questions were put had a significant impact upon the answers received. The apparent unanimity as to the heads of information sought by European countries did not mean the answers were strictly comparable. Many people, for instance, were not sure of their precise age, and occupational descriptions were a minefield of ambiguities. Increasing the number of questions on the census schedule, though often requested, was strongly resisted. Ogle, the Superintendent of Statistics at the General Register Office in Britain, remarked to a parliamentary enquiry in 1890 that the larger the number of questions that are asked, the less accurate are the answers given. The seeking of information on other matters reflected the specific interests of individual countries: what seemed important to some was not to others, for example, ethnicity, legal domicile, physical or medical handicaps.

If the information produced by the census was neither as solid as the figures might suggest, nor strictly comparable either from one census to the next or between different countries, that produced by the registration of births, marriages and deaths was even less so. For, unlike the census which demanded a particular effort, once every ten years or so, the registration system required constant vigilance every day of every year. Civil registration usually came after the start of census-taking and took somewhat longer to reach an acceptable level of accuracy. For instance, while registration in England and Wales began in 1837, the Registrar General estimated that 6.5 per cent of births were not registered in the years 1841–81, though this figure had fallen to 1.8 per cent by the years 1861–70. However even the situation in the 1840s was vastly superior to the situation at the beginning of the nineteenth century, when the Church of England was only managing to enter into its parish registers around two-thirds of births and deaths. These introductory remarks should be borne in mind when reading what follows. For the problem with numbers, upon which all population studies are necessarily based, is that obvious errors do not leap from the page, as in the case of misspellings.

Population Size and Distribution

In spite of these caveats, there is little doubt that we can say more about the population of Europe in the period that concerns us, than about any earlier period. The countries of Europe were converging in the sorts of information at their disposal, as they were in so many other ways. In terms of demography they wanted to know not only how fast their populations were growing, the level of their birth and death rates, the size of their towns and cities, the numbers emigrating, but also how their experience on all these matters compared with that of their neighbours; hence the drive for uniformity in the collection, analysis and presentation of demographic data. The data we receive come, therefore, from political entities, and this has at least two major drawbacks. First these entities change their shape over time, thus making comparison difficult. One thinks, on a minor scale, of the shift of Alsace-Lorraine from France to Germany and back again; or more significantly, the disintegration of the Ottoman Empire in the course of the nineteenth century and of the Austro-Hungarian and Russian empires in 1917–18. Second, if one is seeking, say, the causes of change in population growth rates, in birth and death rates, one's attention is drawn to a variety of socio-economic factors which owe little to political realities. Whether a population is rural or urban, how it earns its living, how

Table 1.1 Questions asked in the censuses of various European states c.1870–1880[a]

Questions	Finland	Sweden	Norway	Denmark	Germany	England, Wales and Scotland	Ireland	Netherlands	Belgium	France	Spain	Italy	Switzerland	Austria	Hungary	Serbia
Date of census	31 Dec. '65	31 Dec. '70	31 Dec. '75	7 Feb. '80	1 Dec. '80	2 Apr. '71	2 Apr. '71	1 Dec. '69	31 Dec. '66	Dec. '76	31 Dec. '77	31 Dec. '71	1 Dec. '70	31 Dec. '80	31 Dec. '80	Dec. '74
1 Surname and first name	✓	✓	✓	✓	✓	✓	✓	✓	✓	✓	✓	✓	✓	✓	✓	✓
2 Sex	✓	✓	✓	✓	✓	✓	✓	✓	✓	✓	✓	✓	✓	✓	✓	✓
3 Age[b]	✓	Y	Y	✓	D	✓	✓	D	D	Y	✓	✓	D	Y	D	✓
4 Relationship to head of family or household	–	✓	✓	✓	✓	✓	✓	✓	✓	✓	✓	✓	✓	✓	✓	✓
5 Civil status	✓	✓	✓	✓	✓	✓	✓	✓	✓	✓	✓	✓	✓	✓	✓	✓
6 Occupation	✓	✓	✓	✓	✓	✓	✓	✓	✓	✓	✓	✓	✓	✓	✓	✓
7 Religion	✓	✓	✓	✓	✓	–	✓	✓	–	–	✓	✓	✓	✓	✓	✓

8 Ethnicity (language spoken)	✓	✓	–	–	–	–	–	–	–	–	–	✓	–	✓	✓	✓c	–
9 Ability to read and write	–	–	–	✓	✓	✓	✓	✓	✓	–	✓	✓	✓	✓	✓	✓	✓
10 Legal domicile	–	–	✓	–	✓	✓	✓	✓	–	–	–	✓	✓	✓d	✓	✓	–
11 Place of birth	–	✓	✓	✓	✓	✓	✓	✓	✓	✓	✓	✓	✓	✓	✓	✓	✓
12 Duration of stay	–	✓	✓	✓	–	✓	✓	✓	✓	✓	✓	✓	✓	✓	✓	✓	–
13 Duration of absence	–	✓	✓	–	–	✓	✓	–	✓	✓	✓	✓	✓	✓	✓	✓	–
14 Usual place of abode	–	✓	–	–	–	✓	✓	✓	–	–	–	–	✓	–	✓	–	–
15 Blind	–	✓	✓	✓	✓	✓	✓	✓	✓	✓	✓	✓	✓	✓	✓	✓	–
16 Deaf and dumb	–	✓	✓	✓	✓	✓	✓	✓	✓	✓	✓	✓	✓	✓	✓	✓	–
17 Imbecile, idiot	–	✓	✓	✓	✓	✓	✓	✓	✓	✓	✓	✓	✓	–	✓	✓	–
18 Insane	–	✓	✓	✓	✓	✓	✓	✓	✓	✓	✓	✓	✓	✓	✓	✓	–

[a] Delegates to the International Statistical Congress in St Petersburg in 1872 considered that these questions were 'essential'. They also put forward other questions that did not carry this label.

[b] D = date of birth; Y = year of birth. Otherwise age was given in years, with confusion sometimes caused over whether this was at last or next birthday.

[c] Mother tongue besides knowledge of that of the country.

[d] Whether one belonged to the 'parish' or not. For foreigners the country of origin to appear in the comments column.

Source: Based on Joseph Körösi, *Projet d'un Recensement du Monde* (Etude de Statistique, Paris, 1881), pp. 42–3.

Society and the State

Table 1.2   The population of various parts of Europe, 1870, 1900 and 1951

Area	1870 (1,000s)	Annual rate of growth (%) 1870–1900	1900 (1,000s)	Annual rate of growth (%) 1900–1951	1951 (1,000s)
European Russia	63,964	1.5	98,380	0.9	158,500
Austria-Hungary	41,233	0.9	53,638	0.3	61,930
Germany	43,465	1.0	59,348	0.4	73,630
France	38,440	–	38,900	0.2	42,160
United Kingdom	31,257	0.9	41,152	0.5	53,242
Benelux	8,689	1.0	11,853	0.9	18,940
Norden	9,438	0.9	12,437	0.8	18,720
Iberia	21,080	0.4	23,974	0.8	36,550
Italy	25,795	0.8	32,346	0.7	47,090
Balkans	4,614	0.9	5,957	1.8	14,910
Europe	287,975	0.9	377,985	0.7	525,672

Source: For 1870 and 1900, Ministère du travail et de la prévoyance sociale, *Statistiques Internationale du Mouvement de la Population d'après les Registres d'Etat Civil. Résumé Retrospectif depuis l'Origine des Statistiques de l'Etat Civil* (Paris, 1907); for 1951, B. R. Mitchell, *International Historical Statistics, Europe 1750–1988*, 3rd edition (London, 1992)

it is housed, what access it has to unadulterated food and fresh water, cuts across political boundaries. Table 1.2 is an attempt to show significant similarities and differences in the population growth of Europe's constituent parts.

The continent as a whole increased its population by around 90 million between 1870 and 1900 and by another 150 million by 1951. If we turn to what I have called Europe's 'constituent parts' (in table 1.2 these are a mixture of regions and states) we see a wide variety of data. Note, for instance, the dramatic difference in the population growth rates of France and Germany; the dramatic fall in the growth rate of the area I have called 'Austria-Hungary' between 1870–1900 and 1900–51 (here, however, as with Russia, which also suffered a decline, although a less severe one, the statistics may be less than wholly reliable; this applies even more so to the Balkans, where the apparent surge of population growth in the years 1900–1951 as against 1870–1900 is probably exaggerated). Some areas maintained relatively high rates throughout the period as a whole, for example, the Benelux and Nordic countries. The Iberian peninsula doubled its annual rate of growth between the two

Table 1.3 The population of Europe, 1870, 1900 and 1951

	1870		1900		1951	
Area	*1,000s*	*%*	*1,000s*	*%*	*1,000s*	*%*
Central and Eastern Europe	105,197	36.5	152,018	40.2	220,430	41.9
Western Europe	131,298	45.6	163,690	43.3	207,322	39.4
Southern Europe	51,489	17.9	62,277	16.5	98,550	18.7
Europe	287,975	100.0	377,985	100.0	526,302	100.0

Source: table 1.2

periods. So although the overall picture is of a decline of the growth rate between 1870–1900 and 1900–51, there is a marked variability in the detail. On the other hand, if we divide Europe into three blocks of territory, namely Central and Eastern Europe (Russia and Austria-Hungary): Western Europe (Benelux, France, Germany, Norden and the UK) and southern Europe (the Balkans, Iberia and Italy), their relative positions are comparatively stable. Central and Eastern Europe on the one hand and Western Europe on the other each held around 40 per cent of the continent's population in 1870, 1900 and 1951, with southern Europe making up the remaining 20 per cent. The apparent rise in the proportion of the population of Central and Eastern Europe (see table 1.3) may be more apparent than real, a product of less than accurate figures.

These changes in growth rates had significant economic, social and political implications. Usually these are discussed within the context of what was happening to the populations of individual states, partly because, as noted already, this is how the statistics are gathered and partly because historians commonly operate within state boundaries. However, the explanation of the rates and of the changes that occurred go beyond state boundaries. Forces summed up in such terms as industrialization, modernization and urbanization affected Europe as a whole. These come to the fore when we come to discuss the mechanisms of change, namely fertility, mortality and migration. Before we turn to these, however, it is worth noting one other feature of the European population, namely its size relative to that of the rest of the world. Down to around 1920 the world's population of European stock was increasing, relative to that of the rest of the world. The figures for the populations of Africa and Asia are notoriously unreliable, but it would appear that whereas they had accounted for around 75 per cent of the world

Table 1.4 Births per 1,000 population in various parts of Europe, 1870, 1900 and 1951

Area	1870	1900	1951
European Russia	49.7	49.1	20.0
Austria-Hungary	41.7	38.4	23.2
Germany	37.9	35.2	16.1
France	24.5	21.4	19.5
United Kingdom	33.8	28.2	16.2
Benelux	33.9	30.1	19.6
Norden	30.6	29.2	18.2
Iberia	35.5	33.1	21.1
Italy	36.9	33.0	18.5
Balkans	34.6	39.5	20.7
Europe	38.4	36.5	19.3

Source: For 1870 and 1900, Ministère du travail et de la prévoyance sociale, *Statistiques Internationale du Mouvement de la Population d'après les Registres d'Etat Civil. Résumé Retrospectif depuis l'Origine des Statistiques de l'Etat Civil* (Paris, 1907); for 1951, B. R. Mitchell, *International Historical Statistics, Europe 1750–1988*, 3rd edition (London, 1992)

population in 1800, that figure had fallen to around 60 per cent in 1920. As we shall see, the expansion of Europe's population outside Europe itself owed much to the massive migration, mostly across the Atlantic, which reached its peak in the years 1870–1914.

Births and Birth Control

The growth of a population in any particular area is determined by two factors: the difference between the number of births and deaths – the so-called *natural increase* – and the difference between the number of those migrating into it and those migrating out – or the *net migration*. We shall look at each of these in turn, beginning with births.

The easiest measure of human fertility to understand, and the easiest to calculate, is the *crude birth rate*. This is simply the number of births occurring in any one year per 1,000 of the mean, or average, population, usually taken as that at mid-year. In 1900 the crude birth rate for Europe as a whole was around 36 per 1,000, that is, for every 1,000 people living at that time, some 36 births occurred annually. This average figure of 36 hid considerable variation across the continent, as table 1.4 shows. Broadly speaking we find high birth rates in Eastern and Central

Europe, with rates of around 40 or more per 1,000, followed by Germany (35), the Iberian and Italian peninsulas (33), Benelux, Norden and the UK (30) and France (21).

How do we account for these differences? Two main factors were involved. The first is related to the age at marriage of women and the proportion of women in the fertile age group who were married. This is because the overwhelming majority of children were born within marriage, although in many countries a considerable proportion of first-born children were conceived outside it. The second is the increasing acceptance of birth control within marriage. As we shall see (and as table 1.4 indicates) this was already having an impact on the birth rates of some countries in the last quarter of the nineteenth century.

Some years ago John Hajnal drew attention to what he called the European marriage pattern. This was characterized by a high age at marriage and a high proportion of people who never married at all. This pattern, he believed, was to be found throughout Europe roughly to the west of a line drawn from St Petersburg to Trieste. This excluded a good 40 per cent of the continent's population (see table 1.3)! By way of example take Sweden, west of the St Petersburg–Trieste line, and Bulgaria to the east of it. If we look at the percentage of women who were single in the age groups 20–24, 25–29 and 45–49 years, we find the situation in Sweden to be 80, 52 and 19 respectively. Corresponding figures for Bulgaria, however, were 24, 3 and 1! Given that, relatively speaking, so many more Bulgarian women were *at risk* of becoming pregnant, in that they were living in the married state, it is not surprising that the crude birth rate in 1900 was 60 per cent higher in Bulgaria than in Sweden.

The different marriage patterns were, according to Hajnal, closely bound up with household formation and composition. Where marriage was late, the newly married couple would usually set up their own household. Even if they moved into the household of the wife's or husband's parent(s), the latter would usually retire and the young couple take over the management of the household. Such a system normally led to the creation of nuclear family households (father, mother and their children, possibly with servants and/or lodgers). In contrast, where marriage was early, the newly married would generally move into an existing household. They would then become part of a larger and frequently complex domestic unit. To give an idea of the two household patterns, take the Essex village of Elmdon in 1861 and Krasnoe Sobakino in Great Russia in 1849. In the former some 73 per cent of households consisted of married couples with or without offspring living with them, and widows/widowers with offspring. The corresponding percentage in Krasnoe Sobakino was 13.3 per cent. If we move from these 'simple family households' to 'multiple family households' i.e. where two or more kin-linked family units were under the same roof, then we find that in Elmdon only 1.7 per cent of households were of this type. In Krasnoe Sobakino the percentage is 80.

Recently Hajnal's thesis has come in for considerable criticism. This has centred not so much on the east–west division Hajnal remarked upon, but rather on what seems a failure to recognize the wide variation in age at marriage, the level of nuptiality, household types and household formation in the area subject to what he called the 'European pattern'. Hajnal himself in a later article seemed to confine his 'European pattern' to northern and north-western Europe, i.e. he excluded Italy and the Iberian peninsula. He did, however, add a new dimension, namely that the institution of service acted as a mechanism to, as it were, keep young men and women out of mischief between their early teens, when they had to leave their childhood homes, and their mid- to late twenties, when they married and set up their own households.

On the question of age at marriage there was undoubtedly very wide variation from one part of Europe to another. Even in areas that seemed, at least at first glance, remarkably similar in terms of economic and social characteristics, the age at first marriage of women could vary from the high to low twenties. The relationship between the age at marriage of men and women could also vary considerably. For instance in the south-east of Norway in the late nineteenth century, ordinary seamen, first mates and ships' captains had median marriage ages, respectively, of 25.9, 27.3 and 30.1. This was to be expected since ships' captains would tend to be older than ships' mates and they, in turn, older than ordinary seamen. However the median age of their wives were, respectively 24.5, 23.5 and 23.8 years.

Although we now know a great deal about age at marriage and the proportions married in the various age groups, our understanding of the mechanisms that led to these statistical outcomes is relatively small. Many factors obviously played their part including what we, at the present time, tend to think of as the *only* factor, or at least the only legitimate one, namely love. Nevertheless economic factors seem to have been of crucial importance. Here are two scenarios.

The son of a Norwegian crofter would leave home in his early teens to work as a living-in farm servant on a farm, usually not far from his birthplace. Often he would move every year or so to another farm. He would get his board and lodging and a very small wage. As he grew older he would acquire skills and gain experience. He would aspire to a croft of his own. Such crofts were provided by farmers for their married labourers, often, but increasingly less so, with some land, in return for labour services. An unmarried labourer could not expect a croft since a farmer would usually expect to receive the labour services of the crofter's wife and children too. Nor could he expect one until his mid-twenties, or later, partly because in many areas all the cultivatable land had been taken up; there was, in any case, a limit to the amount of labour required on any one farm; and a farmer would not want to enter into what could well be a lifetime commitment with a man who had not all the requisite skills and a number of years experience behind him. And there was the wife to consider. A farmer might well consider giving a croft to a competent 25-year-old labourer, but he would think twice about doing so if the man's wife-to-be was too young and inexperienced. This was well understood and various strategies were adopted to ensure that a crofter-to-be married a woman with suitable qualities. For example, fellow farm servants would encourage appropriate liaisons and discourage inappropriate ones. Since farm servants had common sleeping quarters, a covert organization of courtship was not difficult. The farmer's family would also play its part, protecting young girls by keeping an eye on them or making it known that a croft could be available if a particular female farm servant, whose services the farmer did not wish to lose, found a suitable partner. From the crofter-to-be's point of view, a woman, who might well be somewhat older than he was, could be something of a catch in other ways. For example she could have saved up the basic bits and pieces needed to furnish a croft – pots and pans, bed linen, a chair or two – and might even have a cow or a few sheep running with her master's.

The situation for the son of a farmer was quite different. He would normally aspire to a farm of his own. If he were the eldest son that would not be a problem. He would inherit his father's. But unless his father died relatively young or was prepared to retire – and various legal mechanisms were in place for that – he might have to wait a long time not only before he would get a farm of his own but also before he could get married. For few farms could provide more than one livelihood by the late nineteenth century. The situation of younger sons was much more problematic. Depending upon the size of the farm and its labour requirements (these would vary over the life cycle) they would probably go to work on other farms, just like the sons of crofters. Some – an increasing proportion as we shall see – would migrate to the cities, abandoning farming altogether, or even go overseas. Some would emigrate – usually across the Atlantic – with the specific purpose of earning enough to return and buy a farm. Many, of course, were not able to achieve this goal, although a surprising number did so. We know little about them, as return migration has received much less attention from historians than its one-way counterpart. The majority of farmers' sons looked no further than marrying a farmer's daughter who, if not inheriting a farm herself, would be likely to have a dowry which would go towards the acquisition of one. Such women were sought-after from an early age since their prospects were well known. They tended to marry at a younger age than did women who became the wives of crofters, and were usually younger than their husbands. But to put figures on these events (average age at first marriage of farmers marrying spinsters was around 30 years, that of their wives 26: for crofters and their wives 27 and 27, respectively) is to hide enormous variations. For some farmers' sons became crofters; the size of farms varied enormously with some being no bigger than crofters' holdings; some men married widows, some women married widowers. Although in general there were relatively few marriages between the sons of crofters and the daughters of farmers, or between the sons of farmers and the daughters of crofters (although more of the former than of the latter) here too there was very considerable variation across the country. One final feature, the date of the marriage itself, reveals the very strong links between economic factors and marriage as an institution. For marriages did not take place randomly across the year. Rather they were concentrated in those months when the demands of farming or fishing or forestry were at their least, and when the weather was most likely to ensure that guests could travel to and from the wedding most easily (guests could be an important source of income for the newlyweds). Since both the economy and the climate varied across the country, so too did the timing of the marriage ceremony.

No doubt factors such as those described played an important role in determining the age at marriage, its timing and who married who, across the whole of Europe west of Hajnal's St Petersburg–Trieste line. As the continent became more industrialized and more urbanized, so too did the mechanisms of marriage formation. As children became less of an economic resource and more of a consumption good involving increasing outlays on the part of their parents, and as birth control within marriage spread, still further changes occurred. But what was the situation east of the St Petersburg–Trieste line?

We have seen that marriage occurred earlier in Eastern Europe and that a much higher proportion of the population married. Few never married. It would also appear that the characteristic kinship composition of the household of the West (a single conjugal group, usually with children) was rare in Eastern Europe. The timing of marriages, too, seems to be more closely associated with religious beliefs than with economic imperatives. Take the case of Romania in 1872. Marriages in the countryside, where the vast majority of the population lived, were concentrated into January and February, with 64 per cent of all marriages occurring in those two months. November and December accounted for a further 16 per cent. The rest were spread relatively evenly across the year, with the lowest percentage (0.6) occurring in March. The figures point to religious factors playing the dominant role. Certainly the extraordinarily low figure in March (a mere 186 out of 30,041 marriages) points to the influence of Lent and the Eastern Orthodox Church's prohibition of marriages in that period.

Marriage, as just described, served to maintain fertility at widely different levels throughout most of Europe at the beginning of our period. This role, however, was coming to an end. For birth control within marriage was to become the norm. Once accepted by a society there would seem to be no going back. This silent revolution occurred with varying degrees of speed, though in the context of people's time on earth, with amazing rapidity. With the exception of France the change began around 1870. (In France a sustained decline in marital fertility took place in all parts of the country between 1830 and 1880.) In the UK, Scandinavia and Central Europe the change occurred between 1880 and 1920; in Ireland, Eastern Europe and much of inland Spain from 1930 onwards. What this meant in the number of children per marriage can be shown from the case of England. There, marriages entered into in the 1860s and lasting more than twenty years produced an average of six children: those entered into during the First World War, between two and three. The beginnings and the outcome of this process can be seen in table 1.4. By 1900 the impact across the continent as a whole was slight, the fall in the crude birth rate being only from 38.4 per 1,000 in 1870 to 36.5. Had the British used more refined measures and, it must be admitted, had our statistics being more reliable (e.g. the apparent rise in the crude birth rate in the Balkans was probably a reflection of better registration), the impact of the fall in fertility in the United Kingdom, for example, might have emerged more clearly. There can be no doubt, however, of the difference between 1900 and 1951: the latter year being chosen rather than 1945 partly because the demographic chaos in much of Europe in that year was hardly susceptible to good record-keeping and because by 1951 the immediate post-war baby boom (which had also occurred after the First World War) and the re-settlement of wartime refugees had both ended. Note too that by 1951 the various parts of Europe had very much the same crude birth rate, in contrast to the situation in 1870 and 1900.

It has proved easier to describe the fall in fertility than to explain it. A massive project (the European Fertility Project) was started in 1963 under the direction of Ansley J. Coale of Princeton University. The results of the project proved somewhat disappointing, since no clear answers were given as to just why fertility should fall and continue to do so just at that time across a Europe with widely varying socio-economic and cultural characteristics. Two possible reasons for this result were: first, that in order to maintain comparability, only a relatively small number of socio-economic variables were used and no cultural variables; and second, that the 600 or so 'provinces' into which Europe was divided for the purposes of analysis (in England, the county was the unit used) were perhaps too large, and so hid important differences. A later study in Norway which was embedded, methodologically speaking, in the Princeton project, casts some doubt on this explanation. For it examined the fall in fertility (it fell by almost half between 1900 and 1930) in 549 local authority districts (note Norway's population in 1900 was only 2.2 million) using over 100 variables, including both socio-economic and cultural ones. In the event some 63 per cent of the variance in the fall in fertility was explained by just four variables: namely, the percentage of the population of an area occupied in mining and industry in 1900; the percentage employed in trade and transport at the same date; the percentage voting for a continuation of the ban on the sale of alcohol in 1926; and the proportion of women electors participating in the parliamentary elections of 1915–30. Whilst the first two of these signal industrialization, the two cultural correlations appear somewhat bizarre to say the least. Both, perhaps, indicate a more prominent role for women in public affairs. Is it too far-fetched to suggest that, as the bearers of children and their principal carers, women also exerted a greater influence when it came to such private matters as the control of their own fertility? Throughout Europe urbanization and industrialization was gathering pace. Children were no longer as valuable economically as they had been – they were not suited to many of the newer jobs, or their part in them was restricted by law. Compulsory schooling meant they were more expensive to rear. The First World War accelerated these and other factors such as the rise in the service sector, with a dramatic rise in female employment; and a continuing drop in infant mortality. While in some countries the onset of fertility decline preceded the decline in infant mortality in others it came afterwards, though the decline in child mortality, probably as important, occurred earlier and preceded the marital fertility decline almost everywhere. These, and other factors, have been rehearsed many times by those seeking to explain the fall in fertility. The final answers still elude us.

Europeans on the Move

Another factor restricting the growth in Europe's population was emigration. The years 1870–1914 saw the rate of emigration, mostly to North

America, reach its peak. Some 37 millions left Europe for the USA alone. About one-third of these set out from the United Kingdom and Ireland. Italy accounted for about a fifth. In fact the increase in migration from southern and eastern Europe reached its peak on the eve of the First World War, by which time the flow from the 'older' emigrant countries of north-west Europe had diminished. What accounts for this movement? There is no simple answer. Some countries with high rates of population growth also had high rates of emigration, for example Norway, Britain, Germany, Italy: some had low rates, for example, the Netherlands and Denmark. And some countries with low rates of population growth had low emigration, most notably France. As with much else in population studies, the nation state may not be the best framework in which to discuss the causes and mechanics of emigration. To begin with, high rates of emigration were often confined to relatively small areas within a country. For example, south-west England provided a disproportionate number of emigrants, as did the Italian districts of Sicily and Calabria and the Finnish district of Ostrobothnia. Emigration also often started in one region before spreading to others. For example, central and western areas of southern Norway took the lead in the mid-nineteenth century, whereas the north of the country did not experience emigration on any scale until the last quarter of the century.

It would also be wrong to consider emigration in isolation from internal migration. The population of Europe had been mobile geographically for as far back as we are able to study. Much of this was local, circular migration, with many going no further than a day or two's walk from their birthplace. It started in the teenage years as young men and women went to work on farms, or in the towns. Sometimes they never returned, especially those going to the larger towns. Such was the level of mortality that for towns to grow at all they needed fresh drafts of young men and women from the countryside. London, for example, is said to have absorbed half the natural increase of England in the early eighteenth century. Seasonal migration to take in the harvest or participate in the major fisheries also had a long history. Hundreds of thousands moved across Europe. In northern Norway so many men travelled to the fisheries in the months of January to April that the number of women conceiving dipped dramatically during that period.

The significant change that took place in our period was that circular or seasonal migration was now joined by a significant one-way migration from the rural areas to the major cities. These cities expanded as never before and came to dominate most of Europe in settlement terms. Migration to them might be in stages (from countryside to small town, from small town to larger town and so on) but increasingly there was a movement between the larger towns.

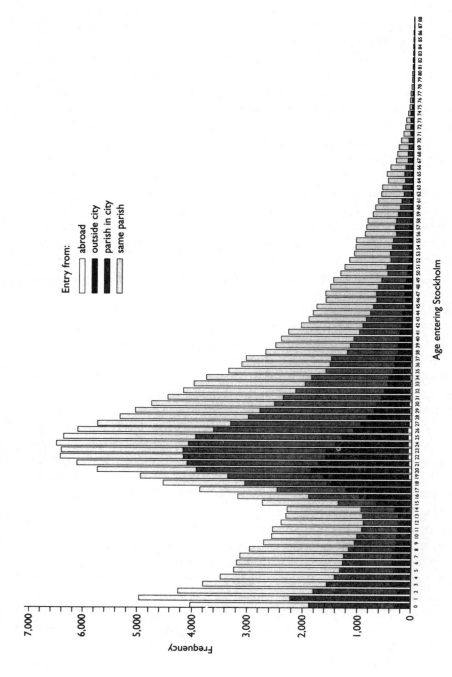

Figure 1.1 Age when movement occurred, by type of migrant, into the parishes of Storkyrkan and Maria, central Stockholm, 1890–1900

Usually the peak age for migration was the later teens and early twenties. Usually migrants were single, or if married only recently so and encumbered by, at most, one or two children. This is exemplified in the migration to and within a couple of parishes in Stockholm in the 1890s. Because Sweden has for a long time kept track of the movement of its citizens within the country, it is possible to trace all the movements as they occurred. Figure 1.1 shows migration in two parishes in central Stockholm from various sources: (1) from abroad (very few), (2) from outside the city, (3) from parishes within the city and (4) from within the same parish. A glance shows that the age pattern of movement was broadly the same, namely a sharp decline from infancy to the early teens, an even swifter rise to a peak in the mid-twenties followed by a sharp fall to the mid-thirties and then a gradual decline with age. Less complete statistics covering migration, emigration and immigration elsewhere in Europe suggest this configuration was widespread.

Why a particular individual or family chose to move to a particular place seems to have been very much part of a planned process. Few seemed to have just 'upped sticks' and left for the great wide yonder. What is called chain migration seems to have been the norm, so called because the links forged between destination and starting point by earlier immigrants served to maintain the flow. Emigrant letters were perhaps one of the most potent forces. Not many of the hundreds of millions that were undoubtedly sent have survived, but those that have often emphasized the economic opportunities awaiting the migrant. A visit to the 'old home' by a successful migrant – whether it be across the Atlantic or to a neighbouring town – was also an inspiration, leading to further migration. A pre-paid ticket was also a common mechanism by which the process of migration was facilitated.

The First World War brought a sharp fall in overseas migration. Nor was it to revive after the war as countries, most notably the USA, legislated against further immigration. The world-wide depression of the 1930s also hit migration across national boundaries, though it continued within countries as urbanization increased and employment in rural areas declined. Significant migration occurred in the United Kingdom, for example, as areas of heavy industry went into depression, whilst new industries and services, especially in the Midlands and southeast, expanded.

The Second World War saw an unprecedented amount of forced migration. There were 7 million forced labourers in Germany by 1944, including 2.7 million from the USSR, 1.7 million Poles, 1.25 million French, around 600,000 Italians and a quarter of a million each of Belgians and Dutch. The following year saw a massive return (around 11 million) of refugees, prisoners-of-war and forced labourers to their home countries.

Table 1.5 Deaths per 1,000 population in various parts of Europe, 1870, 1900 and 1951

Area	1870	1900	1951
European Russia	35.4	31.1	10.0
Austria-Hungary	31.7	25.7	12.7
Germany	27.3	21.9	10.9
France	27.2	21.9	13.3
United Kingdom	21.8	18.4	12.7
Benelux	24.3	18.7	9.8
Norden	18.7	17.7	9.4
Iberia	29.1	27.0	11.7
Italy	30.0	23.8	10.3
Balkans	19.4	23.4	9.1
Europe	29.0	24.7	11.0

Source: For 1870 and 1900, Ministère du travail et de la prévoyance sociale, *Statistiques Internationale du Mouvement de la Population d'après les Registres d'Etat Civil. Résumé Retrospectif depuis l'Origine des Statistiques de l'Etat Civil* (Paris, 1907); for 1951, B. R. Mitchell, *International Historical Statistics, Europe 1750–1988*, 3rd edition (London, 1992)

The Death Rate Falls

If the fall in births and the rise in emigration served to reduce the rate of growth of Europe's population, the fall in the death rate had a more positive effect. Again, like the other demographic variables, the death rate varied considerably across Europe at the beginning of our period. In much of Europe it had been falling from at least the end of the Napoleonic Wars and in some areas before. Table 1.5 shows the crude death rate in various parts of Europe at our benchmark dates of 1870, 1900 and 1951. The crude death rate measures the level of mortality in the entire population. However, the extent of the fall in the number of deaths varied according to age and (much less so) sex. Children experienced the greatest fall in mortality, the elderly the least.

What caused the fall, which, as table 1.5 demonstrates, occurred throughout Europe, albeit at different speeds? This is still the subject of debate in spite of the fact that, as noted earlier, we can chart it far more closely than in any previous period. For instance, we know that deaths from infectious diseases, which in Britain at the beginning of our period accounted for around three-quarters of all deaths, were rapidly approaching negligible proportions by the end. The controversy centres on whether this fall, and the lesser one in deaths from non-infectious diseases, was due to medical intervention, public health measures (e.g. fresh water, sanitary improvements), better housing, or more and better (e.g. less adulterated) food. It is generally admitted that the contribution of hospitals was slight, although not negative as was once thought. The wonder drugs of today are mostly post-Second World War products, though in its day (prior to our period) vaccination against smallpox could be in this category and may well have had a significant impact on mortality, though even this is disputed. Once good sanitation and fresh water became the rule rather than the exception in towns and cities, the gap between urban and rural death rates closed substantially. Not all rural districts, however, had lower death rates than towns. In Austria, for instance, the Alpine areas had the lowest death rates, followed by the cities and behind them the lowland rural areas.

Children under one year experienced the greatest fall in mortality. Again the reasons are not clear. That it tended to parallel the downward shift in fertility would suggest a connection, for example that a trend towards fewer babies, born to younger mothers, gave them a better chance of survival, or that a desire to restrict the number of births mirrored a different attitude to child care, one that laid greater emphasis on the quality rather than the quantity of offspring. The rise of the health visitor and other public and private aids to child rearing probably also played a part. The continuing high incidence of breastfeeding in Britain may account for lower infant mortality there than in much of the rest of Europe.

One cannot leave a survey of mortality without reference to the impact on it of the First and Second World Wars. In England and Wales around one in every fifteen men aged 15–39 years was killed in the First World War and as many as one in six of those aged 20 to 24 years. In France the death rates were double this. Far fewer births occurred than would have been expected. The war also brought a sharp halt to emigration. The major differences between mortality of the First and Second World Wars was that far more people died in the latter and far more of the deaths were of non-combatants; for example, Poland lost 22% of its population, the USSR 14.4%, Yugoslavia 10.8%, Germany 9.0%, though in Western Europe the losses were lower – 1.1% in France, 1.5% in Belgium and 2.5% in the Netherlands.

Conclusion

It will be apparent from the foregoing that so far as European demography in the period 1870–1945 is concerned, there are many questions waiting to be answered. Debates amongst historical demographers of this period can, however, proceed on a firmer foundation of quantitative data than was the case, say, in the controversy over the causes of the rise in Europe's population from around 1750 onwards. We know, thanks to the efforts of government in matters of census taking, the civil registration of births, marriages and deaths and the monitoring of emigration, more or less what happened, be it in terms of population growth, fertility, nuptiality, mortality or movement. Yet we still do not know quite why the changes occurred. Because the statistical data are that much more accurate (it must be remembered that so far as historical demography is concerned the Dark Ages did not end until after the Napoleonic Wars) the kind of explanations put forward to account for, say, the fall in fertility and mortality are more likely to be closer to the truth than for earlier periods. Much work, however, still needs to be done; work that will probably reap the richest rewards at the very local level – the parish, even the street and the individual household.

Appendix 1.1 Populations, crude birth and death rates in European countries in 1870, 1900 and 1951

Countries and regional groupings	1870			1900			1951		
	Population (1,000s)	CBR[a]	CDR[b]	Population (1,000s)	CBR[a]	CDR[b]	Population (1,000s)	CBR[a]	CDR[b]
Europe	**287,975**	**38.4**	**29.0**	**377,985**	**36.5**	**24.7**	**525,672[b]**	**19.3**	**11.0**
European Russia[c]	63,964[d]	49.7	35.4	98,380	49.1	31.1	158,500[d]	20.0[d]	10.0[d]
Austria-Hungary	41,233	41.7	31.7	53,638	38.4	25.7	61,930	23.2	12.7
Austria	20,320	39.8	29.4	25,976	37.3	25.4	6,930	14.8	12.7
Hungary	15,317[e]	46.0[e]	36.1[e]	19,144	39.3	26.9	9,420	20.2	11.7
Romania	4,294	34.4	26.1	6,045	38.8	24.2	16,460	25.1	12.8
Serbia	1,302	44.8	31.7	2,473	42.4	23.5	–	–	–
Czechoslovakia							12,530	22.8	11.4
Yugoslavia							16,590	27.0	14.1
Balkans	4,614	34.6	19.4	5,957	39.5	23.4	14,910	20.7	9.1
Bulgaria	3,154[f]	37.7[f]	18.3[f]	3,744	42.3	22.6	7,260	21.0	10.7
Greece	1,460	28.0[e]	21.9[e]	2,213	35.3	25.2	7,650	20.3	7.5
Germany	43,465	37.9	27.3	59,348	35.2	21.9	73,630	16.1	10.9
Germany	40,803[g]	38.5	27.4	56,046[g]	35.6	22.1	68,880	16.1	10.9
Switzerland	2,662	29.8	25.8	3,302	28.6	19.3	4,750	17.2	10.5
Iberia	21,080	35.5	29.1	23,974	33.1	27.0	36,550	21.1	11.7
Spain	16,201	36.6	31.6	18,566	33.8	28.9	28,090	20.0	11.5
Portugal	4,879[h]	31.9[h]	20.5[h]	5,408	30.5	20.4	8,460	24.6	12.5
Italy	25,795	36.9	30.0	32,346	33.0	23.8	47,090	18.5	10.3

Appendix 1.1 Cont'd

Countries and regional groupings	1870			1900			1951		
	Population (1,000s)	CBR[a]	CDR[b]	Population (1,000s)	CBR[a]	CDR[b]	Population (1,000s)	CBR[a]	CDR[b]
Benelux	8,689	33.9	24.3	11,853	30.1	18.7	18,940	19.6	9.8
Netherlands	3,601	36.1	25.8	5,159	31.5	17.8	10,260	22.3	7.6
Belgium	5,088	32.3	23.3	6,694	28.9	19.3	8,680	16.4	12.4
Norden	9,438	30.6	18.7	12,437	29.2	17.7	18,720	18.2	9.4
Finland	1,754	36.3	18.2[i]	2,697	32.0	21.5	4,050	23.0	10.0
Denmark	1,785	30.5	19.1	2,423	29.8	16.9	4,300	17.8	8.8
Norway	1,735	29.1	16.2	2,200	30.1	15.9	3,300	18.4	8.4
Sweden	4,164	28.8	19.8	5,117	27.0	16.8	7,070	15.6	9.9
United Kingdom	31,257	33.8	21.8	41,152	28.2	18.4	53,242	16.2	12.7
England and Wales	22,501	35.2	22.9	32,249	28.7	18.2	43,810	15.5	12.5
Scotland	3,337	34.6	22.2	4,437	29.6	18.5	5,100	17.8	12.9
Ireland	5,419	27.7	16.7	4,466	22.7	19.6	2,961	21.1	14.3
Northern Ireland							1,371	20.7	12.8
France	38,440	24.5	27.2[j]	38,900	21.4	21.9	42,160	19.5	13.3

Notes: [a]CBR = crude birth rate; [b]CDR = crude death rate; [c]Excluding Poland, Finland, the Caucasus; [d]Estimated; [e]1876; [f]1888; [g]Includes Alsace-Lorraine; [h]1886; [i]In 1869 death rate as high as 77.6 per 1,000; [j]Above average.

Sources: For 1870 and 1900, Ministère du travail et de la prévoyance sociale, *Statistiques Internationale du Mouvement de la Population d'après les Registres d'Etat Civil. Résumé Retrospectif depuis l'Origine des Statistiques de l'Etat Civil* (Paris, 1907); for 1951, B. R. Mitchell, *International Historical Statistics, Europe 1750–1988*, 3rd edition (London, 1992)

2

Prosperity and Depression: The International Economy

Sidney Pollard

Relative Economic Performance of the Major Powers

There are various ways of measuring the economic performance of countries. Most of them begin by adding together the total of all goods and services produced within a period, which forms the 'gross national product' (GNP), which is then divided by the number of the population. The resulting figure of GNP per head would provide an indication of the economic values available on average to the people of that country. Sometimes 'domestic' product is substituted for 'national' product, which ignores the difference which imports, paid for by exports, might make. Since, in general, every cost to one person is an income to another, these estimates can also be expressed as gross national *income* per head. All these 'gross' figures can be converted to 'net' by deducting the cost of capital replacement.

Such measures seek to derive the level of economic values available at any one time. But 'performance' might also be taken to mean how well and how quickly a country is able to raise its national income per head. We would then be looking for the rate of economic *growth* as a useful indicator.

These calculations are difficult and beset with problems if made within one country. The task of comparing the performance of one country with that of another is more complex still. For one thing, price structures differ: for example, what is a franc really worth in terms of pounds? For another, patterns of expenditure differ: thus during this period the British were believed to have spent more on housing and furniture, the French more on food and clothing. Also, practices differ: how, for example, are we to calculate the food produced and consumed on a farm?

These difficulties should be borne in mind when examining table 2.1, which attempts to make the comparison over a long period. The table may look confusing at first sight, but will repay study. There are many uncertainties in detail, and the figures which are based on particularly

Table 2.1 *GNP per capita, 1870–1950, in US$ of 1960*

	1870	1913	1938	1950
Austria-Hungary	*305*	*498*		
Austria		*681*	*640*	721
Belgium	571	894	1,015	1,167
Bulgaria	*220*	*263*	*420*	*423*
Czechoslovakia		*524*	*548*	785
Denmark	340	862	1,045	1,277
Finland	*313*	*520*	913	1,027
France	437[a]	689	936	1,137
Germany	428[a]	743	1,126	*834*
Greece	*250*	*322*	*590*	445
Hungary		*372*	*451*	*560*
Ireland		*611*	*649*	744
Italy	312	441	551	590
Netherlands	506	754	920	1,019
Norway	421	749	1,298	1,652
Poland			*372*	
Portugal	270	*292*	*351*	383
Romania	210	*336*	343	
Serbia/Yugoslavia	*230*	*284*	*339*	*350*
Spain	329	367	337	367
Sweden	246	680	1,097	1,712
Switzerland	549	964	1,204	1,368
United Kingdom	628	965	1,181	1,352
Russia/USSR	250	326	*458*	*585*
Europe	359	534	671	749

[a] In pre-1871 boundaries.
Figures in italics are approximate only.
Source: Paul Bairoch, 'Europe's gross national product: 1800–1975', *Journal of European Economic History*, 5 (1976), pp. 286 and 297

weak data are entered in italics. But overall, the data are likely to reflect reality reasonably well: another estimate, provided by Crafts for the pre-1914 years, reaches broadly similar figures.[1]

Several conclusions emerge from the table. Possibly the most striking is the rapid rise in income, or product, per head, which doubled for Europe as a whole between 1870 and 1950 (and in which, incidentally,

[1] Except for Norway, for which Crafts has much lower figures. N. F. R. Crafts, 'Gross national product in Europe 1870–1910: some new estimates', *Explorations in Economic History*, 20 (1983), pp. 387–401.

Table 2.2   *Gross Domestic Product per man-hour, 1870–1950, in US$ of 1970*

	1870	1913	1938	1950
Austria	0.43	0.90	1.03	1.25
Belgium	0.74	1.26	1.84	2.11
Denmark	0.44	1.00	1.57	1.82
Finland	0.29	0.71	1.15	1.48
France	0.42	0.90	1.69	1.85
Germany	0.43	0.95	1.47	1.40
Italy	0.44	0.72	1.28	1.37
Netherlands	0.74	1.23	1.80	2.27
Norway	0.40	0.82	1.62	2.03
Sweden	0.31	0.83	1.55	2.34
Switzerland	0.55	1.01	1.84	2.21
United Kingdom	0.80	1.35	1.84	2.40

Source: Angus Maddison, *Phases of Capitalist Development* (Oxford, 1982), p. 212

there was another three- to four-fold rise to the 1990s in continental Western Europe). Secondly, the rise in Scandinavia was much faster than elsewhere, while the southern fringe countries of Spain, Portugal, Yugoslavia and Greece were well below the average, widening still further the gap which existed at the beginning. Some of the poorer countries had even by 1950 not reached the level of the most advanced in 1870. Thirdly, there is the effect of war, particularly on the defeated Germany and Italy after the Second World War. A fourth indication, that national averages hide great regional variations, is provided by the estimate for Austria-Hungary for 1913, which may be compared with her constituent parts of Austria, Hungary and Czechoslovakia for the same year.

Behind these changes were changes in productivity, illustrated in table 2.2. Productivity rose much faster than incomes, since some of the gains were absorbed by shorter hours of work. Much of this gain was due to technical improvement, which formed a highly significant factor in the European economy of the period.

Statistical data of this kind may yield useful comparisons and generalizations covering the continent as a whole, but they hide important differences between countries, each of which followed a pattern of development of its own. Among the Great Powers, the United Kingdom, as the first country to have become industrialized, was still the richest country by far in Europe in 1870, and while much of the gap had been closed after two world wars, she was still among the leaders in 1950.

Many observers think that Britain's relative decline, measured by slower growth rates than those of her rivals, began in the last quarter of the nineteenth century; others set the date somewhat later. To some extent, a catching-up process by other countries was inevitable: there was nothing unique in either the resources or the technology which had propelled Britain to the front in the first place. But there were signs that other countries, notably the USA and Germany, were not only catching up, but in some fields were overtaking Britain.

There was a distinct tendency for factors which had been favourable in one period to become hindrances in the following one: there was, in other words, a price to be paid for having been the pioneer. Thus the leading British industries, and those with the best export record, were still those which had borne the weight of the Industrial Revolution, industries sometimes known as the old staples, some of which had little growth potential left: cotton and wool textiles, pig iron, coal mining, steam engine production. By contrast, Britain was lagging in the newer industries of the age, sometimes referred to as those of the 'second industrial revolution', including electrical engineering, chemicals and motor cars. Similarly, because of the earlier industrial successes based on the practical know-how of managers and skills of artisans, Britain was slow to turn to formal, university-based science and technology which had now become necessary for progress.

In the depression years between the wars the old staples in Britain were particularly vulnerable to unemployment and stagnation, in part because there was a decline in the relative demand for their products, and in part because they used technologies which newly industrializing foreign competitors found it easiest to copy. As many of them were geographically concentrated, the regions of their concentration suffered especially badly through lack of employment and social deprivation. Against this, the regions in which the newer, expanding industries were settling, especially the West Midlands and the outer ring of London's suburbs, did relatively well even in the depression years.

The technical lead achieved by Britain earlier in the nineteenth century, her dominant position in maritime trade, and her extensive imperial possessions, had given her economy a shape which differed markedly from the structure of the larger continental economies. Thus she was more integrated into an international division of labour, importing more of her raw materials and exporting more of her manufactures than others. Benefiting from cheap food imports, she had allowed her agriculture to decline further than others, so that by 1910 only 11.5 per cent of her male labour force was employed in agriculture, compared with the European average of 28.3 per cent.[2] Cheap food and the wealth

[2] N. F. R. Crafts, *British Economic Growth during the Industrial Revolution* (Oxford, 1985), p. 62.

accumulated in earlier times were among the reasons for the relatively high standard of living in Britain.

As the earliest industrializers, it was also mostly the British who used their capital to develop railways, harbours, plantations and mines overseas. These made it possible to supply the growing quantities of tropical produce, minerals and increasingly, even such traditional European produce as grain, meat or wool demanded by the European economies. These capital exports generated year by year a stream of profit and interest incomes from abroad, which were used either to pay for imports, or were left abroad to create still more investments there. Shipping services by Britain's merchant marine, much the largest in the world, provided other incomes from abroad, and so did financial services, such as insurance and banking. Collectively these service earnings from abroad came to be known as 'invisible' exports. Much of the foreign capital and British shipping advantage was lost in the First World War, but 'invisible exports' still provided useful foreign earnings even after 1918 and into the post-Second World War period.

Being at the centre of the world's most important trade and payments network, the City of London tended to assume a unique role in the world's monetary system in the period 1870–1914. The gold standard on which the pound sterling was based was adopted almost universally, making international payments relatively easy, and many of these were conducted through holdings and credits in London. London thus developed a kind of balancing role, evening out international economic disturbances, though the stability of the pre-war gold standard system should not be exaggerated. After 1918 both the earnings surplus and the equilibrating role of London were much diminished, though this was not immediately clear to policy-makers who tried in vain to recapture the golden days of the pre-war gold standard. While London's power had waned, no other centre rose to take on its international equilibrating role.

Next to Britain it was France among the Great Powers which trod an early path to industrialization. However, the details of her route, the structure of her economy and her role in international networks were quite different. Although she, too, acquired overseas colonies and engaged in overseas trade, these played a lesser role than in Britain, and were exceeded by her involvement in trade and investment links with the continent of Europe. A number of European countries, including Italy, Spain and some parts of Eastern Europe, came to look to France as their source of capital and modern technology.

Internally, also, the French economy was structurally different from the British. Lacking Britain's large and conveniently located coal and iron resources, French industries tended to concentrate more on consumer goods and on fashion and artistic products in which both the skill of her artisans and the prestige of her leadership in European taste gave her comparative advantages. Nevertheless, many observers have pointed to weaknesses in entrepreneurship, and a tendency toward 'live and let live' within the monopolistic industrial structures of fairly self-contained French regions. There is no doubt that, largely because of the traditions of strong government, the French state took a more active role, especially in the development of the transport network including the railways, than in Britain. Technically, French engineers were always among the most original and innovatory in Europe, especially where the needs of French resources demanded it, such as in textile production and water-power technology.

France has a larger territory than Britain, and her climate is more favourable, and in consequence she remained self-sufficient in food for much longer; in fact, some agrarian products, such as wines and brandies, continued to be among her leading export commodities. This self-sufficiency in food also meant that France was less dependent on foreign trade in general than Britain. There were significant differences between the two countries in the agrarian structure, too. While Britain was, typically, a country of large, capitalistic tenant farmers employing wage labour, France was essentially a country of peasants, working their own or rented family farms with, at most, one or two hired hands on a seasonal basis. The French peasant was said to be very attached to his piece of ground, no matter how modest; at the same time, France had a much lower rate of population increase than other parts of developed Europe, and there was therefore less pressure of population on the land. Both factors tended to inhibit the movement of labour into the industrial towns which marked the typical development path of industrial economies elsewhere.

Much of this traditional picture of the French economy changed in the twentieth century. Heavy industry developed in the north of the country, using local iron ore and some German coal; engineering was built up in the Paris suburbs, as well as elsewhere, and France became the leading motor car producer in Europe; she was also among the leaders in developing hydro-electric power. She was able to stand up to the depression of the 1930s rather better than some of her neighbours.

Of all the major European economies, it was the German which resembled the British most closely, in spite of a number of significant differences. Both were based, in the earlier phases of their industrialization, on coal, iron and engineering, on rapid urbanization, and on exchanges of manufactured exports for food and raw material imports. German industrialization began much later than the British, but unlike

France, which in a sense bypassed the British lead by concentrating of different products, Germany met British competition head-on and by the early twentieth century was defeating it in one country after another, first on the continent of Europe but finally also in traditional British overseas markets. It was notable that German strength also developed in the newer industries, especially in chemicals, pharmaceuticals and electrical engineering, and this was not unconnected with the fact that her universities and technical colleges were among the best in the world. The lost war and losses of territory after 1918 caused only a temporary setback.

Apart from the location on the continent, with her neighbours as obvious trading partners, it was the agrarian structure of the eastern half of Germany which showed the biggest differences from the United Kingdom. East-Elbian agriculture was demesne agriculture in which the large Junker estates, in a region of indifferent soil and climate, produced mostly rye and other grains for export. The region was poor, industrially underdeveloped and socially backward, but in contrast with Ireland, with which there were some obvious similarities, its landlords dominated the policies of the Reich, both in the sense of making sure that their grain economy was protected at the expense of the rest of society, and also in the sense of inhibiting the rise of liberal-democratic government. It was the incongruity between Germany's advanced economic power in the west, and the reactionary political control exercised from the east, which was in part responsible for the economic and social stresses which accompanied the slump and caused the collapse into barbarism after 1933.

Until 1918, the Habsburg monarchy of Austria-Hungary was another major European Power. Straddling central and south-eastern Europe, it exhibited in different parts of its large territory qualities appropriate to both these regions. Thus the Bohemian lands had both modern heavy industry and traditional textile, glass and other consumer industries. Together with the area around the capital, Vienna, their absolute levels of income and growth rates were akin to those of advanced Western Europe. By contrast, the great Hungarian plain was agricultural, and some regions showed a degree of underdevelopment and stagnation normally associated with Eastern Europe and the Balkans. In 1910 the Alpine lands as a whole had a per capita product of 1,089 US dollars of 1970 and the Bohemian lands registered US$ 819; by contrast, Transylvania and Croatia-Slavonia were estimated at US$ 542.[3] After the

---

[3] David F. Good, 'Austria-Hungary', in *Patterns of European Industrialization*, ed. Richard Sylla and Gianni Toniolo (London and New York, 1991), p. 230. Also see table 2.1 above.

break-up of the Habsburg Empire, these differences increased still further in the inter-war years.

The Russian Empire was much the poorest and most backward among the great European Powers. Though the country was well endowed with natural resources, including a vast expanse of land, rich timber supplies and valuable mineral deposits, the great distances, the severe climate of the northern and central provinces, and above all the historical heritage of Tatar invasions, brutal autocracy and personal serfdom until as late as 1861 had delayed her economic development. There were great spurts forward, especially in the 1890s, when the coal, iron and oil riches began to be exploited, much railway mileage was built and general industrial development occurred in St Petersburg, the Moscow region, Poland and other areas. But because of the backwardness of the country, much of this had to rely on foreign capital and on government initiatives. Agriculture, in particular, was still primitive and almost medieval in technology, and the peasants remained poor and in practice tied to the soil until the early twentieth century. Any improvement in their living standard was squeezed out of them by taxes which were designed to force them to yield up their grain, which then formed the major saleable export commodity.

The agony of destruction of the First World War was prolonged in Russia by years of civil war which followed the Bolshevik revolution of 1917, and it was not until about 1928 that planned industrial expansion could begin to exceed the pre-war per capita output. Industrialization was driven forward on the basis of socialist planning at breakneck speed and at the cost of enormous sacrifices, especially on the part of the peasant population. Within a few years a massive heavy industry base was created, together with urbanization, with educational and health services comparable with those of the rest of Europe, and an appropriate transport network. Consumer goods remained in very short supply, but the country had built up sufficient productive resources to be able to withstand the onslaught of the German army, the most powerful war machine the world had seen until that time, in 1941–5, though it did so at enormous human and material cost.

As a centrally directed and planned process, the Soviet industrialization experience was, in technical terms, consciously modelled on the Western pattern, in spite of the fundamental ideological and property rights differences between the Soviet Union and the rest of Europe. But the economic development and growth of the other European countries also showed striking similarities, in spite of the historical and geographical differences between them noted here. The evident tendency to convergence appears to have been based on the real requirements of modern industrial society.

Free Trade and Protection

From the middle of the nineteenth century onward a gradual loosening of protectionist and mercantilist policies in Europe occurred, a move led by the United Kingdom, which stood to gain most from the expansion of international trade. The high point of this movement was reached in the 1860s as a result of a series of bilateral trade agreements between the major countries. These coincided with years of expansion and prosperity culminating in the boom of 1870–3. The countries which lowered their tariff rates and reduced or abolished their import restrictions did so for two main reasons: one was to get the benefits of cheaper or better products from abroad for their people as consumers; the other was the hope of stimulating their producers by the spur of foreign competition. These positive drives reflected a phase of optimism and expansion in the world economy, in spite of temporary crises and wars, especially those fought by Germany, and the American Civil War.

The free-trade phase did not last long. Two major developments contributed to its demise. One was a serious financial crisis ending the boom in 1873–4, followed by years of depression and high unemployment in the later 1870s and the 1880s: many contemporaries were inclined to blame the preceding liberal policies for these ills. The other was the improvements in steamship and rail transport, together with the opening up of the North American plains, which led to a flood of cheap imports of grain into Europe at prices which European farmers, with their much smaller holdings of land and high rents to pay, could not match. To these North American imports were soon added cheap Russian and Indian grain supplies, as well as meat, wool and other products from Australia, New Zealand, the Argentine and other low-cost areas.

The pressure for protection therefore came in the first instance from farmers, whereas earlier tariffs had often been designed to protect manufacturers. However, industrialists were not slow to climb on the bandwagon. A typical case was the German tariff of 1879, often considered to have been the trigger for the general return of protectionism in Europe: it levied import duties on both grain and manufactured goods, the famous 'compact of rye and iron'. Other countries soon followed, the French Méline tariff of 1892 being an outstanding example, and the tendency was for tariff rates to have a general rising trend to 1914, punctuated by occasional tariff wars between individual pairs of countries. At the same time, the typical practice was to have two sets of tariff rates, a lower one for countries with which special treaties had been concluded, and a higher rate for the rest of the world. Only Britain kept to her strict free-trade tradition.

A significant point was that there tended often to be a difference in the objectives of agrarian and manufacturing protection. The former was normally designed to protect the status quo, including the social conditions and structures on the land in the interests of the ruling aristocracies. Tariffs on manufactures, on the other hand, especially when imposed by the more backward countries, were frequently intended as instruments of change and progress. Behind this was the 'infant industry' argument, which maintained that newly established industries needed a period of protection against developed foreign competitors before they were strong enough to stand on their own feet, when they would need protecting no longer. It was a plausible argument, though few of the infants ever seemed to grow up. It should be emphasized, however, that in spite of the general rising tendency of protective barriers, trade in Europe was expanding faster than incomes, thus forming a rising share of the European economy in the decades before 1914.

The post-war settlement following 1918 created numerous new frontiers in Central and Eastern Europe as a number of sovereign states were carved out of the Habsburg and the western parts of the Russian Empire. Typically, these new countries were fiercely nationalistic and economically unbalanced: it was not surprising that they were also protectionist. The Soviet Union was virtually cut off from international trade, and in the West there was no move to a general lowering of tariff barriers, though the newly founded League of Nations made several attempts in that direction. There was therefore a continuing tendency to protectionism.

This was greatly strengthened by the world-wide depression which began in 1929. As heavy unemployment began to affect most advanced countries in the early 1930s, the traditional aim of keeping out foreign goods and pushing the export of one's own received an additional boost from the desire to improve home employment thereby, and to 'export one's unemployment', as it was termed. Clearly, it was much easier to block imports than to force exports on other countries, and the result was ever higher barriers which led to a general decline in trade. Moreover, countries had learned in the war and post-war years to use other methods of protection beside tariff duties. These included quotas, quality specifications, manipulations of the exchange rate as the gold standard collapsed, and currency restrictions on importers. In 1932 even Great Britain, the last champion of free trade, introduced a protective tariff. The overall reduction in trade following these 'beggar my neighbour' policies aggravated the depression still further.

In place of the free movement of goods wherever a market beckoned, governments preferred to conclude bilateral treaties, in which each country used its position as buyer to force its goods on the seller, in effect aiming at balancing the trade with each country in turn. Thus Britain obliged the Scandinavian countries to take her coal, and Germany forced various manufactures on her eastern and south-eastern neighbours. Though there was some loosening of restrictions as conditions improved from 1936 onward, and the Soviet Union began to trade once more with the outside world, compared with the pre-war position Europe was still in a highly protective and restrictive phase when war broke out in 1939.

Trade Cycles and Long Waves

Contemporaries were very conscious of the fact that economic growth did not proceed smoothly, but on the contrary was marked by repeated phases of booms and slumps which came to be known as trade cycles. Britain had experienced these from the late eighteenth century onward, and as other countries industrialized, they not only began to register similar fluctuations, but also saw them increasingly synchronized with those of the rest of the advanced world. From the 1870s onward, these cycles were felt as general European phenomena, though there were always also specific features in each country.

Typically, a cycle would have some years of relatively fast growth, high investment and good employment, leading to a peak when resources became scarce and prices rose, as plans exceeded existing capacity. Usually at that point a crisis occurred in the finance sector and a downturn began, accompanied by bankruptcies and rising unemployment, until the markets were cleared and a new upswing could begin. These cycles, termed 'Juglars' after the French economist who first studied them in detail, had a duration of seven to ten years. Their peaks before the First World War can be dated to 1873–4, 1883–4, 1890, 1900, 1907 and 1913. The war interrupted the sequence to some extent, but a cyclical movement was resumed post-war, with peaks in 1920, 1929 and 1937.

While it is possible to view these cycles as part of a regular system, a kind of immanent heaving of the modern world economy obeying a general law of motion of its own, there are some observers who deny any such regularity. They are more impressed by the differences between the cycles, as well as between the experiences of individual countries, and see each boom and slump as a separate event. There is also a more widespread view that a break occurred as a result of the First World

War, and the cycles thereafter were of quite a different nature from those before 1914.

Thus the 1870s saw a reaction from the over-speculation of the 1870–4 period, which had been particularly marked in Vienna, Paris and Berlin. The 1880s were still depressed, large increases in output being accompanied by low prices and low profits, the 'peak' of 1883–4 being hardly deserving of the name. There followed rapid development in the next two decades, particularly in the developing and industrializing countries of Italy, Austria and Russia, among others, culminating in an exceptionally high level of output and activity in 1913. The type of industry leading the growth phase, the role of the banks and of foreign investment, and the international connections differed in each country, the whole being played out against a background of rising industrial sophistication and international financial integration.

There is yet another movement which may be discerned in addition to the upward trend and the regular seven- to ten-year cycle superimposed on it: that was the sequence of 'long waves' first observed by the Russian economist N. D. Kondratieff.* They were noted originally as price movements – price series being one of the few statistical data available on an international basis before 1914 – which showed a world-wide upward trend to 1873, a decline to 1896, a rise to 1920 followed once more by a decline and a rise from 1936. Linked to a similar wave from 1815 onward, this gave an average duration of some forty-five to fifty years for each Kondratieff long wave.

Again, and particularly in view of the small number of observations, it is possible to doubt the existence of a regular sequence and to view each wave as a singular phenomenon. However, there were some regularities which strengthen the notion of an inherent logic in the long waves.

The first question concerns the price movements themselves. How did they arise? There are two possible sources: changes in the quantity of money, and changes in the number of transactions which the money has to facilitate. As far as money was concerned, the problem of making possible an increasing expenditure by an increasing population in the European economy with a relatively fixed base of metallic money was solved in the long term by extending the use of paper money, bank entries and the like. In the period 1870–1914, however, European currencies were still mainly based on gold, and they were aided by two periods of large gold discoveries in the nineteenth century, which for the time being greatly increased the supply of the precious metals available, leading to price rises. One occurred in the mid-century (California, Australia) and the other in the 1890s (Alaska, South Africa). Both occurred at the end of a period of falling prices when the value of gold had risen to a temporary peak and there was therefore a strong incentive to search for new gold deposits. In the inter-war years the quantity of metal lost in influence on the price level compared with government policies. These tended in a deflationary, price-reducing direction in the 1920s, when countries tried to restore the pre-war gold standard which had been suspended in the war, and were then reversed into an inflationary, job-creating direction after 1933.

From the side of the transactions, it is possible to see in the sequence of price upswing and downswing phases a reflection of activities in the real economy. Price increases were associated with large-scale investments, especially in railways and other infrastructural projects which raised incomes at once but led to cost reductions only in the longer term: these cost reductions then became effective in the following price fall phases. The price increase periods also saw the major wars of the age: the wars of German and Italian unification, the Crimean War, the American Civil War in 1848–73, and the Boer War, the Balkan wars and the First World War, among others, in 1896–1920. Each of these exerted notable inflationary pressures. Conversely, the price phases in turn also influenced the level of prosperity: in inflationary times, booms were longer and more pervasive and slumps were weaker; in deflationary parts of the Kondratieff cycle, the opposite was true: it was then that slumps turned into major depressions, above all in the 1880s and the 1930s.

Some obervers also noted that the long waves tended to coincide with a bunching of important innovations. Thus the boom peaking in 1873–4 was marked by the creation of novel steel-producing capacities and the building of intercontinental and other large railway systems, while the phase after the 1890s saw electricity and motor car innovations. This view is particularly associated with the name of Schumpeter. More recently, Tylecote has put forward the notion of new 'styles' of productive activity characterizing different long waves. Thus the steam transport style was followed by the 'steel and electricity style' of the 1860s and 1870s which, in turn, made way for the 'Fordist' style, introduced in the USA just before the First World War but dominating factory building in Europe in the inter-war years.[4] In each case, technical innovation was accompanied by particular styles of management, employment and financial structure.

The Impact of the World Wars

Most historians would agree that, no matter how pervasive the economic trend and the cycles were on the economic fortunes of Europe,

[4] J. A. Schumpeter, *Business Cycles* (2 vols, New York, 1939); Andrew Tylecote, *The Long Wave in the World Economy* (London and New York, 1991).

the two world wars of 1914–18 and 1939–45 made their own quite distinct impact. In both cases, there were three important aspects to this: one was the sheer destructiveness of each, in human losses and material damage; another was the impetus to technical and organizational innovation in the widest sense, induced by the needs of the military. There was also the effects of the territorial changes of the peace settlements which, though mainly political, also had economic implications.

Compared with earlier conflicts, the First World War exacted a terrifying sacrifice in human lives: there were seven million military and five million civilian casualties in the West, and in Russia as many as sixteen million lives were lost if we include the period of civil war. Adding the victims of the post-war influenza, and of border conflicts and massacres arising out of the war, the total losses amounted to fifty to sixty million people, half of them in Russia. To these have to be added further millions lost through falling birth rates, as well as seven million permanently disabled people in the West alone. The trauma of children who lost their fathers, families who lost their breadwinners, the social costs of disturbances and of the unbalanced sex ratio, though enormous, cannot even be estimated.

Estimates of material losses depend on definitions and vary so widely that no agreed total can be derived, but they may well have come to £50 milliard, including production and investments lost and the direct destruction of fields, houses, means of transport and factories. This represents anything from five to eight years' growth lost to Europe. There was also the less tangible loss of confidence in currencies and government finances, as budgets were unbalanced, inflation became rampant in most countries and moratoria and bankruptcies disturbed trade relationships, especially across frontiers.

Yet where conditions were favourable, as in northern France and Belgium, the effects of the direct destruction were repaired remarkably quickly. Moreover, there were also some economic gains derived from the war, though they came nowhere near to balancing the losses. Above all, scientific and technical progress was spurred on by war needs, in the fields of chemicals, optics and aircraft engineering, among others, and the capacity of such industries as engineering and shipbuilding was greatly enlarged. Mass production methods in factories, social facilities for the large numbers of female workers and more modern systems of accounting and management were installed in many plants for the first time.

Some effects of the boundary changes which resulted from the peace settlements have been noted above. Most of the new nations attempted to foster modernization and industrialization in their economies, though generally with but indifferent success.

The effects of the Second World War on the European economies were in many respects rather similar: human and material losses, disruption of trade, inflationary finance and at the same time rapid technological innovation, this time in such fields as aircraft engineering, rocketry, radar and, ultimately, the nuclear bomb, together with investment and expansion of war-related industries. However, the losses of civilian lives and the material destruction, especially of cities, were very much greater. Direct loss of life probably amounted to around forty million, of which more than half occurred in the Soviet Union, but within those totals this time the civilian casualties, caused by air raids and the extermination policies of the Germans, exceeded the military ones.

In terms of material damage, perhaps ten million houses were destroyed, as well as the majority of railways, bridges etc. in the East, and up to 45 per cent of shipping tonnage in the West. Much farm livestock and farm equipment was also lost, especially in the East, and there was widespread damage to industrial capital all over Europe. While, as in the earlier war, output increases were achieved in war-related industries, consumer goods production was low everywhere, and there were grave shortages of food as well as fuel in the early post-war years. For Europe as a whole, industrial output even in 1946 was only about two-thirds of the pre-war level, the record for agricultural output being somewhat better. But there were enormous regional differences, Great Britain and the Scandinavians (beside the neutral Swiss, Spaniards and Portuguese) having suffered least, while the worst destruction was to be found in Germany and Slavic Eastern Europe.

There were, once more, changed frontiers to be adjusted to, but this time there were also large population movements across Central and Eastern Europe. These had occurred in two phases. The first consisted of the forcible recruitment of servile labour and the large-scale expulsions by the German conquerors of the Slavic population, together with the flight of population ahead of their armies during the war. The second took place after the war, and consisted of the return to their homes of the displaced persons who had been uprooted by the Germans during the war, together with the Germans fleeing or expelled, in turn, from Poland and Czechoslovakia.

The Problems of Post-war Europe, the Great Depression and the Recovery

We may now return to the First World War and its consequences. Not all the after-effects of the war were immediately obvious. The disruption caused to the world's economic development and trading links had gone deeper than had been thought in the attempted rush to normalcy in the years 1918–20. It is generally accepted that the halting and patchy economic recovery of the 1920s and the exceptional depression of the early 1930s were not unconnected with the after-effects of the Great War.

There were complex interrelationships, some of which are not fully understood even today. We may begin with the consequences of war finance. Every belligerent country financed the war partly by borrowing, which led to inflation as well as large claims against the state at the end of the war. Inflation rates differed greatly, as did the ability of governments to return to balanced budgets; and, having gone off gold during the war, European countries achieved their return to a gold base by differing rates of deflation or devaluation of their currency. Though the gold standard was generally restored by 1925–8, the period of adjustment and insecurity had served to interrupt trade and employment.

Two of the largest economies, Britain and Germany, were among those carrying a high level of unemployment even in the 1920s. In the British case, the reason lay in the exceptionally severe deflation induced by the authorities, who were eager to depress prices and raise the value of the pound sterling back to its pre-war ratio with the (gold) dollar. The cost of this vain quest to return to the golden pre-war age in which London would once more be the centre of the world financial system was very high in lost output and employment. For Germany, the causes were somewhat different. For together with Austria, Hungary and several other countries, she had suffered a runaway inflation which in the German case had raised prices a milliardfold when they peaked in 1923, and had led to a widespread loss of both real and nominal capital and savings. With capital scarce, interest rates had to be high to attract foreign, mostly American, capital in the years which followed.

The German case illustrates another post-war problem. The victorious countries were left with large foreign debts, mainly to the USA which had been the main lender, though the United Kingdom had also lent much abroad – more, in fact, than she had received from the Americans. Germany, on the other hand, was left with the obligation to pay large reparations year by year without knowing what the ultimate total was to be, as part of the peace treaty. The German payments to France and Belgium, the main beneficiaries of the reparations, would have allowed them to pay their debts, in turn, to the USA and Britain, but Germany was extremely reluctant to meet her reparation targets: in fact, her hyper-inflation of 1923 was in part induced by governmental policies designed to show that she was not in a position to do so. Ultimately, it was American loans to Germany, largely by private bankers and investors, which provided the foreign currency for Germany to set the cycle of payments going in the later 1920s. But this turned out to be a highly vulnerable arrangement. When the American flow of investments to Germany dried up, first because of overspeculation, and later because of crisis in the USA, the circle of payments was broken, leading to defaults and a banking crisis in Germany which greatly aggravated the slump which set in during 1929.

Another effect of the war was an expansion of production overseas, particularly of foodstuffs, to fill the gap caused by reduced output in Europe. As soon as European capacity recovered, there was therefore a world overcapacity of such produce as wheat, to which were added overproduction of coffee, metals and other commodities. There was also overproduction of coal in Europe and a temporary overcapacity in industries expanded beyond peacetime needs for war purposes, such as shipbuilding.

Several overseas countries had been dependent on the export of these commodities in order to acquire foreign currency with which to pay for imports, and as the demand for them declined, they had to come down in price. To some extent, this was a normal aspect of the downward phase of a long wave: as world prices declined, the prices of food and raw materials fell faster than the prices of manufactures: to use the technical term, the terms of trade between primary commodities and industrial products changed in favour of the latter. The consequences of the opening of the price scissors were serious in the 1920s; they were to become catastrophic in the early 1930s.

As these price changes made Europe's overseas suppliers poorer, they were less able to buy European products. Also, many were indebted to Europeans who had lent them money in the past, and as prices fell, the burden of debt interest and repayment, fixed in terms of money, increased. This led to further poverty and bankruptcies overseas.

In Europe, falling import prices helped to raise real standards of living, at least of those in employment, in the industrial countries. This was a positive effect. But the favourable price movement, and the poverty among Europe's overseas customers, meant that fewer goods could be exported to them, and this aggravated the unemployment problem in Europe: thus, as one set of trading partners worked harder and got poorer, the other set became better off in terms of incomes, but suffered widespread unemployment.

All of these effects had also been observed at similar stages in the trade cycle before 1914, but the lingering consequences of the war greatly aggravated them. There were also additional factors to make the economies more vulnerable and the depression worse. Countries had learned to manipulate their currencies and thus prevent such relief as had in earlier trade cycles been brought about by monetary adjustment. As noted above, they became more sophisticated in obstructing imports.

Also, whereas before 1914 the pressure on employment in Europe could be eased by large-scale emigration to the empty lands overseas, one overseas country after another now closed its borders to free immigration. At the same time, more effective and widespread trade unionism, as well as expanding state welfare provisions, both of which were in part the result of the war and in part called forth by higher unemployment rates and the fear of revolution, meant that the cutting of money wages which in earlier ages had eased the price deflation at certain stages of the trade cycle, had become more difficult.

There was a mild boom in the years to 1929, but by the end of that year a financial crisis, set off by a stock exchange crash of unexampled ferocity in New York, heralded the downturn. The 'depression' set in, marked by unparalleled losses of output and employment. Between 1929 and 1932, the worst year, gross domestic product (GDP) in Austria fell by 22.5%, in Czechoslovakia by 18.2%, in Germany by 15.7% and in France by 11.0%; industrial production declined in the same countries by 34.3%, 26.5%, 40.8% and 25.6%, respectively.[5] In Britain, with losses of 5.8% and 11.4%, and in Scandinavia, the decline was less drastic but still extremely serious by previous standards. Unemployment was worst in Germany, reaching 6 million in 1933, with Britain at 2.3 million, and Italy at 1 million. France peaked in 1936 at under half a million. These were official figures, understating the actual numbers of people seeking work but not registered for one reason or another. Also, the local impact was usually much greater, for example in northern France and the Italian northern industrial cities, in Saxony, the Ruhr or Berlin in Germany, in the Walloon country in Belgium, or in south Wales or the north-east in Britain. There, unemployment rates might reach one-third or even one-half of the potential work force. It should be added that the overall loss of jobs and the decline in production were worse in the USA than in Europe.

The losses did not merely consist of output foregone, and of lower income streams flowing into family households. To suffer poverty was bad enough, but the loss of a job and enforced idleness day after day was, in addition, a traumatic and demoralizing experience for millions of people, aggravated by the recognition that in such a widespread slump there was little hope for most of them of finding jobs soon.

Social and political tensions were inevitable. In Germany, the social fabric was sufficiently damaged to permit a party which denounced the most elementary canons of civilized behaviour to take power; Italy already had a fascist government; and society was also under strain in France and Belgium. Spain, Portugal and much of Eastern Europe

⁵ Derek H. Aldcroft, *The European Economy 1914–1970* (London, 1978), p. 81.

turned to brutal dictatorships as well, though in their case the slump played a less direct part in that development. The mass psychosis deliberately induced by populist parties and governments; the effective use of national hatreds and the charisma of dictatorial leaders; the street violence of paramilitary gangs; the belief that there was a quick fix for economic sufferings but some wicked conspiracy preventing its use – these and other irrational aspects of the political life in the depression years owed much to wartime experiences, but they were also furthered by the new technical means of mass communication, especially the radio and the cheap press.

Recovery began in 1933 in most countries, later in France where the nadir of employment was delayed until 1936. To some extent this was due to the natural effects of the need to replenish run-down stocks and deteriorating capital equipment and housing. Partly it was due to government action: less, perhaps, because that was consciously geared to help the economies towards recovery than because governments ceased their deflationary and other directly harmful policies. In Germany output and employment recovered much faster than elsewhere, largely because of the Hitler government's refusal to listen to orthodox economic opinion, but partly also because of a rearmament drive backed by firm controls over wage levels and imports. Sweden was possibly the only country in which the government attempted to deal with the economic crisis by maintaining rather than by cutting incomes, though it may be going too far to argue, as is sometimes done, that that amounted to a conscious anticipation of a 'Keynesian'* employment policy.

As conditions improved, trading restrictions were eased. The USA, Britain and France agreed in 1936 to abstain from making unilateral changes in the value of their currencies in order to snatch a temporary trade advantage; Germany and the Soviet Union had, in any case, firm government controls over exchange rates and foreign trade. Bilateral trade agreements were increasingly aimed at expanding, rather than restricting trade.

By 1937 a modest boom had developed. Germany's industrial output, driven by rearmament policies, had reached a level of 31.6% over the previous peak of 1929; in the United Kingdom, the peak of industrial production in 1937/8 was 35.4% above 1929; in Sweden it was 53.8%, in Belgium 3.7%, while France was still at 11.8% below the earlier peak. Unemployment had virtually disappeared in Germany, being returned at 2.7% of the labour force in 1937 and 1.3% in 1938, but it was still 5.0% in Italy, 7.7% in the United Kingdom, 3.7% (1938) in France and 13.7% in Austria.[6]

[6] Angus Maddison, *Phases of Capitalist Development* (Oxford, 1982), p. 206.

By traditional standards this was a very weak boom, and it faltered and began to decline again in 1938: unemployment rates rose once more in Belgium and the United Kingdom, as well as the USA, though not elsewhere in Europe. That decline was arrested in the industrialized countries of Europe by rearmament and the rapid conversion to a war economy in 1939.

There was a good deal of post-war planning in the war years in Britain and the USA, as well as among the European governments-in-exile: conscious of the mistakes made in the inter-war years, they were determined to avoid falling into the same errors. On the political plane, a series of international organizations bears witness to that determination. On the economic plane there were positive results, too. On an individual-country basis, Keynesian policies avoided for at least one generation the kind of disastrous unemployment which so damaged pre-war society. On the international plane, organizations beginning with Bretton Woods and GATT and culminating in the European Union represented the attempts to solve economic problems by co-operation rather than by the beggar-my-neighbour methods of the past.

3

The State and the Development of Social Welfare

Rodney Lowe

The growth of government was one of the outstanding features of European society between 1871 and 1945. Its analysis, however, is both frustrating and exciting for the historian. It is frustrating because, as the first section of this chapter will demonstrate, there are no accurate measures of government growth – let alone the evidence to make detailed comparisons between countries. Nonetheless it is exciting because so dramatic a change raises fundamental questions about the nature of each European country; and it has thus attracted, as the second section will show, a wide range of competing interpretations. As with all historical controversies, there is no simple answer. Everyone must decide for themselves which selection of evidence and which explanation is the most convincing.

The development of social welfare is far from the only explanation for government growth. Indeed historians have been slow to acknowledge its significance. They have preferred to concentrate instead on more overt phenomena such as mobilization for war or the drive of totalitarian regimes, such as Germany and the USSR in the 1930s, to control all aspects of society. To an extent such caution is justified because it was only after 1945 that 'welfare states' were established in Western Europe. Consequently it was only then that the defining criterion of membership – or 'citizenship' – of a given country became the right to government-provided social services rather than the duty to undertake military service or to obey national laws. Post-war welfare states, however, merely systematized earlier initiatives by which governments had provided services, such as education, or sought to guarantee a minimum level of subsistence for all through, for example, old age pensions; and it was these initiatives, at the end of the nineteenth century, which had first forced modern societies to reconsider the fundamental question of where responsibility for individual welfare ultimately lay. Did it lie with the individuals themselves, their families, the neighbourhood, charity, mutual associations (such as trade unions),

Table 3.1 Total and central government expenditure as a percentage of GDP

	United Kingdom			Germany			France			Sweden		
	Total gov't	Central gov't	Central %[a]	Total gov't	Central gov't	Central %	Total gov't	Central gov't	Central %	Total gov't	Central gov't	Central %
1890	9	6	62	13	4	34	–	–	–	–	6	–
1913	13	7	55	17	6	35	–	–	–	10	5	52
1924	24	16	67	22	10	45	29	25	84	15	7	49
1930	25	16	63	29	16	54	22	16	73	14	7	48
1938	29	19	67	37	29	79	29	22	76	18	10	54
1950	35	27	77	–	17	54	–	–	–	23	15	70

[a]Percentage of total government expenditure spent by central government.
For Germany, the figures given for 1924 are in fact for 1925; for France, the figures for 1924 and 1930 refer to 1923 and 1929; for Sweden the 1938 figures are for 1936. All figures are rounded up.
Source: P. Flora, *State, Economy and Society in Western Europe* (Berlin, 1983), vol. 1, ch. 8

employers, local government or the central state? If it were not the responsibility of individuals, what obligations did they incur in return for outside help? If this outside help were to be provided by central government, what did this signify not just for the size of government but for individual freedom and for regional or local autonomy?

To make good historians' neglect, sociologists and political scientists have pioneered the collection and analysis of data. Their principal object-ive has been the better understanding of present-day society, and so their main purpose in studying the past has been to find long-term explana-tions for national divergencies within a convergent trend towards greater centralization. Their research has also tended to concentrate on West-ern Europe and on social insurance (which is easily quantifiable) to the exclusion of other 'core' areas of welfare policy such as education, health care and housing. Each of these 'biases' holds dangers for historical ana-lysis. Sweden, for instance, has been accorded 'Great Power' status by many social scientists because by the 1970s it was held to represent an ideal welfare state to which all other countries should aspire. As will be seen, however, the genesis of its exceptional development was as late as 1936 and any attempt to predate this can be misleading. Neverthe-less, this chapter will concentrate on Sweden and the three economic Great Powers of Germany, Britain and France. It is a restricted choice but one that still encapsulates the tension between divergent and con-vergent trends. After all, when government initiatives in social welfare commenced in earnest in the 1880s, Sweden was agrarian and mon-archical, Germany industrializing and autocratic, and France rural and republican, whilst Britain was already urbanized and had a long tradi-tion of parliamentary democracy. Why did governments in such dif-ferent countries embark on an apparently similar course?

The Growth of Government

The size of government is conventionally measured by its share of national resources. This information is presented in tables 3.1–3.3. Table 3.1 provides an estimate of the amount of wealth generated in each country (the gross domestic product or GDP) spent by the four gov-ernments between 1890 and 1950, subdivided by central government and by general government (which includes the expenditure of regional and local authorities). Table 3.2 offers a more moderate estimate of the economic cost of government by expressing its income from taxation as a percentage of GDP. Table 3.3 summarizes the percentage of the labour force employed by government.

Table 3.2 Taxation as a percentage of GDP

	United Kingdom		Germany		France		Sweden	
	Total gov't	Central gov't	Total gov't	Central gov't	Total gov't	Central gov't	Total gov't	Central gov't
1890	7	5	5	3	–	–	9	6
1913	9	7	4	3	–	10	8	5
1925	18	15	15	10	17	16	–	6
1930	18	15	18	12	18	17	–	6
1937	–	15	23	18	–	15	–	9
1950	33	31	19	17	–	–	21	15

For the United Kingdom and Germany the figures given for total government for 1890 and 1913 respectively are in fact for 1891 and 1910. All figures are rounded up.

Source: P. Flora, *State, Economy and Society in Western Europe* (Berlin, 1983), vol. 1, ch. 7

Table 3.3 Public sector employment as a percentage of the labour force

	United Kingdom		Germany		France		Sweden	
	Total gov't	Central gov't	Total gov't	Central gov't	Total gov't	Central gov't	Total gov't	Central gov't
1890	2	1	5	–	3	2	3	–
1910	4	1	6	–	–	3	4	3
1930	6	2	–	4	4	4	5	3
1950	12	6	9	4	9	7	9	9

Figures exclude employment in hospitals, welfare institutions, social security agencies and nationalized industries. All figures are rounded up.
Source: P. Flora, *State, Economy and Society in Western Europe* (Berlin, 1983), vol. 1, ch. 3

These tables have been calculated from the most ambitious international data sets compiled in the 1970s. They nevertheless have major
deficiencies. The relevant data are simply not available for certain years;
hence the absence of any figures until 1890 and the discrepancies noted
at the foot of each table. It is also difficult to select appropriate years.
The statistics for 1913, 1938 and 1945 are distorted by war, or preparation for war, and those for 1930 by economic depression. More 'normal' years from which long-term trends are conventionally calculated are
1910, 1924 and 1937 but data for all four countries are not always available for these years. This is especially true for France, for which a general absence of information reflects the relative backwardness before 1939
of its central administration – which, after all, bore the major responsibility for the collection of such statistics. The year 1950 has been taken
as the concluding date since it is the first year for which the combined
impact of both inter-war and wartime developments can be calculated
for all countries.

Conceptually, there are equally serious deficiencies. In some ways
the tables underestimate the power of government. For example, government greatly influences society through regulation. Trade patterns
can be determined by tariffs, working conditions by factory acts and
the cost of housing by rent controls. Such regulation, however, costs
little money and employs relatively few officials, and so its importance
is hardly reflected by the tables. Moreover, in social welfare many
payments are made in the form of tax allowances (by which government agrees to forgo some of its revenue) rather than cash payments.
Governments, for example, can reduce the cost of parenthood either
by providing a free tax allowance in relation to each child or by paying
a family allowance/child benefit direct to parents. The cost of forgone
revenue, however, has conventionally been omitted from government
accounts whilst that of cash payments has been included; and so government statistics rarely reflect the full cost of family support. Many
other payments go similarly unrecorded.

Conversely the tables can be said to overestimate the importance of
government. Most of the apparent increase in government expenditure
since 1890 has been in the form of 'transfer payments' such as contributory health insurance or old age pensions. Whilst in work, individuals have been encouraged or compelled to put money aside in order
to qualify for benefits when they are unable to work due to ill-health
or old age. Such payments do represent a degree of government control. Workers are forced, often against their will, to be 'thrifty' and to
spread (or transfer) their income throughout their lifetime. The government itself, however, does not spend any money (except in the subsidizing or administration of the schemes). Nor does it dictate how the

benefit should be spent. The more significant figure in economic and political terms, therefore, is the percentage of GDP that government itself consumes in the form of either capital expenditure (such as the building of a hospital) or current expenditure (such as the payment of nurses and doctors to staff it). Such data are not available for the four countries before 1950; but the potential difference they make can be illustrated from the example of Britain. In 1924, as illustrated in table 3.1, government expenditure was equivalent to 24 per cent of GDP. Of this transfer payments accounted for between 12 and 13 per cent. They had risen from a minimal figure (2.2 per cent of GDP) in 1900 to half of government expenditure in twenty years.

The figures for public employment are equally problematic. Because welfare institutions such as hospitals and social insurance agencies in many countries are outside direct government control, their personnel are not recorded as public employees in comparative data. Yet, like the employees of 'private' defence contractors (whose numbers also go unrecorded), their work is essentially dependent on government decisions – be it in the form of subsidies or legislation. Official statistics, in other words, seriously underestimate the consumption by government of national 'human' resources. In any case, what do the figures signify? Politically, public employment might create a significant block of voters with a vested interest in further government expansion. This was a major fear in the 1970s but, as table 3.3 demonstrates, there was no undue cause for alarm before 1950. Economically, public employment can also be damaging if it monopolizes scarce or skilled labour. As was the case in the 1930s, however, government more typically employs under-utilized labour or those outside the 'conventional' workforce such as married women. In such circumstances, it is economically and socially beneficial rather than harmful.

The other statistical evidence which historians require relates to the causes of government growth. The two most expensive categories of expenditure are summarized in table 3.4. This confirms that the permanent enlargement of government was driven by the relentless expansion of welfare expenditure rather than more transitional phenomena such as mobilization for war. Having long overhauled the other largest, traditional components of government expenditure (the administration of justice and debt repayment), expenditure on the social services in all four countries had comprehensively overtaken defence by 1950.

All the data on government growth, therefore, have technical and conceptual deficiencies which make detailed comparisons within countries, let alone between countries, hazardous. Nevertheless they do provide a framework within which broad trends can be identified and certain assumptions challenged. A distinct measure of convergence is evident

Table 3.4 Defence and social service expenditure as a percentage of central government expenditure

	United Kingdom		Germany		France		Sweden	
	Defence	Social services	Defence	Social services	Defence	Social services	Defence	Social services
1890	44	10	–	–	30	7	39	21
1913	54	22	77	5	41	14	41	15
1924	19	27	12	36	29	18	29	22
1930	16	40	9	41	32	26	23	25
1937	32	34	–	–	34	24	23	32
1950	24	40	31	49	21	32	27	39

For Germany, the figures given for 1924 refer to 1925; for France, the figures for 1913 refer to 1912; and for Sweden, the figures given for 1937 are in fact for 1938. The figures for Germany exclude expenditure by social insurance institutions.
Source: P. Flora, *State, Economy and Society in Western Europe* (Berlin, 1983), vol. 1, ch. 8

from the doubling of government expenditure in each country between 1913 and 1938 (table 3.1); from a similar tax-take of around 18 per cent in the three major economic powers in 1930 (table 3.2); and from the employment in the public sector of 9 per cent of the workforce in 1950 in all countries except Britain (table 3.3). Equally, there are clear national divergencies. Expenditure on social services exceeded that of defence in Britain and Germany soon after the First World War but in Sweden from 1930 and in France only after the Second World War. The transition of Britain from a laissez-faire to the most advanced welfare state in the 1940s is illustrated by the government's exceptional tax-take in 1950 and the transformation of the public sector workforce from the smallest to the largest in the four countries. In comparison Sweden, which was to succeed Britain as the leading post-war welfare state, had by far the lowest government expenditure in 1930 and was the most decentralized (table 3.1).

Explaining the Growth of Welfare Policy

A rich variety of theories has been developed to explain the expansion of welfare policy. There are three traditional schools of thought. There is the 'whiggish' interpretation which maintains that it was the inevitable – and desirable – consequence of modernization, as societies sought to adjust to industrialization and urbanization. There is the 'labourist' school which holds that it was the achievement of 'dispossessed' manual workers who either through their industrial power (trade unions) or political influence (as voters in increasingly democratic electorates) were determined to redress the inequities emanating from capitalist economies. Conversely, Marxists argue that welfare policy was a vehicle for class exploitation, with the ruling elite commandeering public resources either to bolster private industry ('social capital') or to bribe people to accept the legitimacy of government, thereby preserving law and order ('social expenditure'). Expenditure on health care, for example, serves both purposes by simultaneously providing industry with a healthy workforce (which it was reluctant to provide out of its own profits) and creating the impression of a fair and caring society.

Each of these theories has its critics. The first cannot explain why leading industrialized countries outside Europe, such as the USA and Japan, have not developed welfare states. The second founders on the fact that working-class or socialist parties rarely enjoyed independent political power before 1950, and that policy advances were often greatest in countries where Labour was weakest. Finally, Marxists have to explain the political and economic advantages which the 'oppressed' have often gained from welfare reforms and the existence of similar policies in Communist countries. Consequently, current wisdom is to reject such general theories and to identify the full range of variables that can influence policy. Then the relative importance of each to individual countries can be determined.

In each country 'modernization', in the form of a population shift from country to town and from agricultural to industrial employment, undoubtedly created a fundamental force for change. Traditional support systems such as the Poor Law broke down, whilst new problems arose such as urban overcrowding and the growing dependence of workers on a precarious cash wage. This led to a common set of social, economic and political pressures. It was soon recognized that society was becoming increasingly interdependent (with, for example, disease spreading from poor to rich suburbs); that poverty was not always the fault of the individual; and that there was a danger of 'free-riders' (people benefiting from public services without directly or indirectly paying for them). Hence on practical as well as humanitarian grounds, there was a need for ever more comprehensive and *compulsory* social services. Economically, it was increasingly accepted that greater state action was required to ensure adequate 'public goods' such as education and health (without which there could not be a skilled and healthy workforce) and to control 'adverse externalities' (such as pollution of the environment by industry). Government, in short, had to make good market failure in both a technical and political sense. In an increasingly complex world, markets often could not deliver services as efficiently as government or as quickly as public opinion demanded. Politically, traditional power structures also came under challenge. The urban concentration of workers resulted in their growing industrial and political strength: as they became unionized and were granted the vote, they threatened – or were seen to threaten – the power and values of the existing elite. Similarly, within the home, male supremacy ('patriarchy') was challenged by the different values and growing aspirations of women.

Each country had to respond to these common pressures in an international environment that was economically and – with two world wars – militarily competitive. Alert to what their rivals were doing, each had to act quickly to maintain internal order and to ensure that its workforce and soldiers were plentiful, healthy, skilled and well motivated. They nevertheless reacted in different ways. Each, after all, was at a different stage of industrialization or urbanization. They were subject at different times to major economic shocks, such as mass unemployment or population decline. The resilience of traditional support

networks varied, as did the prevailing political culture. Differences in
the size of the civil service and in the ability of government to raise taxes
also determined the speed of reform and whether government was to
provide services itself or to subsidize other agencies. Most important
of all, however, was the nature of the political party, or agency, through
which reform was effected. This was determined in part by constitutional factors, such as the nature of the franchise. It depended even more,
however, on broader social issues such as the unity of both employers
and the workforce and of 'right-wing' and 'left-wing' political parties,
because almost invariably the nature and timing of reform was determined by coalitions within these groupings. In defiance of labourist
interpretations, moreover, the decisive influence was rarely wielded by
the urban working class. As one recent analysis has concluded, 'political dominance was, until after the Second World War, largely a question of rural politics. The introduction of welfare states . . . was . . .
dictated by whichever force captured the farmers.'[1] The political allegiance of the emerging middle classes was also important. Assumed by
liberal commentators to oppose state welfare (because it increased their
taxes) and by Marxists to accept it (but only in so far as it guaranteed
internal order) they in fact gradually came to identify it directly with
their own interests. Inflation, depression and demographic change –
including increasing life expectancy, which increased the cost of private pension provision and medical care – combined to undermine
their sense of self-reliance. State welfare, they consequently realized,
could guarantee not just manual workers' but also their own social
security.

Whilst fundamental forces were encouraging convergence, therefore, differences in the social, economic, administrative and political
characteristics of each country caused divergence. Each country reacted
to the initial challenge of modernization in different ways; and these
differences then became entrenched because legislation, once enacted,
proved extremely difficult to reverse. Rather than providing a 'func-
tionally efficient' response to problems, moreover, this early legislation
frequently represented temporary compromises within fragile political
coalitions and had consequences which its authors did not intend. Just as
social scientists are frustrated in their search for general laws by national
divergencies, therefore, so historians in their quest for rational patterns
of development are confronted by seemingly accidental or random factors. This adds to the challenge of summarizing the evolution of social
welfare in individual countries.

---

[1] G. Esping-Andersen, *The Three Worlds of Welfare Capitalism* (Cambridge, 1990),
p. 31.

National Developments

Germany

Germany was both a pioneer of and an exception to the development
of social welfare in Europe. It was Bismarck's* introduction of compulsory national insurance schemes covering sickness (1883), industrial
accidents (1884) and invalidity and old age (1889) that propelled governments in other countries to debate and adopt the principle of social
insurance. The Weimar Republic in 1918 was also the first state to guarantee in its constitution a range of social rights for its citizens. Neither
of these initiatives, however, provided a lasting model for other countries largely because they were the product of a particular battle within
Germany between authoritarianism and liberalism.

After 1871 Germany faced the twin challenge of being a newly created and a rapidly industrializing country. Political power was effectively divided. Absolute power was vested in the Kaiser but its exercise
had to be legitimized by the Reichstag (the national parliament) and
shared with individual states and municipalities (with their own tax-
raising powers) as well as with a wide range of voluntary organizations,
long experienced in the provision of welfare. The tensions within this
untried system were tested to the full by the organization of the new
industrial workforce into unions, which were branded by government
and employers alike as anarchical and unpatriotic because of their rhe-
torical commitment to international revolutionary socialism. As Imperial
Chancellor, Bismarck responded to this crisis with a stick and a carrot.
To suppress unrest, all political organizations of working men were
banned under the Socialist Law of 1878–9 – although candidates of the
Social Democratic Party (the SPD) were allowed to stand for election.
Then, to woo workers' allegiance from the unions to the state, he proposed that all major risks to their income should be covered by a series
of insurance schemes, administered and subsidized by government.

This attempt to construct a 'social monarchy', however, was thwarted
by his lack of a working parliamentary majority. Liberal and Catholic deputies (opposed to enlarged government) united in opposition
with representatives of individual states (hostile to the granting of new
taxation powers to the imperial government). As a result, social insurance assumed a very different form from that originally planned. Rather
than being a unified national scheme, it was fragmented into a thousand
different ones administered by employers, unions and municipalities;
and only invalidity and pensions insurance was subsidized by government. Instead of binding workers to the state, therefore, social insurance

created a large number of autonomous agencies with a
in opposing any further expansion of government. Irom
also the SPD which found these agencies the most effect.
strengthening its organization with the result that – in direct c
Bismarck's intentions – it had become the largest party in the R&
by 1912. The party's acceptance of insurance in 1898, howeve.
signify the triumph of its reformist over its revolutionary wing. 1
its 'incorporation' did contribute to the realization of Bismarck's u&
mate objective: the maintenance of social peace.

Because of its underlying political aim, the scope of pre-war insurance was restricted. It initially covered only industrial workers, since
it was they who posed the revolutionary challenge. In 1911 salaried
workers were included, on more generous terms, but the poor – and
especially those in agricultural employment – remained excluded. Benefits were also limited. Accident insurance was financed and administered
by employers and, in the event, compensation was granted in only 15
per cent of cases. Short-term injury was covered by sickness insurance,
to which workers themselves contributed two-thirds of the cost. Benefits were scarcely above the rate of poor relief. Pensions were equally
low. One major risk to income also remained wholly uncovered at a
national level: unemployment. From the 1890s, municipalities experimented with labour exchanges, job creation and insurance schemes;
but each raised fundamental questions about the respective rights of
employers and labour, with which the imperial government was fearful of becoming involved. Despite Churchill's* claim that Germany
was 'organized not only for war, but for peace',[2] welfare provision at
a national level was therefore limited. Moreover, with its predominant
purpose remaining the reinforcement of the status quo, it appeared
increasingly anachronistic to those countries seeking to relieve social
need and to increase social equality.

A similar sense of anachronism pervaded inter-war developments.
The Weimar Republic sought dramatically to break new ground in
each area of welfare. Hence the introduction, for example, of the right
to membership of works councils, rent control and greater equality
of entrance to gymnasia through the abolition of privileged, private
primary schools. Innovation peaked in 1927 with the introduction of a
scheme of compulsory unemployment insurance. This was to be jointly
financed by employers and workers, but subsidized at times of mass
unemployment by government through emergency loans and a crisis
fund. Social reforms, however, did not win the Republic legitimacy. By
raising unrealistic expectations and creating tensions between federal and

[2] R. S. Churchill, *Winston S. Churchill* (London, 1967), vol. 2, part 2, pp. 862–4.

e governments, they antagonized those sympathetic to the Repub-
's social objectives. By failing to solve the economic crises of hyperin-
ation and mass unemployment, and by creating 'social rights' which
challenged traditional social order, they also branded it as inefficient
and unpatriotic. The term 'wohlfahrstaat' was indeed coined in 1932 as
a derogatory term to describe a country whose economic and political
strength had been destroyed by excessive social expenditure.

The lack of genuine change under Weimar was exposed by the
collapse of unemployment insurance following the onset of mass unemployment in 1928. Employers and unions, despite their joint administration of the scheme, had incompatible aims. The employers' principal
objectives were to reinforce work discipline and to cut social expenditure. Hence their drive to reduce benefit, as a prelude to reducing wages,
and to switch government subsidies from relief to industrial investment,
with the ultimate objective of creating new jobs. The unemployed, in
other words, were to bear the main responsibility for, and the immediate cost of, their own unemployment. In contrast, the unions viewed
joint administration as an extension of industrial democracy. Accordingly, they sought to reduce the insurance fund's deficit by increased
contributions which would have required, above all, employers to accept
direct responsibility for the relief of the unemployed. This fundamental
conflict remained unresolved and precipitated the collapse of parliamentary government.

The ultimate beneficiary of this collapse was, of course, the National
Socialist Party. Once in power the Nazis maintained the momentum of
reform, to the frequent discomfort of more cautious democratic governments abroad. Leisure facilities and working conditions, for example,
were greatly improved under the 'strength through joy' and the 'beauty
of labour' programmes; and generous loans and benefits were targeted
on those who performed 'faithful service to the German people' by
marrying and rearing large families. As labour grew more scarce after
1937, reform escalated to include further insurance 'rights'. As in Bismarck's day, however, welfare policy had an explicit political purpose:
the reinforcement of traditional, hierarchical order. Its main sponsor
was the German Labour Front, the organization charged – after the
banning of independent trade unions – with the 'humanising of class
and labour relations'.[3] Family policy was also designed not to liberate
women but to withdraw them from the labour market. Beneath the
surface, moreover, policy was both ungenerous and pernicious. Autonomous insurance agencies were allowed to survive but only under
'leaders' selected by the party. Contributions remained high and benefits

---

[3] T. Mason, *Social Policy in the Third Reich* (Oxford, 1993), p. 164.

low, whilst funds were depleted by forced loans to government. More notoriously, the education system was used for party indoctrination and the health service to 'purify the race' by the murder not only of racial minorities, such as Jews, but also of the mentally and physically handicapped.[4]

After 1945 liberal opposition to overpowerful government, which had existed in Germany since Bismarck's day, was reinforced by the experience of Nazism. The realization of its principles was also made the more possible by the survival, in however attenuated form, of autonomous insurance agencies and of local government's responsibility for education and social assistance. The foundations of the post-war philosophy of the 'social market' were therefore firmly based on the legacy of the years between 1871 and 1945. This new philosophy maintained that the market was the ultimate source of individual welfare and that government intervention should be restricted to the provision of services (such as education) and the maintenance of good working practices (such as workers' councils) designed to correct traditional market failures, such as the underprovision of public goods and bad industrial relations. Initially regarded as yet another German peculiarity, the concept of the 'social market' has since become a serious alternative to the Swedish model of welfare.

Great Britain

In contrast to Germany, Britain was subject to less intense social and political pressure at the end of the nineteenth century. The earlier onset and the slower pace of industrialization and urbanization had permitted the development of a wide range of non-governmental welfare agencies by both the philanthropic middle classes and workers themselves. Parliamentary government, although elected on a narrower franchise than in Germany, was widely believed to represent the interests of the whole country. A liberal culture also pervaded all sections of society. As José Harris has written:

> The corporate life of society was seen as expressed through the voluntary association and the local community, rather than the persona of the state. . . . More extensive government was widely viewed as not merely undesirable but unnecessary, in the sense that most of the functions performed by government in other societies were in Britain performed by coteries of citizens governing themselves.[5]

[4] M. Burleigh, *Death and Deliverance: 'Euthanasia' in Germany* (Cambridge, 1994).
[5] J. Harris, 'Society and state in twentieth-century Britain', in *The Cambridge Social History of Britain*, ed. F. M. L. Thompson (Cambridge, 1900), vol. 3, pp. 67–8.

These assumptions took their most practical form in strict Gladstonian*
finance which was based on the belief that the role of government was
to provide a legal framework which would enhance – but not subsidies
which might sap – individual independence and responsibility. This
belief was so embedded in government that 'orthodox' finance remained
strong after the First World War, in which Lloyd George's* antics were
widely seen to confirm the corruption and inefficiency of big government, and the subsequent granting of universal suffrage.

It is hardly surprising, therefore, that the concept of social welfare in
Britain remained relatively limited. In contrast to continental practice,
labour policy was rarely regarded as an integral part of government's
welfare responsibilities. There was a flirtation around the time of the
First World War with minimum wages, workers' councils and compulsory arbitration; but government was subsequently happy to accede
to a joint request from employers and unions for a return to non-
interventionist policies. Britain was thus among the last countries to
adopt reforms such as statutory holidays with pay (1938) and insurance
against industrial accidents (1946). Despite the presence of Keynes*
and the exceptional duration of mass unemployment throughout the
1920s as well as the 1930s, there were also few direct attempts by government to create jobs. Family policy, because it was seen to interfere
with free collective bargaining, was likewise restricted. Tax relief for
children was granted early in 1911 and the number of mother and baby
clinics escalated after 1918, but British family allowances were among
the latest and meanest to be introduced (1945).

In the fields of education and health, moreover, government intervention adhered to the original objective of the 1870s: the supplemen-
tation of private provision. By the late 1930s, over two-fifths of beds
were still provided by voluntary hospitals which received only 8 per
cent of their income from government. One-half of elementary schools,
catering for a third of children under fourteen, were also voluntary.
Local government was gradually permitted to expand its services. Once
separately elected boards of guardians were abolished in 1929, for example, it took responsibility for Poor Law institutions and started to
develop a system of public hospitals shadowing the increasingly bank-
rupt voluntary sector. In an attempt to increase educational opportunity, it could also provide secondary schooling after 1902; and by the late
1930s it was paying full scholarships to almost half the children attending fee-paying grammar schools. Nevertheless government intervention
remained limited. Many of local government's powers were permissive
and so were implemented irregularly. Exceptionally, too, there was no
national educational curriculum.

A picture of Britain's welfare services as backward and decentralized would, however, be seriously misleading. Some were in fact pioneering and highly centralized. The 1942 Beveridge* Report, for example, boasted that in the UK social insurance was provided 'on a scale not surpassed and hardly rivalled in any other country in the world'.[6] Britain had introduced the first national system of compulsory unemployment insurance in 1911 and its coverage remained unrivalled throughout the inter-war years. The percentage of the workforce covered by pensions and health insurance was also only exceeded by Denmark and, in the case of pensions, Sweden. Each scheme was highly centralized. Pensions were administered by government from their introduction in 1908. The original intention had been to entrust health and unemployment insurance to non-governmental agencies; but the caution of friendly societies and the weakening of trade unions by mass unemployment resulted in the administration of the former being dominated by a few commercial insurance companies and the latter by government itself. In addition, following a crisis in unemployment similar to Germany's, the most comprehensive national system of relief for the uninsured was introduced in 1934 under the Unemployment Assistance Board. Centralization was also the exceptional feature of housing policy. Other countries chose to subsidize non-governmental agencies but in Britain local government was empowered to build and manage public 'council' housing. By 1939, 12 per cent of housing stock was consequently owned by government whereas the comparable figure for Germany and France was under 1 per cent.

In these two policy areas of social security and housing, therefore, lay the germ of a fundamental change which was to transform Britain from a 'highly localized, amateur, voluntaristic, and intimate' nineteenth-century society into the 'most uniform, centralized, bureaucratic and public' of post-war welfare states.[7] What caused this remarkable transformation? As in Germany, part of the answer unquestionably lies in the use of welfare policy to reinforce the existing political and social order. For example, the burst of reforms under the 1906–14 Liberal government coincided with the rise of the Labour Party and exceptional industrial militancy; and the expansion of unemployment insurance and council housing in 1920 similarly coincided with serious post-war unrest. A reluctance in certain government circles to entrust trade unions with the administration of unemployment insurance and an eagerness

---

[6] W. Beveridge, *Social Insurance and Allied Services* (Cmd 6404) (London, 1942), p. 5.
[7] J. Harris, 'Political thought and the welfare state, 1870–1940', *Past and Present*, 135 (1992), p. 116.

to replace local poor relief with centralized unemployment assistance (once the Labour Party had started to win control of major cities) also suggest a disinclination genuinely to share power.

A conspiratorial explanation is inadequate, however, not least because parliamentary government retained public confidence and policy varied little under Labour governments.[8] Increasing centralization was rather the consequence of practical need and constitutional chance. Even the traditional opponents of state intervention accepted by 1918 that, in practice, government alone had the resources to resolve major social problems. They were thus prepared to accept it so long as it was used to support and not to supplant 'active citizenship' – the willingness of taxpayers to remain personally involved in social problems and the reciprocal willingness of claimants to use benefit as a basis for self-improvement and not dependency. The Labour Party, unlike the German SPD, also came by the 1930s to accept central planning as a means of remedying the 'chaos of capitalism' and of thereby achieving greater equality of opportunity. Constitutionally, central government had a unique opportunity to respond to this ideological change. Its powers were not circumscribed, as in other countries, by a regional tier of government – with the partial exception of Scotland. It closely controlled the legislative and tax-raising powers of local government. Its own powers to raise taxation also commanded a remarkable degree of public acceptance, in stark contrast to the situation in France and Germany.[9] The revenue thus raised might admittedly have been used to subsidize other tiers of government or even non-governmental agencies; but despite the absence of a long-standing administrative tradition (as in Germany) and the genuine reluctance of officials to extend their own powers, the Civil Service opposed this option. Subsidies were seen to weaken public accountability over the expenditure of taxpayers' money and to threaten both inefficiency and corruption.

The consequent irony was that the twin achievements of Gladstonian finance which were designed to force 'coteries of citizens' to solve their own problems – the establishment of an acceptable tax system and the premium on financial probity – became the unwitting vehicle for greater centralization, once it was accepted that neither voluntary associations

---

[8]   Social insurance in Britain was also exceptionally based on flat-rate rather than earnings-related contributions and benefits. This suggests an underlying humanitarian objective to relieve social need rather than a political desire to maintain order through reinforcing status differences between workers.

[9]   This is best discussed in M. J. Daunton, 'Payment and participation: The development of the British welfare state, 1900–1951', *Past and Present*, 150 (1996). Official self-restraint is examined in R. Lowe, 'Bureaucracy triumphant or denied? The expansion of the British civil service, 1919–1939', *Public Administration*, 62 (1984), pp. 291–310.

nor local government had the independent ability to succeed. This was the genesis of the continuing post-war tension between Britain's traditional liberalism and her centralized welfare institutions.

Sweden

Before 1914, Sweden was relatively backward both in economic and political terms. Only 16 per cent of the population lived in towns of over 20,000 people, and government was dependent on the royal appointment rather than a parliamentary majority until 1917. Monarchical government was coming under pressure but, despite the foundation of the Social Democratic Party in 1889 and a general strike in 1909, it was not from the urban working class. Rather it was from small independent farmers, well organized in societies championing teetotalism and dissent against the Lutheran Church. Their predominant ideology was liberalism, which countered any Bismarckian attempt by government to use welfare policy to reinforce the existing power structure. Indeed, so pervasive was this liberalism that the right to poor relief was suspended between 1871 and 1920; and when greater state intervention was later contemplated it was specifically designed to 'help people to help themselves'. Bold initiatives, in any case, were impractical in the 1920s because of unstable coalition government. Until the 1930s, therefore, Sweden tended to be a welfare laggard even in a Scandinavian context, looking for leadership to Denmark.

There was one exception to this rule, which provided a premonition of Sweden's later pre-eminence: the introduction of compulsory, universal pensions in 1913. This was a complex piece of legislation. All citizens were divided into three income bands and required to insure themselves against disability and old age. In return they were entitled to an annual pension worth 30 per cent of their total contributions. A 'living pension' would, therefore, be available only after 47 years. In the meantime there would be a tax-financed means-tested supplement designed to cost no more than the existing Poor Law. There were two main reasons for this pioneering acceptance of the principle of universalism. First, in the Scandinavian tradition, there was a well-established convention whereby investigating committees (consisting of civil servants and representatives of the main political interests) examined in advance any issue on which legislation was to be drafted. Secondly, as a consequence of another Scandinavian tradition (the introduction of compulsory education early in the nineteenth century) there was not only a well-organized but also well-educated body of small independent farmers. The committee system ensured political consensus based on detailed research. The committee which prepared the way for the

1913 Act, for example, was the fourth such committee since 1884 and produced an exhaustive 1,500-page report. The political leaders of the Liberals and the SDP (despite their respective parties' contradictory wish to defend thrift and increase redistribution) felt bound to accept its compromises. It was pressure from the farmers, however, that determined the Act's unique character. They did not want a fully earnings-related system since this would have reinforced the income differential between themselves and industrial workers. Hence the compromise of three income bands. They also wanted to shift the burden of the Poor Law from a tax on land to the general taxpayer. This explains the nature of the supplementary scheme. Above all, however, they did not wish to be excluded from the benefits of welfare reform (as in Germany, and as the SDP evidently wished). The principle of universalism – which later was to be a key feature of Sweden's post-war welfare state – was not, in other words, the achievement of a progressive SDP but of self-interested farmers.

The Act under Liberal pressure was designed to reinforce individual responsibility and therefore was not particularly generous. It was the intention that pensions should be ultimately dependent on insurance contributions and that the supplementary scheme should wither away. In the event the exact reverse happened. Over the next twenty years the supplementary scheme became increasingly generous, whilst the contributory system stagnated. In defiance of labourist interpretations once again, however, it was not the SDP which effected this change. Rather it was the civil service, seeking to defend claimants' right to benefits.

The SDP did start to come into its own in 1932 when it commenced an uninterrupted period of forty-four years in power. Its early reputation was established by a bold and apparently successful attempt to promote individual welfare by reducing unemployment – not by traditional expenditure cuts, but by Keynesian deficit-financed employment schemes, designed to increase aggregate demand. All other areas of policy were gradually reformed. A scheme of voluntary unemployment insurance was introduced in 1934, with additional state subsidies for workers in high-risk and low-paid jobs. In 1936 pensions were made more generous and redistributive. The statutory right was established to a supplementary pension, with its value varying between three regions according to their cost of living. A positive family policy was also introduced, including maternity benefits and loans both to newlyweds and to meet the cost of housing for large families. This burst of reform was not unique. It was paralleled, and even predated, by the programmes of social democratic governments in Denmark and Norway. It also had considerable shortcomings. For example, voluntary insurance was taken up only by 20 per cent of workers and it was not until the special state supplements to the low-paid were halted (ironically at the insistence of the trade unions) that the majority of workers started to join. Family policy was also resented by feminists, who interpreted it correctly as an attempt to keep women in the home, rearing children.

One of the problems for the SDP was that it lacked an overall parliamentary majority. It held power in coalition with the Farmers' League; but on social issues they were frequently in conflict and so compromises had to be reached instead with the Liberals. The League, for example, opposed unemployment insurance in principle (because it benefited only industrial workers) and the condition for Liberal support was the dropping of employers' contributions, which were designed to make the scheme redistributive. The League also opposed variations in the value of pensions (because its supporters were in the lowest cost-of-living regions). This disagreement actually split the Coalition and was made a major issue in the 1936 election, which the SDP won. The Coalition was duly reformed, more firmly on SDP terms. On family policy, however, it was once again in need of Liberal support and this resulted in a greater emphasis on measures to stimulate the birth rate. The radical reputation of the SDP depended, therefore, very much on its positive employment policy. Other areas of policy, partly because of its precarious parliamentary position, were by no means so advanced. This helps to explain why, as illustrated in tables 3.1 and 3.2, Sweden still appeared to be a welfare laggard in the 1930s.

France

France too was a laggard, which perhaps explains the remarkable lack of attention accorded to its welfare system by historians. Under Napoleon III, national pension and accident insurance funds had been set up in 1850 and 1868 respectively. They were reputed to have inspired Bismarck. They did not, however, inspire further action between 1875 and 1940 under the Third Republic. The need for reform was less urgent than elsewhere because the relatively slow of pace of industrialization and the continuing links between many industrial workers and the countryside prevented the worst excesses of urban deprivation and poverty. The demand for reform was muted by debilitating divisions between trade unionists and socialists. A succession of ministries, averaging little more than nine months in office, also provided a weak vehicle for centralized action. In any case, history had alerted all sections of French society to the dangers of strong central government; and the surreptitious subsidy of a complex range of private insurance and savings schemes was their preferred form of relief. This was particularly apparent when an attempt was made in 1910 to introduce a national scheme of pensions and sickness insurance. Within two years it had been thwarted by a court ruling that contributions, compulsorily demanded from employers, were unconstitutional.

Nevertheless there was, as with Sweden, one policy area in which France appeared to be a pioneer: family policy. From the granting of free medical care in 1893 to the introduction of universal family allowances in 1932, provision for children was more generous and comprehensive than elsewhere. However, as in Bismarckian Germany, this was the result less of any progressive urge than of a 'conservative crusade', as is well illustrated by the example of family allowances.[10] Employers championed their introduction and later dominated their administration in order to forestall a general increase in wages. They were supported by the Catholic Church, which sought to preserve the sanctity of family life, and by pronatalists who, since defeat by Prussia in 1870, had been greatly concerned by the size and quality of the French population. Although child poverty was unquestionably reduced by the transfer of resources to parents from all other wage earners, therefore, the fundamental object was not to help children and mothers in their own right. Children were helped as future soldiers, and the allowances were paid to fathers in order to reinforce patriarchal authority. Indeed it was just because the introduction of the allowances did not open a debate – as they did in Britain – over the redistribution of resources between classes and within the family, that legislation was possible.

The legacy of the years before 1945 was not, however, wholly barren. In 1936, the 'popular front' government under Blum* encouraged both sides of industry to agree to the Matignon Award. This established basic rights for workers in relation to pay and working conditions and, as with a similar agreement in Sweden, provided the essential underpinning of future advances in individual welfare. More importantly, it has been argued, a common national attitude towards state welfare was forged throughout all the tortuous pre-war debates and deals, which laid the foundation for rapid legislative advance after 1945. France, it has been written, 'achieved what Britain failed to do . . . social legislation became part of a developing and expanding idea of the state. Though the benefits of welfare were slower to materialize, in both a political and conceptual sense the foundations were more solid.'[11] Reform, in other words, was not handed down from above, impersonally administered and grudgingly received. Rather it formed an integral part of everyday politics, required popular participation and embodied

[10]   S. Pedersen, *Family, Dependence and the Origins of the Welfare State: Britain and France, 1914–1945* (Cambridge, 1993), p. 421.
[11]   D. Ashford, *The Emergence of the Welfare States* (Oxford, 1986), p. 79.

the principle of 'solidarité sociale' – the readiness to accept a need for the redistribution of resources within society. The sense of alienation was minimized.

The rest of Europe

The four countries so far analysed did not, as will have become evident, monopolize welfare initiatives. Other countries, notably in the north-west and east of Europe, were also pioneers. Denmark and Norway, for example, capitalized on the traditional Scandinavian virtues of consensual government, well-educated electorates and a working alliance between social democratic parties and small farmers to outstrip Sweden. To relieve the 'deserving' outside a harsh Poor Law, the Danish government was the first to establish the principle of subsidizing both a non-contributory pensions scheme, administered by local authorities (1891), and the voluntary provision of sickness and unemployment insurance (in 1892 and 1907 respectively). Norway introduced voluntary unemployment insurance even earlier (1906) and uniquely provided additional allowances for the dependants of those claiming sickness insurance after 1909. Following the economic crash of the early 1930s, both countries under SDP-dominated governments also anticipated developments in Sweden by rationalizing existing welfare provision and extending coverage further towards the principle of universalism. Meanwhile the Netherlands, under Catholic-dominated coalitions, was taking decentralized, subsidized provision to its extreme. The country was divided into rival organizations or 'pillars' (based, for instance, on Catholic, Calvinist or socialist interests) and all welfare services were channelled through them. Central government remained weak whilst citizens sought 'sovereignty in their own circle'.[12] This was the origin of the concept of 'subsidiarity', which was so to influence attempts to harmonize European social policy in the 1990s.

Such a concept would have been an anathema to the other major pioneer of European welfare: the inter-war USSR. Social provision had been particularly backward in Russia before 1914, although workers' administrative involvement in limited accident and sickness insurance schemes had been exploited by the Bolsheviks – as by the German SPD – to strengthen their own organization. How far individual social, let alone economic, welfare improved after 1918 must remain conjectural. Foreign experts were greatly impressed by the rapid expansion of education and medical care, and particularly by increased educational

[12]   G. Therbon, 'Pillarization and popular movements', in *The Comparative History of Public Policy*, ed. F. G. Castles (Cambridge, 1989), p. 206.

and employment opportunities for women; but, as in all totalitarian countries, these measures were designed as much to legitimize the state and to boost production as to enhance the quality of individual lives. Italy after 1922 was another totalitarian regime which sought centralized control over all aspects of society. However, the continuing strength of the Catholic Church ensured that here, as in other southern European countries, particular services – and especially education and social assistance – retained some degree of independence from the state.

Conclusion

The growth of central government was, therefore, a predominant feature of all European countries after 1891. It was driven by the social tensions arising from increased industrialization and urbanization, and the need to resolve them at a time when manual workers were acquiring – or threatening to acquire – greater political power. Each country responded by developing welfare services in its own way, influenced by common shocks such as the Paris Commune of 1871, two world wars and inter-war economic depression. Some sought thereby to control the newly enfranchised; others sought to empower them. Some sought to avoid social deprivation either by giving everyone educational skills or by intervention in the labour market; others reacted only after the event with relief policies. Some subsidized existing, voluntary agencies; others replaced them. The choice was determined by the resilience of existing support networks, the nature of national constitutions, the administrative and fiscal capacity of the state, and the temporary balance of power between different social groups at critical moments.

Many major developments were unintended. In Germany, an insurance system designed to maximize loyalty to the state evolved into one which constrained state expansion. Conversely, a fiscal system in Britain designed to minimize state intervention conspired to foster exceptional centralization. In Sweden, the original intention was to base a pioneering system of universal pension on insurance contributions, but it became largely tax-financed. Moreover, universalism – the guiding principle of the post-war Swedish welfare state – was the product not of altruism but of the vested interest of small farmers. Likewise in France, the generous system of family allowances which had been introduced for conservative reasons assumed a very different character in changed circumstances after 1945. The greatest irony of all, however, was that ever more extensive welfare policies emerged out of regimes permeated by liberal principles and a respect for voluntary organizations.

This contradiction alone raises the question of whether the evolution of paternalistic welfare systems (designed to relieve the poor) into solidaristic welfare states (providing common services for all classes) would ever have occurred had it not been for the shock of the Second World War. The development of social welfare before 1945, in other words, did not necessarily determine the creation of welfare states, but it greatly influenced their nature.

4

Leisure and Society in Europe, 1871–1945

Lynn Abrams

Introduction: Transformations in the History of Leisure

> Most of my grandfather's waking hours were fully committed between work in the pit and work on the land. In what time was left he relaxed at home; at weekends . . . he went for a drink. Drinking and gardening brought him into contact with competitive leek growing and flower and vegetable shows. . . . The annual visit of the fair, the village picnic, concerts given by the pit brass band or local male voice choirs, perhaps a trip to the coast, were additional opportunities for enjoyment.[1]

Much has been made by historians of the supposed transformation that occurred in the experience of leisure and recreation towards the end of the nineteenth century. Notwithstanding the evidence from the first decades of the twentieth century cited above, which suggests considerable continuity in the working man's experience of leisure, the final few decades of the previous century appear to represent something of a watershed in terms of the provision and participation in leisure activity in Western Europe. In 1860 *The Times* described developments in modern leisure as 'a great revolution . . . a great displacement of masses . . .'.[2] It has been widely noted that it was in these decades prior to the First World War that leisure and recreational pursuits assumed a character which distinguished them from their pre-industrial antecedents and which was to endure at least until the 1960s.[3] Industrialization, urbanization, capitalist entrepreneurship and state involvement

[1] B. Williamson, *Class, Culture and Community: A Biographical Study of Social Change in Mining* (London, 1982), p. 103.
[2] Cited in P. Bailey, '"A mingled mass of perfectly legitimate pleasures": the Victorian middle class and the problem of leisure', *Victorian Studies*, 21 (1977–8), p. 13.
[3] See H. Cunningham, *Leisure in the Industrial Revolution c.1780–1880* (London, 1980); and J. Walvin, *Leisure and Society, 1830–1950* (London, 1978).

alongside a gradual reduction in working hours and higher wages for industrial work determined that leisure increasingly became distinct from work, that pre-industrial amusements – often seen as barbaric, spontaneous and informal – were left behind by an urban population no less desirous of amusement but constrained by the discipline and environment of the industrial city. According to this view, the pub, the music-hall, the dance-hall and the working-man's club became the favoured locations for leisure in the industrial environment.

During the inter-war era, trends towards rational amusement, mass, commercial entertainment and state involvement in leisure continued, and in some cases were accentuated, until the post-Second World War period when, it has been suggested, the triumph of consumerism over the reduction of worktime brought about the 'dominance of the work-and-spend culture'.[4] Thus, one of the dominant narratives of the history of leisure is contained within a framework which sees the tradition, custom, spontaneity and barbarity of the pre-industrial era, epitomized by sports such as cock-fighting and bear-baiting, customary fairs and wakes and the practice of Saint Monday, being replaced by institutionalized, formalized, regulated and increasingly commercialized leisure of the late nineteenth and twentieth century, characterized by organized spectator sports, the cinema, the dance-hall and the works outing.

A parallel narrative interprets the history of leisure as a story of progress from leisure for the few to leisure for all, or what has been termed the 'democratisation of leisure'.[5] Working people began to believe that they had a right to leisure as entrepreneurs converted popular recreations into commercial activities and governments legislated for reduced working days and public holidays. The emerging seaside resorts and spas which initially catered to the leisured upper and middle classes became accessible to working people for excursions and longer holidays. Organized sports flourished, attracting more spectators than participants. Musical entertainment from the music-hall ditty to Handel's *Messiah* attracted singers and audiences in vast numbers.

A third major current in leisure historiography has been the placing of leisure activities at the centre of analyses of working-class culture and consciousness. Labour historians in Britain, Germany and Russia, and to a lesser extent France, have used working-class leisure as a means of explaining shifts in working-class consciousness and trends in labour politics. While this is not suprising, especially in the case of Germany and Russia, where labour-movement culture assumed great importance in the Social Democrat and Bolshevik task of raising the consciousness

[4]   G. Cross, *Time and Money: The Making of Consumer Culture* (London, 1993), p. 5.
[5]   Walvin, *Leisure and Society*, esp. pp. 60–127.

of the working class, the drawbacks of concentrating on the political impetus behind and consequences of workers' recreations and amusements are plain to see: obfuscation of the lives of workers who were not part of the labour movement, and absence of discussion of activities regarded as non-political, informal and part of the broader working-class community. Similarly, the largely British debate surrounding middle-class attempts to reform popular amusements and the working-class response to that – the social control versus collective class expression debate – addresses the political repercussions of the contest over leisure in the decades before the First World War but has little to say about areas of popular activity hidden from the reformers' gaze such as gambling and street betting, pigeon-racing and billiard halls as well as domestic amusements. In Germany this dichotomy of class expression versus social control has a different resonance since here both the ruling elites and the Social Democratic Party attempted to mould the leisure pursuits of workers. Attempts to lure workers away from popular recreations such as drinking, attending the German version of the penny gaffe, the *Tingel-Tangel*, popular festivals and later the cinema by providing alternative 'rational' recreation not surprisingly failed.

Whilst in a general sense these three approaches – what might be termed the 'taming', 'democratization' and 'labour' approaches respectively – are quite legitimate, from the broad European perspective these frameworks require considerable adjustment to take account of national and regional differences, cultural traditions, religious and ethnic differences and differential rates of economic and social change as well as the political dimension. The picture of a virtual revolution in leisure provision and experience must be qualified by the recognition that for probably the majority of working men and women in Western Europe before the First World War, leisure was still a sporadic and occasional experience, determined by an individual's work, his or her access to disposable income and the pattern of local calendar customs, as the excerpt at the beginning of this chapter illustrates. Also, the political dimension of the relationship between leisure and society which assumed major significance in the 1920s and 1930s in fascist and totalitarian states, and lesser but still considerable influence in all states throughout the period through public leisure provision and sponsorship of voluntary organizations, needs to be taken into account. Moreover, all approaches fail to take sufficient notice of elements of continuity in the leisure experience, the frequent absence of a clear disjuncture between work and leisure and the role of the participants and consumers in adapting traditional leisure pursuits to the industrial environment.

The tendency to emphasize transformative moments in the history of leisure at the expense of longer-term continuities obscures elements of conflict and negotiation which contributed to the complexity of the leisure experience in modern Europe in which the 'traditional' and the modern, the spontaneous and the organized, the rowdy and the disciplined coexisted. In Germany, for example, the survival of the traditional parish fair until at least the First World War, in the face of attempts by employers and local authorities to abolish this inconvenient remnant of a previous age which allegedly disrupted factory production, was in part due to the embracing of the fairs by the working classes and their demand for commercial entertainment and side-shows, which in turn stimulated local trade when the fair came to town. A similar process occurred in England as the traditional wakes of northern industrial towns became occasions for working-class excursions to the seaside. At the same time, festival culture in Germany and Britain was appropriated by local elites who sought to turn what they regarded as 'rough', plebeian occasions such as the Rhineland Carnival and the Shetland Yule celebrations – Up Helly Aa – into 'respectable' and therefore acceptable events characterized by ritualized activities undertaken by civic dignitaries in which the masquerades and 'guising' of the former plebeian events were sanitized, forming just another element of public spectacle.[6] Although one of the traditional purposes of these festivals was the momentary overturning of authority played out through the depiction of a world turned-upside-down, the festivity was nevertheless assimilated into urban recreational culture.

Currents in the historiography of leisure in different European states reflect both broader historiographical traditions – for instance, the history of *mentalité* in France, organized labour history in Germany, the history of labour and class struggle in Britain – and real differences in the organization and experience of leisure activity. In Russia, for example, it has been said that most leisure time, both before and after the revolution, was spent in self-generated entertainment as opposed to organized and institutional leisure activity, even during the Soviet era. The homogeneity of Russian cultural forms, moreover, permitted a high degree of cross-fertilization between folk and high culture.[7] However, it is possible to make some generalizations about developments in leisure provision and experience in Europe between 1871 and 1945 before moving on to a more detailed analysis of the structural and ideological determinants of leisure activity.

---

[6] See L. Abrams, *Workers' Culture in Imperial Germany: Leisure and Recreation in the Rhineland and Westphalia* (London, 1992), pp. 48–50; C. G. Brown, 'Popular culture in twentieth century Scotland: the continuing struggle for rational recreation', unpublished paper, University of Strathclyde, 1995.
[7] R. Stites, *Russian Popular Culture: Entertainment and Society since 1900* (Cambridge, 1992).

Firstly, by the end of the nineteenth century, but especially in the
inter-war era, most workers in industrial and white-collar employment
saw a decrease in the working week tied to the introduction of rationalization and a subsequent increase in the amount of potential leisure
time. In the years following the end of the First World War most Western European countries had introduced eight-hour day or forty-eight-
hour week legislation. Excluded from this positive development were
most agricultural workers and women, whose time was still unstruc-
tured or fractured with little obvious opportunity for leisure after the
completion of paid and unpaid work. These workers were also less likely
to benefit from legislation making provision for paid holidays. By the
eve of the Second World War the number of European workers entitled
to holidays with pay had increased to almost eighty million compared
with just nineteen million in 1926. According to Stephen G. Jones,
'shorter working days and longer holidays heralded a new leisure age',
although one must add the caveat that the shorter working day was
often a reward for more efficient and thus more intensive production.[8]

Secondly, by the end of the First World War the prevalence of 'traditional' or 'rough' amusements had declined, although they certainly had
not disappeared altogether. This was most noticeable in France where
bull-fighting and cock-fighting survived and even prospered well into
the twentieth century as regional customs were updated and commercialized in the urban setting. These amusements were being replaced
by institutionalized leisure such as drinking in public houses, dancing,
music-halls and especially organized sports. Again, rural inhabitants
probably witnessed this development much more slowly. Although
practice undoubtedly lagged behind laws banning public brutal sports
– Cunningham notes that in 1843 the 'Manchester authorities formally
prohibited dog and cock-fighting, bull and badger-baiting, a sign surely
that they still continued'[9] – the difficulty in finding places to hold such
sports meant their decline was almost inevitable.

Thirdly, although arguably leisure had always possessed a commercial element, this feature of leisure provision was accentuated from
around the 1880s, culminating in a full-scale leisure industry providing
entertainment and diversion for the masses amongst whom, with the
appearance of improved transport and communications, were included
rural dwellers. The cinema, spectator sports, fun-fairs as well as cultural
goods such as the radio, gramophones and paperback books and magazines could reach all social groups, forming a new popular culture of
the masses. Finally, as the state increasingly recognized leisure as a

[8] S. J. Jones, 'Work, leisure and unemployment in Western Europe between the
wars', *British Journal of Sports History*, 3 (1986), p. 67.
[9] Cunningham, *Leisure in the Industrial Revolution*, p. 22.

legitimate right of all citizens, it also began to intervene actively in leisure provision, direction and content. Sport and other forms of organized leisure were used by governments for the purpose of forging national unity, the cinema for public information; in the most extreme cases, all forms of popular entertainment in the public sphere were ideal forums for propaganda and instilling ideological conformity, with the National Socialist 'strength through joy' (*Kraft durch Freude*) scheme and the Italian *dopolavoro* movement the best-known examples.

Between 1871 and 1945, then, for much of the population of Western Europe and especially those residing in towns and cities, the *idea* of leisure and the potential activities to be undertaken during leisure time were transformed. New leisure industries consisting of sport, cinema, music-halls and dance-halls, excursions and travel were combined with new leisure facilities such as parks, zoological gardens, libraries and swimming pools often wholly or partially provided by public finance. This was the era of 'mass entertainment' when more people than ever before were able to enjoy active leisure, facilitated by concentrated urban populations, more leisure time and higher real wages as well as improvements in transport and communications and technological invention. At the same time, however, it should be noted that probably the greatest proportion of leisure time was still spent at home. This was particularly the case for married women but also for men and women of the middle classes for whom the progressive domestication of leisure became a reality in the inter-war years. The consumption of mass culture, then, became a major constituent of leisure and that consumption was almost as likely to take place at home as in the public leisure emporium. For example, while around two million people attended the cinema in Germany every day in the 1920s, by 1927 almost four million had access to a radio at home. The number of wireless licences issued in Britain in 1926 was over two million.

Although general trends in the development of leisure provision and opportunity in the industrializing European states can be identified, each country exhibited peculiarities which offer illuminating insights into national cultures whilst not substantially altering the overall picture. These differences are perhaps most noticeable in the realm of organized sport, against a background of a broad shift away from communal, spontaneous and unregulated games towards uniformity, regulation and professionalization. The French obsession with cycling, the British preference for football and the German and Austrian enjoyment of gymnastics suggest that national and cultural factors must be included in any analysis of the development of leisure in Europe. It is suggested that cycling took such a hold on the French people due to a number of factors, not least the mobile nature of cycling races, and especially the longer tours and endurance races which were accessible to a scattered

rural population who were able to spectate for free, and the utility of
the bicycle outside the recreational context. As Richard Holt observes,
'cycling became a craze around the turn of the century but its place in
popular culture rested primarily on its usefulness in everyday life rather
than on the active sporting possibilities it opened up for the common
man.'[10] Cycling as a sport was swiftly commercialized and profession-
alized, epitomized by the Tour de France – first raced in 1903 – which
came to encapsulate not just all the attributes of commercial popular
entertainment but the idea of the nation of France itself. Cycling, it
seems, was peculiarly suited to the political and economic geography
of France.

Schematic accounts of the emergence of modern leisure have recently
been supplemented by studies which seek to provide a more nuanced
picture of the socio-economic and political context within which leisure was experienced. Our understanding of the place of leisure within
modern European society is being refined by studies which place gender, poverty, class and nationalism, to name just a few variables, at the
centre of the analysis. It is clear that access to leisure opportunities was
determined by gender, age and wealth, that the role of the state and
political parties in the provision and direction of leisure activities should
not be underestimated, particularly in the inter-war years, and that mass
commercial culture was only mass in a limited sense of the word, as
the home and consumerism increasingly competed for people's leisure
time and money. In the following discussion the place of leisure in Western European society will be analysed by focusing on three main themes.
Firstly the gendered nature of leisure experience will be discussed, focusing upon the ways in which women's access to leisure opportunities
was restricted by both material and moral constraints. The second theme
will be the elites' use of various forms of leisure activity from festivals
to football in order to bolster a particular sense of middle-class identity
which was regarded as servicing a sense of national unity and identity.
Finally, the politics of leisure, both in terms of state intervention and
direction and the use of leisure and recreation by the European labour
movement, will be considered as one of the main identifying features
of leisure in modern industrial society.

Gender and Leisure

For most of the time her work and her leisure were fused . . . . My
grandfather would have a drink but my grandmother stayed with the

---

[10]   R. Holt, *Sport and Society in Modern France* (London, 1981), p. 102.

children outside. Once a year she went on the Sunday school trip to the seaside. She rarely went for walks . . . . The only occasions when she could step back from the flow of inevitable chores were the great ritual occasions of Easter, Christmas, New Year's Eve and christenings . . . .[11]

Leisure opportunities in this period were clearly structured by gender, as this quotation from a Tyneside mining community illustrates. Men and women did not enjoy equal access to leisure pursuits, partly owing to working-class women's lower living standards, but also because of time and moral constraints placed upon women's enjoyment of leisure which affected middle-class women too. Historians of women have recently drawn attention to the inappropriate and unsatisfactory work/leisure dichotomy for the analysis of women's leisure in the past. Women who undertook paid and unpaid work, who experienced a fracturing as opposed to a clear regulation of time and who probably did not regard paid employment as the pole around which other activities were structured, are to be found on the margins of a leisure historiography that defines leisure as time free from paid work. Most working-class women placed household responsibilities and care of children above all other considerations, so that opportunities for leisure were few and far between, whereas working men's leisure was often prioritized within a family. A man had earned his rest and was permitted to enjoy his leisure – which was dependent upon his wife's household chores. 'My family is an oasis for me, to which I return when the unpleasantness of life overwhelms me' wrote a German toolfitter in 1912.[12] Female workers, on the other hand, describe the home as a second place of work. 'In the evening when my dearest is beside me again what work waits for me', wrote a married textile worker in 1928. 'Cooking, washing, sewing, putting the whole household in order. 14 and 15 hours work are often on the agenda.'[13] Married women, then, serviced men's leisure activities by undertaking most of the housework and child care and by surrendering their wages for the good of the household. Women's access to leisure, therefore, was also restricted by lack of resources. Although it was common in working-class communities for men to hand over their wage-packet to their wife at the end of the week, some retained a significant sum of pocket money, and any bonus or money earned from overtime was often regarded as a man's 'spends' to be spent on drink, a bet or possibly a place in the stand at the Saturday football match. Contemporary observers such as Rowntree in Britain

[11]   Williamson, *Class, Culture and Community*, p. 131.
[12]   A. Levenstein, *Die Arbeiterfrage* (Munich, 1912), p. 277.
[13]   A. Lüdtke (ed.), *Mein Arbeitstag – Mein Wochenende. Arbeiterinnen berichten von ihren Alltag 1928* (Hamburg, 1991), p. 129.

made much of the allegation that working-class men were drinking and gambling their families into destitution. Certainly these predominantly male forms of leisure activity had the potential to be economically and socially dislocative and women could be forced to take extreme action, such as that described by a miner's wife in Duisburg who recollected that 'after the men had got their wages they were often drunk, and the wives sat at home without any money. Many ran straight to the pit and caught hold of their husbands so they didn't end up in the pub.'[14]

Whilst women's experience of leisure throughout the period was restricted by lack of money and time, there were also moral constraints on women's enjoyment of leisure. Notions of respectability and concerns about female sexuality hindered women's access to some forms of amusement and leisure activity. Until the First World War in most of Europe the pub was a 'male republic' with the exception of the presence of barmaids and prostitutes, although it would be misleading to claim that women never entered pubs or never drank. Surveys of pub attendance in England show that between 1900 and 1939 up to 36 per cent of pub customers were female in poor districts, and in Paris the lively *Guingettes* (taverns in the suburbs offering cabaret) attracted both sexes for music, entertainment and drink. If women were permitted inside, however, they were often segregated from the men by being banned from the public bar. While some women did drink they were often subjected to the disapproval of working men as well as middle-class commentators. However, by the 1920s in more middle-class areas it seems that a visit to the pub was becoming a popular activity for couples, who might call in for a drink at the conclusion of an outing.

If a woman visiting a pub was skirting the boundaries of respectability, dance-halls were also regarded with suspicion. Official attitudes towards lower-class dance-halls were prejudiced by the 'association of dancing, music, liquor and sex'; dance-halls were said to be thronged with 'easy women' and the association of women who frequented the dance-halls with prostitutes was a blatant attempt to place controls on female sexuality. Such attitudes were still expressed in the 1920s and 1930s although in the north of England young women attempted to evade their parents' restrictions by taking the so-called Passion Express railway excursion to Blackpool for the Saturday night dance at the Tower Ballroom.

During the inter-war period, with the appearance of large-scale amusements and entertainment establishments, one might have expected the expansion of leisure opportunities for women. However, despite the fact that the end of the war presaged an explosion in demand for amuse-

---

[14] Cited in Abrams, *Workers' Culture*, p. 78.

ment, women throughout Europe were exhorted to find their pleasure within the domestic sphere. At a time of demographic and moral crisis, women were seen primarily as mothers and housewives in the service of the nation, and thus active leisure, or what the proponents of so-called idealized domesticity called 'pleasure-seeking', was regarded as incompatible with women's maternal duties. Although it was almost always the case that women's access to leisure was curtailed upon marriage and motherhood while men continued to 'amuse and enjoy [themselves] with colleagues' and were still expected to 'have some enjoyment out of life – not just work, sleep and food',[15] in the 1920s the home became a place for both rational housework and leisure, and social commentators appeared to emphasize approvingly that for good mothers and rational housewives work and leisure converged. In one German social survey carried out in 1928, in contrast with the active leisure ascribed to men, women's leisure was frequently equated with child care. The leisure activities of one working-class couple with three children were described thus: '[the husband] regularly goes to a football club . . . the wife doesn't like going out . . . she mostly spends her free time with the children.'[16] Indeed, housework was often depicted by advertisers as a joyous and fulfilling activity. This is not to say that there was no easing of the constraints on women's leisure in the inter-war period; but it was mainly young, single women whose opportunities expanded with the appearance of a cinema in every small town. Whilst the level of female attendance at the movies has probably been exaggerated by historians, it is fair to say that the cinema offered a liberating experience for women. There were few barriers to female attendance. It was a relatively cheap form of amusement, it was comfortable, the programme times were convenient for all women – those with young children could attend an afternoon showing – and despite conservative attempts to censure what they regarded as sensational films and those that offended good taste, the movies appeared to offer women in particular some glamour, romance and excitement otherwise absent in their lives. 'The picture-house provides an escape from routine; it is somewhere to rest; somewhere to talk and make friends, and somewhere to make love for those who have no other place to do these things.'[17]

Throughout the period, then, the sexual division of leisure paralleled the sexual division of labour. Women suffered inequality in respect of

---

[15]   A. Salomon, 'Stumme Märtyrinnen', *Die Frau*, 16 (1909), p. 272.
[16]   A. Salomon and M. Baum (eds), *Das Familienleben in der Gegenwart: 182 Familien-monographen* (Berlin, 1930), p. 172.
[17]   Conference on Christian Politics, Economics and Citizenship (1924) cited in A. Davies, *Leisure, Gender and Poverty: Working-class Culture in Salford and Manchester, 1900–1939* (Buckingham, 1992), p. 74.

access to resources and time for leisure constrained by traditional perceptions of woman's role. However, during the inter-war years more
women did enjoy some aspects of commercial entertainment, especially the dance-halls and the cinema and the image of the 'new woman'
in the 1920s – financially independent and sexually liberated – suggests
that at least young single women were able to benefit from the mass
leisure culture of Europe's towns and cities.

Leisure, Class and National Identity

For both the middle and working class, leisure represents a site for the
formation and expression of a class identity and it is at the end of the
nineteenth century that a demarcation between leisure activities begins
to be established, as the middle and upper classes withdrew from former
'popular' recreations, as in the case of many popular festivals, or alternatively, tried to reform and regulate them, in the case of many sports
and musical and dramatic entertainment. At the same time, middle-
class appropriation of certain forms of leisure activity from the 1870s
on was carried out in the service of the national idea.

In Germany this class demarcation is at its most explicit in the realm
of public festivals. National festivals such as Sedan Day – commem-
orating victory over France in 1870 and the consequent unification of
Germany – and the Kaiser's birthday, as well as local events such as the
Bochum May Festival, were commandeered by local elites. Sedan Day,
for instance, was an occasion designed to promote the unity of the new
German Reich, but although envisaged as a truly national occasion
transcending class and confession, was a bourgeois-dominated festival
characterized by mock militarism and civic ritual. Local war-veteran,
militia and shooting clubs celebrated with much flag-waving, marching, cannon-fire and patriotic speeches while the working class was
often left to cheer from the sidelines. Similarly, the traditional Bochum
May Festival was appropriated by the local petite bourgeoisie who
used the event as a means of establishing their identity and staking their
claim to membership of the new German Reich in a town experiencing
rapid and profoundly dislocative industrialization.

The sports arena too, offered the middle and upper classes a forum
for the construction and expression of class identity which was seen
to be coterminous with national identity and interests. In Britain, in
comparison with the German petite bourgeoisie's appropriation of the
'national' festival, sport became associated with national strength and
Victorian virtues such as self-improvement, mutual reliance and discipline. Advocating what came to be known as 'muscular Christianity', the

English public schools were instrumental in disciplining and codifying the games of soccer and rugby football and they thereby 'inculcated the virtues of manliness, selflessness and teamwork'.[18] In turn, this middle-class association of physical exercise and manliness was transmitted to working-class boys via youth organizations such as the Boys' Brigade and the Boy Scouts. In Germany, Austria and France, the middle classes seemed to favour gymnastics, an activity requiring discipline and strength and thus contributing to national preparedness and fostering national unity and patriotism. Richard Holt suggests that the impetus for official encouragement of gymnastics in the French Third Republic stemmed from Social Darwinism and anti-German sentiment. Just as German gymnasts had regarded themselves as a 'regenerative elite' before 1870, after the Franco-Prussian War gymnastics in France became a means of exacting revenge on the victors, and in Holt's words, 'casual keep fit enthusiasts and amateur acrobats [were turned] into a disciplined national force.'[19]

By 1914 what might be termed the middle-class national leisure project, which consisted of middle-class appropriation of certain forms of popular leisure activity, imbuing them with ideals such as military-style discipline and self-control and the association of such activities with national identity and patriotic endeavour, would have run its course but for the renewed interest in leisure adopted by the totalitarian regimes of inter-war Europe. As we shall see below, the relationship between leisure and national identity was to be taken a step further with the state-sponsored leisure programmes of the Nazis and fascists. Arguably this agenda also had a much wider resonance. This is apparent in the national sports which developed in the inter-war years, in the activities of youth groups such as the German *Wandervogel* (rambling) movement and the Boy Scouts and Girl Guides in the United Kingdom, and in the increasing trend towards the nationalization of public culture in the form of national film companies (such as UFA in Germany) and, in Britain, the BBC, which has been called the 'most significant instance of public provision and management of leisure.'[20]

The Politics of Leisure

The role of the state should not be underestimated in any analysis of leisure provision in the late nineteenth and early twentieth century.

---

[18] Walvin, *Leisure and Society*, p. 85.
[19] Holt, *Sport and Society*, p. 46.
[20] S. J. Jones, *Workers at Play: A Social and Economic History of Leisure, 1918–1939* (London, 1986), p. 104.

Starting with attempts to control the operation of commercial entertainment establishments in the mid-nineteenth century through the provision of 'rational recreation' around the turn of the century and overt intervention and provision in the twentieth, public provision and direction of leisure is a constant theme. In inter-war Europe the state not only intervened in the leisure sector in order to provide facilities and opportunities for people to participate in a wide variety of activities by financing parks, swimming pools, libraries and community facilities, but in fascist Italy and Nazi Germany it attempted to use leisure for its own political purposes.

At the same time, leisure became an arena for political conflict and negotiation. For the European left, leisure was a site of intense struggle over control of the non-work time of the working class. While, on the one hand, it was recognized by labour movements that leisure was one means by which the dominant class asserted its hegemony, obtaining the consent of the working class by means of ideological indoctrination (via forms of popular entertainment and recreation), on the other, European labour movements, as well as insisting that all workers should benefit from shorter working hours and improved leisure facilities, also attempted to use working-class recreations as part of a broader socialist cultural policy with the aim of raising the cultural consciousness of the workers and strengthening their commitment to the socialist cause. In Germany and Russia, and to a lesser extent in Britain and France, socialist cultural initiatives comprising the establishment of sporting, recreational and educational clubs, libraries, festivals and musical and theatrical associations, offered workers not just alternative ways to spend their free time, but a 'culture of improvement'. The Bolshevik *Proletkult* was the most ideologically driven cultural movement, professing that art should not only be understood by the masses but be produced by them too in order that it might elevate their feelings and unite the proletariat. In contrast, the French socialist party provided little in the way of recreation for workers. The socialist sports federation (*Fédération Sportive du Travail*) was founded in 1908 with entry restricted to party members and it was not until the inter-war years that sport was recognized as a fertile area of activity and then primarily by the Communists who sought to counter the extensive recreational provision of employers like Peugeot, Michelin and Citroën. The German Social Democratic Party was probably the most successful in terms of the breadth of its leisure provision and the numbers of workers involved. A cradle-to-grave network of clubs and associations (*Vereine*) was affiliated to the SPD, ranging from choral societies, gymnastic associations and cycling clubs to chess and rambling societies and women's and youth groups. With a membership of around 600,000 by 1914, the SPD, which consistently criticized the patriotic, bourgeois and religious festivals of the German Reich, sponsored its own events. Socialist festivals, especially May Day, were conceived as a means of giving 'a public presentation of the alternative culture in symbolic and recreational form'.[21] The socialist festival then, was as much a confirmation of Social Democratic cultural values as it was a signal to the dominant groups in society.

Although the British labour movement was somewhat less successful in creating a labour-movement culture as all-embracing (at least of skilled and 'respectable' workers) as its German counterpart, by the inter-war years recreational activities organized by the co-operative movement, trade unions, Socialist Sunday Schools, local party organizations and agencies affiliated to the Labour Party such as the Workers' Temperance League, the Workers' Travel Association and the British Workers' Sports Federation, suggest a range of activities providing a wide variety of opportunities for cultural and class expression as well as enjoyment. Yet, despite the ideological aims of socialist cultural and leisure policy, it failed to promote a new egalitarianism in leisure, and, moreover, was forced to incorporate many aspects of popular culture into its events in order to attract workers to them. For the majority of the working class this 'culture of improvement' had little relevance to daily lives characterized by short-term need and immediate gratification. By the 1920s and '30s, it has been argued, the labour movement had failed to keep up and come to terms with commercial developments in leisure. In Germany the SPD refused to accept popular cultural forms such as cinema and 'trashy' literature, which they regarded as the 'poison of civilization' and the antithesis of educational improvement. In contrast the Communist Party in Britain and Germany genuinely believed that Marxist sport, film and theatre could help to undermine capitalism. In both countries agit-prop theatre, drama performed on the streets – 'a propertyless theatre for a propertyless class' – was seen as a means of reaching workers, and the German KPD bought in films such as Eisenstein's *Battleship Potemkin* from the Soviet Union in an attempt to counter popular cinema culture.

While the labour movement was attempting to direct working-class leisure activity by promoting respectable recreations imbued with the socialist spirit, state leisure policy had two main aims. Firstly, in the years of leisure expansion before the First World War, controls were imposed on forms of lower-class recreations: for instance licensing regulations were tightened up, police were provided with the powers to prohibit and control leisure activities, and in Britain Acts of Parliament were used to impose countrywide restrictions on particularly

---

[21] Abrams, *Workers' Culture*, p. 54.

troublesome forms of amusement. Betting and gambling, for instance, were prohibited by the 1853 Betting Houses Act and the 1906 Street Betting Act. In Germany, while the Reichstag passed surprisingly little legislation regulating the amusements of the common people, concern at what was regarded as excessive alcohol consumption by the industrial working classes resulted in an imperial decree in 1879 which determined that licences should only be granted if local need warranted another licensed establishment, resulting in a decline in the number of public houses in Germany.

The second aim of state leisure policy was to wean the working classes away from what were regarded as disreputable forms of entertainment by providing alternatives. This was also dealt with in Britain partly through legislation such as the 1850 Libraries Act, the 1906 Open Spaces Act which gave local authorities powers to preserve open spaces 'for the enjoyment of the public' and the 1937 Physical Training and Recreation Act, which provided for the 'development of facilities for, and the encouragement of, physical training and recreation, and . . . the establishment of centres for social activities'. Compared with the 1850 Libraries Act in Britain, in Germany legislation was less important, although the Prussian Ministry of Culture's 1899 circular to all local authorities encouraging the establishment of public, school and mobile libraries, backed up by financial assistance from the Prussian Ministry of Education, gave considerable impetus to what was already a powerful public libraries lobby consisting of organizations such as the Public Library Association and the Society for the Spread of Public Education.

In the late nineteenth century 'rational recreation' had been promoted in the form of public entertainment evenings in Germany and the Penny Concerts in Glasgow sponsored by the Glasgow Corporation. In Germany it was the voluntary associations of the educated middle classes which addressed leisure as part of a much broader concern with the welfare of the working classes. These reformers expounded a philosophy which combined social responsibility with humanitarianism and utilitarianism in an effort to outmanoeuvre working-class radicalism. Their primary aim was to promote harmony between the classes by raising the working class from 'coarse, sensuous enjoyment' which it found in the music-halls and public houses, to 'unadulterated, spiritual pleasures'. Such pleasures were to be found in useful and healthy pursuits, and public parks and libraries were key arenas for the promotion of the reformers' values. For instance, it was hoped that libraries would 'encourage diligence and thrift . . . domesticity and sobriety, awaken [in the ordinary man] his domestic instinct and love of the fatherland and . . . counteract the dissemination of morally damaging and poisonous . . . reading material as well as tavern life and coarse entertainment'.[22]

Throughout Western Europe a combination of legislation and financial and moral support for municipal and local authorities and voluntary organizations stimulated the provision of recreational and cultural facilities. In France in the 1930s, against the background of right-wing manipulation of leisure and especially sport in France's close neighbours, Italy and Germany, the left-wing Popular Front government introduced the forty-hour week and the two-week paid holiday, provided subsidized holiday travel and embarked upon a programme of public building of leisure and sports facilities. Indeed, the first minister for leisure was appointed, heralding official recognition of an area of social life previously neglected. Sports and recreation amenities were generously financed by the government and mass participation in physical activity was officially encouraged. However, the rather naive enthusiasm for the benefits to be gained from sport and recreation expressed by the Popular Front government was to be short-lived. During the Second World War the Vichy government similarly took measures to encourage participation in sport but the agenda was more reminiscent of those of nineteenth-century conservative advocates of rational recreation who saw leisure as a means to social cohesion.

In Germany, Italy and the Soviet Union state intervention in the provision and control of leisure was merely one part of a much broader attempt at social engineering and ideological control. The Soviet All-Union Physical Culture Council established in the Stalin era both provided amenities and managed a massive network of sports teams and clubs. In Germany the 'beauty of labour' (*Schönheit der Arbeit*) and 'strength through joy' (*Kraft durch Freude*) schemes were crude attempts to improve the status and living conditions of workers whose wages were decreasing and whose labour organizations had been destroyed, and indirectly to enhance productivity. Through the provision of social and sports facilities and the opportunity to consume luxury material goods, the National Socialists hoped to destroy traditional class loyalties and replace them with a new loyalty to the nation and the National Socialist state. These schemes were in reality little more than a continuation of traditional paternalistic business practices, epitomized by the Krupp steel company. In the nineteenth century workers at Krupp had been fed the carrot of model company housing, social, recreational and educational facilities, whilst they were being beaten with an anti-union stick. In the 1930s Germany's industrial workers were offered the chance to own their very own 'People's Car' – the *Volkswagen* – by

---

[22]   Abrams, *Workers' Culture*, p. 148.

saving just 5 marks a week, while others were offered holidays and sea cruises to Madeira. While very few went on cruises and no one received a car it has been suggested that the Nazis did succeed in exploiting a 'latent consumerism'. Although the number of workers and their families who went on holiday excursions – maybe to one of the new seaside resorts on the North Sea coast – increased almost five-fold between 1934 and 1938, this was not sufficient compensation for the sustained increase in work intensity demanded by the Nazi government in order to achieve its rearmament objectives.

The Italian fascists arguably went further than the Nazis in the organization of leisure, with the *dopolavoro* movement. By the mid-1930s there were already around 20,000 *dopolavoro* recreational circles throughout Italy, whose aim was to replace the traditional pastimes of the Italian people with organized activity promoted and directed from above. The activities offered to workers – sports, choral singing, drama, excursions and so on – were not simply to fill leisure time which, incidentally, had been increased with the enactment of the eight-hour day in 1923, but were designed to 'instil in workers a consciousness of the nation, a sense of duty, a desire for harmony between labour and capital'.[23] As a form of state interference in popular recreational pastimes, the *dopolavoro* encountered difficulties similar to those that the efforts to introduce rational recreation had several decades previously. The fascists found they had to make intensive efforts to encourage Italians to engage in outside activities sponsored and organized by the OND (*Opera nazionale dopolavoro*) while at the same time intervening in popular community activities such as *bocce* (bowls), dance and music societies and the like in an attempt to 'uplift' the status of these pastimes, imbuing them with the task of forming a new national culture and combating oppositional tendencies which, according to the fascists, flourished within these groups. The attempt to transform *bocce* from a popular working-class street game into a 'truly national sport' is just one example of the fascists' attempt to promote sport as a mass participatory and spectator recreation. Not only did sport have the potential to divert workers' attentions from the class struggle, it also promoted identification with the nation. Although it is doubtful whether either of these aims was fulfilled, one legacy of the fascist obsession with sport was the diversion of funds to finance sports facilities such as local sports fields and football stadia which were badly needed in inter-war Italy.

In Italy and Germany state involvement in leisure provided little that was new. Rather, fascist and Nazi policy tended to shadow and

---

[23] V. de Grazia, *The Culture of Consent: Mass Organization of Leisure in Fascist Italy* (Cambridge, 1981), p. 29.

manipulate existing trends in leisure production and consumption. These regimes did not try to halt the move to mass sporting events and commercial entertainment. On the contrary; they expertly used the new means of communication, the commercial entertainment media and the new desire for material consumption, and along the way may even have expanded access to leisure activities. The Nazis' recognition of the propagandizing opportunities offered by the *Volksempfänger* (people's receiver) resulted in the production of an affordable wireless and the highest ownership of radio sets in Europe; three and a half million sets had been sold by 1939 and listening figures reached just over nine million by 1938. The level of popular consumption of public leisure was fairly low in Italy before the intervention of the state but by the mid-1930s the fascists had opened up access to leisure-time pursuits and introduced Italians from all social classes and regions to sports, excursions, theatrical performances and so on. Indeed, possibly the only aspect of mass popular culture censured by the Italian and German state was the influence of American culture. While James Walvin writes of the pervasive influence of the American presence in the music and art of the inter-war years, in Nazi Germany listening to American jazz music was defined as an oppositional act and all American films were banned.

Some Conclusions

There is no doubt that in the period from 1871 to 1945 the potential for participation in leisure activities by the majority of the population of Western Europe had notably increased and the nature of those recreations had been transformed. Notwithstanding survivals of a 'traditional' or popular culture and long-term continuities in the leisure experience, the general picture is of a leisure that was less bloody and more disciplined, less spontaneous and more organized, and a leisure less consigned to the margins of what constituted political life. However, this transformation did not occur without a struggle. The above survey suggests a period of almost perpetual contest and negotiation between 'rough' and 'respectable', political and popular, the state and society. The advent of 'mass' commercial leisure in the 1920s and '30s may have widened access to leisure and introduced some degree of uniformity which facilitated some greater degree of social mixing in class and gender terms, but the increasing and simultaneous trend towards the domestication of leisure and leisure as consumption reified class differentiation. By the inter-war years time for leisure was generally regarded as a right, irrespective of economic circumstances. Although access to leisure was always determined in part by one's economic resources – a fact brought into stark relief in the depression years when time was no object but hung heavy with no income – by the 1940s and '50s the emergence of a consumer society meant money was arguably the most important determinant of how men and women spent their leisure time.

Part II

Political Movements and Ideologies

5

Conservatism and Nationalism

E. J. Feuchtwanger

Belief in progress was pervasive in the nineteenth century. Even the most trenchant critics of the prevailing state of affairs, for example Karl Marx,* shared this fundamental optimism. Progress would be achieved through the advance of reason, the spread of knowledge and the decline of ignorance. Ever larger numbers of men, and eventually women, would, through enlightenment and education, be able to participate in the political process. The act of political participation would in itself be an educational experience, pushing back the dark forces of superstition and prejudice. This was the view of liberal thinkers like John Stuart Mill.* Reason and rationality reigned supreme. In this prevailing intellectual climate conservatism appeared to be on the defensive. It seemed condemned to fighting a rearguard action through strategies of obfuscation or even sheer repression, but this could no more than delay the onward march of progress.

This commonly though not universally held view of the future turned out to be remarkably wide of the mark. Among the many factors that gave conservatism a new lease of life in the later nineteenth century, and that in consequence created much disillusion with liberalism and progress, was the newly forged alliance between conservatism and nationalism. It replaced the marriage between nationalism and liberalism that had seemed indissoluble ever since the French Revolution. The single most important cause of this realignment of ideologies was the successful unification of Germany by the actions of the conservative Prussian monarchical state under the guidance of Bismarck.* Henceforth nationalism, unrivalled in its capacity for mobilizing masses, was often to be found reinforcing the conservative forces of stability and order. Eventually nationalism would help to precipitate the first total war of the twentieth century, which proved highly destructive of the existing state of affairs.

By 1870 the conservative, monarchical order in Europe had already been under attack for most of a century. The French Revolution and

the Napoleonic era had thoroughly and irrevocably undermined the
ancien régime. The ideological challenge of the revolution had, however, also provoked a counterattack and there was now a broad conservative ideological current which included thinkers as varied as Burke
and Hegel. It was more than a counterattack, for conservative thought
was an autonomous product of Romanticism, just as revolution had
been a consequence of the Enlightenment. Nevertheless, in spite of all
the disillusionment that gathered round the revolutionary project, there
could be no return to the old order and the nineteenth century was to
remain *par excellence* an age of change, seen by the majority as progress.
Liberalism, nationalism, democracy, socialism: these were the ideas in
the face of which conservatism seemed to be forever in retreat. In concrete terms the European conservative order was restabilized after 1815
in the Holy Alliance and the Metternich system, more or less successfully until 1848. After the revolutionary failures of that *annus mirabilis*
the domestic situation in many European states reverted to the pre-
revolutionary condition, but the conservative settlement of 1815 had
been further weakened.

British Foreign Policy and the Tory Party

Britain stood somewhat aside from these developments. She had been
at the heart of the anti-revolutionary coalition during the Napoleonic
period. After 1815 she had continued to support the conservative coalition, the Holy Alliance, led by Austria under Metternich. As early as
1820, when Castlereagh was still foreign secretary, Britain had begun
to disengage from the repressive policies of the continental powers,
which even conservative British policy-makers, themselves committed
to the maintenance of stability, regarded as counterproductive. Under
Canning and even more under Palmerston, British policy shifted to
supporting moderate nationalist and liberal movements. Canning was
a liberal Tory, Palmerston a Canningite Tory, who in the party changes
of the late 1820s moved over to the Whigs. In his later periods in office
between 1846 and his death in 1865, Palmerston used his broadly liberal stance, even if it consisted mainly of rhetoric and gesture, to build
up his support in the British middle-class electorate. The British version of the combination of nationalism with liberalism was the belief,
not confined to the middle classes, in the superiority of the British constitutional and commercial system. This was an article of faith held
across the party-political spectrum. Tory governments did not in principle diverge from the foreign-policy lines laid down by Canning. When
Peel and Aberdeen, as Prime Minister and Foreign Secretary, came to

control foreign policy in 1841 they avoided the playing to the gallery, which had given Palmerston a reputation of blustering and bullying in many European capitals. They tried to maintain an amicable relationship with France, the other liberal Western European power, and sought to prevent differences with France from assuming too high a profile. In so far as there was a distinctive Conservative style in foreign policy, it was almost the reverse of what it became later in the century when Disraeli* donned the mantle of Palmerston. Under the Conservatives the conduct of foreign policy was cautious, pacific and low-key. This became apparent again when the Tories were briefly in office in 1858–9. The Italian *risorgimento* was at this moment the most important issue in Europe. British public opinion was undoubtedly in sympathy with Italian national aspirations and in favour of the liberation from Austrian control of those parts of Italy still remaining under it. Derby and his Foreign Secretary Malmesbury did not swim with this tide and were anxious to avoid the outbreak of war in Italy. Disraeli, as Leader of the House of Commons, fully supported this line. When Palmerston and the Liberals returned to power, their more positively pro-Italian line helped to bridge differences in the party and to bring on board the most important remaining Peelite, Gladstone.* In the 1840s and 1850s the opposition to Palmerston's interventionism and activism did not come so much from the Tories as from his own side of the House, from the group of Radicals around Cobden and Bright, sometimes called the Manchester School. Cobden developed an ideology based on free trade, internationalism and non-intervention. It fitted neatly into his domestic campaign against aristocratic government, which he regarded as the root cause of war and international conflict.

Foreign Policy after Palmerston

After Palmerston's death his policies of robust John-Bullishness went begging for a while. Stanley, later the fifteenth Earl of Derby, who was Foreign Secretary in the Conservative governments of 1866 to 1868 and again in 1874, had more passive and less interventionist instincts than almost any other holder of his office in the nineteenth century. The first Gladstone government between 1868 and 1874 was committed to a policy of retrenchment particularly in defence spending. The Prime Minister subscribed to some but not all of the Cobdenite agenda, but also had his own morally based objections to power politics and imperial acquisitiveness. He believed that Britain's greatness and strength resided above all in the advanced, progressive and productive characteristics of her own society, and not in her world-wide possessions. He believed that European Christian civilization was a historic reality and should impose limits on the national egotism of the states in the European family of nations. He also believed that there was an English-speaking community of nations and regarded without jealousy the rise of the United States as a power. In practice events during the first Gladstone ministry created unease amongst that British public that had applauded the assertion of British power and confidence in the Palmerstonian era. During the Franco-Prussian War, the greatest shift of power in Europe since 1815, Britain was reduced to the role of an impotent bystander. The Paris Commune, which was among the consequences of the war, frightened the middle and upper classes and gave rise to an increasingly conservative mood. Another consequence, Russia's abrogation of the Black Sea clauses of the Treaty of Paris of 1856, seemed to undo some of the achievements of victory in the Crimea. The settlement of the Alabama claims, in the light of future developments a far-sighted move, struck British public opinion as a costly surrender to an upstart power. There was not much the Gladstone government could have done about any of these developments, except perhaps the Alabama claims. Yet they were blamed and Disraeli was given an opportunity to don the Palmerstonian mantle of national assertiveness.

Disraeli's Domestic and Foreign Policies

In 1867 the Tory leader had already put into operation a strategy that was adopted on many subsequent occasions in the face of an apparently irresistibly rising tide of liberalism, democracy and progress. It consisted of the simple device of taking over the enemy's policies and adopting them as one's own. At the time it was referred to as stealing the Whigs' clothes while they were bathing. Many Conservatives shrewdly perceived then and later that often the sting of progressive policies, their threat to stability, could be drawn, when they were implemented under a Conservative aegis. This was, of course, not the sole or even main rationale behind the enactment by a Conservative government of what was arguably the most far-reaching enfranchisement of the nineteenth century. There was also the dawning realization, already demonstrated on the continent by Napoleon III and Bismarck, that the masses were more conservative than many Liberals had anticipated. There had been a Tory working-class element, many of them without a vote before 1867, in some English boroughs, where the locally dominant employers constituted a solidly Liberal faction. There was also a perception that the upper layers of the working class, sometimes called the labour aristocracy, were politically conscious Liberals, while those below them might well be attached to the Tory party. The immediate consequence of the Second Reform Act of 1867 was nevertheless the return of a Liberal majority in the general election of December 1868. In his later years of dominance in British politics Palmerston had operated as a fundamentally conservative consensus politician in domestic affairs. In a rapidly developing industrial and urban society this had created a backlog of demand for legislative reform, and the Gladstone ministry formed after the election of 1868 proceeded to meet some of it. The distinguishing mark of Gladstonian Liberal reform at this stage was a combination of faith in the ability of state action to solve social problems with a fairly strict adherence to individualism and laissez-faire in the methods adopted. Liberals of this period, indeed Gladstone himself, believed there was no moral benefit in doing for a man what he should be doing for himself. On the other hand the Liberal government boldly attacked societal problems, for example the need to provide at least elementary education on a universal basis, often regardless of what would later be seen as party advantage or disadvantage. By the early 1870s this phase of Liberal reform had largely spent itself. As over the management of foreign affairs by the Gladstone government, a degree of disillusionment and fatigue set in. This again, as in foreign affairs, gave the Tory opposition, which had never conclusively emerged from the doldrums since 1846, a chance to assert itself.

Disraeli took the opportunity, in an entirely pragmatic manner, to exploit this momentary constellation. In a number of speeches he sketched in a broad-brush way the programme that was to serve the Conservative Party for many years to come as a strategy of survival in a progressive age. At the core of Toryism, so proclaimed Disraeli, stood the defence of the constitution, the monarchy, the House of Lords and the Church of England. He accused his opponents of being intent on subverting and bringing about the disintegration of these institutions, and they had in fact supplied him with enough ammunition to give some credence to these charges. There was an active republican movement, more positively profiled than it was ever again to be for at least the next century. This was due to the fact that the Queen, in her long withdrawal from public duties following the death of the Prince Consort in 1861, had made herself unpopular. Civil list provision for members of the royal family regularly provoked considerable opposition. Thus republicanism had for the first time since the late eighteenth and early nineteenth century become a cause of some substance, clearly visible on the radical wing of the Liberal Party. It was given encouragement by the establishment of a republic in France. Many on the radical left, having seen a long stride taken towards political democracy in the Reform Act of 1867, regarded the abolition of the hereditary principle and of monarchy as the next logical step on the path to rational progress. As for the House of Lords, not only was it another indefensible example of the hereditary principle, it had already shown itself as an obstacle to progressive reform. It had nearly brought to grief the disestablishment of the Irish Church, for which the Liberals seemed to have been given a clear mandate in the general election of 1868. The House of Lords was to play this obstructive role again on several occasions over the next forty years. The large-scale private ownership of land, still the basis of the peerage, was already coming under attack. Finally the Church of England had always been seen as a bastion of privilege by the large community of Nonconformists, who bulked larger than ever in the revitalized Gladstonian Liberal movement of this period. The disestablishment of the Church of England was an immediate aim of many Liberals from the dissenting sects.

It was therefore natural that Disraeli should reassert the defence of these national institutions as a cardinal aim of Toryism. There was, however, nothing novel about it; nor might it have sufficed as a strategy for survival in the age of progress. The Tory leader therefore claimed that his party had a further aim: social reform to secure the well-being of the people. Admittedly he sketched this aspect of the Conservative programme in the vaguest of terms and briefest of outlines, but the large enfranchisement of 1867 allowed him to assert his own and his party's credentials in this respect with some confidence. This was Tory Democracy, something more in the realm of myth and image than a concrete programme. Disraeli's successors in the party were to make much more of it than he did. Added to this vision of Toryism in the domestic sphere was Disraeli's assertion that in contrast to the Liberal Party, which had tried 'with so much ability and acumen to disintegrate the Empire of England', his party was in foreign affairs the party of national honour and interest and of the maintenance of empire. This was more innovatory than the domestic programme, for, as we have seen, Conservative conduct of foreign affairs had been cautious and non-interventionist. It was also to prove more in tune with the spirit of the times in the Bismarckian and post-Bismarckian age than Gladstonian internationalism. It was to become an integral feature of the Conservative image in British politics for a long time to come.

Bismarck, Prussian Conservatism and German Nationalism

In Britain republicanism would probably have remained an episode, even if Disraeli and others after him had not proclaimed the monarchy as a central feature of the British national self-image. It might merely have been more difficult to organize great national celebrations such as the golden and diamond jubilees of Queen Victoria specifically around the monarchy. On the continent the stakes involved in monarchical government were higher. In France, Louis Napoleon had reclaimed the imperial title in 1852 and had given an influential example of how monarchy could be used to bring popular support to a conservative regime. Even Karl Marx was forced to contemplate the possibility that such a Bonapartist regime might at least temporarily invalidate the transition he had envisaged from capitalism dominated by the bourgeoisie to classless socialism. Such an authoritarian regime, so Marx thought, might, at least temporarily, play an autonomous role divorced from its class basis, even if objectively it was still acting in defence of the bourgeois class interest. Bismarck and perhaps even Disraeli were influenced by Napoleon III, though in Britain the absence of a large independent peasantry and the existence of a constitutional monarchy made the French example less applicable. It was left to Bismarck to demonstrate how a conservative, semi-authoritarian regime centred round a still politically powerful monarchy could be saved by an alliance with nationalism. Bismarck became Prime Minister of Prussia in 1862 because he was seen as the man of last resort to save the monarchy from a humiliating surrender to the Liberal majority that dominated the Prussian parliament. There was also an unfinished nationalist agenda left from the revolutions of 1848. The pressure was again rising for a more unitary constitution to be established for the German-speaking territories of Central Europe than that which had come into being in 1815. Either the non-ethnic, non-national Prussian state would ride this nationalist tiger or else it might well be destroyed by it. It was therefore an obvious strategy when Bismarck sought to meet these internal and external threats by a combination of resistance to Liberal demands at home while appropriating, as opportunity arose, the nationalist agenda abroad. It was the Prussian version of Napoleon III's slogan of order, authority and well-being of the people at home and the pursuit of national dignity abroad. By 1866 and even more by 1871 Bismarck had succeeded sensationally in making the Prussian monarchy, and the Prussian army, the control of which had been the immediate cause of the monarchy's travails when he came to power, into the heroes of German nationalism. The previously irresistible advance of liberal progressivism was called into question. Bismarck's success had not, however, consisted simply in squashing his liberal opponents. He had realized the nationalist aims which were also theirs and he had then displayed relative magnanimity towards them after his triumph. The constitution of the North German Confederation of 1867, after 1871 expanded into the Second German

Reich, comprised many liberal features, such as the rule of law, equal rights for all citizens, some separation of powers and thus limitations on the powers of government. In one respect it went further than many liberals, certainly the Prussian liberals of the 1860s, had wished to go in the direction of democracy, by adopting universal manhood suffrage for the election of the Reichstag. In classical liberal theory the extension of the *pays politique* had to be accompanied by the spread of enlightenment. Bismarck, Napoleon III and Disraeli in passing the Reform Bill of 1867, in their different ways and circumstances, had preempted and outflanked their liberal opponents.

The Market Economy, Free Trade and Economic Nationalism

While liberalism thus suffered a political defeat and conservatism was given a new life-line, economic liberalism continued to rule the roost. In Britain there was never any doubt that the market reigned supreme nationally and internationally. Free trade had split the Tories in 1846 and the split had ushered in the long period of Liberal political predominance. The predicted dire consequences for British agriculture and the position of the landed gentry had been slow in coming. It was not until the late 1870s that the general depression of trade, aggravated for the agrarian sector by the arrival of cheaper agricultural commodities mainly from North America, gave opposition to free trade a new lease of life. There were demands for reciprocity, the use of tariffs as a weapon against countries which put up barriers to British goods. A Fair Trade movement began to make some headway in the Conservative Party in the 1880s. When the agricultural depression became acute in 1879, a Conservative government headed by Disraeli, now Lord Beaconsfield, was in power. Nevertheless the Prime Minister made it abundantly clear in a speech in the House of Lords that a return to the Corn Laws was now no longer practical politics. It was to be another twenty years before the free trade orthodoxy was seriously challenged in the Conservative Party by Joseph Chamberlain's* Tariff Reform Movement. The challenge split the Tories and was a major factor in bringing the Liberals back to power in 1906. It was only in the wake of the Great Depression of 1929 that one can speak of the partial abandonment of free trade by Britain in the Ottawa Agreements of 1932.

In domestic affairs there could also be no question for a long time of departing from the supremacy of the market in Britain, whatever party was in power. The Conservatives, when they became a majority party again in 1874, enacted a programme of social reforms of considerable dimensions. It could be seen as part of a programme of Tory Democracy, of a more popularly orientated Conservatism, of which the Reform Bill of 1867 might be regarded as the first instalment. Consequently later commentators have often seen in these developments the genesis of a conservative form of collectivism, more in tune with the spirit of the times than a liberalism tied to laissez-faire and better able to compete with the fully collectivist socialism that came on the scene a little later. Historians now see little of such a deliberate ideological agenda in the opportunist espousal of parliamentary reform in 1867 and in the cautious and uncoordinated measures of the early years of the 1874 Parliament. Nevertheless Conservative propagandists made effective use of these measures to give substance to the image of popular Conservatism which Disraeli had drawn with broad brush strokes in his speeches of 1872 and 1873. It could be claimed with some justification that the trade union laws of 1875 were significant in avoiding in Britain the kind of collision between the state and organized labour that took place in many other countries.

The attraction of a working-class vote was in any case only one of the tasks facing the British Conservative Party in devising a strategy of survival. It was no less important to make the most of the increasing conservatism of the middle classes. Lord Salisbury,* a member of the high aristocracy, became the most successful Conservative leader of the later nineteenth century, possibly anywhere. It was not without irony that he bestowed upon this bourgeois conservatism, of the value of which to his party he was fully aware, the slightly contemptuous label of 'villa toryism'. It was in some measure due to the increasing domination of the Conservative Party by the middle classes that it was in the end the Liberal Party that responded more successfully to the demands from the manual industrial working class for protection against the rigours of the uncontrolled market.

Bismarck's Move from Liberal to Conservative Economic and Social Policies

British Conservatives were in the long run more successful than their continental counterparts in devising a strategy of survival in the modern age of mass politics. It was, however, Bismarck who had made the decisive moves to detach nationalism from liberalism. In domestic affairs he had, as we have seen, made concessions to the Liberals while retaining the essentials of power. It was above all of great significance for the future that the building of a unified Germany after 1866 and after 1870 took place initially under policies of economic liberalism. Building on

the *Zollverein* which had played an essential role in the process of unification, the new political structure enabled a genuinely unified market
to be completed. Remnants of the old guild order were swept away
and an overall legal framework for a market economy was established.
The necessary legislation resulted from a co-operation between Bismarck's government and that section of the Liberals who had been prepared to collaborate with their former opponent after 1866. This section
adopted the label National Liberal. These Liberals recognized that Bismarck had realized the national aims which had also been theirs, albeit
with methods and instruments they had opposed. This has often been
represented as a second defeat of German liberalism after the failures of
1848. It has been claimed that the German National Liberals sold out
their liberalism in return for their nationalism. In the longer run this
may well have been so, but immediately the National Liberals managed, through their collaboration with Bismarck, to accomplish much
of their economic agenda. The German industrial economy, the rise of
which was speeded by the political-legal framework put in place with
the help of the National Liberals in these years after 1866, is in fact the
one major feature that survived the disasters that overtook Bismarck's
political creation in the twentieth century. Germany remains at the end
of the twentieth century one of the world's leading industrial nations.
The co-operation between Bismarck and the National Liberals, as well
as his brutal disregard of legitimist susceptibilities, drove many of his
former conservative friends into opposition to his policies. Prussian
Conservatives felt that the new Bismarckian Reich was antagonistic to
the values of duty, hierarchy and religion which had distinguished the
old Prussian state.

After 1873 the collaboration between Bismarck and the National
Liberals gradually broke down. The main reason was the end of the great
mid-century economic boom and the onset of what historians have
called the Great Depression. While the concept of an economic depression lasting with minor fluctuations until 1896 is now controversial,
there is no doubt that the bank failures of 1873, starting in the Habsburg
Empire, ushered in an international economic down-turn that particularly affected Germany. The euphoria of the *Gründerzeit* (the time of
the founders of the new Reich) vanished. German liberalism suffered
an ideological and psychological blow from which it never recovered.
Many who considered themselves losers in the new Reich, for example
conservative Prussian landowners, the Junker aristocracy of which Bismarck himself was a member, wanted an end to policies based on the
free market. German heavy industry, still struggling to establish itself
in face of British predominance, became protectionist. A potential alliance of otherwise antagonistic agrarian and industrial interests against

free trade loomed on the horizon. These were some of the pressures that induced Bismarck to disengage from his alliance with the National Liberals.

He also had other, more political and personal reasons. His autocratic instincts inclined him to avoid too much dependence on any party. One feature of his collaboration with the National Liberals had been his anti-Catholic campaign, known as the *Kulturkampf.* The Bismarckian Reich, Kleindeutschland, Germany without Austria, had turned the Catholics, a majority among the German-speaking populations of Central Europe, into a minority. The Catholic Centre Party became the focus for various groups, also including the Polish minority in Prussia and former adherents of the dispossessed Hanoverian dynasty, who felt themselves at a disadvantage in the new Reich. One reason for Bismarck's anti-Catholic campaign may have been that he felt the consolidation of the new German national consciousness required internal enemies, *Reichsfeinde*, to pit itself against. Such tactics became increasingly a feature of Bismarck's style of ruling. In due course and in different ways such tactics also marked conservatism in other countries under the pressure of advancing mass politics. By 1875 Bismarck had to recognize that the *Kulturkampf*, which had cemented his ties with the National Liberals, had run out of steam.

The Threat from Socialism

There were thus many economic and political factors to account for Bismarck's change of course in 1878. The immediate reason was the appearance of organized socialism, a major threat to the survival of conservatism everywhere. In Germany the unified Reich had also led to the foundation, in 1875, of a unified socialist party, which afterwards adopted the title Socialdemocratic Party of Germany (SPD). Although this party was still in its infancy in 1878, two assassination attempts on the Emperor enabled Bismarck to demonize the Socialists as *Reichsfeinde*. He promoted an anti-Socialist Law, which proscribed Socialist organizations and newspapers. This flagrantly anti-liberal measure split the National Liberals and Bismarck thus brought into play a factor that was in many places and circumstances to help the survival of conservatism. The middle classes had been everywhere predominantly liberal in the mid-nineteenth century, but were beginning to feel threatened by the working classes organized in parties and movements dedicated to the supersession of capitalism by some form of socialism. As we have seen in the case of the British Conservative Party there was a more conservative mood among the middle classes. In Germany Bismarck steered a conservative course after 1878 and until his fall from power in 1890. Tariffs were introduced to protect both industry and agriculture. They also provided additional revenue for the Reich, still dependent for much of its income on the separate states. The bureaucracy was cleansed of liberal officials. In the Reichstag, Bismarck allied himself with the Conservative parties and with that section of the National Liberals willing to accept anti-Socialist and anti-laissez-faire policies. Only now can it be said that many German Liberals were willing to abandon most of their liberalism in order to support Bismarck and the existing order. The Centre Party, whose place as the most obvious *Reichsfeind* had, with the end of the *Kulturkampf*, been taken by the Socialists, also became a possible partner for Bismarck in the Reichstag. In its outlook on social and economic problems it was broadly conservative.

In the 1880s the Chancellor embarked upon a series of pioneering social measures, sickness and accident insurance for workers and old-age pensions. He was partly motivated by the paternal instincts of the aristocratic landowner that he was by origin, but also by the calculation that such benefits for the workers would 'take the wind out of the sails of the socialists'. Forward-looking as these measures of welfare were, they, no more than the anti-Socialist Law, could not halt the electoral rise of the SPD. The failure to find a constructive solution to this problem was a factor in Bismarck's fall.

In comparing the fate of conservatism in Britain and Germany in the last third of the nineteenth century, differences in social and economic development need to be borne in mind. Britain was during this period still more urbanized and industrialized than Germany, but these processes had been spread over a long period. In Germany, although industrialization had been underway well before 1870, it was greatly speeded up by the unification, in spite of the economic slump in the 1870s. The breakneck speed of the urbanization and industrialization in Germany imposed greater strains on her society. Bismarck's regime in his last decade in office had been thoroughly conservative, but he did not leave his successors a particularly stable situation. Support for the SPD and membership of trade unions grew by leaps and bounds during the Wilhelmine era. The fact that the Imperial Constitution did not give the Reichstag control over the executive, in that the Chancellor remained the nominee of the Emperor, meant that the SPD, in spite of its impressive electoral showing, could be excluded from any share in the executive government at the national level. In Prussia, two-thirds of Germany in population and area, the three-tier electoral system prevented the SPD from translating its support in the country into seats in the Landtag. The absence of ministerial responsibility and a fully parliamentary system at the Reich level, combined with the three-tier franchise in Prussia and restricted franchises in some other states, meant that politically, Imperial Germany continued to be governed by a pre-industrial elite. The economic and social progress of the country was out of phase with its political development. This produced tensions which the embattled political leaders were tempted to release by pursuing an adventurous and sometimes bellicose foreign policy. Social imperialism took on a particularly acute form in Germany. The deficiencies of Germany's conservative stabilization were fully revealed in the First World War, and the defeat of 1918 precipitated a revolution.

The German case shows that the arrival of an industrial proletariat, often organized by political parties dedicated to a socialist ideology, was becoming the crucial problem for conservatism. Greater political participation by the masses by means of more popular franchises had not, as we have seen, necessarily undermined the conservative position. It seemed more doubtful whether social stability could be maintained and rapid revolutionary change be avoided, when ever larger sections of the population were industrial workers. Apparently the producers of the fast-increasing material wealth of their societies, workers were yet prevented by the distribution of property from enjoying the full fruits of their labours and were in consequence alienated from the rest of society. If this Marxist vision of affairs were to prove even approximately correct, a greater revolutionary challenge to the existing order than ever before was in the making. The various socialist movements in European countries were dedicated precisely to furthering such a development.

The French Third Republic and the Rise of the Extreme Right

The case of France shows even more clearly and rather earlier than Germany the difficulties that might in consequence arise for conservatism. In France the myth of the Revolution could be appropriated for national glory more easily than elsewhere. The regime of Napoleon III had for a time been successful in combining the revolutionary myth, national prestige and social stability. The advance of industrialization and urbanization was, however, slower in France than in Britain and slower than it was eventually to become in Germany. The defeat of 1870 and the long-lasting sense of national humiliation made all problems – the tension between the camp of revolution and the camp of reaction, between clericalism and the secular state, between republicanism and monarchy, between bourgeoisie and a growing proletariat – more acute than ever. The Third Republic established itself largely by default. It was able to become a focus for French patriotism and acquire legitimacy among a majority of the population. The social conservatism of the Republic and the parties that dominated it aroused the hostility of the industrial working class and of many left-wing intellectuals. On the other side of the ideological divide, unreconstructed conservatives, many of them Catholics affronted by the anti-clericalism of the republican parties and opposed to secularism in education and other fields, remained unreconciled to the Republic. Thus there was political instability, shown by the episode of Boulangism* in the mid-1880s, an attempt to overthrow the Republic by a new, more populist Bonapartism.

An even greater crisis came with the Dreyfus* Affair a decade later. Among the anti-Dreyfusards a radical conservatism arose, amounting sometimes to a demand for something like a counterrevolution. This type of conservatism was not only anti-republican, opposed to the revolutionary tradition and to philosophical-ideological positions deriving from the Enlightenment. It was also anti-bourgeois and often anti-capitalist, antagonistic to what it considered the acquisitiveness and corruption of bourgeois society. It hoped to arouse the masses by a national version of socialism, in contradistinction to the cosmopolitan egalitarianism of other socialists. The influence of new trends in philosophy and psychology became apparent. These trends emphasized instinct and non-rational impulses, as well as racial characteristics, allegedly based on biological factors.

Anti-Semitism often marked this radical conservatism, not only because it was an obvious byproduct of the Dreyfus case, but because Jews, or in a more abstract way, the Jewish spirit, were seen as the root cause of many of the modern ills which aroused the disgust of conservatives. Jews were held responsible for plutocratic cosmopolitan capitalism as well as for subversive internationalist socialism. In Germany, too, anti-Semitic parties and trends had arisen in the 1880s and 1890s, which tried to attract groups which found themselves victims of the rapid modernization process noted earlier. Groups such as artisans, small shopkeepers and peasants felt themselves marginalized and fuelled the politics of resentment. In France radical conservatism attained the highest ideological refinement and was linked with names such as Édouard Drumont, Maurice Barrès and Charles Maurras. Here is to be found most clearly the precursor of twentieth-century fascism. Another important influence was the German philosopher Friedrich Nietzsche.* His aphoristic pronouncements on the importance of will and of the superman and on the death of God had wide resonance among intellectuals. This ideological mix was to pose a revolutionary threat to conservatism from the right, as socialism had posed it from the left, even though the dividing lines between traditional and radical or revolutionary conservatism were often fluid. In France the Third Republic emerged if anything strengthened from the Dreyfus Affair. Secularism and anti-clericalism were in the ascendant. The Republic was also able to harness a revived nationalism, intensified by the growing power-political rivalry with Germany in the run-up to 1914.

The Ascendancy of British Conservatism from 1886 to 1906

Britain was again a special case. Circumstances contrived to delay and weaken the threat of socialism, in comparison to Germany and France. The existing political parties, Liberal and Conservative, had mainly defined themselves within the arena of the House of Commons. Successive extensions of the franchise had compelled them to evolve means of organizing a larger electorate. When democratic assumptions began to dominate politics in the final decades of the century, the political parties had to mount at least a pretence of listening to their rank-and-file members. The extensions of the franchise were carried out in such a manner that the monopoly within the political system of the two existing parties was broadly preserved. This was particularly evident in the passage of the Third Reform Bill in 1884. The two parties, the governing Liberals and the Tories as the main opposition, agreed by means of an inter-party conference in November 1884 to adopt a single-member constituency system. In each constituency the first-past-the-post rule was maintained. The representative system thus established, which has remained broadly in existence down to the present, thus makes it difficult for third or further parties to enter the fray. The exception was a regionally based third party, such as existed at the time in the shape of the Irish Nationalist Party. The price the Liberals and Conservatives paid for their agreement of 1884 was a systemic political crisis in the following year over the Irish Home Rule issue. It remained a brief episode. It continued to be difficult for a socialist or labour party to enter politics. When this finally occurred in a significant manner it was through the device of the Labour Representation Committee founded in 1900. It made its major impact through an electoral alliance with the Liberals which remained in force until 1914.

The Labour Representation Committee also highlights another aspect of the rise of labour and socialism specific to Britain. For a long time the development of trade unions predated or overshadowed the political representation of labour. Between the passage of the trade union legislation and the Taff Vale Case the unions found their legal position sufficiently satisfactory to make their leaders disinclined to risk effort and money in promoting a socialist party. Paradoxically the passage of the trade union laws in 1875 proved of little political advantage to the Conservative Party, as the legislation restored the reasonably harmonious relationship between the majority of trade union leaders and the Liberal Party. Thus the Liberal Party retained the allegiance of much of the urban working class. Gradually more collectivist solutions to social problems came into vogue. The Fabians, whose doctrine of permeation prepared them to work with all political parties, converted key figures among the younger generation of politicians, including Tories like A. J. Balfour, to their prescriptions. The election of 1906 brought the Liberals back to power in force. They were helped by their electoral alliance with Labour, but even more by the divisions that had developed within the Conservative Party.

These divisions occurred at the end of a twenty-year period when organized conservatism in Britain had, in defiance of progressive expectations, regained the ascendant. To some extent this was due to accident, personality and the immediate turns and twists of politics. It is possible to interpret the Conservative preponderance more broadly as the result of a continuing successful marriage between conservatism and nationalism. Crucial to the prolonged Conservative hold on power under the leadership of Salisbury was the Liberal split over Irish Home Rule in 1886. The Conservatives managed to mobilize the feeling of threatened nationhood and imperial cohesion across the parties, notably by detaching Liberal Unionists from their party. The disillusion of the Liberal intelligentsia with the whole vision of rational progress also played a role. The mass electorate was not conforming to such expectations. It showed signs of being open to manipulation. Even Gladstone's charismatic leadership was beginning to arouse distrust, not only among Liberal intellectuals but also among high-minded Whigs who had cherished their role as educators of the people and reformers from above. Against this the Tories were able to mobilize just sufficient electoral support to stay in office with their increasingly integrated Liberal and Radical Unionist allies, except for the brief and largely barren Liberal interlude between 1892 and 1895. The Conservatives were able to provide just sufficient domestic reform to compete with their Liberal opponents, themselves restrained by their continuing commitment to laissez-faire and to Irish Home Rule. Increasingly imperialism began to overshadow the political agenda. Even the Liberals could not escape from it and it opened up another fault line in the party, between Liberal Imperialists and Little Englanders. For the Conservatives it was a unifying and positive theme.

Joseph Chamberlain and Social Imperialism

The career of Joseph Chamberlain can be taken as an illustration of the potency of nationalism and imperialism as a conservative force. Even in his days as the most conspicuous leader of the Radical wing of Liberalism he had grown increasingly uneasy with the Gladstonian internationalist stance. He sensed that a working-class electorate was more likely to be enthused by robust patriotism and that it had no sympathy for Irish nationalism. Once he had parted company with the Liberal Party and was committed to making his way with Unionism, he saw his future increasingly not in domestic reform but in the role of imperial statesman. No doubt this was partly due to the fact that as a former radical and nominal Unitarian there were limits on what he could do in domestic affairs within the Tory Anglican fold. He thus chose to be Colonial Secretary when he first had a chance to return to office in a Conservative administration. South Africa became the principal arena for British imperial assertiveness, something that differed much from the way Britain's role was viewed in the days of Palmerston. These developments reached their peak with the Boer War. The first Khaki Election of 1900 showed how successful the marriage of conservatism and nationalism could be in the age of mass politics. But soon there was a reaction against the whole phenomenon of social imperialism. It was a policy over which Salisbury had presided with some reluctance and apprehension and in 1902 he retired from the premiership.

Chamberlain was now free to find a way of continuing the policy of imperial development combined with domestic reform and renewal. He proposed tariff reform as the solution to the multitude of interlocking problems besetting Britain at the beginning of the twentieth century. A customs union would unify the British Empire and enable it to face its rivals, notably the United States and Germany. At home it would make available the resources for social reform and thus deliver 'national efficiency', which might include a more 'eugenically sound' population. There are aspects of Chamberlain's prescription which have led some commentators to label him 'proto-fascist'. It certainly had collectivist, statist, even authoritarian implications, and there were hints of xenophobia and even anti-Semitism. It would be going too far to seek analogies with the radical conservatism of some French intellectuals or with the *völkisch* trends in Germany. It turned out that Chamberlain had underestimated the difficulty of persuading the Conservative Party, let alone the electorate, to adopt tariff reform. British society, even the working class, was perhaps still too libertarian, if not necessarily Liberal in the party sense, to take kindly to such an enhancement of state authority. In more concrete terms, the split in the Conservative ranks caused by tariff reform, combined with the disenchantment with the policy of active imperialism, helped to produce the great Liberal electoral victory of 1906. Even this did not spell the end of the Conservatives as a major force in British politics. In the two elections of 1910 the parties were again much more evenly balanced.

It can thus be argued that conservatism had survived the onward march of liberal progressivism and had successfully entered the mass age in alliance with nationalism. It was, however, increasingly threatened by socialism and the aspirations of the industrial proletariat. Traditional values, such as religion, authority, hierarchy and obedience, the preservation of which had been the object of conservatism, were everywhere being questioned under the impact of modernity. Much in European culture, in the arts as well as in politics, was undermining existing values and pointing towards doubt and disintegration. Expressionism in literature and painting, atonality in music, linked with names like Ibsen, Strindberg, Picasso and Schoenberg, amounted to a fundamental assault on the certainties of the bourgeois age. Some conservatives were thus driven to aspire to a total roll-back of modernity, the French Revolution, the Enlightenment, even the Reformation and the Renaissance. Such aspirations radicalized some intellectuals, notably, as we have seen, in France, to such an extent that they and their successors in other countries would in due course themselves spawn a revolutionary utopian project. Nationalism had for a time and almost universally come to reinforce conservative trends in the most advanced societies of Europe. It was, however, about to plunge Europe into a total war, which was to undermine the status quo more thoroughly than anything since the French Revolution.

The Dilemmas of Liberalism

Eugenio Biagini

The Liberal Climax

A common liberal heritage, in which all European national movements shared, was defined between the age of the Enlightenment and 1848: it consisted of a set of individual freedoms, many of which had first been embodied in the American and the French 'Declarations of the Rights of Man'. Crucial liberal notions were: equality before the law and more equal laws for all, the *Rechtsstaat* (a state based on the rule of law), separation of powers and an independent magistracy, constitutional 'checks and balances' to the powers of the executive, and representative government both at the national and local level.

In the sphere of administration and bureaucracy, there was a common aspiration to replace a system based on aristocratic patronage with one reflecting personal merit and expertise. This ideal of professional competence and fairness translated itself into the effort to spread and improve education, by the introduction of compulsory elementary schooling and the promotion of university learning. In the sphere of public finance, nineteenth-century liberals were great advocates of balanced budgets and a rational fiscal system, with a strong inclination towards free trade. Laissez-faire – an economic system which would require as little interference from the government as possible – was a final goal or an abstract ideal, rather than an attainable objective: as Adam Smith himself had recommended in the final part of the *Wealth of Nations*, most liberals – from William E. Gladstone* (1809–98) in Britain, to Quintino Sella (1827–84) in Italy and Hubert Frere-Orban (1812–96) in Belgium – allowed for a considerable degree of state intervention, at least in areas such as the creation of infrastructures (railways, telegraphs, ports), and the control of 'natural monopolies'. The latter was a rather vague category which could include not only canals and water supplies, but even the regulation of land property, as shown by the reforms carried out in Prussia by Baron Karl vom und zum Stein

(1757–1831) and Prince Karl August von Hardenberg (1750–1822) at the beginning of the nineteenth century, and in Ireland by Gladstone in 1870 and 1881–5.

Last but not least, there was the influence and example of Britain, which European liberals regarded an enormous social and institutional laboratory in which (predominantly) successful experiments had taken place for almost two centuries since the 'Glorious Revolution' (1688–9). Constitutional monarchy and the parliamentary system formed the hard core of the European liberal paradigm. Adam Smith's political economy and 'utilitarian' social reforms, such as the New Poor Law and factory legislation, were fashionable options. The corollary of the British model – an enlightened and capitalist-oriented landed aristocracy – greatly excited liberal fantasies across Europe: however, most observers realized that its creation depended on peculiar historical circumstances, rather than on social and political engineering. Continental liberals tried to translate the British experience into their own national realities, and in so doing produced other viable liberal 'models', such as those embodied in the monarchies established in France ('July Revolution') and in Belgium in 1830. The latter was the main source of inspiration for Italian constitutionalists in 1848.

The events of 1830 also contributed towards creating a liberal strategy adopted, with varying degrees of success, by liberals in the territories of present-day Germany, Austria, Italy, Hungary and Poland between 1830 and 1864. It aimed to achieve political unity and independence for the respective 'national cultures', and to institutionalize the major conquests of the French Revolution of 1789–91. The extent to which these ideas generated a common platform was illustrated by the enthusiastic response evoked in France and Britain by the demands and the struggles of the patriots in Central and Eastern Europe in 1848–9. Though this upheaval of liberal *inter*-nationalism was partly due to Romantic idealism and would not stand the test of *Realpolitik* in 1849, there is little doubt that a recognizably liberal value system was championed by Polish and Hungarian revolutionaries as much as by their supporters in Turin, Frankfurt, Paris or London.

In this struggle liberals confronted what still remained of the *ancien régime*, whose single most important bulwark was probably represented by the churches, especially the Roman Catholic Church in southern Europe. The situation had already been examined – in the 1830s and early 1840s – by the Viscount Alexis de Tocqueville (1805–59), in his studies on democracy in America and France. In the former, the proliferation of democratically organized Protestant sects fostered a liberal culture and strengthened the system of representative government. By contrast, in France the Catholic Church had long since nailed its colours to the mast of the 'divine right' of kings: not only did it seem unable to adapt to the changes inaugurated by the Enlightenment, but it also contributed to constitutional instability by lending its support to the party of reaction and absolutism. While a similar antagonism between church and state could be pointed to in many other European coun-. tries, the case of America was not 'exceptional': rather, it was typical of a broad spread of countries in northern Europe. For, in this respect the main divide was not between the 'old' world and the 'new', but between the Protestant world and the Catholic one. In the former, there was a traditional alliance between moderate liberals and at least some important Christian groups: thus, for instance, in Britain the backbone of the Liberal Party was made up of the Nonconformist Protestants. Arguably, the latter provided a British equivalent of continental anti-clericalism, with the typical call for church disestablishment and secular education: however, liberalism in Britain remained a deeply Christian movement throughout our period. Likewise, in Germany, Norway, and especially Denmark the relationship between liberalism and the Prot-estant churches was positive throughout the nineteenth century. After 1871 the German National Liberals successfully appealed to a Protestant middle-class constituency which a century later would have accounted for much of the Christian Democrat vote.

By contrast, in Catholic countries,[1] as Tocqueville noticed about France, religion and liberalism were on opposite sides of the barricade, very often in the literal sense of the expression. In France the great Revolution had been consistently anti-Catholic (and, in various re-gions, French Protestants had been in the forefront among the Jacobins). Afterwards the confrontation continued for two centuries, through the Third Republic (which disestablished the Catholic Church in 1902), and well into François Mitterand's Socialist presidency in the 1980s. The experiences of Belgium, Spain, Hungary and Italy were similar. Liberal politics in these countries included a good deal of anti-clerical crusading, for which Camillo Benso, Count of Cavour (1810–61) had provided the classical battle-cry of 'A free Church in a free State'. Often, as in France, such conflict extended its long shadows well into the twentieth century.

---

[1] With the exception of Ireland: M. Steed and P. Humphreys point out in 'Identify-ing liberal parties', in *Liberal Parties in Western Europe*, ed. E. J. Kirchner (Cambridge, 1988), p. 421: 'The most obvious explanation is the lack of a secular-clerical cleavage in Irish politics in the late nineteenth century. The coincidence of interest between a non-established Catholic church and the modernizing nation-builders, who would otherwise have been likely to espouse liberalism, in opposing British, Protestant rule produced – uniquely for Western Europe (but similarly to Poland) – an alliance of Catholicism and nationalism which left no place for a secular liberal nationalism.'

In the case of Switzerland this antipathy between Catholics and liberals – and affinity between liberals and Protestants – came to a violent head during the short civil war of 1847: immediately after which the Protestant cantons imposed a liberal constitution on the Catholic ones. Following the cessation of the hostilities, the struggle was resumed in parliament, and led to the 1874 anti-clerical constitutional reform. In the Protestant cantons the Liberal parties and the Calvinist churches were on good terms, a relationship comparable to the Victorian honeymoon between the Scottish Free Kirks and Gladstonian Liberalism in Britain.

Like the Swiss, German Liberals also waged a *Kulturkampf* against the 'dark' powers of the Catholic Church and its 'Black International', in co-operation with the Protestant conservative Otto von Bismarck,* and in the name of economic progress and political and intellectual liberty. At one stage this conflict became so important that, according to Trier's liberal electoral committee, 'Liberal [was] the name for everybody who [was] not a clerical.'[2]

Yet, there was no inherent or inevitable conflict between Roman Catholicism and liberalism, as was illustrated by the example of eminent Catholic liberals such as the French intellectual and politician Alphonse de Lamartine (1790–1869), the Irish patriot Daniel O'Connell (1775–1847) and the Italian novelist Count Alessandro Manzoni (1785–1873) in the years between 1830 and 1848. Rather the contrast was between modernist or neo-Jansenist Catholicism, on the hand, and, on the other, certain aspects of the Catholic tradition – particularly those inherited from the Counterreformation – which by then had been strengthened by Ultramontanism. The latter demanded absolute submission to the pope and rejected *en bloc* the values of the Enlightenment, including both religious toleration and political liberty. The year 1848 saw the culmination of Catholic liberalism: in many cases even abbots, monks and priests took to the streets at the head of revolutionary mobs, and one of them, Vincenzo Gioberti (1801–52), became Liberal Prime Minister of Piedmont-Sardinia in 1849. However, 1849 saw its crisis and demise, when Pius IX (1798–1878) resolutely turned against it (and in consequence was expelled from Rome by a republican insurrection).

After 1849 Ultramontanism became the new orthodoxy, and the Roman Catholic Church moved rapidly towards the anti-liberal philosophy which was to be embodied in the 1864 *Syllabus of Errors*, an outright indictment of constitutional and parliamentary government, democracy, religious tolerance, liberty of thought and expression, modern science and virtually everything else which went under the name

---

[2] J. J. Sheehan, *German Liberalism in the Nineteenth Century* (Chicago and London, 1982), p. 236.

of 'Progress' in nineteenth-century Europe. From then on, until the end of the century, Catholic liberals, including the great British historian Lord Acton (1834–1902) and the Italian Prime Minister Baron Bettino Ricasoli,* found themselves in an awkward position. Some, like the German theologian Ignatz von Döllinger (1799–1890), were excommunicated because of their opposition to the 1870 declaration of papal infallibility.

The 1849 break between Catholicism and liberalism was not really healed for over a century, and deeply affected the nature of liberalism. Though Max Weber's* argument that liberal values depended heavily on the Protestant ethic is only partly defensible, it should not be forgotten that in most Catholic countries liberalism only prevailed after a successful anti-clerical (i.e. anti-Catholic) revolution. In such countries – much more than in Protestant ones – liberalism was affected by (and often confined to) elite pressure groups such as free-thinking intellectuals and the Freemasons.

The long-term political and electoral dimensions of this antagonism are not difficult to assess. On the one hand, right-wing parties (including fascist parties in Italy, Spain, France and South America) could rely on the support of the Catholic hierarchy right up to Vatican II in the 1960s. On the other, Liberal parties in such countries suffered from a systematic lack of popular support, which gradually turned them into predominantly conservative forces. As Tocqueville had prophesied, a difficult relationship with the national religious culture led to electoral vulnerability once democracy had expanded the number of the people involved in the electoral process. By contrast, liberals in Protestant countries generally retained both a broader popular following – usually as a result of their links with aspects of the religious tradition – and a more progressive profile as a centre party midway between the socialists and the conservatives.[3]

This religiously-inspired divide also informed attitudes to women's demands for emancipation and political rights. In the Anglo-Scandinavian countries such demands were incorporated into liberalism from as early as the 1860s: the outstanding examples are Norway, Finland, New Zealand and Australia, where women gained the parliamentary vote before 1914. In Britain John Stuart Mill* managed to build up considerable support for women's rights from as early as 1866–7, his efforts meeting with partial success in 1869, when women were given electoral rights for local government. However, it was only in 1918 that

---

[3] See Steed and Humphreys, 'Identifying liberal parties', pp. 416–19. Their 'Anglo-Scandinavian' (including also the Dutch and German) and 'Continental' camps could easily be renamed – respectively – 'Protestant' and 'Catholic'.

they obtained the right to vote and stand for Parliament, though on a rate-payer qualification (extended to universal suffrage in 1928). The other British Dominions and the United States followed suit. It is remarkable that in all these countries the campaign for women's emancipation was perceived as a Protestant liberal cause. By contrast, in Catholic Europe liberals regarded the women's movement with indifference or even hostility, and nowhere – except in Ireland – were electoral rights for women achieved before the end of the Second World War.

The Crisis of 1870–1, and the Liberal Response to the Challenges of Democracy

The climactic year of confrontation between liberals and Catholics was 1870: as the Vatican Council proclaimed papal infallibility, the Liberal government of unified Italy sent its troops to annexe Rome, the city of the Popes, to the kingdom founded by Cavour. The split between liberalism and Catholicism could hardly have been more complete. This, however, was only one aspect of a multi-faceted European crisis. The Concert of Europe, that informal 'club' of powers which Liberals such as Gladstone had tried to turn into the arbiter and arena for the peaceful solution of international conflict, was fatally undermined by the Franco-German war, and 'national individualism' superseded the principle of collective responsibility established by the Congress of Vienna in 1815. There followed the breakdown of the 'moral consortium' which had represented the counterpart to the free-trade dream of peaceful, ordered and rational progress. A cultural rift also emerged within each of the European countries, as liberals and nationalists began to part company: Disraeli's Crystal Palace speech of 1872 marked the incipient Conservative appropriation of 'patriotism' and imperialism, while in Italy Cavour's heirs and successors, such as Emilio Visconti Venosta (1829–1914) and Marco Minghetti (1818–86), expressed their readiness to 'limit and qualify the practical application of even the principle of nationality, lest it became the cause of a general fire'.[4] It was one of the first instances among European liberals of an important trend, which was to become prevalent after the First World War with the establishment of the League of Nations.

The crisis of 1870 was compounded, in the social sphere, by the events of 1871. The Paris Commune and the ensuing civil war involved the government of Adolphe Thiers,* an old liberal, in a bloody repression,

---

[4] F. Chabod, *Storia della politica estera italiana dal 1870 al 1896* (Bari, 1990), p. 584.

and all over Europe brought home the threat of a proletarian revolution. The 1870s saw the rise both of organized socialist parties, which rejected constitutionalism and parliamentarism as 'bourgeois institutions', and militant anarchism which generated occasional outbursts of terrorism.

In the meanwhile even certainties about economic progress were being shaken: with the onset of the so-called 'Great Depression' in the 1870s the free-trade bonanza of 1850–73 was followed by instability in the international markets caused by a series of trade crises. The United States, the German Empire and Italy, all concerned about their own industrialization, replaced their old free-trade policies with an increasingly aggressive protectionism, which older industrial powers, such as republican France, also adopted. Soon the British Empire remained the last bulwark of economic internationalism.

Though there was more than enough to feel despondent about, liberals showed considerable intellectual vitality in developing solutions to at least some of these problems. The elaboration of theories of mass party politics by liberal intellectuals such as Gaetano Mosca,* Vilfredo Pareto,* Moisey Y. Ostrogorsky,* and Max Weber was one aspect of their response to the challenges of socialism and radical democracy, as well as to the more pressing and realistic threat of a conservative resurgence (illustrated, in the 1870s, by Bismarck's ascendancy in the *Kaiserreich*, MacMahon's presidency in France and Disraeli's* large majority at the 1874 election in Britain).

From the early 1870s, as 'manhood' democracy or extended franchises were adopted in France, Germany and Britain, it became difficult or even impossible to return a working parliamentary majority without a more sophisticated propaganda apparatus. This problem admitted of various solutions, all of which depended to a large extent on the electoral system and nature of the society involved. French Republicans and the Italian 'Sinistra storica' (1877–93) found a feasible strategy in the manipulation of state institutions (such as the Interior Ministry) for 'preparing good elections'. German and British Liberals moved towards the organization of formally democratic parties, with mass organizations structured as hierarchies of representative assemblies, the prototype being the National Liberal Federation (NLF), established in Birmingham in 1877.

In general liberals took an ambivalent attitude to democracy: in some respects they favoured it (especially during the 1848 revolutions), and yet they 'recognized that their position required them to keep democracy at bay'.[5] As W. E. H. Lecky wrote in 1896, they suspected that

---

[5] J. J. Sheehan, 'Some reflections on liberalism in comparative perspective', in *Deutschland und der Westen*, ed. H. Kohler (Berlin, 1984), p. 51.

[d]emocracy destroys the balance of opinions, interests, and classes, on which constitutional liberty mainly depends, and its constant tendency is to impair the efficiency of and authority of parliaments, which have hitherto proved the chief organs of political liberty.[6]

Liberals stuck to the old 'aristocratic' or elitist ideal of citizenship: inherited from the Aristotelian tradition, it had been strengthened, rather than weakened, by the Industrial Revolution and the rise of a 'mass society'. Alexis de Tocqueville, who produced the most brilliant analysis of contemporary democratic trends, was also one of the staunchest defenders of aristocracies (both social and intellectual), which he regarded as essential to the survival of liberty. John Stuart Mill took a more optimistic view and went as far as celebrating the classical Athenian model of direct democracy and participatory citizenship; but in his opinion the ancient system was admirable precisely because it allowed for the selection of real 'aristocrats', namely the philosophers and *rhetores* who dominated the Athenian *ekklesia*.

Whether his analysis of Pericles' Athens was correct or not, Mill's great intuition was that mass democracy did not have to be accompanied by a cult of equality similar to that exhibited by the Americans: in fact, the masses *were* responsive to the appeal of 'aristocratic' leaders, be they Periclean populists (like Gladstone and Mill himself in 1865–73), Bonapartist despots (like Napoleon III and Boulanger*), or even able noblemen of the old school (including Bismarck and Salisbury*). That such emphasis on democratically selected 'aristocratic' leaders was a typical liberal response to democracy was confirmed a generation later by Max Weber, who with his theory of charismatic presidency introduced a strong element of 'aristocratic' rule into his constitutional proposals for the Weimar Republic (see below, p. 122).

German Idealism and the 'New Liberalism'

Whether animated by genuine social concern, or merely worried about the rising tide of democratic demands, most liberals considered programmes and policies more important than propaganda, electioneering or even institutional experimentation. Once the mid-Victorian optimism about economic growth and the efficiency of the market had vanished in the trade mists of the Great Depression, laissez-faire ceased to be a credible strategy. As state intervention increased of its own accord, often in the guise of a series of uncoordinated administrative responses to the pressure of events, liberal reformers felt the need both

[6]   Cited in Sheehan, 'Some reflections on liberalism', p. 52.

for a rationalization of what was happening, and for an intellectual apologia adequate to the levels and quality of social engineering required by a sophisticated industrial society.

Especially from the late 1870s, Hegelian philosophy, in itself one of the most illiberal products of early nineteenth-century thought, inspired many liberal intellectuals and politicians to think afresh about social and economic problems. Throughout Western Europe historians, philologists, philosophers, economists and social reformers found in German theories of the state's 'ethical mission' a fruitful paradigm and a flexible framework. In Germany, France and Britain idealism generated ambitious programmes, amounting to the proclamation of social rights as the necessary integration and fulfilment of the political rights traditionally proclaimed by liberals. Even if Sir William Harcourt's (1827–1904) famous remark – 'We are all Socialists now' – was to be taken with a pinch of salt, the change in liberal attitudes and expectations was considerable. This new climate of opinion was effectively summarized by the German liberal Johannes von Miquel (1828–1901) in 1884:

> We no longer recognize that kind of liberalism which defines progress as the diminution of the state's role, an exclusive reliance on self-help, and the rejection of all public social and economic organizations; which identifies free trade with political freedom; and which will not let the state do anything in economic affairs because the state cannot do everything.[7]

In principle there was no contradiction between classical liberalism and social rights. Indeed, in Britain the path to a theory of social rights had been opened up by J. S. Mill, who had argued that the public good required individual liberty. But even in Britain the impact of German idealism marked a qualitative change: Thomas Hill Green,* the leading light of the Liberal renewal, emphasized the role of the state and adopted an organic, collectivist notion of society within which he elaborated the notion of a socially responsible individualism. The latter was influenced by Kantian logic, and shaped by both the classical ideal of 'civic virtue', and a secularized, but deeply felt, Puritan ethic.

If Mill had been the philosopher and economist of Victorian Liberalism, T. H. Green was to mould the 'New Liberalism' of the Edwardian period. Besides dominating the intellectual debate, he influenced the party leaders H. H. Asquith*, E. Grey*, H. Samuel (1870–1963) and philosopher and political thinker L. T. Hobhouse (1864–1929) whose writing defined the New Liberalism up to 1914. Green's influence was supplemented by the work of economists such as Arnold Toynbee (1852–83) and Alfred Marshall (1842–1924). Their Christian (or Jewish)

---

[7] Cited in Sheehan, *German Liberalism*, p. 189.

idealism and 'compassionate' economics opened the way to the ambitious programmes of social reforms introduced by the Liberal governments of 1905–16: these included a non-contributory old-age-pension scheme (1908), and the first steps towards establishing a public system of insurance against unemployment and sickness.

Parallel elaborations of the notion of social citizenship took place in both Germany and France. The Protestant pastor and eminent social reformer Friedrich Naumann (1860–1919) tried to establish an imperialist version of social liberalism as a popular creed in the *Kaiserreich* at the turn of the century. In the Third Republic, Radicals such as J. Ferry (1832–93), L. Gambetta (1838–82), G. Clemenceau (1841–1924) and L. Bourgeois (1851–1925) led a revival of democratic liberalism which insisted on the ethical mission of the republic, and emphasized public education, 'solidarism', and an ambitious programme of social reforms. However, this programme relied on institutionalized bourgeois paternalism (such as the mutual benefit societies) more than was realistically possible: in fields such as the provision of medical care and pensions the result was disappointing. 'Solidarism' and social rights found their most authoritative theoretician in Emile Durkheim,* the great sociologist who spanned the gap between liberalism and social democracy with a rigorous call to civic virtue and communal values. Self-help and 'the harmony of capital and labour' – ideals which in Britain had been widespread about twenty years before – took on new meaning in *fin de siècle* France, where widespread ownership of property and a strong peasant and artisan culture accounted for a distinctive route to industrialization and economic growth.

The comparative success of this strategy shows that the vitality of old liberal ideals should not be underestimated in assessing the fortunes of European liberalism at the turn of the century. Another illustration of the same truth is provided by the free-trader and labour partnership which characterized left-wing politics in both Britain and Italy during the period 1900–8. In the former the alliance between the Liberal Party and the organized working-class movement (particularly the co-operatives) was a consolidated tradition based on Britain's peculiar position as the greatest world market for consumer goods, as well as the leading exporter of coal, cotton and shipping. When the 'agricultural interests' and some of the industrialists who were most suffering from foreign competition demanded tariff reforms, the working men responded with a free-trade crusade which swept the Liberal Party back into office in December 1905.

In Italy protectionism was identified with state-supported military industries and the 'reactionary bloc' which had produced several governments from 1893 to 1900. Free-trade intellectuals such as Vilfredo

Pareto and Luigi Einaudi (1874–1961) had long tried to create an anti-protectionist popular front similar to the one led by Bright and Cobden in mid-Victorian Britain. Though meeting with only limited and short-lived success, they contributed towards returning Giuseppe Zanardelli (1826–1903) and Giovanni Giolitti* to power with a parliamentary majority of progressive Liberals.

Giolitti was willing to co-operate even with the Socialists, though his main allies were the Radical deputies of the so-called *Estrema* (the 'Extreme Left'). Though the *Estrema* – and especially its Republican wing – produced a popular and democratic alternative to the ruling class's understanding of the meaning and extent of liberty, significantly no liberal theory of social rights comparable to those of Marshall and Green was elaborated in Italy before the mid-1920s.

By then Benito Mussolini* was Prime Minister, the labour movement had been repressed and civil and political liberties severely curtailed. In this context there arose an Italian 'New Liberal' response, first in the shape of Piero Gobetti's (1901–26) call for a 'Rivoluzione liberale'; then with Guido De Ruggiero's (1888–1948) *History of European Liberalism* (1924), which contained also an important prescriptive section; and finally with Carlo Rosselli's (1899–1937) writings on 'socialist liberalism', which culminated in the book *Liberal Socialism* (1930). Though mainly a group of intellectuals, they were considered to be dangerous enough to warrant persecution and exile, while some of their leaders were murdered. In terms of content, Italian 'New Liberalism' was strongly inspired by the British experience, especially by Hobson's 'socialism in liberalism' and the ideas of the early Labour Party, filtered through German idealism.

In Germany, as in France, Italy or Britain the 'New Liberals' and their equivalents strove to create an ethical impetus behind liberalism by attracting the working classes back to its cause. They were unable to accept that the workers – heirs of those artisan radicals who had supported the 1848 revolutions on the continent and Gladstonianism in Britain – were now lost to liberalism. The 'New Liberals' looked forward to a more just society, but also back to the political climate of the first half of the nineteenth century, the climax of liberalism.

A different approach was taken by Max Weber. As the First World War approached he perceived the prospective collapse of the 'liberal ethos' together with the social order on which it was built. He concluded that they could not be propped up without recourse to levels of coercion and repression which he judged to be incompatible with liberalism. As a consequence, he opted for a strategy focusing on institutional and political change, and the creation of a framework 'capable of giving expression to a plurality of points of view and arranging agreement between them'.[8] After the First World War, Weber's main concern was with constitutional legitimation, which could be based on rational, traditional or charismatic grounds (the latter referring to the personal prestige and special gifts of a strong, popularly elected leader). In preparing his draft of the constitution for the Weimar Republic, he strove to blend these three elements with his combination of a limited parliamentary government and a president directly elected by the citizens and endowed with extensive executive powers.

Yet, as Hitler's rise to power was to demonstrate, such formal criteria were in themselves insufficient to guarantee the survival of liberty, let alone of liberalism. Both the Spanish Civil War (1935–9) and the Second World War were to mark decisive revivals of ethical liberalism, from 1940–5 under the leadership of Winston Churchill,* a former 'New Liberal', and Franklin D. Roosevelt,* who had anticipated the Keynesian 'New Deal' of the post-war years. Significantly, this revival of ethical liberalism was not achieved without recourse to coercion on a large scale. Liberal institutions had to be forceably imposed on the peoples of Central Europe: as in the days of the French revolutionary wars and the American Civil War, liberalism – in order to be maintained and defended – required not only ballots, but sometimes bullets.

Liberals and Nationalists

'Make it known that I am shooting all peasants caught carrying arms. Quarter will be given only to regular soldiers. Executions have already begun today.' This was the chilling text of a telegram sent by general E. Cialdini (1811–92) – an Italian Liberal and member of Cavour's majority in parliament – to the governor of Campobasso, in the then inaccessible hills of Molise. It was 20 October 1860. Italy had become a united kingdom only months before. The Piedmontese, fresh from the Austrian battlefields, and incorporating the armies of Tuscany, Emilia and Lombardy, had first proceeded to crush the army of the pope. The next step had been the annexation of the south. Garibaldi had already defeated the bulk of the Neapolitan army, though the last Bourbon king still hung on with his elite forces. The latter were quickly dispatched by Cialdini. But then the real difficulties began.

Thousands of ex-soldiers from the disintegrated southern army took to the hills to join the 'brigands', the social bandits celebrated by E. J. Hobsbawm as 'primitive rebels'. At that time banditry was widespread

---

[8]   R. Bellamy, *Liberalism and Modern Society: An Historical Argument* (Cambridge, 1992), p. 8; see also pp. 164–5.

throughout the Mediterranean basin. In the territories of the former Kingdom of the Two Sicilies these 'brigands' had always been a force to be reckoned with. Though historians have traditionally interpreted banditry in terms of mere social conflict and protest, during the Napoleonic occupation it played an anti-French, almost proto-nationalist, role, similar to that of the *klephts* in the Ottoman Empire or the *guerrillas* in Spain. The perception that the south was 'different' from the north in more than mere socio-economic terms had been suppressed by Risorgimento enthusiasts, only to be reaffirmed in the 1860s. At the time Italian army officers and northern observers resorted to much vocabulary reminiscent of Victorian racism in their descriptions of the southern 'brigands'. The latter referred to the new authorities as 'the Piedmontese', irrespective of actual regional background: according to them the south was being invaded, not liberated.

The *Mezzogiorno* represented the Italian equivalent of what the Irish question was to the British. Even contemporaries – beginning with J. S. Mill and his Italian correspondent, the southern liberal Pasquale Villari (1826–1917) – drew the parallel, and later in the century studies were published comparing the Irish Coercion Acts of 1881–7 with the coercion of the south by Italian governments in the 1860s. The Fenians in Ireland were to the British what the 'bandits' in the *Mezzogiorno* were to the Italian authorities. Rural unrest with proto-national (or national) undertones demanded government by coercion rather than by consent.

As W. C. Lubenow has written, 'British Liberals could admire . . . nationalism without appreciating the ways in which its central features ran contrary to their own state interests.'[9] In a sense, a similar comment could be applied to Italian liberals, and indeed to liberals elsewhere as well. For instance, there were French versions of the same problem: in 1871 the liberal nationalist Thiers had to struggle tooth and nail with the Federalist *Communards*, who seemed hellbent on splitting up France into autonomous cantons. Later, as Eugen Weber has demonstrated (*Peasants into Frenchmen*, 1992), the Third Republic had to 'nationalize' the staunchly reactionary peasants, who had forms of collective allegiance different from those of the 'nation', and many of whom did not speak French any more than Calabrian peasants spoke Italian. In Hungary, the 1848–9 revolution ran into difficulties when the Magyars – both Protestants, such as Lajos Kossuth (1802–94), and Catholics – were deserted by the ethnic and religious minorities. Bavaria in Germany and Tyrol in Austria were always fiercely independent. In

[9]   W. C. Lubenow, 'The Liberals and the national question: Irish Home Rule, nationalism, and their relationship to nineteenth-century Liberalism', *Parliamentary History*, 13, Part I (1994), p. 129.

the United States, despite greater cultural homogeneity, the Civil War involved contrasting forms of national identity, and nowadays some historians would endorse Gladstone's 1862 statement that the Confederate President Jefferson Davis had 'made a nation'.[10]

The point is that there were – and still are – at least two basic forms of 'nationalism', whose aims are incompatible. The one seeks the unification of states and regions with similar cultural and historical heritages into a larger 'nation state'; the other seeks the separation of a region or ethnic group from a broader political unit within which that region or group is considered to be 'imprisoned'. From the second half of the nineteenth century both forms of nationalism were simultaneously in evidence, often in the same parts of Europe. On the continent the encounter between these contrasting forms of collective identity culminated in the suppression of the weaker ones, usually the separatists. In Britain and Ireland neither the Liberals nor the Tories could even contemplate the adoption of large-scale military repression before 1916–21, and, when they did, were unable to carry it out successfully.

Yet, whether they liked it or not, by the 1880s both Liberals and Conservatives had to come to terms with the new realities created by nationalism in its two main Britannic manifestations – that is, Celtic separatism and militant imperialism. Thanks to the ability shown by Lord Salisbury in manipulating the latter without taking it too seriously, the Conservatives went from strength to strength. For their part the Liberals were good at managing and absorbing Celtic separatism, turning a potentially destructive force into an important asset for both the stability of the United Kingdom and the long-term electoral success of their own party.

It is interesting that the one case in which this strategy did not work was Ireland: and yet, even there, Gladstone, followed by Asquith and Augustine Birrell (1850–1933), very nearly succeeded. In 1881–6 a combination of repression and land reform turned a potentially revolutionary movement into a strongly constitutional and parliamentary one. From 1886 the proposal of Home Rule effectively turned the nationalists in Ireland (and the Irish electors in Britain) into staunch allies of the Liberals. By co-opting the party led by the aristocratic Charles S. Parnell,* Gladstone tried to turn a dangerous challenger into a pillar of empire. A similar operation had been successfully carried out in 1840–67 in Canada, a society resembling Ireland in its divisions along historical, religious, ethnic and linguistic lines. However, the First World War – which brought to an end so many liberal experiments throughout

[10] Cf. D. A. Faust, *The Creation of Confederate Nationalism: Ideology and Identity in the Civil War* (Baton Rouge, LA, 1988).

Europe – also fatally undermined the Catholic (liberal) National Party of John Redmond (1856–1918) in Ireland. Following the Easter Rising and its aftermath the 'Canadian' path to Irish self-government was replaced by a new emphasis on 'blood, sacrifice and purification', a rhetoric disturbingly reminiscent of *La Terre et les Morts* of the French and Italian proto-fascist nationalists.

A new notion of 'nation' was also triumphing over older liberal and republican concepts. Romantic nationalists such as the French historian Ernest Renan (1836–92) and the Italian republican Giuseppe Mazzini (1805–71) had upheld an ideal of nation based on a civic religion over-arching national/ethnic origins, and the bureaucratic state. Thus in Renan's famous words

> A nation is a . . . spiritual principle . . . the sharing of a rich legacy of recollections [and] . . . the present consent, the desire of living together, the will to preserve the heritage which has been received undivided. . . . The existence of a nation is . . . a plebiscite of every day, just like the existence of an individual is a perpetual affirmation of life.[11]

Rather different was the vision of the new wave of early twentieth-century nationalists, who emphasized 'geography, race and language, that is . . . those [external] signs which to Mazzini had no intrinsic value'.[12] The contrast between liberal ideals and the rising tide of ethnic nationalism, which Sir Lewis Namier analysed in his study of 1848 in Central Europe, eventually imposed difficult choices on liberals through-out Europe. In Germany an imperialist *Weltpolitik* was adopted by all branches of liberalism. This arose in part from the fact that German liberalism, shaped by the long struggle for national unification, com-bined a strong individualist tradition with an overriding concern for the greatness of the *Kaiserreich*. But it also depended on the fact that even those liberals who had misgivings about aggressive imperialism 'realized that nationalism was a weapon they could not do without'[13] if they were to retain popular support under a democratic electoral system. It was the first step along a road which was eventually to lead many German liberals to endorse Hitler's bid for power in 1933.

The dynamic of events in Italy was similar. There 'Irredentism' claimed the annexation of Trent and Trieste, then in Austrian territory, on purely racial grounds, quite independently of the opinions and aspira-tions of the inhabitants of the provinces in question. Despite Giolitti's attempt to retain the nationalist vote with a vigorous colonial policy

---

[11] From *Le nationalisme française: Anthologie 1871–1914*, Textes choisis et présentés par Raoul Girardet (Paris, 1983), pp. 65–7.
[12] Chabod, *Storia della politica estera italiana*, p. 60.
[13] Sheehan, *German Liberalism*, p. 276.

(1911–12) Liberals and Nationalists were at loggerheads. The Nationalists withdrew their support for the Liberal government only in May 1914. However, the writing had been on the wall for at least five years: in 1909 F. T. Marinetti (1876–1944) had published his *Manifesto futurista*, and in 1910 E. Corradini (1865–1931) produced a new 'philosophy of history' in which struggle between nations (economic and military warfare) replaced the Marxist idea of class struggle as the 'engine of history'. Corradini, Marinetti and the Futurists were but one expression of a wider cultural upheaval, characterized by the exaltation of action as an end in itself. From 1918 social unrest and the fear of a Bolshevik revolution resulted in substantial elements of the old liberal groups endorsing right-wing reactions. In 1922 most of the Italian liberals who had supported Giolitti till 1914 applauded Mussolini's energetic 'revival of national pride and unity', and, even more, his effective repression of labour unrest and socialist 'machinations'.

Though their political aims were completely different, Sinn Fein's military wing belonged to the same generation of European nationalists as the Italian Futurists. They espoused a similar philosophy, with the typical celebration of the regenerative power of violence, blood, sacrifice and death. After the First World War many former notables and party bosses who previously had supported Redmond's National Party, switched allegiance first to Sinn Fein, then to either of the two civil war parties (*Fianna Fail* and *Cumann na nGaedheal/Fine Gael*). This change was accelerated by the fear of a socialist revolution within the traditional agrarian social order: thus militarist republicanism became both the rallying cry of anti-British nationalism, and the effective antidote to militant labour. Though the 'Blue Shirts' (the Irish variety of fascism) did not seize power, in the 1930s Eire, as much as Mussolini's Italy, moved into an era of xenophobic nationalism, dominated by economic 'autarky' and Catholic integralism.

Shouldering the burden of opposition to the wave of totalitarianism was left to 'New Liberals' and liberal-socialists of a younger generation. The members of 'Giustizia e libertà', the movement that Carlo Rosselli founded in France among exiled anti-fascists, were examples of these. They looked forward to a new Risorgimento: an event which Rosselli strove to foster by going to fight for the Republicans in Spain in 1936. There, 'Giustizia e libertà' formed the 'Catalonian battalion' together with Spanish anarchists. As the Italian volunteers faced Mussolini's expeditionary force, 'Giustizia e libertà' gained a foretaste of the stark choice with which they would be faced as the Second World War approached: that between loyalty to country and loyalty to liberal-socialist ideals. It is characteristic of the temper of left-wing liberalism that in 1940 none of the liberal-socialist intellectuals hesitated to put

liberty before nation: to them the Second World War was but the continuation of the Spanish Civil War, i.e. an Italian civil war. 'Today in
Spain, tomorrow in Italy', Carlo Rosselli wrote just a few months before
he and his brother were murdered by Mussolini's agents.

Neither in France nor in Britain did post-war liberalism face such a
serious crisis. In the former Raymond Poincaré* led a vigorous liberal-
bourgeois restoration, combining financial rectitude with progressive
social programmes, and a foreign policy which, under Aristide Briand
(1862–1932), seemed to achieve an effective improvement in relations
with Germany. In Britain, the Lloyd George* post-war coalition (1918–
22) successfully implemented the restoration of peacetime conditions,
though at the cost of prolonging the crisis of the Liberal Party. Though
the latter never recovered its pre-war levels of power, Dangerfield's
The Strange Death of Liberal England (1935) – describing British liberalism as one of the casualties of the Battle of the Somme – was both
influential and misleading. On the one hand, despite internal squabbles
and splits due to rivalries among leaders, the decline of the Liberal Party
was slow and gradual: as late as 1923 they obtained their largest poll ever,
only narrowly missing the right to the royal summons to form a new
government. The Liberal electoral collapse came between 1929 and 1935,
twenty years after the beginning of the First World War, and was due
to shortage of funds and the progressive decay of the party organization, besides competition from the other two main parties. These were
at the time as close as possible to traditional liberalism: the Labour
leader Ramsay MacDonald* was in fact much more of a liberal than a
socialist, while Stanley Baldwin (1867–1947), the Conservative leader,
also appeared to stand within the broad spectrum of old liberalism. As
J. P. D. Dunbabin commented on one occasion,[14] from a continental
point of view, before 1914 Britain had two liberal parties, one of which
called itself 'Conservative'; after 1918 it had three liberal parties, one of
which called itself 'Labour'.

While the situation at home was comparatively stable, it was *colonial*
nationalism which troubled British and French liberals. With armed
revolts (Syria and Iraq) and non-violent movements (India) demanding
independence, European liberals began to accept, as the NLF leader
Ramsey Muir (1872–1941) wrote, that there was 'a natural antithesis
or antipathy between the words "Liberalism" and "Empire"'.[15] Like
their Italian counterparts when confronted with fascism, British liberals

---

[14] At the Churchill College Conference on 'Currents of Radicalism' (Cambridge,
April 1990).
[15] R. Muir, 'Liberalism and the Empire', in *Liberal Points of View*, ed. H. L. Nathan
and H. Heathcote Williams (London, 1927), p. 253.

manifested a strong tendency to split into right- and left-wing groups. Many of the latter had begun to move into the Labour Party in 1916–17, though on liberal, rather than socialist grounds: they were outraged by the abandonment of free trade, by secret diplomacy and by the new wave of imperialism, reinforced by military conscription. Their inspiration came from J. A. Hobson (1858–1940), whose most important piece (*Imperialism: A Study*) had been published in 1902 as an analysis of the forces behind the Boer War. From 1917 both Labour and left-wing Liberals demanded home rule for India as well as for Ireland, and an acceleration of the move towards a more liberal Empire.

Yet, the idea of a 'Liberal Empire' could easily be used for conservative ends as well. Liberal imperialists of various shades argued that liberty was in fact the goal towards which British colonial policy had been moving all the time since 1840, with the aim of establishing representative institutions on the Canadian model first in the 'White Dominions', then in the rest of the Empire. The latter was described as being divided into two groups of colonies: India and Egypt, 'lands of ancient, but somewhat stagnant civilization'; and the African and other 'primitive and backward' colonies and protectorates. As for the former group, Muir maintained that 'the coming of Western influences under the direction of the British power [had] brought an immense series of changes – a great fermentation, an upheaval.'[16] Besides, Muir claimed that 'some of the foundations of liberty . . . [had] been established' in India by the British – meaning the rule of law and personal liberty.[17] Yet, he concluded, 'progress towards organised self-government' was 'the only ultimate justification of our position in India.'[18] By contrast, as regards 'the primitive and backward peoples, mainly in Africa and the Pacific Islands,'[19] Muir still recommended 'the principle of [British] tutelage': the British should regard themselves 'always as the trustees, primarily for their [the primitive peoples'] rights, and, secondarily, for the rights of the whole civilized community to have access to the resources of wealth of the world.'[20] Thus Britain was represented by Liberal imperialists as the spearhead not only of world liberty, but also of economic progress and capitalist civilization.

This theory rested on the belief, not 'in the equality of all nations', but rather 'in a certain hierarchy, no doubt a temporary hierarchy, of races, or, at least, of civilizations;' there were 'peoples not yet able to stand by themselves under the strenuous conditions of the modern

[16]   Ibid., pp. 258–9.
[17]   Ibid., p. 270.
[18]   Ibid., p. 274.
[19]   Ibid., p. 259.
[20]   Ibid., p. 280.

world'. Though British Liberals 'detest[ed] the methods of Amritsar', they 'do not for that reason favour the expulsion of the British from the Sudan nor a great Moslem rising against the Christians, nor a negro rising against the whites. We feel sympathy for Abd-el-Krim as for other brave rebels, but we realise that his success would be a disaster to civilization . . . . We do not want revolution.'[21]

The Quest for Democratic Stability

Undoubtedly Liberals did not want a revolution, either at home or abroad. Much of inter-war liberalism in Western Europe was a quest for stability. In international relations this led to a renewed commitment to a revised and expanded version of the 'Concert of Europe' in the shape of the League of Nations. The first imperative of a liberal foreign policy was 'that Europe shall not again be divided into two camps, which in practice means that the League of Nations shall be substituted for the armed alliances'.[22] Some went far beyond the idea of a 'concert': radical as always, Hobson called for the establishment of 'an International Government, implying the surrender of important elements of sovereignty by individual states'.[23]

Nevertheless, Hobson insisted that the great lesson of the war was that 'justice as well as charity begins at home', and that it was 'impracticable to hope for peace and justice in international affairs unless the conditions for internal peace and justice within the nations have already been substantially obtained'.[24] Social justice and economic recovery were the focus of J. M. Keynes's* thinking. A pupil of Alfred Marshall, Keynes had first risen to notoriety with his acute critique, *The Economic Consequences of the Peace* (1919). Already in the 1920s he had become the most authoritative liberal economist in Britain. Stating his position in 1927, he argued that '[t]here [was] a dual aim before the statesman – a society which is just and a society which is efficient':[25] while confronting this dilemma, Keynes continued, Liberals were 'inclined to sympathise with Labour about what is just, but to suspect that in the blind striving after justice Labour may destroy what is at least as important and is a necessary condition of social progress at all

---

[21]   G. Murray, 'What Liberalism stands for', in *Liberal Points of View*, ed. Nathan and Heathcote Williams, p. 29.
[22]   J. A. Spender, 'Liberal foreign policy', in *Liberal Points of View*, ed. Nathan and Heathcote Williams, p. 93.
[23]   J. A. Hobson, *Confessions of an Economic Heretic* (London, 1938), p. 111.
[24]   Ibid., p. 113.
[25]   J. M. Keynes, 'Liberalism and industry', in *Liberal Points of View*, ed. Nathan and Heathcote Williams, p. 206.

– namely, efficiency.'[26] The task of the Liberals was, then, 'to guide the aspiration of the masses for social justice along channels which [would] not be inconsistent with social efficiency'.[27] Keynes recommended a policy of 'partnership between the State and private enterprise', and of government support for and regulation of 'Trusts and Combines' in place of the old Liberal policy of trying to enforce the greatest possible competition among small-scale industries.[28]

These ideas were embodied in the Liberal manifesto for the 1929 election, *We Can Conquer Unemployment*, signed by the veteran leader David Lloyd George. It called for the mobilization of national resources under state control or supervision: 'Unemployment is industrial disorganization. It is brought to an end by new enterprise, using capital to employ labour. In the present stagnation the Government must supply that initiative which will help to set going a great progressive movement.'[29]

Yet, a major theoretical change in Liberal thinking was underway. Until then the radical Liberal analysis had identified underconsumption – due to maldistribution of national wealth, and consequent widespread poverty – as the main cause of both recurrent trade crises at home and imperialism abroad. According to Hobson there was a financial drive behind imperialism, deriving from the search for new investment markets for British capital, whose 'idle balances' at home depended on slack internal demand and low levels of consumption. The implication was that imperialism was both an economic mistake and a political injustice: sounder economics demanded the development of home markets, by increasing internal demand and levels of popular consumption. In the 1920s Keynes's analysis had shared important aspects with Hobson's, and in his *Treatise on Money* (1930) he elaborated on the Hobsonian theme of the equilibrium between savings and investment. However, with the publication of the revolutionary *General Theory of Employment, Interest and Money* (1936), Keynes argued that there could be no such thing as 'idle balances' or 'uninvested saving': rather, there were often 'unwanted stocks or other losses' which absorbed savings and reduced national wealth. To him 'the root of Hobson's mistake' was

> his supposition that excessive saving caused the actual over-production of capital . . . whereas he should instead have explained 'that a relatively weak propensity to consume helps to cause unemployment by requiring

---

[26] Ibid., p. 206.
[27] Ibid., p. 206.
[28] Ibid., pp. 214–15.
[29] Cited in P. Adelman, *The Decline of the Liberal Party, 1910–1931* (London, 1981), pp. 81–2.

and *not* receiving the accompaniment of a compensating volume of new investment'.[30]

The change from the position he had held in 1930 had important analytical consequences: 'The author of the *Treatise* recognized unemployment as a symptom of disequilibrium, because the economy was not *in balance*. The author of the *General Theory* disclosed the enormity of unemployment at equilibrium, because the economy was at *rest*.'[31] One possible way out – as Hobson had maintained – was through increased consumption; but a much more effective one was through increased investment, which 'should be stimulated either privately or publicly',[32] by lowering interest rates or by public works. Despite the rather common misconception, popularized by Thatcherite propaganda in the 1980s, '[p]ublic investment not deficit finance remained at the heart of Keynes's message.'[33]

The political paradox of the Keynesian revolution was that the Liberals were unable to derive from it any electoral benefit. Yet, theirs were the ideas of the future, which Churchill's wartime coalition and the succeeding Labour governments (1945–51) would implement. In those years, next to Keynes, it was another Liberal, Sir William (later Lord) Beveridge,* who most contributed to reshaping the liberal heritage. Perhaps the last of T. H. Green's disciples, he set the agenda for British, and indeed for Western European, reconstruction. His celebrated 1942 Report proposed the establishment of a comprehensive system of state welfare which included a national health service, family allowances, and a general contributory insurance plan covering unemployment, sickness, funeral expenses and pensions: a scheme operating 'from the cradle to the grave'. Beveridge supplemented his proposal in 1944 with the publication of another report, which envisaged the creation of full employment as a prerequisite for the viability of his welfare system. The liberal theory of social rights was thus extended to comprise 'freedom from Want, Disease, Ignorance, Squalor, and Idleness'.

The impact of the reforms carried out by successive British governments along the lines proposed by Beveridge and on the basis of Keynes's economic analysis was immense: it extended beyond the British Isles to the whole of Western Europe and Canada, where they were imitated during the period 1945–75 (Sweden, New Zealand and Australia had been experimenting with similar reforms from the 1930s).

---

[30] Ibid., pp. 271–2.
[31] P. F. Clarke, *The Keynesian Revolution in the Making* (Cambridge, 1988), p. 281; see also p. 230.
[32] P. F. Clarke, *Liberals and Social Democrats* (Cambridge, 1978), p. 274.
[33] Clarke, *The Keynesian Revolution in the Making*, p. 288.

Thatcherite historians have suggested that Beveridge's schemes were so unrealistically generous as to undermine the performance of the British economy in comparison with that of other countries in the post-war years: however, the main problem with such an interpretation is that by the mid-1950s most other European countries – including dynamic and highly successful economies like West Germany, Norway and Italy – spent a larger percentage of their gross domestic product on social security than the UK.

After 1945 liberalism in Europe retained some of its old paradoxes, such as the fact that within the same ideological framework there were varieties of liberalism spanning the entire political spectrum, from free-market individualism in France, to agricultural and industrial co-partnership in Denmark, to mainline support for the welfare state in Belgium, and devolution and worker participation in Britain. It encompassed both V. Giscard d'Estaing's (1926–) opinion that 'real liberalism . . . recognises the individual as the sole source and exclusive end of all social and political organization', and Jo Grimond's (1913–93) call for 'community politics'. In several instances these divides ran deep within the same society and political system: such was the case in Denmark with *Venstre* and the Radical Party, and in Italy, with the Liberal Party and the more socially oriented Republican Party.

However, all liberals shared important features, embodied in the most significant 'short catechism' of post-war Liberalism: the Oxford *Liberal Manifesto*, prepared by representatives from nineteen countries at the International Liberal Conference in 1947. It proclaimed, among other things, 'equality of rights between men and women', consumers' rights, 'security from the hazards of sickness, unemployment, disability and old age', national self-determination, 'respect for the language, faith, laws, and customs of national minorities', and support for the United Nations, which should be given 'power to enforce the strict observance of all international obligations freely entered into'.[34] In later years the cause of European economic integration and political union was enthusiastically adopted by most European liberals: for many of them it became a moral imperative, adhered to with some of the fervour with which their Victorian forebears had supported free trade.[35]

[34]   'Liberal Manifesto drawn up at the International Liberal Conference at Wadham College, Oxford, April 1947', in F. Bolkstein (ed.), *Modern Liberalism: Conversations with Liberal Politicians* (n.p., 1982), pp. 281–3.
[35]   I am grateful to Cambridge University Press for permission to republish extracts from pp. 10–12 of my introduction to E. F. Biagini (ed.), *Citizenship and Community: Liberals, Radicals and Collective Identities in the British Isles, 1865–1931* (Cambridge, 1996). Special thanks go to P. F. Clarke, J. P. D. Dunbabin and A. J. Reid for their comments on a previous version of this chapter.

Socialist Parties and Policies

Duncan Tanner

The years between 1890 and 1945 were seemingly dominated by nationalism, militarism, fascism, Communism, war and destruction. This chapter explains how and why socialist parties failed to check the challenge of extremism. However, it also discusses and explains the important positive aspects of socialist politics in this period. Whilst extremists on the left and right were reducing politics to base slogans, and whilst confessional, nationalist, liberal and conservative parties in many countries did little to resist the growth of the extremes, democratic socialists reaffirmed a faith in democracy, reform, compassion and decency. They gradually – if belatedly – developed a series of policies designed to create prosperity and security. At different rates in different countries, socialists developed the social and economic approaches on which post-war domestic and foreign policies were based. The left may not have succeeded in preventing the age of extremes, but after 1945 socialists launched successful attacks on the unemployment, insecurity, ignorance, inequality, imperialism and militarism which had made the crafted appeals of a subtle extremism almost unstoppable.

Differing Approaches to the History of European Socialism

At one time most accounts of European labour politics were concerned with institutional developments and with the ideas of the principal political theorists. It was common to contrast an intellectually sophisticated, militant and Marxist-influenced continental socialism with the trade-union based and more moderate British Labour Party. In the 1970s and 1980s, scholars in Britain and America in particular shifted attention to the social history of labour. They focused on class formation, the impact of social factors on socialist support, and the extent to which political and industrial militancy could be explained by variations in class, industrial and labour relations. Generalizations about European socialist politics became more difficult.

In recent years, however, common themes within European socialist politics have received more attention. Social historians have examined pan-European attitudes towards issues such as unemployment and the welfare state.[1] Historians and political scientists in France and Italy have examined the nature of European political parties, noting the parallel responses made by politicians and theorists across Europe to the challenge of a mass democratic system.[2] Several recent studies develop these historiographical changes, and there are now several volumes which contain parallel studies of socialist politics in all the major European countries. These studies generally emphasize social influences on the rise of militancy and on socialist electoral support. There have been few attempts to integrate this with an overview of socialist *political* developments, with an awareness of what the parties hoped to achieve.[3] This chapter shows how socialists with similar aims, facing similar problems and with a similar range of policy alternatives, developed or discussed similar responses. This is not to deny national differences, or to suggest a single 'normal' pattern of development. But it is to argue that core features existed, that socialists were part of the same 'political family' and that the same range of contextual circumstances influenced political developments across Europe. In doing so, it explains the rise and nature of socialist politics, socialist reaction to the politics of extremism and the origins of policies and orientations which were to shape post-war Europe.

The Evolution of Socialist Parties before 1914

Socialist politics did not begin with Marx. Many countries had their own indigenous radical and socialist traditions. The history of France

[1] For example, G. Bock and P. Thane (eds), *Women and the Rise of the European Welfare States, 1880s–1950s* (London, 1991); M. Mansfield, R. Salais and N. Whiteside (eds), *Aux Sources du Chômage 1880–1914* (Paris, 1994).
[2] L. Riall, 'Progress and compromise in liberal Italy', *Historical Journal*, 38 (1995), pp. 205–13; G. Quagliariello, *Politics Without Parties: Moisei Ostrogorski and the Debate on Political Parties on the Eve of the Twentieth Century* (Aldershot, 1996).
[3] S. Berger and D. Broughton (eds), *The Force of Labour: The Western European Labour Movement and the Working Class in the Twentieth Century* (Oxford, 1995); D. Geary, *Labour and Socialist Movements in Europe before 1914* (Oxford, 1989); M. van der Linden and J. Rojahn (eds), *The Formation of Labour Movements 1870–1914: An International Perspective* (New York, 1990).

Table 7.1 Formation of socialist parties

Germany	Socialist Workers Party (SAD)	1875
Spain	Spanish Socialist Workers Party (PSOE)	1879
France	French Workers Party (POF)	1880
Britain	Democratic Federation	1881
	(Social Democratic Federation) (SDF)	1883
Belgium	Belgian Workers Party (POB)	1885
Sweden	Swedish Workers Party (SAP)	1889
Italy	Socialist Party of Italy (PSI)	1892

Source: M. van der Linden and J. Rojahn (eds), *The Formation of Labour Movements 1870–1914: An International Perspective* (New York, 1990)

is peppered with radical events (the French Revolution, the revolutions of 1848, the Paris Commune) which became symbols of the nation's identity. But France was not alone in this respect. In most countries an indigenous radical tradition had a major influence on the nature and evolution of the socialist movement even after the advent of Marxism.

Marx's ideas and sympathizers were certainly instrumental in the formation of the socialist parties which mushroomed across Europe in the 1880s and 1890s (table 7.1). Most of these parties adopted Marxist constitutions. Many (e.g. the Swedish and Italian parties) also followed the organizational structure of the German socialist party, the leading socialist party in Europe before 1914 and the party with the greatest strength and moral authority. Marxism was the ideology of resistance; it described the victory of a workers' creed as a scientific certainty. Yet in reality even party leaders often knew little of Marx's writings, most of which were only available in German or French; and as a result in Spain and Britain the first socialist parties adopted a rigidly deterministic Marxism. Party discipline (echoing the German model) was equally firm. The Second International – set up in 1889 to regulate international socialist action – acted as an ideological policeman and the guardian of Marxist purity.

It was not long before the suitability of such parties and ideas to individual national conditions was challenged. In Spain the anarchists were an important alternative. Industrial or insurrectionary militancy also rivalled socialist politics as a method and ideology (to a lesser degree) in France. But the more important challenge to Marxism came from moderate forms of socialism. In some countries non-Marxist labour organizations had survived the early enthusiasm for Marx's ideas. In Britain, the Fabian society – a London-based group of intellectuals which included Bernard Shaw and Sidney and Beatrice Webb – studied and rejected many aspects of Marxist economics. The Independent Labour Party offered a more actively political (and socialist) alternative, with a greater emphasis on the moral deficiency of capitalism, but the ILP, like the 'Possibilists' in France,[4] were keen to tackle practical political issues, to gain power at local level and to use this power to alleviate poverty. They also opposed the centralization of authority common within organized Marxist parties, preferring a more federal structure and greater local participation.

Neither were such moderate alternatives simply available in countries (like France and Britain) where non-Marxist organizations contested the radical ground. Within theoretically Marxist parties, many realized that Marx's forecast of an inevitable revolution was simplistic or wrong. They abandoned a slavish adherence to Marxist ideas, whilst often maintaining a Marxist rhetoric. Thus in parts of Germany, especially the south, and in areas of Italy, socialists adopted a more moderate approach, diluting Marxism with older influences and ideas.[5] Within Germany, these differences over ideology and strategy came to the fore in the 1890s, when Eduard Bernstein,* an established Marxist intellectual and co-author of the SPD's official programme, redefined Marx's ideas and provided a democratic socialist (or 'revisionist') alternative. Bernstein is often seen as the ideological father of moderate socialist politics.

Nonetheless, Bernstein's significance should not be overstated. Most countries had an equivalent figure, although few wrote in as intellectual a manner, or had such roots in the Marxist tradition. Jaurès* in France, Ramsay MacDonald* in Britain, Turati in Italy and Branting* in Sweden came to similar conclusions, adapted to their local or national conditions. This is hardly surprising. Such people knew one anothers' work. Bernstein had lived in Britain and was accused by German critics of being unduly influenced by British liberal and Fabian ideas. However, similar perspectives resulted more from similar aims and values than from direct contact.

Despite this growing challenge to Marx's ideas, it was politically difficult for many socialists to express their sympathy with Bernstein's

---

[4] D. Stafford, *From Anarchism to Reformism: A Study of the Political Activities of Paul Brousse Within the First International and the French Socialist Movement* (London, 1971). The nature of the rival and more Marxist group, led by Jules Guesde, has recently been reassessed. See R. Stuart, *Marxism at Work: Ideology, Class and French Socialism During the Third Republic* (Cambridge, 1992).
[5] F. Andreucci, 'The diffusion of marxism in Italy during the late nineteenth century', in *Culture, Ideology and Politics*, ed. R. Samuel and G. Stedman Jones (London, 1983), pp. 214–27; R. Fletcher, *Revisionism and Empire* (London, 1984), pp. 24–41.

views. Challenging party traditions was inevitably divisive. Ignaz Auer, the SPD secretary, argued that Bernstein's views on political strategy reflected 'what happens already in nine-tenths of the party, without it being openly admitted', but objected to him raising what was best left unstated.[6] MacDonald in Britain, Jaurès in France and Turati in Italy were attacked for leading their parties towards reformism. Like Branting in Sweden, Jaurès and Turati found it expedient to exaggerate their (genuine) differences with Bernstein. Turati and Jaurès adopted a more orthodox Marxist line on the role of class struggle and on whether socialists should participate in coalition governments with non-socialists or wait until they achieved a clear majority. Indeed, when Bernstein placed this last matter before the International, many revisionists voted against him. A single French socialist party (the SFIO) only came into being in 1905 after Jaurès agreed to accept the German line on nonparticipation in government; the Marxist POF would accept nothing less. Attacking the revisionist drift of domestic politics continued to be a disruptive feature of socialist politics in the years immediately before war. Syndicalists and anarchists criticized revisionism from outside socialist parties. But revisionism was also opposed from within socialist parties. In Germany dissidents like Rosa Luxemburg felt the SPD had taken the wrong direction. In Britain, founding fathers of the party, like Keir Hardie,* agitators rather than machine politicians, felt Labour had become an electoral machine, devoid of socialist purpose. The Italian socialist party came under the control of such radicals, and consequently tensions between moderates, syndicalists and Marxists came to the fore in 1911–12; they were also growing in France by 1914. The First World War and the Russian Revolution were to turn tensions into a substantial split.

It may seem strange that a political party should oppose taking office. Marxists argued that participating in bourgeois coalition governments would prop up a political system which could never benefit workers. They were understandably suspicious of the state and its middle- and upper-class supporters, given the establishment's past tendency to protect its own interests by any means (including making socialist parties illegal). However, bourgeois governments were increasingly showing a willingness to enact reforming legislation, most notably in Britain. This cast doubt on the traditional socialist view that the bourgeois state was an inevitably oppressive force. In such circumstances, socialists who passed over opportunities to use state power for the public good

---

[6] For the party leader August Bebel's reaction, see Bebel to Bernstein, 16 Oct. 1898 and subsequent letters, cited in H. Tudor and J. M. Tudor (eds), *Marxism and Social Democracy: The Revisionist Debate 1896–98* (Cambridge, 1988), pp. 319–31.

might anticipate electoral problems. Moreover, when the very existence of democracy was threatened, as Jaurès thought it was in 1899,
participation in governments of national defence seemed doubly necessary. Even in Italy and Germany – where the state remained a more
oppressive force[7] – socialists sought reforms, like the extension of the
franchise, by bargaining with non-socialist parties. A slice of the loaf
seemed better than no bread at all.

Many socialist parties were less committed to an abstract Marxism
than official rhetoric indicates. Analysis of the material borrowed from
socialist party libraries, for example, shows limited enthusiasm for
Marxist writings and rather more for imaginative fiction and utopian
pictures of the socialist future. Most socialists were motivated more
by moral distaste for the existing order, by hostility to the snobbery,
poverty and limited opportunities which degraded the deserving many
and elevated the undeserving minority. They wanted a world in which
more humane and fraternal relationships would develop, to create a sense
of belonging and community amongst people ravaged by the social
and cultural barbarism which they associated with industrial capitalism. Whilst the struggle for survival dominated people's outlooks, this
was impossible. This ethical socialism often drew on religious language
and motivations. Such people wanted not class conflict but social co-
operation. Only British ethical socialism has been examined in depth.
However, similar ethical motivations can be detected amongst pre-war
socialist leaders in countries like Sweden and Austria.[8]

The role of trade unionism in the growth of political moderation
has attracted some attention. The expansion of trade unionism did not
necessarily lead to the adoption of moderate socialist policies. Some
trade unions – notably in Spain, France and Italy – opposed reformist
socialist parties, which they saw as offering little of practical value
to workers. Union leaders in these countries believed that politicians
invariably became distant from the rank and file and that a historically
oppressive state would never deliver reforms of value. Syndicalists
preached industrial action and suspicion of centralized party and union
structures. Trade unions were not normally directly linked to socialist
parties. Neither was socialist reformism a consequence of trade union
moderation in countries like Britain, where the unions were directly
affiliated to the party. Unions responded favourably to reforming initiatives made by others, rather than initiating the shift themselves.

---

[7]   S. Berger, *The British Labour Party and the German Social Democrats, 1900–1931*
(Oxford, 1994), pp. 25–30.
[8]   L. Kolakowski, *Main Currents of Marxism* (Oxford, 1978), vol. 2, pp. 243–54;
T. Tilton, *The Political Theory of Swedish Social Democracy: Through the Welfare State to
Socialism* (Oxford, 1991), pp. 15–33.

Table 7.2 Electoral support for socialist parties in *c*.1914

	Vote (%)	Seats
Sweden	36.7 (1914)	87
Germany	34.7 (1912)	110
Netherlands	19.3 (1913)	18
Italy	17.7 (1913)	52
France		104
Great Britain	6.4 (1910–Dec.)	42

Sources: M. B. Hamilton, *Democratic Socialism in Britain and Sweden* (Basingstoke, 1988); J. E. Miller, *From Elite to Mass Politics: Italian Socialism in the Giolittian Era, 1900–1914* (Kent, OH, 1990); H. Buiting and S. van Schuppen, 'The implantation of the Social Democratic Labour party in the Netherlands, 1894–1913', *Tijdschrift voor sociale geschiedenis, achttiende jaargang*, 2/3 (1992), pp. 313–32; K. S. Pinson, *Modern Germany* (London, 1966), pp. 601–4; F. W. S. Craig, *British Electoral Facts 1885–1975* (London, 1976)

Electoral and Organizational Expansion before 1914

Socialist parties found it more difficult to expand their support before 1914 than one might think. Marx's enlargened and unified proletariat had not materialized. Social conditions had not created a unified and rad- icalized industrial workforce. The actions of rival parties – their ability to present an attractive programme or party image – also adversely influenced socialist electoral prospects. Some offered reforms; others ex- ploited nationalist, racist or religious prejudices.[9] Socialists were strong- est in Germany, where rival parties were reluctant to embrace reform and where Marxist descriptions of capitalist governments as authoritar- ian and self-serving guardians of the rich seemed most plausible. Social- ism was much weaker, by contrast, in Italy, Britain and France. It was weaker still in Spain, although here the problem was not the existence of popular radical or republican alternatives but a polarized political struc- ture and the grip of traditional values on an underdeveloped economy and a controlled population (see table 7.2 for electoral figures). Organ- izationally the position was not dissimilar. In Germany the socialist party attempted to be a state within a state. It had a huge organizational apparatus, including its own national and local press, a vast member- ship and a supporting network of sporting and cultural organizations, frequently with memberships over 100,000. In Italy, however, local

[9]   E.g. essays in P. Kennedy and A. Nicholls (eds), *Nationalist and Racialist Movements in Britain and Germany before 1914* (Oxford, 1981).

Table 7.3 Membership of socialist parties in *c.*1914

	Party membership (in thousands, to the nearest thousand)
Germany	1,100
Austria	180
France	90
Sweden	84
Italy	37 (1913)
Great Britain	33 (Socialist societies only)
Netherlands	26

Source: Based on S. Berger and D. Broughton (eds), *The Force of Labour: The Western European Labour Movement and the Working Class in the Twentieth Century* (Oxford, 1995), pp. 267–71. However, I have used the more commonly cited figure of 90,000 party members in France, and 1913 figures for Italy, as 1914 figures may be distorted.

socialist branches were formed *after* a national party came into being amongst deputies, and local organization remained weak. In Britain, the socialist ILP (which was affiliated to the Labour Party) had branches in many urban areas by 1914, and was quite strong in the north-west and in Yorkshire. However, whole parts of the country had little active Labour presence. Central Labour Party organization was limited and the party had limited financial resources. In France party membership was insubstantial (table 7.3).

Within every country, socialist support was highly regionalized. Huge areas of southern Italy returned few socialist deputies, the party's support being concentrated in the north. Socialists were weaker in the working-class Catholic areas of the Netherlands and Germany, for example, than in the Protestant areas. Socialists were not the party of the working class (such unity did not exist) but of particular groups and areas. In Germany, Spain, Britain and France, socialists gained substantial support from coalminers, steelworkers and railwaymen, and from the communities which they dominated (unless, as in parts of the Ruhr and Scottish coalfields, religious and ethnic fragmentation cut across occupational groupings and encouraged workers into different political camps).[10] In such areas both the structure and the content of socialist politics seemed attractive and real. At the same time, however, socialists could obtain support from less evidently 'proletarian' occupational groups. In France,

---

[10] A. Campbell, 'The social history of political conflict in the Scots coalfields, 1910–1939', in *Miners, Unions and Politics 1910–47*, ed. A. Campbell, N. Fishman and D. Howell (Aldershot, 1996), p. 155; S. H. F. Hickey, *Workers in Imperial Germany: The Miners of the Ruhr* (Oxford, 1985).

Parisian artisans and agricultural workers from the Mediterranean basin were an important part of the socialists' electoral base, as were agricultural workers in the Emilia-Romagna region of Italy, which supplied more than a quarter of socialist deputies in the 1913 election. In Sweden, where moderate tendencies were strong, the party adapted its programme to the needs of rural workers in 1911, improved its image amongst such groups and gained electorally as a result. Historians of all European countries have used local studies of industrial and community development to explain these patterns of support. Some suggest that particular lifestyles and work patterns fostered both independent thought and traditions of community resistance. Others show how socialists became the voice of communities under pressure, or of people seeking to shape their local environment through interventionist politics. There was no single forward march by the radical champions of the disadvantaged. Industrialization did not create a homogeneous working class with homogeneous interests. On the contrary, workers remained divided, their expectations reduced by poverty, their aspirations blunted by the power of others over their lives. It took a substantial effort, and favourable circumstances, to overcome such disadvantages.

The Impact of War: The Moderate Left

The outbreak of war divided socialist parties. Leading moderates like Bernstein, Jaurès and MacDonald felt that war resulted from an arms race, secret diplomacy or the need to protect empires, and opposed their country's intervention. Jaurès was assassinated for his views. Bernstein and MacDonald left their parties over this issue. Some socialists – like Keir Hardie in Britain – advocated an international General Strike to prevent the pointless and unnecessary destruction of workers' lives. However, this approach – like the subsequent calls for a negotiated peace – did not attract majority support. Most trade union and socialist leaders supported the war effort and even relaxed their hostility to the state. Industrial peace became the norm.

In Britain and France, some trade union and socialist leaders were drawn into the war effort. Albert Thomas, a moderate socialist deputy since 1910, effectively directed the French munitions effort until September 1917. In Britain, Labour and trade union figures played important roles on the home front until 1917, receiving recognition and status for their organizations as a result. However, as war weariness set in, socialists looked to the future and often withdrew from coalitions to campaign for a new future.

In 1918–19 the nationalistic right exploited wartime patriotism to good electoral effect in both France and Britain. However, war also produced a more favourable climate for socialist parties. Full employment amongst men and improved earnings for women and teenagers increased expectations. Those who had made sacrifices hoped for a better future. Some improvements in living standards were seemingly achieved only through state regulation of industry and prices. Even syndicalist union officials in France, hitherto very wary of the state, now saw continuing state regulation as a means of maintaining wages and conditions in less favourable labour-market conditions. The French syndicalist leader Léon Jouhaux and the future German finance minister Rudolf Hilferding* independently argued that capitalism had fundamentally changed.[11] Hilferding described an 'organized capitalism', in which large companies organized into cartels and trusts controlled trade and regularized economic conditions. He argued it would be easier in future for socialists to influence the economy by regulating or nationalizing such organizations, hence ensuring that the power of a technologically more advanced capitalism was exercised for the public good. This faith in the potential power of the state was shared in countries like Britain (where Clause 4 of the new Labour constitution committed the party to public ownership). Moreover, during wartime socialists and trade unionists in Britain and France had moved closer together in discussing their approach to post-war reconstruction. In Britain unions committed more funds to the Labour Party, and a proper – if still weak – national and local organization and policy-making structure was created. In the diverse socialist parties of Sweden, Austria and France, socialist debate in 1918–20 focused on the future role and nature of public ownership. Public ownership seemed to offer a means of creating a reformed capitalist system.

These discussions were not confined to the victorious countries. Moreover, the collapse of autocratic regimes in Germany, the Austro-Hungarian Empire, Russia and Spain meant that socialists could now hope to compete in a democratic context for popular support. Indeed, given the socialists' attitude to participation in the war effort, and their concern for domestic living standards during the conflict, they were now likely to reap electoral benefits. War had fundamentally altered their political world.

Some historians have seen the creation of a mass electorate as the main element in explaining the socialists' post-war success. Socialists in Austria, the Netherlands, Germany and Sweden certainly engaged in mass campaigns for electoral reform before 1914. In some countries (like the Netherlands, Italy and Sweden) pre-war franchise extensions also contributed to partial improvements in the socialists' electoral position.

---

[11] J. N. Horne, *Labour at War: France and Britain 1914–18* (Oxford, 1991), ch. 4; R. Hilferding, *Finance Capital: A Study of the Latest Phase of Capitalist Development*, ed. with an introduction by T. Bottomore (London, 1985).

Yet because the working class was not a united and radicalized bloc, and because rival parties were still attractive, increased enfranchisement did not lead to automatic gains of a pronounced nature. In Britain the Labour Party did not fare well before 1918, despite the fact that working-class men comprised about 70 per cent of the electorate. The franchise was extended in 1918 across Europe (although women did not obtain the vote in every European country). In Britain it now embraced men over twenty-one and most women over thirty. However, it was not electoral reform as such which made greater Labour success possible, but the demise of popular alternative parties and the consolidation of its support during the war. Labour performed well in its heartlands (mainly coalfield constituencies) at the 1918 election, a fact made more significant by the almost total collapse of the Liberals in their former strongholds. Labour became the official opposition in a two-party system, which helped to squeeze the initially still-significant Liberal vote. The creation of a mass democratic system demanded that all parties adapt. In countries where rival parties had previously sheltered behind state power and a restricted electoral system (as in Germany and Austria) socialists had a head start. This, and the circumstances of wartime politics – rather than any 'natural' class appeal to the unenfranchised – were the more important factors in explaining the socialists' post-war success.

Socialist parties were now in a new position. War-induced enthusiasm for state intervention suggested there was a potentially popular 'socialist' means of creating a more efficient economy – and through this the parties' broader social and cultural aims. However, to deliver this new economic prosperity and security, socialists needed to attain office and enact legislation. But the pre-war view of the Socialist International was that socialists should not participate in coalition governments with bourgeois parties. When autocratic monarchies dominated and bourgeois parties were so reactionary, as in Germany, Spain and Austria before 1914, such advice could be followed with ease (it was a less attractive proposition to socialists in France and Britain, where conditions were rather different). However, in 1918 new democratic systems were established. There were many who consequently argued that socialists should abandon Marxist rhetoric, and create and work within a reformed and democratic capitalist system. In Germany, socialists consequently participated in drafting a new constitution and in the immediate post-war governments.

The Impact of War: The Radical Left

The wartime integration of some socialist and trade union leaders into the state apparatus was often bitterly opposed by the parties' more radical elements. In Britain some rank and file trade unionists opposed sacrificing union independence (and sometimes bargaining rights) to the national cause. In Britain the engineering and mining unions, and in France and Germany the metal unions, were particularly prone to strike. Unrest increased dramatically after 1917, as militant union leaders built on discontent over rising prices, food shortages, a sense of unequal sacrifice and war weariness. In Britain the ILP advocated a negotiated peace, as did the new German independent socialist party, the USPD. The Russian Revolution of 1917 created excitement and hope. Anything now seemed possible. In Britain prominent Labour figures like George Lansbury and even former Liberal radicals like Morgan Philips Price and Joseph King were swept up by this enthusiasm, and wrote euphoric accounts of the revolution and the revolutionaries.[12] In Italy during August 1917, and in Austria, Germany and Hungary in 1918, socialists, workers and soldiers even formed workers' councils or soviets.

Revolutionary activity was soon defeated. Most people, including moderate socialists, saw further conflict as a threat to stability and normality, rather than an opportunity for sweeping change. This resulted in socialist leaders supporting anti-revolutionary police action in Germany. Internal party tensions escalated. When the Soviet Union called for the formation of Communist parties across Europe there was a huge response. In France around two-thirds of socialist party members joined the Communist Party (PCF) in 1920. There was considerable popular support for Communist parties in France, Italy and Germany, and for radical socialists in Norway, Austria and elsewhere.[13]

Discontent continued to rage across Europe in the immediate post-war years, as unemployment rose dramatically following the collapse of war-induced demand. In Britain and France, vast numbers of working days were lost through strikes in the mining, iron and steel and shipbuilding industries. In Italy opposition went further and resulted in the famous *biennio rosso*, the occupation of factories by workers' councils, in 1919–20. In Austria and Italy, discontent was fiercely resisted by the nationalist right, who benefited from the perceived threat to stability and order. In Britain, the press and middle-class groups argued that militant trade unionists were exploiting and terrifying poor and hard-working people, who lacked their ability to take what they wanted.[14] The right also gained considerable support in Germany and France.

[12]   G. Lansbury, *What I Saw in Russia* (London, 1920); J. King, *Bolshevism and Bolsheviks* (London, 1919); M. Philips Price, *Reminiscences of the Russian Revolution* (London, 1921).
[13]   For Norway, S. S. Nilson, 'Factional strife in the Norwegian Labour party 1918–24', *Journal of Contemporary History*, 16 (1981), pp. 691–704.
[14]   R. I. McKibbin, 'Class and conventional wisdom: the Conservative party and the 'public' in inter-war Britain', in his *Ideologies of Class* (Oxford, 1990), pp. 272–3.

Politics had thus begun to polarize by 1920, with moderate socialists left to negotiate a middle way between the two extremes.

Moderate Socialism and the Challenge of Peace

Building on pre-war revisionist debates, several leading socialists re- acted to the new conditions by rejecting Marxism and its core idea of a class struggle, whilst accepting the need to intervene substantially in economic and social affairs, to reform capitalism and create a just and efficient social and economic system. In the 1920s, they sought the means to turn ideological aims into tangible results.

The most successful party in this respect was the still-understudied Swedish Social Democrats. Having rejected the Marxist idea that economic changes within capitalism would inevitably bring about a situation with massive radical potential, Swedish socialists thought it necessary to outline the values which should form the basis of a social- ist state and the policies which would create a new economic and social order. For the leading Swedish writer and politician Ernst Wigforss, socialism was about equality, freedom, fraternity and security. Building on such views, the party leader from 1928, Per Albin Hansson, aimed at 'the breaking down of all the social and economic barriers that now divide citizens'. The tools of change were to be a socialized market economy, redistributive taxation, an elaborate welfare system and sup- port for proto-Keynesian ideas. The result was electoral progress, cul- minating with a major victory in 1932. This was followed by forty-four years of uninterrupted socialist rule, in which Sweden developed a powerful economy and the world's best welfare system.

There were parallel instances of intellectual adaptation in other coun- tries. In Britain theorists like G. D. H. Cole and R. H. Tawney, and politicians like Ramsay MacDonald, undertook a similar reformulation of socialist ideas (although this had begun before 1914). The Belgian socialist Hendrik de Man* wrote a massively successful book (it was translated into eleven languages) which provided his party with an intellectual basis for the rejection of Marxism. It also led to the devel- opment of party programmes throughout the Low Countries which were designed to make capitalism work more effectively through plan- ning and other forms of state regulation.[15] In Germany, Hilferding's 1925 Heidelberg programme made it clear that the SPD was now a revisionist party. The SPD's adoption of a rural programme in 1927

---

[15] H. de Man, *The Psychology of Socialism* (London, 1928); E. Hansen, 'Depression decade crisis: social democracy and *planisme* in Belgium and the Netherlands, 1929– 39', *Journal of Contemporary History*, 16 (1981), pp. 293–322.

was part of an attempt to define an economic and social strategy for the whole nation. Building on their pre-war doubts about the causes of war, socialists also continued to attack the arms race, militarism and imperialism, seeking to reduce arms and promote international co-operation.

Despite these changes, most socialist parties continued to believe that the wasteful and inefficient international capitalist economy needed to be regulated and controlled if it was to create and distribute wealth in a fair and acceptable manner. State regulation and control of industry consequently remained high on their agenda. Events in the 1920s – the growth of even larger firms, the extension of international agreements between companies, and the growing importance of international banking – led many socialists to believe that state regulation of companies and banks which already had enormous power over the market could remove the cycle of booms and slumps which so adversely affected ordinary people. Many socialists in Germany, Britain and France expressed a desire to promote new technology and industrial modernization (under state direction) as a means of further improving the capacity for wealth creation.

Socialists also extended and improved their social and welfare policies in the 1920s, whilst socialist-dominated state and town councils introduced a range of reforms. The Swedish socialists again led the way, with Gustav Möller's 1928 pamphlet, *Security for the Swedish People*, providing a commitment to the creation of a complete welfare state and a rationale for the party's whole approach. In Germany, socialists were responsible for the creation of a strong state insurance system, and for the workers' councils which were designed to foster good industrial relations. Socialist town and city councils across Europe also provided a range of social services, both in old established industrial centres and on the new municipal housing schemes which were being established in the suburbs.

Socialist parties continued their organizational expansion in the 1920s. The Swedish and German parties led the field, with reorganized and expanded activities. In Sweden party membership had tripled to around 200,000 by the mid 1920s and increased to around 350,000 in the 1930s. In Britain, Labour Party membership grew, albeit to less substantial levels, with local parties and newspapers being founded in large numbers between 1922 and 1929. Whilst party membership in all countries consisted largely of workers, there was some increase in the number of middle-class and women members, these two groups together comprising 40 per cent of the German socialist party by the end of the 1920s (although see below for the limited scope and impact of this change). In the process of organizational expansion, party discipline and the power of party leaders was tightened, to the disquiet of some activists. Equally,

Table 7.4 Socialist and labour party electoral support in the 1920s and 1930s

	Date of election and % share of the vote						
Germany	1920	1924	1924	1928	1930	1932	1932
	21.6	20.5	26	29.8	24.5	21.6	20.4
Great Britain	1922	1923	1924	1929	1931	1935	
	29.7	30.7	33.3	37.1	30.8	38.0	
Sweden	1920	1921	1924	1928	1933	1936	
	29.7	36.2	41.1	37	41.7	45.9	

Source: M. B. Hamilton, *Democratic Socialism in Britain and Sweden* (Basingstoke, 1988); H. Buiting and S. van Schuppen, 'The implantation of the Social Democratic Labour party in the Netherlands, 1894–1913', *Tijdschrift voor sociale geschiedenis, achttiende jaargang*, 2/3 (1992), pp. 313–32; K. S. Pinson, *Modern Germany* (London, 1966), pp. 601–4; F. W. S. Craig, *British Electoral Facts 1885–1975* (London, 1976)

the diversity of local socialism became less apparent, as national leaders sought to create uniform programmes and party images.

In Britain, Sweden and Germany electoral results show an expansion of support across the 1920s, partially as a result of increased success outside the party's working-class heartlands (table 7.4). In all three countries, socialists were the largest single party by the end of the 1920s. In Britain nearly 75 of the 288 Labour seats were won for the first time in 1929, including many in London and the south-east where light industry and the service sector dominated.[16] The SPD also managed to extend its support in the rural and Catholic areas which had hitherto resisted its appeals, although the extent of its progress should not be overstated.

The Limits of Socialist Progress

Despite these changes, socialist parties did not become 'People's' parties in the 1920s, nor did the obstacles to their expansion disappear. Confessional parties – and Catholic unions – continued to take a substantial portion of their potential working-class support in countries like the Netherlands and Germany. Communists competed – sometimes very successfully – for a further portion of the old socialist vote. Neither were social trends encouraging. Trade union membership generally fell across the 1920s, and employment in Britain and France shifted away from the industries which had supplied a substantial portion of the socialists'

[16] D. M. Tanner, 'Class voting and radical politics: the Liberal and Labour parties, 1910–31', in *Party, State and Society: Electoral Behaviour in Britain since 1820*, ed. M. Taylor and J. Lawrence (London, 1997), pp. 120–1.

vote to newer industries, often located in very different areas. In France
in particular, socialist support stagnated.

French historians have paid particular attention to the social constraints
on socialist progress. Noiriel has suggested that in France the old working class shrunk during the 1920s and 1930s, whilst a new working class
was being created. Industries changed; large numbers of immigrants
were brought into the workforce; labour management became stricter,
and the size and nature of companies altered.[17] Huge new housing estates
were created on the outskirts of cities or in new areas. The Communist
Party (like socialist parties in Austria, the Netherlands, Germany and
Britain) managed to put down roots in these new municipal housing
complexes, but the French socialist party stagnated. Its urban base was
shrinking.

A second emphasis – especially amongst German and British historians
– is the failure of socialists to adapt more successfully to the enfranchisement of women. They suggest that in the period before 1930, women
were probably less likely to support socialist parties than men, with
confessional parties, or in Britain the Conservative Party, being more
attractive.[18] In both Britain and Germany, socialist parties attempted to
involve and promote women within the party organization, and were
fairly successful in this respect compared to socialists in France and
Italy. If the radical left produced the most prominent women socialists
(Rosa Luxemburg and Clara Zetkin*) it was the neglected German
revisionist Lily Braun who produced the most articulate case for 'fem-
inizing' her party.[19] However, neither the SPD nor the Labour Party
was especially receptive to such ideas. Party leaders saw welfare programmes as the prime means of mobilizing the 'women's vote'. In
Britain networks of women's committees were established and women
party members outnumbered men in some constituencies by the end of
the 1920s. But there were considerable tensions between the advocates
of more feminist demands and concerns (on matters such as family
allowances and birth control) and the views of party loyalists.[20]

[17] G. Noiriel, *Workers in French Society in the 19th and 20th Centuries* (New York,
1990), ch. 4.
[18] H. L. Boak, 'Women in Weimar Germany: the "Frauenfrage" and the female vote',
in *Social Change and Political Developments in Weimar Germany*, ed. R. Bessel and E. J.
Feuchtwanger (London, 1981); M. Pugh, *Women and the Women's Movement in Britain
1914–1959* (London, 1992), pp. 141–53.
[19] A. G. Meyer, *The Feminism and Socialism of Lily Braun* (Bloomington, 1985).
[20] M. Savage, *The Dynamics of Working Class Politics* (Cambridge, 1987), pp. 195–
7; and D. M. Tanner, 'The Labour party and electoral politics in the coalfields', in
Miners, Unions and Politics, ed. Campbell *et al.*, p. 81. On family allowances and birth
control, S. Pedersen, *Family, Dependence, and the Origins of the Welfare State: Britain and
France, 1914–45* (Cambridge, 1993); and P. M. Graves, *Labour Women: Women in
British Working Class Politics 1918–39* (Cambridge, 1994).

Nationalism was a further obstacle to socialist progress. Austro-Marxists like Otto Bauer had challenged Marx's hostility to nationalism before 1914, and provided a fuller and better understanding of its relationship to socialism. Socialists in the Low Countries and the United Kingdom had also adapted to and utilized separatist sentiments and cultural diversity.[21] Yet after 1914 attempts to recognize diversity were marginalized as more uniform national programmes emerged. In addition to losing opportunities to gain ground in such areas, socialist support for reason, international arbitration and trade with the USSR, like their opposition to imperialism and militarism, could easily be misrepresented by right-wing critics.

The development of a cross-class appeal in the 1920s was not universal, nor was it universally popular. In Britain Labour's radical wing was concerned about the party leaders' moderation and about their willingness to form and preserve governments with bourgeois support at the expense of implementing the party's full programme. In Spain, however, leading socialists like Largo Cabellero even expressed doubts about the possibility of 'carrying out the work of socialism within the framework of bourgeois democracy'.[22] Anarcho-syndicalist parties and trade unions made more strident criticisms. In France, where socialist support and membership was becoming progressively less dependent on the urban proletariat, the party was increasingly opposed to moderating its demands and strategy. Léon Blum,* party leader for most of the inter-war years, believed that war had accentuated 'fortune and misery (and) concentrated capitalism as well as the industrial proletariat'. In doing so it 'proved that class antagonism really is the law of contemporary society'.[23] A traditional socialism had been partially reaffirmed.

When socialists participated in governments and moderated their policies in the 1920s, they were condemned by traditional socialist advocates of non-participation in government. They were also punished by the voters when the coalitions failed. Complicity with the government's repression of unrest ensured that the majority socialists in Germany lost support during the 1920 election, to the USPD's benefit. The SPD subsequently became more cautious. Instead of joining coalitions, it supplied support to bourgeois cabinets, especially when the Republic and social stability were in danger (as in the crisis of 1923). Having joined a 'Grand Coalition' in 1928–30 to defend Weimar democracy against the right, socialists were forced to accept tax and spending plans which

[21]   See for example D. Howell, *A Lost Left: Three Studies in Socialism and Nationalism* (Manchester, 1986).
[22]   A. Smith, 'Spain', in *The Force of Labour*, ed. Berger and Broughton, p. 187.
[23]   Horne, *Labour at War*, p. 367.

sat poorly with their own aims. The party again suffered at the polls and at the hands of Communist critics.

Other socialist parties were even more reluctant to accept political office. In France and Austria, socialists took no part in government during the 1920s. In Austria this seemed to work, in that unity was maintained (a Communist Party existed but was very weak) and electoral support increased. The party used municipal power to demonstrate what socialism could achieve. In 'Red Vienna', socialists established huge housing estates and erected a system of municipal provision which sought both to protect and educate workers.[24] It was a massive exercise in social engineering. But the strategy – like the German SPD's ambivalent approach to government – did little to defend the Austrian Republic against the growing threat from the right, to create the idea that the democratic left could defend the interests of the whole nation. This is not to blame socialists for the collapse of democracy. If socialists participated in governments which made harsh decisions, this risked handing support or power to the extremists. If they did not try to defend democracy, but let bourgeois coalitions try and fail, the right might win by default. When the SPD resigned from the Grand Coalition in 1930 rather than face this dilemma, Hilferding likened the decision to that of a man driven to suicide by his fear of death. He failed to recognize that taking full responsibility for an economic crisis was itself suicidal – unless the party had a programme which could guide it out of the crisis.

Crisis and Reconstruction

From 1930 socialists faced two major and extraordinary problems: an economic crisis which resulted in the collapse of the world economy and the growth of a right-wing extremism which led to world war.

By the late 1920s, the German and British economies were heavily reliant on foreign capital for investment and on foreign exports for their prosperity. The Wall Street crash, the collapse of the world economy and the growth of tariff barriers caused both loans and exports to dry up. Unemployment increased and countries had great difficulty in balancing their budgets. The currency plummeted. Massive inflation of the kind which decimated Germany in 1923 loomed once again.

The advice of most economic experts was to ride out the crisis by reducing expenditure and stabilizing the currency. In the longer term, securing the home market by introducing tariffs or attempting to restore international confidence and trade were the preferred options. Hilferding

[24]   H. Gruber, *Red Vienna: Experiment in Working Class Culture, 1919–34* (Oxford, 1991).

admitted there was no socialist solution to the crisis. Caution during the crisis should be followed by economic modernization under state direction once it had passed.[25]

However, it was difficult for socialists to make the cuts in expenditure which most economists argued were vital to prevent financial ruin. SPD ministers resigned from the Grand Coalition in 1930 because the party could not agree to cuts in unemployment benefit. Similar problems caused the collapse of the Labour government in 1931 and the formation of the National Government under the Labour leader, Ramsay MacDonald. Socialists had a programme for long-term economic restructuring, but faced a short-term crisis, to which the parties' leaders and financial experts had no answer.

Elements outside the socialist leadership suggested an alternative approach. In Britain, the economist Maynard Keynes* inspired the Liberal Party's programme, *We can conquer unemployment*, in 1929. Related programmes were advanced by elements within every major European socialist party. Most of these programmes suggested public expenditure as a means of job creation. They often incorporated tariff protection and credit control. Such proposals, however, were untested and seemed to imply that capitalism and the market were redeemable, when many socialists assumed the opposite. Socialist leaders were unwilling to take the economic risk or the political gamble involved in adopting these untried and heretical ideas, for both conservative parties and left-wing critics were waiting to pounce. It was only in Sweden, where attempts at making capitalism deliver the economic and social goods were already well-established, that new ideas were utilized and socialism prospered. In countries like Britain and Germany, socialists accepted the orthodox economic 'solutions' advanced by the economic traditionalists and paid the political and electoral price (see table 7.4).

The failure to adopt these new ideas had one further consequence. Moderate socialists who had wanted to fight the Depression, and in France to create an alliance of anti-fascists, became disillusioned by their party's lack of resolve. In France the 'neo-socialists' left, as did renegade Labour MPs like Oswald Mosley* in Britain. Many of the French neo-socialists, like Mosley in Britain and the anti-Marxist reformer Hendrik de Man in Belgium, eventually ended up in or supporting extreme right-wing organizations. Advocates of social change and the erosion of class conflict, they increasingly saw a planned, corporate economy and national service as the answer to their country's social and economic problems.

[25] H. James, *The German Slump: Politics and Economics 1924–1936* (Oxford, 1986), ch. 9; and R. Breitman, *German Socialism and Weimar Democracy* (Chapel Hill, 1981), ch. 7.

The economic crisis was accompanied in some countries by fear of a nationalist/fascist backlash. Unlike many liberal and nationalist elements in Germany and elsewhere, socialists did not accept the need to dissolve democratic powers or incorporate the far right into government. They also and rightly recognized that fighting the far right on the streets (like the Communists) simply allowed fascist parties to present themselves as champions of law, order and stability – a strategy which allowed the NSDAP in Germany to mop up support from the smaller middle-class and nationalist parties. Neither could socialist paramilitary groups defend the Republic by military means (as the Austrian experience of 1934 proved[26]).

Socialists were in a near-impossible situation. The non-fascist right was firmly opposed to taking a tougher stand against fascism, seeing it as a protection against Communism. Even if socialists formed governments and asked the police and army to act, they were hardly reliable allies. Communists were unwilling to form an anti-fascist alliance. The USSR argued that capitalism was collapsing. Communist parties should lead the fight against capitalism's militant champions, not support socialists. These 'social fascists' were rivals and enemies who were propping up the system. Only later did the Communists support a 'Popular Front' against fascism.

The obstacles to effective socialist action became apparent in France and Spain in the later 1930s. When the socialist-dominated French 'Popular Front' government of 1934 advanced a radical programme, Communist 'allies' claimed it was too moderate, whilst right-wing opponents attacked it as economically disastrous. An investment strike saw millions of francs exported abroad. This curtailed the 'Blum experiment'. Similarly, the government's reluctance to intervene against fascism either at home or in Spain brought hostility from the Communist Party, without appeasing the socialists' critics. The government collapsed, leaving the socialist party weaker than ever. The lesson seemed to be that participation in government at a time of political polarization could only bring disaster.

In Spain the position was hardly better. When the dictatorship of Primo de Rivera collapsed in 1930, republicans formed a government with socialist support. The new government's attacks on landowners and the Church aggravated the right, but failed to satisfy the socialist rank and file, let alone the anarchists. Disunited, the left was defeated at the polls in 1933. A section attempted revolution in Asturias the following year. A 'Popular Front' coalition won the election in 1936, but

---

[26] In 1934 Socialist paramilitaries bravely resisted a shift to authoritarian rule by Chancellor Dollfuss, but were easily defeated.

its unity was fragile. The country collapsed into civil war because the right could not accept the return of another reforming government; but even in war, the left could find no unity.

Economic crisis and the triumph of the far right halted the development of socialist politics across Europe. But where socialist parties survived, they continued to develop and to learn from the political failures of the 1920s. In Britain Labour was routed at the polls in 1931 and a major re-examination of policy ensued. Capitalism had collapsed. Its failure to revive suggested that the market could not cure all economic problems. Think-tanks sprang up like mushrooms. Keynesian ideas and economic planning became features of intellectual debate, whilst the social and medical consequences of long-term unemployment became a central concern. Nonetheless, the policy changes should not be overstated.[27] Labour was simply discussing the concrete means of delivering long-established ends. The central role of the state in restructuring both the economy and social attitudes was receiving attention but ethical concerns and motives remained to the fore.

In electoral terms, socialists took some time to recover from the slump. Only in Sweden (where attention to social and welfare policies produced a range of concrete policies) did the process of expansion continue uninterrupted. In the 1930s, party leaders in Britain, Sweden and the Netherlands tried to develop an approach which was more sensitive to middle-class and professional opinion, with some success. However, socialists had not achieved the dominant and dynamic position which they were to gain after 1945. Wartime circumstances and wartime governments helped to produce popular expectations which socialists seemed the most likely to realize. In broad terms if not in details, the socialist programmes of 1945 were a product of two decades spent searching for a New Jerusalem. But it was only after 1945 that socialists had the support and the will necessary to try and turn these ideas into realities.

Exceptional Pathways versus Similar Patterns of Development?

No two socialist parties have identical histories. Socialist parties built on past national traditions and addressed current national problems;

---

[27] M. Durbin, *New Jerusalems: The Labour Party and the Economics of Democratic Socialism* (London, 1985); M. Francis, 'Economics and ethics: the nature of Labour's socialism, 1945–51', *Twentieth Century British History*, 6 (1995), pp. 220–43. For a Dutch parallel see L. M. van Voss, 'The Netherlands', in Berger and Broughton (eds), *The Force of Labour*, p. 52.

their fortunes and their approaches varied accordingly. But to go beyond this and suggest that all countries have a unique pattern of political development which reflects its particular experience of class formation, is a different matter.[28] Neither is it helpful to identify a 'natural' model of socialist party development and deviant pathways.

Common social and economic influences can be detected which evidently had a considerable impact on the electoral and political development of socialist parties across Europe. As Berger and Broughton's recent and excellent collection of essays also clearly and directly argues, the development of European socialist politics has been guided and restrained by a range of common influences and themes; the importance of war, the nature of the state, the existence of social fragmentation and of regional success. Berger points out, for example, that reformist socialism was the dominant tendency within socialist parties where the state and its non-socialist rivals accepted reform (as in Sweden and Britain), whereas more radical variants of socialism were adopted where capitalism showed itself to be less amenable (as in Spain).

Yet as D. S. White has suggested, there was also a re-evaluation of socialist politics across Europe in the 1920s which itself introduced common themes.[29] This chapter has extended his argument, suggesting that political similarities were not just a function of social forces or the state's actions. Because socialist parties had similar roots and socialist politicians similar aims, because socialists lived in the same world and faced similar problems with a similar range of available solutions, their politics developed along broadly similar lines. Parallel political aims and parallel outcomes could occur in radically different social and economic settings. Socialists were not all pragmatists. Their intentions, and the limitations of their political and ideological environments, were important influences on the pattern of socialist politics before 1945. The errors and indecisions of socialist politicians, like their successful rethinking and reformulations of policy and ideology, should be seen as important contributions to the pattern of socialist politics between the wars.

---

[28]   For Britain, see T. Nairn, 'The figures of descent', *New Left Review*, 161 (1987), pp. 20–77 (a restatement of a famous earlier article). There is a good discussion of German 'exceptionalist' or 'Sonderweg' historians in Berger, *The British Labour Party and the German Social Democrats*, pp. 10–17. See also I. Katznelson and R. Zolberg (eds), *Working Class Formation: Nineteenth Century Patterns in Western Europe and the United States* (Princeton, NJ, 1986).
[29]   D. S. White, 'Reconsidering European Socialism in the 1920s', *Journal of Contemporary History*, 16 (1981), pp. 251–72.

The Rise of European Feminism

Martin Pugh

The intellectual origins of the modern women's movement are to be found in the late-eighteenth-century Enlightenment. Women, it was argued, were rational human beings like men, and with the same fundamental rights and capacity for self-government. Influential expressions of such views were published by the English feminist Mary Wollstonecraft in *A Vindication of the Rights of Woman* (1792) and the German, Theodore Gottlieb von Hippel in *On the Civil Improvement of Women* (1794). Indeed, on the outbreak of the French Revolution thirty-three of the famous *cahiers de doléances* expressed female grievances. However, this proved to be a brief manifestation of feminism. The 1792 constitution banned women from public life, and the women's clubs were dissolved by the Convention in 1793. Eventually, the French Revolution led to Napoleon's Civil Code of 1804, which was widely implemented throughout Europe during the following century. In effect it confined women to a subordinate role within marriage. Wives enjoyed no legal rights; they surrendered control over their property, income and children to their husbands, and were largely denied access to divorce.

As a result the cause of female emancipation became closely associated with the growth of liberalism during the nineteenth century. The release of individual talents, the opening up of autocratic government and the removal of artificial barriers seemed to indicate the way ahead for women. Such thinking was articulated in John Stuart Mill's* famous work, *The Subjection of Women* (1869), in which he argued:

> what is called the nature of woman is essentially an artificial thing – the result of forced repression in some directions, unnatural stimulation in others.

However, the claim that women's potential was suppressed by a combination of law and custom conflicted with a formidable body of belief, widely accepted by women as well as by men, that Nature or God had designed the two sexes to perform distinct roles in society and equipped them with quite different attributes and mentalities. Perhaps not surprisingly a number of nineteenth-century feminists went some way to accepting this diagnosis, that is to say, they agreed that women were fundamentally different by reason of their typical life experiences, but they disputed the implications of the separate spheres ideology. Some feminists emphasized that women, as mothers, made a vital contribution to the stability of the state, and that they acquired skills and interests that were, in fact, very relevant to the political sphere. Others argued that because women were naturally less violent and more self-sacrificing than men, their influence would be a civilizing and improving one. Tactically this was shrewd for it helped to win women allies within the world of politics and the churches, and also forced men to face up to some of the inconsistencies in their arguments.

The Emergence of a Women's Movement

However, while the case for female emancipation was of long standing, an organized feminist movement was slow to appear. It began in the United States in the 1840s and in Britain in the 1850s. Although the emphasis varied over time and territorially, campaigns for emancipation concentrated on four main areas: first, economic issues including access to education and the professions; second, reforms affecting marriage such as equal divorce and the retention of income by wives; third, an attack on the double standard in sexual morality; and fourth, the formal rights of citizenship, notably the parliamentary vote.

Yet for many years the women's movement failed to mobilize widespread support. It consisted largely of small, urban, middle-class pressure groups, although alliances with sympathetic politicians made it less marginal than this suggests. In most countries – though Germany is something of an exception – it proved difficult to attract working-class women. This was partly because most were trapped by the daily burdens of domesticity and lacked the institutional means, such as trade unions, which brought men into public life. Where ordinary women did participate in organizations they were religious or philanthropic in character and likely to reinforce conventional ideas about women's role. Moreover, feminists often found it hard to accept that many working women saw marriage and motherhood as the chief goal in life, despite the hardships, and took pride in performing their role well. The legal disabilities under which women laboured seemed to be of little immediate relevance to them.

Thus, analysis of 'first wave' feminism has underlined the centrality of middle-class women activists. Participation was frequently associated with a background in Protestant religion, higher education, family involvement in liberal political and moral causes, and the positive support given by the fathers of feminists. Those middle-class women who remained unmarried experienced most acutely the effects of the prevailing ideology, for they were denied access to the professions and thus to the means of independent support. In spite of this, most feminists were, in fact, married women who often enjoyed the support of their husbands in their feminist campaigns.

In the early period feminism concentrated less on winning the vote than in the Edwardian era, and rather more on moral issues. For example, women in several countries had participated in the campaigns against the slave trade and in temperance organizations. By the 1870s the issue of prostitution had come to occupy a central place. The classic example was the campaign in Britain led by Josephine Butler for the repeal of the Contagious Diseases Acts. Introduced in the 1860s, this legislation allowed the military authorities to license prostitutes and compel them to submit to medical inspection and hospitalization. In Germany and France the state also used the police to regulate a system of prostitution. Not surprisingly the stubborn defence by influential men of their own privileges led some women towards a more radical critique of sexuality and marriage. The Swedish feminist, Ellen Key,* argued that women should be free to end marriage if they were not satisfied, and should be entitled to half the assets and income of their partnership. Her views were influential in Germany where the League for the Protection of Mothers was founded in 1904. It contended that marriage was oppressive to woman and that the state had failed to reward mothers for their work; women ought to enjoy access to birth control, easier divorce and the legalization of free unions.

However, feminists in other countries, including Britain, took a more negative view about sexuality and marriage. As the odds were so heavily weighted against women they argued that women should avoid marriage in favour of a life of independence and self-respect. This was articulated in a famous book by Cicely Hamilton, *Marriage as a Trade* (1908), in which she claimed that women usually married out of necessity, giving their bodies in return for board and lodging. An even more controversial attack on marriage came in 1913 with Christabel Pankhurst's* *The Great Scourge*, which suggested that as most men suffered from venereal disease women should shun marriage altogether. It was not until towards the end of the First World War, when attitudes were influenced by Marie Stopes's *Married Love* (1918), that a more positive view of women's sexuality, and thus of sexual relations within marriage, came to be widely adopted by feminists in Britain.

National Variations

The strength of the women's movement in the late nineteenth and early twentieth century unquestionably lay in north-western Europe and its colonial offshoots, that is in Scandinavia, Germany, Britain, the United States and Australasia. Clearly the Protestant and Anglo-Saxon societies, with their comparatively liberal political culture and parliamentary systems, offered the best conditions for feminism; conversely, in the Catholic-dominated societies of southern Europe and in the autocracies of east-central Europe women's movements were slower to emerge and generally weaker. Of course, things were more complicated than this division suggests. Germany, for example, enjoyed the right social conditions for a women's movement, but suffered from an illiberal political system. France is also an interesting case. Intellectually the French contributed a great deal to the women's movement throughout the century, and actually launched the word 'feminism' in the 1890s. Yet French women failed to win the vote until the end of the Second World War, decades after their counterparts elsewhere in northern Europe; and feminism there remained essentially a movement of writers, journalists and academics, marginal to the main political parties and relatively isolated from the population.

It was in the countries of Scandinavia that women's organizations enjoyed the greatest sympathy from ordinary women, were best integrated into the political system and won the earliest successes. For example, Finland granted women the vote in 1906 and Norway in 1913. Part of the explanation lies in the fact that both countries had been under foreign rule and the women's claim to citizenship was thus effectively carried forward with the broader struggle for national self-determination. The Finnish Women's Association, founded in 1884, was unique in carrying its campaign into the rural areas, where most of the people lived. The rejection of proposals for the women's vote by the Russian authorities in 1897 neatly united the national and feminist causes and as a result the grant of the vote was not controversial. In Norway the Association for the Promotion of Women's Interests was also founded in 1884. As women already enjoyed many legal and economic rights the movement was largely a moderate and middle-class one concentrating on temperance, moral reforms and, from 1890 onwards, the vote. As elsewhere in Scandinavia its success was partly due to effective links with the male political system, in particular the Radical

Liberals who wished to promote the break with Sweden. It is significant that the Norwegian Labour Party had 25,000 female members by 1909, for example. Campaigns for women's enfranchisement built up during the 1890s and 1900s, and the achievement of independence in 1905 paved the way for the women's vote in 1913.

The two other Scandinavian states developed women's organizations much earlier but encountered greater opposition. In Sweden the Association for Married Women's Property Rights dated from 1873 and the Fredrika-Bremmer-Society from 1884. Since Swedish women already enjoyed many rights, including freedom to engage in trade and other occupations and the local government vote, the movement concentrated on educational reforms, temperance and other moral issues at first; not until 1902 was a Swedish Women's Suffrage Association formed. In Denmark the cause was pioneered by the Danish Women's Association in 1871. During the 1880s two developments influenced its fortunes. First it was stimulated by the spread of Josephine Butler's campaign against legalized prostitution which in turn led Danish feminists to see the parliamentary vote as a more urgent goal. Second, the cause became associated with the fortunes of the Left-Liberals and, after 1900, with the Social Democrats. By the 1900s the women's suffrage societies enjoyed 23,000 members, a large total in a population of only 1.5 million. By 1912 their political allies had given feminists a majority for the suffrage in the lower house; only the opposition of Conservatives entrenched in the upper house delayed women's enfranchisement until 1915. In some ways the movement in the Netherlands was similar. The Dutch also developed an active movement, and their two suffrage organizations, formed in 1894 and 1907, had 19,000 members by 1913. Thus the vote became a major issue in the Netherlands but the reformers were checked by the Conservatives who held power from 1909 onwards.

In Britain the women's movement evolved from a well-established tradition of Liberal-Nonconformist radicalism, based upon middle-class families committed to prolonged campaigning by parliamentary methods. Under the leadership of women such as Barbara Leigh Smith the pioneers founded the *English Women's Journal* in 1858 and the Society for Promoting the Employment of Women in 1859. The movement at first developed into a series of overlapping single-issue campaigns and pressure groups focusing on married women's property, higher education for women, entry into the medical profession, abolition of the Contagious Diseases Acts and raising the age of consent. On virtually all these issues the feminists had considerable success, partly because they enjoyed much male support in Parliament from the Liberals, and in the churches.

However, the emphasis shifted towards winning a parliamentary vote as the key to further reforms. The campaign had begun during the crisis over the Second Reform Act in 1866–7 when J. S. Mill first proposed women's suffrage to Parliament. However, the National Society for Women's Suffrage and its successor, the National Union of Women's Suffrage Societies (1897), were criticized for their tactics. Both of its leaders, Lydia Becker and, from 1890, Millicent Fawcett,* believed in gradually building up support amongst MPs, avoiding party politics, and accepting a limited measure of suffrage. In fact they succeeded in winning the municipal vote in 1869; and by 1897 they had achieved a majority of support in the House of Commons.

However, by comparison with the Scandinavian countries the feminists in Britain suffered from a more complicated relationship with the political parties. Though the Liberals provided the original supporters, the Liberal Party, led by anti-suffragists like W. E. Gladstone* and, after 1908, H. H. Asquith,* refused to adopt a woman's suffrage policy. Many feared that a limited suffrage would give extra votes to wealthy women, while others increasingly saw women as under the influence of the churches. This diagnosis seemed to be corroborated by the growing sympathy for enfranchisement amongst the Conservatives from the 1880s onwards. Similarly, many socialists felt wary about enfranchising women, arguing that real emancipation for women depended not on a vote for a few middle-class ladies but on the wider transformation of society along socialist lines.

It is worth noting that similar reservations emerged in Belgium where the much larger Catholic community provoked wide opposition to women's suffrage. Socialists in Belgium believed that women would add to the strength of the clerical vote, and the liberals refused to include women in their franchise bills.

In the context of the British and Belgian women's movements the difficulties faced in France are more readily comprehensible. Organized feminism was revived during the 1860s by Maria Deraismes and Léon Richer, who founded the newspaper *Le Droit des Femmes* (1869) and the Association Pour le Droit des Femmes (1871). However, this women's movement was not only very moderate in methods but was hampered by the fact that its leaders were themselves primarily republicans and only secondarily feminists. Understandably, but unfortunately, the supporters of the new Third Republic were fearful about disloyalty to the political system, and it was in this perspective that they viewed women. Even Richer said of them: 'They are in great majority reactionaries and clerics. If they voted today, the Republic would not last six months.'

French feminism never really overcame the conservatism of the republicans entrenched in the senate, or the influence exerted by the Catholic Church over ordinary women. Not surprisingly the caution of the women's movement provoked a more radical approach. During the 1890s Hubertine Auclert* tried to persuade the French to follow the British example by placing more emphasis on the parliamentary vote; she also adopted relatively militant tactics such as refusing to pay taxes. But Auclert was widely denounced as hysterical, and on the whole French feminists kept to their moderate line. Thus it was not until 1901 that a suffrage bill was even introduced into the Chamber of Deputies; seven days before the outbreak of the Great War the first mass rally took place, but the whole issue was swiftly buried in the national crisis.

In Italy feminists struggled even more to establish effective organizations in a society in which they were easily outflanked by the broader appeal of the Catholic Church. The legal system discriminated very severely against women in Italy; for example, adultery was an offence for women but not for men, and the courts regularly annulled marriages if the husband claimed that his wife had not been a virgin. However, women's organizations confined themselves to attempts to open the professions to women, close brothels, gain maternity leave and win the vote. They established 'For Women' in 1898, the National Council of Italian Women in 1903 and a Catholic body, the Union of Women, in 1908. However, they enjoyed little support from the political parties and remained much more marginal than feminist movements in northern Europe.

By contrast, in Germany many women were quite closely connected with a political cause, socialism. This helped to give feminism more of a working-class dimension than elsewhere, but also had the effect of dividing the cause along lines of social class. Originally the German Social Democratic Party (SPD) had been anti-feminist, partly because of its Marxist ideology and partly because it saw women as a threat to men's wages. But Clara Zetkin* and others argued that women and men were simply the common victims of capitalism; and that the employment of women was part of the necessary development of capitalism in its climactic stage. Thus, the SPD modified its position by advocating protective legislation for women in 1871, taking up women's suffrage in the Erfurt Programme (1891) and proposing equal pay in the Gotha Programme (1896). By 1913 the party had 141,000 female members.

However, there was a price to be paid. Zetkin and the other feminist-socialists were essentially conflating women's interests with those of working-class men: they showed little interest in winning the vote, for example. It is doubtful whether the SPD was really feminist; rather it happily mobilized women as allies in the campaign against an autocratic system.

Inevitably a middle-class feminist movement developed separately from the SPD; it comprised the Bund Deutscher Frauenvereine (1894) and the German Union for Women's Suffrage (1902). During the 1900s this movement became more radical, campaigning against the state regulation of prostitution and in favour of contraception and the legalization of abortion. This, however, was a symptom of its isolation from the political mainstream in Germany. In an autocratic system with a waning liberalism there was simply not the basis for the kind of women's movement that existed in Britain. Ultimately, German women had no way of achieving enfranchisement for themselves until German men had overthrown the whole system created by Bismarck.

This was even more true in the other great imperial states – the Habsburg Empire and tsarist Russia. In the former there was no effective parliament to which a women's movement could appeal; and indeed feminist organizations were banned. Austria especially suffered from the lack of a middle class and the dominance of Catholicism, though in Bohemia the more liberal Czech nationalists gave some support to female enfranchisement.

In Russia the severe punishment meted out for political criticism and the virtual absence of independent political institutions made the development of organized feminism all but impossible. The backwardness of the economy and the limited size of the middle class also limited the scope for recruiting feminists. It has been suggested that the abolition of serfdom in 1861 helped to stimulate the movement by encouraging some gentry families to sell land and move to the towns, in the process losing their ability to support their unmarried daughters and other female relatives. Such feminists as there were in Russia came from the intelligentsia and Jewish families concentrated in St Petersburg and Moscow, and their chief interest was in expanding access to higher education for girls.

However, the government regarded women's education as subversive and from time to time closed down courses for women. As a result feminists often abandoned women's causes in order to concentrate on revolutionary activity. The defeat of Russia by Japan in 1905 and the revolution of the same year greatly stimulated feminist organization. The younger radicals formed the All-Russian Union of Equal Rights for Women, which had 10,000 members by 1906 and took to petitioning the Duma. However, the police and murder squads effectively intimidated so many feminists that the Union's membership fell to 1,000 by 1908. The liberal interlude created by the revolution was already coming to an end, and with it the hopes of reform for women.

International Feminism

To emphasize the national differences in the strength and character of feminist organizations is not to deny that they reflected the dilemmas and grievances common to women throughout the Western world. An international movement was therefore a natural development accelerated by improvements in communications during the nineteenth century which facilitated the movement of individuals and ideas across national frontiers. At the very least the knowledge that women in the United States and Australasia were engaged in the same struggle boosted the morale of small groups of beleaguered feminists in Europe. Moreover, it was in some of these far-flung territories that the early breakthrough was made. New Zealand, for example, enfranchised all adult women in 1893, and both feminists and politicians subsequently travelled to Europe to argue from direct experience that the fears of the anti-suffragists were groundless.

However, it was through the medium of books and journals that feminist ideas circulated most widely. For example, Mill's *The Subjection of Women* was translated into French, German, Swedish, Danish, Polish and Italian. The work of August Bebel, *Women in the Past, Present and Future* (1878) went through fifty German editions up to 1909 and was widely translated; and the main works of the Swede, Ellen Key, *The Strength of Women Misused* (1896) and *The Century of the Child, Love and Marriage* (1900), were widely read in North America and Europe. Nor should one forget the indirect influence of dramatists such as the Norwegian, Henrik Ibsen, whose play *A Doll's House* was written in 1879 and first performed in Britain in 1889. It helped to focus public attention on marriage and the injustices suffered by married women in the 1890s, and was instrumental in awakening the feminism of such women as Elizabeth Robins. The stage also proved to be a means of reaching men who were unlikely to read feminist tracts; David Lloyd George,* for example, admitted that it was Ibsen who had first made him recognize the force of the women's case.

In addition almost any 'international' congress or conference enabled feminists to win attention from the press and the public more readily than a local gathering; this was true even when most of the delegates at such conferences were drawn from the host country. The first attempt at a permanent organization was the short-lived International Association of Women (1868–71). In 1888, the American suffragists Elizabeth Cady Stanton and Susan B. Anthony established the International Council of Women. Though dominated by Americans, by the 1890s it had attracted representatives from fourteen countries and set up national councils in Germany, Britain, Sweden, Italy, Denmark, the Netherlands and New Zealand. Most European states were included by the early 1900s. Under the Presidency of such respectable figures as the English Liberal, Lady Aberdeen, the ICW represented the moderate-philanthropic side of feminism. Those who favoured a more radical approach met at Berlin in 1904 to found the International Women's Suffrage Alliance which had suffrage societies in twenty-one countries by 1911. The IWSA met more frequently than the ICW, showed more urgency about winning the vote, and placed more emphasis on campaigns to defend women's role in the labour force.

However, apart from improving contact and morale these organizations achieved little. The outbreak of war in 1914 had the effect of focusing their activity more effectively. While women in many countries withdrew to support their own national cause, the more left-wing feminists found themselves coming together in recognition of the fact that the devastation being inflicted upon Europe was peculiarly the work of men. Thus, a conference of women from twelve countries, mostly connected with the IWSA, met at the Hague in 1915 to set up the Women's International League for Peace and Freedom. Its immediate object was to campaign for a negotiated peace settlement to the war.

For several years this was a highly unpopular cause, and governments obstructed the attendance of women at international conferences. However, by 1917 they were winning converts by means of the Women's Peace Crusades which capitalized effectively on the disillusionment caused by the prolongation of the war, the heavy casualties and food shortages. After 1918 the WILPF was overtaken by much larger pressure groups, notably the League of Nations Union, in which women participated extensively. In Britain women became prominent in organizing the Peacemakers' Pilgrimages in the 1920s and in conducting peace celebrations during Armistice Weeks, when they sold white poppies and laid wreaths of white poppies at war memorials. Throughout the inter-war period the cause of disarmament and the settlement of international disputes by arbitration fostered women's consciousness of their own distinctive contribution to politics, and also gave them prominence in the traditionally male preserve of defence and foreign affairs.

Winning the Vote and the First World War

Between 1900 and 1914 the women's campaigns began to be dominated by the question of the parliamentary vote especially in the United States, Britain and Scandinavia, though to some extent in France and Germany as well. One can identify several common features that paved the way for success. First, women obtained a formal footing in the system, often by gaining a local government vote. Second, they built up alliances with liberal and/or socialist parties. Third, they usually won over a majority in the lower houses of the European legislatures, though they were still obstructed by the upper houses.

The British case represents a partial variation on this theme in the sense that suffragists became frustrated with and alienated from the Edwardian Liberal governments between 1906 and 1914. The antagonism towards both Liberal and Labour parties explains the adoption of militant tactics by the Women's Social and Political Union, led by Mrs Emmeline Pankhurst and her daughter Christabel, from 1905 onwards. Militancy was not unique to Britain, but it was certainly a distinctive feature of the campaign. Its adherents hoped to mobilize public opinion on a massive scale, thereby bringing effective pressure to bear on the government to introduce its own legislation for women's suffrage. Their methods included heckling ministerial speeches, interventions to secure the defeat of government candidates at by-elections, attempts to enter the chamber of the House of Commons, hunger strikes when in prison, the breaking of windows, setting fire to post boxes and other attacks upon public and private property.

Though highly successful in winning publicity and thus pushing the issue up the political agenda and stimulating the participation of women in the campaign, the Pankhursts' methods failed to force the government's hand. This was partly because they had alienated the labour movement. As a result they never enjoyed the working-class support that might have made the authorities take them seriously. The destruction of property irritated MPs, some of whom withdrew their previous support for women's suffrage; but it was never on a sufficiently large scale to constitute a major threat to property or the political system. By 1914 the Pankhursts had antagonized many feminists and become trapped in a battle from which neither side could retreat without loss of face. As a result they quickly accepted the government's offer of release from prison on the outbreak of war and suspended their campaign. Like feminists in many countries the Pankhursts moved to the right during the war and never recovered their previous campaigning spirit.

It has traditionally been believed that women's role in the war effort decisively changed opinion in their favour and led politicians in several countries to enfranchise them at, or soon after, the end of the First World War. However, such a neat explanation does not appear very convincing when seen in the continental context. In the first place, in Finland, Iceland and Norway enfranchisement preceded the war. In the second place, countries such as Sweden and Denmark granted the vote without being involved in the conflict.

Table 8.1   The enfranchisement of women

Finland	1906
Iceland	1908, 1911
Norway	1913
Denmark	1915
Russia	1917
Britain	1918, 1928
Austria	1918
Germany	1919
Netherlands	1919
Poland	1919
Sweden	1919–21
Czechoslovakia	1919–20
Belgium	1920, 1948
Spain	1932
France	1944
Italy	1945
Portugal	1945
Hungary	1945
Yugoslavia	1945
Romania	1946

In the third place, as table 8.1 shows, there were a considerable number of countries in which women continued to be denied the vote in spite of their participation in their country's cause. 'It is humiliating', complained one Frenchwoman, 'to think that we are Frenchwomen, daughters of the land of the revolution, and that in the year of grace 1919 we are still reduced to demanding the "rights of women".' Feminist tactics at this stage were to emphasize their patriotism, their special role in tackling moral and social issues, and the example now being set by other European states in extending the vote. But they had allowed their loyalty to be taken for granted, and they continued to be reluctant to adopt mass lobbying techniques as women had done elsewhere. There is thus little basis for the view that the war had a radicalizing effect on French women; rather it probably strengthened support for their traditional role as mothers. Certainly it made little impact upon the conservatism of small-town and rural France on which the politicians relied for their support; and they continued to make female anticlericalism an excuse for doing nothing to disturb the status quo.

Finally, we come to those countries in which the war did make some impact on the women's cause, not so much by changing attitudes towards women or their role, but, more indirectly, by undermining the political system which obstructed women. In Russia, for example, although women strongly backed the national cause by work in hospitals, factories and farms, they exercised no influence until the revolution of February 1917 overthrew the tsarist regime. Then they successfully petitioned the Provisional Government, which issued a new electoral law enfranchising men and women at twenty years. When the Bolsheviks came to power later that year the women's movement was effectively obliterated.

The fall of the other imperial autocracies also created favourable opportunities. From the ruin of the Habsburg Empire emerged the states of Austria, Czechoslovakia and Poland whose new constitutions enfranchised women in 1918–19. In Germany women had been fully involved in wartime work, but suffered from a decline in their institutional position within the SPD; the party actually lost 60 per cent of its female members during the war, and Clara Zetkin effectively lost her influence within the party. However, what eventually mattered was the revolution of 1918 which overthrew the imperial system and brought the Socialists to power at last; they both gave women the vote and enshrined equal rights within the new constitution.

In Britain the women's campaign was largely abandoned during wartime on the assumption that no government would take up the question of the vote. In fact, the politicians found themselves obliged to do so in order to ensure that the men who were fighting were enabled to vote. This entailed devising an all-party compromise on the franchise in which a vote for women aged over thirty years was included. Although the war brought no fundamental change in the British system, it clearly helped women by replacing the pre-war government under the anti-suffragist Asquith with a coalition government led by a more sympathetic Prime Minister, Lloyd George. But these short-term shifts should not be mistaken for any fundamental change in women's roles as a result of wartime employment. For politicians, trade unionists and women themselves, wartime work in munitions factories had always been seen as purely temporary, and feminists largely failed to defend women's gains. If anything, by leading to the death of three-quarters of a million British males the war had the effect of concentrating thoughts upon women's conventional role as wives and mothers during the post-war decade.

Inter-war Feminism

Perhaps because women succeeded in winning the vote in so many countries around 1919 there has been a temptation to see this as a peak followed by anti-climax and decline. This is, of course, an over-simplification if only because in several states progress towards winning the vote was still continuing. In Italy, for example, it was only the senate that blocked enfranchisement by failing to ratify a vote by the lower house in 1919 and 1920. Similarly in France the Chamber of Deputies held its first debate on the question in 1919; it backed women's suffrage in 1919, 1925, 1932 and 1935 only to be overruled by the senate. By this time the Catholic Church had begun to throw its weight behind the proposal on the basis that its interests would probably be strengthened by a female electorate.

However, it cannot be denied that the women's cause suffered from two major developments between the wars: the prolonged economic depression and the rise of fascist regimes to power. Moreover, where feminists had been successful in winning the vote they now had to face new dilemmas. Should they modify the aims and agenda of the movement? Should they try to work within the political system or maintain wholly independent women's organizations? And how were they to mobilize the newly enfranchised, but by no means feminist, women? As the veteran English suffragist Millicent Fawcett put it: 'I shall retire and watch you all floundering.'

In one sense her prognostication proved correct. Women found themselves universally being forced out of their wartime role in the labour force so that jobs could be reserved for returning soldiers. Nowhere did the movement effectively challenge the prevailing view that married women had no claim to employment if their husbands were in work; nowhere did governments dissent from the trade unionist belief in the concept of the 'family wage' for each male head of household.

On the other hand, the women's movement enjoyed considerable scope for influencing policies affecting motherhood. 'If one gets rights for killing men,' declared the French feminist Leonie Rouzade, 'one should get more rights for having created humanity.' Politicians were, of course, receptive to pressure in this area because for several decades they had been worried by the decline in the birth rate. France, Germany, Italy and Russia all began to award women gold medals for the production of a given number of children. Child allowances or family allowances were variously introduced in France (1932), Germany (1935), Italy (1936), Spain (1938), Britain (1945), Norway (1946) and Sweden (1947). Indeed it is now clear that the influence of women was one of the most important forces in the development of the welfare state in post-1918 Europe, especially in Scandinavia where feminism had always been more positively aligned with traditional ideas on women's role. In Britain the women's pressure groups won a variety of material benefits of this kind including maternity payments (1911), maternity and infant welfare clinics (1918) and widows pensions (1925), as well as other feminist reforms such as equal divorce (1923), equal guardianship (1925) and equal suffrage (1928).

The achievement of health-and-welfare measures encouraged some feminists such as Eleanor Rathbone,* the President of the National Union of Societies for Equal Citizenship in Britain, to develop what became known as the 'New Feminism'. It placed less emphasis on equal rights and more on issues that affected the ordinary wife and mother including family allowances and the provision of advice on birth control. However, this proved divisive. Equal rights feminists argued that New Feminism represented a betrayal because it helped to perpetuate the idea of woman as essentially wife and mother. This was one of the reasons for the organizational fragmentation of the movement between the wars. Amongst the many new bodies were the Women's Citizens Association (1917), the Six Point Group (1921), the Open Door Council (1926) and the Townswomen's Guilds (1929). The Open Door Council encapsulated the dilemmas of inter-war feminism most acutely. Founded by equal rights feminists in order to resist the trend towards protective legislation which excluded women from employment on grounds of health and safety, it was condemned by trade unions and socialists as a mere middle-class pressure group interfering with the lives of working-class women. This split between the middle classes and the labour movement which was common throughout Europe undoubtedly weakened feminism in this period, and it encouraged governments in their view that women's organizations did not represent the mass of ordinary women.

Feminism and Fascism

'We want men who are men and women who are women.' The words of the British fascist leader, Sir Oswald Mosley,* underline the conservative nature of fascist thinking. Inevitably, in the rural, Catholic societies of southern Europe where women's organizations had been relatively slow to develop, the seizure of power by fascists decisively checked any further progress. To take an obvious example, in Spain the victory of the Republicans brought the brief enfranchisement of women; but after winning the civil war of 1936–7 General Franco* simply withdrew voting rights generally. In fact Spanish women did not finally win the vote until 1975.

In Italy the relationship between women and the fascist regime was more complicated. Though Mussolini* was personally hostile to women's rights and in particular refused demands for the parliamentary vote, he judged it politic to avoid alienating women. In 1925 he granted them a local government vote, though this proved to be an empty gesture since local elections were abolished.

Fascist ideology placed great emphasis on the family and, thus, on women as 'the guardians of the hearth', an approach which fitted neatly with Catholic views. The Pope fully shared the desire to maintain a patriarchal society, and his encyclical of 1930 pronounced that the true equality of the sexes was to be found only within marriage. However, as Mussolini was only too well aware, Italy's birth rate had fallen from 37–38 per thousand population in the 1860s to 31 by 1914. He desperately wanted Italy to avoid the pattern now established in the industrialized countries, and he therefore tried to keep the population in the rural areas where the birth rate stayed higher.

In aid of this objective the regime paid 'family allocations' based on the number of children, gave priority in employment to men with children and removed female employees unless they were war widows. It also tried to spread its propaganda by organizing the Fasci Femminili and, in rural districts, the Massaie Rurali or Rural Housewives; by 1939 they had, respectively, 500,000 and one million members. However, these efforts enjoyed little success. By 1931 the Italian birth rate had fallen further to 25 per thousand. Women continued to withdraw from agriculture while increasing their share of higher education. On the other hand, feminism as a political force was rapidly marginalized in the struggle between socialism and fascism; and the long-term effect of Mussolini's rule was to demoralize the cause in Italy.

In Germany fascist objectives were similar. 'In my state', pronounced Hitler,* 'the mother is the most important citizen.' He professed to regard the very idea of female emancipation as an invention of Jewish intellectuals. After the supposed decadence of the Weimar regime, 'true women' were to return to their vocation – rearing families and strengthening the Aryan race.

However, the implementation of this thinking was complicated by the insistence of some Nazi women on participating in the movement. As early as 1923 they had organized the German Women's Order of the Red Swastika, followed in 1926 by the German Women's Battle League. In 1931 the leadership attempted to reassert its control by amalgamating the two organizations in the NS-Frauenschaft whose membership had reached 3.3 million by 1939. While asserting the primacy of marriage and motherhood the NS-Frauenschaft accepted the social and economic progress already made by German women. When the Nazis came to power in 1933 the existing women's organizations were either dissolved or absorbed into the Deutsches Frauenwerk which

recruited six million members. In this way a women's movement effectively ceased to exist in Germany, and women were virtually excluded
from public life. Yet on the whole they were neither greatly antagonized nor enthused by the Nazi movement. When women won the
vote they had not used it to support either the left or the Nazis, but
favoured the Centre Party and the German National People's Party,
both of which upheld traditional gender roles.

However, though rather conservative, German women largely de-
fied official efforts to influence their role in the home and the work-
place. For example, although the Nazis fulfilled their promise to dismiss
married women from jobs as doctors, teachers, civil servants and judges,
the proportion of women in employment actually rose from 34.3 per
cent in 1933 to 36.7 per cent in 1939. Even amongst married women
the number in employment increased by two million between 1933
and 1939, no doubt an indication of a booming economy. Above all
the Nazis wanted to reverse the unusually steep fall in the birth rate
from 38–39 per thousand in the 1870s to only 15 in 1932. To this end
they offered tax relief for large families, imposed higher taxes on child-
less couples, and gave interest-free loans to married couples if the wife
stopped work; a quarter of the loan became a gift for each child born.
By 1939 the birth rate had risen to 20 per thousand, but this was due
less to government incentives than to the fact that more people were
marrying; the average family size in Germany continued to fall. Thus,
while on the one hand organized feminism disappeared, on the other
hand fascist propaganda was too much at cross purposes with economic
change and social attitudes to be capable of influencing women's role
significantly.

The Second World War and Beyond

In some ways the outbreak of the Second World War revived the flag-
ging fortunes of the women's movement. By creating severe shortages
of labour it helped to reverse the effects of the inter-war depression, and
by creating food shortages it gave ordinary housewives a new importance in the eyes of governments. Above all, the widespread expectation
that the civilian population would become the target of intensive bombing gave a fresh impetus to policies designed to promote the welfare
of women and children.

Yet the most important effect of the war was its indirect political
implications; by destabilizing and destroying many regimes it helped to
weaken the obstacles to change for women. The most obvious symptom of this was the enfranchisement of women before or shortly after

the end of the war: France in 1944, Italy, Portugal, Hungary and Yugo-slavia in 1945 and Romania in 1946. In France, for example, the whole political system was swept away by the dramatic German advance in May 1940. Strictly speaking women were given the vote not by a par-liamentary decision but by a decree issued by General de Gaulle in August 1944 on behalf of the new provisional government. The con-sequences of this breakthrough were, however, limited. Women voted for the first time in October 1945 when thirty-five female deputies were returned out of 545. But this 6 per cent share of the representa-tion subsequently fell to 3.6 per cent in 1951 and 1.6 per cent in 1958. The French state merely continued its pro-natalist policies by extending cash maternity allowances and free medical care to mothers in 1946. Although the constitution of the Fourth Republic was amended in 1946 so as to give women equal rights in law, this turned out to be a mere formality.

In Germany the war exposed the contradictions in Nazi attitudes towards women. Although the government felt obliged to urge women to take up the jobs vacated by men, Hitler shrank from the full mobil-ization of women for ideological-demographic reasons. Not until 1943 were German women aged 17 to 45 required to report for work, but even then middle-class women frequently evaded their duty, while working-class women began to abandon employment because their income was subtracted from their welfare benefits. As a result, by September 1944 only 14.9 million women were employed in Germany compared to 16.4 million in May 1939. Notwithstanding the national crisis the Nazi regime had simply failed to tap the potential of its female population.

In Britain the dramatic defeat of the National Government and its replacement by a three-party coalition under Churchill* in May 1940 created new opportunities for women. The loosening of party discip-line in Parliament led the women MPs of all parties to draw together to defend women's interests especially over employment; for the first time something like a women's party came into existence. By 1941 the government had decided, albeit reluctantly, to impose industrial con-scription on women, and this stimulated the formation of an Equal Pay Campaign Committee whose efforts eventually won equal pay for teachers and civil servants in 1954.

However, the pressure exerted by women MPs was not backed by any large movement in the country; in this sense the war largely failed to reverse the decline of the 1930s. As a result the election of 1945 brought only a marginal increase in the number of female MPs to twenty-four. Moreover, politicians' thinking continued to be dominated by conven-tional assumptions. This is underlined by the spate of social reforms following the war. For example, the enactment in 1945 of family allowances paid directly to mothers reflected the concern to boost the population rather than the original feminist idea of giving a wage for the housewife's work. Although some feminists rightly hailed such innovations as the National Health Service as a major gain for women, the welfare state was far from being feminist; on the contrary, it recognized a woman's rights to benefits in so far as she was married to a man rather than treating her as an independent person.

Consequently, 1945 appears less as a launching-point for the women's movement than as the end of a cycle of growth and decline. The campaigns by women's pressure groups that had developed during the last thirty years of the nineteenth century reached a climax with the pre-1914 struggle for the vote. After this success women had achieved a limited footing in politics and extensive reforms for mothers and wives, but had been checked by the economic depression and, in view of the difficulty in recruiting from the younger generation of women, had gone into a decline by the 1930s. By the end of the Second World War the first-wave feminists had passed from the scene leaving a somewhat marginalized women's movement. The feminist dilemma was symbolised by the publication in 1949 of Simone de Beauvoir's famous work *The Second Sex*. Though an inspiration to feminists later in the century it did little to revive the movement at the time. Simone de Beauvoir herself encapsulated the problem in her own life: between the wars she had been a feminist more by establishing herself in a career than by campaigning for feminism. By the late 1960s she was to be overtaken by a new generation of young, well-educated women who took for granted political rights, professional employment and a radical view of women's sexuality; in tackling the unfinished business of feminism they also rediscovered the earlier history of their movement.

9

Revolutionary Europe

James D. White

The Roots of the Revolution: The Nationalities

The fact that the Russian Empire was an unwieldy conglomeration of territories inhabited by a nationally variegated population created tensions which grew increasingly acute with the passage of time. By the start of the First World War the total population of the Russian Empire was over 178.4 million people. Of these the single largest group was formed by the Russians, who made up 43.4% of the total. They were followed by the Ukrainians who constituted 17.5% and the Turkic-speaking peoples (10.6%), who predominated in Central Asia.

Belorussians made up 10.6% of the population, these being followed by the Poles with 5.8%, the Finns with 4.5% and the Jews with 3.9%. Lithuanians and Latvians each formed just over 1% of the Russian Empire's population, and Estonians under 1%. The other national groups, of which there were over a hundred, each constituted a small fraction of the total.[1]

Some peoples, such as the Finns, the Poles and the Jews had possessed a strong sense of national identity even before they were incorporated into the Russian Empire. But from the latter part of the nineteenth century the impact of nationalism in Western Europe was increasingly felt. National movements appeared among the Ukrainians, Latvians, Lithuanians, Estonians and other groups, which demanded recognition of their respective nations and a degree of autonomy to pursue their own affairs.

The tsarist government, however, was moving in exactly the opposite direction. For administrative convenience and to remove the security threat that national aspirations might cause, particularly on the country's borderlands, the government tried to extend the practices of Russia

---

[1] Population figures are taken from A. Suvorin (ed.), *Russkii kalendar' na 1916 g.* (Petrograd, 1916), pp. 81–4. They are projections from the 1897 census.

proper to all other parts of the empire. This policy of 'Russification' made Russian the language of administration, justice and education, and it was imposed with particular severity in Poland, Lithuania and the Ukraine.

The Jews in Russia suffered special discrimination by the tsarist regime. Not only were they restricted in where they could live, but also in what professions they could enter and in what numbers they could receive higher education. Their safety was constantly threatened by pogroms, carried out by local mobs with the connivance of the authorities.

The policy of 'Russification' alienated the nationalities of the Russian Empire from the government and ensured that national groups would be well represented in the revolutionary movement. National grievances were to be one of the driving forces behind the 1905 revolution and were to be renewed in the 1917 revolution and its aftermath.

The Roots of the Revolution: The Peasants

The Russian Empire at the start of the twentieth century was overwhelmingly an agrarian country, with over 85 per cent of the population living on the land and over three-quarters making their livelihood from agriculture. Serfdom had been abolished from most territories of the Russian Empire during the nineteenth century. But different sets of regulations for different parts of the empire had left some peasants in a better economic situation than others. Although some managed to prosper in the post-Emancipation era, many found themselves worse off. They were likely to have less land than had been available to them as serfs. And since their former masters were allowed to retain as their private property such amenities as forests, meadows and streams, peasants henceforth had to pay for the cutting of timber and the grazing and watering of livestock.

From the time of the Emancipation the peasants were burdened with various types of financial exactions. They had to pay redemption dues for the land as well as the poll tax and *zemstvo* (local government) dues. Arrears in these payments became so great that in 1886 the poll tax had to be discontinued and the redemption payments reduced (these latter being abolished entirely in 1905). The loss of revenue from the poll tax was compensated for by the introduction of indirect taxation on goods such as matches, kerosene, tea, tobacco, liquor and sugar, items which figured prominently in the budgets of the poorer sections of the population. Some historians have argued that if the peasants were able to purchase goods of this type they could not have been all that badly off.

It is not an argument, however, that is supported either by contemporary accounts or detailed statistical analysis.[2]

Under the 1861 legislation the peasant allotments were owned not by individuals, but by the village community, the *mir*. This was a traditional Russian institution, which provided mutual aid for its members, made decisions affecting the households which composed it, kept the peace, and tried to maintain the solidarity of interests within the community as a whole. In many provinces, especially in central Russia, the *mir* periodically redivided the land among the peasant households to ensure that each had a fair share. But the inter-mingling of small strips of land characteristic of peasant farming made improvements in agricultural technique difficult, and the practice of re-allocating the strips also acted as a disincentive to improving the land.

With little advance in farming techniques and a rapidly increasing population, the economic situation of the peasants, particularly those in Russia's central provinces, deteriorated noticeably in the 1870s and 1880s, culminating in the famine of 1891–2. In the view of the peasants, the only hope of amelioration was to acquire more land, in particular the land belonging to the landowners' estates.

Peasant discontent erupted in 1905, the kinds of action varying according to geographical area. It might involve the illegal cutting of timber, unauthorized grazing of cattle, strikes of farm labourers for higher wages or the refusal to pay taxes, as well as the seizure of estates. The unrest was especially virulent in the impoverished provinces of central Russia, where the *mir* was often the institution which organized the peasant disturbances.

In 1906, after ruthlessly pacifying the countryside, the Prime Minister Petr Stolypin* passed legislation which encouraged individual peasants to consolidate their scattered strips of land into a single holding which would be owned privately and would no longer be subject to redivision. The project had moderate success, particularly in those areas in the western provinces where communal ownership was already weak. But in central Russia the communal form of landownership continued to predominate, and any peasants who separated out under the Stolypin legislation were generally deeply resented by their neighbours. Peasant rebellions were now directed not only against the landowners but also against the 'separators' as well.

---

[2] See J. Y. Simms, Jr, 'The crisis in Russian agriculture at the end of the nineteenth century', *Slavic Review*, 36 (1977), pp. 377–98; Simms's conclusions are endorsed in R. Pipes, *The Russian Revolution 1899–1919* (London, 1990), pp. 105–7. They are contested in S. G. Wheatcroft, 'The 1891–92 famine in Russia: towards a more detailed analysis of its scale and demographic significance', in *Economy and Society in Russia and the Soviet Union 1860–1930*, ed. L. Edmondson and P. Waldron (London, 1992), pp. 51–3.

The Impact of Industry

Until the end of the nineteenth century, industry in Russia had been mostly small-scale and connected with agriculture. The entrepreneurs were either gentry who had set up factories on their estates, or merchants of peasant origin who traded in handicraft goods produced in agrarian communities in various parts of the country. By the middle of the nineteenth century merchant entrepreneurs, such as the Guchkovs and the Morozovs, had established a thriving textile industry in Moscow.

Russia experienced an upsurge in industrial development in the last decades of the nineteenth century. It was led by a boom in railway construction, the most spectacular project being the building of the trans-Siberian railway (1891–1905). Besides being of strategic importance, railways were intended to facilitate the transport of grain for export, the chief means by which Russia paid for her imports.

The desire to maintain a favourable balance of trade also led to the erection of high tariff barriers. Foreign companies, however, responded to these by setting up branches inside the country. When Count Serge Witte* was Minister of Finance (1892–1903) he actively encouraged foreign firms to invest in Russia. Industrial growth was especially rapid during the 1890s. In the decade between 1887 and 1897 the number of industries increased by 26.5%, the number of workers by 59.2% and the value of production by 112.82%.[3] Industrial development in Russia, however, was patchy and confined to a few geographical areas such as the capital cities, the Baltic provinces, the Ukraine and the Urals. Workers were recruited mainly from the peasantry, and often divided their time between industrial and agricultural work. Skilled workers, who worked full time in industry, were a small minority in the total Russian workforce.

Wages in Russian industry were in general low and apt to be paid irregularly. They might not even be paid in money, but in vouchers which could be exchanged for goods at the company store. The working day was likely to be from ten to fifteen hours, in conditions that were often dangerous and insanitary. Workers were often housed in cramped lodgings, or in barracks hurriedly and cheaply built in the vicinity of the factory by the employers.

Strikes by industrial workers began to multiply in Russia from the 1870s onwards. Usually these were for higher wages, shorter hours, and for the removal of particularly objectionable factory foremen and supervisors. In the revolution of 1905 the strike movement took on a

[3] P. I. Lyashchenko, *History of the National Economy of Russia* (New York, 1949), p. 526.

mass character, and in St Petersburg the body established to lead the strike was the St Petersburg Soviet, of which Leon Trotsky* became the chairman.

The Political Order

Despite attempts during the nineteenth century to liberalize Russia's system of government, the autocratic regime survived into the twentieth century. Consequently, the responsibility for ruling the vast multinational empire at a time of complex social and economic change fell on the shoulders of Nicholas II. This task of manoeuvring the country through the difficult transition to a modern industrial nation required qualities and abilities that neither the tsar nor his entourage possessed.

The autocratic form of government was oppressive because it refused to countenance any institution or initiative which did not have official sanction. A strict censorship operated, making the open discussion of political and social issues impossible. The behaviour of the population was monitored by the secret police. The autocratic system found support among the more conservative landowners, particularly those who received subsidies from it. But it was deeply unpopular among Russia's intelligentsia, which was denied freedom of expression and the protection of the law. The business community, too, resented the degree to which any economic activity was surrounded by arbitrary regulations.

As there was no representative government, there could be no political parties in the Western sense, competing for election to power. Groups formed in opposition to the government were necessarily illegal, and could only hope to enact their programmes if the autocracy were overthrown. The first political parties were consequently revolutionary ones. At the turn of the century there were two such parties: the Social Democrats and the Socialist Revolutionaries. The Social Democrats thought of the workers as the driving force behind the coming revolution. The Socialist Revolutionaries, on the other hand, looked to all exploited groups in society for their support, and were prepared to use terrorist methods against the authorities. In 1903 the Russian Social Democratic Labour Party (RSDLP) split on the issue of how party membership was to be defined, the Bolsheviks favouring a more restricted, and the Mensheviks a more open membership. Lenin wanted to make the Bolshevik Party the 'vanguard' of the workers' movement, but this wish was not fulfilled until after the Bolsheviks took power.

To counter the revolutionary upsurge, in October 1905 the tsarist government established a new legislative body, the Duma. This fell considerably short of being a parliament in the Western sense, because government ministers were responsible not to the Duma, but to the tsar. Though their powers were severely limited, the four Dumas which met between 1906 and 1917 gave the country some experience of constitutional government.

New political parties fought elections to the Dumas, among them two liberal parties which were committed to constitutional government: the Constitutional Democrats (Kadets) led by Paul Miliukov, and the Octobrists led by Alexander Guchkov. Being the more radical, the Kadets were continually at odds with the government. The Octobrists, on the other hand, the dominant party in the Third Duma, tried to co-operate with Stolypin in return for a package of liberal reforms. Conservative resistance, however, blocked any reform except Stolypin's agrarian reform, thus letting slip the opportunity for an orderly modernization of the country.

The First World War: The Effects of the War

Russia's involvement in the First World War had a profound effect on the country, putting severe strains on its economy, its society and its political system. The initial effect of the war, however, was to create a climate of national unity, as the country rallied round its government in a time of crisis. Industrial and agrarian unrest, which had been on the increase since 1912, abated, and there was promise of civil peace while hostilities continued. But the unprecedented scale of the war and its unexpected duration aggravated the country's most serious underlying problems and gave a new intensity to old antagonisms.

Between 1914 and 1916, thirteen million men were drafted into the armed forces, most of them peasants. Although there had been under-employment in agriculture, the massive recruitment of young, able-bodied men was to leave the countryside, especially the landed estates, short of workers to provide food for the army and the towns. Agriculture became increasingly an occupation for women and for those either too old or too young to serve in the army. The shortage of labour was to some extent alleviated by using prisoners of war or refugees, where these were available.

Industry responded to the war by switching from its normal peace-time output to the production of munitions. As more workers were needed to fulfil orders for military contracts, many women and youths from the countryside were drawn into industry, thus exacerbating the labour shortage in agriculture. Industry's success in effecting the change from civilian to military production was itself to cause a serious problem for the Russian economy. It created a shortage of articles for domestic consumption, so that peasants with grain to sell had little incentive to do so, since there would be nothing to buy with the money they received. This difficulty, which first appeared during the war, was to last well into Soviet times.

Even when they were available, there were considerable problems in transporting foodstuffs to their intended destinations, as Russia's railway system was in a critical state. Trains which were needed to carry grain were being used to carry troops and military equipment. A great deal of pressure was put upon the transport system and on accommodation in towns when the Russian army retreated from Poland and the Baltic provinces in the summer of 1915. A mass of refugees fled to provinces in the Russian interior, where they had to be settled and catered for.

Coping with the upheaval the war had brought about was beyond the power of the government and its agencies. It was consequently forced to tolerate the existence and to accept the help of various voluntary bodies which were established during the war, and which tended to be liberal in political complexion. The earliest of these were the Union of Towns and the Union of Zemstvos, which took on the task of caring for wounded soldiers. Voluntary organizations also came into being to look after the welfare of refugee communities. The most important of the voluntary organizations, however, were the War Industries committees, which were created in 1915. They were dedicated to mobilizing the country's industry for the war effort, and were formed in all the major towns. They consisted mainly of businessmen, but might also include professional people and representatives of local government. A Workers' Group was set up to enlist the support of the labour movement. The chairman of the Central War Industries Committee was Alexander Guchkov, who, like many liberals, believed that the government was not pursuing the war effectively enough, and that the support given to the government during the war by the voluntary organizations was not being rewarded by concessions on the part of the regime. At the end of 1916 Guchkov began to organize a palace coup to depose the tsar.

The war provided the opportunity for national groups to make a contribution to the military effort and by this to create a debt of gratitude, the desired reward being autonomy or even independence. To this end, in 1915 the Latvians established Rifle battalions, which fought with distinction on the Northern Front. Czech and Polish formations of a similar kind appeared in Russia during 1917.

The war had brought new and serious divisions which cut across socialist party organizations. Some socialists supported the war, while others, the 'defencists', supported it conditionally, in so far as it was a war to defend one's own country against foreign aggression. A minority of socialists, which included Lenin* and Trotsky, took an 'internationalist' position and demanded that the war be brought to an end as soon as possible. Trotsky thought this should happen by a general peace agreement; but Lenin believed that Russia should withdraw from the conflict immediately, even if it meant a German victory. Both Lenin and Trotsky, however, were convinced that the war would inevitably lead to a socialist revolution.

The Provisional Government

At the end of February 1917,[4] mass demonstrations took place on the streets of Petrograd, which the garrison troops were unable and unwilling to disperse. The tsarist regime was brought to an end, and in its place a Provisional Government headed by Prince G. E. Lvov was formed, consisting mainly of liberal politicians like Miliukov and Guchkov, but also including the Socialist Revolutionary Alexander Kerensky. During the February revolution the Petrograd Soviet was also established, a body headed by members of the Menshevik and Socialist Revolutionary parties. In the weeks that followed local soviets were set up in many towns up and down the country. Although the Petrograd Soviet enjoyed popular support and was the body with real power in the capital, its leadership gave its conditional support to the Provisional Government, and from April onwards participated in governmental coalitions. This situation of 'dual-power' lasted until the Bolsheviks took power in October.

The position of the Provisional Government was inherently weak because it was intended to rule the country only until the Constituent Assembly met. This caretaker status prevented it from embarking on any far-reaching programme of reform. Its situation was further undermined by the need to placate the Soviet on all major policy issues.

Where the Provisional Government was most successful was in dismantling the tsarist regime's apparatus of repression. It quickly introduced such civil rights as freedom of speech, freedom of the press and freedom of assembly, and set about releasing the political prisoners who had been convicted under the old regime. Ironically, however, measures of this kind guaranteed that opponents of the Provisional Government would have unprecedented opportunities to campaign against it.

The Provisional Government failed to take effective action to tackle the major problems facing the country at that time. These included

---

[4] Dates up to 14 February 1918 are given according to the Russian calendar, which was thirteen days behind the Western one.

such questions as the war, the agrarian situation, industrial relations, supply difficulties and the aspirations of the nationalities.

The Provisional Government initially emphasized its determination to fight the war to a victorious conclusion and to acquire the Straits and Constantinople. Such declarations brought it into conflict with the overwhelmingly defencist Soviet, and the Foreign Minister Paul Miliukov was forced to resign in April. In the months that followed the February revolution it became increasingly unfeasible to continue fighting the war, as public opinion turned against it and discipline in the army deteriorated. Immediately after the February revolution measures were taken to democratize the army in the hope of increasing the soldiers' motivation to fight. But desertions increased steadily, especially as the land was appropriated by the peasants, and soldiers returned to their native villages to take part in the redivision.

Following the unsuccessful offensive on the South-Western Front in June the Provisional Government, then headed by Alexander Kerensky, tried to restore discipline in the army. Kerensky appointed as the army's Commander-in-Chief General Lavr Kornilov, who was to become the rallying-point for right-wing opinion in the country. Kornilov attempted a *coup d'état*, but this failed, and in the aftermath military discipline crumbled and desertions multiplied. Kerensky was compromised by his association with Kornilov, and as the Provisional Government was discredited the Bolsheviks began to enjoy an unprecedented popularity.

Despite the urgent need for agrarian reform, the Provisional Government postponed the issue until the Constituent Assembly met. As a result, peasants took matters into their own hands and from March onwards agrarian disturbances became common. Land was seized both from landowners and from those peasants who had separated out from the commune under the Stolypin legislation.

Agrarian disturbances aggravated the government's problem of supplying food to the towns and the army. A rationing system was introduced for grain, and plans were made to extend state regulation to the production and distribution of a range of goods of prime necessity. Measures for controlling the economy, however, were opposed by the Moscow industrialists, who exercised considerable influence over the Provisional Government.

Pressure from the business community also prevented the Provisional Government from legislating to introduce an eight-hour day for industrial workers. The economic dislocation of the country caused the workers great hardship, as the real value of their earnings declined and scarcities worsened. To protect their interests, workers formed factory committees, which took an increasingly active part in running the enterprises, so encroaching on the functions of management. Hunger compelled many workers to return to the countryside, where they hoped to share in the redivision of the land.

From its inception the Provisional Government was confronted by the nationalities' demands for independence or autonomy. Some of these the government was prepared to concede, as in the case of the Finns and the Poles. But other requests received a less sympathetic response, as the government intended to maintain the integrity of the Russian Empire. Despite the significant degree of autonomy conceded to the Ukraine in June, the Ukrainians in company with other national groups perceived the Provisional Government as being unduly resistant to their national aspirations.

The Bolshevik revolution

The part played by the Bolsheviks in the events of 1917 has been distorted by the ideological doctrines and factional struggles of Soviet times. The Bolshevik Party contended that its rule was legitimate because it had led the victorious proletarian revolution. The corollary was that it had not led any unsuccessful revolutions. Any failure of that kind would have undermined the idea of the party's infallibility. Hence, between 1920 and 1930 the Soviet leadership emphasized the contrast between the February and the October revolutions. In February the proletariat had not been victorious, and clearly the Bolsheviks had not provided leadership; whereas the October revolution, reputedly planned and organized by the Bolsheviks, had brought the proletariat to power. During the 1920s, when Soviet materials on the Russian Revolution were first published, the official doctrine was that the February revolution was spontaneous and leaderless and that the October revolution was led by the Bolsheviks. This pattern of events has become the most widely accepted interpretation of the 1917 revolutions ever since.

In fact Bolshevik activities in 1917 do not conform to the neat scheme of a spontaneous February and a well-organized October revolution. A more critical appraisal of the evidence reveals that there was substantial Bolshevik involvement in the February revolution,[5] and that the October insurrection was not the well-planned and well-executed seizure of power that both the Bolsheviks and their adversaries later claimed it to be.

[5] See J. D. White, 'The Sormovo-Nikolaev Zemlyachestvo in the February Revolution', *Soviet Studies*, 31, no. 4 (1979), pp. 475–504; M. Melançon, 'Who wrote what when?: proclamations of the February Revolution in Petrograd, 23 February–1 March 1917', *Soviet Studies*, 40, no. 3 (1988), pp. 479–500; J. D. White, 'The February Revolution and the Bolshevik Vyborg District Committee (In Response to Michael Melançon)', *Soviet Studies*, 41, no. 4 (1989), pp. 602–24.

In the February revolution the Bolsheviks had been eclipsed by the Mensheviks and the Socialist Revolutionaries, who took the initiative in forming the Petrograd Soviet. In the first weeks of the new regime, therefore, the Bolsheviks were relegated to the margins of Russian politics. What was to bring them eventual success was the policy propounded by Lenin on his return to Russia in April: to dissociate themselves from the Provisional Government, to oppose the war, and to demand that all power pass to the Soviets. By the autumn, when warweariness, hunger and disillusion with the Kerensky regime had become widespread, the Bolshevik promises of 'peace, bread and land' had a powerful and broad appeal.

The prospects of success, however, brought about divisions within the Bolshevik ranks. A section represented by Zinoviev and Kamenev wanted to use the party's popularity for electoral campaigns; Lenin favoured using pro-Bolshevik troops in Finland and Kronstadt to encircle Petrograd and seize power by force; Trotsky believed the Bolsheviks could come to power peacefully at the forthcoming Second Congress of Soviets, if Kerensky could be prevented from bringing fresh troops into the capital. The serious differences of opinion threw the Bolshevik Party into considerable disarray on the eve of taking power.

Polemics between Trotsky and Stalin* in Soviet times about who deserved most credit for leading the October revolution and who was the best Leninist have overshadowed the question of how exactly the Bolsheviks came to power. Both Soviet and Western histories of the October revolution have tended to focus on developments in Petrograd.[6] But at the time, the Bolsheviks were very conscious of the fact that it would be pointless to control the capital if troops could be brought from the Northern Front to restore order. A successful insurrection would have to secure the approaches to Petrograd.

The organizational means of achieving this was to establish a network of Military Revolutionary Committees between the Northern Front and Petrograd, which would ensure that no Provisional Government troops would be able to reach the capital. This process was set in motion by Trotsky on 11 October, the day after the Bolshevik Central Committee had managed to agree in principle to prepare for an armed insurrection. The position was made more secure when power passed to the Soviet in Reval (Tallinn) on 23 October.

The Petrograd Military Revolutionary Committee sent out its representatives to take control of strategic points throughout the city, so that by the afternoon of 25 October Trotsky could report that during

---

[6] This point is made in A. Ezergailis, *The Latvian Impact on the Bolshevik Revolution* (New York, 1983), p. 221.

the previous night the power of the Provisional Government had been destroyed and that it only remained for the broom of history to sweep it away. By the following morning the Winter Palace had been captured and the members of the Provisional Government arrested.

The Brest-Litovsk peace

The first act of the Bolshevik Party on coming to power was to issue decrees on Peace, Land and Workers' Control. In this way it signified that it offered a solution to the three major problems which the Provisional Government had failed to tackle, and that in doing so it was acting in the interests of the people at large. The move was intended to give the Bolshevik government legitimacy and popularity. It would also ensure that any future coalition partners could only be those who would accept the three fundamental directions in policy. Only the Left Socialist Revolutionaries were prepared to do this, but the coalition with them turned out to be short-lived. In this way the promulgation of the three decrees laid the foundations of one-party rule.

Initially the Bolshevik government also considered itself to be 'provisional' because the Constituent Assembly was still scheduled to be convoked. Elections to the Assembly were in fact held in November, and the first and only meeting took place on 5 January 1918. The Socialist Revolutionaries received 40% of the vote, the Bolsheviks 24%, the Kadets 5% and the Mensheviks 2%. The Bolsheviks unceremoniously dissolved the Assembly, arguing that, since the elections had taken place after the Socialist Revolutionary Party split into right and left wings, they poorly reflected the political alignments in the country. They also maintained that in any case the Soviets were superior to parliamentary assemblies as democratic institutions.

Despite Lenin's stated intention before October 1917 to smash the state machine, once in power the Bolsheviks expected to take over the existing ministries and obtain the co-operation of civil servants. This proved to be difficult, as white-collar workers of all kinds staged a stubborn and prolonged strike. The Bolsheviks took urgent measures in response to combat this and other forms of resistance to their rule. A special committee for this purpose was set up headed by Feliks Dzierzyński. It was known as the Cheka and was to become infamous as an instrument of oppression throughout the entire Soviet period. Freedom of the press and other civil rights were early casualties of the Bolshevik regime.

The Bolsheviks also originally intended to leave industrial enterprises in private hands and collaborate with their existing owners and managers. In the event the necessary co-operation was not forthcoming and the Bolsheviks were forced to nationalize some of the factories, with large-scale nationalization of industry taking place in the summer of 1918.

On taking power, the Bolsheviks believed that the Russian Revolution would be accompanied by revolutions in all the belligerent countries, so that the war would quickly come to an end. The Decree on Peace called upon the proletariat of Britain, France and Germany to bring about peace in this way. The appeal, however, did not produce any such result, and the Bolsheviks were forced into negotiating with the Central Powers at Brest-Litovsk.

The Germans and their allies demanded substantial territorial concessions as a price for peace. The Russians tried to prolong the negotiations in the hope that the international revolution might come to their aid. Eventually the Germans responded by advancing along the entire length of the front and forcing the Soviet government to accept dictated terms. By the Treaty of Brest-Litovsk signed on 3 March 1918, the Germans gained the Ukraine and the former Baltic provinces.

The civil war

The Treaty of Brest-Litovsk provided the context in which the Russian Civil War ignited. The treaty inflicted such deep humiliation on the country that even within the Bolshevik Party there was a substantial section of the membership which believed that it was better to fight the Germans – even if it meant defeat – than to accept the terms. The hopelessness of this attitude, as Lenin repeatedly pointed out, was that there was nothing to fight the Germans with; the Russian army had disintegrated. Moreover, signing the treaty left the Bolsheviks politically isolated. By that time they had alienated the other socialist parties by a number of their actions and policies, such as the dissolution of the Constituent Assembly, the repressions of the Cheka, the ending of press freedom and the curtailment of civil rights. Their regime was under serious threat when on 6 July 1918 the Left Socialist Revolutionaries assassinated the German ambassador Mirbach and staged an anti-Bolshevik uprising. The rebellion was only quelled because the Latvian Riflemen took the side of the Bolshevik government. The revolt of the Czechoslovak legion in Siberia in June of 1918, however, had placed an effective fighting force in the hands of the Mensheviks and Socialist Revolutionaries and opened a front of the civil war in the east.

Russia's withdrawal from the war created the conditions in which the Allied Powers intervened in the civil war on the side of the Whites, the intention being to renew the Russian war-effort against the Germans. Though foreign powers such as France, Britain, the USA and

Japan sent troops to Russia, they took relatively little part in the actual fighting, but contributed supplies, weapons and ammunition. Despite the apparent odds against them the Reds managed to emerge victorious in the civil war. To what was this success due?

An important factor was that the character of the civil war changed during its course. The 'democratic' opposition to the Bolsheviks was replaced by leaders, such as Admiral Kolchak in the east and General Denikin in the south, whose rule was as dictatorial as that of the Bolsheviks. They wished to return the land to its former owners and keep the integrity of the Russian Empire. In this way the Whites' objectives in the war necessarily antagonized the peasants and the non-Russian nationalities.

Deep personal and political divisions and rivalries existed within the White camp, whereas the Reds were relatively united under the Bolshevik Party. Though the Reds were surrounded by White armies, the geographical separation of the anti-Bolshevik forces made co-ordinated efforts difficult. The Reds had the advantage that they controlled the industrial regions of the country, while the Whites were mainly based on the agrarian periphery.

But whatever advantages they possessed, the Reds would have been defeated if they had not been able to succeed on the battlefield. Trotsky, the War Commissar, and Vacietis, his Commander-in-Chief, built up the Red Army as a disciplined and efficient fighting force.[7] Trotsky managed to induce former tsarist officers to take up posts as 'military specialists' in the Red Army, and encouraged the promotion of talented commanders such as Budienny, Frunze, Tukhachevsky and Voroshilov.

The export of revolution

The Treaty of Brest-Litovsk had prohibited Russia from conducting propaganda activities on territory occupied by Germany and its allies. This prohibition could be circumvented, however, if the political propaganda were conducted by ostensibly independent local Bolshevik organizations. Consequently, in the course of 1918 a number of new Communist parties were formed in the Ukraine, Belorussia, Latvia, Lithuania and Estonia, Finland and Poland. These outwardly independent organizations carried on a campaign of propaganda and terrorism against the German forces in the occupied territories of the former

---

[7] Vacietis states that when he became Commander-in-Chief he modelled units of the Red Army on the Latvian Rifle Division. J. Vacietis, *Latviesu strelnieku vesturiska nozime* (Riga, 1989), p. 189.

Russian Empire. The activities of the organizations were co-ordinated in Moscow by the Commissariat of Nationalities headed by Stalin.[8]

By 1918, as the tide of the war turned against them, the Central Powers began to succumb to the same kind of social and national tensions as had overtaken Russia. During the spring and summer of 1918 the Austro-Hungarian Empire disintegrated as Poles, Czechs, Slovaks, Serbs, Croats and Slovenes formed themselves into the independent states of Poland, Czechoslovakia and Yugoslavia. In October rioting broke out on the streets of Budapest and the pro-Entente aristocrat Count Mihály Károlyi was installed as Prime Minister. Democratic reforms were carried out and Hungary was declared a republic.

In Germany the prospect of military defeat and fear of popular unrest persuaded the Kaiser in September to issue a proclamation instituting parliamentary government. The liberal Prince Max of Baden was appointed Chancellor to implement the democratic reforms. At the same time a request for an armistice was sent to President Wilson. Among the terms of the armistice Wilson offered was the demand that German troops evacuate occupied Russian territory.

At the beginning of November a naval mutiny at Kiel spread to other parts of Germany. Workers' and soldiers' councils similar to the soviets in Russia were set up with great rapidity. On 9 November the Kaiser was forced to abdicate and Germany was declared a republic. On the following day a Council of People's Commissars headed by Friedrich Ebert, and consisting of Independent Socialists (who had opposed the war) and Social Democrats (who had supported it) took control in Berlin. The Spartakists, led by Rosa Luxemburg and Karl Liebknecht, stood aloof from the new government, as they favoured a socialist republic on the Russian model. This was something the Social Democrats were determined to prevent, an objective facilitated by the Independents' withdrawal from the government on 28 December.

On 11 November soldiers' councils sprang up in the German armies in the Russian-occupied territories. They collaborated with the local Soviet authorities to effect an orderly return home to Germany. This allowed the Red Army under Vacietis to advance rapidly into the Baltic area and, with the help of the respective national Communist groups, temporarily to establish Estonian, Latvian and Lithuanian Soviet governments.

At a congress opening on 30 December and attended by Soviet Russia's emissary Karl Radek, the Spartakists constituted themselves into the Communist Party of Germany. On 6 January 1919, against Radek's

---

[8]   J. D. White, 'National Communism and world revolution: the political consequences of the German military withdrawal from the Baltic area in 1918–19', *Europe-Asia Studies*, no. 8 (1994), pp. 1349–69.

advice, the Spartakists attempted an armed uprising in Berlin, seizing newspaper and telegraph offices but no centres of power. The rebellion was quickly crushed by Ebert's government with the help of volunteer units (*Freikorps*) from the old army. Luxemburg and Liebknecht were arrested and murdered on the way to prison. On 6 February the Constituent Assembly met at Weimar and formed a government of which Ebert became Prime Minister.

The wave of reaction which followed the failed Spartakist uprising had repercussions in the German armies then evacuating the Baltic area. The soldiers' councils were dissolved and the withdrawal from the occupied territories was temporarily stopped, thus halting the advance of the Red Army westwards. The Poles took advantage of this situation to take over some of the German positions in Lithuania.

At the beginning of January 1919, when it seemed that the Russian Revolution was about to be exported through the Baltic area into Germany and beyond, Lenin decided to form the Third or Communist International (Comintern). Its first congress was held in March, and its nucleus was formed by the Communist parties that had been established in the occupied territories after Brest-Litovsk. The main Communist party from abroad was the German Communist Party, but it was the Russians who dominated the new International.

As the Comintern was being formed, a Soviet republic was being established in Hungary. In the face of Allied demands that Hungary cede Transylvania to Romania, Count Károlyi resigned on 20 March and handed over power to the Hungarian Communists led by Béla Kun. The regime lasted until June when Hungary was invaded by Romanian and Czechoslovak forces. A Soviet regime was also set up in Bavaria in April, but this was quickly and ruthlessly crushed by the *Freikorps*.

In June of 1920, at the time the second congress of the Comintern met, another occasion arose when the Russian revolution might be carried into Western Europe. This was after the Reds' victory in the civil war when Józef Pilsudski's Poland invaded the Ukraine and was driven back by Tukhachevsky to the outskirts of Warsaw. Lenin saw the Red Army's victory as a chance to set up a Soviet regime in Poland. But the fortunes of war were reversed when the Poles rallied and put the Red Army to flight.

The results of the revolution

The changes which the revolution and the civil war brought about in Russia did not solve the country's long-term social and economic problems, but altered somewhat the form which they took. Thus, the landlords had been eliminated as a distinct social group, and their land had been given to the peasantry. This did nothing to improve the productivity of agriculture, and while it might have ended the age-old conflict between landlord and peasant, it opened up a new one between the peasantry and the state. The state needed the grain the peasants produced, but the peasants had little incentive to sell it at the prices offered.

The revolution eliminated Russia's capitalist class, and ended for the time being the country's slow and difficult progress towards market relations. It severed existing trading patterns, and ended foreign investment in Russia. It left an economy with imbalances and lacking any obvious direction of development.

The revolution gave recognition to national identity, and in the case of the Finns, the Poles and the Baltic peoples it had given them, for a time at least, independence. Though subscribing to the nineteenth-century belief that national differences would eventually disappear, the young Soviet regime gained considerable political capital from the tactic of espousing the cause of national self-determination.

The most visible outcome of the revolution was to place in power a government which claimed to represent the interests of the working class, and which justified its policies in ideological terms, implying that these policies were the embodiment of socialist or Communist principles. Terminology and ideas taken from Marx,* Engels and their followers entered the vocabulary of politics, administration, education and science.

The predilection of the Soviet regime to present everything in ideological terms tends to obscure the fact that a great deal of continuity remained between pre-revolutionary and post-revolutionary Russia. The basic fabric of Russian society remained the same. The revolution in the countryside reversed the Stolypin reform and gave new vitality to the peasant commune and to egalitarianism at the expense of individual initiative and responsibility. The collectivism and conformity of the Soviet regime were not imposed by ideology, but were the habits of traditional Russian society. The expectation that all initiative would come from the state rather than from the population was another feature of tsarist Russia which was retained in Soviet times. And the all-pervasive imposition of petty formalities on the common people by a privileged and corrupt bureaucracy, a phenomenon thought of as being characteristically 'Stalinist', was described by visitors to Russia in the civil war period.[9] They were descriptions, moreover, which had striking parallels in nineteenth-century accounts of Russian politics and society.[10]

---

[9]   Examples would include A. Berkman, *The Bolshevik Myth* (New York, 1925; rpt. London, 1989); E. Goldman, *My Disillusionment in Russia* (New York, 1923); B. Russell, *The Practice and Theory of Bolshevism* (London, 1920).
[10]   D. Mackenzie Wallace, *Russia* (London, 1878); E. B. Lanin, *Russian Characteristics* (London, 1892).

Models of Communism

The fact that from its inception the Soviet regime felt impelled to justify its own existence and the policies it introduced in terms of Marxist theory has led to the belief that the Bolsheviks did in fact implement a programme inspired by Marxist ideology. E. H. Carr, for example, wrote that it was 'this element of self-consciousness' that made the Russian Revolution unique in modern history. The Russian writer Alexander Tsypko, from a different perspective, argued that collectivization and all the other disastrous economic policies implemented in the Soviet Union and in other socialist countries were inspired by the ideas of Karl Marx.[11] Contemporary writings on the subject, however, reveal a fact which is of cardinal importance for explaining the evolution of the Soviet regime. It is that on coming to power the Bolsheviks were extremely vague about what a socialist (or Communist) society was, and that their ideas on how to achieve one varied over time.

From the First World War to the early 1920s the Bolsheviks believed that socialism had matured within the capitalist system, and that the new order would simply emerge from the ruins of the old. They had been encouraged in this belief by Rudolf Hilferding's* book *Das Finanzkapital*, published in 1910, which argued that the formation of monopolies and trusts had prepared the way for an economy that was centralized and that could be monitored through the banking system. Hilferding had also maintained that the economies of individual countries were becoming increasingly integrated, with the implication that when the collapse of capitalism came it would be on an international scale.

Before coming to power Lenin had envisaged the future socialist economy as a matter of keeping track of the goods and services needed by the population by using the banks as 'accounting' or 'book-keeping' agencies. The idea was incorporated in the Bolshevik Party programme of 1919, but in the following year Nikolai Bukharin recognized that actual events had proved it impracticable.

The absence of any *a priori* model of socialism, in conjunction with the assumption that what was taking place was the working out of world-historical laws, created the impression among the Bolsheviks that the economic realities which confronted them were phenomena of 'socialism' or 'Communism'. During the civil war the collapse of market relations, inflation, the direct exchange of goods and the requisitioning of grain were all interpreted as signifying the imminent emergence of a Communist society.

---

[11]   E. H. Carr, *1917: Before and After* (London, 1969), pp. 8–9; A. Tsypko, *Nasilie Izhi ili Kak zabludilsia prizrak* (Moscow, 1990), *passim*.

As early as 1918 some Bolsheviks had convinced themselves that the peasants preferred to cultivate the land collectively and in large units.[12] Thus, when Soviet republics were established in the Ukraine, the Baltic states and Hungary in 1919, large estates were not divided up, but kept intact as state farms. The policy was repeated in Poland in 1920. But in all cases it was unpopular and was subsequently recognized to be a mistake.

When the New Economic Policy was introduced in 1921 it was thought to be a retreat from Communist policies of the civil war period. Later, however, attitudes to NEP changed, and it became widely held that the way to achieve socialism was through the development of market relations. In 1924 Stalin signalled an end to the belief in an integrated international economic system when he unveiled his theory of 'socialism in one country'.

The idea that a socialist economy was a planned economy was first voiced by the ex-Bolshevik Alexander Bogdanov in 1921.[13] In the early 1920s this conception of socialism was taken up by the Soviet regime, the earliest plans incorporating the principle that all the sectors of the economy should be co-ordinated and developed in a balanced way. Stalin's intervention, however, politicized planning, making its objective not balanced economic growth, but the crude maximization of output.[14]

In 1929 difficulties with grain deliveries prompted Stalin to order the forced collectivization of agriculture, and by so doing to bring NEP to an end. From the 1930s collectivized agriculture and five-year plans gave characteristic form to the Soviet economic system. This model of socialism was the one with which the Soviet Union entered the Second World War, and the one which was replicated in the Eastern Bloc countries in the post-war era.

The international setting

The revolution in Germany and the establishment of Soviet regimes in Hungary and Bavaria suggested to many statesmen that Bolshevism might spread westwards. The establishment of the Comintern and the rhetoric of its chairman Zinoviev implied that this was the intention of the Soviet regime, despite the calls of its Commissar for Foreign Affairs Chicherin for normalization in international relations.

---

[12]   D. Götze, ed., 'Briefe Clara Zetkins an Julian Marchlewski', *Beiträge zur Geschichte der Arbeiterbewegung*, no. 6 (1978), p. 862.
[13]   A. A. Bogdanov, *Tektologiia: Vseobshchaia organizatsionnaia nauka* (Moscow, 1989), vol. 1, p. 273.
[14]   L. S. Rogachevskaia, 'Kak sostavlialsia plan pervoi piatiletki', *Voprosy istorii*, no. 8 (1993), pp. 149–52.

At the end of the civil war Soviet Russia found itself isolated in the international arena, able to establish normal diplomatic relations only with the Baltic countries and other small neighbouring states. The breakthrough came in 1922 with Germany, upon whom the Treaty of Versailles had imposed harsh terms, and which, like Russia, was isolated diplomatically. At Rapallo, Soviet Russia resumed diplomatic relations with Weimar Germany and agreed to future economic co-operation between the two countries. One outcome of this agreement was that German military engineers were allowed to test on Soviet territory types of weapon that were forbidden to Germany by the Treaty of Versailles. This co-operation lasted until the Nazi party came to power in Germany in 1933.

In the inter-war years Soviet leaders suspected that it would only be a matter of time before the Western Powers would renew their efforts to overthrow the Bolshevik regime and unleash war on the Soviet Union. The conviction that war was imminent was a powerful incentive for the Soviet Union to industrialize rapidly and to collectivize its agriculture.

In the 1930s, faced by the rise of fascism in Europe and Japanese militarism in the East, Soviet diplomacy tried to establish a common front with the Western democracies for collective security against possible aggression. The Comintern accordingly abandoned its earlier doctrine of 'class against class' and called on its constituent Communist parties to establish popular fronts with all political forces opposed to fascism and Japanese militarism. As part of this campaign the Soviet Union in 1938 intervened on the Republican side in the Spanish Civil War. However, the proposed alliance between the Soviet Union and the Western democracies for collective security did not materialize, and Stalin opted in August 1939 to conclude a non-aggression pact with Nazi Germany.

The Soviet government would subsequently argue that it had no choice in this matter; but the case has been made that Stalin had consistently favoured a pro-German orientation in Soviet foreign policy and regarded the Molotov–Ribbentrop Pact not as a temporary expedient but as part of a long-term strategy.[15] Whatever Stalin's motives may have been for making it, there is one respect at least in which the Molotov–Ribbentrop Pact had a long-term significance. In assigning to the Soviet sphere of influence eastern Poland, the three Baltic states and Bessarabia, it anticipated the time following the Second World War when the sphere of Soviet domination would be enlarged enormously in Central and Eastern Europe and the Soviet model of Communism would be extended to the countries of the Eastern Bloc.

[15] M. Heller and A. Nekrich, *Utopia in Power* (London, 1986), pp. 322–68.

10

European Fascism

Richard Thurlow

One Fascism or Many?

Fascism is the great political boo word of the twentieth century. The Second World War, which was caused by fascist imperialism, led to the premature death of over thirty million Europeans, including four to six million Jews who were murdered by the Nazis and their collaborators. Yet, while universal horror is expressed at the consequences of fascism in its most bestial form, there is very little agreement on the nature of the term. At one pole are those who argue that fascism, as a nationalist creed, was not for export, and that the Italian movement was a unique phenomenon.[1] Others distinguish between the original movement (usually with a capital F, as in this chapter) and generic fascism, a concept which links together a variety of inter-war European political movements. Few, however, still adhere to the extreme view of the Comintern in the 'Class against Class' period from 1928–33, that everybody who did not adhere to Bolshevik revolutionary discipline, was, objectively, helping the establishment of fascism, or was a 'social fascist'.

The lack of consensus on a definition has not deterred the use of fascism as a heuristic label. There is no agreement on whether fascism possessed a coherent political ideology, if it was a movement of the right or left, or the extent to which fascism and Nazism were two sides of the same coin. Disagreement is still expressed about the origins of fascism, whether it was confined to Europe, or if it, finally, disappeared in 1945. Some historians still adhere to the 'political thug' interpretation, while others see fascism as a system of ideas, which, despite its anti-rationalism, was as complex as liberalism or Marxism. There is also a

---

[1]   G. Allardyce, 'What Fascism is not: thoughts on the deflation of a concept', *American Historical Review*, 84, no. 2 (1979), 367–88. AHA forum response, S. Payne, 'Reply', ibid., pp. 389–91.

need to distinguish between fascism as movement and fascism as regime. This first section will argue that the concept of fascism is a useful one; that it needs to be distinguished from forms of right-wing authoritarianism, and other revolutionary creeds; and that fascist movements possessed common characteristics, but that national cultural traditions made them variegated in practice.

Although many of the earlier surveys of European fascist movements emphasized national characteristics, and their links to an extreme right political tradition, several recent interpretations have highlighted the revolutionary, ideological and left-wing roots of fascism, or have suggested a synthesis.[2] At the academic crossroads is Stanley Payne. He argued that although fascism was a nationalist creed dependent on different cultural traditions, there were, nevertheless, common features to fascist movements. He stressed three criteria in a Weberian ideal-type definition: the 'fascist negations', ideology and goals, and style and organization. Fascism was anti-liberal, anti-socialist, anti-Communist and anti-conservative; it was a charismatic movement organized under the leadership principle, whose aim was to establish a national corporatist, national syndicalist or national socialist state; and it was totalitarian in character.[3] This definition has now been revised to incorporate more recent interpretations of the positive ideas of fascism as a 'third way' revolutionary ultra-nationalism, with a vitalist doctrine which positively encouraged violence both as end and means.

Zeev Sternhell has argued that fascism was an anti-materialist ethical revision of Marxism, which aimed at destroying the alleged decadence of inter-war Europe, by restructuring society through modernization, the leadership of technocratic elites, and the operation of a planned economy. For Sternhell fascism was 'neither right nor left'.[4]

Roger Griffin, like Payne, has developed a Weberian ideal-type, but his interpretation is not a list definition of characteristics, but is based on underlying structural beliefs. He argues that fascism was a reaction to a perceived cultural despair about the decadence of inter-war society. It was, at root, a manic, revolutionary palingenetic doctrine whose mythic core advocated renaissance, or rebirth, through a populist ultra-nationalism. The phoenix thus became a prominent symbol of fascist movements. The Sorelian myth was an important key to understanding fascism, with its emphasis on the psychological roots of action, the

[2]   E. Weber (ed.), *Varieties of Fascism* (New York, 1964); S. J. Woolf (ed.), *Fascism in Europe* (London, 1981); E. Nolte, *Three Faces of Fascism* (London, 1966).
[3]   S. Payne, *Fascism: Comparison and Definition* (Madison, WI, 1980); S. Payne, *A History of Fascism 1914–45* (London, 1996), p. 14.
[4]   Z. Sternhell, 'Fascist ideology', in *Fascism: A Readers Guide*, ed. W. Lacqueur (Harmondsworth, 1979).

contempt for bourgeois values and the purifying function of violence; nationalism, however, in the fascist version, replaced the function of class conflict and the general strike. The heterogeneity of fascist roots meant it could spawn a variety of different forms.[5]

Roger Eatwell has highlighted the key role of synthesis in his spectral syncratic theory of fascism. The dialectical method emphasizes the convergence of doctrine within fascism of ideas taken from both the extreme right and the revolutionary left. The four key syntheses identified are, first, between a view of man constrained by nature, and the need to create a 'new man'; secondly between a commitment to science and a vitalist belief in the power of the will; thirdly between the faith and service of Christianity and the heroism of classical thought: and fourthly between a belief in modern technology and private property, with state management to create full employment and public welfare. He has recently emphasized the national roots of fascism, particularly with the conditions for the success or failure of the movement.[6]

Such interpretations emphasize the conscious role of ideology in fascist articulation of their beliefs. The utopian vision of the hodge-podge of fantasies that was fascism, suggested that it was often a ragbag of ideas spawned in the political underworld. It was not the intellectual force of ideas which led to the rise of fascism, but rather the collapse of the old order, and the inability of authoritarian and liberal forms of government to cope with the forces unleashed by the First World War. Fascism was to represent an alternative revolution to the threat posed by Communism. It would sweep away the values of traditional elites, while maintaining property relationships. In practice collusion with elites proved essential to the rise of fascism in both Italy and Germany.[7] Yet, while the fascist new man was to become a figure of ridicule in the Italian establishment, the insidious permeation of Nazi values into German society and the virtual conquest of much of Europe made Hitler's* crazy beliefs far more significant.

While commonly seen as a right-wing movement, fascism was a late-comer to European politics and searched for political space in which to develop.[8] It needs to be differentiated from the reactionary, moderate, radical and extreme right. Fascism was an attempt to create a new world, not a reversion to an imaginary utopian past. It was a revolutionary movement, which aimed to change the nature of man, not to preserve

---

[5] R. Griffin, *The Nature of Fascism* (London, 1991); R. Griffin (ed.), *Fascism: A Reader* (Oxford, 1995).
[6] R. Eatwell, 'Towards a new model of generic fascism', *Journal of Theoretical Politics*, 4, no. 2 (1992), 161–94; R. Eatwell, *Fascism: A History* (London, 1995).
[7] M. Blinkhorn (ed.), *Fascists and Conservatives* (London, 1990).
[8] J. Linz, 'Some notes towards a comparative study of Fascism in sociological historical perspective', in *Fascism: A Readers Guide*, ed. Lacqueur, pp. 13–78.

the constitution or conserve the national heritage. Like the radical right it was a mass movement, but had its own agenda, rather than being manipulated by elites, or becoming the tool of Bonapartist generals. It was differentiated from the extreme right by its willingness to use political democracy to its own advantage.

With the image of an activist right-wing mass movement, and its own view as an alternative revolution, fascism can be seen as a 'third way' synthesis of left and right ideas, which varied in the different national contexts. Part of the difference between Italian fascism and German Nazism proved to be the failure of the former, and the success of the latter, in setting its own political agenda. Fascism, despite the bombastic propaganda, proved to be a stillborn alternative revolution; Nazism came much closer to establishing its horrific vision of the future of Germany, and of Europe.

Fascism was a broad-ranging European phenomenon of the inter-war period, with many rivulets and tributaries leading backwards to the French Revolution and the intellectual attack on liberalism, positivism and rationalism at the end of the nineteenth century, and forward to the revival of integral nationalism after the Second World War.[9] Nazism and Fascism were the exceptions rather than the rule. Most national fascisms were the outgrowth of small, often persecuted, minority sects which made little political impact, except as a reflection of Italian Fascism, and increasingly in the 1930s, Nazism.

Those fascists who were to emerge from political oblivion did so mainly as a result of collaboration with the Nazis during the Second World War. The name of the Nasjonal Samling leader, Quisling,* in Norway, was to become a term of abuse, denoting treachery in most European languages. Fascist movements, with varying degrees of accuracy, were to be perceived as a Nazi 'fifth column' in most states during the Second World War. Somewhat ironically, the most notorious collaborators, such as the Frenchmen Marcel Deat and Jacques Doriot, the Englishman John Amery and the Belgian Leon Degrelle,* objected to being labelled as fascists.

Fascism was usually associated with regimes and movements which combined beliefs in integral nationalism, dictatorship, elitism, futurism, racism, anti-Semitism, anti-feminism, youth, planism, corporatism, totalitarianism, militarism and imperialism, as well as an implacable hostility to the alleged decadence of a pluralist political system and to the values of bourgeois society. It was against, in Sir Oswald Mosley's* words, the 'united muttons' of the 'old gangs' of European society.[10]

---

[9] N. O'Sullivan, *Fascism* (London, 1983); L. Cheles, R. Ferguson and M. Vaughan (eds), *The Far Right in Europe*, 2nd edn (London, 1995).
[10] O. Mosley, *The Greater Britain* (London, 1932), pp. 178–9.

Yet between fascist movements there were important variations. Italian Fascism and German Nazism will be examined separately, but all fascist movements had cultural idiosyncrasies. Thus the British Union of Fascists, probably the movement most coherent in its beliefs and least successful in its political impact, was pacifist, relatively feminist, and after 1934, engaged only in defensive violence.[11] In Belgium, separate Walloon and Flemish fascist movements were divided between working for a fascist Belgium, Burgundy or Flanders, and whether the electoral or paramilitary path was the route to power. The most important, Rex, began as a radical right Catholic monarchist party and ended as Nazi collaborators.

In Eastern Europe fascists adopted a more leftist tinge. The virulent political anti-Semitism of the Arrow Cross in Hungary was for the most part tolerated by the authorities, as it focused resentment on a convenient scapegoat and deflected the vaguely socialistic calls for land reform. Hungary was also notable for the Turanian myth; a Central European variant of the Nordic-Aryan man. The Iron Guard in Romania developed a mystical fascism. The Thunder Cross in Latvia was to be distinguished by its militant anti-Communism. Several national fascisms, including Mussolini's* and Mosley's, were not originally anti-Semitic, but later adopted it, as a result of Nazi influence, or as a reaction to the perceived hostility of some Jews.

Fascism exhibited many traits in different national contexts. The writings of 'fellow travellers of the right' increased the diversity of such ideas and helped provide a gloomy prognosis for the future of Europe in the 1930s. Their significance should not be overrated, however. Fascism is only of continuing interest as a reflected afterglow of the 'achievements' of the Nazis. Yet it would be equally a mistake to see the different fascist movements simply as a mirror of Nazi actions, or to judge them purely in the light of the Holocaust. There were many fascisms, most of them insignificant; but all of them struggled for an alternative revolution, and the creation of a new man, even if these concepts meant different things in various national contexts.

The Circumstances Conducive to Fascist Movements

The emergence of fascism in inter-war Europe can only be explained as a consequence of the devastating impact of the First World War. It is true that the roots of fascism were laid in the period before 1914,

---

[11]   R. Thurlow, *Fascism in Britain* (Oxford, 1987), pp. 92–118; R. Thurlow, *The Secret State* (Oxford, 1994), pp. 173–213.

and some consideration needs to be given to these developments; but the ideas, frustrations, resentments and movements which were to coalesce in various permutations in inter-war Europe, and which came to be regarded as fascist, can only be understood as a reaction to the trigger of the seminal crisis of the old order. It was the collapse of the Hohenzollern, Habsburg and Romanov dynasties in Central and Eastern Europe, the mass slaughter on the Western Front, the Bolshevik revolution in October 1917, the consequences of the peace treaties and the failure of the post-war political and economic order, which precipitated the rise of fascism.

Without these developments fascism would have remained on the political fringe, if anybody had even been bothered to invent it. The birth of fascism had its origins in the political underworld of pre-1914 Europe, amongst those who failed to appreciate the spread of liberalism, the triumph of nationalism and the process of state-building in Western Europe during the nineteenth century. For those who became alienated from the 'soulless' triumph of materialism in Bismarckian Germany, the political corruption of the age of *trasformismo* and the deterioration of public order in liberal Italy, the instability of the Third Republic in France, and the perceived decline in Britain, fascism was to provide one of the solutions to the crisis. These factors were all potential sources of trouble, if the age of progress and the triumph of industrialism were to be questioned.

The intellectual origins of fascism can be found in the revolt against rationalism at the end of the nineteenth century. The dominance of liberalism, rationalism and positivism was increasingly questioned by a generation of intellectuals who emphasized the irrational sources of human conduct, and the relationship between feelings, values, emotions and intellect.[12] From their different perspectives and disciplines, Freud, Bergson, Nietzsche,* Sorel, Kidd, Pareto* and Mosca argued that basic instincts rather than reason determined human action. Second-level popularizers and propagandists could easily turn such insights into political form, which could later be developed by fascists. Thus in Germany, intellectuals like Paul de Lagarde, Julius Langbehn and Moeller van den Bruck could apply such influences to Volkish thought, to create proto-fascist ideas which found deep cultural resonance on the far right. There is a direct link, via the pseudo-science of Houston Stewart Chamberlain, between the influence of Nietzsche, Wagner and Social Darwinism, and Hitler.

In Italy such magpie intellectualism was also evident with the influence of Sorel, Nietzsche, Pareto and the Italian syndicalists, on the young

[12]   H. Hughes, *Consciousness and Society* (London, 1959).

Marxist, Benito Mussolini. Zeev Sternhell has argued that the fascist ideology was deeply implanted in French culture by the 1930s, that its origins were to be found in the writings of Maurice Barrès in the 1880s, and in the Boulanger* crisis. Feelings and values were to represent a truer source of conduct for fascists than reason. To the bourgeois, as George Valois, the founder of Le Faisceau put it, 'brandishing his contracts and statistics: two plus three makes . . . nought, the barbarian replies, smashing his head in'.[13]

Fascism was a product of the chaos following the First World War. Political violence was to be the catalyst which enabled Mussolini's Fascist party to kick its way into the headlines after November 1920, and to give its name to a generic phenomenon. Over much of Central, Eastern and southern Europe state authority had collapsed following the armistice and the failure to lift the economic blockade, until the signing of the peace treaties in 1919–20. The revolutions in Budapest and Munich, the Spartacist revolt in northern Germany and the advance of the Red Army to the gates of Warsaw, led to paramilitary groups of ex-soldiers being formed, such as the *freikorps* in Germany, and the 'Men of Szeged', in Hungary, as proto-fascist resistance in the face of the collapse of state authority.

Although social stability was restored through the emergence of monarchical, militarist or presidential forms of authoritarian government, following the failure of Woodrow Wilson's brave new world of implanted liberal democracies in much of Europe, in Italy the authorities failed to take the initiative. Here, the passivity of the state in the face of revolutionary socialist attempts to organize the labour market in the countryside, which were designed to establish the framework for the eventual collectivization of agriculture, led to landowners in the Po Valley employing Fascist *squadristi* to destroy the power of socialist trade unions. This they successfully did through a brutal campaign of murder, intimidation and castor-oil politics. The state decreed that the authorities should take an even-handed approach to control political violence between Fascists and socialists. The Carabinieri turned a blind eye to Fascist violence and arrested the socialist victims. It was this, more than anything else, which turned an obscure extremist sect, that won only one seat at the 1919 general election fought on a universal suffrage/proportional representation franchise, and only thirty-eight seats in 1921, into an effective political force.

Mussolini, who disapproved of the independent initiative of the local Fascist warlords, the Ras, turned the situation to his advantage, after being forced to drop a pacification pact with the socialists in 1921. By

[13]   Sternhell, 'Fascist ideology', p. 357.

a combination of daring and political skill, his 'Janus-faced' strategy of negotiating deals to become part of a national parliamentary bloc, while maintaining what was in effect a private army, enabled him to make use of the collapse of state power. This occurred in 1922, when a combination of Mussolini's political bravado and state failure to oppose the 'march on Rome' by the ill-equipped Fascist *squadristi*, opened the door for the offer of the premiership. A mixture of deft manoeuvres, blackmail and political violence was to turn Mussolini from a coalition leader into a Fascist dictator.

Fascism triumphed in Italy as a result of the collapse of state authority. Although the 'fascists of the first hour' were defined by their attendance at the meeting at San Sepolcro, Milan, in 1919, Italian Fascism was born in the interventionist crisis in 1915. Here a noisy mass movement encouraged the backstairs intrigue which brought Italy into the war. This proto-fascist alliance included, on the left, national syndicalists and the ex-revolutionary socialist, Mussolini, as well as Marinetti's Futurists, the right-wing Nationalist Association and the romantic poet-adventurer, D'Annunzio. The 'mutilated peace', and the refusal of the allies to implement all the clauses of the Treaty of London (1915), led D'Annunzio to seize power in Fiume for fifteen months (September 1919–December 1920) and to establish a plebiscitary government which was to influence the style of fascism.

The failure of the state to gain for Italy all the perceived fruits of victory, the weakness of central authority, the collapse of law and order, the inability to check the growth of unemployment and inflation, and the threat of Communism, created the lethal mixture of acute anxiety and frustrated rising expectations, which was the background to Fascism's rise to power. The success of Mussolini in consolidating that power led to the export of fascism elsewhere. Although not mimetic movements, Le Faisceau in France and the British Fascisti took their inspiration from Mussolini's success in Italy, although both were based on national traditions. Fascism was also admired by the fledgling National Socialist Workers' Party (NSDAP) in Germany, whose failed Munich beer hall *putsch* in 1923 attempted to imitate Mussolini's route to power.

The conditions for the rise of Nazism in Germany were even more complex. It was caused by national resentment at the harsh terms of the Versailles peace treaty, the failure both of democracy in the Weimar Republic (1918–30) and of the more authoritarian period of presidential power after 1930. It was the inability of liberalism and social democracy, as well as Prussian conservatism and authoritarianism, to find an effective answer to the deepening economic and social crisis caused by the collapse of the international financial system in 1930–1, which in

1932 led over 30 per cent of Germans to vote for the Nazis in the two general elections and for Hitler for president.

Hitler eventually came to power as the result of backstairs intrigue, in January 1933. Like Mussolini, who passed the Acerbo law (1923) to enable the Fascists to claim two-thirds of the parliamentary seats, Hitler neutralized the Reichstag by passing an Enabling Act (1933) which effectively gave him the power to rule by decree. Unlike the Italian Duce, he was then able to become the Fuehrer, with no theoretical limitation on his power, by combining the posts of Chancellor and President. As Hindenburg,* on his deathbed, had already signed a decree justifying the Night of the Long Knives, on 30 June 1934, Hitler found it much easier to survive multiple political murder, than Mussolini had following the Matteotti crisis in 1924. Hitler came to power as a result of economic, social and political crisis. Waiting in the wings were the Communists: 'after Hitler, us', they confidently proclaimed. Hitler easily outsmarted both his rivals and the German establishment, and used the Reichstag fire to destroy the Communists. Although Communists and socialists together easily outnumbered the Nazis, the deep division between reformists and revolutionaries left the route open for the Nazis to seize power.

Thus Europe's potentially most powerful nation succumbed to the political virus of the most radical form of fascism. The ideology of Nazism made it a party of the lunatic fringe, based on waste-paper basket ideas. However, Germans did not vote for Hitler because they believed in a world conspiracy of Jews, or were Nordic racists. Nazi success was due to frustrated rising expectations engendered by the failure of other governments to restore German confidence after the debacle of 1918. The successive cycles of crisis and recovery, following defeat and the 'stab in the back' myth, the humiliation of Versailles, the threatened Communist revolution in 1919–20, the great inflation of 1919–23, followed by the stability of 1924–9, the catastrophe of the banking collapse and the inexorably rising mass unemployment after 1930, led to growing support for the Nazis. Nazism appeared to many as possessing a dynamism which offered the only non-Communist solution to the crisis; it did indeed take the credit for recovery, beefing up several of the economic programmes already in place, and followed a foreign policy which restored national pride and led to war, once it achieved power. The evidence suggests that the self-image as a *volkspartei* was not too far wide of the mark, although Protestant rural agricultural areas and traditional middle-class urban communities disproportionately supported the Nazis, while blue-collar workers were underrepresented.

Yet nowhere outside Germany and Italy were political conditions to be suitable for the rise of fascism. Many of the economic and social factors, especially the paralysis engendered by the economic depression of the 1930s and the fear of Communist revolution, particularly in Central and Eastern Europe, were general problems. Mimetic Nazism, however, proved to have little attraction outside Germany; Scandinavia, the supposed home of the Nordic/Aryan man, had minuscule fascist parties.

Military and monarchical dictatorship used repression to suppress fascism in much of Europe, or incorporated fascist movements into conservative ruling coalitions, thereby emasculating them. In Romania Corneliu Codreanu,* the leader of the Iron Guard, was 'shot while trying to escape' by King Carol's government. The victory of Franco* in the Spanish Civil War owed much to the crucial support given him by Hitler and Mussolini; it owed little to Spain's native fascist group, the Falange, which had marginal political support, even if it did play a role in destabilizing Spanish politics in the 1930s. Franco's upgrading of the Falange into the Nationalist political party in 1937 was a cynical manoeuvre. It was a means by which, through persuasion and a head-banging exercise, fascists, conservatives, and Alfonsine and Carlist monarchists could be controlled by the military. Franco proved that political murder was no totalitarian monopoly. He was a product of the extreme right, who upheld Catholic values and landlord power in rural Spain. His vicious regime was not fascist; it was no attempted alternative revolution.

Fascism and Nazism

Italian Fascism and German Nazism were separate but related movements whose mythic core, propaganda, and style possessed many common attributes. The analogy was somewhat confused by the fact that Italian Fascism more approximated a national socialism than Nazism despite its name, the implementation of radical ideological goals was further advanced in Nazi Germany than in Fascist Italy, and Mussolini failed to make Italians 'Believe, Obey, Fight'. The two movements also influenced each other, with Italian influence paramount in the 1920s, and the Nazis dominating 'the brutal friendship' after 1935. The abject performance of Italy in the Second World War ensured vassal status for Mussolini, long before his reincarnation as leader of the doomed Salò republic between 1943 and 1945, when his attempted return to socialist roots was ignored, both by the Nazis and by those Italians fortunate enough to evade the security apparatus of the regime.

Yet although Fascism and Nazism were at root two sides of the same coin, there were differences which have led some historians to see them as separate phenomena. Fascism was a voluntarist, idealist creed dependent on the human will and a Lamarckian view of evolution. The transmission of acquired characteristics to future generations, reinforced by indoctrination, was central to the educational propaganda of Italian Fascism. Nazism was more deterministic. It was a ragbag of voluntarist and pseudo-scientific nostrums that were subordinated to a materialist racial hierarchy, which avoided dilution only by natural selection and the application of strict Social Darwinist principles. Fascism was racist, but it based its beliefs on ethnocentrism and cultural differences, not on biology or skin colour. The use of chemical warfare against the unfortunate Abyssinians in 1935 showed that Mussolini's Fascism was as bestial for Africans as Nazism was for defeated nations deemed inferior (practically everybody; although West Europeans were treated better than Slavs, whilst Jews, Communists and some minority groups were subject to genocide).

Nazism was the more brutal in its anti-Semitism; not all fascisms persecuted the Jews, although the Nazis found some of their most enthusiatic accomplices to murder from amongst the ranks of national fascisms. Italian Fascism only adopted anti-Semitism after 1938, and only then half-heartedly. There were exceptions, like Roberto Farinacci, but Italians took even less notice of official anti-Semitic policy than most fascist propaganda. The Italian army, for example, sabotaged official attempts to co-operate with the implementation of the 'final solution' in areas under its jurisdiction.

Fascism and Nazism, depite their differences, were alternative routes to modernization. They were attempts to escape from a perceived spiritual and material crisis in Italy and Germany by creating a new society. They failed because the utopian nature of the enterprise and their imperial ambitions led them into an eventually overwhelming conflict with a combination of their enemies. Totalitarian controls, propaganda and finding national solutions to the economic and social problems of inter-war Europe gave them the appearance of being successful in the 1930s. Both used the past to invent the future; Mussolini tried to indoctrinate his countrymen with the spirit of the Roman centurion, and to recreate 'mare nostrum', to turn the Mediterranean into a great Italian sea. Hitler used the spirit of the German forests, the Teutonic knights, Frederick Barbarossa and Frederick the Great, to justify the revision of Versailles, the bringing of all ethnic Germans within new state borders, and the implementation of *lebensraum*, with the conquest of a new European empire, as the basis of the thousand-year 'Third Reich'.

While looking backwards to create the spirit of the future, the attempt to support the traditional social structure was always subordinate to that modernization so necessary to defend the state. In Italy the 'Battle of the grain' led to the sacrifice of peasant farmers, to the gain of capitalist agriculture. In Germany, giving priority to rearmament meant the transfer of resources from agriculture to industry, and the relative decline of the small farmer, who had provided disproportionate support in the Nazi rise to power. Economic nationalism and the growing international crisis were other forces which made modernization and self-sufficiency a priority in both Italy and Germany; despite the illiberal and reactionary ideology, the necessity for more tanks, ships, guns and planes widened the propaganda gap between theory and reality in both Fascist Italy and Nazi Germany.

Italian Fascism had always been imbued with the modernization myth; both left- and right-wing influences saw the necessity of modernization for a resurgent Italy. National Syndicalists had emphasized productivism and the managerial revolution in industry, as well as the implementation of a corporate state. Nationalists had stressed the need for an empire to enable self-sufficiency. Futurists worshipped the machine and the avant-garde. Mussolini liked to be photographed driving a sports car, or at the controls of a tank. Draining the Pontine marshes, building the *autostrada* and making the railways run on time were other real and propaganda achievements of modernization in Fascist Italy.

Nazi Germany's 'reactionary modernism' was more problematic. If *Hitler's Table Talk* is to be believed, the Nazis' eventual aim was to turn back the clock and create vast *latifundia* in Eastern Europe, where German peasant farmers were to supervise Slavic slaves in a de-urbanized society. This horrific vision masked the realities of the needs of war; nevertheless, the barbarities of the invasion of the Soviet Union represented the destructive preparatory work for this project.

The Fascist and Nazi states also exhibited interesting contrasts. Whereas it took Mussolini seven years to move from coalition government to personal rule, it took Hitler just seven months. Between 1922 and 1945 Mussolini showed little continuity in either tactics or strategy. Mussolini was an opportunist, who consistently manipulated factions and interest groups to his own advantage. During the Matteotti crisis in 1924, Mussolini supported the intransigent Ras and *squadristi*, and threatened a further revolution. For most of his period in power Mussolini sided with vested interest groups, and subordinated the Fascist militia to the army and the security police. There was no Fascist revolution, merely constant propaganda that a 'Fascist new man' was being created in Italy. Hitler also co-operated with traditional elites while he consolidated power; but after the Night of the Long Knives and the death of Hindenburg in 1934, the introduction of the personal oath of loyalty, and the combination of the posts of Chancellor and President, gave Hitler the leverage he needed to establish greater power than was the case with Mussolini.

While Mussolini postured, Hitler rebuilt the German state. Mussolini was Italian Prime Minister for longer than anybody else in the twentieth century, yet Fascism made little lasting impression. The triumph of Fascism proved to be little more than the manipulation of Mussolini to keep himself in power. Mussolinism in practice meant opportunism and expediency. There were numerous U-turns in economic and social policy, with laissez-faire economics being jettisoned for protectionism and autarky, and syndicates replaced by corporations, although neither made much difference to control in industry. The turn to imperialism in 1935 was an attempt to solve domestic problems with foreign adventures. It was an expensive failure, as Abyssinia was more costly to subdue than its value to the Italian state, particularly as little in the way of mineral wealth was discovered. It also drove Mussolini into the fated alliance with Hitler.

The problem was that Italy was a nation weak in resources, which even with Mussolini's bravado made her little more than a mouse trying to roar. Nazi Germany possessed the material and human resources to make her potentially the most powerful state in Europe. Hitler's policies in maximizing her production potential, in escaping from the Versailles system and in the foreign policy successes between 1935 and 1939 completed and extended the old nationalist dream of the Greater German Reich, with the reoccupation of the Rhineland in 1936, the Anschluss union with Austria in 1938 and the incorporation of the Sudeten Germans after the Munich settlement. If Hitler had not embarked on further conquests after 1938, he would have been regarded by many as one of the greatest German statesmen in history.

There was also an interesting contrast in personal style of rule. While propaganda depicted a highly efficient engine of state in Italy and Germany, the reality was different. Mussolini found difficulty in sorting the wheat from the chaff and in devolving routine administration. There were also wholesale changes in personnel, which had little to do with policy, and much to do with the manipulation of rivals and Mussolini securing his personal position. The Fascist party was subordinated to the state, and neither state nor society was effectively transformed.

The Hitler state was a propaganda myth; not a well-oiled Nazi machine, but a behemoth, with overlapping jurisdiction, unclear responsibilities and separate party and state agencies competing for influence. The accumulation of power was based on Social Darwinist principles, rather than administrative competence or the rule of law. 'Working towards the Fuehrer' meant ruthless behaviour and political backstabbing, as well as trying to second-guess what Hitler intended. Hitler never lost the bohemian habits of his failed art student days in Vienna before 1914. Apart from foreign policy, military matters and architecture, he was not interested in routine matters of state. He hated taking any sort of decision, and apart from issues that could not be avoided, policies were decided at lower levels of the administration.

The Nazi state was based on feudal principles; with an oath of allegiance to the Fuehrer, and bigwig barons who jealously guarded their own fiefdoms from encroachment by rivals. Those who gained extra power were the most cunning, ruthless and radical; men like Himmler,* Goebbels* and Goering; or efficient administrators who made the system work when it was threatened with collapse, like Albert Speer; or men who controlled access to Hitler, like Martin Bormann.

If the means of government were inefficient in Fascist Italy and Nazi Germany, it was not surprising that the alternative revolution permeated slowly into state and society. The development of fascism was more insidious in Germany than Italy, however. In spite of Gentile's educational reforms, the control of social life through the *dopolavoro* (after work) organization, Mussolini's bluster and the choreography of numerous rallies, Fascism made little permanent impact on Italian life. In Germany the Nazis were more successful. By infiltration, or creating parallel institutions, the old elites were undermined. Some historians and sociologists argue that defeat completed the destructive side of Hitler's alternative revolution, by sweeping away the last vestiges of imperial Germany and creating the conditions for radical change after 1945, in the occupied zones.

If Fascist Italy and Nazi Germany ultimately collapsed and left few permanent domestic legacies, Europe became divided into two armed camps, and Germany was divided for forty-six years, when the anti-fascist coalition noisily disintegrated during the Cold War. Ultimately, both relied on the use of force and secret police to retain power, although the Gestapo and the SS were more ruthless than the OVRA was in Italy.

Why was Fascism Less Successful in France and Britain?

Fascism in France and Britain failed to make much impact, apart from the direct influence of Nazism on occupied and Vichy France between 1940 and 1944, and in the Channel Islands. Nazi invasion, rather than the growth of native fascist sentiment, caused this development. Vichy France was the product of the extreme right, albeit with fascist trappings. Native fascism was not the gravedigger of the Third Republic, merely one of many political influences which made French political history so complex in the 1930s. In Britain, fascism was even less of a problem. Apart from a brief period in 1934, when Lord Rothermere's *Daily Mail* said 'Hurrah for the Blackshirts', Sir Oswald Mosley's attempt to revolutionize British politics fell on deaf ears; his enemies in the establishment and on the left viewed him with loathing, and the media ignored the movement or treated it with ridicule, apart from political violence which was seen as being instigated or provoked by the BUF.

In both France and Britain, except perhaps for the large demonstration by the extreme right in Paris on 6 February 1934, the anti-fascism of the Popular Front and the United Front caused more difficulties for the authorities than native fascism. The problem of definition makes it difficult to judge the size of the fascist threat in France. If all the movements of the extra-parliamentary extreme right are labelled 'fascist', then possibly a million 'fascists' resisted the Popular Front between 1936 and 1938. If the 'alternative revolution' or palingenetic model is used, then there were no more than 60,000. At no stage were there more than 50,000 members of the BUF, and for much of the period between 1935 and 1939, probably less than 9,000 first-division members. Other Nazi mimetic, or Colonel Blimp organizations, had minuscule membership.

While the impact of the First World War had severely weakened both France and Britain, they were on the winning side, and dictated the peace terms. Whilst the war led to the growth of Italian Fascism and Nazism in Germany, France and Britain looked backwards to restore the pre-1914 world in a much-changed political environment. Although this proved impossible, politicians worked for the incorporation of new forces within the structures of the old: hence the acceptance of the conventions of parliamentary government by the Labour Party in Britain, and the failure of political extremism after the extension of the franchise and the establishment of parliamentary democracy, in both countries.

Whilst there were challenges to the British state from labour unrest (1919–27) and the Irish troubles (1919–23), these were contained by the authorities. There was no credible revolutionary threat from the left, apart from in the vivid imagination of Special Branch, MI5, brass hats and some right-wing politicians. Given the dominance of Baldwinian conservatism in inter-war politics, there was no political space to encourage the growth of credible right-wing extremism in response to a largely nonexistent revolutionary threat. In France, the revolutionary tradition made extra-parliamentary agitation more problematic: the weakness of coalition governments, and the emergence of a much stronger Communist party than in Britain, meant that in periods of social unrest, the right was more prone to dabble in street politics. Yet despite the weakness, corruption and ineptitude of French governments, the Third Republic survived because both the right and left were bitterly divided, the military remained in barracks and the political police kept the authorities well informed of developments. The radical right, like Colonel François La Rocque's Croix de Feu, was, despite its use of palingenetic imagery, counterrevolutionary and socially conservative. The fascists, like Georges Valois's Le Faisceau, Bucard's Francistes and Jacques Doriot's Parti Populaire Français, were revolutionary, neo-socialist and desired an accommodation with Nazi Germany. The left was bitterly divided between reformists and revolutionaries, Stalinists and Trotskyists. Only in the 'two waves' of 'fascism', from 1924–6, and 1933–9, did the conservative parliamentary right attempt to manipulate street politics. But the emergence of stronger right-wing governments of Poincaré* (1926) and Daladier* (1938) focused attention back on the National Assembly.

Whereas in Britain careful state management of fascism and Communism managed to marginalize political extremism, and avoided the aura of persecution and martyrdom, the banning of extreme right-wing demonstrations by Léon Blum's* Popular Front government in 1936, and the internment of fascists and Communists in 1939–40, helped accentuate the fault-lines in French society. In Britain, the Public Order Act (1936) and the internment of fascists in 1940, caused far fewer problems, because the BUF was isolated and in the 'fifth column' scare did not evoke popular sympathy. In fact interning fascists strengthened, not weakened, national consensus.

In both Britain and France the objective conditions for the growth of political extremism were not present. Although both suffered from the slump in the 1930s, neither experienced catastrophic decline: both had sluggish growth patterns throughout the inter-war period based on new industries. Fascism was seen by many as a foreign import, while the aggressive behaviour of Mussolini, and in particular Hitler, was seen as threatening the national interests of Britain and France in the 1930s. Although the economic recovery of Germany was viewed favourably in the 1930s by some right-wing commentators, as was the destruction of the labour movement, this was perceived as being attained by the unacceptable undermining of political democracy and the rule of law, the creation of a police state and a society built in the shadow of the concentration camp.[14]

[14] I would like to thank Dave Baker, Roger Eatwell and Roger Griffin for their comments on this article.

Part III

Diplomacy, Defence and War

European Diplomacy, 1871–1914

Keith Wilson

From the conclusion of the Franco-Prussian War until the outbreak of the First World War the diplomacy of the European Powers was formulated in response to two sets of developments. The first set were revolts against Ottoman rule in Eastern Europe and the rivalry these independence and nationalist movements inspired between the multinational Austro-Hungarian and Russian empires for domination of that region. The second set of developments arose from the rivalry between the established imperial powers of Great Britain, Russia and France for the maintenance and extension of their extra-European positions; from the mid-1880s, and to an even greater extent from the late 1890s, this competition for extra-European influence was increased by the determination of Germany to emulate these three Powers and establish an extra-European presence for itself.

In 1871 the German states south of the river Main, which had constituted an intermediary system and source of rivalry both between Prussia and Austria and between the North German Confederation and France, became part of the German Empire. The German annexation of the French provinces of Alsace and Lorraine, insisted on by the Prussian generals in order to increase the defensibility of the new German Empire, was the last change of frontier in Western Europe. That there should be no further German gains at the expense of France was a view reinforced by the line protective of France taken by Russia and Great Britain in the course of the 'war-scare' of 1875. To this Prince Otto von Bismarck,* who as Chancellor dominated the making of the foreign policy of the German Empire until the accession of Kaiser Wilhelm II* in July 1888, was easily reconciled. The Austro-Hungarian Empire, for its part, quickly reconciled itself to the loss of its position in German affairs. Even French politicians, privately if not publicly, reconciled themselves to the loss of Alsace and Lorraine; in the mid-1890s a French Minister for Foreign Affairs was to deter a Russian strike upon Constantinople by making French compliance and support dependent

1865: Prussia

1866: Territory acquired by Prussia

1867–71: Limit of North German Confederation

1871: Limit of German Empire

Map 11.1 The unification of Germany

upon the quid pro quo of the restoration of the lost provinces – an undertaking which he knew full well the Russians would reject. Changes in the map of Europe were to occur in 1878, 1908, 1912 and 1913. All these changes were to be in the Balkans, the region to which Austria-Hungary had effectively been consigned by the creation of the German Empire.

One must be prepared for inconsistencies, contradictions, apparent anomalies. For instance, the German Empire assiduously avoided Austro-Hungarian overtures for an exclusive alliance throughout the 1870s, only to seek one herself in 1879. As Germany was, in 1879, the supplicant, the alliance that was made was made on Austro-Hungarian, rather than German, terms. Again, the isolation of France was a tenet of German policy from 1871 to 1890. Then, the Germans quite explicitly envisaged, and risked, a Franco-Russian alliance. In 1885–6 the British sought an alliance with Germany against Russia. On the other hand, in 1887 and throughout the 1890s and into the 1900s, they refused Italian, Austro-Hungarian and German blandishments to join the Triple Alliance.

The record of European diplomacy is at least as much the record of what did not happen as of what did. It is, in these years anyway, at least as much a study of failures as of successes. Austria-Hungary's failure to secure an alliance with Germany until 1879 has already been mentioned; she also failed to set up an Austro-German-British alliance in 1879–80. Germany, having provided the context in which a Franco-Russian alliance could be concluded, spent much of the next twenty years trying to break up that alliance, and failed to do so; she also tried, and failed, throughout the decade from 1904 to 1914 to detach Britain from France and Russia and to secure British neutrality in a European war. Lord Salisbury,* the British Prime Minister and Foreign Secretary for all but twenty months from 1887 to 1900, failed to secure a German alliance in 1885–6, and also failed to realize his grand strategic vision of a settlement of Anglo-Russian differences at the expense of the Ottoman and Chinese empires. Hanotaux, one of only two Frenchmen to act as Minister for Foreign Affairs for any serious length of time, failed to achieve, through the creation of a crisis with Britain on the Nile, his aim of a Franco-Russian-British alliance. Russia failed to establish a large and pro-Russian Bulgarian state in 1877–8; and in 1912 failed to restrain the Balkan League of Bulgaria, Serbia and Greece from attacking the Ottoman Empire. The Italians failed consistently from the early 1880s to get German and Austro-Hungarian or British support for their policy of altering the status quo in the Mediterranean in their interests at the expense of France and the Ottoman Empire. The Ottoman Empire failed to secure an alliance with Britain in 1908–9 and 1911.

On Alliances and Alignments

In his book *Europe Re-shaped 1848–1878* John Grenville wrote, in the chapter on Napoleon III: 'In studying the course of international relations, historians tend to pay too much attention to the making of friends and too little to the choice of enemies; but really the choice of enemies dictates which friends a country seeks.' So far as the years 1871 to 1914 are concerned, this is a dictum which must be applied with care. There were relatively enduring friendships; there were also relatively enduring enmities. But the choice of enemies did not always govern the selection of friends.

One might cite, as examples of enduring friendly relationships, the Dual Alliance between Austria-Hungary and Germany, signed in October 1879, which lasted until November 1918; the Triple Alliance of Germany, Austria-Hungary and Italy, signed in May 1882, which lasted until July 1914; the Austro-Hungarian–Romanian Alliance, signed in October 1883, which lasted until the spring of 1914; and the Franco-Russian understanding of August 1891, transformed into an alliance by the approval in December 1893 of a draft military convention drawn up in August 1892, which lasted until 1917. One might cite, as examples of enduring animosities, Austro-Russian rivalry; Anglo-Russian rivalry; and the poor relations obtaining between France and Great Britain from the occupation of Egypt in 1882 until that problem was removed by the Anglo-French Agreement of April 1904.

Yet within the large periods of animosity there were shorter periods of friendship, and within the large periods of friendship shorter periods of animosity, or lack of support, or absence of co-ordination in policy-making. Great Britain, who in 1877–9, 1885–6, 1892–3 and 1900–5 had to contemplate war with Russia, was nevertheless (or perhaps consequently) on relatively good terms with her from the conclusion of the Anglo-Russian Conventions of September 1907 until the outbreak of the Great War in 1914. Austria-Hungary collaborated with Russia in relation to the future of the Ottoman Empire at conferences at Reichstadt in July 1876 and in the Treaty of Budapest of January 1877; they had an agreement on Balkan affairs which lasted from May 1897 until the Austro-Hungarian annexation of Bosnia-Hercegovina in October 1908. In the mid-1890s the French did not want to see their ally Russia seize Constantinople and become a Mediterranean power. In the late 1890s the Russians had no wish to fight Britain in the interests of France's Fashoda policy. Neither Austria-Hungary nor Italy supported Germany's Morocco policy at the Algeciras Conference of February 1906. Germany knew nothing, in advance, of Aehrenthal's* decision to annex Bosnia-Hercegovina in October 1908; her line in the ensuing crisis was designed as much to regain a degree of control over Austro-Hungarian policy as for any other purpose. From 1882 Germany and Austria-Hungary constantly obstructed and thwarted the designs of Italy. In the last years of peace Germany and Austria-Hungary were pursuing completely contradictory policies in regard to the Balkans.

Grenville's dictum, that the choice of enemies dictates which friends a country seeks, may apply to Andrassy's* bid for a German alliance in the 1870s, and to Kalnocky's* treaty with Romania in October 1883. It may apply to Italy's wish for an alliance with the Central Powers, who might help her to challenge the French position in the Mediterranean. It may also apply to the series of agreements negotiated by the French Minister for Foreign Affairs, Delcassé,* between 1900 and 1905; certainly he claimed a retrospective credit to this effect. It does not apply to Bismarck's overture to Andrassy in 1879, as Bismarck made it clear that he was hoping to re-establish friendly relations between both Austria-Hungary and Germany and what he hoped would be an only temporarily hostile Russia. It does not apply to Russia's decision to ally with France in the early 1890s: the Russians were already contemplating concentrating their energies along what they regarded as the line of least resistance – towards Central Asia and the Far East; they had already developed something of an inferiority complex as far as Western Europe, and Germany in particular, was concerned, and had no wish to make an enemy of the latter. Sometimes the dictum applies both ways: in 1901 the British decided on an alliance with Japan, a likely enemy of Russia, who was their own rival; they had no wish to make an enemy of France, however, and the terms of the alliance made it clear that it was up to the French whether they made themselves into enemies. From the British point of view the main motive was to bring Russia to the negotiating table; a secondary motive, ignored in practice by the Japanese, was to exercise restraint over Japan. In 1877–8, was Great Britain the friend of the Ottoman Empire and therefore the enemy of Russia, or the enemy of Russia and therefore the friend of the Ottoman Empire, or was it not rather the case that there was no *arrière-pensée* in the making of the two choices simultaneously?

The alliances which, from 1879, became a feature of the diplomatic landscape had certain characteristics. Their duration was fixed at three or five years; they were also renewable. The Austro-Serbian alliance of June 1881 was unusual in being specified to last for ten years; in 1889 it was prolonged until 1895. The renewal of those alliances which were renewed led to a fear, on the part of their members, of losing their allies. For this reason alone some alliances became institutionalized, self-perpetuating. This process also owed something to the varying degrees of integration of military planning to cater for certain contingencies, as between certain allies. The terms of these treaties of alliance specified, without exception, the secrecy of the arrangements made. In effect, the degree of secrecy maintained varied considerably. It was no secret amongst the Chancelleries and Foreign Offices of the European Powers that certain alliances had been concluded. What was not always so well known was the precise wording of the complete texts. The German Emperor Wilhelm I insisted in 1879 on showing a copy of the preamble of the Austro-German alliance to the tsar of Russia. In 1887 Salisbury, who had known of this alliance since 1879, having been told of it by the Austrians, although not of the precise way in which it was aimed at Russia, insisted that Bismarck show him the full text, which Bismarck was happy to do. Perhaps only the 'Reinsurance treaty' between Germany and Russia of June 1887 was kept truly secret; certainly the possibility of the discovery of its existence by Austria-Hungary, and the adverse consequences on German–Austro-Hungarian relations of such a discovery, was given by the vast majority of the German diplomatic establishment in 1890 as a reason for not renewing it. Some alliances were so little a secret that they produced, or inspired, others. The Russians allowed themselves to join the DreiKaiserBund in June 1881, for instance, because they were afraid of an attack on them by the new Germanic bloc; their becoming part of this Bund was in no sense a counter-alliance – it was designed to neutralize the Dual Alliance, and give the latter a negative and defensive character which it might not otherwise have; for the Russians, this was a reinsurance treaty too. Another example is the rather public renewal, in May 1891, of the Triple Alliance. So disappointed were the Russians with the realization that the Triple Alliance would continue to exist – a disappointment compounded by heavy Italian hints that the British had now joined it – that a distinct impetus, acknowledged in the letters of August 1891 between the Russian Foreign Minister Giers* and the French Foreign Minister Ribot,* was given to the creation of the Franco-Russian alliance.

As alliances increased their longevity, and passed through the hands of numerous ministers and officials who registered more or less well the obligations, commitments and implications to which their increasingly distant predecessors had agreed, the originally defensive character which all these alliances had was increased by the inhibiting effect of a confusion springing from a lack of certain knowledge as to where anyone stood and of what was ruled in and what was ruled out. This confusion, or doubt, helps to explain why the post-1878 status quo lasted as long as it did – until 1912. How could there be anything other than confusion and uncertainty when members of one 'group' were quite able to make agreements with members of another 'group', as Germany did with Russia over the Baltic in 1908 and over the Baghdad Railway at Potsdam in 1910, and as France did with Germany over Morocco in 1909; when the Dual Alliance, which in the minds of Haymerle* and Kalnocky* was directed against Russia, co-existed from 1881 to 1887 with the DreiKaiserBund, which consisted of Russia, Germany and Austria-Hungary; when Italy in July 1902 concluded with France an agreement completely at variance with the terms of the Triple Alliance, renewed only a few days earlier; or when Italy again, this time in 1909, made promises to Russia as regards the Dardanelles which she went on flatly to contradict in a secret agreement with Austria-Hungary? The phrase 'the international anarchy', as a description of the diplomacy of these years, was coined by Lowes Dickinson under the impression that the groups were cohesive; the real international anarchy was in their lack of cohesiveness.

That said, there was a certain thrust, and a certain bias, in the alliances concluded in the early 1880s. Only one of these, the DreiKaiserBund, was not anti-Russian. The Austro-German alliance of October 1879 was anti-Russian; so was the Austro-Serbian alliance of June 1881, which was concluded at precisely the same time as the DreiKaiserBund; so was the Triple Alliance of May 1882; so was the Austro-Hungarian–Romanian alliance of October 1883, which was later adhered to by Germany. The most striking feature of all this diplomatic activity is that it was Austro-Hungarian in conception and in execution. The first of the alliances, the Dual Alliance, was not, in Bismarck's view, intended to be the foundation-stone of an anti-Russian system. So far as he was concerned, it was a temporary measure, perhaps embarked upon as a result of a failure of nerve on his part; it was designed, and to some extent was successful in this, to concentrate the Russian mind on returning to the fold of the three Northern Courts in such a way that in future both Russia and Austria-Hungary would defer to Germany, as had not been the case in the 1870s. It was the Austro-Hungarian Foreign Ministers Haymerle and Kalnocky who pressured Bismarck into links with Italy (which would enable Austria-Hungary to concentrate all the Dual Monarchy's forces against Russia), and who pressed ahead with alliances of their own with Serbia and Romania, dragging Germany after them into the latter. If any 'system' was set up at this time, it was not only an anti-Russian one, but an Austro-Hungarian manufactured one. The DreiKaiserBund was, in a sense, an effort on Bismarck's part to balance the thrust of Austro-Hungarian policy.

The anti-Russian bias of the existing alliances was increased in 1887, not only by the non-renewal of the DreiKaiserBund but by the conclusion of the Anglo-Austro-Hungarian-Italian Mediterranean Agreements in February and December, in origin an Italian initiative. In a sense, once again, Bismarck's conclusion of the Reinsurance treaty with Russia in June 1887, midway between the two Mediterranean Agreements, was designed to reassure Russia and to balance this anti-Russian thrust on the part of other Powers. As he said in March 1887, having accommodated himself to the prospect raised by the Italians:

> England and Italy with Austria as regards Constantinople form a counterweight which will deter Russia from any sort of provocative action.

If, at the same time, France is held in check by us, such a combination
will result in a balance of power which for us would be the best pledge
of peace.[1]

Bismarck was not the only statesman of this period to welcome this
kind of a balance between alliances. N. K. Giers, who was Russian Foreign Minister for thirteen years, from 1882 to 1895, had the same outlook. Until 1890 he maintained a link with Germany, and was indeed
in that year prepared to extend the Reinsurance treaty for another six
years. In his view, Russia occupied a pivotal position: a Russo-German
connection to some extent neutralized the power of the Germanic bloc;
if Russia withdrew from European affairs the equilibrium on which
peace depended would be lost. Within a year of taking office he had
contemplated a Russo-French combination as a counterweight to Germany. Hence, when in 1890 the Germans refused to renew their link
with Russia, Giers looked to a treaty with France to restore the equilibrium thrown out of balance by Germany's shift away from Russia
and her attempts to secure an agreement with Britain.

The fact that Great Britain avoided, though not always for want of
trying, the conclusion of any alliance in the 1880s and 1890s, and could
therefore be portrayed as constituting a 'bloc' in her own right, gave
some Englishmen, after Salisbury's time, the impression that England
was 'the balancing power' and could therefore preserve peace through
the uncertainty of others as to what her attitude would be and as to
which 'side' she would join. Lord Salisbury himself was never subject
to this delusion. Throughout his time Britain leant distinctly towards
the Triple Alliance, and remained a member of the anti-Russian bloc
through the Mediterranean Agreements, which Salisbury was prepared
to renew in 1897, although he was not prepared to convert them, as
Austria-Hungary pressed him to do, into something more in the nature
of an alliance. The Mediterranean Agreements rescued Salisbury from
a truly nonsensical obligation which he had undertaken in July 1878 –
a guarantee of Ottoman possessions in Asia, an obligation which Britain alone, or with just the Ottoman Empire, was completely unfitted
and incompetent to carry out, but an obligation undertaken, as were all
those in the other alliances already discussed, in the direction of deter-
ring or at least delaying developments which would result in clashes of
empires and the destruction of all the fabrics of which Western civilization was composed.

---

[1] Bismarck to Prince Henry VII of Reuss, 11 March 1887, in *Die Grosse Politik der
europäischen Kabinette 1871–1914*, ed. J. Lepsius, A. Mendelssohn-Bartholdy and F.
Thimme (Berlin, 1922–7), vol. 4, no. 901.

The Impact of Balkan Developments

In September 1872 the Russians announced to the Austro-Hungarians that in the event of a rising on the part of the Christian subjects of the Ottoman Empire they would not tolerate the forcible intervention of Austria-Hungary, and that if such intervention occurred 'it would become the starting point of a conflict between us.' This was the Russian Foreign Minister Gorchakov's* way of coming to terms with what might be the new, re-orientated Austria-Hungary, the Austria-Hungary that had come to terms with its exclusion from the affairs of Germany. Just such a rising began, in July 1875, in Bosnia. This rising raised the question not only of the future of the western Balkans but of the Balkan region as a whole. For if Bosnia secured autonomy, as the Russians suggested it might, the Bulgarians might also insist on such a status, and even a series of declarations of independence by the vassal states of the Ottoman Empire might follow. A year after the Bosnia revolt began there was a palace revolution in Constantinople. This produced Sultan Abdul Hamid II,* who was to rule, and control Ottoman foreign policy, until 1909. Immediately afterwards, Serbia and Montenegro declared war on the Ottoman Empire. Their declarations of war led to a series of meetings and agreements between Austria-Hungary and Russia. At Reichstadt in July 1876 the agreement was that both would maintain neutrality; that if the Ottoman Empire lost, Russia would take Bessarabia, and Austria-Hungary Bosnia; that there would be autonomous regimes in Bulgaria, Rumelia and Albania; that if the Ottoman Empire won (which was the most likely outcome) there would be no change in the status quo. The Ottoman Empire did defeat Serbia; but their victory only increased the internal pressure on the Russian government to intervene. At Budapest in January 1877 Andrassy limited any Russian intervention: if Russia confined any military operations to the eastern Balkans, Austria-Hungary would be neutral and would try to prevent mediation by disavowing the Triple Treaty of April 1856 under which Austria, France and Britain had promised to maintain the independence and integrity of the Ottoman Empire; Bulgaria would get autonomy; and Austria-Hungary might, if she wished, occupy Bosnia. At Budapest in March 1877 Andrassy successfully insisted that if the Ottoman Empire collapsed completely, the agreement made at Reichstadt the previous year would govern the situation.

These agreements between Austria-Hungary and Russia, following the initiatives taken by the Bosnians, Serbs and Montenegrins, sanctioned a Russo-Turkish war and considerable changes in the Balkans at the expense of the Ottoman Empire. They signalled the end of the

Map 11.2 The European empires in 1870

'Crimean System' set up in 1856. The changes sanctioned by Austria-Hungary, however, were as nothing compared to those which the Russians, who declared war on the Ottoman Empire in April 1877, were contemplating by December of that year, as their armies finally advanced, following stiff resistance at Plevna, upon Constantinople. On the conclusion of an armistice at the end of January 1878 Andrassy declared, 'Russia has played us false. Gorchakov wants to settle the whole Eastern Question by a coup like that of 1871 [when Russia denounced the clauses of the Peace of Paris neutralizing the Black Sea; Russia, had, however, taken no steps to build herself a fleet there]. For us is reserved the endorsement and the humiliation.'[2] Neither the Austro-Hungarians nor the British were prepared to endorse the Treaty of San Stefano, concluded between Russia and the Ottoman Empire on 3 March 1878, under the terms of which so large an autonomous Bulgaria, with access to the Aegean, was set up – a Bulgaria, moreover, which Russian forces would occupy for two years and whose government they would supervise during that time; Montenegro was not only recognized as an independent state, but almost trebled her territory; Russia annexed Bessarabia, and also made extensive gains in the southern Caucasus. War between Austria-Hungary and Great Britain on the one side, and Russia on the other, was only averted by the prospect of just such a variation on the Crimean War configuration. Russia, exhausted by her efforts against the Ottoman Empire, agreed that the Treaty of San Stefano be referred to a congress of all the European Powers, which a reluctant Bismarck was prevailed upon to host at Berlin.

By the Treaty of Berlin, of 13 July 1878, Bulgaria was constituted an autonomous principality under the suzerainty of the Sultan. Ottoman rule was restored in Macedonia and a new province of Eastern Rumelia was set up between the old Bulgaria and the Ottoman dominions proper. On the other hand Russia made gains in southern Bessarabia and in the Caucasus; a Russian army of 50,000 men was allowed to occupy Bulgaria and Eastern Rumelia for nine months; and Montenegro, Serbia and Romania became independent states. Austria-Hungary was allowed to occupy and administer Bosnia and Hercegovina, with the exception of the Sandjak of Novi-Bazar, a strip of land which ran between Serbia and Montenegro.

The developments which began in July 1875 and which ran up to and through the Russo-Turkish war and the extremely contentious Congress of Berlin, produced the Austro-German alliance of October 1879

---

[2] F. R. Bridge, *From Sadowa to Sarajevo: The Foreign Policy of Austria-Hungary 1866–1914* (London, 1972) p. 87.

which in turn produced, as already stated, the DreiKaiserBund of June 1881. They also produced the Austro-Hungarian system of alliances, built up between 1881 and 1884, the British guarantee of the Ottoman Empire in Asia, and a British interpretation of the rules governing exit from and access to the Black Sea which was at variance with that of every other power and remained so for over thirty years. Further developments, in the shape of a revolt in Eastern Rumelia in September 1885 which led to a union between that province and Bulgaria and the end of Russian influence there, produced the break-up of the DreiKaiserBund and its replacement by the Mediterranean Agreements and the Reinsurance treaty.

In the mid-1890s revolts in the Ottoman province of Armenia raised once more the whole question of the future of the Ottoman Empire in Europe, still a substantial area despite the large losses inflicted on it by the Congress of Berlin. A general revolt against the power of the Sultan on the part of the peoples of the Balkans still subjects of the Ottoman Empire, was envisaged. The prospect that would ensue, of a return to, or an escalation of, the rivalry between Russia and Austria-Hungary for control of the power vacuum that would result, however, was one reason for the agreement concluded in May 1897 by the Austro-Hungarian Foreign Minister Goluchowski* and his Russian counterpart Muraviev.* The two Powers agreed that changes in the status quo were not to be encouraged, but that, should the maintenance of the status quo become impossible, both discarded in advance all idea of conquest and would establish any new order of things in the Balkans on agreed lines. One of these agreed lines was that Austria-Hungary could convert her existing rights to occupy and garrison Bosnia and Hercegovina into annexation of these provinces. Apart from this, and the establishment of an independent Albanian state, the remaining territory of the Ottoman Empire would be equitably partitioned between the existing small Balkan states, in such a way as to safeguard the principle of the present equilibrium between those states.

At the time that this agreement was being made, Ottoman armies were inflicting a series of defeats upon the Greek army, the Ottoman Empire having declared war on Greece on 24 April 1897. The Ottoman victories demonstrated that the demise of the Ottoman Empire was not as imminent as had been feared. The appreciation of this fact, together with increasing German interest in the Ottoman Empire, symbolized by the start of the Baghdad Railway project, together with a considerable diplomatic effort on the part of all the Powers to keep matters relating to Macedonia from getting out of control, helped the situation in the Balkans to hold until October 1908. The situation was then changed, not as a result of revolt within the Ottoman Empire or action on the part of one of the smaller states but, as in 1877, through the action of a Great Power. In October 1908 the Austro-Hungarian Foreign Minister, Aehrenthal, announced, prematurely in the opinion of his Russian counterpart Isvolsky,* whose country's corresponding compensation had not been finalized, the annexation of Bosnia and Hercegovina. This announcement coincided with Bulgaria's declaration of its independence. The action of Aehrenthal not only enraged Serbia; it ended the era of Austro-Russian collaboration and abstention, and opened a new one of opposition, resentment, suspicion and antagonism.

The final contribution of the Balkan region to European diplomacy in the years 1871 to 1914 will be dealt with in more detail later. Suffice it to say at this stage that these final touches were initiated not by a Great Power, but by the now-independent small Balkan Powers. Early in 1912 a series of alliances and military conventions was concluded between Bulgaria and Serbia, Bulgaria and Greece, and Serbia and Montenegro. One observer commented, with a degree of accuracy: 'For the first time in the history of the Eastern question the small states have acquired a position of such independence of the Great Powers that they feel able to act completely without them and even to take them in tow.' On 8 October 1912 Montenegro declared war on the Ottoman Empire. Bulgaria, Greece and Serbia followed suit on 17 October. Within a month the Ottoman Empire in Europe had practically ceased to exist.

The Impact of Extra-European Developments

What European diplomacy produced, and what produced European diplomacy, are questions to which the answers are complicated by the extra-European interests and aspirations of most of the European Powers. In the case of the revision of the Franco-Russian alliance in 1899 both areas made a contribution. The duration of the original alliance had been geared to that of the Triple Alliance of Germany, Italy and Austria-Hungary, and its object had been the maintenance of peace. In August 1899 the connection with the life of the Triple Alliance was broken, and the object was re-formulated so as to include the preservation of the balance of power in Europe. Two prospects inspired these changes. One was that the Habsburg Emperor since 1848, Franz Joseph,* would die and that the Austro-Hungarian Empire would disintegrate. The other was that Germany, now clearly in pursuit of a position in the world commensurate with that which she occupied in Europe, would become a Mediterranean Power by annexing enough of the former Habsburg dominions to create a state of sixty million inhabitants stretching from the North Sea to the Adriatic. Delcassé, who believed the

German fleet was intended for the Mediterranean, and Muraviev, who was concerned at the growth of German influence throughout the Otto-man Empire as far as the Persian Gulf, therefore made sure that the Franco-Russian alliance would outlive the Triple Alliance, be still in existence should Austria-Hungary disintegrate, and be prepared to pre-vent Germany from taking up certain positions which would allow her to dominate the continent and challenge France in the Mediterranean generally and in North Africa in particular, as well as Russia in the Middle East and Asia.

In other cases the developments were more purely extra-European. The Russian drive, continued from the 1860s into the 1870s, to incor-porate the khanates of Central Asia into the Russian Empire and press as a result more closely upon the frontiers of Persia, Afghanistan and India, had as much if not more to do with British policy towards Rus-sia in Europe and the Ottoman Empire•as any other single factor. The British occupation of Egypt in 1882 so alienated the French, despite their having been invited to participate, that they were on bad terms with the British for over twenty years, and on the verge of war in 1893 and 1898. During that time, in order to get her way in Egyptian affairs, Britain gravitated substantially towards the Triple Alliance Powers. The British reconquest of the Sudan was a development of a diversionary expedition, undertaken following a request from Kaiser Wilhelm II only weeks after his telegram of congratulation to President Kruger, in order to relieve pressure on the Italians in Abyssinia. Only the prospect of a German presence in Morocco, another power vacuum which France had earmarked for exploitation, brought Delcassé to the negotiating table in 1903. The Sino-Japanese War of 1894–5, which raised the question of the future of China, and the Spanish–American War of 1898–9, which produced an American presence in South-East Asia, both led to searches for appropriate alliances and alignments. The British first sought an alliance with the United States of America, which rebuffed them. They then sought an agreement with Germany before finally settling upon an alliance with Japan which, or so they hoped, would permit them to pursue their pretensions and protect their existing interests in the Far East. The British war in South Africa against the Boer Republics, which coincided with a fast-moving Far Eastern situation and was the great-est shock to the British psyche since the Indian Mutiny, allowed the Russians to make massive gains in Persia and re-emphasized Russian impregnability and the Russian threat to India. As a result, the British re-embarked on Salisbury's well-trodden road to St Petersburg, this time via Paris. Only defeat in her war with Japan of 1904–5, however, brought Russia to consider coming to terms, as she did in 1907, with Great Britain. And only the weakness of Russia that was a result of that defeat in the Far East and the revolution in Russia that followed, enabled Austria-Hungary to get away, without a war, with Aehrenthal's annexation of Bosnia and Hercegovina in 1908–9. As a result of the Russo-Japanese War, Russia was far less of a factor in the European balance of power than she had been hitherto, certainly in the eyes of the French who, feeling exposed, made overtures to Great Britain in January 1906 for an alliance which the French Ambassador to London mistakenly believed had been offered to him by Lord Lansdowne* in May 1905. The French were rebuffed. Although they persisted, and played their part in smoothing the path towards an Anglo-Russian agreement, they continued to be rebuffed. Unsurprisingly, after another experience of German pressure over Morocco in the summer of 1911, during which they were consistently advised by the British to make the necessary concessions to Germany, the French in 1912 and 1913 insisted, in yet another modification of the Franco-Russian alliance, that the Russians commence building a system of strategic railways on the German-Russian frontier which would when complete deter Germany from attempting to put such pressure on them ever again. Arguably, this policy of Poincaré's,* like his insistence on the impenetrability of the existing 'blocs', backfired. As the period ended, the prospect of the collapse of the Portuguese Empire in Africa and South-East Asia presented the possibility of Anglo-German agreement which the majority of the British cabinet were inclined to pursue; and the Russians made a nuisance of themselves in Persia in order to bring Great Britain into a common front with themselves and France to counteract, on a diplomatic plane, the growing influence of Germany at Constantinople.

On the Wars of 1914

'Some day', observed a British Foreign Office official in 1913, 'Serbia will set Europe by the ears.' When war eventually came, however, it was the product of the actions of Great Powers rather than small ones. The ball was set rolling by Italy, Austria-Hungary and Germany – in that order. The Italian attack on the Ottoman Empire, in September 1911, with a view to acquiring the North African province of Libya, was, in retrospect, a greater watershed than any of the great watersheds already mentioned in passing – the Congress of Berlin, the dismissal of Bismarck, the Russo-Japanese War, the Austro-Hungarian annexation of Bosnia and Hercegovina. For it was the weakness of the Ottoman Empire that was exposed by the Italo-Turkish war that inspired Bulgaria, Serbia and Greece to combine as they did in 1912 to make gains

Map 11.3 The Balkans, 1912–1914

for themselves at its expense. The outcome of the first Balkan war of October–November 1912, combined with the outcome of the second Balkan war of June 1913, in which Bulgaria was defeated by her former allies Serbia and Greece together with Romania, created a situation of enormous complexity, full of potential for further, and larger, wars.

Serbia remained the ally of Greece, which was on the worst possible terms with the Ottoman Empire. Her other ally, Romania, was completely antipathetic to Bulgaria, resentful of the Austro-Hungarian sympathy towards the Bulgarian attack on her in 1913, and increasingly aware that 55 per cent of the population of Transylvania was Romanian, under Magyar rule within the Austro-Hungarian Empire. On 12 June 1914 the Greeks delivered an ultimatum to Constantinople, demanding an end to atrocities against Greeks in Smyrna, Crete and elsewhere. The Ottoman Empire, on this occasion, complied; it was within weeks rather than months of being in a position to declare war itself, with or without Bulgaria as an ally. On the occasion of the Greek ultimatum, Kaiser Wilhelm II of Germany remarked: 'We shall shortly see the third chapter of the Balkan Wars in which we shall all be involved.'

Although as a result of the first Balkan war it was the Ottoman Empire that had lost the most territory, it was the Austro-Hungarian Empire that had lost most in terms of position, prestige and potential. For, in November 1912, Serbia had doubled in size, and many times multiplied the threat that its existence posed to the integrity of Austria-Hungary and to the latter's domination of the eastern coast of the Adriatic. From November 1912 Austria-Hungary tried, and failed, to improve its position diplomatically. Its only success was the creation of Albania. Austria-Hungary did not manage to gain Bulgaria as an ally; most seriously of all, it appeared, in the spring of 1914, to have lost its ally since 1883, Romania – the Balkan state upon whose allegiance and loyalty Austria-Hungary's existence as an empire primarily depended. Although from October 1913 successive Austrian Crown Council meetings had discussed 'the Serbian threat', at the time of the assassination of the Archduke Franz Ferdinand* it was upon retrieving Romania that all Austro-Hungarian diplomatic efforts were focused. Franz Joseph's argument for action against Serbia, which he embodied in a memorandum for Kaiser Wilhelm II sent to Berlin at the beginning of July, was that only the employment of force against Serbia would return Romania to the Austro-Hungarian fold, and re-establish the security of the Habsburg Empire.

A resolution of Austria-Hungary's Serbian problem had been pressed upon the Habsburg Empire by the German Empire since early in 1913. Here we come to the second of the wars that broke out in July–August 1914, the German–Russian war. The German Empire had convinced itself that the balance of power in Europe depended on the balance of power in the Balkans, and furthermore that the first Balkan war had altered the Balkan balance of power in favour of the Slavs and against the German Powers. In December 1912 the Kaiser began to use a particular vocabulary. He began to speak of 'the final struggle between the

Slavs and the Teutons', of 'the struggle of the Teutons against the Slav flood'. He went on to write:

> if we are to take up arms it will be to help Austria, not only to defend ourselves against Russia but against the Slavs in general and to remain *Germans. Id est* there is *about to be* a racial struggle between the Teutons and the Slavs who have become uppish. . . . It is a question of the existence of the Teutons on the European Continent. . . . The question for Germany is to be or not to be. . . .[3]

In October 1913 he described the Balkan wars as 'not passing phenomena created by diplomatic activity but a World Historical Process of the same order as the migrations of nations which in this case took the form of a strong Slav advance'.[4]

In December 1912, following a special council convened by the Kaiser, the German decision-making hierarchy began to prepare the German public, through the press, for the German-Russian war which they now believed to be inevitable, and which they believed their only chance of winning lay in fighting before the Russian military improvements and increases begun in 1912 were completed, as they would be by 1918. An Army Bill, which only days before the outbreak of the Balkan war had been considered by the General Staff to be unnecessary, was drafted and then passed into law in April 1913. The Germans also commenced to lay the diplomatic framework for their war with Russia. One element in this framework was the freeing of their ally Austria-Hungary from concern about Serbia, so that the Austro-Hungarian war effort could be concentrated upon Russia.

Unity between Serbia and Austria-Hungary was a policy assiduously pursued by the Germans for the last eighteen months of peace between the European Powers. According to the Germans, this unity could be achieved, and the problem of Serbia solved, in one of two ways. If the carrot failed, there was always the stick. In March 1913 the Kaiser said that he considered a combination of Serbia, Romania and Greece under Austro-Hungarian leadership a natural and good one. At army manoeuvres in Silesia in mid-September he told the Chief of the Austro-Hungarian General Staff that 'it would be better to see Serbia united with Austria than for Austria to have as its neighbour a south Slav state which would at all times stab it in the back.' The Kaiser pursued the

[3]   F. Fischer, *War of Illusions: German Policies from 1911 to 1914* (New York, 1975), pp. 161, 165, 190–1.
[4]   Report by Berchtold, 28 October 1913, in *Österreich-Ungarns Aussenpolitik von der Bosnischen Krise 1908 bis zum Kriegsausbruch 1914*, ed. L. Bittner, A. Pribram, H. Srbik and H. Uebersberger (Vienna, 1930), vol. 7, no. 8934.

matter further with the Austro-Hungarian Foreign Minister, Berchtold,*
at the end of October. As the German ambassador in Vienna reported
to the Chancellor, Bethmann-Hollweg:*

> The Emperor Wilhelm II remarked that Austria-Hungary must do every-
> thing to establish, if at all possible *à l'aimable*, an economic and political
> understanding with Serbia, but if that could not be achieved by peaceful
> means more energetic methods must be employed. Somehow or other
> Serbia must in all circumstances be made to join forces with Austria-
> Hungary, particularly in the military sphere; so that in case of a conflict
> with Russia Austria-Hungary will not have the Serbian army against it
> but on its side. He added that it could be assumed with certainty that for
> the next six years Russia would be incapable of taking military action.[5]

In December 1913 the Austro-Hungarian military attaché in Berlin
reported another conversation with the Kaiser, in which the latter had
said that 'the Serbs must be harnessed before the car of the Austro-
Hungarian Monarchy – in one way or another'; and that it could not be
a matter of indifference to Germany whether twenty divisions of the
Austrian army were earmarked for operations against the southern Slavs,
or not. In March 1914, at a meeting in Berlin which included Foreign
Minister von Jagow, his deputy Zimmermann, and Colonies Minister
Solf, the Kaiser advised a former Austro-Hungarian Minister of Trade
'to conclude a customs alliance with Serbia and in the end a military convention'. On 16 and 17 June, in conversation with the Archduke Franz
Ferdinand, the Kaiser maintained that it was vital for Austria-Hungary
to take energetic steps against Serbia, arguing once more that Russia was
by no means ready for war and that she would probably not oppose
such an action.

German support and encouragement for Austro-Hungarian action
against Serbia at the beginning of July 1914, then, may best be seen as a
continuation of a policy consistently pursued and pressed upon Austria-
Hungary for at least the previous eighteen months. The assassination
of the Archduke merely caused the Germans to agree that the Serbs
were, as the Austrians had always maintained, irreconcilable, and not
to be won over or won round by the means suggested in Germany's
interests by the Kaiser in particular.

Thus far, it has been maintained that the Austro-Hungarian declaration of war on Serbia was the third of the Balkan wars; and that, from
the German point of view, this move was seen as a clearing of the
decks, as a freeing of Austria-Hungary's back – a move designed to

---

[5] Tschirschky to Bethmann-Hollweg, 28 October 1913, cited in F. Fischer, *War of Illusions*, p. 225.

improve the position of the German Powers for a war at some unspecified point before 1918 against Russia. What happened in July 1914 was that the German calculation, or assumption, that Russia was not ready for war and would not oppose the action of Austria-Hungary, proved to be mistaken. Fearful of what would otherwise happen to Austria-Hungary, whose rulers deliberately ignored last-minute German attempts to make them see the situation in a European as opposed to a Balkan perspective, the Germans in turn deliberately misinterpreted the Russian mobilization, which all of them knew would take at least six weeks to complete, as an act of war, instead of the diplomatic move to buy time for negotiations which it really was. The German–Russian war, intended but not fixed for the future, was thereby brought forward, and followed by four days, instead of by four months, or four years, the Austro-Serbian war which was designed to increase in it the chances of Teutonic victory over the greatest of the Slavonic Powers.

Another war was brought forward in 1914. This was the third of the wars that broke out at this time – the German-English war. At the turn of the century, when Germany had embarked seriously on an extra-European policy (*Weltpolitik*) it had commenced to equip itself with a navy one *raison d'être* for which was that this might, in the end, be used to compel the British Empire to make colonial concessions to the German Empire. Chancellor von Bülow* admitted in a memorandum of 29 March 1900 for the Bavarian representative von Lerchenfeld that the Imperial Government was basing its naval calculations upon a probable war with England. In 1903 Bethmann-Hollweg, then occupying the highest administrative office in Prussia, described the Kaiser's intentions in this way: 'His basic and primary idea is to destroy England's position in the world to the advantage of Germany.'

This German outlook was heavily conditioned by the animosity of France and Russia towards Great Britain which was such a feature of the international scene at the turn of the century. As relations between France and Russia, on the one hand, and Great Britain on the other, improved the long-term aims of Germany did not change. Rather, the Germans tried to spoil Franco-Russian-British relations in a bid to return themselves to the relatively advantageous diplomatic position they had enjoyed, in addition to being the strongest single Power on the continent. The untroubled position of Germany on the continent of Europe ended, precisely, in October 1912. The recovery of Russia, and the 'Slav threat' given apparent substance by the victories of the Balkan League over the Ottoman Empire, presented the Germans with an unexpected European problem, the solution of which was to be found in a deviation from, or interruption of, *Weltpolitik*. The Germans believed they had to deal with the 'Slav threat', had to secure their European position, had to readjust in their favour the balance of power which they thought had recently changed against them. Only when this had been accomplished could they concentrate on *Weltpolitik* again, and take on, ultimately, Great Britain, if events demonstrated that the latter was prepared neither to yield nor to come to terms. Hence the necessity for the German–Russian war. Essentially, this was a nuisance, something to be got out of the way quickly in order to return to the longer-term business of acquiring an extra-European empire at Britain's expense, or with her assistance.

In July–August 1914 the Germans made only a very half-hearted effort to secure British neutrality. They were half-hearted in this respect for two reasons. In the first place, they did not regard British power as sufficient to deter them from their war with Russia, even though this entailed that they should first invade and defeat France, Russia's ally. Such power as Britain had could not, in their view, be brought to bear quickly enough to affect the outcome of either campaign. As Jagow had told his ambassador in London in February: 'We have not built our fleet in vain, and in my opinion people in England will seriously ask themselves whether it will be just that simple and without danger to play the role of France's guardian angel against us.' In the second place, the British had recently demonstrated their recalcitrance, their indisposition to make concessions, by refusing at French insistence to ratify agreements with Germany on the Portuguese colonies and on the Baghdad Railway, and by commencing negotiations for an Anglo-Russian naval convention. Bethmann-Hollweg described this latter development, all details of which reached him through a German spy in the Russian embassy in London, as 'the last link in the chain' of British 'encirclement' of the German Empire. The Germans, therefore, might as well have their war with England at the same time as their war with Russia. At the very least, with the help they fully but misguidedly expected from both Austria-Hungary and Italy, they would defeat Britain's two friends, France and Russia, and re-establish a British isolation of which they could hope to take advantage.

Imperial Pretensions

The wars of July–August 1914 overlapped and intermingled. Two of them, and arguably all three of them, came before their time. It was on the attitude of Russia that the Germans miscalculated, and it was this miscalculation that brought forward both the German–Russian war and the German–English war. Despite being pressed by the French from mid-1912 to build strategic railways that would relieve the German pressure on France and reduce the necessity for the sort of concessions France had made in the Agadir crisis of 1911, the Russians were not considering an attack upon the Central Powers. Even after the successes of the Balkan League, which Russia had been unable to restrain from attacking the Ottoman Empire, the policy of Russian Foreign Minister Sazonov was to preserve the status quo in the Balkans. However, from October 1912 there was a growing appreciation on the occasions when foreign policy was discussed in the councils of the tsar, of two things. One of these was the extent to which the occupation of the Straits area and the dominance of the Balkans as a whole represented an ultimate goal of Russian policy. The other was the extent to which the collapse of the Ottoman Empire, the schemes for compensation or for a sharing of influence put forward by Austria-Hungary, and the growth of German influence at Constantinople, were regarded as constituting a threat to this 'historic striving' on Russia's part, and to the application of the principle of 'the Balkans for the Balkan peoples'. The situation was compounded by the realization, as a result of the closure and threat of closure of the Straits since September 1911, of the value to the Russian economy of the free and unrestricted use of this waterway. Not only were the Russians afraid of the establishment of a causeway of Teutonic influence from Berlin through Vienna to Constantinople, Asia Minor, Mesopotamia, the Persian Gulf and the Indian Ocean (as were the British also), but they became adamant that they would fight rather than see the Bosphorus and the Dardanelles fall under the control of a hostile Power, great or small. Following a decision to this effect in January 1914, and the acquisition in February of German memoranda which stressed a German desire to control the Straits, even at the cost of European war, should the Ottoman Empire collapse, Sazonov told the British ambassador in April that whilst Russia would never take aggressive action against an independent Ottoman Empire, she would have to act against an Ottoman Empire that became a dependency of Germany and Austria-Hungary. Given that the Russians fully expected Austria-Hungary itself to break up – something that would have done much to ease the situation in which the Russians were finding themselves, in the not-too-distant future and certainly on the death of Franz Joseph – there was something here in the nature of a race against time.

Although Austria-Hungary's policy in attacking Serbia in July 1914, with a view to re-creating a Balkan constellation amenable to herself by redistributing Serbia amongst the other Balkan states, was defensive in that she was attempting to break out of what she perceived as encirclement by states sympathetic to Russia, it was also aggressive. The more long term the view taken of it, the more aggressive it was. For not only was Austria-Hungary trying to change the situation produced by the two Balkan wars, she was also intending to use a new status quo as a springboard from which to establish her own influence and exclude that of Russia from the whole area. Whilst Russian policy was defensive, in that it was geared to maintaining the present status quo in physical terms (for the defection of Romania from Austria-Hungary would certainly strengthen Russia's diplomatic position), it too was aggressive in the long term, in that she too was determined exclusively to exploit and enjoy the resources of the Balkan region and beyond.

What sharpened and made explicit this rivalry was the almost complete expulsion from Europe, in October 1912, at the hands of Serbia, Greece, Bulgaria and Montenegro, of the Ottoman Empire. Balkan nationalism, and the military incapacity of the Ottoman armies, created a new context in which the wars of 1914, the wars of the immediate and of the more distant future, merged into the Great War. This merging took place because no Great Power, no regime, no body of ministers, was prepared to curb its imperial inclinations, tendencies or pretensions – whether these related primarily to Eastern Europe, as in the cases of Austria-Hungary and Russia, or whether they related primarily to regions outside of Europe altogether, as in the cases of Germany, France and Great Britain. Great Britain, when examined closely, is found to have gone to war at this time only because her Prime Minister and Foreign Secretary insisted that she should do so, and threatened to resign and consequently ruin the political fortunes and future of the Liberal Party if she did not. H. H. Asquith's* and Sir Edward Grey's* reason for insisting on this course of action was that the maintenance of the British Empire depended on the maintenance of good relations with the Russian Empire.

12

European Imperialism, 1871–1945

David Omissi

'The past is a foreign country: they do things differently there.' Empire is one of the ways in which the world of a century ago did things differently from our own. Today, the independence of African and Asian polities is taken for granted, and their delegates sit in the United Nations as a matter of right. But in 1900, it was Europeans who ruled India, most of Africa and South-East Asia, and countless other territories around the world. Britain, France, Spain, Italy, Holland, Belgium, Germany, Portugal and the USA – all had their colonial empires (as did Russia, in a continental sort of way).

Empire meant much more than mere political facts, however. In the high imperial epoch, colonial domination was widely thought right and fitting, or at least inevitable. It was usual to believe – certainly in Europe – that the black, yellow and brown races were destined to be ruled by whites, or, in some extreme cases, simply to die out. Intelligent, thoughtful Europeans accepted empire, and the racism that went with it, as part of their working assumptions about the world. Many of the colonial peoples themselves had imbibed the view of their colonizers, and found political independence hard to desire, or even to imagine. Imperialism, in short, was a habit of mind. As the historian John Julius Norwich remarked of his thirties' childhood, 'we were all imperialists then.'

But, on closer examination, the contrast between the post-imperial present and the imperial past seems perhaps less stark. Everywhere legacies of empire endure. The distribution of the world's peoples is in part a silent witness to the imperial age – from the voluntary settlement of whites in the New World, to the forced migration of millions of African, Chinese and Indian slaves and labourers. With the expansion of Europe came the spread of English, French, Spanish and Portuguese as international languages. The current boundaries of most African and Asian states were set by European imperialists, often ignoring the wishes of their inhabitants in the process. Many of the world's major cities are graced by former colonial buildings – relics of the lost certainties of an imperial age, and often now home to institutions of government, law and education which were founded, in their original form, as part of the colonial project. Although European empires have passed away, our world remains very much a world shaped by empire.

Colonial Expansion

In the 1870s, most European powers had empires or were in the process of acquiring them. The oldest was the Portuguese empire on the East and West African coast, then largely gone to seed, but which would later revive, eventually outliving many of its rivals. France had a long-standing commercial interest in West Africa and the Levant, and from the 1830s had conquered and settled Algeria. Over the centuries, the Dutch had picked up an empire in the East Indies, acquired originally for its lucrative spice trade. And tsarist Russia was expanding eastward, mainly at the expense of the Muslim states of Central Asia.

But it was Britain, industrially dominant, that was easily the world's most important colonial power, holding an immense variety of territories in every continent. 'Great Britain' was itself, of course, a multi-ethnic imperial construct, dominated by the English, with the Scots as equal, if junior, partners. These two major groups were joined by others – the Welsh, the Manx, the Channel Islanders – who owed various forms of allegiance to the Crown. Ireland occupied an especially ambivalent place within this curious polity. Constitutionally part of Britain, Ireland was also its oldest colony. It took the Irish themselves more than a century from the Union of 1801 to decide (almost) finally whether they were partners in British imperialism, or victims of it.

Of less dubious loyalty were the 'New Britains' – the colonies created by white settlement. These included those North American colonies that had stayed loyal (most of them unified as the Canadian Confederation in 1867) and Australia – once a dumping ground for convicts, now becoming a major area of European settlement, its Aboriginal inhabitants violently displaced as more and more gold-rushing whites arrived from the 1850s. In South Africa, Cape Colony had been grabbed from the Dutch during the Napoleonic Wars; although British settlers were dominant, much of its population was of Dutch or African stock. New Zealand was conquered from the 1840s; white settlement and European diseases soon reduced the indigenous Maoris to a minority. These settler colonies were linked to the mother country by language and sentiment, ties reinforced by a steady trickle of emigrants. All these territories enjoyed, or would soon obtain, responsible government, which involved taking control over internal affairs, while accepting imperial direction of foreign relations and defence.

Very different were the non-white dependent territories. The most ancient of these were the West Indies – remnants of the once-vital Atlantic sugar trade, now decayed and neglected, the largest of them, Jamaica, still reeling from the rebellion of 1865. There was the island of Ceylon; a few trading posts in West Africa; and a scattering of colonies, ports, islands and coaling stations across the coasts and oceans of the world – including nodal points of empire such as Malta, Aden and Singapore. These territories were not considered suitable for self-government, and were ruled mostly by autocratic governors appointed from London.

Above all, there was India – the crown jewel of empire – where one-fifth of humanity lived under British sway, this huge population alone entitling India to first rank among the colonial territories. Sixty years of aggression from the 1790s had brought almost all the subcontinent under British control. India had been acquired and was ruled by the East India Company – a joint-stock venture, overseen by Parliament – until 1858, when it passed directly to the British Crown as a legacy of the 1857 'mutiny'. For much of the century, Russian expansion seemed to threaten Indian security; but India was an endless source of soldiers; and the Indian Army, led by white officers, became the chief arm of British imperialism in Asia, projecting imperial power around the fringes of the Indian Ocean, and beyond.

This Empire was very much an empire overseas. In the mid-nineteenth century, Britain controlled the lion's share of world trade and shipping. It was therefore vital to protect the sea lanes on which the Empire depended. Britain's warships dominated the oceans of the world; in the 1880s, the Royal Navy was greater than all other navies combined. The mid-century threat from France had faded, and the Royal Navy policed the Gulf, the African coast, the Indian Ocean and the China Sea without serious rival. In an age of steam-powered, armoured warships, British naval predominance expressed British industrial might. Although under challenge from the later 1890s (especially from Germany), even then Britain still maintained the largest navy in the world.

In addition to this vast (and expanding) 'formal' empire, some historians have identified a hidden or 'informal' empire exercised through a mixture of economic pressure and naval power. Empire, according to this account, was not confined to the bits coloured red on the map. Just as important were the areas which Britain did not claim to rule, but from which other major players were excluded, and in which Britain wielded economic power without legal responsibility. Britain, as the world's leading exporter of manufactures, could impose trade on its own terms with weaker states (who also depended on British capital for infrastructural projects). This 'imperialism of Free Trade' was allegedly exercised in China, Iran, West and East Africa and, above all, in Latin America.

Certainly there was some blurring of the boundary between empire and influence; but this 'informal empire' hypothesis does not seem credible. In the first place, informal empire assumes a high level of economic dependence; but this was rarely, if ever, the case. Admittedly, the gates of China may have been forced in the Opium Wars of the 1840s; but China was too vast ever to be economically dependent on Britain. The contrast with the formal empire of India, which was much more fully opened to British trade, is instructive. Even in Latin America, the volume of trade was simply not great enough to create dependence, and local governments retained much freedom of action. Arguably, Latin American states even benefited from the economic connection with Britain; for example, by obtaining development capital for railway building. And the 'Monroe Doctrine' of the United States largely prevented serious British political intervention in Latin America.

Either way, it is hard to deny that there were important changes in attitudes to empire from the 1870s – the beginning of the so-called 'new imperialism'. In the last decades of the nineteenth century, colonial expansion seemed to step up a gear. In some circles, empire became a subject of intense debate; and imperial rhetoric became more important in political discourse. Benjamin Disraeli* tried to position the Conservatives as *the* party of empire, implying that the Liberals would weaken Britain's hold on her overseas possessions. He encouraged Queen Victoria to assume the title 'Empress of India' in 1876; and his premiership also witnessed British imperial expansion in Afghanistan and Burma. Disraeli's great political rival, the Liberal leader William Ewart Gladstone,* was anti-imperialist – in the sense that he thought Britain should try to avoid new acquisitions – but even he did not give up any overseas territory.

The chief evidence for a 'new imperialism', however, was the 'scramble for Africa' – 'one of the most remarkable events in the history of the world', according to a contemporary observer. 'Scramble' is probably too dramatic a word: the European take-over of Africa was more gradual and episodic than that. But it was still without precedent: the powers of one continent conquering another in the space of barely twenty years. All major, and some minor, European states were involved. The French, for example, acquired a vast empire in West Africa, Morocco and Madagascar. It is possible to overstate the novelty of this 'new imperialism' – there was some continuity with what went before; and most European powers were building on existing footholds. But

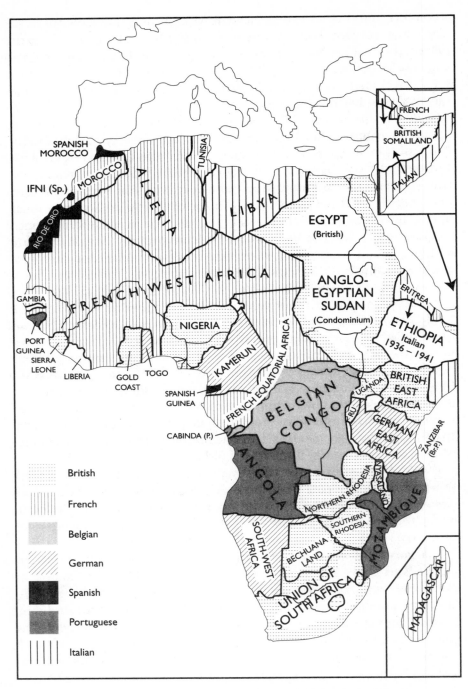

Map 12.1 European rule in Africa, 1914

it was certainly 'new' in that new imperial powers became involved. Germany occupied Togo, Cameroun, South-West Africa and Tanganyika; Italy took over Eritrea and Libya; and Belgium joined the colonial club in the guise of King Leopold's personal empire in the Congo. By 1912, Liberia and Ethiopia were the only African states to retain their independence.

Why did this happen? There seem to be as many theories as there are historians; and this brief chapter can only outline some of the basics. It is first worth noting that the Partition followed a period of growing European activity overseas – by traders, settlers, officials, missionaries and soldiers. One important aspect of this activity was explorers' growing interest in Africa from the 1850s to the 1870s, an interest which has been seen as a 'prelude to partition'. By adding tantalizing details to the map of what was then known (at least to Europeans) as the 'dark continent', and by bringing back exotic tales of riches and savagery, explorers arguably made the European public, and politicians, more 'Africa-minded'.

Explorers may have encouraged, but it was politicians who decided. Some historians of the Partition have therefore stressed the diplomacy of imperialism – explaining the non-European activities of colonial powers largely in terms of European diplomacy; an argument which highlights the activities of the political elite. The German Chancellor, Otto von Bismarck,* explained his own mid-1880s 'colonial bid' in these terms. He wanted to heighten colonial tensions in order to keep potentially anti-German powers (such as Britain, France and Russia) apart *in Europe*. His map of Africa, he famously remarked, had France on one side, Russia on the other, and Germany in the middle.

But diplomats did not operate in a cultural vacuum; even Bismarck was not a completely free agent. Policy-makers worked within the confines of a political and cultural context. If Bismarck was generally indifferent to the imperial enthusiasms of the age, the same was not true of his overlord, Kaiser Wilhelm II* (or, for that matter, the voters). The Kaiser, jealous of the British Empire, was anxious that Germany be taken seriously as a world power; he saw 'a place in the sun' as an essential attribute of this status. The French public, in turn, were fitfully interested in empire, which they saw largely as a question of national prestige; and the Italians, conscious of their relative weakness, wanted colonies in order to be fully accepted as a Great Power.

Related explanations have asserted the primacy of domestic politics in the making of foreign policy. According to the theory of 'social imperialism', the elite used imperial expansion to defuse domestic tension, to avoid social reform, or to preserve the social order. This has been argued most persuasively in the German case: German imperialism was an attempt to export social tensions. The growth of an organized industrial working class posed problems for Germany's semi-feudal social and political order. Winning a 'place in the sun' could defuse such tensions, or distract attention from them. Elements of this thinking have also been associated with Benjamin Disraeli and Cecil Rhodes.* Disraeli saw imperialism as one way of dealing with social disorder and the problems arising from the expansion of the British franchise in 1867, while Rhodes believed imperial expansion was the best way of averting social revolution.

But there was much more to imperialism than that; colonies were not just useless trappings of Great Power status, or a means to keep order at home. There was often thought to be big money at stake in empire, and several commentators have seen links between capitalism and imperialism. The discovery of massive diamond and gold fields in South Africa encouraged imperial enthusiasts to believe that other parts of the continent would yield similar treasures. These hopes (however misplaced) created pressure to annex in order to lay down claims for the future, and to preempt other resource-grabbing imperial powers. Africa was also seen as a potential source of new markets. From the early 1870s, some sectors of the European economy suffered a 'Great Depression'. Optimists thought that African markets would soak up surplus European goods and revive the economy.

This economic outlook informed the imperialist programme of Joseph Chamberlain,* Conservative Colonial Secretary from 1895 to 1903. Chamberlain spoke for a body of opinion that foresaw the imminent end of free trade. In the future, he thought, the major powers would become self-sufficient imperial economic blocs – raw materials coming from their empires, while the home country provided manufactured goods and a stream of migrants. Chamberlain dreamed of an imperial economic union of Britain and the white dominions, ruled over by an imperial parliament. His grand vision foundered because of the Dominion's mistrust of imperial centralization. In terms of more practical politics, he campaigned for tariff reform – using preferential tariffs to create a British imperial trading bloc. At election time, however, the prospect of the 'dear loaf' – tariffs on food – put voters off.

Apart from figures like Chamberlain, governments often turned out to be rather reluctant imperialists. Hard-headed politicians did not want to be drawn into paying for far-away colonies of whose worth they knew nothing. Evidence for this can be seen in the revival of chartered company imperialism in the 1880s – a sort of 'imperialism of private enterprise'. In several areas of Africa, governments took over only when company imperialism had faltered. Moreover, much British expansion in this period was arguably defensive – involving attempts to firm up areas of informal influence; or to preempt newer colonial powers such as Germany, or more aggressive ones such as France; or to create a defensive glacis to protect existing territory.

Governments did, however, have to react to the major pressure groups who had vested interests in imperial expansion – the *Deutsche Kolonialverein*; the Navy Leagues in Britain and Germany; the Royal Colonial Institute; and the *parti colonial* in France. German steel manufacturers were understandably keen to see an expansion in the Navy. The British aristocracy and upper middle classes found 'outdoor relief' in the running of the Empire. Such elites relished the chance to become viceroys, governors and army officers, exercising a taste for autocratic benevolence and lavish display that was less affordable in the industrial democracy at home. All these groups sought to nudge governments in an imperial direction.

But did anyone outside the elites really care about imperialism? Was imperialism just the passion of a vocal minority, or was it a more popular habit of mind? Working-class attitudes to empire are difficult to measure. There was certainly propaganda saturation: in late-Victorian Britain one could not pick up a bottle of Worcester sauce or a pack of cigarettes without being bombarded with positive images of the Empire – all-powerful, benign, gorgeously exotic and, of course, supreme at sea. Imperial themes ran through most forms of popular entertainment: the music-hall, adventure stories, children's literature and the uniformed youth organizations. On occasion, there were great displays of popular imperial enthusiasm, not least at Queen Victoria's Diamond Jubilee in 1897; and the outcry over the death of General Gordon in the Sudan suggests that imperial issues could excite the public, if in a shallow and ephemeral way.

Popular culture provides important evidence that people were well-disposed towards empire, and would respond positively to images of it. But against this must be set a picture of astonishing ignorance. Most people had no idea where, or what, the Empire was. At the turn of the century, opinion polling was in its infancy; but a Colonial Office survey of public opinion in 1951 is very illuminating. Even at that date none of those interviewed could distinguish between a Dominion and colony; and more than half could not name a single British colony. (Three per cent suggested the United States; one man tried Lincolnshire.) Ignorance was not the same thing as indifference, of course; but domestic political issues were almost always dominant at election time. Although it was vaguely assumed that the Empire helped to make Britain rich and great, efforts to mobilize the public around specific imperial issues generally met with scant success.

Probably more significant than the popular imperialism of the metropolis was 'peripheral sub-imperialism' – the pressure for expansion on or near imperial frontiers. India, for example, was a long-standing imperial power in its own right. The Government of India gradually extended its influence throughout the Indian Ocean region in the nineteenth century – establishing a protectorate over Aden, for example, and annexing Burma. Much of Britain's empire on the fringes of the Indian Ocean was essentially a footnote to the Indian Empire, and was acquired largely by Indian troops.

These sub-imperial urges were not confined to India. French expansion in West Africa also owed much to the imperialism of 'the man on the spot'. Generals humiliated by defeat in the 1870 war with Prussia could gain fame and promotion overseas by annexing ever more African territory – most of it pretty useless semi-desert and jungle, but which looked impressive coloured blue on the map. (French generals justified their insubordination by appealing to the need to stabilize turbulent frontiers.) In the expanding settler society of South Africa, Cape mining magnates and politicians such as Cecil Rhodes pursued their own imperial agendas. (Rhodes dreamed of a Cape-to-Cairo railway on an all-red route.) These frontier imperialisms might receive tacit government support, or could drag reluctant governments in after them.

One should also remember that new technologies were making colonial conquest easier and cheaper. In the later nineteenth century, the balance of technical power between Africa and Europe shifted decisively in the latter's favour. The telegraph transformed communications; and better steamships made it easier to trade with, and to dominate, the world overseas. Above all, there was the machine gun, which dramatically cut the military cost of colonial conquest. African states had previously survived partly because they could put up effective military resistance. But even the most resolute African armies were helpless before the Maxim gun, which, in most cases, they had not got. With machine guns, even the smallest European expedition wielded massive, and highly mobile, firepower. The massacre of the Mahdist army at Omdurman in 1898, with barely any loss to the Anglo-Egyptian forces, is one chilling illustration.

Once the first wave of annexations was over, almost all the colonial empires in Africa faced 'post-pacification' revolts – the Shona-Ndebele rebellion in Southern Rhodesia (1896–7) and the Abushire (1888–9) and Maji-Maji (1905–6) risings in German East Africa being some of the best-known examples. Some sought to restore the pre-colonial *ancien régime*; several were strongly religious in form. These risings were all easily crushed, with varying degrees of severity; but they were not entirely futile. In the first place, they forced the imperial powers to pay more heed to indigenous interests, if only to avoid future trouble. Secondly, they could also inspire more modern, and more effective, resistance movements. Mass nationalism was later to draw on the rhetoric and the example of earlier risings.

But even where they did not resist, Africans were not simply passive spectators to the partition of their continent. They also took the initiative. Some influential African interests were convinced that Europeans had something of benefit to offer them, which created a 'scramble for protection' amongst African polities, anxious to draw European Powers into local conflicts in order to win powerful benefactors. African elites, however, often did not realize what the implications of this were, and usually overestimated their ability to manage the resulting European intrusion.

Despite the cheap and easy successes in Africa, there were European voices raised against imperial expansion. In Britain, dissent became most vocal during the South African War of 1899–1902 (a conflict in which the British absorbed the Boer Republics of Southern Africa, for a mix of economic, strategic and political motives). Expecting a quick, cheap victory, the British instead found themselves entangled in a long and messy guerrilla war. Unpalatable stories kept coming home from Africa – of embarrassing defeats, and of Boer women and children dying in barbed-wire concentration camps. British public opinion turned against the war in its later stages, and there was even a small pro-Boer movement which found some echo amongst the left wing of the Liberal Party.

Around the same time, imperial expansion came under more general intellectual attack from the left-wing thinker J. A. Hobson. In his book *Imperialism: A Study* (1902) he argued that annexation served the interests only of 'capitalists'. According to Hobson, investors were able to get a better return on their money overseas, especially in the colonies, so that is where their money went; they influenced British foreign policy to further their sectional interests; and colonial annexation was largely a device for protecting investments. The South African War was thus a 'capitalists' war' – a battle to secure for a few rich men the profits from the Rand gold reserves. Hobson argued for more investment at home, to raise working-class living standards and purchasing power.

His economic analysis (although influential in left-wing circles) was seriously flawed. The links between finance capital and empire were much more tenuous than he allowed. There was in fact very little British investment in tropical Africa. Most British investment overseas went to the Americas, while French and German capitalists looked to Europe, especially Russia. Businessmen wanted to make money, not empire. But Hobson's work was a symptom of a growing disquiet about imperialism, especially on the political left. For example, Joseph Conrad's contemporary novella, *Heart of Darkness*, was a thinly-disguised attack on the brutality of the Belgians in the Congo. There was also wider public concern about the human and financial costs of empire, which fed into the striking Liberal victory in the 1906 British general election.

Most Liberals generally agreed with most Conservatives over imperial policy, but there was a slight change in tone after 1906. Power was devolved (if only to the whites) in the former Boer Republics, and the provinces were encouraged into a self-governing Union of South Africa in 1910. There was also reform in India. For several decades India had been developing a home-grown leadership able to challenge British rule. As early as 1885, Indian intellectuals had formed the Indian National Congress as a forum for the discussion of public affairs. Although elitist, and not at first anti-British, Congress was seen by some as the potential nucleus of a more dangerous movement. This came with the *swadeshi* campaign of economic boycott in Bengal, itself a response to the partition of the province in 1905 (seen by nationally-minded Indians as a ploy to fragment legitimate political opposition). The Liberals responded with cautious reforms in 1909, which aimed to make the Government of India more responsive to Indian opinion.

Colonial Encounters

The new imperialism, like the old, undoubtedly featured violence and brutality. But the pattern of exchange between Europeans and the colonized world was not simply one of conquest, domination and resistance. It also involved varied cultural exchanges – some fruitful and enriching, others producing stark bafflement or hatred on both sides.

Admittedly, force was sometimes seen (particularly by military men) as the only language that non-Europeans could understand. Imperial policing was always much more heavy-handed than police work in the metropolis, and the casual loss of civilian life at the hands of trigger-happy policemen was a feature common to all non-white colonial territories. The police were the most visible manifestation of the colonial state, and the one that most nearly touched the life of the people. In most areas, the military were also drawn into the maintenance of order, which tended to give colonial rule a particularly coercive aspect. When faced with unrest, armed force was always the last, and often the first, resort of the colonial state.

But empire did not live by force alone. Despite the massive imbalance in power between state and subjects, imperial rule could not have relied simply on coercion. It would have been too controversial at home. It would have provoked too much expensive resistance (and Treasury constraints were always a major limit to colonial power). And any attempt to rule by force would have exposed the imperial bluff – for the colonial empires rested on fragile military foundations, and surprisingly little armed force was needed to control most imperial territories.

Furthermore, European manpower was too expensive and too thinly spread to allow a white monopoly of the coercive apparatus. Every imperial power had to rely on indigenous recruits to its armed forces (and often to the lower reaches of its bureaucracy as well). This dependence restricted the colonizers' freedom of manoeuvre, for no colonial state could afford to alienate the indigenous communities upon whom its power depended.

Imperial rulers therefore had to strike bargains with their subjects, and win allies amongst them. The imperial connection could bring great benefit to useful indigenous military communities – like the middle peasantry of the Punjab who formed the backbone of the Indian Army, and the Yaos of Nyasaland who served with distinction in the King's African Rifles. Colonial states also tried to involve the indigenous in routine administration. In many areas, the colonial elite exercised their power indirectly, through local figures of authority – Malay sultans, African chiefs, and the Indian princes whose often inept autocracy relied on British support. Colonial rule depended as much on collaboration as on coercion.

But empire was more than a pragmatic mixture of threat, bluff and promise. There was a sincere belief in some imperial quarters that empire was good for its subjects. Colonial rule, it was thought, would eventually raise Africa and Asia to European levels of civilization, or (where that was impossible) would stamp out the worst barbarities of 'primitive' existence. Lord Curzon (Viceroy of India, 1899–1905) was not alone in seeing the British Empire as 'an instrument for the good of humanity'. Admittedly, much of this rhetoric was humbug, but some of it was quite sincere. European imperialists sought to export their culture, values and institutions as part of a 'civilizing mission'. There were certainly some major humanitarian achievements – slavery was abolished in the British Empire in 1833, for example (although arguably for economic motives) and for decades afterwards the Royal Navy worked hard to stamp out the vestiges of the traffic in humans.

The civilizing mission cost money, however, and most of the tropical colonies were too poor to do anything much more than raise taxes and keep order. But in some areas, empire could act as an agent of development. The Government of India, for example, was relatively wealthy, and was ambitious in contemporary terms. Educational progress in the later nineteenth century included the establishment of Indian universities (the first three founded, ironically enough, in 1857, the year of the mutiny). Technology was turned to beneficial ends: steamships plying the Ganges opened the interior to wider commerce; and, from the 1880s, vast schemes of irrigation brought fertility to millions of previously arid acres. A network of canals disciplined the waters of India's great rivers, and helped protect the peasantry from years of dearth. (Grants of newly-fertile land were also a useful means of rewarding allies of the Raj, such as the peasant-soldiers of the Punjab.)

But it was the railway which was the most spectacular achievement of imperial engineering – opening up the interior of South Africa, and crossing the great Canadian prairies. Railways were the largest single investment of the age; and the fact that the capital was often British gave the metropolis an important lever over the colonies of settlement. Railways were of especial importance in India. Although built mainly to serve the interests of British commerce and security, railways still made India more prosperous. Railways stimulated Indian engineering, eased internal trade and linked the subcontinent more closely to the world economy. Railways joined the jute and cotton fields to the mills of Bombay and Calcutta, and to the coal mines which fuelled them. Admittedly, by creating a trade in grains, the railways made the rural poor more dependent on market fluctuations, but they also made famine relief easier.

In a similar way, colonial medicine was frequently invoked to justify imperial rule. Western medicine, it was argued, clearly benefited indigenous peoples by eradicating the great killer epidemics – cholera, yellow fever, malaria, dysentry, bilharzia and plague. The successes of tropical medicine became an important legitimizing imperial myth. Marshal Lyautey, the architect of French power in Morocco, even claimed that medicine was 'the sole excuse for colonialism'.

But a closer look at colonial medicine produces a more ambiguous picture than imperial rhetorics might allow. In the first place, imperialism was responsible for the spread of disease, through the epidemiological unification of the world. European diseases more than decimated the indigenous population of Australasia; and imperial armies were a major vector of cholera in nineteenth-century India. The Great War, in moving millions of men around the world, created conditions ideal for the spread of influenza, the pandemic of 1918–19 killing perhaps twice as many as the war itself.

Secondly, the medical benefits of empire were very unevenly spread. Europeans were keen, first of all, to protect themselves, their soldiers and their interests. The security of *European* health was the first medical priority of most colonial governments. Hence the emergence of 'enclavist' medicine, in which Europeans and those close to them were protected, while the rest were left largely to fend for themselves. Growing medical knowledge encouraged segregation, with whites withdrawing into medically secure compounds while the slums and shanty towns remained at the mercy of disease. Furthermore, colonial governments might be reluctant to sanction medical intervention, fearful that the violation of indigenous bodily taboos could provoke civil unrest. Successful mass inoculation was generally a feature of the twentieth century, by which time imperialism was arguably in retreat.

The belief in the civilizing mission was expressed perhaps most clearly in the work of European missionaries. The very idea of the mission implied raising an inferior civilization to higher standards; and in the imperial context this could mean imposing Western values on non-Western societies. Missionary activity often enshrined the belief that the light of Truth shone more brightly on Europe than it did on the 'dark corners of the earth'. Missionaries set up schools and hospitals, and attacked what they saw as un-Christian institutions such as polygamy and slavery. Their proselytism could act like a solvent on indigenous culture, weakening powers of ideological resistance to empire. Indeed, missionaries working ahead of imperial political frontiers might well call for state intervention to protect themselves or their converts, or to obtain secular backing for the word of God.

But missionaries were not mere ideological commissars of imperialism. They could also be vocal critics of imperial brutality and excess. Their relationship with deeply racist settler societies, suspicious of Christian egalitarianism, could be very fraught. Missionaries, it must be remembered, were often using imperialism to pursue their own, quite separate, agendas – creating an 'invisible empire' of the Godly, which was marginal or even hostile to the more prosaic ambitions of the secular imperialists. Missionaries, frankly, could be a damn nuisance to hard-headed empire-builders. Furthermore, because Christianity was a religion of the book, missionaries encouraged indigenous literacy, despite its sometimes disturbing political implications. Translating the Bible involved missionaries in the respectful study of non-European languages, while some missions adopted indigenous customs to distance their spiritual message from specifically Western values. If missionaries had simply been the *parti colonial* at prayer, they would hardly have won converts.

The missionary encounter was merely one aspect of a much wider cultural exchange associated with imperialism. Empire brought with it 'imperial studies' – such as Indology and Orientalism – which contributed much of value to a scholarly understanding of colonized societies. But colonial knowledge was saturated with the desire to dominate. Early anthropology, for example, served the needs of colonial administration, which sought to understand its subjects in order to control them. The vital importance of 'knowing the natives' was one inspiration behind the flood of census data, settlement reports and handbooks that was so prominent a feature of later colonial rule. Much of this literature, especially at the less scholarly end, was infused with unflattering stereotypes about the 'unchanging East' which helped to boost imperial self-esteem. Similar cultural materials, of a more popular kind, were important in shaping Europeans' sense of who they were, largely by constructing an idea of who they were not. By generating cultural contrasts between 'East' and 'West' – between the primitive and the rational, the spiritual and the material, the black and the white – empire helped to reinvent Europe.

This sense of difference was taken to extremes in the racism that flourished from the later nineteenth century, as Europeans became more contemptuous of other societies. Social Darwinists – those who applied Charles Darwin's evolutionary theories to human society – came to see an important biological distance between the colonizers and the colonized. The harsh doctrine of the 'survival of the fittest' (not, incidentally, Darwin's phrase) was eagerly adopted by Social Darwinists, who predictably saw 'fitness' in white skin. Pseudo-sciences such as phrenology – basically the study of bumps on the head – were deployed to 'prove' that Europeans were more intelligent than others, and hence destined to rule over them. As late as the 1930s, one British writer felt able to remark that 'the mass of the people of India have neither martial aptitude nor physical courage.' He ascribed this to:

> prolonged years of varying religions, of early marriage, of premature brides and juvenile eroticism, of a thousand years of malaria and hookworm, and the deteriorating effect of aeons of tropical sun on races that were once white and lived on uplands and on cool steppes. (George MacMunn, *The Martial Races of India*, 1911)

This sort of racism informed the increasing social distance between colonizers and their subjects that was typical of later British imperialism – a distance expressed in myriad ways. Colonial clothing became more rigidly European, and imperialists made a point of being overdressed. Solar topis became *de rigeur* protection against the largely imaginary 'perils of the midday sun'. The earlier practice of adopting indigenous customs or dress ('going native', as it was now contemptuously termed) was frowned upon as corrosive of colonial authority. Social exclusiveness was reinforced by the private space of the all-white colonial club – an institution bitterly attacked in George Orwell's anti-imperial novel *Burmese Days*. These reserved British habits contrasted with the more easygoing, but perhaps more brutal, relations between colonizers and subjects in the French, Portuguese and Dutch empires.

Social distance, however, could coexist with relations of a more intimate kind. There was a wide range of sexual encounters between Europeans and their subject peoples. In explaining this, one must never forget the sheer misery of empire – the heat, the dust, the boredom and the loneliness. Sex with indigenous peoples (like intemperate drinking) was one of the dubious consolations of imperial power, an indulgence which helped to make the 'White Man's Burden' bearable. Europeans, especially the tightly-buttoned British, perhaps found in empire some sexual opportunities that were denied them at home. The white elite enjoyed the comforts of oriental mistresses; the rank and file made do with the coarser pleasures of the regimental brothel; while homosexuals could follow their secret star in the more expansive spaces of empire.

Some of these relationships may have contained genuine respect, affection and mutual benefit. Love can, with difficulty, cross barriers of culture, colour and religion. More practically, indigenous prostitutes were at least making money out of the colonial encounter; and some gained wealth and independence from their trade. But the element of exploition cannot be gainsaid. Almost all relationships between colonizers and others were saturated with inequalities in power: sexual relations were no different. Rape and sexual violence were as much facets of empire as the mission hospital and the law court.

Colonial Retreat?

Even at the meridian, imperialists knew that at some point the sun had to set. The great imperial poet Rudyard Kipling sounded his own warning, in the poem 'Recessional', published in the year of Victoria's Diamond Jubilee:

> Far-called, our navies melt away;
> On dune and headland sinks the fire:
> Lo, all our pomp of yesterday
> Is one with Nineveh and Tyre!
> Judge of the Nations, spare us yet,
> Lest we forget – lest we forget!

Reproduced by permission of A.P. Watt Ltd
on behalf of The National Trust

Historians still dispute when and why imperial decline began; but few deny that the Great War of 1914–18 marked a major test of empire.

The causes of the war lay in Europe, and the fiercest fighting happened there. But the war was also an imperial conflict. Important campaigns took place in Africa, and minor ones in the Far East. The entry of Ottoman Turkey into the scale spread the conflict to Egypt, Palestine,

Iraq and Syria. And when peace was made, accounts between Germany and the Allies were partly settled in the loose change of voiceless colonies.

For the French and British at least, imperial systems worked during the war much as imperial optimists had hoped. The French, for example, had long planned to rely on troops raised in West Africa – the so-called *force noire* – to counter Germany's greater reserves of manpower; and African troops indeed fought with distinction on the Western Front (to the bitter disgust of German racists).

Even more than the French, the British Empire struggled almost as a single power. Efforts to make the War Cabinet truly imperial, with the addition of Dominion and Indian representatives, did not come to much; but the Empire succoured Britain in countless other ways. Regiments were raised all over the Empire, making a crucial difference on the Western Front and elsewhere. The early white volunteers included many recent migrants from Britain, and these brave and loyal soldiers became the finest shock troops of the imperial army. Of more prosaic importance were the Chinese, Indian and African labourers who carried supplies and built roads. The Empire was also a great source of food – of Canadian wheat, New Zealand butter and Australian meat. Despite their cunning and skill, German submariners were never able to cut these essential imperial lifelines. By 1918, Germany was starving, Britain was not; and the Empire was one reason for this decisive difference.

The outcome of the Great War was also a dramatic success for imperialism. The major colonial powers – Britain and France – emerged tired but victorious. Their dependent empires grew. In the former Ottoman Middle East, a whole new region was incorporated into empire. Syria and Lebanon passed to French control. Britain gained Iraq, Transjordan and Palestine (making the defence of India more secure). The British Empire in 1920 was larger, and more triumphant, than ever before. And, by absorbing former German territories in East Africa, the route from Cairo to the Cape was at last all red.

Victory also removed one irksome colonial rival. By the punitive Treaty of Versailles of 1919, Germany was prohibited from holding colonies. Flushed with a costly success, the Allied Powers deemed that the Germans were not civilized enough to perform the imperial mission. Germany's African territories were rudely partitioned between Britain, France, Belgium and South Africa, while Australia and New Zealand picked up a scattering of Pacific islands.

The international situation in the 1920s was therefore peculiarly favourable to empire. The two main anti-colonial powers (the Soviet Union and the USA) both withdrew into different forms of isolation. Germany was kept weak by treaty, while diplomacy sweetened Italy and Japan. An agreement of naval limitation, signed at Washington in 1921, averted an incipient building race with Japan and the USA in the Pacific – a race which Britain would doubtless have lost. Instead, the Royal Navy retained equal first place with the American fleet until the early 1940s.

But success, although real, was fragile. Victory was rapidly followed by a four-year 'crisis of empire' – a general tremor running through the imperial system. Between 1918 and 1922, there were great troubles in Ireland, India, Egypt and Mesopotamia. The white Dominions rapidly disbanded their wartime armed forces; the British army was stretched too far, and politicians seemed unwilling to heed military advice to 'govern or get out'. Nationalists had been encouraged during the war, with bold promises made in India, in Egypt, and to the Arabs of the Ottoman Empire. They now wanted to cash their post-dated cheques, and would do more than quibble if they bounced. Inflation, repression and the extractive demands of the war had alienated the peasantry in Egypt and India. The postponment of Irish Home Rule in 1914, and the execution of the rebels of 1916, had embittered many Irish Catholics.

Faced with popular unrest, the British conceded what they had to, in order to retain what they could. Independence, hedged with many safeguards, was granted to Egypt and Ireland in 1922. Declarations of liberal intent in India culminated in the 1919 Government of India Act, which offered Indians limited self-government in the provinces and more say at the centre. These reforms sought to associate educated Indians with government, and thereby to draw the sting of their grievances. But the nationalists had won an important victory, gaining a political arena in which they could audibly criticize official policy. Despite the concessions at the top, the popular troubles in India continued into the early 1920s.

The picture, however, was not simply one of steady decline from the high point of global victory. Empire recovered from its crisis, after a fashion. True, there were revolts in Morocco and Syria against the French, besides riots in Palestine (directed against Jewish immigrants) and intermittent troubles in India. The British had to abandon the ideas of formal imperial unity they had aired before and during the war. Nevertheless, from the mid-1920s, the colonial empires enjoyed a belated, ten-year honeymoon – less disturbed by uncertainties and inter-imperial rivalries than they had been in the 1890s, and less troubled by internal dissent and a hostile international climate than they would be in the 1940s.

But the wider imperial purpose was beginning to falter. The appearance of renewed power, tranquillity and certainty has to be qualified.

Map 12.2 British imperial territories in 1939

Malta
Cyprus
Palestine
Iraq
Kuwait
Transjordan
Egypt
Qatar
Trucial States
Aden Protectorate
Nepal
Bhutan
India
Burma
Hong Kong
North Borneo
Maldives
Malaya
Brunei
Nigeria
Sudan
British Somaliland
Ceylon
Uganda
Kenya
Seychelles
Zanzibar
Chagos Is.
Singapore
Northern Rhodesia
Tanganyika
Bechuanaland
Nyasaland
Sarawak
Papua New Guinea
Gilbert Is.
Ellice Is.
Solomon Is.
Fiji
New Hebrides
Tonga
South West Africa
Southern Rhodesia
Mauritius
Swaziland
Basutoland
South Africa
Australia
New Zealand

Territory under British rule

Territory under dominant British influence

In ways difficult to measure, the Great War struck a heavy blow at European pretensions to be more civilized than the rest of the world. So much imperial self-esteem drained away in the squalid butchery of Verdun and the Somme. The conflict had left ten million dead and twenty million seriously wounded, most of them Europeans. It was certainly war, but it was not especially magnificent.

There was accordingly something bashful about post-war imperial rhetoric. The naked old colonialism had to be decently draped in the new language of the League of Nations (partly to save the anti-colonial blushes of the American President, Woodrow Wilson). The former German and Ottoman territories were transferred to the Allied Powers not as colonies but as Mandates of the League – meaning that they were held in trust until they could join the ranks of the independent nations. Nationalists might complain, with some reason, that new Mandate was but old Empire writ large. But independence was envisaged from the very start. Iraq achieved it in 1932, although successor regimes remained very much clients of the former colonial power.

Furthermore, metropolitan intellectuals were turning against empire. Its claims and postures were increasingly seen as ridiculous, at least by the over-educated. The Wembley Exhibition of 1924–5 was greeted with derision. 'I bring you to see the wonders of the Empire, and all you want to do is go on the dodgems,' mocked the playwright Noel Coward. George Orwell was another of these high-powered dissidents. An Old Etonian servant of empire, he was disgusted with what he saw as colonial policeman in Burma, and came home to write several attacks on the corruption and brutality of empire.

Opposition, moreover, was not confined to dissident Europeans. Imperialism, by accident or design, opened Western education to at least some of the indigenous. As a by-product of this process, a new generation of men were acquiring the tools with which to challenge colonial rule on its own intellectual terms. It was difficult to study at a Western-style university or law school without imbibing some liberal ideas – democracy, representative government, national self-determination and social justice. Applied to empire, these doctrines were highly subversive. In general, the Western-educated accepted the bureaucratic structure and boundaries of the colonial state. But they would later turn Western ideas against autocratic colonial rule; and they would use the infrastructure created by the colonial state – railways, roads, the post, the press – in mounting their anti-colonial campaigns.

At this stage, imperialists saw these men – Jawaharlal Nehru,* Ho Chi Minh,* Jomo Kenyatta and Kwame Nkrumah among them – as little more than deracinated, irresponsible rabble-rousers. They could afford to be dismissive, for nationalism as yet had little influence on imperial political life. Most colonial powers were repressive enough to maintain order in their colonies, and no dangerous mass movements had emerged. The exception was India, where the the London-educated lawyer M. K. Gandhi had developed a distinctive non-violent means of mass protest, which he called *satyagraha* – 'soul force' or 'truth force'. His methods were effective in winning support in India, and in gaining world esteem. His (mainly) peaceful campaigns of civil disobedience in the early 1930s undermined the legitimacy of the Raj even if they brought little in the way of immediate political change.

Gandhian protest combined modern and traditional forms. Gandhi indigenized nationalism in order to make it culturally accessible to the peasants and workers whose own discontents he sought to harness. Affecting the style of an Indian holy man, he adopted a simple life which created the impression that he shared the poverty of the peasants. His strategies were effective. The people who came to hear him speak, or to watch him tour, projected onto his person their own social and economic concerns, understood through the medium of popular Hinduism. Stories circulated about him – how the bullets of British soldiers had passed harmlessly through his body, and how a man who insulted him found his eyelids stuck together.

Gandhi's ability to raise sporadic mass movements certainly worried the rulers of British India. Unless they were prepared to govern simply by whip and by club, they had to accommodate nationalism. The most extensive concession was the 1935 Government of India Act, which sought to entangle Indian politicans in the routine business of provincial government. The Act granted provincial self-government, with a restricted franchise. But no real power was transferred at the centre, where the provisions for 'dyarchy' – dual Indian and British control – were never implemented. The Viceroy remained in charge of defence, foreign policy and communications. Even these limited concessions, however, outraged diehard defenders of the Raj like the Conservative maverick Winston Churchill,* to whom Gandhi was nothing but a 'seditious Middle Temple lawyer, posing as a fakir'.

While nationalists were winning some political ground, empire was paradoxically becoming more rather than less economically important. The Depression of the 1930s encouraged all European states to adopt protectionism, using their colonies as a bulwark against the tides of global economic failure. Tariff reforms stimulated inter-imperial trade, until, by the later 1930s, over 40 per cent of British trade was with the Empire. The gradual establishment of the 'sterling area' – in which most British imperial territories agreed to fix their currencies in relation to the pound – achieved a measure of economic co-ordination. From the 1930s to the 1960s, the British were to try and construct an imperial economy from the wreckage of an economy that had actually worked.

What picture, then, emerges of empire in 1935, at the time of King George V's Silver Jubilee? In Britain, the anniversary occasioned an outburst of popular royalist and patriotic sentiment that took more sophisticated observers by surprise. Imperialism may have failed as an intellectual construct, but few people listened to intellectuals. In a deeper sense, empire seemed as solid as ever – white-painted battleships still rode at anchor at Valetta or 'Gib'; solar topis were still totemically wedged in place. No imperial elite foresaw the imminent transfer of power to non-white dependent territories. Most thought that relations with the colonies would evolve constitutionally – the bonds would loosen, certainly, but ties of affection and shared values could replace those of autocracy and raw military power.

The global crisis of 1935–45 smashed these brittle illusions. From the mid-1930s, the international climate drastically worsened from the point of view of Britain and France. Japan turned hostile, Mussolini became expansionist, and Hitler plotted to overturn the verdict of Versailles. The League of Nations – by then essentially an Anglo-French colonial club – was exposed as a hollow sham by the Japanese invasion of Manchuria in 1931, and by Mussolini's attack on Abyssinia in 1935. Britain and France alone could not confidently face the combination of Japan, Italy and Germany. None of the three would be appeased.

War came first in Europe, with Germany. It began in minor key, then became a sequence of calamities. It is hard to overestimate the impact of the conflict on the power, prestige and self-esteem of the major colonial players. The *Wehrmacht* overran Belgium, Holland and France in a few weeks in 1940. The British army was forced off the continent for three years, in the shambolic retreat from Dunkirk. Ten months after invading Poland, Germany had become dominant in Europe, with more successes to come.

As the war became global, the sorrows of empire came in battalions. After hammering the American fleet at Pearl Harbor in December 1941, the Japanese conquered the British, Dutch and French empires in the Far East. This shattered European imperial prestige – the secure appearance of perpetually unshakeable power – perhaps beyond repair. The colonial peoples of South-East Asia had seen white men as they had never seen them before – scuttling, in panic, and defeated by Asians. Above all, there was the fall of Singapore, Britain's most important fortress East of Suez, where 130,000 troops trudged into captivity in the largest capitulation in British imperial history. In the spring of 1942, it must have seemed in Asia that final British defeat was likely. As Joseph Goebbels put it, the British were 'on the toboggan'.

The Japanese tried to portray themselves as liberators, attempting to rally their new subjects with the slogan of 'Asia for the Asians'. They encouraged the limited development of self-government in the conquered areas of South-East Asia – the 'Co-prosperity Sphere' as it was somewhat euphemistically named. The Allies replied in kind: desperate to win, they were willing to support even Communist resistance movements in Malaya and elsewhere, painfully aware that anti-Japanese resistance could easily turn against resurgent European imperialism. The price of victory, it seemed, might be empire itself.

Empire was losing the propaganda war as well. Under pressure from his anti-colonial American associates, Churchill signed the Atlantic Charter of August 1941, which promised the right of all peoples to self-determination. Churchill never meant it to apply outside Europe – 'I have not become the King's First Minister in order to preside over the liquidation of the British Empire' – but the American public were not going to fight for the old colonialism. As in the first war, imperialists had to make promises to survive. In April 1942, India was offered a post-war constitution-making body. The main Indian parties rejected the offer, and the British had then to face the mass disturbances of the 'Quit India' movement.

As the war progressed, the colonial powers were becoming more minor players in world politics. France, Belgium and Holland remained occupied; and even Britain was becoming a junior partner to the USA at sea and the USSR on land. The US Navy overtook the British fleet by 1943, and was massively superior by the end of the war. Australia and New Zealand felt betrayed by Britain's failure to send (as promised) a main fleet to Singapore, and they began looking to the USA for protection. In the Asia-Pacific theatre, Americans were taking most of the crucial strategic decisions, and victory was won mainly by American air and sea power. By 1945, the USA and the USSR had emerged as rival superpowers; both, in their different ways, were hostile to the old colonial order. Britain, on the other hand, ended the war exhausted, and heavily in debt to the USA, and even to India.

All these pressures were undermining the imperial system. But, despite the disasters, the British Empire functioned surprisingly well during the war – in some ways more effectively than in 1914–18. The Indian Army grew to two million men, the largest volunteer army in history. Dominion and colonial troops fought with distinction in many theatres. A training scheme in Canada meant that the Dominions and colonies provided almost 40 per cent of RAF aircrews. Despite the losses in the Far East, most imperial territory was successfully defended. The Axis attempt to break through to the Nile was defeated at Alamein, and the Japanese invasion of India was driven back. To a remarkable extent,

Churchill was able to impose his will on Allied strategy. The policy of 'Italy first' meant a massive British presence in the Mediterranean and Middle East, creating a suitable basis for the post-war reconstruction of British power in the region.

The balance-sheet of empire in 1945, therefore, looked healthier than it had done three years earlier. Much of Africa remained peacefully under colonial rule. There were to be major riots in Accra (in the Gold Coast) in 1948, but mass nationalism lay in the future. The war had affected colonial Africa much less than it had the empires in South-East Asia and the Middle East. Even Algeria, in the 1950s the scene of the bitterest war for independence, remained tranquil. Nationalist intellectuals had little influence. The dominant metropolitan ideology of state intervention lent itself easily to a policy of colonial development, especially in Africa. The British hoped that, by boosting the African economy, British colonies could earn dollars selling their produce to the USA, thereby creating a market for British goods. (Ironically, the disruption caused by this 'second colonial occupation' created much of the unrest of the early 1950s.)

In the Far East, France and Holland, defeated in 1940, sought to reassert their self-esteem through empire. Both powers proved willing to fight imperial wars to restore the imperial system. The Dutch soon had to admit defeat in Indonesia. In Vietnam, anti-Japanese resistance became anti-French almost at once. The French tried to suppress the Viet Minh nationalist movement, losing a nine-year war in the process. Attempts to restore the colonial order in South-East Asia (and later in Algeria) would eventually prove costly, unpopular at home and futile.

The British were more ambivalent about their Asian inheritance. The victory of the Labour Party at the polls in July 1945 showed that welfare, housing and jobs were the major electoral concerns. The public seemed largely indifferent to empire. Labour politicians were certainly willing to shed imperial burdens which had become too costly or tiresome to bear. Palestine is a notable example. The Arab–Jewish conflict, which Britain had done so much to create, was by the mid-1940s slipping beyond Britain's ability to police. The British turned over the problem to the United Nations, and withdrew with great loss of face in 1948.

Above all, there was the loss and partition of India, accepted with barely a murmur by the British public. The exhausted British had to honour their wartime promise of self-government, and get out before mass unrest spread to the army, or turned into civil war. The creation of the successor states of India and Pakistan was accompanied by the deaths of perhaps 180,000 people, and the displacement of millions more. But the 'transfer of power' was packaged as a great success by

Lord Louis Mountbatten, the last and most flamboyant Viceroy, who returned even more popular a hero than when he went out. Skilful public relations turned an ignominious scuttle into a supreme act of statesmanship, making the transfer look like the fulfilment, rather than the abdication, of Britain's imperial responsibilities in the subcontinent. And, apart from a few Tory backbenchers (such as the youthful Enoch Powell) most people frankly did not give a damn.

But, despite these losses, the imperial idea was far from dead in the later 1940s. The USA increasingly saw the British Empire as a useful bulwark against Soviet Communism. The British and French were both anxious for a 'seat on the top table', and the search for Great Power status would involve imperial pretensions as well as atomic research. Ernest Bevin (Labour's Foreign Secretary) wanted Britain still to play the imperial policeman in the oil-rich Middle East, which was becoming a new focus of empire to replace India. Despite the loss of Palestine, he maintained British bases in the Suez Canal Zone. Iraq under an unpopular monarchy remained a British client state, a useful source of oil, and an advanced base against the now hostile Soviet Union. British politicians of both main parties remained largely indifferent to European union until the later 1950s. The imperial habit of mind was to die hard.

13

The First World War as Total War

Gerard J. DeGroot

The First World War was not a distant campaign fought by professional armies, but a conflict which involved societies to a level unprecedented in the history of war. Civilians worked for the war, starved for the war and suffered deep emotional strain because of the war. It was virtually impossible for a citizen of one of the combatant nations to avoid losing a relative or close acquaintance. Beyond the direct experience of loss, war also fundamentally changed work patterns, diet, health, entertainment and the availability of goods and services. Propaganda machines encouraged citizens to make ever greater sacrifices for the war. But for most civilians the actual combat remained remote: confined to the lines of trenches on the various fronts. In this sense, the First World War was not as total as the Second World War,[1] when the fighting front was extended to the streets of London, Berlin, Stalingrad and Rome and civilians found themselves in the serried ranks of wartime casualties.

In the 1960s, some historians (chief among them Arthur Marwick) were struck by the apparent connection between war and social change in the twentieth century. Perhaps unconsciously affected by the temper of the sixties, they saw a great ferment of change – much of it positive – caused by war's disruption. War, they argued, encouraged women towards emancipation, governments towards social responsibility, and workers towards consciousness and assertiveness. Class and gender divisions consequently crumbled.

Thirty years later, with the millennium approaching, these excessively sanguine theories of war and society seem as incongruous as the clothes we wore back then. Twentieth-century social change does not seem as distinct, nor progress as direct. War had some profound (even positive) effects, but it is reckless to postulate an all-embracing theory of war and its effect upon society. In more stable societies, like Britain

---

[1] The word 'total' is supposed to be an absolute; one should not refer to degrees of totality. But for the purposes of this chapter, that linguistic rule will be relaxed.

and France, forces of conservatism and tradition were probably equal to the challenges of war. Germany, Italy and Russia seem to have been more deeply affected by the social consequences of war, but one could argue that the changes apparent in those countries were not born of war but only stimulated by it. When we study the First World War we need to be aware not just of the forces of change, but also of the countervailing forces which constrained or absorbed change. Progress was profound, but so was the power of convention, tradition, authority, repression and nostalgia.

Industrial Policy and the State

All the combatant nations expected a short war. This expectation was based on two premises: (1) that war itself had not fundamentally changed despite the advance of military technology and the increased size of European armies and (2) that modern industrialized economies would not be able to withstand a prolonged war. Economists and political theorists argued that the economic dislocation caused by a pan-European war would force combatants to opt for a negotiated peace if military victory did not come quickly. Strategic plans were formed according to this premise. Count von Schlieffen, originator of the plan to defeat France within six weeks (so that the German army could turn and meet the advancing Russians in the nick of time) argued that long wars

> are impossible at a time when a nation's existence is founded on the uninterrupted continuance of its trade and industry; indeed a rapid decision is essential. . . . A strategy based on attrition is unworkable. . . .[2]

Thus, all of the combatant nations were prepared for a short war, not a long one. Existing stockpiles of ammunition and supplies were considered sufficient to preclude the necessity of a massive shift to a war economy. Existing munitions factories would cope with demand merely by working at peak production.

Both France and Germany planned for a land campaign of strictly limited duration, in other words, a conflict like the short Franco-Prussian War, not like the long American Civil War. Germany, for instance, did not anticipate that armaments consumption would *increase* as the war progressed; therefore no steps were taken to convert factories outside the armaments industry to munitions production. Russia and Austria-Hungary, also wedded to 'short war' preconceptions, were nevertheless

[2]   G. Hardach, *The First World War 1914–1918* (Harmondsworth, 1987), p. 55.

Table 13.1 Relative strength of the Great Powers in 1914

	Population in millions	Military expenditure in £ 1913–14 (in millions)	Troops	Battleships	Submarines	Tonnage of merchant ships (in millions)
The Allied Powers						
France	40	37	1,250,000	28	73	2
Britain	45	50	711,000	64	64	20
Italy	35	10	750,000	14	12	1.75
Russia	164	67	1,200,000	16	29	0.75
Serbia	5	1.25	195,000			
Romania	7.5	3	420,000			
Belgium	7.5	2.75	180,000			
Greece	5	0.75	120,000			
USA	92	30	150,000	37	25	4.5
The Central Powers						
Germany	65	60	2,200,000	40	23	5
Austria-Hungary	50	22	810,000	16	6	1
Bulgaria	5	1.5	340,000			
Turkey	20	8	360,000			

unprepared even for a limited contest, due to the weaknesses in their economies. Britain, her eyes open to opportunity, devised a strategy of 'business as usual' under which her army would make a minimal contribution to the fighting, while the Royal Navy applied an economic blockade upon the Central Powers. Meanwhile, Britain would make money out of the war by being the arsenal and financier of the Entente, and her businessmen would commandeer German export markets disrupted by the blockade.

Hindsight tells us that twentieth-century total wars produce full employment, full production and inflation caused by increased demand for scarce goods. Yet faith in the logic of a short war meant that the combatants were preoccupied by worries over recession and unemployment due to a trade slump, a fall in demand and uncertainty in the stock markets. They therefore anticipated that government would have to intervene to reassure the business community and to guard against social unrest. Thus, in Britain, steps were taken to prevent a run on gold and to protect food supplies and distribution. Likewise, in Germany, new laws anticipated a currency crisis, not a munitions crisis. These preparations were not entirely unwarranted. At least initially, war's disruption did cause unemployment to rise, in Germany as high as 20 per cent in the first months of the war. A similar pattern occurred elsewhere. In fact, male unemployment explains in part the enthusiasm for military enlistment.

But before governments could sufficiently mobilize to deal with these problems, the war had solved them. The failure of the German Schlieffen Plan, the French Plan XVII and the Russian invasion of Central Europe forced acceptance of the inevitability of a long and costly war. Economies and societies proved more adaptable than pessimistic economists had predicted. The belligerents began to address the problem of how to balance the needs of the military (in munitions and men) against those of civilian society and industrial production. An expanded role for the state in the economy became inevitable. The state would (or should) plan, co-ordinate and oversee the war economy. The extent and nature of government intervention differed from country to country, depending as it did on levels of preparation, degrees of crisis, willingness (or ability) of the state to assume autocratic control and the strength of countervailing political ideologies. But nowhere was state expansion fuelled by an ideological shift in attitudes toward government and the economy. The growth of the state was accepted only as a pragmatic response to the war crisis.

Every state has a maximum level beyond which its military forces cannot grow. This level is determined not only by population size but also by industrial configuration, balance of trade, access to raw materials, wealth (or ability to borrow), access to surplus labour, willingness of citizens to make sacrifices for the war effort, and by competing commitments. A country cannot, much as it might wish, allow unrestricted military expansion, for eventually the requirements of its gargantuan force will no longer be able to be met by the productive capacity of its ever-shrinking civilian population or by its ability to purchase commodities abroad. Britain mobilized 12.5% of her men for the forces, Germany 15.4% and France 16.9%. Yet these figures should not be taken as a relative measure of each nation's commitment to the war. The differences are explained by the interplay of capabilities and commitments within each country. Each mobilized an army (and navy) near to its maximum potential size.[3] But each arrived at this level of commitment not through careful planning and adjustment but through blind groping in the dark. No country knew its own capabilities until it stumbled upon them. Thus, the shift to a war economy was in no sense smooth; problems were attacked on an *ad hoc* basis according to the principle of the squeaky wheel.

For instance, France did not immediately build huge, specially constructed and highly efficient munitions factories once her shortage of armaments became apparent. Instead, she tried at first to make do by converting existing factories, paying little attention to economies of scale. She then began slowly to concentrate on larger undertakings with greater specialization and division of labour. When this did not solve her problems, she reluctantly accepted the inevitable necessity of large purpose-built government-run factories. As the war escalated, so too did the pace of government intervention and mobilization. Escalation matched escalation as each nation squeezed the last man and the last gun from civilian society. For example, the Hindenburg* Programme of 1917 was Germany's response to the prodigious British shell production revealed on the Somme in 1916. Yet British firepower on the Somme was a response to the frustrations experienced in 1915 against superior German defences.

When it became apparent that existing armaments factories could not keep pace with wartime demands, the state turned in desperation to private industry. Industrialists found themselves in an enviable position: war allowed them to be both patriotic and rich. Most German armaments firms enjoyed at least a doubling of profits during the war. 'Profiteering' understandably annoyed the working class, for whom

---

[3] It could be argued that some countries mobilized armies of a size larger than the capacity of the home front to supply. This was certainly the case with Russia, due to her industrial backwardness. It was probably also the case with Germany in 1918, when desperate situations inspired desperate measures.

war meant sacrifice, not good fortune.[4] The extent to which businesses were controlled depended on the authority and assertiveness of the state and its sensitivity to the workers. In Russia and Italy, a phenomenal level of corruption existed: businessmen landed huge advances for supplies often never delivered. Britain, more sensitive to the image of profiteering, did introduce an excess profits duty early in the war. But clever accountants usually found ways around the rules. Germany waited until 1918, when the workers were already dangerously restless. One does not need to be a Marxist to notice that the co-operation of business during the war was won with a carrot, that of the workers with a stick.

Since the first priority was the survival of the nation, armies usually got the first call on manpower. Combatants rushed headlong toward economic catastrophe by forcing every seemingly available man into uniform. They were aided in this effort by the willingness of the population to serve. At least during its first year, this was a popular war, and a sense of duty ran deep, as was evident in the British response to the call by War Minister Herbert Kitchener for volunteers. Unfortunately, the more successful Kitchener was at raising an army, the more of a failure he was, by implication, at equipping it. The shell shortage of May 1915 arose in part because the government failed to pay sufficient attention to the industrial implications of a large citizen army.

This was, to use the German term, a *Materialschlacht*, a conflict of materials as much as of men. During the Battle of the Marne of September 1914 (a contest tiny compared to those which followed), more artillery shells were used than during the entire Franco-Prussian War. Before 1914, France planned for a munitions output of 10–12,000 shells per day. She eventually had to produce 200,000 per day. Even industrially backward Russia produced 150,000 shells a day. In both France and Germany munitions crises arose during the first months of the war. France's industrial capacity was seriously depleted by the loss of industrially important areas to the Germans. The captured territory represented 16.3% of her industrial capacity and 21.1% of her industrial labour force. The Longwy–Briey area alone was responsible for 64% of France's pig iron production, 58% of steel and 40% of coal. Germany likewise found herself in desperate straits when the Allied blockade cut supplies of essential raw materials like nitrogen. She consequently established the Kriegsrohstoffabteilung (War Raw Materials Department), or KRA, within the War Ministry, which oversaw procurement and distribution of raw materials and encouraged the development of

---

[4] The word 'profiteer' entered common usage in Britain during the war, to describe a social ill which did not exist before it.

substitutes. But almost all supply problems in every combatant country were essentially manpower problems. If coal was scarce it was because miners had left the pits to join the army. If farmers became soldiers, fields did not get tilled and food supplies dwindled.

The Problem of Manpower

Mobilizing the reserves (as in France, Germany, Russia and Austria-Hungary) or calling for volunteers (as in Britain) meant removing men from civilian production. The economy could not long withstand this drain upon human resources. There was some flexibility within the system: luxury goods did not need to be made, services could be cut back and bureaucracies culled of labour. But eventually, everywhere, shortages of labour began to develop in industries essential to the war effort: raw materials, food production and especially munitions. The situation was so critical in France that in September 1914 the armaments industry was given a higher labour priority than the armed forces. But by that time it was too late, since so many skilled workers were already in uniform. By the end of 1915, over 500,000 skilled men had to be called back into industry. Germany, likewise, recalled 1.2 million workers in September 1916 and 1.9 million the following July. Shortages of labour were all the more acute because of the unexpectedly massive losses on the fighting fronts. The war, like some ruthlessly efficient blast furnace, consumed men (essentially a non-renewable resource) at a prodigious rate. In the first four months of the war, France lost 455,000 men killed or missing, another 400,000 wounded.

There were three principal ways to attack labour shortages: firstly, by managing output; secondly, by transforming production processes and labour practices so as to make more efficient use of workers; thirdly, by tapping sources of surplus labour. These three methods were used to varying degrees in all the combatant countries, as need dictated.

Controlling output meant determining what could be produced in what quantities. It also meant controlling imports and exports in a manner most suited to economic efficiency and the needs of the war. In other words, market forces would no longer determine what was produced or imported. Early in the war, shoemakers might have made gentlemen's fine riding boots if a market existed, even if that meant fewer boots for the infantry. Governments gradually asserted control over industries deemed non-essential. Under the Hindenburg Programme, these industries were not technically shut down, but they were deprived of labour and raw materials. But whilst in theory it was possible for a government to control the type and quantity of goods produced, in practice manifold difficulties arose. Governments often lacked the expertise, confidence or will to intervene, especially since those with power (the industrial oligarchy) often stood most to lose from expanded state authority and were most inclined to resist it. In managing output, governments usually appealed first for voluntary restraint, then turned to polite cajoling and only reluctantly resorted to regulating producers.

Production could be made more efficient through scientific improvements which increased output per labourer. Across Europe, the war inspired industrial modernization. Assembly lines were introduced, standardization was imposed, labour became more specialized and the pace of electrification quickened. The construction of huge factories allowed combatants to exploit economies of scale. Improvements in the transportation network also reduced inefficiencies caused by delays. In Britain, for instance, productivity improvements brought by industrial expansion and technological modernization meant that an 18-pounder high explosive shell cost the government 32s in January 1915, and by the end of the year just 12s 6d. Much of the new technology introduced already existed before the war, as was the case with Bessemer converters for the steel industry. But producers had not previously been motivated to introduce it. This was particularly the case in Britain where supposedly secure imperial markets had encouraged inefficiency. The importance of productivity improvements can be gauged by the fact that while production increased massively during the war, the size of the industrial labour force actually declined in Germany and increased by just 100,000 in Britain.

But science could achieve only so much. By far the greatest manpower savings were achieved through radical changes in the management of labour. In the half-century before the war, trade unions had amassed significant power for the individual worker by carving out small monopolies for individual trades. Agreements with employers regarding which skilled workers could perform which specific tasks protected workers from being undercut by non-union labour, but in the process introduced massive complexity and inefficiency into production. The relaxation of these agreements paved the way for dilution, by which unions accepted (or were forced to accept) that previously skilled trades could be performed by semi-skilled or non-skilled labour. This did not mean that skilled men were suddenly made redundant and sent to the front, but rather that production processes were reorganized so that the skilled worker only performed tasks which genuinely required skill. The rest of his duties were either mechanized or performed by a less skilled worker.

Governments sought not only to manage but also to control labour. Since the worker is most powerful when labour is scarce, shortages during the war played into the hands of the unions and should have increased their power. But government intervened by introducing new laws limiting the unions' ability to exploit the situation. Both Britain and Germany passed laws restricting the worker's right to change jobs.[5] The Patriotic Auxiliary Service Law in Germany was the most comprehensive measure of worker control introduced by any nation during the war. It required all males aged between 18 and 60 to accept essential war jobs, if they were not already in military service. Universities were to be closed down, the Sunday holiday was to be abandoned and women encouraged into war work. In the same way, under the terms of the Munitions of War Act, passed in Britain in 1915, the government assumed wide powers to control labour, in the process restricting the freedom of the worker. Wartime governments also introduced compulsory bargaining legislation and prohibitions on the right to strike. Conscription was occasionally used to rid workplaces of troublesome agitators. These rulings played into the hands of the employers, contributing to a rise in working-class consciousness and antagonism between classes. Coercive laws nevertheless could not stop determined workers from striking; in all the combatant countries industrial action increased during the war, as the initial mood of co-operation evaporated.

Conscription was in theory a way to manage labour. It was not simply about moving men into the trenches; it also allowed governments to select those men whose removal from the workforce would be least detrimental to war production. Unfortunately, governments seldom used these powers well – as revealed by the occasional need to recall skilled men from the front. Industrial conscription, acting in tandem with military conscription, might have allowed a better management of labour and a balancing of civilian and military requirements. But attempts to introduce industrial conscription in Britain and Germany ran aground because of doctrinal objections and fears of working-class rebellion.

The unions sacrificed much, but at the same time gained some concessions. The Patriotic Auxiliary Service Law recognized the trade unions and confirmed the workers' rights of association. In Britain, unions were brought into the management process, for instance in determining which workers should be reserved for civilian work. Governments also made promises about an eventual return to pre-war practices. Greater and more comprehensive government control reduced the power of labour but at the same time made the workers more cohesive as a group. Divisions between various crafts and between the

---

[5] Germany, unlike Britain, accepted higher wages as legitimate grounds for changing jobs. But this merely encouraged wage inflation.

skilled and less skilled were reduced. Though the workers felt some-what emasculated by the war, at the end of it they presented a more united front.

Dilution and the various laws controlling labour paved the way for the introduction of substitute workers, many of them unskilled itiner-ant male labourers who suddenly found themselves in secure, relatively well-paid employment. Workers in non-essential industries were either directed by their governments into war work, or were enticed by the higher pay in that work. Combatants also turned to juveniles, the dis-abled, the retired and returned servicemen for manpower. Germany even tried to force men from occupied areas in Belgium and Poland to work in war industries, a programme more controversial than successful.

The most significant new source of labour in the war industries was women, who proved efficient at the exacting processes involved in munitions making. 'If the women working in the factories stopped for twenty minutes', the French General Joseph Joffre once remarked, 'France would lose the war.'[6] Yet contrary to myth, the women who entered industry were almost all working class, and most already had jobs, or at least were not without job experience. In other words, waged labour was nothing new for them; the female labour force did not increase to the extent which is often carelessly presumed. What was different was the *type of jobs* they performed. The proportion of women to men in German industry was 22% in 1913, and 35% in 1918. The cor-responding figures for Britain are 26% and 35%. Most of these women would have worked (or expected to work) in traditionally female employment (domestic service, food processing, millinery, light indus-try) which was disrupted by the war. Most found better pay and more secure employment in war industry. German women, for instance, saw their average earnings rise by 158% during the war, compared to 112% for men. But the conditions were hard and sometimes danger-ous and the work by its very nature temporary. Though these women gained some status and self-esteem through participation in the war effort, real progress was strictly limited since nearly everyone accepted that after the war these women would give up their jobs to returning soldiers and would return to pre-war patterns of employment.

The improvisation of a war machine was everywhere chaotic. Gov-ernment intervention, lacking plan or direction, could be misdirected and contradictory. But there is no doubting the industrial expansion which each country underwent in order to meet its army's voracious appetite for munitions. British defence expenditure expanded from £91 million in 1913 to £1.956 billion in 1918, the latter figure being 80

[6] M. Ferro, *La Grande Guerre* (Paris, 1969), p. 292.

per cent of all government expenditure. In 1914, 91 artillery pieces and 300 machine guns were produced. In 1918, the figures were 8,039 and 120,900, respectively. But the most impressive achievement was perhaps that of France, given her loss of industrially important territory in 1914. Starting from a much higher base than Britain, France still managed to increase her rifle production 290-fold and machine gun production 170-fold. One has to conclude that the war inspired in France an industrial surge which should have occurred forty years earlier.

Mobilizing Minds

Since civilians were involved in the war effort as never before, their energies had somehow to be inspired and channelled. Propaganda designed to encourage ever greater effort was improvised by governments and concerned individuals. Civilians were constantly reminded of their relationship to the war: thus it became patriotic to use less fuel, waste less food, refuse to go on strike, collect scrap metal, be optimistic and, of course, volunteer for the forces. Millions of posters reminded citizens of the correct behaviour.

At the same time, civilians had to be persuaded that their country's cause was just and that the war was going well – in other words that the sacrifices had justification. Mythic images were frequently used to remind citizens of the purpose of their struggle. These, of course, bore little relation to reality: British posters idealized a green and pleasant land foreign to those who knew only dark satanic mills. Convincing the population of the nobility of their cause also meant reminding the people of the enemy's evil. The German people were told that the war was Russia's fault, the French that it was Germany's. German invaders were accused of atrocities by Belgian, French and British propagandists, while the Germans claimed that the British blockade killed the infirm, the old and babies. Tales of raped nuns, women with their breasts cut off and babies impaled on bayonets were told in every language, and bore a remarkable similarity to stories from previous wars.

The two main objects of propaganda often worked against each other. Reports that the war was going well acted against pleas for redoubled effort. The problem was all the more acute because the combatants had so little experience in mobilizing minds. Efforts were often crude, counterproductive, disorganized and *ad hoc*. Private propaganda organized by concerned patriots often worked against the efforts of official agencies. It is difficult, in the end, to assess the effectiveness of propaganda campaigns. The Germans claimed that British propaganda was instrumental in their defeat. But, since this allegation dovetails nicely with the 'stab in the back' thesis popularized by Adolf Hitler, one needs to be wary of according it much credibility. Much propaganda was based on a poor understanding of civilians' commitment to the war. War encourages citizens to believe the best about their country; patriotism rises in direct relation to a perceived threat. Both British and German workers declared an industrial truce at the start of the war, without government persuasion. In Britain, the most impressive surge in support for the war came not as a result of any propaganda campaign, but because of the startling success of the German offensive of spring 1918.[7] This suggests, in turn, that censorship – the other tool of those assigned to manipulate public opinion – has dubious utility, based as it is on the misguided assumption that the public can not be trusted with bad news. Yet all governments assumed sweeping powers over the press.

The cinema, which had experienced a massive surge in popularity in the decade before the war, was an important tool in the manipulation of morale. Films and newsreels could keep the public informed, encourage greater effort, and keep people entertained and happy. There was also a gradual recognition that concerts, dance-halls, pubs and clubs were useful in keeping the people content when they were not working. But this recognition was not without its exceptions. Sporting contests, because they drew fit men away from the forces, were curtailed, some would argue unjustifiably. Licensing hours and the potency of beer were also limited. Fearful of grain shortages, the German government outlawed the consumption of spirits, but beer (or what passed for beer) continued to be produced. Full prohibition might have meant a more sober population and even a better-fed one (since grain used for beer would make bread) but the threat of widespread discontent gave governments cold feet.

Because the First World War was not truly total in the sense that civilians did not (with few exceptions) come under attack, a chasm of experience developed between the home front and the fighting front. Soldiers felt deep antagonism toward civilians who, they felt, could never understand the horror of the trenches. This chasm was both an advantage and a disadvantage for those who had to mobilize minds. When it came to the soldiers' suffering, ignorance was perhaps bliss. But, as the Second World War would demonstrate, sacrifices shared tend to be more easily endured. It was impossible to establish a truly

---

[7] It is well to remember that the poet Rupert Brooke, out of fashion on the eve of war, gained in popularity because he articulated the British sense of heroic mission. The war inspired a collective craving for bad patriotic poetry and sugary, sentimental songs. For every Wilfred Owen there were ten romantic rhymers who have deservedly been forgotten.

co-operative war effort if the worst experience of war – death and injury – remained a forbidden zone for most civilians.

Housing, Food and Health

Total war is unhealthy. While soldiers are killed, civilians starve. Those most vulnerable – the poor, elderly and very young – are the most common victims. These assumptions, though generally valid, need careful qualification. During the First World War, deprivation was not universal. Improvements in living standards were not uncommon. Some people emerged from the war healthier than they entered it.

That said, in the area of housing decline was the rule. Towns caught in the path of opposing armies were often completely destroyed, with a resultant tide of refugees. France lost 290,000 houses in the battle areas, and absorbed over 900,000 refugees, 150,000 from Belgium. But far more important was the effect of war on housing in areas untouched by combat. The need for labour meant that the construction industry virtually ground to a halt. Since working-class housing was already in a poor state before the war, the situation became even more appalling during four years of forced neglect. At the same time, a housing shortage developed in areas affected by the wartime industrial boom. Workers left towns and villages, converging on cities where the housing shortage was already acute. Rampant overcrowding resulted, with a consequent rise in diseases associated with poor housing – tuberculosis, bronchitis, rheumatic fever, etc. Governments, preoccupied with winning the war, could do little to alleviate poor conditions beyond promising improvements when victory came.

The food supply was everywhere severely restricted. Before the war, France was nearly self-sufficient in most commodities and was a net exporter of food, as was Italy. Germany produced 90% of the food she consumed. Austrian industry and Hungarian farms had a symbiotic relationship which rendered the Dual Monarchy virtually self-sufficient in food. Russia was the largest exporter of agricultural products in the world. Yet all these countries suffered drastic food shortages during the war. In Germany, conditions deteriorated to such an extent that civilians were allotted rations well below subsistence levels. The cereal ration was 64% of pre-war consumption, that of meat 18% and fats just 12%. Austria's agricultural production was 41% of pre-war levels, Hungary's 57%. The country to fare best was ironically Britain, who before the war could feed herself from home production only 125 days out of a year. Her salvation was her navy, which insured a reasonably steady flow of food imports. Yet, for a short period, Britain nearly went the way of the other combatants. At the height of the German U-boat campaign in 1917, Britain was reduced to just a few days' supply of sugar and a week or so of meat.

Food production fell drastically (by approximately 33% across Europe) mainly because of the shortage of farm labour. France, once the larder of Europe, imported 639,000 tons of food in 1917. Her grain harvest that year was down by 40%. (Granted, 20% of France's pre-war wheat crop, 26% of her oats and nearly 50% of her sugar beets came from areas occupied by Germany during the war.) Gripped by a short-war mentality, no combatant foresaw a food problem, and therefore nothing was done to stop the exodus of farm labourers into factories and the military. Agricultural production was affected in other ways. Horses were commandeered by armies. Farm machinery could not be replaced when it broke down, since tractor factories were making military vehicles. Chemicals used for fertilizers were suddenly needed for explosives manufacture. (Though German agriculture was nearly self-sufficient before the war, one-third of the fertilizers and chemicals used were imported.) The British blockade caused disastrous shortages in Germany and Austria-Hungary. The Central Powers made use of the farm production of allies and of captured areas, but transportation and manpower problems prevented those countries from producing the surplus Germany imagined she would be able to exploit. These were backward economies which had trouble feeding their own people, much less Germans. Nor did German-occupied areas of France and Belgium yield much of value; civilians there were fed by their compatriots who were allowed to cross battle-lines with food convoys.

The more serious the food situation, the more inclined governments were to intervene. Government intervention dealt with two concerns: supply and consumption. In the first category, the automatic response was to increase imports. Germany got some food from Scandinavia, Holland and Switzerland, but the Allied blockade prevented her looking further afield. Because the Entente theoretically had access to the rest of the world (as long as U-boat losses could be controlled), its food shortages did not reach crisis proportions.

At home, steps could be taken to secure replacement farm labour. Britain, for instance, encouraged women to work on farms, though with only limited success. Germany was forced to use 900,000 prisoners of war on her farms, a number roughly equal (in number, not productivity) to her agricultural labour force during peacetime. France used women, children, prisoners and old men, but still had to recall 300,000 soldiers to work the farms. The fertilizer problem was partially resolved by the development of new sources of nitrogen. Pasture was converted to arable land, thus increasing grain production at the expense of meat.

Ersatz substitutes for coffee, eggs, milk, butter and a host of other commodities were found, much to the disgust of the consumer. In Germany,
some 11,000 such substitutes were registered with the government.
We can trace the process of adaptation in food production through the
wartime history of the humble loaf of bread, the staple of the working-
class diet. As the war progressed, the milling process became less wasteful, with the loaf darker and less digestible. Rye, oats, barley, even
woodshavings and fine sand were added, while fat, salt and sweetening
were removed. By the end of the war the loaf would probably have
made better artillery ammunition than food.

Consumption could be controlled by making food less appealing:
tinned fish instead of fresh, brown bread instead of white, etc. The British recognized that fresh bread was more appetizing, therefore regulations were passed stipulating that bread could not be sold unless it was
at least eight hours old. But governments mainly controlled consumption of food through price fixing and rationing. Both measures were
adopted reluctantly and less than wholeheartedly since they benefited
the consumer at the expense of the producer. (Though it has to be said
that farmers everywhere had a good war.) Price fixing was designed to
cool the temper of the workers, who found that their wages did not
keep pace with food price rises. Average real wages declined by 15%
in Britain, 23% in Germany, 33% in Italy and by as high as 57% in
Russia during the war. Germany started fixing the prices of potatoes,
sugar and grain in 1914, France in the following year. Britain did not
tamper with prices until 1917, when workers showed signs of serious
discontent. Price fixing could, however, result in the opposite of the
effect intended. In Germany, controls on the price of milk and grain
simply persuaded farmers to reduce production of both commodities
in favour of meat, the price of which was not controlled. Milk became
virtually unavailable outside the black market, a phenomenon repeated
whenever the price of a commodity was fixed.

Rationing was adopted in France and Britain to reduce worker discontent, since without it food simply went where the money was. In
Germany, the problem was much more serious, and rationing had to
be adopted (as early as January 1915 for bread) in order to prevent widespread starvation. Russia, whose export market dwindled because of the
war, found herself with a food surplus in rural areas. But, because inflation hit manufactured goods harder than agricultural produce, farmers
lost much of their purchasing power and thus simply refused to sell
their produce. Food shortages in urban areas, already serious because
of the collapse of the transport system, therefore worsened.

Government controls sometimes led to an improvement in nutritional
standards. Less refined food saved labour and production costs, but

also meant a more nutritious (if less desirable) end product. Wholewheat bread (even with sand and woodshavings added) was more nutritious than the pre-war white loaf. Shortages of meat sometimes led to a reliance on more nutritional fish (usually tinned), beans and pulses. Consumption of butter and sugar declined drastically, leaving the consumer unhappy but healthier. Shortages of sugar and grain forced reductions in the potency and availability of alcohol, with attendant beneficial effects. Rationing often meant that the very poor were provided access to a quantity of food they had not previously enjoyed. The losers in this homogenization of dietary standards were the better-off, who were denied access to an amount of food which their money would ordinarily have bought. But, lest one assume that diets were democratized, it should be emphasized that rationing seldom lived up to lofty ideals. A black market, in which only money talked, did thrive.

These unanticipated improvements occurred only in those countries (particularly Britain) where food shortages did not reach a point of crisis. No amount of tinkering with consumption or production could alter the fact that Germany did not have enough food to feed her population. It is no wonder, therefore, that food riots were common in the later stages of the war. Generally speaking, in every combatant country, workers found that wages did not keep pace with inflation; therefore living standards tumbled. Italian food production declined by only 10 per cent during the war, but since workers were already seriously impoverished before 1914, nutrition standards could ill afford even this slight drop in production. But not all workers suffered equally or indeed absolutely. Many who had struggled to feed families due to unsteady, poorly-paid employment suddenly found themselves earning unheard-of wages in secure jobs. Often a family enjoyed the benefits of more than one income, as the mother or an older child found jobs in war industries. The removal, to the forces, of the male breadwinner meant the loss of his income, but it often also meant that the biggest drain on family income was now fed, clothed and housed by the state. Thus, in some cases, the amount of money spent on food per family member actually increased during the war, with a resultant rise in health standards.

Dietary changes, full employment, disintegration of the housing stock, etc. meant that families were buffeted in different directions as far as health standards were concerned. Much depended on the individual family's unique circumstances. German wage rates in war industries rose by 142% during the war, but by just 68% in civil industries. Productivity improvements (in all countries) meant that semi-skilled workers on piece rates often earned more than skilled workers on time rates – up to 33% more in Rhineland munitions factories. If the family had children of working age, if war-related work was available and capricious illness kept at bay, the war might have meant improved health. If, however, father was away at the front and mother had to look after a number of small children in a damp and dingy flat on an income ravaged by wartime inflation, the result might mean serious diet-related illnesses and even death. What is certain is that Europeans were neither universally nor uniformly enfeebled by the war.

Health statistics are, however, notoriously bad at measuring grief and stress, and the physical ailments associated with these mental conditions. A woman whose family income rose because of the war and who was suddenly able to feed her family better would not necessarily have felt that the war had been good to her. She might still have had to deal with constant, corrosive anxiety if a loved one was in danger at the front. Or, worse, she might have to confront the death of one close to her – a husband, father, lover or son. Given the rigidly patriarchal structure of European societies, this often meant the depletion of the very core of her identity.

War and Society – the Long-term Consequences

Those who believe that total war fundamentally altered the complexion of society usually focus on two groups: women and the working class. Women, so the argument goes, gained personal esteem and societal recognition by moving into jobs vacated by men. This was supposedly converted, after the war, into political gains, be they concrete reforms like enfranchisement or ethereal ones like gender equality. The workers likewise supposedly made gains through their contribution to the war. Wartime shortages of labour increased the power of the working class, at the same time making it more cohesive and assertive. Government was forced to negotiate with trade unions on a more equal basis. A mixing of the classes (especially in the trenches) is supposed to have led to greater harmony between classes and an 'inspection effect' – greater awareness of working-class conditions and greater desire to effect improvements.

These positive effects have been grossly exaggerated. Take the case of women. During the war, they were but temporary men – cheap labour. The differential between male and female wages in Germany narrowed as a result of the war, but by 1918 women's earnings in industry were still only 50–60 per cent of those of men. The fact that women could be paid so much less for basically similar work increased antagonism between the sexes and, needless to say, did nothing for gender equality. Women never attained the status of skilled workers, the real source of power in the labour hierarchy. Without that status, they were expendable, in the same way that unskilled or semi-skilled men were before the war. Women who took up male jobs understood that they were to surrender these jobs at war's end and were often the first to defend this proviso. Very few had their consciousness raised to an extent that they rejected the usual pattern of a working-class woman's life: work, followed by marriage, followed by a family. Most, in fact, appear to have welcomed a return to that status quo. Thus, though their sense of self-worth may have risen during the war, very few found opportunities after it to take advantage of their greater self-esteem by charting a different course for themselves.

There is also a serious flaw in the argument that women can gain status in society by taking up men's jobs. Status in a patriarchal society is calculated according to a male-orientated measure of importance. If a job becomes essentially 'woman's work', its status declines, a decline highlighted by the lower pay attached to it. This is particularly obvious if one looks at clerical work, a predominantly male occupation before the war. Wartime labour shortages resulted in more women becoming clerks and secretaries, with the result that the status of these jobs declined. Few men wanted to return to clerical work after the war, therefore these cast-off jobs were left to women, who were paid less.

War reinforces the fundamentally masculine role of warrior and the feminine role of helpless maiden. Women, as sweethearts, lovers or prostitutes, satisfy the sexual and romantic fantasies of men home on leave, roles not conducive to gender equality. War also renders societies more conservative by encouraging a nostalgia for a mythical past of prosperity and security. This has a particularly profound effect upon women, who become the icons of tradition – those who keep the home fires burning. During the war, motherhood took on added importance as lives became more precious. Women were encouraged to play closer attention to the needs of their children and were encouraged to have more of them to make up for the loss of life. Deprivation among children was blamed on maternal neglect rather than on poverty. Whilst there was a great deal of male pressure behind this cult of motherhood, one suspects that many women welcomed a return to a nurturing role – a role in which they were acknowledged to be proficient. In comparison to the home, the noisy, dirty, tedious factory had few attractions, other than pay. Thus it is no surprise that immediately after the war Europeans felt a common desire to rebuild through the family, as evidenced by rising marriage and birth rates. It is safe to assume that women were willing partners in this regeneration.

Advances made by workers after the war depended upon retreat by women, therefore it is difficult to imagine how both groups could have benefited from the war. The workers feared that the introduction of female industrial labour would permanently erode union power and depress wages. In fact this did not happen. The number of female industrial labourers in Britain after the war was lower than the number before the war, a statistic duplicated in Germany. But, while male workers won this concession, a return to their pre-war status should not be confused with progress.

Advancements made by workers were dependent upon the shortage of labour. No matter how much the worker's consciousness may have been raised by the war, his power was, as always, subject to the vagaries of the trade cycle. Thus, while the immediate post-war boom seemed to offer opportunities for the newly assertive working class, when boom turned to bust, the workers were enfeebled. Whatever else might be said about the turbulent inter-war years, they were not a time of notable worker solidarity or power.

It is difficult to imagine how a war so lucrative for the business class and so hard on the workers (who sacrificed lives and rights) should be seen as a time of brilliant progress for the latter. In any case, class consciousness is not exclusive to the working class. The middle class also had its consciousness raised by this war. Those on fixed incomes were badly hit by inflation. Others felt that they were unfairly asked, through ever-increasing taxes, to bear the cost of the war. Since this war was particularly deadly for those with the misfortune to be officers, the middle class also suffered disproportionately high death rates. A sense of adversity forced this once-amorphous class to become more cohesive and combative. The middle class emerged from the war determined to gain back what they had lost. The most profound example of this assertiveness was their objection to funding (through taxes) the social improvements which the workers felt were their due reward for war service. In Britain, middle-class assertiveness took the form of groups like the Middle Class Union and the opposition to the General Strike. In more volatile Germany, it took the form of support for the Nazi party.

Inter-class antagonism was far more significant than cross-class camaraderie. The latter was supposedly encouraged in the trenches. But that is a distinctly romantic fantasy stimulated by the writings of Wilfred Owen and Erich Maria Remarque. It is difficult to imagine how an authoritarian, status-conscious, highly rigid institution like the military could possibly be the furnace for a social revolution. In the army, deference to social betters was established policy – one important element to the maintenance of discipline. Nor did the working-class soldier derive extra status or self-esteem from the trench experience, where lives were so cheap and easily wasted.

We end with the psychological effects of this war – a subject seldom seriously studied, perhaps because of the difficulties in measuring their extent. Across Europe, the losses caused by the war were prodigious. France lost 1.3 million men, Russia and Germany nearly 2 million, Italy 500,000 and the British Empire almost a million. Demographers argue that post-war baby booms and changes in emigration patterns quickly rectified these losses. But not in the hearts of those who suffered a loved one's departure. The Lost Generation was made up not of those who died but of those condemned to go on living. It is well to bear in mind the scourge of ubiquitous death when considering the apparently positive benefits of total war.

14

Warfare and National Defence

David French

Contrary to the widely held expectation, the war which broke out in Europe in August 1914 was not over by Christmas. In the ensuing four years Europe underwent a war not equalled in terms of duration, intensity and destructiveness since the French Revolutionary and Napoleonic Wars a century earlier. Approximately ten million men died in combat and about the same number died from the indirect consequences of the war. The German, Austro-Hungarian, Russian and Ottoman empires were toppled and even the victor Powers were left with deep psychological scars. This dreadful outcome was the result of a combination of military, economic and political developments which had taken place in the preceding half-century.

War Plans and Military Innovation before 1914

In the Franco-Prussian War of 1870–1 Prussia's short-service conscript soldiers had defeated the long-service professionals of the French army and created a powerful new German state in the heart of Europe. In the following decades each of the European Great Powers opted to ape the victorious Prussians and base their form of military organization upon short-service conscripts. Young men at about the age of twenty were enlisted for a period of compulsory military training which usually lasted for two to three years. They were then released into the reserve, ready to be called up in the event of a national emergency. Consequently, by August 1914 each of the Great Powers was able to mobilize an army numbered in millions. The only exception to this was Britain which, because of its world-wide empire, had continued to rely upon long-service professionals.

Armies numbered in millions would have become military dinosaurs, immobile and starving, but for the fact that in the second half of the nineteenth century Europe experienced the 'railway revolution'. The

Table 14.1 Battle deaths 1914–1918

	No. of deaths
The Allied Powers	
France	1,400,000
Britain	900,000[a]
Italy	615,000
Russia	1,700,000[b]
Serbia	45,000
Greece	5,000
Romania	335,000
Belgium	13,000
USA	50,000
The Central Powers	
Germany	1,800,000
Austria-Hungary	1,200,000
Bulgaria	90,000
Turkey	325,000

[a] Includes India, Australia, New Zealand, S. Africa and Canada.
[b] In addition there were 1,500,000 Civil War deaths 1917–20.

railways not only transformed the European economy, they also revolutionized the way in which Europe could make war by making it possible to mobilize and transport hundreds of thousands of soldiers quickly from their places of mobilization, deep in the interior, to the frontiers. But if the railways determined how each belligerent would mobilize its army, they were also one of the reasons why their war plans failed in the opening weeks of the war. As each army enjoyed roughly the same degree of mobility, none of them was able to steal a march on its enemies and wrest an advantage from the possession of superior strategic mobility. It was a similar story when the troops disembarked from their trains and prepared to engage each other on the battlefield. For their tactical mobility on or near the battlefield, armies relied, as they had always done, on marching men and horses.

However, science and industrialization had multiplied the lethality of the weapons soldiers used on the battlefield. By the early twentieth century every Power had armies which were equipped with breach-loading rifles, machine guns and artillery pieces firing cylindro-conical bullets or shells which were propelled by smokeless powder. The effect of these developments was to increase enormously the range, volume and accuracy of fire which troops could deliver. Pre-war military thinkers were not blind to the lethality of modern weapons but they found it difficult to produce a solution to the problem of how men were to cross the zone of enemy fire and close with the enemy. Hitherto armies had tried to control soldiers' fears by moving them in dense masses in the hope that the foolhardy would encourage the timid to go forward. But in the era of smokeless powder and long-range rifle fire, men advancing in close order would be slaughtered; yet if they tried to advance in open order, they might become so dispersed that their officers would lose control of them and the advance would grind to a halt as, seeing their comrades shot beside them, the survivors went to ground. Camouflage was one possible solution, and it was not coincidental that in the late nineteenth century most European armies shed the brightly coloured uniforms they had worn for the past two hundred years in favour of khaki or grey in an attempt to make themselves less conspicuous. But camouflage alone would not stop a bullet. The victory of the Japanese army in Manchuria in 1904–5 seemed to suggest that high morale was the best solution and that victory would go to the troops who had been inculcated with a stoicism which amounted almost to a contempt for death.

The war plans of the Great Powers, which had been in constant preparation for many years before 1914, had one theme in common. Convinced by the Prussian experience in 1870 that the side which attacked first would win, each Power planned to take the offensive against its enemies immediately after the declaration of war. Not one of them recognized that it might be wiser to remain on the defensive, absorb the enemy's initial blow and then mount a devastating counterattack. In 1890 the Germans rejected Bismarck's policy of isolating France by remaining on good terms with Austria and Russia. When in 1894 France and Russia became allies, the German General Staff believed that they faced the nightmare possibility of a two-front war. Confronted by the vast open spaces of Russia, the German generals concluded that a quick victory in the east could not be achieved. They therefore planned to defeat France first before turning against Russia. Confronted by powerful French fortifications along the Franco-German frontier, Count Alfred von Schlieffen, the Chief of the General Staff from 1891 to 1906, decided to outflank them by advancing through neutral Belgium. France was to be crushed within six weeks so that the German army could then turn eastward to defeat Russia. The French and Russians had no intention of waiting passively for these blows to fall upon them. Fearful of being overrun by the Germans, the French placed growing pressure upon their Russian allies to hasten their own mobilization plans so that they could mount a rapid strike against East Prussia and thus take some of the pressure off the French army. Until about 1910 the Russians were reluctant to agree, for, like the Germans, they too faced a two-front war, against both Germany and Germany's ally, Austria-Hungary; but eventually they obliged. The Austrians also had their own offensive plans, for a war against Serbia or Russia, but not both at once, and even the British General Staff planned to send its army to northern France, although their plans were not endorsed by the Cabinet until after the war had begun.

Tactics and Strategy in the Great War

On 3 August 1914 Germany declared war on France and two days later Britain declared war on Germany. Publicly the British did so to preserve Belgian neutrality, but in private the British government was determined to ensure that Germany did not defeat France and Russia and secure its own hegemony over Europe. Each nation threw huge numbers of men against its enemies in a vain attempt to break down their resistance. All they succeeded in doing was to produce horrifyingly large casualty lists and to demonstrate the superiority of the defence over the offence. Between 25–30 August the Russian advance into East Prussia was repulsed by the newly appointed commander of the German Eighth Army, General Paul von Hindenburg* and his Chief of Staff, General Erich Ludendorff,* at Tannenberg. Early in September the German advance through Belgium and northern France was brought to a halt outside Paris when the French Commander-in-Chief, General Joffre, mounted a counterattack on the river Marne. Even the Serbs succeeded eventually in repulsing the Austrians after they had temporarily occupied the Serbian capital, Belgrade. By the end of 1914, there was a tactical stalemate on both the Eastern and Western fronts. In France and Flanders, and in Poland and Galicia, the troops of all of the armies reacted in the same way: they tried to make themselves safe by digging field entrenchments.

This minimized their casualties, but it did not promise to bring the war to a satisfactory conclusion. By Christmas of 1914 two alliances were confronting each other. The Entente alliance consisted of France, Russia, Britain, Belgium and Serbia; it was joined by Italy in May 1915. They were opposed by the Central Powers, comprising Germany and Austria-Hungary, joined by the Ottoman Empire in November 1914 and further reinforced by Bulgaria in October 1915. But merely adding extra soldiers to each alliance did not solve the fundamental problem of how each side was to attain its objectives. Between 1915 and 1917 both alliances mounted a series of great offensives designed either to effect a clear breakthrough in the enemy defences, to wear down their opponents' powers of resistance by killing their soldiers, or to bring succour to an ailing ally. In September and October 1915 the British and French mounted an autumn offensive to show their commitment to Russia shortly after the German and Austrian armies had conquered Russian Poland. Between February and July 1916 the German Commander-in-Chief, General von Falkenhayn, mounted an offensive against the French fortress of Verdun which was designed to bring France to the peace table by exhausting French military manpower. The operation only came to a halt when a British army under Sir Douglas Haig* and a French army under Marshal Foch* attacked across the river Somme between July and November 1916. Initially they hoped rapidly to break through the German line. When it was apparent that they could not do so they switched instead to trying to exhaust German manpower.

In April 1917 the new French Commander-in-Chief, General Nivelle, mounted a disastrous offensive on the Chemin des Dames which failed to do more than dent the German defences but caused a large part of the demoralized French army to mutiny. Most French soldiers were willing to hold their trenches against the Germans, but they adamantly refused to take part in any further futile and costly assaults. Nivelle's successor, General Pétain,* was willing to acquiesce and decided to avoid any more major offensives until the arrival of a huge American army in 1918 or 1919 gave the Entente an overwhelming superiority and made their victory certain. The British, however, were not content to be so patient, and morale in the British army remained sufficiently high to enable Haig to launch a long-cherished offensive from the Ypres salient between July and November 1917 designed to clear the German army away from the Belgian coast. These battles have passed into European folklore as the epitome of military madness, when an entire generation of young men was sacrificed in return for a few square miles of mud. The combination of quick-firing field artillery, machine guns, trenches and barbed wire seemed to have given a decisive tactical advantage to the defence over the offence.

The most imaginative attempt to break this stalemate was undertaken by the British, who sent first a fleet and then troops to the Dardanelles in an effort to knock out Germany's ally, Turkey, open a supply route to Russia, and persuade the Balkan neutrals to join the Entente alliance and open a new front against the Central Powers. But that attempt, too, failed, when the British found the Turks to be a much more formidable enemy than they predicted. In March 1915 a purely naval attack against the shore batteries which barred the passage up the Dardanelles to the Turkish capital, Constantinople, foundered when half a dozen Allied battleships were sunk or damaged by a hidden minefield, an episode which spoke volumes about the inability of even the world's greatest navy to project its power close inshore. A month later British, Australian, New Zealand and French troops were landed on the Gallipoli Peninsula in an effort to destroy the batteries which covered the minefields, only to find themselves the victims of the same kind of tactical conundrum which already ruled on the Western Front. In January 1916, after nine months of costly stalemate, the last remaining Allied troops were finally evacuated.

A second Anglo-French amphibious campaign was begun in October 1915 when both countries sent troops to the Greek port of Salonika in an attempt to open a route through Greece to assist Serbia, about to be crushed by a combined offensive mounted by German, Austrian and Bulgarian troops. Their assistance came too late to save the Serbs, but the Anglo-French force, later reinforced by Italian, Serbian and Russian troops, remained at Salonika for the rest of the war. Ostensibly the Allied force was to operate in conjunction with the Russians to place pressure on Bulgaria; in reality they were there so that the French, who were always more enthusiastic about the campaign than the British, could reduce Greece to the status of a French satellite and so strengthen their post-war influence in the eastern Mediterranean. But the British had their own post-war ambitions in the Levant, and in 1917 and 1918 directed their own efforts towards conquering Palestine, while at the same time taking great care to exclude their allies from any share of the spoils.

On the Eastern Front, however, where the ratio of soldiers to space was much lower than in the west, armies still retained the ability to break through their enemies' defences. The Germans demonstrated this against the Russians at Gorlice-Tarnow in May 1915 and proceeded to conquer most of Russian Poland as a result. The Russian General Brusilov did it in June 1916 when he inflicted about half a million casualties on the Austrian army. However, the cost of his victory, coming on top of the losses the Russian army had already suffered, was prohibitive. The Germans were able to despatch sufficient troops to sustain their ally, while in the winter and spring of 1917 the morale of the Russian army, beset not only by heavy casualties but by inflation and news of the hardships their families were suffering at home, slumped. When the garrison of Petrograd mutinied in March 1917 it paved the way for the collapse of the tsarist regime and the establishment of a Provisional Government. However, after one more half-hearted offensive in July 1917, the remnants of the Russian army disintegrated, the Bolsheviks were able to seize power in November 1917, and in March 1918 they signed the peace treaty of Brest-Litovsk with the Central Powers.

Both sides also tried to employ new military technologies to break the stalemate. Primitive aircraft were employed by each of the Powers in August 1914. Initially they were used purely for reconnaissance duties. Later, equipped with various signalling devices, including primitive wireless sets, they acted as airborne spotters for the artillery, pinpointing targets and correcting their aim. Aircraft equipped with bombs and machine-guns attacked enemy troops, while the smaller and more agile machines – 'scouts' in First World War parlance, later rechristened 'fighters' – attempted to protect friendly airspace. The Germans also employed lighter-than-air Zeppelins and heavier-than-air *Gotha* bombers in a primitive strategic bombing campaign directed against the civilian population in Britain, in the hope that mass panic would ensue and compel the British government to make peace. It did not; it merely reduced the distinction between combatants and civilians, thus adding a new dimension to the horrors of war, and in 1917 encouraged the British to established the Royal Air Force as the world's first independent air force so that they could retaliate in kind. At Ypres in April 1915 the Germans were the first belligerent to employ poisonous gas, although their example was quickly followed by their enemies. Britain's major contribution to the new technologies of war was the tank, the first of which were employed during the Battle of the Somme in September 1916. But each of these new weapons failed to have a decisive impact. This was partly because of their own inherent technological limitations and partly because they were initially employed in small quantities and as an adjunct to conventional warfare, rather than massed together in sufficient force to achieve a major breakthrough.

The longer the war continued, and the longer grew the casualty lists, the more determined most of the belligerent populations became to ensure that something positive came of it. Until 1917 any government which had suggested that the time was ripe for a compromise peace would have been swept away by a wave of public indignation. The issues at stake, the political and economic dominance of the whole of Europe and the redistribution of colonial power outside Europe, were of such magnitude as to make a compromise peace impossible until one or other of the warring coalitions no longer possessed the means to continue fighting. The Russians wanted Constantinople and guarantees for their Slav clients in south-eastern Europe that would have brought about the collapse of the Habsburg Empire. The Germans wanted massive territorial acquisitions and an empire stretching from Belgium to Baghdad. The French wanted the return of Alsace-Lorraine, forfeited to Germany in 1871, and the British wanted colonial spoils in Africa and the Middle East and the destruction of 'Prussian militarism', a clever catch-phrase for the destruction of the existing regime in Germany and its replacement by a more democratic one.

The enthusiasm which permeated the belligerents persisted for a surprisingly long time. It would be too mechanistic to attribute this simply to the ability of Europe's elites to manipulate their peoples through the use of mass propaganda techniques. But the effect of their enthusiasm is not in doubt. It made possible something which pre-war thinkers had predicted would be impossible, a long war. Despite the fact that young men of military age were everywhere called to the colours, the remaining men, and growing numbers of women, were willing to come forward to take their places in the factories and fields, to grow food and to produce the munitions which the armies needed in order to continue fighting. Everywhere civilians tightened their belts, were subjected to rationing and witnessed growing government controls over more and more aspects of social and economic life as an increasingly large proportion of national resources was harnessed to support the war effort. As this process continued, the very nature of war itself was transformed. Strategy was no longer merely a matter of attempting to concentrate the maximum number of guns, shells and soldiers at the vital point on the battlefield. Instead it became an exercise in striking the correct balance between meeting the needs of the fighting front and ensuring that the civilian population had enough resources so that their enthusiasm for the continuation of the war was not undermined by serious hardships. The First World War was the first total war of the industrial age.

Naval Warfare

The war at sea was also gripped by a tactical stalemate, for sea fighting had also been subject to the same industrial revolution that had transformed fighting on land in the second half of the nineteenth century. Ironclads and later steel-hulled steam-powered ships armed with rifled cannon took the place of wooden sailing ships powered by the wind and armed with smooth bore guns. The first major seagoing warship driven entirely by steam and not by sail, the British *HMS Devastation*, was launched in 1871. Each successive generation of battleships was bigger, faster and more heavily armed and armoured until the process reached its pre-war culmination in 1906 with the launching of *HMS Dreadnought*, the first all-big-gun battleship to be powered by steam-turbines, rather than the more conventional reciprocating engines. But although steam battleships were tactically far more powerful than their wooden predecessors, their greater tactical power was bought at the cost of a reduction in strategic flexibility. Sail-powered wooden fleets had been able to keep at sea almost indefinitely. Their operational capabilities were constrained only by the health of their crews, the need to replenish their food supplies and to repair storm damage. By contrast, steam-powered warships were so hungry for coal that they had to return to port every few weeks to replenish their fuel supplies. The cost of being a major naval power therefore rose, for if a state wished to project its naval power much beyond its own coastal waters, it had to possess a series of naval bases and coaling stations across the globe.

By 1914 all of the belligerents, but especially Britain and Germany, had invested much money and national pride in their fleets of Dreadnoughts. But the very magnitude of that investment made a rapid decision in the war at sea unlikely, for neither side felt that it enjoyed a sufficient numerical advantage to make victory certain, and was reluctant to gamble its entire investment on the outcome of a single battle. The German High Seas Fleet had been created as an expression of Germany's Great Power status and as a tool to blackmail the British into granting them political concessions. It had not been designed to win a war on its own, and the German admirals had no intention of obliging the Royal Navy by prematurely seeking a major battle in the North Sea. They preferred instead to try to reduce the size of the British Grand Fleet by a process of attrition, employing mines and U-boats to sink isolated British vessels. When the two fleets did finally stumble across each other at Jutland in May 1916 the result was a tactical victory for the Germans, in that they sunk more British ships than they lost, and a strategic victory for the British, in that their numerical superiority and the blockade of the Central Powers both remained intact. Although the High Seas Fleet did venture out of port several times after Jutland, it never again sought a fleet action, and when it was ordered to make a final attack in October 1918, its crews mutinied.

In February 1917 the Germans switched the focus of the naval war from the surface of the sea to underneath the waves. They declared unrestricted U-boat warfare in the hope that they could sink so many Entente merchant ships that Britain would sue for peace before the USA, which was bound to be enraged when its own ships were sunk, declared war and made its weight felt on the Western Front. Their gamble failed. The Germans had miscalculated. They had too few submarines to impose a watertight blockade on the British Isles, and the British, by a combination of rationing tonnage and, belatedly, introducing convoys, were able to maintain enough of their overseas trade to continue fighting. From the Entente's point of view the one positive result of the campaign was that it precipitated America's entry into the war in April 1917.

The Defeat of Germany

This proved decisive, although not in the way some commentators have suggested. American troops did not play a determining role in the battles on the Western Front in 1918. Indeed, the first American army was not activated in France until August 1918. But the knowledge that the USA had the potential to deploy a huge new army in 1919 was crucial in persuading the Germans that they had to act decisively and attack in order to win the war quickly in 1918. That in turn allowed France and Britain to break German military resistance, the linchpin of the Central Powers' coalition. By the end of 1917 the only things sustaining the resistance of Germany's allies and the German people was the knowledge that one of their mightiest enemies, Russia, was suing for peace, and the hope that the Germans might soon be able to deliver a knock-out blow against the French and British armies on the Western Front before they were overwhelmed in 1919 by the arrival of an unbloodied American army. Therefore between March and June 1918 the Germans mounted a series of offensives in France and Flanders which came close to dividing the British and French armies and driving the former into the sea. But ultimately they failed. The French and British were just able to absorb the German attacks and the German army, in making them, lost nearly a million men. Germany could no longer make good such losses, for they came on top of the horrendous losses of previous years. In 1916 alone the army had lost 282,000 men at Verdun, 500,000 on the Somme and 350,000 on the Eastern Front.

By the autumn of 1918 Germany had not only run out of men, but its soldiers and their families had run out of hope. Burdened by the certain knowledge that if the war continued into 1919 they would be hopelessly outnumbered, and made hungry and depressed by the Allied blockade, the resistance of much of the army disintegrated. A division of the Prussian Guards jeered at a division of Württembergers about to launch a counterattack, accusing them of being strikebreakers who were prolonging the war. Officers discovered increasing numbers of men who refused to obey orders and who preferred to desert rather than entrain for the front. When, beginning in August, the British and French armies, and in September the American army, began to counterattack and drive the Germans back beyond the start line of their spring offensive, the morale of the German army in the west finally broke. Allied and Bolshevik propaganda only served to weaken German resistance after the ordinary soldiers recognized that the tide of battle had turned decisively against Germany. Contrary to the post-war myth propagated by the German right, the home front did not stab the army in the back.

Morale at home only began to disintegrate after soldiers returning from the front told their compatriots that the army had been defeated in France. In November 1918 Germany underwent a socialist revolution which toppled the Kaiser and forced the high command to seek an armistice. The war ended when the German home and fighting fronts collapsed.

Lessons of the War

'Never again' was not the lesson which Europe's soldiers drew from their experiences between 1914 and 1918. Rather, their guiding light in the inter-war period was 'Never again in the same old way.' But beyond that each of the former belligerents drew different lessons depending upon their own wartime experiences. The one thing they had in common was that they devoted their attention to those factors which they thought had contributed most to their victory or defeat, and in particular looked for ways to avoid another expensive and lengthy war of attrition.

Air warfare had originated in the First World War as an ancillary to the war on land. But, as the range and carrying capacity of aircraft multiplied rapidly during the war, it became apparent to some airmen that aircraft might be more than just the eyes of the artillery: they might soon be a substitute for it, and a substitute capable of carrying destructive power far beyond the enemy's front line. Aircraft might possess the ability not just to kill soldiers at the front but also destroy guns and the factories which produced them. The lesson which the exponents of strategic bombing, like Sir Hugh Trenchard in Britain and Colonel Giulio Douhet in Italy, drew from the First World War was that wars were no longer won by armies in the field, for as long as they had the men and munitions they needed they could resist almost indefinitely. In the future, wars would be won and lost when the will to resist of the entire nation was broken, and the quickest way to do that was to direct air attacks against civilian targets far behind the enemy's lines. Strategic air bombardment could, they claimed, win wars by itself without the need to raise and commit huge armies to a war on the ground.

Some military thinkers in Russia, Britain and Germany believed that tanks and mechanization would enable them to avoid another attritional stalemate. In the 1920s and 1930s prophets of tank warfare such as Basil Liddell Hart and J. F. C. Fuller in Britain, Charles de Gaulle in France, Marshal Tukhachevski in the USSR and Heinz Guderian* in Germany, predicted that the new war would be fought by entire divisions composed of tanks. Such formations would be capable of breaking through the enemy's defences and paralysing his resistance by destroying his lines of communication and headquarters. But only in Germany was this vision put into practice in the opening phase of the Second World War. By 1932 the Red Army had over 2,000 tanks and was developing a doctrine of deep strategic penetration. But in the late 1930s Russia's plans for a large mechanized army were stifled by a combination of the Great Purges, which robbed the army of many of its best officers, and a misleading reading of the experiences of the Spanish Civil War. The defeat of the Francoist forces at the battle of Guadalajara in March 1937 seemed to indicate the superiority of the anti-tank gun over the tank. The British army in the 1920s was in the forefront of tank development. In 1927 it established the first completely mechanized brigade in any army, the Experimental Mechanized Force, and in the second half of the 1930s it became the first all-motorized army in the world. But further developments were blocked, largely because politicians fought shy of embarking on another continental land war at a time when memories of the grievous losses Britain had sustained in the last one were still fresh in the electorate's mind. They preferred instead to pursue a national strategy which suggested that Britain should fight the next European war using a mixture of economic blockade, air bombardment and the French army.

Only in Germany did the exponents of mobile armoured warfare have a significant influence over national strategy. The main lesson which German strategists drew from their experiences between 1914 and 1918 was that wars had to be made swift and decisive because Germany could not hope to win a protracted war of attrition fought on two fronts. The limitations placed upon the German armed forces and arms industry by the Treaty of Versailles further encouraged German planners to turn to mechanization as the best way of multiplying the effectiveness of the forces they were allowed. Although the Germans were forbidden by the terms of the Treaty of Versailles to possess tanks, they got around this restriction by secretly co-operating with the Soviet Union in the 1920s and conducting experiments with tanks in Russia. This meant that after Hitler* came to power in 1933 and flaunted the Versailles treaty, armoured-warfare enthusiasts like Guderian were able quickly to create an effective armoured force within the expanded German army. The German panzers also had the inestimable advantage that the German air force, the *Luftwaffe*, was willing to co-operate closely with them. Under its first Chief of Staff, General Weaver, the *Luftwaffe* had toyed with the idea of undertaking strategic air bombardment missions, but following Weaver's death in 1936, it switched its role to providing close air support for the army.

German Methods in the Second World War

The effectiveness of the Germans' Panzer divisions in 1940 owed much to the fact that the main lessons which the French drew from the First World War were very different. The French did have some officers like Charles de Gaulle and Jean Estienne, who advocated that the army should invest heavily in armoured divisions. But their ideas were rejected because their insistence on the need for a small, highly professional army ran directly counter to France's historic commitment to a 'nation in arms' drawn from the whole people. The majority of French officers and civilian strategists concluded that the war had shown that battles were won by devastating firepower and that the offence could only prevail if it had an overwhelming superiority in men and munitions. To ensure that the Germans could never enjoy such a superiority, the crux of French policy in the 1920s and 1930s was to create an impregnable series of defences along the Franco-German frontier, the Maginot line, in the expectation that concrete would minimize France's casualties. But their design was vitiated by four factors. They overlooked the fact that battles were decided not just by weight of firepower but also by speed and mobility. The Maginot line could be outflanked because it did not extend along the Franco-Belgian frontier to the Channel; it could be enveloped from the air because the French were too slow to invest in airpower; and if it was pierced or outflanked the French lacked sufficient mechanized and armoured formations to mount an effective counterattack.

The combination of Panzer divisions and close air support gave the German army an advantage which it did not lose until 1942. The German army had fewer tanks than the British and French in the summer of 1940, and qualitatively the French probably had the edge over their enemies. But the Germans enjoyed three advantages which proved decisive. They employed *Stuka* dive-bombers of the *Luftwaffe* in close co-operation with their panzers as flying artillery to demoralize enemy soldiers and to destroy stubborn pockets of enemy resistance. They used their tanks *en masse*, concentrating them in nine Panzer divisions, rather than scattering many of them in small groups amongst their infantry divisions as the French did. And they had a command and control system which allowed their generals to direct their forces towards their objectives with a speed which left their opponents bewildered. The same *blitzkrieg* tactics proved to be equally successful in the Balkans in 1941, in the North African desert in 1941–2 and in Russia until the battle for Moscow in December 1941.

But eventually the new technologies proved to be incapable of living up to the expectations of their exponents and bringing the war to a rapid and decisive conclusion. On land, by the end of 1942 Germany's enemies had discovered that by copying the Germans and forming their own armoured divisions, by equipping their infantry with lavish quantities of anti-tank guns and mines, and by employing sufficient fighters to shoot down the German *Stukas*, they could stop the panzers in their tracks. The belligerents also discovered that tanks created almost as many problems as they solved. Panzer divisions consumed enormous quantities of supplies. In 1914 a typical infantry division required about 100 tons of supplies each day. Much of that was accounted for by fodder for its transport horses which in the spring and summer was easily found in nearby fields. But tanks and the myriad of lorries and gun tractors which accompanied them could not live off the land so easily. They needed large quantities of spare parts and petrol if they were to function. In 1940 a German Panzer division used 300 tons of supplies daily. Four years later in Normandy, a typical American armoured division needed 1,000–1,500 tons each day. Paradoxically, therefore, although tanks increased tactical mobility, they did so at the cost of constraining strategic flexibility. Armies were now accompanied by an enormous 'tail' of workshops, supply lorries and petrol tankers, all of which proved to be very vulnerable for any army which did not enjoy air superiority, as the British and American air forces demonstrated in the Normandy campaign in the summer of 1944. Their fighter-bombers wrought so much havoc amongst the German divisions advancing from central France to the battlefield that eventually the Germans could only carry out road and rail movements under cover of darkness.

Air Power

The inter-war exponents of strategic bombing had based their predictions on the assumption that, to use the phrase of the British Prime Minister, Stanley Baldwin, the bomber would always get through. But by the late 1930s that was no longer necessarily the case. The British were the first nation to create an effective air-defence system. Ground radar stations detected incoming bombers when they were as much as forty miles from the coast. The first primitive radar sets could only discover the range and direction of the raiders; later, more advanced equipment could also ascertain their height and speed. Ground-to-air radio-telephones then enabled controllers on the ground to pass this information to squadrons of fast monoplane fighters, the Spitfires and Hurricanes of Fighter Command, in sufficient time for them to take off and intercept the raiders before they had reached their targets. The system did not always work perfectly, but when it did, as the experience

of the Battle of Britain in 1940 demonstrated, it was sufficiently effective to enable the British to inflict an unacceptably heavy rate of losses
on the *Luftwaffe*.

Ironically the British failed to learn the lesson of their own experience. In 1939–40 the heavy losses British aircraft suffered in daylight
raids on Germany compelled Bomber Command to confine its attacks
to the cover of darkness. But until the adoption of four-engined aircraft, the Stirlings, Halifaxes and Lancasters, and of better night navi-
gation and bomb-aiming aids in 1943–4, RAF bombers had considerable
difficulty in finding, never mind destroying, their targets. In February 1942, in a tacit admission that the RAF was incapable of precision
night attacks, it was ordered to direct its weight against entire cities in
an effort to undermine the morale of the German civilian population
either by killing them or by rendering them homeless. But even this
switch of objectives did not produce a rapid victory. By then the Germans, too, had developed a technologically sophisticated air-defence
system which could exact a very high toll on the RAF. German civilian
morale did not crack under the weight of Allied bombing. In 1943 the
Commander-in-Chief of Bomber Command, Sir Arthur Harris, insisted
that he could destroy Berlin from the air, thus defeating Germany and
rendering a landing by the Allied armies in north-west Europe unnecessary. But, despite repeated large-scale raids between November 1943
and March 1944, which left much of the city in ruins, German resistance continued and Bomber Command's losses were so high that it
eventually had to be withdrawn and its aircraft switched to targets in
France in preparation for the D-Day landings. The United States Army
Air Force suffered similarly unacceptably heavy losses when they sent
unescorted heavy bombers into German air space in daylight during
1943. They only managed to reduce their losses to acceptable levels when
they deployed long-range fighter escorts to protect their bombers. For
most of the war, Allied attempts to win the war by attacking 'pinpoint' targets such as ball-bearing factories similarly failed. The planners
failed to take account of the fact that the Germans could find alternative sources of supply, that the bombers failed to hit their targets, and
that the targets were so heavily defended that the cost of attacking
them was prohibitive.

The strategic bombing offensive cost the lives of 100,000 British,
Commonwealth and American aircrew and perhaps between three-
quarters of a million and one million Germans. It was a major mis-
application of resources. Airpower might have been better devoted to
assisting the Allied navies in countering German U-boat attacks on
Britain's trans-Atlantic communications or in providing more direct
air support for their armies. Strategic bombing may have prevented the

German economy from producing larger quantities of munitions, but whatever contribution the bomber offensive made to the defeat of Germany, it did not fulfil the dreams of some of the more visionary exponents of aerial bombardment: it did not obviate the need for sustained and costly land campaigns. The war in the air, like the war on the ground, degenerated into a war of attrition.

The war at sea resumed almost at the point where it had ended in 1918. After the fall of France in June 1940 the Germans began to try to impose an economic blockade on Britain using U-boats and a handful of surface raiders. The Royal Navy retaliated in two ways. It attempted to protect merchant shipping by sailing in convoys and it concentrated most of its major vessels in home waters as a deterrent against German surface raiders which might attempt to break out into the Atlantic, where they could create havoc amongst the Atlantic convoys upon which Britain depended for its economic survival. It soon became apparent that the war at sea would be won or lost as much in the air and in the laboratories as on or below the surface of the sea. Off the coast of Norway in 1940, and off the coast of Crete in 1941, the *Luftwaffe* demonstrated the vulnerability to air attack of warships operating without friendly air cover. Similarly in May 1941 a handful of obsolete British Fleet Air Arm Swordfish torpedo bombers played a vital part in damaging the German battleship *Bismarck* and so slowing its progress that the battleships and cruisers of the Royal Navy were able to sink it. The sinking of the *Bismarck* marked the end of German attempts to use heavy ships in the battle of the Atlantic, although its sister ship, the *Tirpitz*, continued to menace the convoys which the British were despatching to Russia's Arctic ports until it was sunk by the RAF in November 1944.

Airpower also played a vital role in containing the U-boat menace. In the First World War U-boats had usually operated singly and attacked submerged. Between 1939 and 1942 they preferred to attack in groups – 'wolf packs' – and to operate on the surface and at night, when Allied escort warships could neither see them nor detect them with the sonar devices they used to track submerged U-boats. These tactics were devastating. In 1941 the Allies lost 3.6 million tons of shipping, of which U-boats accounted for 2.1 million tons. However, such losses were not fatal. The British were able to keep going by reducing their imports to essentials, building more ships in their own shipyards and purchasing others from the USA. And in the spring of 1943 the Allies finally found an effective response to the U-boats with a combination of surface escorts equipped with radar and very long-range aircraft able to fly patrols across the whole of the Atlantic from bases in Britain, Iceland and Canada. The Allies now had the ability to detect U-boats either on the surface or submerged by both day and night, and once they were detected they could be attacked and driven away from the convoys. A third essential element in the Allies' armoury was their growing ability to pinpoint the position of hostile submarines by breaking the enciphered wireless messages which they used to talk to their bases in France and Norway. In 1944 and 1945 the submarines continued to inflict losses on Allied merchant shipping, but they were now incapable of doing so on a sufficient scale to prevent the build-up of the American army in Britain in preparation for the D-Day landing in June 1944.

On land, between 1942 and 1945 the British and American armies fighting in North Africa, Sicily, Italy and north-west Europe played a major role in wearing down the resistance of the German army. But without a doubt the heaviest cost of fighting and winning the land campaign fell upon the Red Army. Between 1941 and 1945 the Germans never deployed less than two-thirds of their land forces on the Russian front. While Britain lost approximately 350,000 dead during the war, and the USA lost 274,000, the Soviet Union lost a staggering twenty million. Germany's losses were approximately six-and-a-half million. Hitler mounted operation *Barbarossa* in June 1941 in an attempt to gain *lebensraum* ('living space') for his people, to provide Germany with the resources it needed to escape from the clutches of the British blockade and to extirpate what he believed was a Jewish/Bolshevik menace to European civilization. He hoped to win the campaign swiftly in a series of gigantic battles of encirclement and annihilation. In fact, although the Soviet Union lost millions of men and much territory, the regime did not collapse and the army continued fighting. The battles which progressively crippled the German army were not fought by the British and American forces under Montgomery* and Eisenhower* in North Africa or in north-west Europe. They were fought in front of Moscow between December 1941 and January 1942, at Stalingrad between September 1942 and January 1943 and at Kursk in July and August 1943.

This pointed to the fact that the major lesson of the Second World War in Europe was the same as that of the First World War, namely that any major conflict between coalitions of industrial powers was bound to degenerate into a war of attrition. Between 1939 and 1941 Germany did gain some significant advantages by being the first of the Powers to utilize masses of tanks and aircraft, and to co-ordinate their movements by radio and wireless telegraphy. But the effect of these advantages was limited. By avoiding being defeated both Britain (with the assistance of the USA, following America's entry into the war) and the USSR were able to copy the Germans' innovations. Having done so they were able to use their vastly superior industrial and economic potential to outbuild and eventually outfight the Axis Powers. In the final outcome, both world wars were won by the coalition which possessed the greater industrial potential and the ability to mobilize it for the purpose of fighting the war.

15

Appeasement

P. M. H. Bell

Any consideration of appeasement must begin with an attempt at definition. The word has acquired so many meanings that it is difficult to use with precision. Which states practised a policy of appeasement, and over what period of time? To what parts of the globe did it apply – only to Europe, or to Asia and the Pacific as well? What colour or resonance does the word carry with it? It has been used at different times to imply extremes of virtue on the one hand and of cowardice or foolishness on the other.

The British naturally associate the policy of appeasement principally, or even exclusively, with their own country, and especially with Neville Chamberlain* in his dealings with Hitler.* But France too pursued a policy of appeasement, with Georges Bonnet* as its most prominent exponent. Less obviously, it can be argued that the Soviet Union was among the appeasers, and that the biggest single act of appeasement was the Soviet–German pact of August 1939, which accepted German control over a far larger area of territory than that conceded by Britain and France at the Munich conference in September 1938.

As to dates, Paul Kennedy has argued that some form of appeasement formed a continuous strand in British foreign policy from the 1860s onwards, in that there was a strong tendency to seek for peaceful, negotiated solutions to problems rather than to adopt a stance of confrontation or conflict.[1] There is some truth in this, though it is a generalization so broad as to be unhelpful for most purposes. Another starting-point has been found in 1919, when Lloyd George,* the British Prime Minister, argued strongly for a moderate peace with Germany in his Fontainebleau memorandum of 25 March, and when his friend and adviser the South African General Smuts actually used the

---

[1] P. M. Kennedy, *Strategy and Diplomacy, 1870–1945; Eight Essays* (London, 1983); see ch. 1, 'The tradition of appeasement in British foreign policy, 1865–1939'.

word 'appeasement' in a letter to Lloyd George on 26 March.[2] In the 1920s, British policy was frequently directed towards revising the Treaty of Versailles in Germany's favour (notably by scaling down reparation payments), and towards bringing Germany back into the concert of Europe (for example, by treating her as an equal partner at international conferences). From the Locarno Treaty of 1925 onwards, the French Foreign Minister Aristide Briand directed his actions towards recon-ciliation between France and Germany, often using the word *apaisement* to describe his objective. Another version of the time-scale covered by appeasement takes the Manchurian crisis of 1931 as its starting-point, regarding the passive reaction by other powers to the Japanese occu-pation of Manchuria as the beginning of a phenomenon which then extended through the decade of the 1930s. Yet another interpretation, particularly common in Britain, attaches the policy of appeasement tightly to the years 1938–9, and to the policy pursued by Neville Cham-berlain, with the Munich agreement of September 1938 as its centre-piece. Some writers have claimed that this period should be extended right through the phoney war of 1939–40, taking the policy of ap-peasement up to the time of the fall of Chamberlain and Churchill's* assumption of office on 10 May 1940.

Turning to geography, appeasement is usually regarded as a Euro-pean policy, directed towards meeting the claims of Germany (and to a lesser degree Italy), with the ultimate aim of reaching a lasting set-tlement of European problems. Other interpretations include the Far East and Pacific within their scope, extending the term to include British, French and American policies towards Japan.

The psychological and moral implications of the word 'appeasement' have been even more varied. At the time of the Munich agreement, at the end of September 1938, it was not thought incongruous to apply to Neville Chamberlain the words of one of the Beatitudes, 'Blessed are the peace-makers.' Letters flooded in to Chamberlain with heart-felt thanks for his achievement in saving the peace of Europe.[3] Yet at the same time Churchill saw Munich as a surrender to the threat of force. '£1 was demanded at the pistol's point. When it was given, £2 were demanded at the pistol's point. Finally, the Dictator consented to take £1.17s.6d. and the rest in promises of good will for the future.' In 1948 Churchill presented, as the theme of the first volume of his war memoirs, 'How the English-speaking peoples through their unwisdom,

[2]   W. K. Hancock, *Smuts: The Sanguine Years, 1870–1919* (Cambridge, 1962), p. 512.
[3]   K. Feiling, *The Life of Neville Chamberlain* (London, 1946), pp. 370–81, gives some-thing of the flavour.

0 100 200
Miles
Lost by Germany 1919
Saar: League of Nations control 1919 – 1935
Demilitarized Rhineland 1919 – 1936
Austria-Hungary until 1918
Plebiscite areas
Former territory of Imperial Russia
NORWAY
SWEDEN
FINLAND
Oslo
Stockholm
Helsinki
Leningrad
ESTONIA
LATVIA
Riga
LITHUANIA
Memel
Vilna
Minsk
USSR
DENMARK
Copenhagen
North Sea
Baltic Sea
Kiel
Danzig
Free City
EAST PRUSSIA
HOLLAND
GERMANY
Berlin
Poznan
Warsaw
POLAND
BELGIUM
Aachen
Bohn
Coblenz
Mainz
Saar
Weimar
Saxony
Breslau
Prague
Cracow
Lvov
CZECHOSLOVAKIA
Alsace-Lorraine
Bavaria
Munich
Vienna
AUSTRIA
Graz
Budapest
HUNGARY
Transylvania
Cluj
Bessarabia
FRANCE
SWITZERLAND
Trent
Slovenia
ROMANIA
Trieste
Bucharest
YUGOSLAVIA
Croatia
Belgrade
Sarajevo
Bosnia
Serbia
ITALY
Adriatic Sea
BULGARIA
Sofia
Montenegro
ALBANIA
Macedonia
GREECE
TURKEY

Map 15.1 European frontiers, 1919–1937

carelessness and good nature, allowed the wicked to rearm.'[4] Again, there has been a marked contrast between those who saw appeasement as a simple reaction against the horrors of war (for example, Daladier,* the French Premier from 1938 to March 1940, had been an infantryman during the Great War, and did not want others to endure a repetition), and those who have seen it as a policy of farsighted calculation – the best means, for example, of saving the British and French empires, or a deep-laid plot to turn Germany eastwards against the Soviet Union, so that the Nazi and Communist giants might tear one another apart and leave Britain and France as spectators. Virtue approaching saintliness; cowardice or foolishness; simplicity verging on naivety; strategems worthy of Machiavelli – all these have been attached to the apparently plain word 'appeasement'. Surely they cannot all be correct.

We must start, therefore, with a working definition. Great Britain and France were the countries most closely associated with a policy of appeasement. To include the Soviet Union would have a certain logic, but would cast the net too widely for a single essay. The central scene of the policy was Europe, and its core was the British and French attempt to reach a permanent settlement with Germany, which would bring stability to Europe by means of negotiation and limited concessions. It is important to stress the words *limited concessions.* Appeasement is sometimes referred to as a policy of 'peace at any price', but this was never true for either Britain or France. It was a policy of peace at a limited price, to be paid if possible by someone else – for example, by Czechoslovakia in 1938. As to dates, the period to be examined will be that between 1935 and 1939, though with a backward glance to the First World War and the Treaty of Versailles, and a forward look at events during the phoney war and the summer of 1940. It is in the second half of the 1930s that the central events related to the policy of appeasement took place: the acceptance of the growth of German power and territory, from open rearmament in 1935, through the occupation of the Rhineland in 1936, to the *Anschluss* with Austria and the Czechoslovakian crisis in 1938. Here lies the heart of our subject.

The widely different resonances of the word itself must be reduced to the simple, workaday assumption, which was widely made at the time, that it was possible to find terms which would satisfy German aspirations (themselves often seen as legitimate) and so secure peace and stability in Europe without involving any fundamental damage to British or French interests. This was not saintly, nor was it unduly cowardly. It meant accepting the growth of German power and the

[4] W. S. Churchill, *The Second World War*, vol. 1, *The Gathering Storm* (London, 1948), p. 256 (speech in the debate on Munich), p. ix (theme of the volume).

expansion of German territory, up to a point, as being preferable to a policy of opposing German claims at the risk of friction and perhaps war. In the event, what happened was that the British and French permitted the growth of German power to a point where, if it was to be resisted at all, it could only be at the cost of a great war; but that was far from being their intention.

The Main Events

The principal events of the period 1935–9 may be rapidly summarized. In March 1935 Germany openly denounced the disarmament clauses of the Treaty of Versailles, which had imposed a limit of 100,000 on the strength of the army, to be raised by voluntary recruitment, and forbidden the existence of any air force at all. In practice, these restrictions had long been evaded, with greater or lesser degrees of concealment. But now the German government announced the introduction of conscription and the formation of an army of thirty-six infantry divisions; the first three Panzer divisions followed in October. Also in March 1935 the Germans declared publicly that a military air force (the *Luftwaffe*) was already in existence. At that time, its strength was some 2,500 aircraft, though a large proportion of these were trainers. The British and French made formal protests against these breaches of vital sections of the Treaty of Versailles, but left it at that. The British Foreign Secretary, Sir John Simon, carried on with a visit to Berlin which had been arranged before the German announcements. Moreover, in June 1935 the British government, acting solely on its own account and without consultation with France, concluded a naval agreement with Germany, accepting a German fleet of 35 per cent of the strength of the Royal Navy, and even agreeing that the Germans had the right to build up to equality in submarines if they thought it necessary. This too was in breach of the Versailles treaty, which had forbidden Germany to possess warships of over 10,000 tons, or to have any submarines at all. In short, the British took the lead in accepting the rearmament of Germany, which from 1935 onwards was pursued at great speed, especially in the air. The Nazis shrewdly seized on the *Luftwaffe* as a means of strking terror into the hearts of potential opponents; and their success in this regard had considerable effects on the policy of appeasement.

In October 1935 Mussolini,* the Italian dictator, launched an invasion of Ethiopia. The links between this event and appeasement were by no means straightforward. The French government was willing to accept Italian expansion in Africa as the price of retaining Italy as an ally against Germany in Europe; that is, in crude terms, to appease one country in order to oppose another. The British government, at least in principle, claimed to oppose the Italian action in Ethiopia in order to maintain the authority of the League of Nations and the concept of collective security. Britain therefore took the lead in imposing limited economic sanctions on Italy. But at the same time the British worked secretly with the French to find terms which would give Mussolini most of what he wanted in Ethiopia, while saving some fragment of territory and independence for the Emperor of Ethiopia, Haile Selassie. These negotiations culminated in what is commonly known as the Hoare–Laval pact of December 1935, which was a characteristically 'appeasing' proposal, in that it accepted the growth of Italian territory at someone else's (i.e. Ethiopia's) expense. In the event, the Hoare–Laval proposals were leaked to the French press, denounced by a vocal section of British public opinion and rapidly abandoned. The Italians went ahead anyway with the military conquest of Ethiopia. This set a precedent for successful military adventure. The episode also provoked dissension between France and Britain, because the French had broadly speaking been willing to accept the Italian action, and felt that the British had thrown away the advantages of that policy without putting anything effective in its place. Over Ethiopia, policies of resistance to aggression (economic sanctions) and appeasement (the Hoare–Laval agreement) had both been tried, but neither had been carried through.

For the French and British, Ethiopia was far away. But the next event to shake the structure of international relations was close to home. In March 1936 the Germans moved troops into the Rhineland zone, which had been demilitarized under the terms of the Versailles Treaty, confirmed with Germany's free agreement by the Treaty of Locarno in 1925. Demilitarization meant that Germany must not station any armed forces in the Rhineland, nor construct any fortifications there, leaving the French an open door through which they could march into Germany in case of need. The closing of that door by military occupation, and later by the building of the fortifications known as the Siegfried Line, destroyed the ability of France to come to the help of her allies in Eastern Europe, and undermined the whole basis of French policy in Europe. Its consequences for Britain were less immediate, but in the long run highly significant – after all, Stanley Baldwin, the Prime Minister at the time, had earlier declared that the British frontier no longer lay on the white cliffs of Dover but on the Rhine. Yet both France and Britain accepted the German occupation of the Rhineland, and its progressive fortification, with no more than formal protest.

The Treaty of Versailles expressly forbade the union of the new state of Austria with Germany; and in the 1920s and early 1930s France and Britain several times reaffirmed their support for Austrian independence.

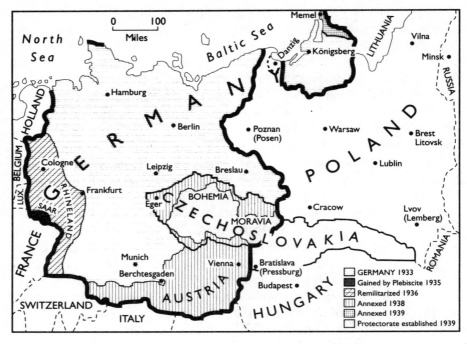

Map 15.2   The expansion of Germany, 1935–July 1939

On 11 March 1938 the government of Austria was taken over by nominees of Germany, under pressure exercised from Berlin – often by the simple device of threatening telephone calls. On the 12th, German troops entered the country unopposed, with bands playing and often welcomed with flowers. On the 13th Hitler proclaimed the annexation of Austria to Germany. In three days a sovereign European state, supposedly safeguarded by treaties and other declarations, vanished from the map. Austria's nominal protectors made no move. Italy was the country most closely concerned, and had defended Austria in an earlier crisis; but Mussolini was now in league with Hitler. France and Britain delivered protests at Berlin, but separately and without conviction. In Britain especially there was a strong belief that the prohibition of union between Austria and Germany had been an error and an injustice, running contrary to the principle of self-determination.

The German annexation of Austria left the state of Czechoslovakia, another creation of the peace settlement in 1919, with the head of its long, slender shape in the jaws of a German nutcracker. The country contained a minority of rather over three million German-speakers (about one-fifth of the total population), who themselves included a substantial Nazi element. The Sudeten German Nazi party, under guidance from Berlin, agitated first for autonomy within the Czechoslo-vakian state, and then for separation from it and union with Germany. This agitation threatened to destroy Czechoslovakia if it succeeded by disruption from within, and carried the danger of European war if it led to German armed intervention from without. France had a treaty of alliance with Czechoslovakia; and if France were drawn into war Brit-ain would be bound to follow. To avoid this danger, both the British and French governments put intense pressure on the Czech govern-ment to make concessions to the Sudeten Germans. Finally the British Prime Minister, Neville Chamberlain, took the bold initiative of flying to meet Hitler to find a solution through the ceding of territory by Czechoslovakia to Germany. An extraordinary fortnight of diplomatic activity in late September 1938 culminated in the Munich conference on 29 September. Hitler, Mussolini, Chamberlain and Daladier, with a Czech delegation in attendance to await their country's fate, decided on the transfer of a horse-shoe shaped slice of territory from Czecho-slovakia to Germany. At the beginning of November, Poland annexed Teschen, and Germany and Italy together (without a word from France and Britain) handed another large strip of territory to Hungary. The Czechoslovakian crisis, and especially the Munich agreement, are gen-erally regarded as the apogee of the policy of appeasement, because on this occasion it was not a question of the British and French simply accepting the growth of German power and territory, but of them tak-ing the initiative to ensure that Hitler got what he wanted. When people refer to appeasement, it is usually Munich that they have in mind.

While these events were taking place in 1938, certain more long-drawn-out processes were also under way. Civil war broke out in Spain in July 1936, continuing until the end of March 1939. The major Powers, and several lesser ones, signed an agreement pledging non-intervention in this war. Germany and Italy, and to a lesser degree the Soviet Union, openly disregarded the non-intervention agreement, while Britain and France stood by and watched while the war was won by General Franco's Nationalists with German and Italian support. This amounted to a form of continuous appeasement. The policy also had a number of other aspects. For much of the 1930s, and especially between 1936 and 1938, Britain tried to formulate a policy of colonial appeasement, which might allow Germany to recover some of the colonies she had lost in the peace settlement of 1919, or perhaps take a share in some form of joint administration over parts of central Africa. A complicated proposal along the lines of joint administration was put to Hitler by the British government in February 1938, only to be brushed aside as irrelevant. The British also discussed schemes of economic appeasement, either on a limited scale, by conceding a German sphere of economic influence in Central Europe (which the Germans were creating for themselves anyway), or more grandly by bringing Germany back into the world economic system and weaning her away from her policy of autarky or self-sufficiency. There was a widespread feeling that if only the Germans could be made fat and contented through economic prosperity they would not be prone to military adventures and aggression. These ideas led to various discussions between the British and German governments, which reached no conclusion. A proposal for a coal cartel between British and German producers was approaching fruition in March 1939, but was then abandoned.

These events and schemes form the body of what is known as the policy of appeasement. On most reckonings, the catalogue of concessions to Germany came to an end in March 1939, when Germany seized most of what remained of Czechoslovakia, throwing the tail-end (Ruthenia) to Hungary. Hitler's claim that he sought only to unite German-speaking peoples within the Reich was exposed as a lie, and a vital basis of the policy of appeasement was destroyed. A reaction then set in. The British and French distributed a string of guarantees across Eastern Europe (to Poland, Romania and Greece), designed to act as a deterrent against any further German expansion. The change of mind was not absolutely convincing, and there was much suspicion that Chamberlain in Britain and Bonnet in France still hankered after another Munich at the expense of Poland in 1939. Even after Britain and France declared war on Germany in September 1939, there were movements for a compromise peace (stronger in France than in Britain). In May 1940, faced with a successful German offensive in the west and the imminent intervention of Mussolini on the German side, the French government proposed an attempt to buy Italy off with an offer of territorial concessions in Africa and the Mediterranean; which may perhaps be regarded as the last, useless kick of the policy of appeasement.

When these events are set out this baldly, the extent of Germany's gains between 1935 and 1939 and the paucity of any concessions made in return become strikingly apparent. What after all did the Germans concede? The Anglo-German naval agreement limited the size of their fleet, but it could be broken at any time; and in any case the limits comprised as much as the Germans wished to build at that period. Germany did not actually attack Czechoslovakia in September 1938. This was a real concession, which Hitler later regretted bitterly, resolving that he would not again be deprived of a war by an interfering British politician. Even so, merely to abstain from war would not normally be regarded as much of a concession, or a fair *quid pro quo* in a bargain. Apart from these two cases, which were of dubious value, the traffic was all one-way. At first sight, there is a good deal of explaining to be done. What were the motives behind the policy of appeasement, and why was it pursued in face of such apparent lack of success?

The Motives behind Appeasement

The most obvious motives probably remain the most important. There was a profound reaction, in both France and Britain, against the appalling experience of the war of 1914–18. It now requires an effort of imagination to understand the full depth of that emotion; but anyone who looks at the war memorials in every town and village from the north of Scotland to the Pyrenees can catch something of its force. It is above all impressive to visit the immense war cemeteries in Flanders, or to stand in a tiny French village and read a list of twenty or thirty killed, often with the same names recurring. The figures of some 1,327,000 French military deaths and 723,000 for the United Kingdom are still appalling, and were more so at the time. 'Never again' was a sentiment shared on both sides of the Channel. Everyone was therefore determined that the causes of the Great War must be understood and avoided in the future. Among these causes, in the understanding of many people in the 1930s, were the pre-1914 alliance system, arms races and economic competition. Thus British statesmen frequently said that alliances would only make Germany feel threatened; that the Anglo-German Naval Agreement of 1935 was better than the naval rivalry before 1914; and that Germany must be assured of access to raw materials for her industries and markets for her exports.

Alongside this revulsion against the last war and its perceived causes there lay a dread of the next. This fear was particularly powerful in France. The French population had suffered a sort of biological disaster in the war of 1914–18, not only through the casualties but through the tremendous fall in births during the war years. This gap in the French population (the total 'deficit' was reckoned at some 1,770,000) moved on inexorably as the years passed. School classrooms were part-empty. By 1935 there were fewer men reaching the age of call-up for military service. Later still there would be fewer men and women to marry and raise the next generation. France could not afford another catastrophe of this kind.

The British were haunted by similar fears. Their casualties had been smaller than the French, but no-one wanted to see another Somme or Passchendaele. A new terror was added with the fear of aerial bombardment. In 1934 Stanley Baldwin told the House of Commons that 'the bomber will always get through' – a simple phrase which made a deep impression on the public mind. In 1936 the Joint Planning Committee of the Chiefs of Staff estimated that London might suffer 20,000 casualties in the first twenty-four hours of a future war against Germany, rising to 150,000 within a week. The dread of air attack possessed the minds of both layman and expert. Behind such fears lurked others, amorphous but terrible. In 1928 a leading authority on war and politics wrote that the next war would be waged through 'agencies and processes of destruction wholesale, unlimited, and perhaps, once launched, uncontrollable. . . . Death stands at attention, obedient, expectant, ready to serve, ready to shear away the peoples *en masse*; ready, if called on, to pulverise, without hope of repair, what is left of civilisation. He awaits only the word of command.'[5] The words carried all the more weight because their author was no pacifist, and was indeed known to relish war when he was engaged in it – Winston Churchill. His prediction proved very close to the mark. Later generations, which have lived under the threat of nuclear war, should not find it difficult to appreciate the fears of their predecessors in the 1930s.

Revulsion against war was accompanied by a reaction against the Treaty of Versailles of 1919. This was much stronger in Britain than in France. During the 1920s the view took root in the British mind that the peace treaty had been harsh and unjust towards a beaten foe. Reparations, as J. M. Keynes* argued in *The Economic Consequences of the Peace* (first published in 1919), were both unjust and unworkable. Disarmament, which should have been applied to all countries, was imposed solely upon Germany. The principle of self-determination, which many held sacred, was imposed when it could damage Germany but disregarded when it would help – for example, the Austrians were not allowed an official plebiscite on union with Germany. If all this (or even half of it) were true, then it followed that the Treaty of Versailles should not be enforced but revised in Germany's favour. Reparations were scaled down, and there was some relief in Britain when they were effectively abandoned in 1932. Germany should be allowed equal rights in armaments. German-speaking people in Austria or the Sudeten areas of Czechoslovakia should be allowed to join Germany if they wished to do so. These propositions had the force of truths universally acknowledged. To oppose German claims on such matters ran counter to instincts of justice and fair play, as well as creating friction and incurring the risk of war at some stage.

These deep-seated psychological motives for the policy of appeasement were reinforced by others which partook more of the nature of

[5]   Ibid., p. 33, quoting from the same author's *The Aftermath*, written in 1928 and published in 1929.

calculation. There were important strategic constraints on French and British policy. From the end of the war of 1914–18, the French high command worked on the assumption that at some time there would be another war against Germany. In such a war, France would be inferior in numbers and economic resources, and would have to stand on the defensive for a prolonged period – a concept which found practical (indeed literally concrete) expression in the Maginot line, the fortified zone along the French frontier with Germany. The French army was committed to a defensive strategy and permeated by a defensive frame of mind, which in practice ruled out certain options in foreign policy – for example, a rapid strike into the Rhineland in 1936, or an offensive to help the Czechs in 1938. It was also vital for France to have allies, to counterbalance German superiority; and this meant that French policy was often constrained within the limits of what Britain would accept. Single-handed French action was ruled out – the last time it was attempted was in the occupation of the Ruhr in 1923, which came to be seen as an unhappy venture, not to be repeated.

The British too worked under severe strategic constraints, of which the gravest were those arising from Britain's world position. The British Empire in the 1930s was at its greatest territorial extent, covering about a quarter of the land surface of the globe. To defend it was beyond British economic and military resources. There were four zones of particular anxiety: the defence of the United Kingdom; the Mediterranean and Middle East; India; and the Far East and Pacific. In the 1930s there were threats from Japan in the Pacific, Italy in the Mediterranean, and Germany at home; and in the background loomed a potential danger from the Soviet Union in India. It is not surprising that in 1937 the Chiefs of Staff argued powerfully that it must be the prime task of foreign policy to diminish the number of Britain's enemies. Three major enemies were too many, and their threats too widely spread, to be coped with. This was one of the most cogent reasons for a policy of appeasement. Was it not sensible to appease, even in the sense of buying off, one or more of these enemies? The logic is so powerful that the surprising thing is, not that such a policy was attempted, but that it was not pursued with even greater determination than it was.

Another important constraint on British policy in the 1930s lay in the strategic concept of 'limited liability'. After the experience of the 1914–18 war, the British had no wish to send another great army to the continent. The Committee of Imperial Defence actually warned its members in 1934 against using the words 'expeditionary force'. It would be better to confine British efforts in any future war to a limited strategy of naval blockade, aerial warfare, a small army and economic assistance to a continental ally (i.e. France). This concept, of which Neville

Chamberlain was a strong advocate, placed restraints on British policy by ruling out options involving land warfare on any large scale. Indeed, in September 1938, when there was a serious danger of European war over Czechoslovakia, Britain could only offer to send two divisions to France – fewer troops, in terms of numbers, than were at that time operating in Palestine to combat an Arab revolt.

In addition to these general strategic constraints, there were also specific inhibitions arising from French and British assessments of German strength at particular times. Perhaps the most dramatic case was the French General Staff's estimate of the German forces in the Rhineland zone in March 1936. They produced fairly accurate figures for the army units involved (10,000 troops, plus 23,000 armed police incorporated as infantry), but then produced an extraordinary total of 235,000 auxiliaries, supposedly organized into fifteen divisions. They then proceeded to argue, on the basis of these inflated figures, that they could not take even limited military action in the Rhineland without calling up something like a million French reservists – facing the government of the day with an alarming political as well as military problem. Again, in January 1938 French Air Force intelligence attributed to the *Luftwaffe* a strength of 2,800 first-line aircraft, as against 1,450 French, which were also of poorer quality. British estimates of German air strength were too low in 1934–5, when the Air Staff underrated the rate of German aircraft production; but by 1938 this complacency had given way to exaggeration of German airpower. In September 1938 (at the height of the crisis over Czechoslovakia) the RAF estimated the combat-ready German bomber force at 1,019, while the actual figure in August was 582.[6] In August a *Luftwaffe* report had concluded that, without bases in the Low Countries, the bombing of England was impossible. But the effect of the RAF's inflated estimate of German bomber strength was to reinforce in the government's mind the existing fears of aerial bombardment, and so give an added impulse to the desire to find an agreement which would avoid war.

Strategic constraints were accompanied by economic constraints. In France, 1935 saw the worst point of the economic depression of the 1930s, and the French economy remained stagnant until the end of 1938, when German steel production was almost four times greater than that of France. French governments were acutely conscious of their industrial weakness in face of Germany, and also of their need for a British alliance to provide them with economic support. British problems were

[6]   J. A. Gunsburg, *Divided and Conquered: The French High Command and the Defeat of the West, 1940* (Westport, CT, 1979), p. 53. E. L. Homze, *Arming the Luftwaffe: The Reich Air Ministry and the German Aircraft Industry, 1919–39* (Lincoln, NB, 1976), p. 241.

even more acute. To adopt a policy of confrontation with Germany, incurring the risk of war, would demand substantial rearmament; but any large-scale rearmament programme would mean increasing imports of the necessary raw materials, while at the same time diminishing the capacity to pay for them by means of exports. This would in turn cause a crisis in the balance of payments. Even if these problems could be overcome, there were limits on the industrial resources available for rearmament – for example, large-scale aircraft production needed factories, machine tools and skilled labour which could not be found overnight.

Behind these various economic inhibitions on British policy there lay a final crucial consideration. It was considered virtually certain that an all-out war would lead to national bankruptcy, in the sense that the country would no longer be able to pay for its imports. This situation had been faced before, during the Great War, but on that occasion the British had been saved from disaster by loans from the United States. Next time there would be no American loans, which fell under a double prohibition. First, under the Johnson Act of 1934 the United States would make no loans to any government which had defaulted on its previous debts – which included Britain. Next, under United States neutrality legislation, enacted at different times between 1935 and 1937, no loans (whether private or governmental) were to be made to any belligerent country. The same prohibitions would also apply to France, so that both countries faced the daunting prospect of having to supply and finance a great war from their own resources. It was a powerful argument for avoiding such a war if at all possible.

These three categories of motive (emotional, strategic and economic) together constituted a strong case for preserving the peace and trying to reach an agreement with Germany by making some concessions to German demands. There were also other motives at work. In France there prevailed, from 1936 or 1937 onwards, a sort of paralysis of will. French diplomats reported on the European situation with their customary lucidity. The outlines of impending doom could be clearly discerned. Yet no-one could decide how to avert it. If France chose to resist the advance of German power, if necessary by force, she would be involved in a war which could at best only result in another victory like that in the Great War; and France could afford no more victories like that. On the other hand, if the French continued to acquiesce in the German advance, the best that they could hope for was that the tiger would eat them last – after, say, Czechoslovakia and Poland. The problem seemed insoluble by rational means, and there was no-one of the stature of Clemenceau or (in later times) de Gaulle to disregard reason.

A very different state of affairs prevailed on the other side of the Channel. Neville Chamberlain possessed a steely political will. When he became Prime Minister in May 1937 he was determined to impart a new drive to British foreign policy, which he thought Baldwin had allowed to drift. Alastair Parker has shrewdly reminded us that, in all the talk of constraints on British policy, it is too easy to forget that Chamberlain actually *wanted* to follow a policy of appeasement.[7] The constraints were real, but Chamberlain was not constrained into his policy. It was what he wanted to do, and he was a very tough and determined man. In this sense, the old caricature of a feeble 'man with an umbrella' is thoroughly misleading.

There were other elements at work. There was some active sympathy with Nazism as a political doctrine and form of government – more in France, where there were a number of near-fascist groups, than in Britain, where Oswald Mosley* never had much of a following and where the 'fellow-travellers of the Right' were not very influential. There was a good deal of hostility towards the Soviet Union and Communism – this time more in Britain than in France, where the slogan that one should have 'no enemies on the Left' was still powerful. The 1930s were a period of intense ideological debate and vibrancy in Europe, and such attitudes and prejudices counted for something in the making of policy.

Finally, there was one motive behind the whole policy of appeasement which is so obvious that it can easily be missed. Those who pursued the policy *believed that it would work*. They thought that Hitler could be appeased: that he was a rational statesman with limited aims – probably the absorption into Germany of the various German-speaking populations in neighbouring countries. This optimism was always stronger among British leaders than among French – perhaps because French politicians all had some training in philosophy, and were inclined to take political theories more seriously than the pragmatic British. It has often been asserted that, if only British and French ministers had read Hitler's *Mein Kampf*, they would have known what to expect, and changed their policies accordingly. In fact, the British and French Embassies in Berlin provided perfectly competent summaries of *Mein Kampf*. The problem was not to know what Hitler had written in the 1920s, but what he was going to do in the 1930s. On the whole, the British tended to think that Hitler the Chancellor would be different from Hitler the prisoner. They often believed that Hitler represented a moderate strand in Nazism, and that if he were displaced it would be

---

[7]   R. A. C. Parker, *Chamberlain and Appeasement: British Policy and the Coming of the Second World War* (London, 1993).

by someone more extreme. In France, even Daladier, who declared from time to time that Hitler's appetite would only grow through being fed, and that the real issue in 1938 was not the frontier of Czechoslovakia but the fate of Europe – even Daladier never pursued his own arguments to their logical conclusion. An absolutely vital premise of the policy of appeasement, on both sides of the Channel, was the assumption that it had a good chance of working. In fact, of course, it did not work. It is time to look at the other side of the argument, and turn to the case against appeasement.

The Case against Appeasement

The fundamental case against appeasement is extremely simple. It failed. The policy was intended to avoid war, but war came. It was intended to achieve a European settlement while preserving basic British and French interests, and above all the security of the two states. In June 1940, France lay defeated and two-thirds occupied by the Germans. The German army stood at Calais, and appeared to have a good chance of reaching Dover. German bombers were based within easy range of London. The policy of appeasement had ended in utter disaster. In these circumstances, the fact that it was also dishonourable stood out all the more starkly. To sacrifice small states – for example, Czechoslovakia – to the maw of Nazi Germany might have been acceptable if the sacrifice had attained its objective; but when it did not, the policy stood doubly condemned as dishonour plus disaster.

From this verdict there can be no appeal. Appeasement failed the acid test: it did not work. But there is another, and more elaborate, aspect to the case against, which may be summarized as the assumption that there was available another policy, simple to devise and straightforward to apply, which could have saved the world from war and from the curse of Hitler. Not for the first time we must go back to Churchill for the most forceful statement of this view. In the Preface to *The Gathering Storm* he wrote: 'One day President Roosevelt* told me that he was asking publicly for suggestions about what the war should be called. I said at once "The Unnecessary War". There never was a war more easy to stop than that which has just wrecked what was left of the world from the previous struggle.'[8] The application of a firm, consistent and courageous policy of resistance to German demands would have cut them short at an early date, and probably have got rid of Hitler into the bargain.

[8] Churchill, *The Gathering Storm*, p. viii.

From this line of reasoning there has resulted much discussion of 'lost opportunities' when such results might have been achieved. The favourite occasion has been the German occupation of the Rhineland in March 1936. Looking back, it was widely assumed that an immediate French intervention ('police action' was a favourite description) would have resulted in an immediate German retreat. Even before March 1936 was out, Pope Pius XII told the French Ambassador at the Vatican that if France had moved 200,000 troops into the Rhineland they would have done everyone a great service. Hitler himself later encouraged the idea of a lost opportunity in the Rhineland by saying that if the French had marched the Germans would have had to withdraw with their tails between their legs. But at the time his instructions were that the troops must withdraw fighting step by step, and it is likely that they would have stood firm on the Rhine itself. The 'lost opportunity', if there was one, was not to stop Hitler *without* war but *by* war; by serious military operations, not a promenade.

Another much-canvassed occasion has been the Czechoslovakian crisis of 1938, where two 'might-have-beens' are envisaged. One is that, through a combination of a firm stance against Germany and suitable encouragement to conspirators against Hitler within Germany, Hitler might have been overthrown. The other scenario is for a war against Germany, waged by Czechoslovakia, France, Britain and perhaps the Soviet Union, and resulting in a much easier and less costly victory than that achieved in 1945 after nearly six years of struggle. Such speculations are of unending interest, and battles fought on paper can produce whatever results their manipulators require. There could, of course, have been no certainty of an Allied victory, and one shrewd and well-informed study estimates that the Czech resistance would have lasted no longer than that of Poland in 1939, though German casualties might well have been much higher than in Poland.[9]

Another strong candidate for a lost opportunity to stop Germany is found in the negotiations for a three-power alliance between France, Britain and the Soviet Union in the summer of 1939. The argument is that such a coalition would have been so powerful that even Hitler would have been deterred from further territorial expansion, and contented himself with consolidating the gains which he had made in 1938 and March 1939. There has been a strong consensus in historical writing on this affair that the British wrecked these negotiations by a combination of tardiness, incompetence and anti-Soviet prejudice. (Such

---

[9]   W. Murray, *The Change in the European Balance of Power, 1938–1939* (Princeton, NJ, 1984); see ch. 7, and especially pp. 217–34.

accusations are not levelled against the French, who wanted to press the talks forward with all speed and ruthlessness.) The case against the British conduct of the negotiations is indeed strong; for example, they repeatedly affirmed that certain points were unacceptable, only to accept them some time later. But it is by no means certain that a three-power agreement was there for the taking if the British had only shown reasonable determination and competence. The question is whether an alliance was available at a price which the British government was willing or able to pay. Stalin* wished to strengthen his borders by securing a large sphere of influence in Eastern Europe, notably in eastern Poland and the Baltic states. The British were in no position to deliver such a sphere of influence, even if they had wanted to do so. Hitler was, and did. The essence of the German–Soviet agreement of 23 August 1939 lay in a line on the map delimiting German and Soviet spheres. The case, like the others, must remain hypothetical; but it is at any rate highly questionable whether the great three-power anti-German coalition was in fact within reach.

In general, the idea of lost opportunities which has played a large part in the case against appeasement looks a good deal weaker than it once did. Certainly in 1936 and 1938 it appears that the true choice was between immediate war and the likelihood of a worse war later. Yet a war postponed might be a war averted; and the choice might well be rephrased as one between war now and a chance of peace later. It was Churchill himself who was to say, several years later and in a different context, that 'jaw-jaw is better than war-war.'

With the passage of time, the 'lost opportunities' case against appeasement has come to look much weaker. The anti-appeasers themselves are doubtless also due for reassessment. The reputation of Eden* as an opponent of appeasement, which arose from his resignation as Foreign Secretary in February 1938 (which meant that he took no reponsibility for the fate of either Austria or Czechoslovakia) has been severely damaged in recent years. Even Churchill's record has been sceptically reviewed, with questions about the accuracy of his information relating to German rearmament and the soundness of his proposals for a 'Grand Alliance', which probably put too much faith in the Soviet Union. In France, there has been a new biography of Daladier, which puts him more firmly in the anti-appeasement camp, without fully explaining his swings between resistance and capitulation. Paul Reynaud* awaits a biographer; yet it was he who most pungently summed up the true basis of the case against appeasement. In June 1940, when Pétain* was arguing the case for an armistice with Germany, and thinking in terms of a rational discussion round a negotiating table, Reynaud told him

sharply that things were not like that any more. 'Hitler is Gengis Khan!'
he exclaimed. The author of this vehement and accurate remark deserves
to be remembered.[10]

Argument without End

Appeasement has retained a remarkable hold on historical scholarship,
and in large part on the public mind. This is partly through its connection with the Second World War, which even fifty years after its
close still commands attention and arouses controversy. The debate on
appeasement is part of the wider debate on the origins of that war. Did
Britain and France, by trying to appease Hitler, open the way to war and
bring catastrophe upon Europe and the world? Or did they, by demon-
strating beyond doubt that Hitler was unappeasable, lay the basis for
the implacable resistance which eventually brought him down? Either
argument can be sustained, and has been. But the questions go further
and deeper, touching the long-term fate and the national identities of
France and Britain.

In France, appeasement was the prelude to the defeat of 1940. Discussion of foreign policy in the late 1930s is carried on in the shadow
of the most shattering event in recent French history. The titles of
Jean-Baptiste Duroselle's massive histories of French foreign policy
in the relevant period tell the story in themselves: *La décadence, 1932–
1939*, and *L'abîme, 1939–1945*. Through decadence (of which appeasement was a part) to the abyss. It is no coincidence that some of the
most acute and profound observations on French appeasement, and its
end in the decision to go to war in 1939, are to be found in a study of
the events of 1940 – Jean-Louis Crémieux-Brilhac's *Les Français de l'an
40*.[11] These events, which themselves led to the German occupation,
the Vichy regime, collaboration and resistance, are still living issues in
France. Professional historical writing has made some headway with
them, but they remain acutely sensitive in the public mind. Appeasement forms a part of a fitful debate on France in the Second World

[10]   On Eden, see D. Carlton, *Anthony Eden: A Biography* (London, 1981), for a critical
account; David Dutton, in *Anthony Eden: A Life and Reputation* (London, 1997) provides a perceptive and balanced reassessment. On Churchill, see D. C. Watt, 'Churchill
and Appeasement', in *Churchill*, ed. R. Blake and W. R. Louis (Oxford, 1993), ch. 12.
E. Du Réau, *Edouard Daladier, 1884–1970* (Paris, 1993) contains much new material.
Reynaud's remark is quoted in P. M. H. Bell, *A Certain Eventuality: Britain and the Fall
of France* (Farnborough, 1974), p. 57.
[11]   J.-B. Duroselle, *La décadence, 1932–1939* (Paris, 1979); and *L'abîme, 1939–1945*
(Paris, 1982). J.-L. Crémieux-Brilhac, *Les Français de l'an 40*, vol. 1, *La guerre, oui ou
non?*, vol. 2, *Ouvriers et soldats* (Paris, 1990).

War, which has certainly not been concluded and in some respects has scarcely begun.[12]

For Britain, the events associated with appeasement did not end in the catastrophe of defeat but in the sudden renaissance and glorious defiance of 1940. Yet appeasement and defiance alike have become part of the story of British decline in the twentieth century. In July 1940 a hastily-written little book of some 120 pages was published under the pseudonym of 'Cato', which concealed a trio of authors, one of whom was Michael Foot, later leader of the Labour Party. Its title was *Guilty Men*, and its cast list of the guilty was headed by the name of Neville Chamberlain. The charge was one of having led Britain to the verge of defeat (the opening scenes of the book are set on the beaches of Dunkirk) by appeasement in diplomacy and by neglect in armaments. Appeasement, therefore, was one of the causes of Britain's decline and (almost) fall. Some fifty years later John Charmley stood this interpretation on its head, by arguing that in fact Chamberlain's policy of appeasement was the last hope of arresting, or at least postponing, Britain's decline as a Great Power. According to Charmley, the fatal blow to Britain was the Second World War, which led to national bankruptcy, economic and political subordination to the United States, and, in the not-very-long run, the loss of Empire. Therefore Chamberlain, in trying to avoid that deadly conflict, was pursuing a policy which would have preserved British power. Between these two radically different diagnoses lie many historical discussions in which the decline (or sometimes collapse) of British power is a recurrent theme. The subject itself has been something of an obsession for politicians, journalists and historians.[13] While the debate on British decline continues, appeasement is not likely to vanish from the historical agenda.

In addition to these considerations, the word appeasement has acquired a life of its own, by frequent repetition and appeal to analogies during later crises in international affairs. Repeatedly statesmen argued that appeasement had failed in the 1930s, and led to a terrible war. Therefore resistance to an aggressor rather than an attempt to negotiate with him was the best and ultimately safest course. President Truman applied this line of reasoning when deciding in 1950 to oppose the North Korean

---

[12] For example, the best studies we have on Bonnet and Gamelin are by British historians: A. P. Adamthwaite, *France and the Coming of the Second World War, 1936–1939* (London, 1977); M. S. Alexander, *The Republic in Danger: General Maurice Gamelin and the Politics of French Defence, 1933–1940* (Cambridge, 1992).

[13] J. Charmley, *Chamberlain and the Lost Peace* (London, 1989); and *Churchill: The End of Glory* (London, 1993). See also C. Barnett, *The Collapse of British Power* (London, 1972). The *International History Review*, 13, no. 4 (1991) devoted the whole number to articles on 'The decline and fall of Great Britain'.

attack on the South. Anthony Eden in Britain and Guy Mollet in France appealed to the same analogy when deciding to use force against President Nasser of Egypt after he nationalized the Suez Canal in 1956. In the 1960s the United States government invoked the precedent of appeasement, and especially the Munich conference, to explain and justify the war in Vietnam. Much later, in 1991, similar arguments were used in the United States, Britain and France at the time of the Gulf War. Saddam Hussein of Iraq was cast as Hitler, with Kuwait as a sort of Austria or Czechoslovakia. It is significant that these very different episodes involved both Democratic and Republican presidents of the United States; Conservative prime ministers in Britain (Eden and Major); and Socialist leaders in France (Guy Mollet as Premier in 1956, François Mitterrand as President in 1991). Appeals to the appeasement analogy spanned political differences with ease. This is partly because of the appealing simplicity of the idea, but even more because of the moral element which has become firmly embedded in the appeasement debate. After appeasement had become indelibly stained with dishonour as well as disaster, the idea of a reversion to such a policy became abhorrent right across the political spectrum. The issue here is not whether the analogy was universally valid, or whether the appeal to the precedent of the 1930s was always justifiable or useful; but only that the appeal was made, and was widely accepted. Appeasement has been not merely a subject of historical study, but a part of current political discussion. This remained true during the prolonged crisis in the former Yugoslavia in the early 1990s, when references to precedents in the 1930s – to appeasement and Munich – were frequent in both the British and French press. The political echoes of the appeasement debate still persist; and as long as that is the case, the subject will continue to exercise a particular magnetism.

Where do we stand now? Appeasement is under review and revision, as it always has been. There is a sense in which all history is revisionist history, and the rise of so-called 'revisionist schools' is no more surprising than the presence of waves on the sea. There were contemporary debates in parliaments and the press in 1938, after the Munich conference. The *Guilty Men* thesis attracted replies during the war – Quintin Hogg declared that *The Left was never Right*. After the war, many of the participants stated their case in their memoirs – Hoare, Simon, Halifax* in Britain; Reynaud and Bonnet in France, among a host of others. In Britain, the introduction of the Thirty-Year rule for access to government records meant that in 1968 documents from 1938 became available to historians; and valuable collections of private papers often (though not always) followed the same rule. In France the opening of the archives was less systematic, but over the years the files of the Quai d'Orsay, and of some individuals, have been opened for research. The result of this has been, over something like a quarter of a century, an increasing grasp of detail and of the process of decision-making which had previously been impossible. There has also been a marked change of emphasis and attitude. Historians who work long hours on government documents absorb, almost without noticing it, a frame of mind similar to that of the politicians and officials they are studying. The fierce, and often essentially political, attacks on appeasement tended to give way to explanations of the policy, and of the constraints within which hard-pressed governments had to work.

At the same time, and simply with the passage of the years, there was a change from the generation of historians who had been closely involved in the events themselves to others who had no memory of the 1930s, and so progressively to other generations putting different questions. In Britain, the stronger the case for appeasement has come to seem, through the examination of government documents, the more attention has shifted to the question of why the policy was changed. After all, if the motives behind the policy were as powerful as they now appear, why was it abandoned?

This process of revision and rethinking will not come to an end, except in the unlikely event of the subject falling into complete oblivion or (more simply) out of fashion. The great wave of new evidence in Britain has probably passed, but in France there is certainly fresh documentation to be opened and exploited. New interpretations can confidently be expected, if only because each generation writes its own history. It may even come about that, at some stage, appeasement will cease to be a political subject and become solely a matter for the historians – like, for example, the Peloponnesian War. Thucydides, writing his history of that war, declared that: 'My work is not a piece of writing designed to meet the taste of an immediate public, but was done to last for ever.'[14] It was a daring claim, but he has yet to be proved wrong. We have yet to see who will be the Thucydides of the policy of appeasement, capturing both its events and its essence for readers far in the future.

---

[14] Thucydides, *History of the Peloponnesian War*, trans. Rex Warner, revised edn (London, 1972), p. 48.

16

The Second World War

A. W. Purdue

The very term 'the Second World War' imposes a significance and meaning which may misrepresent the years and events described by it. Should the war be seen as separate from the First World War or as the second military phase of a European war, a Thirty Years' War? Is the designation 'world war' apposite for the first two years of the conflict when it was confined to Europe and North Africa?

What is undeniable is that the years 1939–45 saw warfare on a massive scale over much of the globe, enormous loss of life and the mobilization of entire economies and populations for war. Its immediate results were equally momentous: a great movement of populations, the total defeat of Germany and Japan, the redrawing of frontiers and a new world order dominated by the USA and the USSR. It is scarcely surprising that historians, especially European historians, who continued to live in a 'post-war' and 'cold war' world, should have made far-reaching claims for the war as a historical turning-point.

The war, it has been variously claimed, brought about the end of a Europe-dominated world, made for fundamental social change and led to the formation of the European Union. Whether the war was such a turning-point can be contested. Major developments may well have simply been speeded up by the war or even slowed down while others, which once seemed so obvious and fundamental, may be seen to have been short-term consequences, even temporary blips. Assumptions made at the height of the Cold War or even in the late 1980s can look dated after the collapse of Communism and of Soviet power in Eastern Europe and the reunification of Germany, while the thesis of the relationship between the war and social change has come to be widely questioned.

Britain alone was involved in both the long and the broad war, a combatant throughout all its years and with her armed forces fighting in both Asia and Europe. Yet Britain was a power and, indeed, a Great Power, that had desperately sought to avoid a war, for her resources did not match her commitments which were dangerously stretched around the world. Although horror at the prospect of another war had played a part in British appeasement of Germany, Neville Chamberlain's* foreign policy had been based upon a realistic assessment of Britain's military and economic strength. A war, Chamberlain feared, could mean the decline of the British economy and the demise of the British Empire. To fight a war in the Pacific or a war in Europe would be very difficult; to fight both would invite disaster. By the spring of 1939, however, Chamberlain's policy of limited accommodation of German ambitions was seen to have failed. The British guarantee to Poland at the end of March represented not a reversal of this policy but a recognition that the threat of force had to be part of it and that, if this failed to guide Hitler* towards compromise, war might be unavoidable. With this change British public opinion, opposed even to re-armament for most of the thirties, was reluctantly in tune.

The British and French declarations of war on Germany of 3 September 1939 initiated a conflict that the two allies had sought to avoid over an ostensible issue that neither the governments nor public opinion felt strongly about, the territorial integrity of Poland. In reality they went to war to prevent the domination of Europe by Germany and, in Britain's case, out of frustration after successive humiliations in the course of attempting to contain German ambitions within a peaceful and orderly revision of the Treaty of Versailles. France, seared by the loss of life in the First World War, defensive in her military posture and deeply divided politically, went hesitantly to war, the last-minute waverings of her government overcome only by Poland's refusal to compromise and Britain's new-found determination. The German government clearly desired a war in 1939, but what sort of war: a war with Poland or a war with Britain and France as well? Although Hitler despised Chamberlain as a weakling, he seems to have felt thwarted by him and to have considered that he had been outmanoeuvred by him at the time of Munich. The British Prime Minister had conceded so much as to give Hitler virtually all of his demands without his having to invade Czechoslovakia, but Hitler felt cheated of his war. The revision of Versailles was obtainable, indeed had largely been obtained, without war, but the ethos of National Socialism demanded the exercise of force. The war Hitler wanted in 1939, as in 1938, was a limited one, which is not to say that his plans for conquest were limited, merely that he was not yet ready for a great war.

It seems most unlikely that the author of *Mein Kampf* had simply the aspiration, shared by nearly all German politicians and generals, of revising Versailles. Whether he sought a greater Germany that would include most of Eastern Europe or was bent on world domination, whether he

Table 16.1 Relative strength of the Great Powers in 1939

	Defence expenditure as % of national income (1937)	Share of world manufacturing output (1938) (%)	Troops	Aircraft	Battleships	Submarines
Germany	23.5	13.2	1,500,000	4,500	5	36
Italy	14.5	2.9	850,000	2,000	4	82
Japan	28.2	3.8	approx. 1,000,000		9	60
USSR	26.4	17.6	1,300,000	1,500	4	38
Britain	5.7	9.2	154,000	2,800	19	71
France	9.1	4.5	700,000	2,500	5	76
USA	1.5	28.7	166,000	2,500	15	84

had a consistent and coherent programme or was an opportunist who took advantage of events to pursue flexible goals, are questions which are unlikely ever to be definitively answered. If, however, Hitler had expected to fight a great war in 1939, it seems obvious that he would have attuned his armament and economic strategy to this end. Either Hitler planned for short furious wars and developed a *Blitzkrieg* economy, which provided armaments in 'width' rather than 'depth' and did not necessitate a decline in the standard of living, or he was planning for a major war but his economic planning got out of phase with his foreign policy, with the major war being planned for the mid-1940s but coming earlier because of Britain's and France's unexpected resolution.

Hitler had brought security to the east by the pact with Stalin* of 23 August and confidently expected a short limited war with Poland. Momentarily taken aback by the information that Britain and Poland had signed an alliance and that he would not have Italian support, he called off the invasion of Poland planned for 25 August and steeled himself to launch the offensive on 1 September, still hoping that Britain and France would back down. 'What now?', he is supposed to have said to von Ribbentrop when he received Britain's declaration of war.

There was of course little that Britain and France could do to assist Poland, which was defeated and partitioned within the month by Germany and the Soviet Union. What then were the Allied war aims? They were to use a combination of a blockade of Germany and a build-up of Anglo-French military strength to force Germany to the conference table; if the enemy remained obdurate, then an invasion of Germany would take place once Allied strength was maximized and German strength weakened by shortages of supplies. On paper at least there was something to be said for this, as Allied arms production was proceeding faster than Germany's and the German economy was believed to be overheated and short of raw materials. Germany's policy was designed to avoid a long stalemate which was not in her favour, and an attack on France was planned as early as November 1939 although it did not take place until May 1940. The overwhelmingly successful German offensive from April to June of 1940, which saw first Denmark and Norway overrun and then a devastating offensive against Holland, Belgium and France, ending with the French surrender on 22 June, owed much to the professionalism of the German army and little to the balance of men and weaponry. Its effect was to give Hitler all that the Kaiser's government and generals had hoped for in 1914. For Britain it posed the question Hitler had put to von Ribbentrop in the previous year, 'What now?'

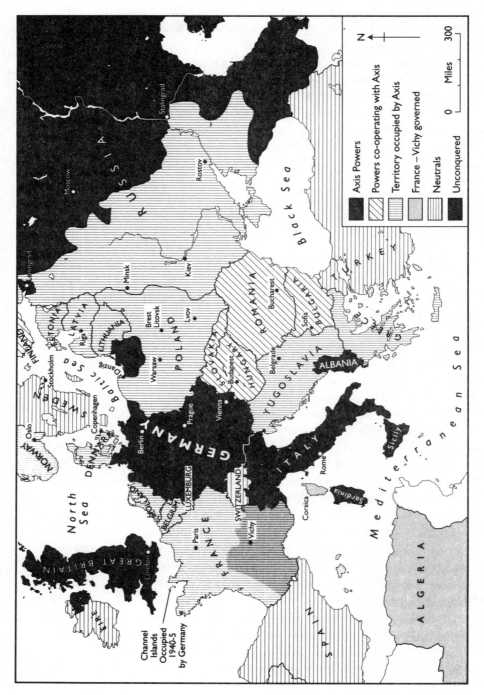

Map 16.1 The German mastery of Europe, 1942

For Winston Churchill* the answer was to fight on, confident in the example of misty parallels in the past and in eventual American intervention. He had succeeded Chamberlain as Prime Minister in April after a vote of confidence in the government had resulted in a number of Conservatives voting against Chamberlain and many abstaining. The vote of confidence came over the failure of the British in Norway and, as Churchill bore considerable responsibility for this, there was irony in his having benefited from its political effect. From early in the war, he became an icon for its determined and spirited prosecution which made him impervious to the dreadful record of his military initiatives in this as in the previous war.

The great significance of Churchill's becoming Prime Minister lay in his ability to rally and encourage the nation in the wake of Dunkirk and the fall of France, in that it ensured that Britain continued the war. But to what end? If by the end of 1940 and after the Battle of Britain a German invasion of Britain seemed less likely, the chances of a successful British invasion of a German-occupied Europe were slim indeed, while, as Mussolini* had overcome his hesitations and brought Italy into the war in May, there was an additional threat to British interests in the Mediterranean. No responsible government could have totally ignored the possibility of peace negotiations with Germany, but Churchill made sure that little serious discussion took place, arguing that any German peace terms would demand a disarmed and humiliated Britain. That Halifax,* Butler and Chamberlain were prepared at least to explore what Hitler had to offer is not surprising; that Churchill refused to do so is a tribute to his stout heart and optimism but not to his appreciation of the realities of the situation. Britain, it is true, was not alone, for she had loyal and substantial support from the Empire. The Empire provided invaluable troops for the war in Europe but at the same time provided hostages to fortune in the event of a war with Japan. Britain, as the events of the summer and autumn of 1940 were to show, could survive, but without new allies she could not hope to win.

Churchill's resolution and rhetoric sustained the British people, but what sustained Churchill was his confidence that the USA would come into the war. That confidence was not well founded. Roosevelt* did not want to see Britain defeated, but then he had not wanted to see France defeated. Congress would not permit an American entry into the war even had Roosevelt been determined on it; and there is little to suggest he was. A much-lauded agreement gave Britain fifty obsolete destroyers in return for leases of air and naval bases in the Caribbean and Newfoundland. By the end of 1940 Britain, increasingly dependent on imports from America, was virtually out of dollars and, although the Lend-Lease agreement of March 1941 maintained the flow of supplies,

Britain paid a high price in her compromised independence for limited support from a neutral USA.

However, Churchill's policy was vindicated by two decisions by Adolf Hitler, the first rash and the latter almost inexplicable: the decision to invade Russia while Britain remained undefeated and when Germany's ally, Italy, had opened new fronts in the Balkans and Mediterranean; and the German declaration of war on the USA after the Japanese attack on Pearl Harbor.

The invasion of Russia, 'Operation Barbarossa', began on 22 June 1941. It had originally been planned for 7 May but was delayed by the need for German troops to be sent to assist with Italy's ill-judged military initiatives that had resulted in reverses in Libya and Greece and a pro-British *coup d'état* in Yugoslavia. It has been agreed that the delay in beginning Barbarossa was damaging to its chances of success, but the Germans nevertheless made rapid progress and by late November stood before Leningrad and Moscow. For all Germany's early victories, Hitler's invasion of Russia reduced the pressure on Britain enormously at the paradoxical price of an alliance with the Power which had joined with Germany in partitioning Poland, for whose integrity Britain had supposedly gone to war.

If the failures of one ally caused the delay of Barbarossa, it was the neglect of another, Japan, which enabled the Russians to transfer troops from Manchuria to the west in the knowledge that there was little chance of a Japanese invasion of the Soviet Union. Thrown into battle at a crucial phase in December, these troops were decisive in halting the German advance.

That Hitler's world view was essentially Eurocentric is suggested by his relations with Japan. The Japanese had signed the Anti-Comintern Pact in 1936 but were shocked to learn of the Nazi–Soviet Pact of August 1939. At the same time aggressive but fearful of encirclement, Japanese military planners hovered between a southern expansion, which could bring war with the Western colonial powers and the USA, and a push northwards from Manchuria against the Soviet Union, the policy favoured by opinion within the army. Despite the Tripartite Pact between Germany, Italy and Japan in the autumn of 1940, German–Japanese co-operation did not improve and, ignorant of Hitler's planned invasion of Russia, the Japanese signed a neutrality pact with the Soviet Union in April 1941. A Japanese attack on the Soviet Union co-ordinated with Barbarossa would greatly have aided Germany but Hitler did little to encourage one.

The combination of Germany's lack of encouragement for a northwards push by Japan and an American embargo on oil supplies, which Roosevelt had initially intended to limit but not to prevent, led to Japan's desperate gamble of war with Britain and the USA which began with the attack on Pearl Harbor, 7 December 1941.

The rapid fall of Malaya, Singapore and Hong Kong showed what little capability Britain had to fight a war to protect her empire while fighting Germany as well. The silver lining was that Churchill's fond hopes were realized and with the German declaration of war on the USA of 11 December, America was now a British ally. It is, however, far from certain that America would have entered the European war had it not been for Germany's declaration. That declaration can be seen to have destroyed Germany's chances of winning the war and is hard to explain on any rational basis.

Despite the depressing sequence of defeats in the Pacific, there were considerable grounds for confidence after December 1941 that Britain would, along with the USA and the USSR, emerge on the winning side of the war. Whether she would emerge as a Great Power was another question. The price for the 'Grand Alliance' with America was steep, the surrender of an independent strategic and foreign policy and in the long run the demise of the British Empire and Great Power status. No doubt, from the position of 1941, it was a price worth paying, considering the alternatives.

Home Fronts

The term 'total war' is often used to describe both the First and the Second World War. The term embraces not only the extent of the conflicts and the scale of the destruction but the total mobilization of resources and populations of industrialized states with the effect that economies and civilians, even if far from the battle lines, were as much part of the war as the armies themselves. Whether we can make a neat distinction between the great wars of the twentieth century and previous conflicts is debatable; the impact of the Thirty Years' War of the seventeenth century on the civilian population of Germany was devastating, while the Napoleonic Wars saw not only the French a nation at arms, but the British as well. Nevertheless, the world wars, in the scale of the conflict, in the close connection between economic and military effectiveness and in the lack of constraint of the participant powers, can, with some justification, be seen as 'total wars'.

Such wars, it has been argued, demand the participation of all sections of society and test its institutions, and are therefore catalysts of social change. The support of disadvantaged groups or classes is secured by rewarding them with improved or relatively improved incomes and living conditions so that war has a levelling and egalitarian effect. The social impact of modern war stretches across social strata to gender as women are required, at least temporarily, to take on new roles to replace men drafted into the armed forces, and there is debate as to whether such a development has had a permanent effect on the position of women in society. Yet, as we shall see, the social effects of war were by no means uniform across the powers involved in the Second World War.

The myths and realities of the war and especially the year of 1940 have become central to the image of modern Britain. The home front became for a while the war front as the Battle of Britain was followed by the 'Blitz' and invasion was expected. Perhaps due to the rich rhetoric of Churchill, Britain's lone stand against Germany immediately became part of the collective imagination by which nations exist. Yet considered closely there is not one image of Britain in its 'finest hour' but rather two, not entirely consistent, images. The concept of the 'People's War', with its egalitarian and collectivist connotations, jostles that of a more martial and traditional war waged by an island race sustained by its sense of history. Contemporary films such as *Britain Can Take It* give us the 'all in it together' message and the emphasis on the need for social change as well as victory, as in *Dawn Patrol*; but they also give us the depiction of gallantry in *Ships Have Wings*, in which rank and class seem naturally synonymous.

One incontestable result of the war was the expansion of government and of government power. The war required not only the mobilization of the economies and populations of industrialized states for the war effort but, for pluralist and liberal societies, the suspension of their norms in relation to civil society and civil liberties. It had been with great reluctance and much soul-searching that the 'liberal England' of 1914 had gone down this path. The Britain of 1939 had been prepared for total war and went to war with the assumptions of 1918 rather than 1914, which were that civil liberties, private property and consumers' needs should be sacrificed to the war effort. Nor was there any substantial challenge to the assumption that the state had the right to control the media, not only in order to censor the dissemination of information, but to use propaganda to reinforce national morale. Such assumptions were strengthened by the widespread popularity of the notion of central planning among left and centre circles during the thirties.

By 1939 conscription was already in place, ration books printed and a formidable array of special powers were quickly taken by the government, including the national registration of all citizens, exchange controls and conscription of labour. The Emergency Powers Act of May 1940 gave the government virtually unlimited powers. In 1941 income tax was raised for the third time since the beginning of the war to 10/- in the pound. By July 1940 many basic foodstuffs such as meat, butter and sugar were rationed. Late in 1941 conscription was extended to include women. Britain's siege economy saw the greatest subordination of economy and society to the war effort of any country but the USSR.

To what extent did the war have an egalitarian influence? Certainly full employment, high taxation and rationing point to a degree of levelling, but when a large percentage of the population is in uniform, with ranks upon sleeve or shoulder, hierarchy can be said to be firmly intact. To a considerable extent different sections of society fought separate but parallel wars, though they endured common hardships, and the degree of social mixing depicted in many accounts of the war has been exaggerated. Nor were the many separate wars just a matter of class: the leftist documentary film-makers of the thirties found government employment in the Crown Film unit as naturally as country gentlemen moved into cavalry regiments and Oxford dons into Intelligence. The various peer groups of British society found their own wars. The enthusiastic receptions accorded to the King and Queen in the bombed East End of London are where the images of a people's war and a war fought by a society with its normal hierarchy and social distinctions meet: a people's monarchy or a monarchist people?

The needs of the war demanded the mobilization of women as well as men. In Britain women were conscripted and directed to war work, whether in the armed forces, where they fulfilled an essentially auxiliary role, or in industry or agriculture. Some historians have seen this as a great breakthrough for female independence; and many women undoubtedly found the experience rewarding and liberating, while films of the period like *The Gentle Sex* and *Millions Like Us* encouraged such attitudes. In fact women's war work was seen by most contemporaries, including the great majority of women, as necessary but undesirable.

Contemporary propaganda and post-war nostalgia have depicted a universal dedication to the war effort, at once cheerful and selfless. It did not always seem so to merchant seamen who brought ships through dangerous waters only to find that striking dockers would not unload them. The home front saw strikes, absenteeism and low productivity per person as well as heroism and fortitude, the black market as well as equal shares.

Historians have, however, pointed to a shift in public opinion and, perhaps more importantly, in influential opinion during the early years of the war. The defeats of the first half of 1940 did much to destroy the reputations of the Conservative politicians who had led Britain during the pre-war years. The *Guilty Men* thesis cleverly indicted their domestic policies along with their foreign policies and their handling of the war effort. Although the composition of Parliament remained the same, a new middle ground arose in government with the inclusion of the Labour Party in the coalition and the increased influence of more left-wing Conservatives. Historians have written of the growth of a new political consensus in favour of greater state welfare on the back of a planned economy. The economic views of John Maynard Keynes and the social reformist ideas of William Beveridge underpinned the new consensus.

Churchill, who had been in the political wilderness during the thirties, was exempt from the criticism of the old Conservative establishment but was not interested in the new consensus on home affairs. It was Churchill's weakness as it was his strength that he was interested in one thing at a time. He was interested in the war and its prosecution and quite content to leave domestic matters to Labour cabinet ministers like Ernest Bevin at the Ministry of Labour, Herbert Morrison at the Home Office and, later on, Hugh Dalton at the Board of Trade.

Churchill had promised the British people 'blood sweat and tears' but soon other voices were promising a 'New Jerusalem' of family allowances, a free health service and expanded national insurance. The Beveridge Report with its talk of conquering the five giants of Want, Disease, Ignorance, Squalor and Idleness was published in 1942 and raised great expectations of benefits after a war which was as yet far from won.

If Britain's move to an economy and society geared to total war represented a suspension of peace-time norms, this was not the case with the USSR. It may, indeed, be argued that the USSR's war economy represented little real change from peacetime, for its command economy was already almost totally dedicated to the needs of the state rather than the individual, and the overwhelming share of GNP taken up by state spending was directed to heavy industrial production including armaments. Thus, despite weaknesses in the Russian army due to the purging of nearly all its generals and colonels and the obsolescence of many of its tanks and aircraft, the Soviet economy could move to a ruthless concentration on the production of armaments with greater ease than other European Powers.

Just as the move to a war economy required no essential change in Soviet economic doctrine, so it was hardly necessary for the USSR to tighten its control of the lives of its population. The Soviet state, forged by the traumatic process of enforced industrialization and agricultural collectivism, proved resilient; a major achievement was the transfer of entire factories to eastern areas of the USSR. The population was kept in order by fear, close supervision and by the loyalty of new technological and administrative elites for whom the regime provided education and social advancement. A society formally dedicated to equality developed in an inegalitarian direction during the war years as the support of crucial elite groups was ensured by special privileges. In the USSR women were already working in manual and heavy industrial occupations which in the West were seen as the province of men. The big change came in agriculture, where more and more work on collective farms was done by women replacing the male labour taken by the armed forces; but agricultural labour for 352 days a year on an inadequate diet was no breakthrough for feminism.

What was found necessary in the face of invasion was a change in propaganda. Patriotism and the defence of Mother Russia rather than socialism and the advancement of world Communism became the themes of radio, newspapers and particularly films. Sergei Eisenstein's film *Ivan The Terrible* enlisted even that unsympathetic tsar to the war effort, while the portraits of great tsarist generals were now found in public buildings.

In contrast to Britain and the USSR, Germany did not effectively mobilize her entire resources for the war effort until 1942. As we have seen, the German economy was perceived by the Allies at the beginning of the war to have many weaknesses, and it may well be that even the level of peacetime rearmament at the existing pace could not have been maintained. There were labour shortages, a foreign exchange crisis and a deep reluctance to diminish the popularity of the regime by cutting back consumer expenditure. It has indeed been argued that the Nazi regime had to go to war or reduce an armaments programme which was overheating the economy. The victories of 1939 and 1940, however, gave the regime the resources of conquered territories and new labour supplies. At the same time failings in the German economy were disguised by the pact with the USSR which enabled Germany to take imports from Eastern Europe without interference.

Here is, perhaps, a paradox: the state which had been taken as a model of totalitarianism and the rhetoric of whose leaders was full of words like 'planning', 'corporatism' and 'autarchy' allowed its business interests, its workers and consumers to enjoy a greater degree of 'business as usual' than any other European belligerent. Whether this was because the regime was over-confident, reluctant to endanger its internal popularity or whether the move to a full war economy was simply slowed by inefficiency in a Third Reich with too many competing authorities and interest groups impeding economic mobilization is debatable. It is clear, however, that a full mobilization of national resources for the war effort only came with the appointment of Albert Speer as Minister of Armaments and Munitions in February 1942. By this time, after the *Wehrmacht* had failed to knock out the Russians and the Americans were in the war, there was a dawning realization that Germany was in for a long and desperate struggle. Speer established a centralized organ of control, the Central Planning Board, and by 1943 he had complete control of the economy. The production of armaments and munitions soared because of more effective planning, an embargo on the production of luxury commodities, the intensified exploitation of conquered territories and the conscription of foreign labour.

German society, it is now – often reluctantly – conceded, had become more egalitarian and in some respects more modern under the Third Reich. German workers had seen their standard of living increase during the late thirties, and the Nazi ethos had seen the crumbling of the traditional social hierarchy. Despite the regime's declared belief in women as mothers and wives, there had actually been more employed females in Germany at the beginning of the war than in Britain, but no great effort was made to increase the female workforce. In 1943 women under 45 were ordered to register so that they could be directed to work but only a small minority were directed to employment, and the profile of the female workforce remained substantially unchanged, with large numbers continuing to be employed in domestic service.

Public support for the war effort seems to have remained consistently high until the very end of the war. As with Britain the impact of bombing on civilian morale did not have the demoralizing effect that was confidently expected. Up until 1943 morale in Germany was underpinned by hopes of success; if in the last two years of the war, it was sustained more by fear of defeat and of Russian invasion, this proved just as effective in maintaining cohesion. Government propaganda reflected the changing fortunes of war moving from an emphasis on the Nazi 'new order' to patriotic appeals to German history.

Morale, in general, seems to have depended on factors buried deep in national psyches and traditions as much as in contemporary political structures. While Italy combined an ineffective war economy, for which little preparation had been made, with a rapid deterioration of morale, Japan, a cohesive society, had similar economic problems but both military and civilians remained patriotic and defiant long after victory had ceased to seem likely.

For Britain and to some degree the USSR there were really two home fronts – their own, and one far from the threat of bombing, in the United States. Increasingly as the war progressed, the British economy became dependent on the American economy. Under Lend-Lease, raw materials, machine tools and food were provided by the USA while a quarter of the munitions needed by British and Empire forces came from across the Atlantic.

This brings us to that central development, the emergence of the USA as the superpower with a capacity for productivity which put her in a different league to other combatants. If Germany, belatedly moving into top gear, more than doubled her arms production, outdistancing Britain and almost equalling the Soviet Union by 1943, her efforts looked puny compared to the achievement of the USA, which between 1941 and 1943 increased her production by a factor of eight. The enormous superiority of the United States in its productive capacity was to be the major determinant of eventual Allied victory.

The Road to Victory

From the end of 1941 the war was genuinely a world war in the sense that the conflict stretched around the globe. It can be argued, however, that there were actually two wars, one in Europe (though it spilled over into North Africa and the Middle East) and the other in the Pacific, linked by the involvement of Britain and America in both. Clearly the fortunes of war in the Far East had their effects upon the war in Europe and vice versa, the demands of the European theatre most importantly limiting the resources the Western Allies could devote to the war with Japan; but there was little co-ordination between Japan and her nominal allies, Germany and Italy, while until after the war against Germany was won, the USSR honoured her neutrality pact with Japan.

Japan's initial success was considerable: between December 1941 and May 1942 she took all the American, British and Dutch islands in the Pacific and gained control of the entire mainland coastline from Manchuria to the frontiers of India. Japan was perhaps too successful for the good of her own original strategy, which was to seize Malaya and the Dutch East Indies with their rubber and oil, and enough further territory to make feasible the defence of their expanded and now economically self-sufficient empire, a Greater East Asia Co-prosperity Sphere. The Imperial Japanese Navy had always based its war plans on the notion of defeating numerically superior American fleets close to the home islands. Early success prompted the Japanese to attempt to extend their conquests and overextend the navy, which penetrated into the Indian Ocean, inflicting losses on British ships but losing carrier-aircraft, and far into the south-eastern and mid-Pacific, meeting a setback at the Battle of the Coral Sea in May 1942 and then suffering major defeat in June at the great naval encounter of the war, the Battle of Midway. Japan was now on the defensive with a seriously weakened navy.

The length of the Pacific war was determined not only by the tenacity and military ability of the Japanese, inferior in numbers and armaments to their opponents, but by America's decision to give the war in Europe first priority. Against much civilian and military opinion, Roosevelt strongly favoured a 'Europe first' strategy, allocating the greater part of the US army and airforce to the European theatre and anxious to launch an attack on German-occupied Western Europe.

The great land battles of the war were taking place within the Soviet Union, and Stalin's demands that the Western Allies take some of the pressure off the Soviet forces by invading France were insistent. The very need to invade France owed much to the help Stalin had given Hitler in 1939 and 1940, but Stalin's demands gained vocal support from sections of Western opinion. An invasion of France did not, however, promise success in the circumstances of 1942. In Western Europe Germany's position was secure: she controlled the northern European coast from the Pyrenees to the North Cape; sympathetic governments were in office in the defeated countries; and resistance movements were no great problem. German U-boat successes in the Battle of the Atlantic continued to impede the build-up of US forces in Britain. Only when the German forces in France were weakened and when sufficient US military might was available would an invasion be feasible.

The outcome of the war in Eastern Europe remained in doubt until the middle of 1943. The German offensive of the summer of 1942 enjoyed initial success but ended in February 1943 with the surrender of twenty German divisions at Stalingrad. The failure of the attack on Kursk in July 1943 marked the end of any possibility of German victory over Russia which, by the early months of 1944, had a six-to-one manpower superiority on the Eastern Front.

The enormous casualties on the Eastern Front caused many contemporaries and subsequently historians to conclude that here was where the war was won and lost. The Soviet Union withstood the main force of Hitler's armies but whether Russia alone could have defeated Germany is questionable. The immense economic superiority of the USA, which expanded its armaments production on a scale which dwarfed that of other Powers, suggests that even if, as in the First World War, Russia had been defeated, an Allied victory would have resulted in the long term.

As it was, the Soviet Union received immense amounts of supplies from the USA and the Red Army's manoeuvrability owed much to the fact that the Soviets received more trucks from America than the Germans were able to produce. Bombing raids by British and American aircraft destroyed German munition factories and supply trains, though without making a major impact on production. If American and British actions in North Africa and Italy kept only a limited number of German divisions from the Eastern Front, the five divisions engaged in North Africa in the winter of 1942–3 constituted a powerful force, while the invasions of Sicily and then the Italian mainland in July and September 1943 were both a major distraction and a considerable psychological setback for Germany. It is untrue that there was no second front before the D-Day landings of June 1944; but there was no decisive blow against Hitler's grip on Western Europe until then.

What were the Allies fighting for except to defeat Germany? The USA entered a war in which her allies had been fighting for survival. It was a war against fascism only in that Italy and Germany were respectively Fascist and National Socialist states. Britain had gone to war to prevent further extensions to German power, not to overthrow the Nazi regime; while the Soviet regime, as unsavoury as its Nazi opponent, had been on good terms with its adversary before June 1941. Britain and the USSR were bound together by a common enemy and fought to survive and to defeat that enemy. Beyond that, Britain's objective was security; a power without expansionist ambitions, she wanted to remain a Great Power, to keep her empire and see a stable Europe. The USSR also sought security but, like tsarist Russia, sought it in expanded frontiers and a dominant position in adjacent states; as the military position improved, wider ambitions and world Communism were to come back on the agenda. The 'my enemy's enemy' principle was perhaps good enough for two states fighting for survival, but US entry into the war and, after Stalingrad, the prospect of eventual victory raised the question of war aims.

Relations between Britain and the USA bore some similarity to those between the two Powers in the First World War with the important difference that Britain was now much the weaker and more junior partner. In 1941 Roosevelt and Churchill had signed the Atlantic Charter, a high-minded and woolly document impeccably liberal and internationalist in sentiment, which Woodrow Wilson would certainly have approved of. Churchill managed to convince himself that references to the right of all peoples to choose their form of government and to international free trade did not apply to the British Empire or to Imperial Preference. There was, however, a basic incompatibility between Churchill's desire to preserve the Empire and remake a European balance of power on the one hand and Roosevelt's opposition to the British Empire and his distrust of Britain's worldly approach to international relations involving spheres of influence and a balance of power on the other.

Churchill realized that Britain's influence upon the Soviet Union was likely to decline as the latter's position improved. He sought early agreement with Moscow and was prepared to pay the price of accepting Russia's June 1941 borders. Later, from a weaker position, he sought in 1944 to come to an agreement with Stalin on spheres of influence in Eastern Europe. Roosevelt was in no hurry, confident that the USA would be far stronger at the end of the war and in a position to exert great influence on the future of Europe. Though Roosevelt had no illusions that the USSR was sympathetic to his own vision of a new world order based on self-determination, free trade and a United Nations, he placed high hopes on establishing close relations between himself and Stalin and on the containment of the USSR by international institutions and US military and economic strength. Unlike Churchill, he was disinclined to conflate military strategy and political aims, and was content to leave aside the question of future territorial and political arrangements and the post-war balance of power. To Stalin, and at times to Britain too, Roosevelt's idealism and US self-interest seemed to march in step.

Parallel to increasing Allied success in the war came a series of conferences from 1943 to 1945 which attempted to reconcile the military policies of the Allies with an agreed programme of post-war settlements in Europe and Asia. There were, however, only two wartime conferences at which all the three main Allied leaders met: Teheran in December 1943, and Yalta in February 1945 when Germany was all but beaten. Central to any consideration of the shape of post-war Europe were the fates of Germany and Poland. From 1942 it had been agreed that Germany would be offered only unconditional surrender and at Yalta it was agreed to divide the country into four separate zones, the whole to be co-ordinated by a Control Council at Berlin. The post-war hostility between the USSR and her allies was to translate this into a division into West and East Germanies that would endure for nearly half a century.

At both Teheran and Yalta Poland provided a major cause of dissension. Britain had ostensibly gone to war for Poland and the Polish government-in-exile was based in London while the Soviet Union had not only invaded Poland in 1939 but had behaved with great barbarity there; yet the Poles were to be 'liberated' by the Red Army. At the Teheran conference in December 1943 it was agreed that the eastern Polish frontiers would be redrawn in Russia's favour while Poland would be compensated to the west at Germany's expense. At the Yalta conference of 1945 an ostensible compromise (in reality a Soviet victory) made the Russian-based Polish Communist Committee the nucleus of a Polish provisional government while Stalin promised there would be free elections after the war. Between these two conferences the USSR, which had in 1939 massacred much of the Polish officer corps at Katyn, had in 1944 allowed the Germans to crush the Warsaw rising while Soviet forces paused a few miles away. The fate of Poland pointed to the Soviet Union's determination to dominate East and Central Europe and to the inability of the Western Allies to do anything to oppose a Soviet dictation wherever the Red Army had 'liberated' territory.

As the Allied armies closed in on Berlin from east and west, relations between the Soviet Union and the Western allies deteriorated once it became apparent from Soviet treatment of conquered territory that the promises of free elections given at Yalta were worthless. By the time of the German surrender of 7 May Truman, who had become President on Roosevelt's death, had come to realize that where the armies met political systems also met. As Stalin put it early in 1945: 'whoever occupies the territory also imposes on it his own social system.'

By the end of the war in Europe only Burma, the Philippines and a number of islands had been wrested from the Japanese. The main strength of the Imperial Army had not been engaged and fierce resistance in Okinawa, invaded in April, pointed to the costs in Allied casualties of an invasion of the home islands. It has been suggested that President Truman's decision to use the new secret weapon, the atomic bomb, was made in order to demonstrate its destructive power to the Russians. It is more likely that Hiroshima and Nagasaki were bombed in August to avoid a costly invasion, though any worry it caused in Moscow was probably welcomed. On 14 August the Japanese surrendered unconditionally and the war, which had begun with a German army with largely horse-drawn supply trains invading Poland, ended in the Far East with the new weapon of mass destruction, the fear of which would dominate the post-war world.

The Effects of the War

The last year of the war saw or exposed its worst horrors: the 'conventional' bombing of Tokyo and Dresden caused as much death and destruction as the atomic bombs dropped on Japan, while Allied victory revealed the cruelty and inhumanity of Japanese treatment of prisoners of war and, most shocking of all, the 'Holocaust', as the Nazis' cold-blooded murder of six million European Jews came to be known. If confident assumptions about human progress had been called into question by the First World War, then one effect of the Second World War was to confirm pessimism. Neither the unsatisfactory expedient of trying war criminals, nor the inauguration of a new world organization, the United Nations, to replace the discredited League of Nations could draw a line between the present and the past.

Though the war had begun as the second active stage of a European civil war, it left Europe weaker and less central to world affairs. Not only was Western Europe heavily dependent on the USA, but the influence of the European Powers was on the wane in the Middle East, Asia and even Africa. It seems probable, however, that the war revealed

Table 16.2   War deaths 1939–1945

	Military	Civilian
Germany	3,500,000	800,000
Italy	330,000	80,000
Japan	1,500,000	500,000
USSR	7,500,000	2,500,000
Britain	397,000	62,000
France	210,000	107,000
USA	292,000	

rather than caused the weakening of European power and influence. The transfer of Western technology to the Far East was already advanced, while isolationism and economic depression obscured the true extent of American power.

The division of Europe largely on the lines where the armies of the Western allies and the Soviet Union met was to be frozen by the Cold War into an ideological separation that was to last for some forty-five years. This outcome of the war was also the position from which its significance was assessed.

An obvious consequence of the war was the death and destruction it caused. Over fifty million lost their lives and about the same number were uprooted from their homes, permanently or temporarily. Europe saw a great movement of people and, whereas Versailles had attempted to fit frontiers to peoples, now people were moved to fit frontiers. Eastern Europe moved west as the Soviet Union took over areas of Poland, and Poland received eastern areas of Germany.

However, European economic recovery proved to be swift and social stability returned surprisingly quickly. By 1950 European output of almost every commodity was to be above pre-war levels. The outstanding success story was that of the zones of Germany occupied by the Western Powers. The German Federal Republic, as it became, demonstrated with its economic miracle that half of Germany had the potential to become the strongest economic power in Europe. West Germany's success was to be paralleled by that of her ex-ally, Japan.

The movement for European unity gained strength in the post-war period under the vision of Christian Democratic and Social Democratic politicians. There were also, however, hard-headed reasons for this development: French realization that close economic bonds were a more practical means of coming to terms with Germany's latent power than political and military opposition was important, while the common economic institutions set up under German hegemony after 1940 provided an unacknowledged precedent.

For Britain the war was a disaster that victory only temporarily obscured. Victory, with British troops ubiquitous in Western Europe, the Mediterranean and throughout the Empire, disguised weakness: an economy drip-fed by American supplies and aid; a political independence qualified by economic dependence; and a World Power status and empire that the next decade would erode. A new political consensus saw a Labour government elected with a Conservative opposition little inclined to deny its central tenets, that a mixed economy could under government direction provide welfare benefits and greater prosperity for the British people, retain Great Power status, hang on to the essence of the Empire and play a leading role in Europe. Government took responsibility for an ambitious welfare state but experienced great difficulty in providing the economic growth to pay for it. There were too many straws for the back of the British economy.

Did the war substantially alter European societies? Did it, alternatively, simply speed up social change or even slow it down? Some historians have argued that major socio-economic changes were taking place in Britain, France and Germany in the late 1930s and that changes attributed to the war can be discerned before it: the interventionist state, an improvement in the relative position of the working classes and a modest increase in social mobility, the Americanization of popular culture and the dawning of the consumer society. The evidence, like that for changes in the position of women, who gained the vote in post-war France but, for the most part, returned to their pre-war roles as in other Western European societies, is susceptible of contrary interpretations.

The Second World War raises in acute form the perennial tension in historical interpretation between arguments for continuity and for change. Was the war a great turning-point in European history? No great effort of imagination is required to see that the consequences of a victory for Nazi Germany would have been considerable yet, in the extended conflict from late 1941, the logic of numbers and economics was always against this. The Cold War perspective gave the war the appearance of a distinct turning-point ushering in a divided Europe in which ideological differences overlaid more complex and traditional rivalries. But from today's perspective the continuity of European history is more apparent.

Chronology of Events
1870–1945

1870	July	France declares war on Germany
	September	The French surrender at Sedan
		The Third Republic is proclaimed
	October	Russia renounces the 'Black Sea' clauses of 1856
1871	January	William I, King of Prussia, is crowned Emperor of Germany at Versailles
	May	Treaty of Frankfurt transfers Alsace and Lorraine to Germany
		Fall of the Paris Commune
	July	Beginning of the *Kulturkampf* against the Catholic Church in Prussia
	October	Britain annexes the Kimberley diamond fields in South Africa
1873	October	Alliance of the three Emperors (Germany, Russia and Austria)
1874	February	British Conservatives win a parliamentary majority for the first time since 1841
1875	July	Revolt breaks out in Bosnia and Hercegovina
	November	Britain buys Suez Canal shares
1876	May	Massacres of Bulgarians by the Turks
	July	Serbia and Montenegro declare war on Turkey
1877	January	Queen Victoria is proclaimed Empress of India
	April	Russia declares war on Turkey
		Britain annexes the Transvaal
1878	March	Turkey surrenders. Treaty of San Stephano creates 'Big Bulgaria'
	June	Congress of Berlin revises San Stephano
		Britain acquires Cyprus
	October	Socialists are outlawed in Germany
1879	July	Germany introduces tariffs
	October	Austria and Germany form the Dual Alliance
		Britain invades Afghanistan

1880	October	Expulsion of Roman Catholic Orders from France
1881	February	British troops defeated at the Battle of Majuba Hill
	March	Assassination of Tsar Alexander II of Russia; succeeded by Alexander III
	August	Pretoria Convention restores the Transvaal under British suzerainty
1882	May	Italy joins the Dual Alliance
	July	British begin bombardment of Alexandria
	September	British occupy Egypt and the Sudan
1884	January	Abolition of the Poll Tax in Russia
	April–August	Germany occupies S. W. Africa, Togoland and Cameroon
		Britain establishes protectorates over Basutoland, the Somali coast, Nigeria and New Guinea
1885	February	Death of General Gordon at Khartoum
		Germany annexes Zanzibar and Tanganyika
		King Leopold of Belgium establishes the Congo State
	September	Eastern Rumelia unites with Bulgaria
	December	Foundation of the Indian National Congress
1886	April	Defeat of the first Irish Home Rule Bill leads to split in British Liberal Party
1887	June	Reinsurance Treaty agreed between Russia and Germany
	October	Failure of *coup d'état* by General Boulanger in France
1888	March	Death of the Emperor William I
	June	Death of the Emperor Frederick; succeeded by William II
	October	France floats Russian loan
1890	March	Dismissal of Bismarck as German Chancellor; replaced by Caprivi
	July	Anglo-German Convention: Britain exchanges Heligoland for Zanzibar
	October	German Social Democrats adopt new programme at Erfurt
1891	May	Construction of the Trans-Siberian Railway begins
1892	August	Franco-Russian military convention is drafted
		Germany adopts the Schlieffen Plan
	November	Caprivi introduces new military law to expand German army
1893	July	German Army Bill is passed
	December	Tsar Alexander approves Franco-Russian military convention
1894	January	Franco-Russian Alliance comes into force
	August	Nicholas II succeeds as Russian tsar
	December	Trial of Dreyfus in Paris

1896	March	Italy defeated at the Battle of Adowa in Abyssinia
	July	German Reichstag passes Civil Law Code
	October	Publication of the Russo-German Reinsurance Treaty
1897	June	Diamond Jubilee of Queen Victoria
		Tirpitz appointed German Naval Secretary
	December	Russia occupies Port Arthur
1898	February	Joseph Chamberlain proposes Anglo-German alliance
	March	First German Navy Bill is passed
	July	France occupies Fashoda
1899	August	Second trial and pardon of Dreyfus
	October	Outbreak of war between Britain and the Boers
	December	Germany secures Baghdad Railway concessions
1900	February	Foundation of the British Labour Party
	July	Second German Navy Bill is passed
	October	Bülow appointed German Chancellor
1901	December	Negotiations for an Anglo-German alliance are broken off
1902	January	Anglo-Japanese Alliance is signed
	May	The Peace of Vereeniging ends the South African War
1903	May	Joseph Chamberlain launches campaign for tariff reform
	November	Russian Social Democratic Workers' Party splits into Mensheviks and Bolsheviks
1904	February	Japanese fleet attacks the Russians at Port Arthur
	April	Britain and France sign an entente
1905	January	Revolution breaks out in St Petersburg
	March	Germany challenges French claim to Morocco: William II lands at Tangier
	April	Anglo-French military convention
	May	Japanese naval victory over Russia at Tsushima
	June	Delcassé resigns as French Foreign Minister
	August	Proclamation of the Duma in Russia
	September	Norway becomes independent from Sweden
		Russia cedes Port Arthur to Japan under the Treaty of Portsmouth
1906	January	Algeciras conference on Morocco
		Moltke appointed Chief of German General Staff
	July	The first Duma meets in Russia
1907	June	Introduction of women's suffrage in Norway
	August	Anglo-Russian Convention is signed
1908	July	Rising of the Young Turks
	October	Austria annexes Bosnia and Hercegovina

1909	July	Bethmann-Hollweg becomes German Chancellor
	November	Rejection of Lloyd George's budget by the House of Lords
1911	July	German gunboat, *Panther*, arrives at Agadir
	September	Italy declares war on Turkey and seizes Tripoli
1912	February	Haldane's mission to Berlin to seek a reduction in naval building
	March	The French proclaim a protectorate over Morocco
	October	First Balkan war breaks out
1913	February	Second Balkan war breaks out
	May	Third Balkan war begins
	October	Treaty of London resolves First Balkan war
		German–Turkish military convention is agreed
1914	June	Assassination of Archduke Franz Ferdinand at Sarajevo
	July	Austria sends ultimatum to Serbia and declares war on her
		Germany declares war on France and Russia
	August	Germany invades Belgium
		Britain declares war on Germany and Austria
		Battle of Tannenberg
	September	Battle of Marne checks German advance on Paris
	November	First Battle of Ypres
		Britain declares war on Turkey
1915	February	Germany and Britain declare a blockade of each other's ports
	April	Allied troops land at Gallipoli
	May	Italy declares war on Austria
		Cunard liner, *Lusitania*, is sunk by the Germans
1916	January	Allies evacuate Gallipoli
	February	Battle of Verdun begins
	April	Easter Rising in Dublin
	June	Battle of Jutland
	July	Battle of Somme begins
	December	Lloyd George becomes Prime Minister
1917	January	Germany announces unrestricted submarine warfare
	March	Russian Revolution overthrows the tsar; Provisional Government under Prince Lvov
	April	USA declares war on Germany
		Lenin returns to Russia
	July	Third Battle of Ypres (Passchendaele) begins
	November	Bolshevik revolution in Russia
1918	January	President Woodrow Wilson announces the 'Fourteen Points'
	March	Treaty of Brest-Litovsk ends Russo-German War
	June	British Labour Party adopts new constitution with socialist clause
	November	Surrender of Austria and Germany
	December	Lloyd George wins general election

1919 January   Revolution breaks out in Berlin
                Peace Conference opens in Paris
      February   Mussolini founds the Fasci del Combattimento
      April   Amritsar massacre in India
      June   Treaty of Versailles is signed
      August   New German constitution inaugurates the Weimar Republic

1920 January   American Senate votes against joining the League of Nations
      August   Gandhi inaugurates Non-cooperation campaign
      November   First assembly of the League of Nations
                Expulsion of General Wrangel from the Crimea effectively ends the counterrevolution in Russia
      December   Ireland is partitioned
                German reparations payments are settled

1921 March   New Economic Policy introduced in Russia
                Anglo-Soviet trade agreement is signed
      November   Disarmament Conference meets in Washington

1922 January   Cannes Conference postpones German reparations payments
      February   Washington Naval Agreement between USA, Britain and Japan
                Anglo-Japanese Alliance lapses
                Britain abandons protectorate over Egypt
      April   Treaty of Rapallo between Russia and Germany
      September   Chanak crisis brings Britain and Turkey close to war
                American protectionist tariff comes into force
                Franco-Polish military convention is agreed
      October   Collapse of the Lloyd George Coalition at the Carlton Club meeting
                Mussolini's March on Rome
      November   Mustafa Kemal proclaims Turkish Republic

1923 January   The French occupy the Ruhr
                Agreement reached on repayment of British war debt to USA
      September   Primo de Rivera assumes dictatorship of Spain
      November   Hitler's coup in Munich fails
                German currency is stabilized

1924 January   First Labour government in Britain
                Alliance between France and Czechoslovakia
      August   London Conference accepts the Dawes Plan on German reparations

1925 April   Britain returns to the Gold Standard
      July   The French evacuate the Ruhr and Westphalia
      December   Locarno Treaties signed in London

1926 January   France and Britain evacuate the first Rhineland zone
      May   General Strike in Britain
      September   Germany joins the League of Nations
      November   Imperial Conference in London grants equal status to the Dominions

1927	May	'Black Friday' in Germany – breakdown of the economic system
1928	April	Equal franchise won by women in Britain
	May	Left-wing victory in German elections
1929	August	ˈThe Young Plan further reduces German reparations
	October	Wall Street 'Crash' in New York
		The Irwin Declaration promises India eventual Dominion status
1930	March	Civil Disobedience begins in India
	April	London Naval Treaty is signed
	September	107 Nazis returned in German elections
	November	Round Table Conference on India begins
		Statute of Westminster defines the status of British Dominions
1931	July	German Danatbank goes bankrupt; banks close until 5 August
	August	Collapse of Labour government in Britain; formation of National Government
	September	Britain is forced off the Gold Standard
		Second Indian Round Table Conference
	December	Republican constitution declared in Spain
1932	February	World Disarmament Conference opens in Geneva
	March	Britain adopts general tariff policy
	April	Hindenburg re-elected German President
	July	230 Nazis returned in German elections
	October	Foundation of the British Union of Fascists
1933	January	Hitler becomes German Chancellor
	May	Suppression of trade unions in Germany
	October	Germany leaves Disarmament Conference and League of Nations
1934	July	Murder of Dollfuss in Austria
1935	March	Germany repudiates the military clauses of the Treaty of Versailles
	April	Stresa Front formed by Britain, France and Italy
	June	Anglo-German Naval Agreement is signed
	August	Government of India Act is passed
	October	Mussolini invades Abyssinia
	December	Hoare–Laval Pact is revealed
1936	February	Popular Front wins Spanish elections
	March	Germany remilitarizes the Rhineland and denounces the Locarno Treaties
		London Naval Conference between USA, Britain and France
	July	Outbreak of Spanish Civil War
	November	Germans and Italians recognize General Franco's regime in Spain
	December	Abdication of King Edward VIII

| 1937 | February | Congress wins a majority in Indian provincial assemblies |

1938	March	Austria is annexed by Germany
	May	Hitler and Mussolini meet in Rome
	September	Munich settlement allows annexation of the Sudetenland by Germany

1939	March	Germany invades Bohemia and Moravia
		Britain and France give guarantee to Poland
	April	Hitler renounces the Anglo-German Naval Agreement
		Britain gives guarantees to Romania and Greece
	August	German–Soviet Pact of Non-aggression
	September	Germany and Russia invade Poland
		Britain and France declare war on Germany

1940	April	Germany invades Denmark and Norway
	May	Churchill replaces Chamberlain as British Prime Minister
		Germany invades the Low Countries and France
	June	France capitulates
		British troops are evacuated from the Continent
	August	Battle of Britain begins
		Start of London Blitz
		Tripartite pact between Germany, Italy and Japan

1941	March	Introduction of Lend-Lease arrangements between the USA and Britain
	June	Germany invades the Soviet Union
	August	Churchill and Roosevelt announce the Atlantic Charter

1942	February	Singapore falls to the Japanese
		Japanese invade Burma
	May	Britain and the Soviet Union sign twenty-year treaty
	June	Tobruk falls to Axis Powers
	October	Battle of El Alamein
	December	Publication of the Beveridge Report

1943	January	Churchill and Roosevelt hold Casablanca Conference
	February	German forces surrender at Stalingrad
	July	Allies invade Sicily
		Mussolini is forced to resign
	October	Britain, USA and the Soviet Union agree to set up the United Nations
	November	Churchill, Roosevelt and Stalin meet at Teheran Conference

| 1944 | June | Allied forces enter Rome |
| | | Allied troops land in Normandy |

| 1945 | January | Russian troops enter Warsaw |
| | February | Churchill, Roosevelt and Stalin meet at Yalta |

April	Mussolini is killed
	Hitler commits suicide
May	Germany surrenders
July	Landslide Labour victory in British general election
	Potsdam Conference begins
August	Japan surrenders

Biographies

Abdul Hamid II (1842–1918), Sultan of Turkey 1876–1909.

Aehrenthal, Alois Baron (1909 Count) Lexa von (1854–1912), Imperial and Royal Ambassador at St Petersburg 1899–1906; Foreign Minister 1906–12.

Andrassy von Csik-Szent-Kiraly u. Kraszna-Horka, Julius Count (1823–1890), Hungarian Minister-President 1867–71; Imperial and Royal Foreign Minister 1871–9.

Asquith, Henry Herbert (1852–1928), Chancellor of the Exchequer 1905–8; Prime Minister 1908–16; Leader of the Liberal Party 1908–26. He was responsible for the 'Super Tax' on incomes over £5,000, old age pensions and reform of the House of Lords in 1911.

Auclert, Hubertine (1848–1914). French feminist. Auclert founded the Droit de la Femme in 1878 and edited the newspaper *La Citoyenne* from 1881 to 1892. Her object was to stimulate French feminism by making the vote the first priority, followed by access to the professions, equal pay and equal divorce. She adopted more militant tactics than most of her countrywomen, including street demonstrations, lobbying of politicians and withholding taxes. But by the 1890s she had become damaged by disputes with the moderates, lost influence and became a rather isolated figure.

Bebel, Ferdinand August (1840–1913). Craftsman (woodworker) by trade, politician by career. Friend of Marx, founding father of the SPD and the author of the most-read socialist books in Germany, he was a shrewd and adaptable political leader rather than a theorist. Reichstag deputy 1871–81 and 1883–1913. Party leader for much of this period.

Berchtold von u. zu Ungarschitz, Fratting u. Pullitz, Leopold Count (1863–1942), Imperial and Royal Ambassador at St Petersburg 1906–11; Foreign Minister 1912–15.

Bernstein, Eduard (1850–1932). Working class and Jewish background. Friend of Engels and Kautsky and co-author of the German Social Democratic Party's 1891 Erfurt Programme. Also editor of the party newspaper before being exiled to Britain when Bismarck introduced anti-socialist legislation. Rejected much of Marx's views and accepted the permanency of capitalism. Returned to Germany 1901, but his 'revisionism' rejected by party conference. Opposed socialist support for the war effort and briefly left the party over this. A parliamentary deputy in 1902–6, 1912–18, 1920–8, he was concerned with the ideological and strategic direction of the socialist party, rather than everyday politics.

Bethmann-Hollweg, Theobald von (1856–1921), German Chancellor and Minister-President of Prussia 1909–17.

Beveridge, William Henry (1879–1963). Civil servant, social reformer and academic. A major formative influence on British social policy during the twentieth century, Beveridge's ideas were a mixture of interventionist Liberalism and turn-of-the-century National Efficiency. From 1908 he acted as a civil servant advising the government on unemployment insurance. Between 1919 and 1937 he served as director of the London School of Economics. He became a household name as a result of his role in the Second World War when he chaired an inter-departmental committee on social insurance. This culminated in the famous 'Beveridge Report' of 1942 which proposed a comprehensive state scheme to secure the welfare of the British population. In combination with his *Full Employment in a Free Society* (1944) this helped to create a popular consensus over economic and social policy immediately after the war. Beveridge's ideas were largely implemented by the Attlee government and maintained subsequently by the Conservatives.

Bismarck-Schönhausen, Otto von (1815–98) came from a land-owning Junker family on his father's side and from the Prussian high bureaucracy on his mother's. In his youth he became known as the 'wild Junker' and found it difficult to settle down in a civil service career. He had a spell running the family estates and partly under the influence of his future wife Johanna von Puttkamer experienced a religious conversion. His first incursion into politics was as a member of the United Diet in 1847 and during the revolution of 1848. He acquired a reputation as an extreme reactionary. In 1851 he re-entered official service in the important post of Prussian Ambassador to the German Diet in Frankfurt. It fell to him to maintain Prussian interests in Germany against Austria. He developed into an exponent of *Realpolitik* and moved away from the dogmatic conservative legitimism of his friends in the Prussian court. In 1859 he was relegated to the Prussian Embassy in St Petersburg, but as the constitutional conflict between the Prussian liberals and the King escalated he was talked about as a potential foreign or prime minister. The call came in September 1862 when Bismarck was able to convince the king that he could save the monarchy's prerogatives. After an unpromising start, when he was execrated among liberals throughout Germany, his unification of *Kleindeutschland* turned him into a hero. After 1870 his main concern in foreign policy was to maintain the status quo in Europe to ensure the survival of the new Reich. He was, however, not above using the threat of war to further his aims at home and abroad. By introducing a tariff which protected both agricultural and industrial products in 1879 he hoped to stabilize support for the regime as well as strengthen the economy. However, in domestic affairs he found it increasingly difficult to control the dynamic social and economic forces unleashed by the establishment of a unified Germany. His long political survival meant that the German political system, which he himself largely created, did not adapt sufficiently to changing circumstances. Ultimately Bismarck's hold on power depended on the Emperor, and when the young Wilhelm II succeeded to the throne in 1888 his days were numbered. After his fall in March 1890 he became his own best propagandist and in his *Reflections and Reminiscences* gave his version of the events in which he had played so great a role.

Blum, Léon (1872–1950). Parisian. Came from a bourgeois and Jewish background. Educated at the elite École Normale Supérieure and the Sorbonne. A lawyer by training, and with a legalistic outlook on some matters, he also enjoyed a sophisticated and cultured lifestyle and wrote books on literature, socialism and marriage. Entered parliament in 1919. Like Jaurès (whom he admired), emphasized the need to synthesize Marxism and morality and refused to be called a reformer. A party unifier, who doubted his abilities as an inspirational leader, Blum was still no pragmatist. He held firmly to his convictions when tried by the Vichy regime in 1942.

Bonnet, Georges (1889–1973). Member of the French Radical Party. Ambassador in Washington, 1936–7; Minister of Finance, 1937–8; Foreign Minister in Daladier's government, April 1938–September 1939; Minister of Justice, September 1939–March 1940.

Bonnet fought in the First World War. As Foreign Minister under Daladier, he was the leader of those who sought to 'appease' Hitler by making concessions, and in 1938 played a leading part in putting pressure on Czechoslovakia to abandon the Sudetenland. In December 1938 he welcomed Ribbentrop, the German Foreign Minister, to Paris and signed a joint declaration affirming good relations between France and Germany; he was widely thought to have offered Germany a free hand in Eastern Europe. In the war crisis at the beginning of September 1939 he tried hard to secure a Munich-type settlement, through a conference to be convened by Mussolini, and was prepared to do almost anything to avoid war. During the German occupation of France he took refuge in Switzerland, and after the war he returned to politics under the French Fourth Republic. He wrote a number of somewhat contradictory volumes of memoirs; see particularly *De Munich à la guerre: La défense de la Paix* (revised edn, Paris, 1967).

Boulanger, General Ernest Jean (1837–91). After a military career in Algeria and Cochin China, Boulanger took part in the wars of 1859 and 1870 and fought against the Paris Commune in 1871. When he was Minister of War in 1886 Boulanger seemed to have Bonapartist aspirations and appeared in the 14 July parade on a black horse. Though sacked as a minister in 1887 and put on the retired list by alarmed politicians in 1888, he became increasingly popular and was elected as deputy for a succession of constituencies. In January 1889, however, he failed to organize the expected coup and thereafter his star was on the wane; he shot himself in Brussels after the death of his mistress.

Branting, Karl Hjalmar (1860–1925). Born Stockholm. Founding father of Swedish Social Democracy, active from its origins in the 1880s, its first deputy, and a major influence on its future direction. Party leader from 1907. Prime Minister 1920, 1921–3, 1924–5. Formed alliances with Liberals and set Swedish party on a reformist pathway. Nobel Peace Prize 1921.

Bülow, Bernhard (1899 Count, 1905 Prince) von (1849–1929), Ambassador at Rome 1893–7; Secretary of State at the Wilhelmstrasse 1897–1900; German Chancellor 1900–9.

Chamberlain, Arthur Neville (1869–1940). Minister of Health 1923, 1924–9; Chancellor of the Exchequer, 1923–4, 1931–7; Prime Minister, 1937–40; Lord President of the Council, 1940.

Neville Chamberlain came from a prominent Birmingham political family, being the son of Joseph Chamberlain and the half-brother of Austen. His early political experience was in home affairs, where he was a reforming Minister of Health. As Chancellor of the Exchequer in the governments headed by MacDonald and Baldwin in the 1930s he became a dominant figure in many aspects of policy, notably on questions of rearmament, where the Treasury played a leading role. When he became Prime Minister in May 1937 he played an active role in foreign policy, and during the Czechoslovakian crisis of 1938 he took the lead, flying to meet Hitler on three occasions in September. He reluctantly but determinedly led Britain into war in September 1939, and remained as wartime Prime Minister until he resigned after the House of Commons debate; he sat in Churchill's War Cabinet until illness forced him to resign in October 1940. He died the next month.

Chamberlain, Joseph (1836–1914). British businessman, social reformer and imperialist, associated with campaigns for tariff reform and imperial unity. Raised in a

Liberal and Nonconformist atmosphere, Chamberlain began his career with the family business in Birmingham. In 1874, at 38, he retired with a substantial fortune. After carrying out social reforms as Mayor of Birmingham, he entered Parliament in 1876. He broke with Gladstone in 1886 over the latter's advocacy of Irish Home Rule; as a Liberal Unionist, he became Colonial Secretary in 1895 in the Conservative Cabinet of Lord Salisbury. An enthusiastic supporter of the Boer War, he resigned his Cabinet post in 1903 to campaign (unsuccessfully) for preferential tariffs on imperial goods.

Churchill, Sir Winston (1874–1965). Churchill had a long political career behind him when he became Prime Minister in 1940. He had been successively a Conservative, a Liberal and then a Conservative again and had held cabinet office under Asquith, Lloyd George and Baldwin. An opponent of Neville Chamberlain's policy of appeasement and an advocate of rearmament in the late thirties, he was brought into the cabinet on the outbreak of war in 1939 and became Prime Minister of a Coalition government amidst the series of German successes in the spring of 1940.

He was able to convince the British people that the war should be continued and that victory was possible. Strongly pro-American, he did much to forge and maintain the alliance with the United States. Though widely perceived as a great wartime leader, he and the Conservative Party were defeated at the 1945 general election after the ending of the Coalition, and Clement Attlee became Prime Minister of a Labour government. Churchill became Prime Minister again from 1951 to 1955.

Codreanu, Corneliu (1899–1938). With Horst Wessel and Jose Antonio Primo de Rivera the most important fascist 'martyr'. In the 1920s he developed a highly mystical and virulently anti-Semitic form of Romanian ultra-nationalism. It adopted a fascist form with the creation of the paramilitary terrorist organization, the Legion of the Archangel Michael (1927) and the Iron Guard (1930). These were persecuted by the regime of King Carol I and Codreanu was murdered in prison in 1938. Carol was forced into exile in 1940, and his successor, General Antonescu, followed the advice of Hitler, crushed the Legion, and turned Romania into a Nazi puppet state.

Daladier, Edouard (1884–1970). Member of the French Radical Party. Premier (Président du Conseil) 1933, 1934; Minister of Defence, 1936–8; Premier and Minister of Defence, April 1938–March 1940; Minister of Defence, March–May 1940.

Daladier served in the infantry during the First World War. As Minister of Defence in Léon Blum's Popular Front government, he promoted French rearmament and eased relations between the government and the army. As Premier during 1938 he adopted an ambiguous position during the Czechoslovakian crisis, sometimes advocating resistance to German demands and correctly predicting the future course of German aggression, but repeatedly falling back on a policy of urging the Czechs to surrender in order to avoid war. In 1939 he took a much firmer line, against both Italy and Germany, and led France into war in September. He resigned as Premier in March 1940, but remained Minister of Defence in Reynaud's government until May. He was arrested by Pétain's government in August 1940, and charged at the Riom trial (1942) with causing the defeat of France. He was deported to Germany in 1943. He survived the war, and resumed political life under the Fourth and Fifth Republics.

Degrelle, Leon (1906–94). The most significant fascist survivor after 1945. Leader of Rex, the greatest threat to Belgian democracy in the 1930s. This was a radical right Catholic party heavily influenced by Charles Maurras, which became steadily Nazified by 1939. A charismatic speaker, he became notorious for his collaborationist activity in the war. Degrelle formed the Legion Wallonie, which fought, with some distinction, on the eastern front for the Nazis against the Soviet Union. He escaped to Spain in 1945, and became a significant influence in attempts to develop the 'Eurofascism' idea after 1945.

Delcassé, Théophile (1852–1923), French Foreign Minister, 1898–1905 and August 1914 to October 1915; Minister of Marine 1911–13; Ambassador at St Petersburg 1913–14.

de Man, Hendrick (1885–1953). Born Antwerp. Wealthy and cultured background. One-time director of education in the Belgian socialist party, he was critical of pre-war socialist practice, and of Marxist ideology, although in a manner very different from that of the revisionists. Later a professor of social psychology at Frankfurt University, he was concerned with the moral appeal and value of socialism, and with human motives. In the 1930s he produced plans for tackling unemployment, initially within the Belgian socialist party. By late 1930s concerned to create a new socialism, with an emphasis on responsibility and authority. President of Belgian socialist party by 1939; Minister without Portfolio, Government of National Unity. Sympathetic to Germany up to 1940, he engaged in pragmatic co-operation whilst the Germans destroyed his corporatist dreams, until retiring in 1941. Tried in Belgium for treason in 1944, but lived bitterly in Switzerland until 1953.

Disraeli, Benjamin (1804–81), Earl of Beaconsfield, was born into a Jewish family, but baptized into the Church of England at the age of twelve. His father was a man of letters, still known for his collection of literary anecdotes and sketches, *The Curiosities of Literature*. Benjamin gained early notoriety as a writer of scandalous society novels, but he also acquired debts which bedevilled his career for a long time. He had amorous involvements and suffered episodes of depression. He had political ambitions and attached himself to Lord Lyndhurst, a Tory Lord Chancellor. He eventually succeeded in getting elected for Maidstone in 1837. Two years later he married Mary Anne, the wealthy widow of Wyndham Lewis, his colleague in the representation of Maidstone. In the 1841 Parliament he gathered round himself a group of young aristocrats known as Young England, advocating a romantic Toryism based on harmony between the upper and working classes. He published his two major novels *Coningsby* and *Sybil, or The Two Nations*. As the rift between Peel and the Conservative back benches deepened, Disraeli became the most articulate spokesman of the anti-free-traders. The party split of 1846 left the Protectionist rump short of political talent and gave him the opportunity to emerge as a major figure. By 1849 he was recognized, with some reluctance, as the leader of the Protectionist Tories in the Commons and was sustained in that position for next twenty years by Lord Derby, the leader in the Lords. Disraeli continued to be much distrusted in his party for his eventually successful attempts to drop protection and his unsuccessful efforts to link up with other groups to form a viable government. Liberal disunity over parliamentary reform in 1866 gave him the chance for a major political achievement, the passage of the Second Reform Bill the following year. He became briefly Prime Minister in February 1868, but when this was followed by heavy electoral defeat in December 1868 his continuance as leader was again in doubt. His aim to turn the Conservatives into a majority party was at last crowned with success in 1874. He emerged from the Near Eastern crisis of the middle 1870s with an apparent diplomatic triumph, in spite of the campaign against his policies conducted by his great rival Gladstone. In the last two years of his premiership economic and agricultural depression, as well as humiliating imperial setbacks, turned the electoral tide against him and he was heavily defeated in the election of 1880. The myth of Disraeli as the maker of modern democratic Toryism, or Tory Democracy, remained potent after his death.

Dreyfus, Alfred (1859–1935) was the Alsatian Jewish officer on the French General Staff at the centre of the Affair named after him. Treason discovered in the Ministry of War in 1894 was blamed on him and he was sentenced to imprisonment on Devil's Island. His family worked for his rehabilitation and his innocence became clear with the suicide of another officer in 1898. Although Dreyfus bore his ordeal with dignity, he showed little personal awareness of the great political issues that were fought out over his case. He was finally rehabilitated in 1906.

Durkheim, Emile (1858–1917). An alumnus of the Ecole Normale, Durkheim became a professor at the Sorbonne in 1902. An eminent sociologist and anthropologist, he elaborated a communitarian defence of liberalism. In works such as *Le suicide* (1897) and *Formes élémentaires de la vie religieuse* (1912) he emphasized the extent to which individual development depends on social environment, and explored questions such as the social nature of moral knowledge, and the normative relation between the private and the public.

Eden, Robert Anthony (1897–1977). Minister for League of Nations Affairs, 1935; Foreign Secretary, December 1935–February 1938; Dominions Secretary, September 1939–May 1940; Foreign Secretary in Churchill's War Cabinet, December 1940–5, again Foreign Secretary, 1951–5; Prime Minister 1955–January 1957.

Eden fought as an infantry officer in the First World War. He made his ministerial career at the Foreign Office, becoming Foreign Secretary for the first time at the age of 38. Under Baldwin and Chamberlain, he took part in the policy of 'appeasement', in the sense of trying to reach agreement with Germany over the Rhineland in 1936 and adopting a non-intervention policy towards the Spanish Civil War. He resigned in February 1938, more on questions of timing and method than on an issue of principle. His resignation removed him from any responsibility during the Czechoslovakian crisis of 1938, though from the back benches he made only cautious criticisms of government policy. Through his wartime association with Churchill, and glowing references in Churchill's memoirs, Eden gained a reputation as an opponent of 'appeasement' which he did not entirely deserve. Two volumes of *The Eden Memoirs* refer to these matters: *Facing the Dictators* (1962), and *The Reckoning* (1965).

Eisenhower, General Dwight D. (1890–1969). A gifted staff officer who saw no active service during the First World War, Eisenhower was chosen to command a series of Allied expeditions, beginning with the Anglo-American invasion of French North Africa in 1942–3 and culminating in the Allied invasion of north-west Europe in 1944–5. His detractors argued that he had little idea of how to command troops in battle. But he showed himself to be the outstanding soldier-diplomat amongst the Western Allies, able to harness the services of such difficult and antagonistic characters as the British Field Marshal Montgomery and the American General George Patton, to the Allied war effort. He served as President of the USA from 1952–60.

Fawcett, Millicent Garrett (1847–1929). English suffragist leader. Fawcett's work on behalf of women's causes stretched from the late 1860s to 1920s; she was especially important as the President of the National Union of Women's Suffrage Societies from 1897 to 1918. An unexciting but convincing speaker, Fawcett adhered rigidly to non-violent tactics and to patient pressure applied to politicians. Under her leadership NUWSS withstood the onset of militancy in the Edwardian period, adopted an alliance with the Labour Party in 1912, survived the divisions of wartime and re-emerged as the National Union of Societies for Equal Citizenship.

Foch, Marshal Ferdinand (1851–1929). Foch made his reputation as a resolute field commander in the opening battles of the First World War, during which he rose from command of a corps in August to an army group by the end of the year. When his patron, the French Commander-in-Chief General Joffre, was dismissed in December 1916, he was temporarily eclipsed by Nivelle, only to be appointed Chief of Staff of the French army in May 1917, following the fiasco of the Nivelle offensive.

In March 1918, during the crisis in Anglo-French relations provoked by the initial success of the Germans' spring offensive, he was appointed to co-ordinate the operations of all of the Allied armies on the Western Front.

Franco, Francisco (1892–1975). The longest lasting of the 'Great Dictators', the Spanish 'Caudillo' was an extreme right ultra-nationalist, whose reactionary governments were as brutal as any fascist or collaborationist regime. He became leader, mainly through the death of others, of the military and nationalist revolt which led to the Spanish Civil War (1936–9). The military aid given by Mussolini and Hitler was instrumental in Franco's victory and the establishment of his regime (1939–75). Franco avoided the fate of Hitler and Mussolini by remaining a 'non-belligerent' in the Second World War.

Franz Ferdinand, Archduke (1863–1914), heir-apparent to the Habsburg monarchy 1894–1914; his assassination at Sarajevo on 28 June 1914 triggered the outbreak of the First World War.

Franz Joseph I (1830–1916), Emperor of Austria 1848–1916.

Giers, Nicholas Karlovich (1820–95), assistant to Russian Foreign Minister 1876–82; Russian Foreign Minister 1882–95.

Giolitti, Giovanni (1842–1928). A lawyer and a civil servant by training, Giolitti entered the Italian parliament in 1882 as a member of A. Depretis' centre-left liberals. Treasury Minister in 1889–93, he was one of the leaders of the opposition to the conservative reaction of 1898–1900. When the liberals formed a government under G. Zanardelli in 1901, Giolitti was Minister of Internal Affairs, and, from 1903, Prime Minister. Giolitti dominated the first fifteen years of the century (l'età giolittiana): it was an age of economic growth and liberal reforms, including the introduction of universal male suffrage (1913). Giolitti supported the labour movement and invited the socialists (PSI) to join the government. However, when the revolutionary current gained control of the PSI, Giolitti sought to strengthen his majority with the support of the Catholics and the Nationalists. In opposition in 1914–18, he favoured neutrality, but was unable to prevent Italy's intervention in the First World War (1915). In office again in 1919–21, Giolitti tried to implement radical social reforms as a response to post-war labour unrest. After recommending a repressive response to blackshirt outrages, in 1922–4 he hoped that it would be possible to turn fascism into a constitutional movement. Soon disillusioned, from 1924 he became an outspoken opponent of Mussolini.

Gladstone, William E. (1809–98). Perhaps the most famous nineteenth-century liberal statesman, Gladstone entered politics as a staunch conservative. Educated at Eton and Oxford, a loyal member of the Church of England, he served under Sir Robert Peel in 1834. At the Board of Trade in 1841–5, and as Colonial Secretary in 1845–6, he supported 'liberal' reforms such as the repeal of the Corn Laws and devolution for Canada. However, his conversion to liberalism took place between 1852 and 1859, and was occasioned by the beginning of the constitutional phase of the Italian Risorgimento, which he enthusiastically supported. Chancellor of the Exchequer in 1852–5 and 1859–66, he was the architect of the 'social contract' of mid-Victorian Britain. In 1866–7 he was one of the leaders of the movement for electoral reform, and in 1868 led the Liberals to a landslide victory. In office until 1874, he presided over many important reforms, but failed to obtain a majority at the next election. A convinced supporter of an 'inter-nationalist' approach to foreign policy, in 1876 he led a popular agitation in support of Bulgarian independence. In 1879–80 his electoral campaign in Midlothian inaugurated a new phase in British electoral techniques. In office again in 1880–6, he tried to solve the Irish question by implementing a scheme of self-government similar to the Canadian one. However, his proposal was rejected by the electorate in 1886 and only insufficiently supported in 1892. He retired in 1894.

Goebbels, Joseph (1897–1945). A brilliant propagandist and orator, despite being a physical cripple. He became the most dedicated acolyte of Hitler after 1926. Responsible for building the Nazi party in Berlin before the rise to power, he became Minister for National Enlightenment and Propaganda in 1933. In this post he successfully provided the political co-ordination between people and government. The choreographer of the Third Reich, his most valuable work was in the elections of 1930–3, the sinister anti-Semitic propaganda, and his mixture of terror and exhortation to the population to defend the Nazi regime in its final days. Committed suicide, after murdering his children, in Hitler's bunker.

Goluchowski von Goluchowo, Agenor Count (1849–1921), Imperial and Royal minister at Bucharest 1887–93; Foreign Minister 1895–1906.

Gorchakov, Prince Alexander Mikhailovich (1798–1883), Russian Minister for Foreign Affairs 1856–82; Chancellor 1867–82.

Green, Thomas Hill (1836–82). A Fellow of Balliol College and White's Professor of Moral Philosophy at Oxford, Green was a receptive scholar of German idealism and the founder of the neo-Kantian or neo-Hegelian school of thought in Britain. His teaching – with its strong emphasis on civic virtue and a common citizenship – was the most powerful philosophical influence in the British Isles during the last quarter of the nineteenth century. His works include *Prolegomena to Ethics* (1883) and *Lectures on the Principles of Political Obligation* (1901).

Grey, Sir Edward (1862–1933), Parliamentary Under-Secretary for Foreign Affairs 1892–5; Foreign Secretary 1905–16. A prominent Liberal Imperialist, Grey was regarded from an early stage as being hostile towards Germany.

Guderian, General Heinz (1888–1954). After serving on the Western Front in the First World War, Guderian became one of the leading exponents of mechanization and armoured warfare in the German army between the wars. He played a key role in establishing the first Panzer divisions and led a Panzer Corps in the invasion of Poland in 1939 and of France in 1940. However, having disobeyed one of Hitler's orders, he was dismissed at the end of 1941 after the opening stages of the invasion of Russia. He returned to active service following the disaster at Stalingrad, first as Inspector General of Armoured Troops and subsequently as Chief of the General Staff, only to be dismissed again in March 1945, a few weeks before the end of the war.

Haig, Field Marshal Sir Douglas (1861–1928). In December 1915 Haig succeeded Sir John French as the Commander-in-Chief of the British armies in France. On the Somme in 1916 and at Ypres in 1917 he fought two of the most costly and controversial battles of the war because he was convinced he could force the German army to exhaust its manpower if he continued to attack them. In the eyes of historians his reputation has never recovered and these battles have eclipsed the more successful campaign he waged between August and November 1918, which finally broke the German army's resistance.

Halifax, Lord (Edward Wood) (1881–1959). Viceroy of India, 1926–31; Lord President of the Council, 1937–8; Foreign Secretary, February 1938–December 1940; Ambassador to the United States, December 1940–6.

Halifax served in the First World War. As Viceroy of India, he negotiated successfully with Gandhi, an experience which had some effect on his later dealings with Hitler – a very different personality. While Lord President, he visited Germany in November 1937, meeting Hitler and holding out the prospect of accepting German claims in Austria, the Sudetenland and Danzig. He succeeded Eden as Foreign

Secretary in February 1938, and worked closely with Chamberlain during the Czechoslovakian crisis that year, until he changed his mind and opposed the terms demanded by Hitler at Godesberg. From that point, and through into 1939, he took a stronger line than Chamberlain; so that his association with 'appeasement' was less close than was once believed. When Chamberlain resigned in May 1940, there was a real chance that Halifax might have been his successor, but he refused. He stayed on as Foreign Secretary in Churchill's War Cabinet until December 1940, when he was moved to Washington. He published his memoirs, *Fullness of Days*, in 1957.

Hardie, James Keir (1856–1915). One of the founding fathers of British socialism, Hardie inspired devotion in his lifetime and became a legend after his death. The illegitimate son of a Scottish coal miner, he became the champion of the unemployed, a crusader for moral causes, who always seemed to rest on the side of principle. He was less successful as a party leader or in Parliament, where he represented West Ham (1892–5) and Merthyr (1900–15). No political theorist, in later years he was also eclipsed as a political leader by machine politicians. He then oscillated between a belief in unity and a desire to restate his credentials as a radical icon. Lived an active and committed life, sacrificing his health and his family for his reputation and his cause.

Haymerle, Heinrich Ritter (1876 Baron) (1828–81), Imperial and Royal Ambassador at Rome 1877–9; Foreign Minister 1879–81.

Hilferding, Rudolf (1877–1943). A doctor by profession, and perhaps the most distinguished political economist of his generation. Author of many works, especially *Finance Capital (Das Finanzkapital)* (1910). Grew up in Austria, but lived in Germany from 1906. Taught at the SPD education college and edited the party newspaper. Joined USPD. Reich Finance Minister 1923, 1928. Following Hitler's accession, fled Germany for Switzerland and France.

Himmler, Heinrich (1900–45). A Nordic racist and petty bourgeois chicken farmer, he became one of the more sinister figures in Hitler's Germany. Appointed head of Hitler's bodyguard, the SS, in 1929, he was ultimately responsible for its diversification into many areas of military, security and economic organization, including SS armoured divisions, concentration camp management, forced labour and political and military intelligence. The SS arranged the mass murders of the Night of the Long Knives, of the Holocaust and of civilians on the Soviet front. Himmler committed suicide after capture in 1945.

Hindenburg, Field Marshal Paul von (1847–1934). Brought out of retirement in 1914, Hindenburg, together with his Chief of Staff, Ludendorff, was responsible for repelling the Russian invasion of East Prussia at Tannenberg in August 1914. He then went on to expel the Russians from Poland and Galicia in 1915. In August 1916 he became Chief of the General Staff and *de facto* supreme commander. Although he could not prevent Germany from losing the war, he still retained enough prestige to be elected President of the Weimar Republic in 1925, a post he held until his death in 1934.

Hitler, Adolf (1889–1945). Before 1914 a bohemian drop-out in Vienna, he rose to become Chancellor of Germany in January 1933, and the Fuehrer by 1934, with few theoretical limitations on his power. Hitler joined the National Socialist Workers Party in 1919, and had become its leader in 1921. He was imprisoned in 1923 for his part in the Munich beer hall *putsch*. His successful foreign policy included the remilitarization of the Rhineland (1936), the Anschluss (1938), the destruction of Czechoslovakia (1938–9) and the invasion and conquest of Poland (1939). These actions led to the Second World War. Nazi imperialism saw the extension of the

German Empire to include most of continental Europe by 1942. Hitler committed suicide after the German defeat in 1945.

Ho Chi Minh (1890–1969). Founder of the Indochina Communist Party (1930) and its successor, the Viet Minh (1941), and President of the Democratic Republic of Vietnam (North Vietnam, 1945–69). Born to a poor rural family, he worked as a sailor before doing various manual jobs in Europe. He picked up socialist ideas in France, and was an early member of the French Communist Party, founded in the wake of the Russian Revolution. Persecuted by the authorities, he several times visited the USSR. In September 1945, in the wake of Japan's defeat, he declared Vietnam independent – recognized by the French authorities only after the First Indochina War (1946–54). His thinking fused nationalism with Communism, and he was an advocate of the revolutionary potential of the peasantry.

Isvolsky, Alexander Petrovich (1856–1919), Russian Minister at Copenhagen 1903–6; Foreign Minister 1906–10; Ambassador at Paris 1910–17.

Jaurès, Jean (1859–1914). Born into a farming family. A brilliant scholar and a university lecturer in philosophy, Jaurès was respected, even revered, by many contemporaries. An ethical socialist, concerned with justice and dignity, he was also a French patriot whose socialism was rooted in French tradition. Originally an independent deputy, who accepted that individual socialists should rally to the defence of the Republic when it was threatened by the right, he nonetheless accepted the majority's criticism of this view. Jaurès was a reformer but did not side with Bernstein. Assassinated for his anti-war views in 1914.

Kalnocky von Köröspatak, Gustav Count (1832–98), Imperial and Royal Ambassador at St Petersburg 1880–1; Foreign Minister 1881–95.

Key, Ellen (1849–1926). Swedish feminist, teacher and author. Key was an early advocate of sexual liberation for women. Her publications, including *The Strength of Women Misused* (1896) and *The Century of the Child, Love and Marriage* (1900), led to her being attacked as a supporter of free love. In fact she adopted a very positive view of motherhood, but wanted women to enjoy more freedom within marriage and more support from the state. She felt that feminists in Britain put too much emphasis on winning the vote and employment.

Keynes, John Maynard, Baron (1883–1946). British economist. Attacked the high level of reparations imposed on Germany after 1919, as well as the return to gold at the old parity in Britain in 1925. His book *General Theory of Employment, Interest and Money* (1936) revolutionized economic thinking and employment policies in many countries. Also made important contributions to the international monetary arrangements after 1945.

Kondratieff, Nicolai Dmitrievich (1892–1936). Russian economist, founder and first director of the Moscow Konyunkturnyi Institute. Developed a theory of long cycles in works published 1922–8 (one English version: *Long Wave Cycle* (1928)). Perished in Stalin's *gulag*.

Lansdowne, Henry Charles Petty-Fitzmaurice, 5th Marquess (1845–1927), Viceroy of India 1888–94; Secretary of State for War 1895–1900; Foreign Secretary 1900–5; Minister without Portfolio 1915–16.

Lenin [Ulianov], Vladimir Ilich (1870–1924). Founder of the Bolshevik Party and first head of the Soviet government. Lenin was born in Simbirsk, the son of a school inspector. His brother Alexander was executed in 1887 for an attempt on the life of Alexander III. He studied first at Kazan and then at St Petersburg universities, graduating in Law in 1891. In 1895 Lenin founded the revolutionary group the Union of Struggle for the Liberation of the Working Class, but in the same year he was arrested and exiled to Siberia. After his release in 1900 he moved abroad and began to edit the Social Democrat newspaper *Iskra*. In 1902 Lenin published *What Is To Be Done?*, a pamphlet in which he advocated the creation of a party of disciplined professional revolutionaries. When the Russian Social Democratic Labour Party split into Bolshevik and Menshevik wings at its Second Congress in 1903, Lenin became the leader of the Bolsheviks. Lenin was still abroad when the 1905 revolution broke out in Russia, and only returned to St Petersburg in November. In 1907 he was again abroad engaging in polemics with fellow Social Democrats and in 1916 published his book *Imperialism the Highest Stage of Capitalism*, which argued that modern finance capitalism prepared the way for socialism.

During the First World War, when most European socialists advocated 'peace without annexations or indemnities', Lenin called upon the workers to turn the imperialist war into a civil war, even if this meant a German victory. In January 1917 Lenin could foresee that the tsar might be deposed and replaced by a government of Miliukov, Guchkov and Kerensky. When the February revolution broke out Lenin was in Switzerland; he returned to Petrograd with German help in April 1917. In his 'April Theses' he set out the tactics which the Bolshevik Party followed in regard to the war, the Provisional Government and the Soviets. Following the July Days Lenin went into hiding in Finland. From there after the failure of the Kornilov revolt he began to agitate in favour of seizing power by an armed uprising. When the Bolsheviks did come to power on 25 October Lenin became the party Chairman. Despite considerable opposition from inside and outside his party, he favoured making immediate peace with Germany. On 30 August 1918 he was shot and wounded by a Socialist Revolutionary terrorist. Though he never fully recovered his health, he framed many of the Soviet state's economic, social, military, nationality and cultural policies. He died in Gorki in January 1924.

Lloyd George, David (1863–1945). British Liberal Prime Minister and world statesman. At home Lloyd George played a key role in the implementation of the 'New Liberalism' in the form of taxation of wealth in the 'People's Budget' of 1909 and social reforms such as old age pensions and insurance for health and unemployment. He first rose to prominence as an opponent of the war in South Africa (1899–1902). However, he proved to be a vital supporter of British plans for participation in the First World War, partly by throwing his political weight behind Grey's policy. As a result of dissatisfaction with the war effort Lloyd George rose to the premiership in December 1916. He introduced many changes in the system of government and presided over victory in 1918. At the peace settlement he often supported the French against the more liberal inclinations of President Woodrow Wilson, and consequently bore some of the responsibility for the harshness of the Treaty of Versailles; he was quick to accept the need to revise it. He remained in office until 1922 only by means of Conservative support; subsequently his divisive role within the Liberal Party and his alienation from Labour during the war effectively kept him out of power.

Ludendorff, General Erich (1865–1937). As a General Staff Officer, Ludendorff was responsible for the capture of the key Belgian fortress of Liege in August 1914. He was then transferred to the Eastern Front to act as Chief of Staff to Hindenburg. After defeating the Russians at Tannenberg the two men worked together as a team, first controlling the German war effort in the east and, between August 1916 and October 1918, acting as effective dictators of Germany. In 1923 he took part in Hitler's abortive Munich beer hall *putsch*.

Lyautey, Louis-Hubert-Gonzalve (1854–1934). French statesman and soldier, founder of the French Empire in Morocco, and devoted believer in the civilizing virtues of colonialism. An outstanding student at the St-Cyr Military Academy, Lyautey served in Algeria in the 1880s, and in Tonkin and Madagascar in the 1890s. He is best remembered for his resident generalship in Morocco from 1912, where he conquered the country and established its colonial administration. He briefly served in France as Minister of War (1916–17) before returning to Morocco until his resignation in 1925. He was a member of the Académie Française from 1912, and was made a Marshal of France in 1921.

MacDonald, James Ramsay (1866–1937). Son of a farmworker and a ploughman. Illegitimate. Largely self-educated, but still Labour Party's most important political and ideological strategist. An advocate and promoter of informed policy debate. As party Secretary from 1900 to 1910, he was closely involved with expanding organization. Subsequent posts included party Treasurer 1912–14, Chairman of the parliamentary party (leader) 1911–14 and 1923–31, and Prime Minister in 1924 (the first-ever Labour government) and in 1929–31. An ILP socialist, rather than a trade unionist, MacDonald had firm principles (he resigned as leader when the party supported the war) but was a depressive and egotistical character who found internal strife hard to tolerate. He became distanced from his party and disillusioned with its apparent inability to discuss matters rationally and fraternally. Formed a National Government during the economic crisis of 1931 and was expelled from the party.

Marx, Karl (1818–83). German philosopher and economist, the most influential socialist thinker in the twentieth century. In his writings, which combined Hegelian philosophy with Smithian economics, Marx sought to demonstrate that once capital had begun to circulate it would inevitably spread to every country and would create a world market. Having reached its point of culmination, capitalism would then collapse and give way to a socialist society. In this way, Marx intended to prove that socialism was not a utopian aspiration, but the certain outcome of historical development. Marx's project, however, remained incomplete and only the first volume of *Capital* was published in his lifetime. The fragmentary and ambiguous nature of Marx's literary legacy left it open to various interpretations, and in this way it was able to inspire a wide variety of socialist movements. The Bolshevik seizure of power in 1917 and the foundation of the Soviet state – ostensibly embodying Marxist principles – ensured that the type of Marxism propounded by Lenin would gain the widest currency throughout the world.

Méline, Félix Jules (1838–1925). French politician, president of the Chamber of Deputies 1888–9. Protectionist, played a leading part in the French protectionist legislation of 1888–1902.

Mill, John Stuart (1806–73). Philosopher, economist, political and social reformer, he was the son of the Utilitarian thinker James Mill. After a long career at the East India Company, J. S. Mill retired in 1858, and devoted his time and energy to intellectual and political activities. In 1859 he published his classical essay *On Liberty*, which he had written in co-operation with his wife Harriet Taylor. An ardent advocate of women's political and social emancipation, he sat in Parliament in 1865–8. His last campaign was in support of land tenure reform. His works include *A System of Logic* (1843) and *Principles of Political Economy* (1848).

Montgomery, Field Marshal Sir Bernard (1887–1976). After commanding a division during the Dunkirk campaign in 1940, Montgomery served in several posts in Britain before being given command of 8th Army in North Africa in August 1942. He gained the first major Commonwealth victory over the Germans at Alamein in November 1942. He then went on to command the British troops which invaded Sicily and Italy before commanding all Allied ground forces during the Normandy landings in 1944. His unbounded conceit earned him as many enemies amongst the upper echelons of the Allied high command as his professionalism and concern for their welfare earned him admirers amongst the soldiers who served under his command.

Mosca, Gaetano (1858–1941). Italian jurist and political scientist, studied in Palermo and taught at the universities of Palermo, Rome and Turin. He is best known for his theory of the 'ruling minority' (*classe politica*), which was further developed by V. Pareto. A conservative liberal in politics, was made a life senator in 1919, and became a bitter opponent of fascism in the 1920s. His works include *Sulla teorica dei governi e sul governo parlamentare* (1884) and *The Ruling Class* (1939).

Mosley, Sir Oswald (1896–1980). The 'Leader' of the British Union of Fascists (1932–40). Ex-Conservative MP (1918–22); ex-Labour MP (1926–30); ex-New Party MP (1930–1). Chancellor of the Duchy of Lancaster in 1929–30. Mosley formed the BUF because he felt the party system could not reverse the economic and political decline of Britain. After initial growth to 40,000 members by July 1934, the BUF almost collapsed. It became blamed for increased political violence and anti-Semitism in the 1930s, although it made a slow recovery advocating 'Mosley and Peace' (1937–40). Mosley was interned from June 1940 to November 1943.

Muraviev, Count Michael Alexandrovich (1845–1900). Russian Foreign Minister 1896–1900.

Mussolini, Benito (1883–1945). Ex-revolutionary socialist and editor of *Avanti*, he formed the fascist party (PNF) in 1919. After the fascist 'march on Rome' in 1922, he became Prime Minister of a coalition government. Used the murder of socialist deputy Matteoti, as the excuse to turn Italy into a one-party 'totalitarian' state. Remained Prime Minister until 1943, when the king withdrew his support after the Allied invasion. Freed from arrest by Otto Skorzeny, he was installed as Nazi puppet ruler of the Italian Social Republic (1943–5). Shot by partisans as he tried to escape to Switzerland, his body was strung up on a lamppost in Milan.

Nehru, Jawaharlal 'Pandit' (1889–1964). Leading Indian nationalist, and first Prime Minister of independent India (1947–64). Born to a family of Kashmiri Brahmins, Nehru was educated at Harrow, Cambridge and the Inner Temple. Nationalist by political temperament, he was associated with the Indian National Congress from 1919, becoming its President in 1929. He was imprisoned by the British eight times for nationalist activity between 1921 and 1945. By the 1930s he was widely seen as the heir-apparent of his mentor, M. K. Gandhi. Unlike Gandhi, he advocated modernization, and socialism adapted to Indian conditions.

Nietzsche, Friedrich (1844–1900). Born in the Prussian part of Saxony and became Professor of Classical Philology at the University of Basle in 1869. He was a disciple of Richard Wagner, whose musical dramas he saw as harbingers of a revolutionary culture of the future. Nietzsche's friendship with Wagner ended when the composer's last work, *Parsifal*, showed a reversion to Christianity. Among the concepts that emerge from his writings is the notion of Christian ethics as 'the morality of the slave', as against the 'master morality' of the Superman. Nietzsche's great influence derives from the fact that he contradicted some of the fundamental assumptions of the liberal age of enlightenment and reason, as well as of Christianity. His ideas were, however, often distorted for political ends. For the last ten years of his life he suffered from mental illness and was for a time confined in an asylum.

Norman, Montagu, Baron (1871–1950). English banker, Governor of the Bank of England 1920–44. Bears much responsibility for the return to gold in 1925 and the deflationary policies to keep it in being to 1931. Helped to prop up some of the new countries of East-Central Europe by British loans.

Ostrogorsky, Moisey Y. (1854–1919). Russian political scientist, studied at St Petersburg and Paris. An international expert on British and American politics, in 1906 was elected to the Duma, becoming one of the leaders of the (liberal) Constitutional Democratic Party. His publications include a treaty on the rights of women (1892) and the masterly *Democracy and the Organization of Political Parties* (2 vols, 1902), which examined oligarchic tendencies in Western democracies.

Pankhurst, Christabel (1880–1958). English suffragette leader. The daughter of Dr Richard and Mrs Emmeline Pankhurst, Christabel became the dominant figure in the Women's Social and Political Union between 1903 and 1914. She was instrumental in the break with the labour movement and pioneered militant tactics in 1905 when she interrupted a meeting of Sir Edward Grey and received a prison sentence for assault on a policeman. She fled to Paris to escape further imprisonment in 1912 but returned on the outbreak of war in 1914. Her work on behalf of the coalition government was rewarded with the official nomination by Lloyd George as candidate for Smethwick in 1918. However after her narrow defeat she abandoned women's causes for lecturing tours in the United States, where she preached on the Second Coming of Christ.

Pareto, Vilfredo (1848–1923). Italian economist and political scientist. Born in Paris, and studied in Turin and Florence. He applied mathematics to economic analysis, and his *Manuale d'economia politica* (1906) laid the foundation of modern welfare economics. His *Trattato di sociologia generale* (1916), which had a major impact on modern political thinking, elaborated a theory of elites and class formation.

Parnell, Charles Stewart (1846–91). Charles Stewart Parnell was born on 27 June 1846 of Protestant landowning stock in County Wicklow. He inherited Avondale, the family seat in County Wicklow, and lived the traditional life of a landowner, but took an active interest in the well-being of his tenants. In entering politics in 1874 he was following family tradition. After unsuccessfully contesting County Dublin as a Home Ruler he was elected for Meath in 1875. He came to wider notice by joining John Biggar in tactics of obstruction to highlight Irish grievances, breaking away from the cautious line followed by Isaac Butt, the Home Rule leader. Renewed agrarian unrest, the New Departure, linking the constitutional with the revolutionary advancement of the Irish cause, and the emergence of a more aggressive Irish Nationalist Party at Westminster after the election of 1880 made Parnell the 'uncrowned king of Ireland'. As President of the Irish National Land League, later of the Irish National League, he was the champion of the people in Ireland. As chairman of the Irish parliamentary party he pursued the alleviation of the agrarian problem and the establishment of an autonomous government in Dublin by constitutional means at Westminster. He reached the height of his influence in British politics when the election of 1885 left the eighty-six Irish Nationalists holding the balance of power in the Commons. After the failure of Gladstone's first Home Rule Bill in 1886 Parnell continued his alliance with the Liberals. An attempt to discredit him failed spectacularly when letters published in *The Times* in 1887 claiming a link between Parnell and terrorism, a matter subjected to investigation by a Special Commission, were exposed as a forgery in 1889. Parnell's visit to Gladstone at Hawarden in December 1889 marked a high point in the Liberal–Nationalist alliance. Less than a year later the Home Rule cause received an all-but-fatal blow, when Parnell's longstanding liaison with Mrs O'Shea was exposed in an undefended divorce case brought by Captain O'Shea. For the Liberals, with their large Nonconformist following, cooperation with Parnell became untenable. The Irish Nationalist Party split, only a minority continuing to accept Parnell's leadership. The stricken leader fought on passionately, in his speeches often reverting to the revolutionary strand in Irish nationalism. Worn out by the struggle, he died on 6 October 1891. Parnell, reserved and withdrawn as a person, was a remarkably charismatic leader, whose myth remained potent after his death.

Pétain, Marshal Philippe (1856–1951). Pétain established his reputation as one of the outstanding soldiers of the First World War by his successful defence of Verdun in 1916. Appointed Commander-in-Chief of the French army in May 1917, he nursed its morale back to health in the succeeding year and enabled it to withstand the German offensive in the spring of 1918. Following the defeat of the French army in 1940 he was called upon to conclude an armistice with the Germans and then presided over the Vichy regime, although growing senility meant that he was little more than a figurehead. He was tried and sentenced to death by his countrymen after the war, but the sentence was commuted to life imprisonment.

Poincaré, Raymond (1860–1934). A lawyer by training, Poincaré was elected to the National Assembly in 1887 as a deputy for the *Union des Gauches*. After a successful career in the lower chamber, he became a senator (1903–13). He was Minister of Public Education (1893, 1895), Finance Minister (1894–5), Prime Minister (1912–13), President (1913–20) and Foreign Minister (1922–4). Though he led France through the First World War to the reconquest of Alsace-Lorraine, he pursued a policy of stability in international relations as well as in home affairs. In 1926 he became Prime Minister for a further term, leading a government of National Union till he retired in 1929.

Quisling, Vidkun (1887–1945). Founder and leader of the Norwegian Nasjonal Samling, which never obtained more than 2 per cent of the vote in the 1930s. Notorious for his seizure of power, his name became part of the vocabulary of most European languages, denoting collaboration and treachery. Hitler tended to ignore his devoted disciple, and German control was mainly administered by a Council of State, or by the military. Shot as a traitor in October 1945, for plotting to bring about the Nazi invasion of 1940, for treasonable behaviour on seizing power on 9 April 1940 and forming a government on 1 February 1942, and for persecution of Jews and execution of Norwegian citizens.

Rathbone, Eleanor (1872–1946). English feminist and politician. Rathbone emerged into public life via local government, philanthropy and work for the National Union of Women's Suffrage Societies, whose President she became in 1918. Charitable activity in Liverpool during the First World War led her to campaign for the 'endowment of motherhood' – better known as Family Allowances. She played a major role in propagating the New Feminism during the 1920s and became elected as an Independent Member of Parliament for the Combined English Universities from 1929 until her death.

Reynaud, Paul (1876–1966). Leading member of the Democratic Alliance, a small centre party in the French Third Republic. Held several ministerial posts in the 1930s. Minister of Finance in Daladier's government, November 1938–March 1940; succeeded Daladier as Premier (Président du Conseil), March 1940; resigned 16 June 1940.

In the mid-1930s Reynaud was a supporter of de Gaulle's ideas on armoured forces. He became an energetic Minister of Finance under Daladier, stimulating industrial production and improving the financial position; he came into conflict with the Left by doing away with the forty-hour week introduced by the Popular Front. During the Czechoslovakian crisis he advocated a strong line against Germany, and emerged as a determined opponent of Nazi Germany. Becoming Premier in March 1940 he attempted to prosecute the war with vigour. At the time of the French defeat in June 1940 he wanted to continue the war from North Africa, but in the event resigned and was succeeded by Pétain. He was imprisoned by the Pétain government in September 1940, and deported to Germany in 1942. He returned to political life after the war. He wrote two versions of his memoirs, *La France a sauvé l'Europe* (2 vols, Paris, 1947) and *Au Coeur de la mêlée* (Paris, 1951).

Rhodes, Cecil (1853–1902). Financier, statesman and empire builder in South Africa. The son of a vicar, Rhodes was educated at home because of his poor health. He went to Africa to farm in 1870, but soon succumbed to 'diamond fever'. After great prospecting success, he bought up many holdings, becoming the world's leading mineral magnate by the 1880s (and vastly wealthy). He entered South African politics, dreaming of reconciliation between Afrikaans- and English-speakers, of a Cape-to-Cairo railway, and even of the peaceful recovery of the United States by the British Empire. Prime Minister of Cape Colony from 1890; but the abortive 'Jameson Raid' on the Transvaal in 1895 resulted in his resignation and the failure of most of his plans. He bequeathed a fortune to found the Oxford scholarships which still bear his name.

Ribot, Alexandre (1842–1923). French Foreign Minister, 1890–93; Finance Minister 1914–17; Prime Minister, March to September 1917.

Ricasoli, Bettino (1809–80). Head of one of the oldest Italian families, Baron Ricasoli took part in the 1848 revolution in Florence. After 1849 he travelled extensively in Europe before returning to his estates in Tuscany, where he experimented with the most advanced agricultural technology of the time. In 1859 he led Tuscany through a bloodless revolution and piloted its annexation to the kingdom of Sardinia, in order to form a new Italy. Nicknamed 'the Iron Baron' because of his moral integrity and political inflexibility, he became Prime Minister after Cavour's death in 1861, and then again in 1866–7. His priorities were the building of a national railway network and the struggle against banditry in the south. A Jansenist Catholic, he pursued a policy of 'A Free Church in a Free State'.

Roosevelt, Franklin D. (1882–1945). A Democratic politician and statesman, Roosevelt came from a patrician New York family. Despite being partially paralysed by poliomyelitis, he was elected governor of New York in 1928 and President of the United States in 1932. He was President from 1933 until his death in 1945. His first term of office was characterized as the 'New Deal', the reform programme by which Roosevelt strove to devise policies which would bring the United States out of the Depression. He was re-elected in 1936, 1940 and 1944.

Though he won in 1940 on a platform of non-intervention in the war, he was opposed to a German domination of Europe and he initiated aid to Britain via the 'Lend-Lease' programme. When, after Pearl Harbor, the USA was at war with Japan and Germany, he devoted himself to the prosecution of the war, travelling to the series of wartime Allied conferences and little inclined to leave strategic decisions to his generals. He was committed to an Allied invasion of Europe, which eventually took place with the D-Day landings on the French coast. Though he worked closely with Churchill, he was often suspicious of British policies, feeling that his desire for a liberal world order, and Britain's imperial interests, did not coincide. He hoped to establish good personal relations with Stalin that would avert clashes in framing the post-war world. He died in April 1945 shortly after the Yalta Conference and less than a month before the German surrender.

Salisbury, third Marquess of (1830–1903), was as Lord Robert Cecil a younger son in need of earning his living as a writer. He wrote many articles for the *Quarterly Review* and *Saturday Review*. While not amounting to a systematic political philosophy, his writings continue to give him a considerable reputation as a conservative intellectual. He was suspicious of all orthodoxies, sceptical of the possibility of progress and pessimistic about human nature. He was a devout High Anglican. He sat for fifteen years from 1853 for the family borough of Stamford without having to face an election. As Viscount Cranborne he was the most prominent Conservative opponent of the Reform Bill of 1867 and resigned from the Cabinet. Having succeeded to the Salisbury title in 1868 he remained Disraeli's most formidable opponent in the Conservative Party until a reconciliation was effected with his entry into the 1874 Cabinet as Secretary of State for India. The Eastern crisis drew him closer to Disraeli, in spite of his High Church position which made him sympathetic to the Christian minorities in the Balkans. From 1878 to 1880 he served as Foreign Secretary and was a principal architect of the Berlin settlement. From this date he remained one of the chief makers of British foreign policy for the rest of his career. As Tory leader in the Lords after Beaconsfield's death he emerged as the strongest Conservative personality, overshadowing Sir Stafford Northcote, the leader in the Commons. He defeated the more extravagant claims of Lord Randolph Churchill to a leading position in the party and was chiefly responsible for the adoption of the single-member constituency system in the Third Reform Bill of 1884. After the fall of the second Gladstone government in June 1885 he formed the first of his four administrations. His second, after the defeat of the Home Rule Bill, was a coalition of Conservative and Liberal Unionists and ushered in a long Conservative ascendancy. Salisbury, although a shy and aloof man, proved a shrewd party manager and lost something of the fear of modern mass politics that had earlier motivated him. He presided with some reluctance over the active imperialism at the end of the century. He relinquished his tenure of the Foreign Office in 1900, which since 1885 he had almost always combined with the premiership. Ill-health forced his resignation in 1902 and he was succeeded by his nephew A. J. Balfour. He was the longest-serving Prime Minister of the nineteenth century and the last to sit in the Lords.

Schacht, Hjalmar (1877–1970). German banker, president of the Reichsbank 1923–9 and 1933–9; Economics Minister 1934–7. Instrumental in ending the hyper-inflation of the Mark in 1923. His tight monetary control provided a framework for the German recovery and rearmament of the 1930s.

Stalin [Jugashvili], Iosif Vissarionovich (1879–1953). Bolshevik leader and head of Soviet government. Stalin was born in the Georgian town of Gori, the son of a cobbler. He was educated at the Orthodox seminary in Tiflis and joined the local Social Democratic group *Mesame Dasi* in 1898. He then worked as a political organizer and agitator for the Social Democrats in Transcaucasia. When the Social Democratic Party split in 1903, Stalin, unlike most Georgians, who sided with the Mensheviks, joined the Bolshevik wing. In 1912 he moved to St Petersburg and became an editor of the Bolshevik newspaper *Pravda*. Stalin was repeatedly imprisoned and exiled, and was in Siberia at the time of the February revolution. He returned to Petrograd on 12 March 1917 and resumed the editorship of *Pravda*. His advocacy of qualified support for the Provisional Government and for a defensive war attracted Lenin's criticism in April. After the Bolsheviks took power Stalin became Commissar for Nationality Affairs. During the Civil War he organized the defence of Tsaritsyn (later renamed Stalingrad). In 1922 he became General Secretary of the Russian Communist Party's Central Committee. In 1923 he published an essay on Leninism outlining the theory of 'socialism in one country'. He presided over the industrialization of the USSR and initiated the collectivization of agriculture. During the 1930s, especially in 1937–8, Stalin ordered the mass imprisonment and execution of perceived 'enemies of the people', including many from the generation that had been active in the Russian Revolution.

Stolypin, Pyotr Arkadievich (1862–1911). Russian politician, Prime Minister and Minister of the Interior 1906–11. His reforms were designed to permit the Russian peasantry to free itself from the obligations to the village community and work their own individual holdings.

Thiers, Adolphe (1797–1877). French statesman, journalist and historian, Thiers was close to Lafayette and a life-long admirer of parliamentary monarchy on the British model. Under the July Monarchy (1830–48) he was Minister for Internal Affairs (1832–4) and briefly Prime Minister in 1840. Exiled after Louis Napoleon's *coup d'état* (1851–2), he returned to parliamentary life in 1863 as a deputy of the Orleanist liberal party. After Napoleon's fall, Thiers became head of the executive (1870–1) and then President of the Republic (1871–7). Always hostile to revolutions, he was the architect of the bloody repression of the Paris Commune in 1871.

Trotsky [Bronstein], Lev Davydovich (1879–1940). Leading figure in the Russian revolutionary movement and prominent member of the Soviet government.

Trotsky was the son of a fairly prosperous Jewish farmer from Yanovka in the Ukrainian province of Kherson. For his membership of a workers' circle in Nikolaev he was exiled to Siberia in 1898. He managed to escape and joined Lenin in London in 1902. Trotsky was the delegate of the Siberian Social Democrats at II Congress of RSDLP in 1903, at which he sided with the Mensheviks against Lenin. He returned to Russia and played a prominent part in the 1905 revolution as Chairman of the St Petersburg Soviet. On 3 December 1905 he was arrested and again exiled to Siberia, but he escaped *en route* and made his way abroad. He broke with the Mensheviks, and established a group, the Mezhraionka, which attempted to unite both wings of the RSDLP.

During the First World War Trotsky edited the newspaper *Nashe slovo* in Paris, but was deported from France for anti-war agitation. In New York he edited the Russian-language newspaper *Novyi mir*, in which he published commentaries on the February revolution in 1917. On his way back to Russia he was detained in Canada by the British authorities and only arrived in Petrograd on 5 May 1917. Along with Mezhraionka Trotsky joined the Bolshevik Party in July. After the July Days he was arrested and imprisoned until 2 September. On 25 September he was elected Chairman of Petrograd Soviet and played a prominent part in setting up the network of Military Revolutionary Committees during October. Trotsky became Commissar for Foreign Affairs and led the Soviet delegation at the Brest-Litovsk peace negotiations. He served as Commissar for Military Affairs during the Civil War. From 1923 onwards Trotsky became a critic of the increasing centralization of the Soviet regime. He was expelled from the Communist Party in 1927 and deported from the USSR the following year. In exile Trotsky continued to criticize the Stalin dictatorship. In exile too he published his monumental *History of the Russian Revolution* (1931–3). He settled in Mexico in 1937 and on 20 August 1940 was assassinated by one of Stalin's agents.

Weber, Max (1864–1920). Eminent German sociologist. Weber hailed from a family which combined a strong Calvinist tradition with a firm commitment to political liberalism. Educated at Heidelberg, Göttingen and Berlin (under T. Mommsen), he held teaching positions at Berlin, Freiburg, Heidelberg and Munich. His contributions to the methodology of the social sciences (with the concept of the ideal-type), and to the study of religion, politics and economics (*The Protestant Ethic and the Spirit of Capitalism*, 1904–5) were highly influential. His two-volume treatise, *Economy and Society*, has reshaped Western sociological thought.

Wilhelm II (1859–1941). German Emperor and King of Prussia 1888–1918.

Witte, Serge Yulievich, Count (1849–1915). Russian politician, Minister of Finance and Transport 1892–1903; Prime Minister 1903–6. Attempted to speed the modernization of Russia by encouraging foreign investment, putting the rouble on a gold standard and expanding the railway network.

Zetkin, Clara (1857–1933) German Marxist-feminist. Author of an influential pamphlet, *The Question of Women Workers and Women at the Present Time* (1889), Zetkin regarded employment as the necessary precondition for women's emancipation. She helped to persuade the German Social Democrats to organize women and founded the International Socialist Women's Congress in 1907. She opposed the First World War and was gaoled as a pacifist. In 1918 Zetkin helped to found the German Communist Party and became a member of the Reichstag from 1920 to 1932.

Zhukov, Marshal Georgi (1896–1974). After serving as a cavalry NCO in the tsarist army, Zhukov rose rapidly through the ranks of the Soviet army in the inter-war period. He gained experience of armoured warfare fighting the Japanese in Manchuria in 1939 and in 1941 Stalin appointed him Chief-of-Staff of the Red Army. During the Second World War he played a prominent role either in planning or in commanding Soviet forces, in nearly every key battle, fighting in front of Moscow in 1941 and planning the Soviet victories at Stalingrad and Kursk in 1942 and 1943. In 1945 he commanded the Soviet forces which captured Berlin.

Guide to Further Reading

1 Population: Patterns and Processes

Introduction

As with all academic disciplines, most advances in historical demography first see the light of day in the journals. The first port of call, then, are the bibliographies that cover the subject. Our subject is well served by the *Population Index*, which not only lists books and articles from throughout the world, but also provides very informative summaries of them. *The International Bibliography of Historical Demography* is also excellent and, as its name suggests, is devoted solely to the history of population. Next are journals devoted solely to population, namely *Population Studies*, *Annales de Démographie Historique* (most articles in French though each has a summary in English and the tables and graphs which almost always accompany articles in this discipline are easy to follow, with a dictionary if necessary), *Journal of Family History* (especially good on marriage, family and household), *Social History of Medicine* (not surprisingly, very good on factors related to mortality and morbidity), *Local Population Studies* (lives up to its name, with a wide coverage based on micro-level studies). Additionally the subject is covered quite regularly by journals such as the *Economic History Review*, *Continuity and Change*, *History*, *Journal of Interdisciplinary History*, *Social Science History* and, judging by its first issue, the *International Journal of Population Geography*. Other articles will be found in the bibliographies of the books discussed below.

Population size and distribution

D. S. Goyer, *The Handbook of National Population Censuses* (New York, 1992) is a very useful guide to the differences between and the changes made in the censuses of each individual European country from the origin of census taking to the present day. The standard reference work for statistics of population size, age, sex and marital structure, birth, death and marriage rates is B. R. Mitchell, *International Historical Statistics: Europe 1750–1988*, 3rd edn (London, 1992). Two works in French produced around the turn of the century go into much greater depth than Mitchell. J. Bertillon, *Statistique Internationale Résultant des Recensements de la Population Executés dans les Divers Pays de l'Europe pendant le XIX Siècle et les Epoques Précédentes, Etablie Conformément au Voeu de l'Institut International de Statistique* (Paris, 1899) is a major source of data (it is used by Mitchell) from the various censuses carried out by European countries up to the end of the nineteenth century. Doing a similar job for the registration of births, marriages and deaths, with a full commentary on its strengths and weaknesses, as regards both coverage and quality, is Ministère du travail et de la prévoyance sociale, *Statistique*

Internationale du Mouvement de la Population d'après les Registres de l'État Civil. Résumé Retrospectif depuis l'Origine des Statistiques de l'État Civil (Paris, 1907).

Two recent works that provide both data and commentary on the fortunes of Europe's population down to the present day are A. Blum and J.-L. Rallu, *European Population*, vols 1 and 2 (Paris, 1993), and J.-C. Chesnais, *The Demographic Transition: Stages, Patterns and Economic Interpretations. A Longitudinal Study of Sixty-Seven Countries Covering the Period 1720–1984* (Oxford, 1992). An earlier, still useful and probably more accessible short account is by D. V. Glass and E. Grebanik, 'World population, 1800–1950', in *The Cambridge Economic History of Europe*, ed. H. J. Habakkuk and M. Postan, vol. 6: *The Industrial Revolutions and After: Incomes, Population and Technological Change* (Cambridge, 1966), part I, pp. 56–138.

Births and birth control

A. J. Coale and S. C. Watkins (eds), *The Decline of Fertility in Europe* (Princeton, NJ, 1986) brings together in a single volume the various national studies done under the aegis of the Princeton Project. S. C. Watkins, *From Provinces into Nations* (Princeton, NJ, 1991) uses data from the Project to explore the thesis that in terms of marriage and fertility the national has come to predominate over the local community. 'Villages have babies', she wrote, 'in the sense that those who had them – men as well as women – were influenced by what others in the community were doing and saying. In the nineteenth century, perhaps earlier, these communities were largely local i.e. other men and women in the village. By 1960 the communities were largely national' (in S. C. Watkins, 'Social networks and social science history', *Social Science History*, 19, no. 3 (1995), pp. 295–311. Both these use more refined measures of fertility, nuptiality etc. than the crude rates used above. These are not, however, particularly difficult to understand. J. R. Gillis, L. A. Tilly and D. Levine (eds), *The European Experience of Declining Fertility, 1850–1970: A Quiet Revolution* (Oxford, 1992), pursues the theme pioneered by Cook and Watkins. Hajnal's articles are to be found in J. Hajnal, 'European marriage patterns in perspective', in *Population in History: Essays in Historical Demography*, ed. D. V. Glass and D. C. Eversley (London, 1965) and in J. Hajnal, 'Two kinds of pre-industrial household formation system', *Population and Development Review*, 8, no. 3 (1982), pp. 449–94. The latter is also to be found in R. Wall, J. Robin and P. Laslett (eds), *Family Forms in Historical Europe* (Cambridge, 1983). This book explores the social structure of marriage and fertility as did its more famous predecessor, P. Laslett and R. Wall (eds), *Household and Family in Past Time: Comparative Studies in the Size and Structure of the Domestic Group over the Last Three Centuries in England, France, Serbia, Japan and Colonial North America with Further Materials from Western Europe* (Cambridge, 1972). For a multi-faceted critique of the Hajnal thesis see the articles (all of them!) in the *Journal of Family History*, 16, no. 1 (1991). For a detailed study of marriage in one country see E. Sundt, *On Marriage in Norway*, trans. Michael Drake (Cambridge, 1981; first published 1855).

Europeans on the move

D. Baines, *Emigration from Europe 1815–1930* (Cambridge, 1991) is a good place to start the subject, being one of a series now published by the Cambridge University Press for the Economic History Society and intended for students wanting an up-to-date overview. Other excellent accounts are to be found in C. Erickson, *Leaving England: Essays on British Emigration in the Nineteenth Century* (London, 1994); W. Nugent, *Crossings: The Great Transatlantic Migration 1870–1914* (Bloomington, 1995); L. Page-Moch, *Moving Europeans: Migration in Western Europe since 1650* (Bloomington, 1992);

and for an account of that tragic sub-set of migrants, A. C. Bramwell (ed.), *Refugees in the Age of Total War* (London, 1988). Its main focus is on pre-1945 refugees.

The death rate falls

It was remarked above that new insights usually appear first in the journals. It is here too that the cut and thrust of debate finds its finest expression. One such recent debate has been about the causes of the fall in infant mortality (i.e. deaths of children under one year of age). Here are some contributions, in order of date: S. Szreter, 'The importance of social intervention in Britain's mortality decline *c.*1850–1914: a re-interpretation of the role of public health', *Social History of Medicine*, 1 (1988), pp. 1–37: R. I. Woods, P. A. Watterson and J. H. Woodward, 'The causes of rapid infant mortality decline in England and Wales, 1861–1921', Part I, *Population Studies*, 42 (1989), pp. 343–66 and Part II, *Population Studies*, 43 (1989), pp. 113–32; S. Guha, 'The importance of social intervention in England's mortality decline', *Social History of Medicine*, 7 (1994), pp. 89–113: S. Szreter, 'Mortality in England in the eighteenth and nineteenth centuries: a reply to Sumit Guha', *Social History of Medicine*, 7 (1994), pp. 269–82; a dozen articles covering various European countries under the title 'La Mortalité des enfants dans le passé' in *Annales de démographie historique 1994*, pp. 7–214; E. Garret and A. Reid, 'Thinking of England and taking care: family building strategies and infant mortality in England and Wales, 1981–1911', *International Journal of Population Geography*, 1 (1995), pp. 69–102; N. Williams and C. Galley, 'Urban-rural differentials in infant mortality in Victorian England', *Population Studies*, 49 (1995), pp. 401–20.

2 Prosperity and Depression: The International Economy

The best elementary introduction to the European economy 1870–1945 will be found in Carlo M. Cipolla (ed.), *Fontana Economic History of Europe* (London, 1973), vols 4–6. There are chapters to cover individual countries as well as on main themes, each written by an expert.

Aldcroft, Derek H., *The European Economy 1914–1970*, London, 1978. Much the best short introduction to the post-1918 period.

Aldcroft, D. and Ville, S., eds, *The European Economy, 1750–1914: A Thematic Approach*, Manchester, 1994. A more up-to-date introduction than Cipolla's, concentrating, as the subtitle implies, on themes rather than countries.

Berend, I. T. and Ranki, G., *The European Periphery and Industrialization 1780–1914*, Cambridge and Paris, 1977. A good account of the smaller countries which are often neglected in European surveys.

Henderson, W. O., *Britain and Industrial Europe*, Liverpool, 1954. Examines the contribution of Britain to the economic development on the continent.

Kaser, M. C. and Rodice, E. D., eds, *The Economic History of Eastern Europe, 1919–1975*, Oxford, 1984. Covers an elusive subject with exceptional clarity.

Kindleberger, C. P., *The World in Depression, 1929–39*, London, 1973. A clear account of a complex issue.

Landes, David S., *The Unbound Prometheus*, Cambridge, 1969. A classic study, emphasizing technical change and entrepreneurship.

Maddison, Angus, *Phases of Capitalist Development*, Oxford, 1982. Traces the economic growth of a number of advanced countries on the basis of comprehensive statistics.

Milward, A. and Saul, S. B., *The Development of the Economies of Continental Europe: 1850–1914*, London, 1977. Much the most comprehensive study, with good accounts of the smaller nations as well as the Great Powers.

Mitchell, B. R., *European Historical Statistics 1750–1970*, London, 1975. Provides wide-ranging, indispensable basic statistical information.

Pollard, Sidney, *Peaceful Conquest: The Industrialization of Europe 1760–1970*, Oxford, 1981. Industrialization and modernization are seen as spreading from one or more centres to the rest of Europe, with emphasis on regional developments.

Sylla, Richard and Toniolo, Gianni, eds, *Patterns of European Industrialization*, London and New York, 1991. Another collective volume. Experts on the economic history of each country examine the validity of the theory of Alexander Gerschenkron on European industrialization.

Tipton, Frank B. and Aldrich, Robert, *An Economic and Social History of Europe*, 2 vols, London, 1987. A good introductory text which puts the economic development in its social and political setting.

Trebilcock, Clive, *The Industrialization of the European Powers 1780–1914*, London, 1981. Compares the development of individual countries.

Tylecote, Andrew, *The Long Wave in the World Economy*, London and New York, 1991. A recent re-statement of the Long Wave doctrine, emphasizing periodic changes in 'style'.

3   The State and the Development of Social Welfare

As mentioned in the text, the development of social welfare before 1945 has been largely ignored by historians. Much of the raw material required for analysis, however, was collated between 1973 and 1986 in a series of ambitious projects headed by Peter Flora. This resulted in a two-volume statistical compilation, P. Flora (ed.), *State, Economy and Society in Western Europe, 1815–1875* (Berlin, 1983–6); and a three-volume, incomplete history of individual countries, P. Flora (ed.), *Growth to Limits* (Berlin, 1986). General conclusions were reached in P. Flora and A. J. Heidenheimer, *The Development of Welfare States in Europe and America* (New York, 1981). Among the most stimulating and recent conceptual analyses are P. Baldwin, *The Politics of Social Solidarity* (Cambridge, 1990) and G. Esping-Andersen, *The Three Worlds of Welfare Capitalism* (Cambridge, 1990).

Amongst individual countries, Britain is the best analysed. The standard, introductory texts are D. Fraser, *The Evolution of the British Welfare State* (Basingstoke, 1984) and P. Thane, *The Foundations of the Welfare State* (Harlow, 1982). The latter includes some brief international comparisons. The broader issue of government growth is covered in greater conceptual and empirical detail by R. Middleton, *Government versus the Market* (Cheltenham, 1996). Comparative work with Britain provides the best introduction to the history of other countries. For Germany, these include W. J. Mommsen, *The Emergence of the Welfare State in Britain and Germany* (London, 1981) and the excellent monograph, E. P. Hennock, *British Social Reform and German Precedents* (Oxford, 1987). For Sweden there is H. Heclo, *Modern Social Politics in Britain and Sweden* (Yale, 1984); for Denmark, D. Levine, *Poverty and Society* (New Brunswick, NJ, 1988); and for France, D. E. Ashford, *The Emergence of the Welfare States* (Oxford, 1986). Other individual studies are T. Mason, *Social Policy in the Third Reich* (Oxford, 1993) and S. E. Olsson, *Social Policy and Welfare State in Sweden* (Lund, 1990).

One of the more exciting approaches to social welfare is through gender history. A broad introduction is provided by G. Bock and P. Thane, *Maternity and Gender Policies:*

Women and the Rise of European Welfare States, 1880s–1950s (London, 1991). Good individual studies are S. Pedersen, *Family, Dependence and the Origins of the Welfare State: Britain and France, 1914–1945* (Cambridge, 1993) and S. Koven and S. Michel, *Mothers of a New World: Maternalist Policies and the Origins of Welfare States* (London, 1993).

On individual policies, A. Power, *Hovels to High Rise* (London, 1993) provides a basic introduction to European housing policy since 1850, whilst Appendix F of the 1942 Beveridge Report, *Social Insurance and Allied Services* (London, Cmd 6404) summarizes insurance practice then current in other countries.

4 Leisure and Society in Europe, 1871–1945

Recent years have seen leisure emerge as a mainstream theme in social and economic history. There is no shortage of both general studies of leisure in the modern period and more specific analyses of recreational activities. As a starting point, on the reduction of the working day see G. Cross, *Quest for Time: The Reduction of Work in Britain and France, 1840–1940* (Berkeley, CA, 1989) and S. J. Jones, 'Work, leisure and unemployment in Western Europe between the wars', *British Journal of Sports History*, 3 (1986), pp. 55–80. For a survey of British leisure historiography see P. Bailey, 'Leisure, culture and the historian: reviewing the first generation of leisure historiography in Britain', *Leisure Studies*, 8 (1989).

On the history of leisure in Britain see R. Malcolmson, *Popular Recreations in English Society 1700–1850* (Cambridge, 1973); H. Cunningham, *Leisure in the Industrial Revolution c.1780–1880* (London, 1980); J. Walvin, *Leisure and Society, 1830–1950* (London, 1978); J. Walton and J. Walvin (eds), *Leisure in Britain* (Manchester, 1983); J. Lowerson and J. Myerscough, *Time to Spare in Victorian England* (Sussex, 1977). From the perspective of class struggle in the pre-First World War period see P. Bailey, *Leisure and Class in Victorian England: Rational Recreation and the Contest for Control* (London, 1978); G. Stedman Jones, 'Working-class culture and working-class politics in London 1870–1900', *Journal of Social History*, 4 (1977), pp. 460–501 and E. Yeo and S. Yeo (eds), *Popular Culture and Class Conflict 1590–1914* (Brighton, 1981).

On the inter-war period see S. J. Jones, *Workers at Play: A Social and Economic History of Leisure, 1918–1939* (London, 1986) and A. Davies, *Leisure, Gender and Poverty: Working-Class Culture in Salford and Manchester, 1900–1939* (Buckingham, 1992) which not only includes women and young people in its analysis but makes excellent use of oral history.

The rest of Europe is less well served by studies in the English language. On popular leisure in Germany see L. Abrams, *Workers' Culture in Imperial Germany: Leisure and Recreation in the Rhineland and Westphalia* (London, 1992). The efforts of the organized labour movement to influence the leisure activities of the working class in Germany have been comprehensively studied. See the special issue of *Journal of Contemporary History*, 13 (1978) which focuses on workers' culture and on the Weimar Republic; and W. L. Guttsman, *Workers' Culture in Weimar Germany: Between Tradition and Commitment* (Oxford, 1990). On France there is C. Rearick's examination of leisure and entertainment, *Pleasures of the Belle Epoque: Entertainment and Festivity in Turn-of-the-Century France* (New Haven, 1986) and J. Beauroy (ed.), *The Wolf and the Lamb: Popular Culture in France from the Old Regime to the Twentieth Century* (Saratoga, NY, 1976). Similarly, the leisure of the Russian population has not been thoroughly examined although R. Stites's *Russian Popular Culture: Entertainment and Society since 1900* (Cambridge, 1992) provides a lively account of popular music, cinema, circus and popular fiction.

Individual forms of leisure, especially drinking, cinema and sport, have attracted broad coverage. The choice of works detailing alcohol consumption and its place within popular and working-class culture is tremendous. A selection includes: B. Harrison, *Drink and the Victorians: The Temperance Question in England 1815–72* (London, 1971); D. E. Dingle, *The Campaign for Prohibition in Victorian England* (London, 1980); J. Roberts, *Drink, Temperance and the Working Class in Nineteenth Century Germany* (London, 1984); G. Brennan, 'Beyond the barriers: popular culture and the Parisian Guingettes', *Eighteenth Century Studies*, 18 (1984–5).

Cinema has been widely discussed within the context of the emergence of a mass entertainment industry, particularly after the First World War. Cinema in Britain has been fairly comprehensively covered by J. Richards. See his *Best of British: Cinema and Society 1930–1970* (Oxford, 1983), *The Age of the Dream Palace: Cinema and Society in Britain 1930–1939* (London, 1984) and J. Richards and D. Sheridan (eds), *Mass Observation at the Movies* (London, 1987). On the reception of film by the British working class see S. J. Jones, *The British Labour Movement and Film 1918–1939* (London, 1987). Paul Monaco's *Cinema and Society: France and Germany during the Twenties* (New York, 1976) is a comparative examination of the age of the movies while D. Welch, 'Cinema and society in Imperial Germany, 1905–1918', *German History*, 8 (1990), pp. 28–45, traces the early history of the cinema industry in Germany.

The development of sport from its origins in community games to the modern spectator sport has a comprehensive history. For Britain, R. Holt's *Sport and the British: A Modern History* (Oxford, 1989) provides a general survey, and G. Jarvie and G. Walker (eds), *Scottish Sport in the Making of the Nation: Ninety Minute Patriots* (Leicester, 1994) places emphasis on sport and national identity. For France see R. Holt, *Sport and Society in Modern France* (London, 1981). Particular sports have also received attention. On football see T. Mason's comprehensive study *Association Football and English Society 1863–1915* (Brighton, 1980) and J. Walvin, *The People's Game: A Social History of British Football* (London, 1975). On gymnastics and other sports in France there is E. Weber's 'Gymnastics and Sports in *Fin-de-Siècle* France: Opium of the Classes?', *American Historical Review*, 76 (1971), pp. 70–98. On the labour movement and sport see R. Wheeler, 'Organised sport and organised labour: the workers' sport movement', *Journal of Contemporary History*, 13 (1978), pp. 191–210; and on 'muscular Christianity' see J. A. Mangan, *Athleticism in the Victorian and Edwardian Public School* (Manchester, 1981).

The relationship between leisure and the state in the 1920s and 1930s is dealt with by S. J. Jones for Britain in his *Workers at Play*. Elsewhere, notably in Italy and Germany, where the state intervened more forcibly, information in the English language is rather sparse. On fascist Italy, V. de Grazia's *The Culture of Consent: Mass Organisation of Leisure in Fascist Italy* (Cambridge, 1981) provides comprehensive coverage of the *dopolavoro* movement but there is nothing similar for Nazi Germany's 'strength through joy' scheme. Information can be found in T. Mason, *Social Policy in the Third Reich* (Oxford, 1993). On the Nazis' use of radio see K. Lacey, *Feminine Frequencies: Gender, German Radio and the Public Sphere 1923–1945* (Ann Arbor, MI, 1996).

Women's experience of leisure in the past is yet to be fully explored but in addition to Davies's *Leisure, Gender and Poverty* there are a number of sociological studies which incorporate a historical perspective, especially R. Deem, *All Work and No Play: The Sociology of Women and Leisure* (Milton Keynes, 1986); E. Wimbush and M. Talbot (eds), *Relative Freedoms: Women and Leisure* (Milton Keynes, 1988); E. Green, S. Hebron and D. Woodward, *Women's Leisure, What Leisure?* (London, 1990).

Finally, on mass, commercial and consumer culture in the twentieth century see A. Briggs, *Mass Entertainment: The Origins of a Modern Industry* (Adelaide, 1960); R. Williams, *Dream Worlds: Mass Consumption in Late Nineteenth Century France* (Berkeley, CA, 1982); G. Cross, *Time and Money: The Making of a Consumer Culture* (London, 1993).

5 Conservatism and Nationalism

British conservatism

Blake, Robert, *Disraeli*, London, 1966.

Blake, Lord and Cecil, Hugh, eds, *Salisbury: The Man and his Policies*, New York, 1987.

Coleman, Bruce, *Conservatism and the Conservative Party in Nineteenth-Century Britain*, London, 1988.

Feuchtwanger, E. J., *Disraeli, Democracy and the Tory Party: Conservative Leadership and Organization after the Second Reform Bill*, Oxford, 1968.

Foster, R. F., *Lord Randolph Churchill: A Political Life*, Oxford, 1981.

Green, E. H. H., *The Crisis of Conservatism: The Politics, Economics and Ideology of the British Conservative Party, 1880–1914*, London, 1995.

Hanham, H. J., *Elections and Party Management: Politics in the Time of Disraeli and Gladstone*, London, 1959.

Hanham, H. J., *The Nineteenth Constitution: Documents and Commentary*, Cambridge, 1969.

Jay, Richard, *Joseph Chamberlain: A Political Study*, Oxford, 1981.

Marsh, Peter T., *The Discipline of Popular Government: Lord Salisbury's Domestic Statecraft, 1881–1902*, Hassocks, 1978.

Marsh, Peter T., *Joseph Chamberlain: Entrepreneur in Politics*, New Haven/London, 1994.

Pugh, Martin, *The Tories and the People 1880–1935*, Oxford, 1985.

Shannon, Richard, *The Age of Disraeli, 1867–1881: The Rise of Tory Democracy*, London, 1992.

Smith, Paul, *Disraelian Conservatism and Social Reform*, London, 1967.

Smith, Paul, ed., *Lord Salisbury on Politics: A Selection from his Articles in the Quarterly Review 1860–1883*, Cambridge, 1972.

Weintraub, Stanley, *Disraeli: A Biography*, London, 1993.

Conservative foreign policy

Bourne, Kenneth, *The Foreign Policy of Victorian England 1830–1902*, Oxford, 1970 [documents and commentary].

Cain, P. J. and Hopkins, A. G., *British Imperialism: Innovation and Expansion 1688–1914*, London, 1993.

Eldridge, C. C., *England's Mission: The Imperial Idea in the Age of Gladstone and Disraeli, 1868–1880*, London, 1973.

Grenville, J. A. S., *Lord Salisbury and Foreign Policy: The Close of the Nineteenth Century*, London, 1970.

Millman, Richard, *Britain and the Eastern Question, 1875–1878*, Oxford, 1979.

Swartz, Marvin, *The Politics of British Foreign Policy in the Era of Disraeli and Gladstone*, Basingstoke, 1985.

Bismarckian Germany

Blackbourn, David and Eley, Geoff, *The Peculiarities of German History: Bourgeois Society and Politics in Nineteenth-Century Germany*, Oxford, 1984.

Carr, William, *The Origins of the Wars of German Unification*, London, 1991.

Crankshaw, Edward, *Bismarck*, London/Basingstoke, 1981.

Eley, Geoff, *Reshaping the German Right: Radical Nationalism and Political Change after Bismarck*, New Haven/London, 1980.

Feuchtwanger, E. J., *Prussia: Myth and Reality. The Role of Prussia in German History*, London, 1970.

Gall, Lothar, *Bismarck: The White Revolutionary*, 2 vols, London, 1986 and 1987.

Guttsman, W. L., *The German Social Democratic Party 1875–1933*, London, 1981.

Hamerow, T. S., *The Social Foundations of German Unification*, 2 vols, Princeton, NJ, 1969 and 1972.

James, Harold, *A German Identity 1770–1990*, London, 1989.

Mommsen, W. J., *Imperial Germany 1867–1918: Politics, Culture, and Society in an Authoritarian State*, London, 1995.

Morck, Gordon, 'Bismarck and the "Capitulation" of German Liberalism', *Journal of Modern History*, no. 43, 1971.

Röhl, J. C. G., *Germany without Bismarck: The Crisis of Government in the Second Reich*, London, 1967.

Sheehan, J. J., *German Liberalism in the Nineteenth Century*, Chicago/London, 1978.

Wehler, H.-U., *The German Empire 1871–1918*, Leamington Spa, 1985.

6   The Dilemmas of Liberalism

General

A useful starting point is M. Steed and P. Humphreys, 'Identifying Liberal parties', in *Liberal Parties in Western Europe*, ed. E. J. Kirchner (Cambridge, 1988), pp. 396–435. Parallel national histories of liberalism are offered by the classical G. de Ruggiero, *The History of European Liberalism*, trans. R. G. Collingwood (London, 1927), and the recent work by R. Bellamy, *Liberalism and Modern Society: An Historical Argument* (Cambridge, 1992). An interesting and usually underestimated aspect of liberal thought is studied by E. L. Forget and R. A. Lodell, *The Peasant in Economic Thought: 'A Perfect Republic'* (Cheltenham, 1995).

Free trade and economic policies

H. C. G. Matthew, 'Disraeli, Gladstone and the policy of mid-Victorian budgets', *The Historical Journal*, 22, no. 3 (1979), pp. 615–43; B. Hilton, *The Age of Atonement: The Influence of Evangelicalism on Social and Economic. Thought 1765–1865* (Oxford, 1988); A. Howe, 'Towards the "hungry forties": free trade in Britain, c.1880–1906', and F. Trentmann, 'The strange death of free trade: the erosion of "Liberal consensus" in Great Britain, c.1903–1932', in *Citizenship and Community: Liberals, Radicals and Collective Identities in the British Isles 1865–1931*, ed. E. F. Biagini (Cambridge, 1996), pp. 168–92 and 193–250 respectively; P. F. Clarke, *Liberals and Social Democrats* (Cambridge, 1978) and *The Keynesian Revolution in the Making* (Cambridge, 1988).

Anti-clericalism

See the articles on Spain, France and Italy in the issue of the *European Studies Review* devoted to anti-clericalism, 13, no. 2 (April 1983). On Nonconformist Protestantism as a form of anti-clericalism in Britain, see D. W. Bebbington, *The Nonconformist Conscience* (London, 1982); and the chapter on 'Anticlericalism' in E. F. Biagini, *Liberty, Retrenchment and Reform: Popular Liberalism in the Age of Gladstone 1860–80* (Cambridge, 1992). The literature on the *Kulturkampf* in Germany is very extensive: a starting point can be D. Blackbourn, 'Progress and piety: Liberals, Catholics and the state in Bismarck's Germany', in *Populist and Patricians: Essays in Modern German History* (London, 1987), pp. 143–67. See also F. Spotts, *The Churches and Politics in Germany* (Middletown, CT, 1973). Protestants in Catholic countries were virulently anti-clerical: on the French case see W. Doyle, *The Oxford History of the French Revolution* (Oxford, 1990), pp. 7, 9, 36, 138, 142, 144–7, 410–1; and the relevant chapter in P. Nord, *Republican Moment: Struggles for Democracy in Nineteenth-century France* (Cambridge, MA, 1995).

Britain and Protestant Europe

J. Vincent, *The Formation of the British Liberal Party 1859–1867* (London, 1966); J. Parry, *Democracy and Religion: Gladstone and the Liberal Party, 1867–1875* (Cambridge, 1986) and *The Rise and Fall of Liberal Government in Victorian Britain* (London and New Haven, 1993); Biagini, *Liberty, Retrenchment and Reform*; H. C. G. Matthew, *Gladstone*, 2 vols (Oxford, 1986–95); M. Barker, *Gladstone and Radicalism: The Reconstruction of Liberal Politics in Britain, 1885–94* (Hassocks, 1975); M. Freeden, *Liberalism Divided: A Study in British Political Thought 1914–1939* (Oxford, 1986). On the Scandinavian countries: V. Wåhlin, 'The growth of bourgeois and popular movements in Denmark ca. 1830–1870', *Scandinavian Journal of History*, 5 (1980), pp. 151–83; L. Svåsand, 'The early organization society in Norway: some characteristics', ibid., pp. 185–96; H. Stenius, 'The breakthrough of the principle of mass organization in Finland', ibid., pp. 197–217; S. Rokkan, 'Norway: Geography, Religion and Social Class', in *Party System and Voter Alignments*, ed. S. M. Lipset and S. Rokkan (New York, 1967); J. Y. Leiphart and L. Svåsand, 'The Norwegian Liberal Party: from political pioneer to political footnote', in *Liberal Parties*, ed. Kirchner, pp. 304–25; A. H. Thomas, 'Liberalism in Denmark', ibid., pp. 279–303. On the Swiss Confederation see G. A. Craig, *The Triumph of Liberalism: Zurich in the Golden Age, 1830–1869* (New York, 1988); A. G. Imlah, *Great Britain and Switzerland 1830–1860* (London, 1966); D. L. Seiler, 'Liberal parties in Switzerland', in *Liberal Parties*, ed. Kirchner, pp. 356–75. On the Netherlands see W. Werkade, *Democratic Parties in the Low Countries* (Leiden, 1969); and H. Daalder and R. Koole, 'Liberal parties in the Netherlands', in *Liberal Parties*, ed. Kirchner, pp. 151–77. On Germany see J. J. Sheehan, *German Liberalism in the Nineteenth Century* (Chicago and London, 1982); K. H. Jarausch and L. E. Jones (eds), *In Search of a Liberal Germany: Studies in the History of German Liberalism from 1789 to the Present* (New York, Oxford, Berg, 1990); D. Beetham, *Max Weber and the Theory of Modern Politics* (Cambridge, 1985); W. Mommsen, *Max Weber and German Politics 1890–1920* (New York, 1967); R. Dahrendorf, *Society and Democracy in Germany* (New York, 1967).

Catholic Europe

On France see J. P. T. Bury and R. Tombs, *Thiers 1797–1877: A Political Biography* (London, 1986); and J. P. T. Bury, *Gambetta and the Making of the Third Republic* (London, 1973); J. M. Mayeur and M. Reberioux, *The Third Republic from Its Origin to the Great War* (Cambridge, 1984). For later developments see 'Interview with Jean F. Denieau', in *Modern Liberalism: Conversations with Liberal Politicians*, ed. F. Bolkstein (n.p., 1982), pp. 7–36; and J. Frears, 'Liberalism in France', in *Liberal Parties*, ed. Kirchner, pp. 124–50. Belgium is a classic, though understudied, case: see 'Interview with Jean Rey', in *Modern Liberalism*, ed. Bolkstein, pp. 203–4; and C. Rudd, 'The Belgian Liberal parties: economic radicals and social conservatives', in *Liberal Parties*, ed. Kirchner, pp. 178–212. For the Italian experience see A. Lyttelton, 'Landlords, peasants and the limits of Liberalism', in *Gramsci and Italy's Passive Revolution*, ed. J. A. Davis (London, 1979); A. Mastropaolo, 'Electoral processes, political behaviour, and social forces in Italy from the rise of the left to the fall of Giolitti, 1876–1913', in *Wählerbewegung in der europäischen Geschichte*, ed. O. Busch (Berlin, 1980), pp. 97–124;

C. Seton-Watson, *Italy from Liberalism to Fascism 1870–1925* (London, 1967); R. Bellamy, *Modern Italian Social Theory* (Cambridge, 1987). See also G. Pridham, 'Two roads of Italian Liberalism: the Partito Repubblicano Italiano (PRI) and the Partito Liberale (PLI)', in *Liberal Parties*, ed. Kirchner, pp. 29–61.

Nationalism and liberalism

On the concert of Europe see H. C. G. Matthew, *Gladstone 1875–1898* (Oxford, 1995), esp. pp. 7–30, 122–5; and W. N. Medlicott, *Bismarck, Gladstone and the Concert of Europe* (London, 1956). For British attitudes to the Italian Risorgimento see D. E. D. Beales, *England and Italy, 1859–60* (London, 1961) and his 'Garibaldi and England: the politics of Italian enthusiasm', in *Society and Politics in the Age of the Risorgimento*, ed. J. Davis and D. M. Smith (Cambridge, 1991). For the Greek parallel see G. Koliopoulos, *Brigands with a Cause: Brigandage and Irredentism in Modern Greece 1812–1912* (Oxford, 1987); and *Kolokotrones: the Klepht and the Warrior: An Autobiography*, trans. E. M. Edmonds (London, 1892). On the much less violent French case see the classical work by E. Weber, *Peasants into Frenchmen: The Modernization of Rural France* (Stanford, CA, 1992). On the British case see T. W. Heyck, *The Dimensions of British Radicalism: The Case of Ireland 1874–95* (Urbana, IL, 1974). On Liberal imperialism see H. C. G. Matthew, *The Liberal Imperialists: The Ideas and Politics of a Post-Gladstonian Elite* (Oxford, 1973). On national conflicts in Central Europe see L. Namier, *1848: The Revolution of the Intellectuals* (London, 1946), which documents the temptations of imperialism and ethnic nationalism; R. F. Leslie, *Reform and Insurrection in Russian Poland 1856–1865* (London, 1963); A. Walicki, *Philosophy and Romantic Nationalism: The Case of Poland* (New York, 1982), esp. parts 1 and 2; S. A. Blejwas, *Realism in Polish Politics: Warsaw Positivism and National Survival in Nineteenth Century Poland* (New Haven, 1994).

The 'New Liberalism' and social liberalism

General: J. T. Kloppenberg, *Uncertain Victory: Social Democracy and Progressivism in European and American Thought, 1870–1920* (Oxford, 1986). The British case: I. M. Greengarten, *Thomas Hill Green and the Development of Liberal-Democratic Thought* (Toronto, 1981); M. Richter, *The Politics of Conscience: T. H. Green and His Age* (London, 1964); P. F. Clarke, *Lancashire and the New Liberalism* (Cambridge, 1971); S. Collini, *Liberalism and Sociology: L. T. Hobhouse and Political Argument in England 1880–1914* (Cambridge, 1979); M. Freeden, *The New Liberalism: An Ideology of Social Reform* (Oxford, 1978). On the German case: J. Sheehan, *The Career of Lujo Brentano: A Study of Liberalism and Social Reform in Imperial Germany* (Chicago, 1966); W. Mommsen, *The Political and Social Theory of Max Weber* (Cambridge, 1989). On France: S. Elwitt, *The Third Republic Defended: Bourgeois Reform in France, 1880–1914* (Baton Rouge, LA, 1986); W. Logue, *From Philosophy to Sociology: The Evolution of French Liberalism, 1870–1914* (Chicago, 1983). On Italy: C. Rosselli, *Liberal Socialism*, ed. with an introduction by N. Urbinati (Princeton, NJ, 1994); R. Bellamy, 'History and Liberalism in an Italian "New Liberal theorist" ', *Historical Journal*, 30 (1987), pp. 191–200.

The age of fascism and antifascism

C. Maier, *Recasting Bourgeois Europe: Stabilisation in France, Germany and Italy in the Decade after World War One* (Princeton, NJ, 1975) and K. O. Morgan, *Consensus and Disunity: The Lloyd George Coalition Government 1918–22* (Oxford, 1979). On Italy: C. Rosselli, *Liberal Socialism*, A. Lyttelton, *The Seizure of Power: Fascism in Italy 1919–29* (London, 1973); P. Corner, 'Liberalism, pre-Fascism, Fascism', in *Rethinking Italian Fascism*, ed. D. Forgacs (London, 1986), pp. 11–20.

7 Socialist Parties and Policies

Accounts of socialist politics in several countries

Berger, S. and Broughton, D., eds, *The Force of Labour: The Western European Labour Movement and the Working Class in the Twentieth Century*, Oxford, 1995. Chapters on most larger European countries, with a concluding thematic overview. Some chapters concentrate on the post-1945 period.

Geary, D., *Labour and Socialist Movements in Europe before 1914*, Oxford, 1989. Chapters on origins and development of socialist politics in Britain, France, Germany, Russia, Italy and Spain, with particular attention to the impact of social/economic influences. Chapters by major British authorities on these subjects.

Geary, D., *European Labour Politics from 1900 to the Depression*, London, 1991. Integrated pamphlet-length analysis, with helpful bibliography.

Graham, H. and Preston, P., eds, *The Popular Front in Europe*, Basingstoke, 1987. Country-by-country analysis of Popular Front activity.

Linden, M. van der and Rojahn, J., eds, *The Formation of Labour Movements 1870–1914: An International Perspective*, New York, 1990. Chapters on most socialist parties, largely written by authorities from these countries.

Wrigley, C., ed., *Challenges of Labour: Central and Western Europe 1917–20*, London, 1993. Country-by-country analysis of radicalism and unrest in this important period.

Interpretative overviews

Cronin, J. E., 'Neither exceptional nor peculiar: Towards the comparative study of labour in advanced society', *International Review of Social History*, 38 (1993), 59–75. Less helpful than the title suggests.

Linden, M. van der, 'The national integration of European working classes', *International Review of Social History*, 33 (1988), 285–311. Useful but rather sweeping account.

White, D. S., 'Reconsidering European socialism in the 1920s', *Journal of Contemporary History*, 16 (1981), 251–72. Valuable introduction.

Britain

Howell, D., *British Social Democracy*, London, 1976. Still the best of the many broad overviews, although in need of revision.

McKibbin, R. I., *The Evolution of the Labour Party 1910–1924*, Oxford, 1983. Interpretation of 'rise of Labour' now being questioned, but a reliable account of the institutional changes.

Tanner, D. M., *Political Change and the Labour Party 1900–18*, Cambridge, 1990. The most detailed explanation of the Labour Party's expansion to 1918.

Tanner, D. M., 'Class voting and radical politics: the electoral expansion of the Labour party 1910–31', in *Party, State and Society: Electoral Behaviour in Modern Britain*, ed. M. Taylor and J. Lawrence, London, 1996. Extends Tanner (1990), incorporating recent research and views on the 1920s.

France

Judt, A., *Socialism in Provence 1871–1914: Study in the Origins of the French Left*, Cambridge, 1979. Classic local study, with broader implications than this might indicate.

Judt, A., *Marxism and the French Left: Studies on Labour and Politics in France 1830–1981*, Oxford, 1986. Excellent essays, but a patchy rather than comprehensive analysis.

Magraw, R., *The History of the French Working Class*, vol. 2, Oxford, 1992. Some coverage of party politics, but strongest on trade unions and labour conditions before 1914.

Noiriel, G., *Workers in French Society in the 19th and 20th Centuries*, New York, 1990. Discussion of class, communities and social change. Complements Magraw by concentrating on twentieth century.

Williams, S., ed., *Socialism in France from Jaurès to Mitterand*, London, 1983. Not a full history, but contains work by major French-language authorities.

Germany

Fletcher, R., ed., *Bernstein to Brandt: A Short History of German Social Democracy*, London, 1987. Brief essays by major authorities, including aspects not covered in older studies.

Guttsman, W. L., *The German Social Democratic Party: From Ghetto to Government*, London, 1981. Conventional but detailed institutional analysis.

James, H., *The German Slump: Politics and Economics 1924–1936*, Oxford, 1986. Revisionist account, with important implications for assessments of socialist politics.

Other countries

Heywood, P., *Marxism and the Failure of Organised Socialism in Spain, 1879–1936*, Cambridge, 1990. Emphasizes the absence of a clear analysis of the problems on the left, and explains the comparative strength and eventual triumph of reformism.

Miller, J. E., *From Elite to Mass Politics: Italian Socialism in the Giolittian Era, 1900–1914*, Kent, OH, 1990. Institutional analysis which attempts to explain internal tensions and the weakness of the party as a mass organization.

Tilton, T., *The Political Theory of Swedish Social Democracy: Through the Welfare State to Socialism*, Oxford, 1991. Account of major individuals and their contribution to policy/ideas. Explains how Swedish socialism was different and successful.

Comparative studies

Berger, S., *The British Labour Party and the German Social Democrats, 1900–1931*, Oxford, 1994. Argues many features of German socialist party development are also evident in the UK.

Hamilton, M. B., *Democratic Socialism in Britain and Sweden*, Basingstoke, 1988. Insufficiently integrated but still useful study of parallel changes in socialist politics.

Horne, J. N., *Labour at War: France and Britain 1914–18*, Oxford, 1991. Conventional portrait of British Labour politics, but good examination of wartime changes in French socialist and trade union opinion.

Pedersen, S., *Family, Dependence, and the Origins of the Welfare State: Britain and France, 1914–45*, Cambridge, 1993. Unusual comparative study of social policy between the wars – most accounts concentrate on economic policy. Socialist opinion and policy features prominently.

Collections of material by leading socialists

Barker, B., ed., *Ramsay MacDonald's Political Writings*, London, 1972. Extracts from most of his major books.

Beetham, D., ed., *Marxists in the Face of Fascism*, Manchester, 1983. Includes extracts from socialists. Helps explain why many socialists could not work with the Communist Party.

Bottomore, T. and Goode, P., eds, *Austro-Marxism*, Oxford, 1978. The contribution of an important and influential intellectual centre to the discussion of central political issues.

Goode, P., ed., *Karl Kautsky: Selected Political Writings*, London, 1983. Extracts from the 'Pope of Socialism', selected and introduced by a major authority.

Tudor, H. and Tudor, J. M., eds, *Marxism and Social Democracy: The Revisionist Debate 1896–98*, Cambridge, 1988. Excellent and revealing source for this key episode.

Key biographies and biographical studies

Geary, D., *Karl Kautsky*, Manchester, 1987. Good short biography of this important and misjudged German theorist and leader.

Goldberg, H., *The Life of Jean Jaurès*, Madison, WI, 1962. Still the major English-language biography of the pre-war French socialist leader and philosopher.

Marquand, D., *Ramsay MacDonald*, London, 1977. The fullest and best biography of the British Labour leader.

Nationalism and feminism

Bryson, V., *Feminist Political Theory*, Basingstoke, 1992. Useful brief chapters on the main socialist feminists and their views.

Evans, R., *Comrades and Sisters: Feminism, Socialism and Pacifism in Europe 1870–1945*, Brighton, 1987. Good general overview, especially strong on Germany, by the leading authority.

Pugh, M., *Women and the Women's Movement in Britain 1914–1951*, Basingstoke, 1992. Less detailed on Labour women than other recent texts, but more astute and balanced.

Schwarzmantel, J., *Socialism and the Idea of the Nation*, Brighton, 1991. Helpful on the tensions between socialism and nationalism, although weaker on historical examples.

Sowerwine, C., *Sisters or Citizens? Women and Socialism in France since 1876*, New York, 1982. One of the few studies on this theme.

8 The Rise of European Feminism

Useful source books in English are: Candida Ann Lacey, *Barbara Leigh Smith Bodichon and the Langham Place Group* (London, 1987); E. O. Hellerstein, L. P. Hume and K. M. Offen, *Victorian Women* (Brighton, 1981); Patricia Hollis, *Women in Public: The Women's Movement, 1850–1900* (London, 1979); Jane Lewis, *Before the Vote Was Won* (London, 1986); Sheila Jeffreys, *The Sexuality Debates* (London, 1987); Jane Marcus, *Suffrage and the Pankhursts* (London, 1986); Dale Spender, *Time and Tide Wait For No Man* (London, 1984). There is an excellent, short analysis of feminist ideology in John Charvet, *Feminism* (London, 1982). There are also several comparative studies including Olive Banks, *Faces of Feminism* (Oxford, 1981); Jane Rendall, *The Origins of Modern Feminism: Women in Britain, France and the United States, 1780–1860* (London, 1985); and a short but comprehensive study of women's organizations up to 1920 in Richard Evans, *The Feminists* (London, 1977).

On France, James McMillan, *Housewife or Harlot: The Place of Women in French Society, 1870–1940* (Brighton, 1981) argues that the First World War made little positive impact on women. See also Steven Hause, *Women's Suffrage and Social Politics in the French Third Republic* (Princeton, NJ, 1984); and Karen Offen, 'Women, citizenship and suffrage with a French twist 1789–1993', in *Suffrage and Beyond: International Feminist Perspectives*, ed. C. Daley and M. Nolan (Auckland, 1994).

For Germany the period from the late eighteenth to late twentieth century is covered in Ute Frevert, *Women in German History* (Oxford, 1989); on the pre-Nazi era see W. Thonnessen, *The Emancipation of Women: The Rise and Decline of the Women's Movement in German Social Democracy, 1863–1933* (London, 1969); and Richard Evans, *The Feminist Movement in Germany, 1894–1933* (London, 1976). On women under fascism see

Jill Stephenson, *The Nazi Organisation of Women* (London, 1981); Tim Mason, 'Women in Nazi Germany 1925–40', *History Workshop Journal*, 1 (1976), pp. 74–113; and Tim Mason, 'Women in Germany 1925–40: family, welfare and work', *History Workshop Journal*, 2 (1976), pp. 5–32.

For an introduction to the movement in Britain P. Levine, *Victorian Feminism* (London, 1987) is useful. More specialist studies are Sheila Herstein, *A Mid-Victorian Feminist: Barbara Bodichon* (Yale, 1986), and an important analysis of the social background of first-wave activists by Olive Banks, *Becoming a Feminist* (Brighton, 1986). Two famous accounts by contemporaries are still useful if biased: Ray Strachey, *The Cause* (London, 1978) and E. Sylvia Pankhurst, *The Suffragette Movement* (London, 1977). Modern accounts which tend to play down the significance of militancy are Andrew Rosen, *Rise Up Women: The Militant Campaign of the Women's Social and Political Union, 1903–14* (London, 1974) and Martin Pugh, *Votes for Women in Britain, 1867–1928* (London, 1994). The dilemmas faced by feminists in Britain after the vote was won are examined in Brian Harrison, *Prudent Revolutionaries* (Oxford, 1987); Martin Pugh, *Women and the Women's Movement in Britain, 1914–1959* (London, 1992); and Joanna Alberti, *Beyond Suffrage: Feminists in War and Peace, 1914–28* (London, 1989).

Little is available in English on the Italian movement, but see Evans, *The Feminists*, and a useful article: Alexander De Grand, 'Women under Italian Fascism', *Historical Journal*, 19 (1976), pp. 946–68.

Useful on the movement in Russia are: Linda Edmondson, *Feminism in Russia 1900–1917* (London, 1984), and Gail Lapidus, *Women in Soviet Society: Equality, Development of Social Change* (Berkeley, CA, 1978).

Feminism in the Scandinavian countries is best approached via the general account in Evans, *The Feminists*. More detailed analyses of the early success of Nordic women are available in the following articles: Ida Blom, 'The struggle for women's suffrage in Norway, 1885–1913', *Scandinavian Journal of History*, 5 (1980), pp. 3–22; Riitta Jallinoja, 'The women's liberation movement in Finland: the social and political mobilisation of women in Finland, 1880–1910', *Scandinavian Journal of History*, 5 (1980), pp. 37–49; and Gunnar Quist, 'Policy towards women and the women's struggle in Sweden', *Scandinavian Journal of History*, 5 (1980), pp. 51–74.

9 Revolutionary Europe

General and reference works

Acton, E., *Rethinking the Russian Revolution*, London, 1990. A useful guide to what has been published on the 1917 revolution, though the author's categorization of historians is artificial.

Carr, E. H., *The Bolshevik Revolution*, 3 vols, London, 1950. This is a thematic treatment of the subject. Volume 1 deals with politics; volume 2 with economics and volume 3 with external relations.

Carr, E. H., *The Russian Revolution from Lenin to Stalin 1917–29*, London, 1979. A condensed version of the author's fourteen-volume history of the Soviet Union from 1917 to 1929. It is an informative and readable introduction to the period.

Edmondson, L., and Waldron, P., eds, *Economy and Society in Russia and the Soviet Union 1860–1930*, London, 1992. A collection of essays on various aspects of Russian and Soviet economic history.

Fitzpatrick, S., *The Russian Revolution*, Oxford, 1982. A stimulating interpretative essay on the Russian Revolution and the early Soviet period.

Hosking, G., *A History of the Soviet Union*, London, 1985. A good general narrative history.

Pipes, R., *The Russian Revolution 1899–1919*, London, 1990. An extensive treatment of the Russian Revolution's political aspects from a markedly anti-Bolshevik perspective.

Pipes, R., *Russia under the Bolshevik Regime 1919–1924*, London, 1995. The continuation of the author's history of the Russian Revolution in the same anti-Bolshevik spirit.

Schapiro, L., *The Russian Revolution and the Origins of Present-Day Communism*, London, 1984. A short history of the Russian Revolution dealing mostly with political developments.

Shukman, H., ed., *The Blackwell Encyclopedia of the Russian Revolution*, Oxford, 1988. Information on events, institutions and personalities of the revolutionary period.

Pre-revolutionary Russia

Bartlett, R., *Land Commune and Peasant Community in Russia*, London, 1990. A collection of essays on various aspects of the *mir*.

Bonnell, V. E., *The Russian Worker: Life and Labor under the Tsarist Regime*, Berkeley, CA, 1983. A collection of workers' memoirs.

Crisp, O., *Studies in the Russian Economy before 1914*, London, 1976. A collection of essays on the economic history of tsarist Russia.

Eklov, B. and Frank, S., eds, *The World of the Russian Peasant*, Boston, 1990. A collection of essays on Russian peasant society.

Falkus, M. E., *The Industrialisation of Russia 1700–1914*, London, 1972. A brief economic history of tsarist Russia, including much statistical material.

Gatrell, P., *The Tsarist Economy 1850–1917*, London, 1986. An economic history of Russia and its various interpretations.

Hosking, G., *The Russian Constitutional Experiment: Government and Duma 1907–1914*, Cambridge, 1973. A study of the Russian State Dumas, the Third in particular.

Johnson, R. E., *Peasant and Proletarian: The Working Class of Moscow in the Late Nineteenth Century*, Leicester, 1979.

McCauley, M., *Octobrists to Bolsheviks 1905–1917*, London, 1984. A useful collection of documents and materials.

Rogger, H., *Russia in the Age of Modernization and Revolution (1881–1917)*, London, 1983.

Siegelbaum, L. H., *The Politics of Industrial Mobilization in Russia, 1914–17*, London, 1983. A detailed treatment of the War Industries Committees drawing upon archival sources.

Stone, N., *The Eastern Front 1914–1917*, London, 1975. An erudite and original study of the Russian war effort.

Weber, M., *The Russian Revolutions*, trans. and edited by G. C. Wells and P. Baehr, Cambridge, 1995.

The Russian Revolution and the Civil War

Abraham, R., *Alexander Kerensky: The First Love of the Revolution*, London, 1987. A sympathetic but scholarly biography of Kerensky.

Berkman, A., *The Bolshevik Myth*, London, 1989. The memoirs of a Russo-American anarchist covering 1920–1, first published in 1925 and reflecting the increasingly repressive nature of the Soviet regime.

Bone, A., *The Bolsheviks and the October Revolution*, London, 1974. An invaluable first-hand source on the Bolshevik party during the October revolution and the Brest-Litovsk peace negotiations.

Chamberlin, W. H., *The Russian Revolution*, 2 vols, New York, 1935. The first general history of the Russian Revolution and Civil War in English, but still of value.

Cohen, S., *Bukharin and the Bolshevik Revolution: A Political Biography 1888–1938*, New York, 1973. This is one of the best biographies of a key figure in early Soviet history. It is strong both on the factual and theoretical aspects.

Daniels, R. V., *The Conscience of the Revolution*, Cambridge, MA, 1960. A study of the opposition movements of the early Soviet period; it brings out the element of continuity between them.

Daniels, R. V., *Red October: The Bolshevik Revolution of 1917*, London, 1968. A detailed and readable study focusing on the period of the October revolution.

Davies, N., *White Eagle, Red Star: The Polish-Soviet War, 1919–1920*, London, 1972. One of the few studies in English devoted to the Russo-Polish War.

Dobb, M., *Soviet Economic Development since 1917*, London, 1966.

Ferro, M., *The Russian Revolution of February 1917*, trans. J. L. Richards, London, 1972. A detailed work by a French historian.

Ferro, M., *October 1917: A Social History of the Russian Revolution*, trans. N. Stone, Boston, 1980. The part played by the workers, soldiers and peasants in the Russian Revolution.

Figes, O., *Peasant Russia, Civil War: The Volga Countryside in Revolution*, Oxford, 1989. Making wide use of archival sources, this is the best study in English of the Russian peasantry during the Civil War period.

Fitzpatrick, S., *The Commissariat of the Enlightenment: Soviet Organisation of Education and the Arts under Lunacharsky*, Cambridge, 1970. A study of early Soviet cultural policies, focusing in particular on the Commissariat of Education and its chief, Anatole Lunacharsky.

Frankel, E. R., *Revolution in Russia: Reassessments of 1917*, Cambridge, 1992. A collection of essays on various aspects of the Russian Revolution, such as political power and mass action, nationalities, and historiographical questions.

Hasegawa, T., *The February Revolution*, Seattle and London, 1981. The most detailed history of the February revolution, written by a Japanese historian.

Katkov, G., *Russia 1917: The February Revolution*, London, 1967. A well written and ingenious interpretation of the February revolution.

Katkov, G., *The Kornilov Affair: Kerensky and the Break-Up of the Russian Army*, London, 1980. An account of the Kornilov Affair based on Kornilov's version of events.

Keep, J., *The Russian Revolution: A Study in Mass Mobilization*, London, 1976. A book which concentrates on the workers' and peasants' movements during 1917–18.

Keep, J., *The Debate on Soviet Power: Minutes of the All-Russian Central Executive Committee*, Oxford, 1979. An excellent first-hand source on the first weeks of Bolshevik rule.

Lincoln, W. B., *Red Victory: A History of the Russian Civil War*, New York, 1989. Strong on personalities; excellent bibliography.

Malle, S., *The Economic Organisation of War Communism 1918–1921*, Cambridge, 1985. Abundant factual material.

Mawdsley, E., *The Russian Civil War*, Cambridge, 1987. One of the few histories of the Russian Civil War in English; it has a good bibliography.

McCauley, M., ed., *The Russian Revolution and the Soviet State 1917–1921: Documents*, London, 1975. A good collection of some of the main documents of the period.

Nove, A., *An Economic History of the USSR*, Harmondsworth, 1992. A lively treatment of the economic aspects of Soviet history, including the period of the Revolution and the Civil War.

Rabinowitch, A., *Prelude to Revolution*, Bloomington, 1968. A detailed examination of the July Days and the part played in them by the Bolsheviks.

Rabinowitch, A., *The Bolsheviks Come to Power*, London, 1979. A great many sources have been used to put together this account of the October revolution, but it is too focused on events in Petrograd.

Read, C., *From Tsar to Soviets: The Russian People and their Revolution, 1917–1921*, London, 1996. A social history of the Russian Revolution.

Reed, J., *Ten Days that Shook the World*, New York, 1919. A famous and highly readable account of the October revolution by an American journalist, but not all of it is completely factual.

Rigby, T. H., *Lenin's Government: Sovnarkom 1917–1922*, Cambridge, 1979. An institutional history of the early Soviet period.

Schapiro, L., *The Communist Party of the Soviet Union*, London, 1963. A history of the Russian Communist Party from its foundation to the 1960s.

Schapiro, L., *The Origin of the Communist Autocracy*, London, 1977. The author traces the process by which Soviet Russia became a one-party state.

Serge, V., *Memoirs of a Revolutionary 1901–1941*, Oxford, 1963. Memoirs of a Russo-Belgian sympathizer of Trotsky first published in French.

Smith, S. A., *Red Petrograd: Revolution in the Factories, 1917–18*, Cambridge, 1983. A well-researched account of a key aspect of the workers' movement in 1917–18.

Sukhanov, N. N., *The Russian Revolution 1917*, Oxford, 1955. The most detailed and colourful memoirs of a participant in the 1917 revolution. They were first published in 1922–3 in Berlin.

Trotsky, L. D., *The History of the Russian Revolution*, London, 1934. There are many editions of this classic work.

Wheeler-Bennett, J. W., *Brest-Litovsk: The Forgotten Peace*, London, 1938. Although written before the Second World War, this is still the best treatment of the subject.

White, J. D., *The Russian Revolution 1917–1921: A Short History*, London, 1994. An account dealing with the various aspects of the Russian Revolution and Civil War period.

Wildman, A. K., *The End of the Russian Imperial Army*, 2 vols, Chicago, 1980. An examination of the impact of the Russian Revolution on the army.

Williams, B., *The Russian Revolution 1917–1921*, Oxford, 1987. A concise treatment of the period which does include a discussion of cultural developments.

The international revolution

Claudin, F., *The Communist Movement: From Comintern to Cominform*, Harmondsworth, 1975. A perceptive analytic history of the Comintern and Cominform by a Spanish former Communist.

Dukes, P., *October and the World: Perspectives on the Russian Revolution*, London, 1979. An examination of the international impact of the Russian Revolution.

Harman, C., *The Lost Revolution: Germany 1918 to 1923*, London, 1982. The German revolution from a Trotskyist viewpoint.

Hulse, J. W., *The Forming of the Communist International*, Stanford, CA, 1964. A scholarly treatment of the foundation of the Comintern.

Nettl, J. P., *Rosa Luxemburg*, Oxford, 1969. A scholarly study of the life and times of Rosa Luxemburg.

Ryder, A. J., *The German Revolution of 1918*, Cambridge, 1967. The best work in English on the subject.

The Soviet Union 1921–1940

Conquest, R., *The Harvest of Sorrow*, London, 1986. An account of the forced collectivization of Soviet agriculture.

Deutscher, I., *Stalin: A Political Biography*, 2nd edn, London, 1964. The most readable biography of Stalin.

Getty, J. A., *Origins of the Great Purges*, Cambridge, 1985. A thoughtful examination of the purges using archival material.

McCauley, M., *The Soviet Union since 1917*, London, 1981. A concise history of the Soviet Union.

Medvedev, R., *Let History Judge*, London, 1972. A Soviet historian's attempt to explain the Stalin era.

Nove, A., ed., *The Stalin Phenomenon*, London, 1993. A collection of essays on Stalinism.

Trotsky, L. D., *The Revolution Betrayed*, London, 1937. Trotsky's classic critique of the Soviet system under Stalin.

10 European Fascism

Allardyce, G. R., 'What Fascism is not', *American Historical Review*, 84, no. 2 (1979), 367–88. The case against generic fascism.

Arendt, H., *The Origins of Totalitarianism*, London, 1961. Brilliant but overstated comparison between Nazism and Stalinism.

Aycoberry, P., *The Nazi Question*, London, 1981. A stimulating survey of the literature.

Blinkhorn, M., ed., *Fascists and Conservatives*, London, 1990. Interesting essays on collusion, or not, between elites and national fascisms.

Broszat, M., *The Hitler State*, London, 1981. Structuralist analysis of the diffusion of power in the Nazi state.

Burleigh, M., ed., *Confronting the Nazi Past*, London, 1996. Important essays on the social history of the Third Reich.

Cassels, A., *Fascist Italy*, 2nd edn, Arlington Heights, IL, 1985. The best short survey of Italian Fascism.

Childers, T., *The Formation of the Nazi Constituency 1919–33*, London, 1986. Good essays on who supported the Nazis.

Conway, M., *Collaboration in Belgium*, New Haven, 1993. Impressive study of how Rex became ardent Nazis.

Corner, P., *Fascism in Ferrara*, Oxford, 1975. Why Italian Fascism became a significant force.

Eatwell, R., 'Towards a new model of generic fascism', *Journal of Theoretical Politics*, 4, no. 2 (1992), 161–94. An important interpretation of the nature of fascism.

Eatwell, R., 'Fascism', in *Contemporary Political Ideologies*, ed. R. Eatwell and S. Wright, London, 1993, 169–91. Fascism as a synthesis of left and right.

Eatwell, R., *Fascism: A History*, London, 1995. An interesting study of fascism's success in Italy and Germany, but failure elsewhere.

Eatwell, R., 'On defining the "Fascist minimum": the centrality of ideology', *Journal of Political Ideologies*, 1, no. 3 (1996).

Felice, R. de, *Interpretations of Fascism*, Cambridge, MA, 1977. A thoughtful survey.

Forgacs, D., ed., *Rethinking Italian Fascism*, London, 1986. Important revisions of the nature of Mussolini's Italy.

Gregor A. J., *Interpretations of Fascism*, Morristown, NJ, 1974. Interesting, particularly on Marxist and modernization theories.

Griffin, R., *The Nature of Fascism*, London, 1991. Successfully incorporates an impressive range of movements within a model of generic fascism.

Griffin, R., *Fascism: A Reader*, London, 1995. By far the best book of documents and readings on generic fascism.

Hayes, P., *Quisling*, Newton Abbot, 1971. Political biography of the notorious Norwegian fascist leader.

Hiden, J. and Farquaharson, J., *Explaining Hitler's Germany*, 2nd edn, London, 1989. A useful survey of the literature on the nature of Nazi state and society.

Kershaw, I., *The Nazi Dictatorship*, 3rd edn, London, 1993. The best textbook on Nazi Germany.

Koch, H., ed., *Aspects of the Third Reich*, London, 1985. A useful selection of intentionalist and structuralist/functionalist articles on Nazism.

Larsen, S. et al., *Who were the Fascists?*, Bergen, 1980. The most comprehensive collection of essays on the sociology of European fascism.

Lyttleton, A., *The Seizure of Power*, London, 1973. How Mussolini became the Italian Duce (1922–5).

Mack Smith, D., *Mussolini*, London, 1981. Classic biography of Mussolini as opportunist and political thug.

Mommsen, H., *From Weimar to Auschwitz*, Cambridge, 1991. Seminal essays on structuralist interpretation of Nazism.

Mosse, G. L., ed., *International Fascism*, London, 1979. Important articles on Fascism, most of which were first published in the *Journal of Contemporary History*, 1976.

Muhlberger, D., ed., *The Social Basis of European Fascism*, London, 1987. Much useful material on who were the fascists, which emphasizes the wide social class recruitment of most fascist parties.

Nolte, E., *Three Faces of Fascism*, London, 1966. Important, but ignores social and economic factors, and fascism was not against transcendence.

O'Sullivan, N., *Fascism*, London, 1983. Backward linkages of the ideas and style of fascism to the enlightenment and the impact of the French Revolution.

Payne, S., *Fascism: Comparison and Definition*, Madison, WI, 1980. Influential Weberian ideal type definition which emphasizes the fascist negations, and style.

Payne, S., *A History of Fascism 1914–45*, London, 1996. A magisterial synopsis of its subject covering an encyclopaedic range of movements with a good discussion of the major theories of fascism.

Preston, P., *Franco*, London, 1994. Seminal biography of the Spanish dictator. Brilliant, but a depressing read.

Prowe, D., 'Classic fascism and the new radical right in Western Europe', *Contemporary European History*, 3, no. 3 (1994), 289–313. An important article which discusses the relationship between interwar fascism and the post-1945 radical right.

Rogger, H. and Weber, E., eds, *The European Right*, London, 1965. Good essays on fascism, the radical right and authoritarianism in Europe in the nineteenth and twentieth centuries.

Sternhell, Z., *Neither Right nor Left*, Berkeley, CA, 1986. Controversial, iconoclastic but stimulating study of French 'fascist' ideas in the 1930s.

Sternhell, Z., 'Fascism', in *The Blackwell Encyclopaedia of Political Thought*, ed. D. Miller Oxford, 1987, pp. 148–51. Useful short analysis of fascist ideas, but fails to discuss Nazism.

Sternhell, Z., *The Birth of Fascist Ideology*, Princeton, NJ, 1994. A major work, but needs to stress the impact of the First World War, and German roots.

Thomas, H., *The Spanish Civil War*, 3rd edn, London, 1977. Still the major narrative history of its theme.

Thurlow, R., *Fascism in Britain: A History 1918–85*, Oxford, 1987. A study of an unsuccessful fascism.

Turner, H. A., ed., *Reapprasials of Fascism*, New York, 1975. A useful collection of stimulating essays.

Weber, E., ed., *Varieties of Fascism*, New York, 1964. A survey of fascisms with documents. Still a good introduction to the subject.

Woolf, S. J., ed., *The Nature of Fascism*, London, 1968. Interesting essays on some general themes of national fascisms.

Woolf, S. J., ed., *Fascism in Europe*, London, 1981. Good essays on national fascisms.

11   European Diplomacy, 1871–1914

On 1871–1914

Anderson, M. S., *The Eastern Question 1774–1923*, London, 1966.

Bourne, K., *The Foreign Policy of Victorian England 1830–1902*, Oxford, 1970.

Bridge, F. R., *From Sadowa to Sarajevo*, London, 1972.

Fuller, W. C., *Strategy and Power in Russia 1600–1914*, New York, 1992.

Geiss, I., *German Foreign Policy 1870–1914*, London, 1976.

Geyer, D., *Russian Imperialism: The Interaction of Domestic and Foreign Policy 1860–1914*, Leamington Spa, 1987.

Gillard, P., *The Struggle for Asia, 1829–1914*, London, 1977.

Howard, C. H. D., *Britain and the casus belli 1822–1902*, London, 1974.

Ingram, E., 'The defence of India 1874–1914: a strategic dilemma', *Militargeschichtliche Mitteilungen*, 14 (1974).

Jelavich, B., *Russia's Balkan Entanglements 1809–1914*, Cambridge, 1991.

Lowe, C. J., *The Reluctant Imperialists: British Foreign Policy 1878–1902*, London, 1967.

Lowe, C. J. and Marzari, F., *Italian Foreign Policy 1870–1940*, London, 1975.

Taylor, A. J. P., *The Struggle for Mastery in Europe 1848–1918*, Oxford, 1954.

Yasamee, F., 'Abdulhamid II and the Ottoman defence problem', *Diplomacy and Statecraft*, 4 (1993).

On 1870–1880

Bagdasarian, N., *The Austro-German Rapprochement 1870–1879*, London, 1976.

Jelavich, B., *The Ottoman Empire, the Great Powers, and the Straits Question, 1870–1887*, Bloomington, IN, 1973.

Langer, W. L., *European Alliances and Alignments 1871–1890*, New York, 1931.

Medlicott, W. N., *The Congress of Berlin and After*, London, 1938.

Millman, R., *Great Britain and the Eastern Question 1875–1878*, Oxford, 1979.

Morris, P., 'The Russians in Central Asia 1870–1887', *Slavonic and East European Review*, 53 (1975).

Rupp, G. H., *A Wavering Friendship: Russia and Austria 1876–1878*, Cambridge, MA, 1941.

Schroeder, P., 'The lost intermediaries: the impact of 1870 on the European system', *International History Review*, 6 (1984).

Stojanovich, M., *The Great Powers and the Balkans 1875–1878*, Cambridge, 1939.

Sumner, B., 'Russia and Pan-Slavism in the 1870s', *Transactions of the Royal Historical Society*, 4th series, 18 (1935).

Sumner, B., *Russia and the Balkans 1870–1880*, Oxford, 1937.

Waller, B., *Bismarck at the Crossroads*, London, 1974.

On 1880–1890

Brown, M. L., *Heinrich von Haymerle*, Columbia, SC, 1973.

Fuller, J. V., *Bismarck's Diplomacy at its Zenith*, Cambridge, MA, 1922.

Greaves, R. L., *Persia and the Defence of India 1884–1892*, London, 1959.

Hinsley, F. H., 'Salisbury and the Mediterranean Agreements of 1887', *Historical Journal*, 1 (1958).

Jelavich, C. and B., *Tsarist Russia and Balkan Nationalism*, Berkeley, CA, 1958.

Kennan, G., *The Decline of Bismarck's European Order: Franco-Russian Relations 1875–1890*, Princeton, NJ, 1979.

Langer, W. L., *European Alliances and Alignments 1871–1890*, New York, 1931.

Lowe, C. J., *Salisbury and the Mediterranean 1886–1896*, London, 1965.

Medlicott, W. N., 'The Powers and the union of the two Bulgarias, 1885', *English Historical Review*, 54 (1939).

Medlicott, W. N., 'Bismarck and the Three Emperors' Alliance 1881–87', *Transactions of the Royal Historical Society*, 4th series, 27 (1945).

Taylor, A. J. P., *Germany's First Bid for Colonies 1884–5*, London, 1938.

Yasamee, F., *Ottoman Diplomacy: Abdulhamid II and the European Great Powers 1878–1888*, Istanbul, 1996.

On 1890–1900

Andrew, C., 'German world policy and the re-shaping of the Dual Alliance', *Journal of Contemporary History*, 1 (1966).

Andrew, C. and Kanya-Forstner, A. S., 'Hanotaux, the Colonial Party and the Fashoda Strategy', *Journal of Imperial and Commonwealth History*, 3 (1974).

Greaves, R., 'British policy in Persia 1892–1903', *Bulletin of the School of Oriental and African Studies*, 28 (1965).

Grenville, J. A. S., *Lord Salisbury and Foreign Policy*, London, 1964.

Kennedy, P. M., 'German world policy and the Alliance negotiations with England 1897–1900', *Journal of Modern History*, 45 (1973).

Langer, W. L., *The Franco-Russian Alliance*, Cambridge, MA, 1929.

Langer, W. L., *The Diplomacy of Imperialism 1890–1902*, New York, 1935.

Lieven, D., 'Pro-Germans and Russian foreign policy 1890–1914', *International History Review*, 2 (1980).

Lowe, C. J., *Salisbury and the Mediterranean 1886–1896*, London, 1965.

Martel, G., *Imperial Diplomacy*, London, 1986.

Maxwell, M., 'A re-examination of the role of N. K. Giers as Russian Foreign Minister', *European Studies Review*, 1 (1971).

Rich, N., *Friedrich von Holstein*, Cambridge, 1965.

Röhl, J. C. G., *Germany without Bismarck*, London, 1967.

Sanderson, G. N., *England, Europe and the Upper Nile 1882–1899*, Edinburgh, 1965.

Wilson, K. M., *Empire and Continent*, London, 1987.

On 1900–1914

Andrew, C., *Théophile Delcassé and the Making of the Entente Cordiale*, London, 1968.

Berghahn, V. R., *Germany and the Approach of War in 1914*, London, 1973.

Bridge, F. R., 'Isvolsky, Aehrenthal and the end of the Austro-Russian entente 1906–1908', *Mitteilungen des Oesterreichischen Staatsarchivs*, 29 (1976).

Cohen, S., 'Mesopotamia in British strategy 1903–1914', *International Journal of Middle Eastern Studies*, 9 (1978).

Edwards, E. W., 'The Japanese Alliance and the Anglo-French Agreement', *History*, 42 (1957).

Edwards, E. W., 'The Franco-German Agreement on Morocco, 1909', *English Historical Review*, 78 (1963).

Friedberg, A. L., *The Weary Titan: Britain and the Experience of Relative Decline 1895–1905*, Princeton, NJ, 1988.

Kehr, E. (ed. G. A. Craig), *Economic Interest, Militarism and Foreign Policy*, Cambridge, 1965.

Kent, M. R. (ed.), *The Great Powers and the End of the Ottoman Empire 1900–1918*, London, 1984.

Lambi, I. J., *The Navy and German Power Politics 1862–1914*, London, 1984.

Liu, K.-C., 'German fears of a quadruple alliance 1904–5', *Journal of Modern History*, 18 (1946).

Long, J., 'Franco-Russian relations during the Russo-Japanese war', *Slavonic and East European Review*, 52 (1974).

Rich, N., *Friedrich von Holstein*, Cambridge, 1965.

Rolo, P. J. V., *Entente Cordiale*, London, 1969.

Wilson, K. M., 'The question of anti-Germanism at the Foreign Office before the First World War', *Canadian Journal of History*, 18 (1983).

Wilson, K. M., *The Policy of the Entente: The Determinants of British Foreign Policy 1904–1914*, Cambridge, 1985.

Winzen, P., 'Prince Bülow's Weltmachtpolitik', *Australian Journal of Politics and History*, 22 (1976).

On 1910–1914

Askew, W. C., *Europe and Italy's Acquisition of Libya 1911–1912*, Durham, NC, 1942.

Bestuhev, I. V., 'Russian foreign policy, February to June 1914', *Journal of Contemporary History*, 1 (1966).

Bridge, F. R., 'Tarde venientibus ossa: Austro-Hungarian colonial aspirations in Asia Minor 1913–14', *Middle Eastern Studies*, 6 (1970).

Crampton, R. J., *The Hollow Détente: Anglo-German Relations in the Balkans 1911–1914*, London, 1980.

Fischer, F., *War of Illusions: German Policies from 1911 to 1914*, New York, 1975.

Helmreich, E. C., *The Diplomacy of the Balkan Wars*, New York, 1938.

Jelavich, B., 'Roumania in the First World War: the pre-war crisis, 1912–1914', *International History Review*, 14 (1992).

Kaiser, D., 'Germany and the origins of the First World War', *Journal of Modern History*, 55 (1983).

Keiger, J. F. V., *France and the Origins of the First World War*, London, 1983.

Spring, D. W., 'Russia and the Franco-Russian Alliance 1905–1914: dependence or interdependence?', *Slavonic and East European Review*, 66 (1988).

Thaden, E. C., *Russia and the Balkan Alliance of 1912*, University Park, PA, 1965.

Turner, L. C. F., *The Origins of the First World War*, London, 1970.

Wedel, O. H., *Austro-German Diplomatic Relations 1908–1914*, Stanford, CA, 1932.

Williamson, S. R., *Austria-Hungary and the Origins of the First World War*, London, 1991.

Wilson, K. M., 'Imperial interests in the British decision for war, 1914: the defence of India in Central Asia', *Review of International Studies*, 10 (1984).

Wilson, K. M., *The Policy of the Entente 1904–1914*, Cambridge, 1985.

Wilson, K. M. (ed.), *Decisions for War, 1914*, London, 1995.

Zotiades, G. B., 'Russia and the question of Constantinople and the Turkish Straits during the Balkan Wars', *Balkan Studies*, 11 (1970).

12 European Imperialism, 1871–1945

Overviews

Cain, P. J. and Hopkins, A. G., *British Imperialism: I Innovation and Expansion, 1688–1914*, and *II Crisis and Deconstruction, 1914–1990*, London, 1993. At the centre of much debate.

James, L., *The Rise and Fall of the British Empire*, London, 1994. The most recent popular history.

Louis, W. R., ed., *The Oxford History of the British Empire*, Oxford, forthcoming. These five volumes will contain essays by many leading imperial historians.

Marshall, P., ed., *The Cambridge Illustrated History of the British Empire*, Cambridge, 1996. Perhaps the best starting point for the British Empire, and one of the main sources for the current chapter.

McDonough, F., *The British Empire, 1815–1914*, London, 1994. Very basic, but a minor miracle of compression.

Morris, J., *Pax Britannica*, London, 1968–78. This three-volume work is the most vivid and readable of the popular histories.

Porter, P., *The Lion's Share: A Short History of British Imperialism, 1850–1983*, London, 1984. The liveliest of the older textbooks (originally published in 1975).

Thornton, A. P., *The Imperial Idea and Its Enemies: A Study in British Power*, London, 1959. A witty and memorable classic.

Area studies

Brown, J., *Modern India: The Origins of an Asian Democracy*, Oxford, 1994. An elegant and readable standard introduction.

Oliver, R. and Atmore, A., *Africa Since 1800*, Cambridge, 1994. A standard work, now in its fourth edition.

Sarkar, S., *Modern India, 1885–1947*, 1989. A detailed textbook, with a lot of 'history from below'.

Smith, C. D., *Palestine and the Arab-Israeli Conflict*, New York, 1992. A balanced and judicious overview.

Worden, W., *The Making of Modern South Africa: Conquest, Segregation and Apartheid*, Oxford, 1994.

Yapp, M. E., *The Making of the Modern Near East, 1792–1923*, and *The Near East Since the First World War*, London, 1987 and 1991.

Colonial expansion

Cottrell, P. L., *British Overseas Investment in the Nineteenth Century*, London, 1975.

Eldridge, C. C., ed., *British Imperialism in the Nineteenth Century*, London, 1984.

Förster, S., Mommsen, W. J. and Robinson, R., eds, *Bismarck, Europe and Africa: The Berlin Africa Conference 1884–1885 and the Onset of Partition*, Oxford, 1988.

Gallagher, J. A. and Robinson, R. E., 'The imperialism of Free Trade', *Economic History Review*, 6 (1953). Original statement of the 'informal empire' hypothesis.

Headrick, D. R., *Tentacles of Progress: Technology Transfer in an Age of Imperialism, 1850–1940*, New York and Oxford, 1988. Highlights the growing technical and military dominance of Europe.

Kennedy, P. M., *The Rise and Fall of British Naval Mastery*, London, 1991. Originally published in 1976, this is a very readable overview.

MacKenzie, J. M., ed., *Imperialism and Popular Culture*, and *Popular Imperialism and the Military*, Manchester, 1986 and 1992. Collections of essays suggesting that imperial values permeated popular entertainments.

Porter, A., *European Imperialism, 1860–1914*, London, 1994. The best brief introduction to the debates about the later nineteenth century. It also contains a very useful annotated bibliography.

Price, R., *An Imperial War and the British Working Class*, London, 1972. Argues that 'popular imperialism' was confined mainly to the lower middle class.

Ranger, T. O., *Revolt in Southern Rhodesia, 1896–7*, London, 1967. A classic study of a 'post-pacification revolt'.

Semmel, B., *Imperialism and Social Reform: English Social-Imperial Thought, 1895–1914*, London, 1960.

Thompson, A., 'Informal Empire? An exploration in the history of Anglo-Argentine relations, 1810–1914', *Journal of Latin American Studies*, 24 (1992), 419–36. Succinctly reviews the debate, and concludes that 'informal empire' is not persuasive.

Warwick, P., ed., *The South African War: The Anglo-Boer War, 1899–1902*, London, 1980.

Colonial encounters

Anderson, D. M. and Killingray, D., *Policing the Empire: Government, Authority and Control, 1830–1940*; and *Policing and Decolonisation: Nationalism, Politics and the Police, 1917–65* Manchester, 1991 and 1992.

Arnold, D., *Police Power and Colonial Rule: Madras, 1858–1947*, Delhi, 1986. A seminal monograph.

Arnold, D., *Colonizing the Body: State Medicine and Epidemic Disease in Nineteenth-Century India*, Berkeley, CA, 1993.

Arnold, D., ed., *Imperial Medicine and Indigenous Societies*, Manchester, 1988.

Hyam, R., *Empire and Sexuality: The British Experience*, Manchester, 1990.

MacKenzie, J. M., *Orientalism: History, Theory and the Arts*, Manchester, 1995. Replies persuasively to Said's *Orientalism*.

Omissi, D. E., *The Sepoy and the Raj: The Indian Army, 1860–1940*, London, 1994.

Porter, A., 'Religion and Empire: British expansion in the long nineteenth century', *Journal of Imperial and Commonwealth History*, 20 (1992), 370–90. A survey of the relationship between missionaries and the state.

Said, E., *Orientalism*, London, 1978. Passionately argues that Orientalist perceptions of the East were saturated with racism and the desire to dominate.

Colonial retreat?

Ageron, C.-R., ed., *Les chemins de la décolonisation française, 1936–1956*, Paris, 1986.

Amin, S., 'Gandhi as Mahatma: Gorakhpur District, Eastern UP, 1921–2', in *Subaltern Studies III*, ed. R. Guha, Delhi, 1984. A brilliant essay on popular perceptions of Gandhi.

Betts, R. F., *France and Decolonisation, 1900–1960*, London, 1991. A manageable overview.

Brown, J. M., *Gandhi: Prisoner of Hope*, Oxford, 1989. The standard biography.

Darwin, J., 'Imperialism in decline? Tendencies in British imperial policy between the wars', *Historical Journal*, 23 (1980).

Darwin, J., *Britain and Decolonisation: The Retreat from Empire in the Post-War World*, London, 1988. The standard account for the British Empire, extending further back in time than its title suggests.

Hargreaves, J., *Decolonization in Africa*, London, 1988. The earlier chapters have material on imperial policy up to 1945.

Hasan, M., ed., *India's Partition: Process, Strategy and Mobilization*, Delhi, 1994. A collection of essays on the end of empire in India, with a useful historiographical introduction.

Holland, R., *European Decolonization, 1918–1981*, London, 1985. A comparative introduction to the end of empire.

Owen, N., '"More than a transfer of power": Independence Day ceremonies in India, 15 August 1947', *Contemporary Record*, 6 (1992), 415–51. Shrewdly dissects the public relations of decolonization.

Atlases

Bayly, C., ed., *Atlas of the British Empire*, London, 1989.
Porter, A. N., ed., *Atlas of British Overseas Expansion*, London, 1991.

13 The First World War as Total War

A number of good general books on the domestic consequences of the war are available. Gerd Hardach's *The First World War 1914–1918* (Harmondsworth, reprinted 1987) deals with the war's consequences on the world economy, and therefore makes some very useful comparisons. See also J. M. Winter and Richard Wall (eds), *The Upheaval of War: Family, Work and Welfare in Europe, 1914–1918* (Cambridge, 1989), for a diverse collection of essays. The British home front is covered in great depth in Trevor Wilson's mammoth *Myriad Faces of War* (Cambridge, 1986), and, more manageably, by Gerard DeGroot in *Blighty: British Society in the Era of the Great War* (Harlow, 1996). For Germany, see Gerald Feldman, *Army, Industry and Labour in Germany 1914–1918* (Princeton, NJ, 1966); for Austria-Hungary, A. J. May's *The Passing of the Hapsburg Monarchy* (Philadelphia, 1966); for France, Jean-Jacques Becker's *The Great War and the French People* (Leamington Spa, translated edn 1985) and J. Cruickshank, *Variations on Catastrophe* (London, 1982). See also D. Mitrany, *The Effect of the War in South-Eastern Europe* (London, 1936).

The Marwick thesis, now out of favour, can be found in Arthur Marwick, *War and Social Change in the Twentieth Century* (London, 1974), *Britain in the Century of Total War* (London, 1968), and *The Deluge: British Society and the First World War* (London, 1965). Stefan Andreski's *Military Organization and Society* (London, 1968) ploughs a similar furrow.

For the relationship between the state and industry, Kathleen Burk's edited collection *War and the State* (London, 1982) is excellent. R. J. Q. Adams studies the British munitions industry in *Arms and the Wizard* (London, 1978). Two books by David French, *British Economic and Strategic Planning, 1905–1915* (London, 1982), and *British Strategy and War Aims, 1914–1916* (London, 1986), provide useful insight into how economic policy affected war strategy, and vice versa. Manpower problems are examined in Keith Grieves, *The Politics of Manpower* (Manchester, 1988). The collection of articles edited by Ian Beckett and Keith Simpson, *A Nation in Arms* (Manchester, 1985), is useful on the characteristics and demographics of Britain's army. Similar books pertaining to the other combatants which are written in English are not plentiful. But, for Germany, see R. Armeson's *Total Warfare and Compulsory Labour* (Den Haag, 1964) and for Russia, Z. O. Zagorski's *State Control of Industry in Russia during the War* (London, 1928); his *The War and the Russian Government* (New Haven, 1929) is also helpful. For France, Gerd Krumeich's *Armaments and Politics in France on the Eve of the First World War* (Leamington Spa, translated 1984) sets the scene nicely.

Harold Lasswell's *Propaganda Techniques in the World War* (London, 1938) is dated but still useful. Michael Sanders and Phillip Taylor focus specifically on Britain in *British Propaganda during the First World War* (London, 1982), but still make comparisons with other countries. Broader, if shorter, studies include Alice Marquis, 'Words as weapons: propaganda in Britain and Germany during the First World War', *Journal of Contemporary History*, 13 (1978) and E. Demm, 'Propaganda and caricature in the First World War', *Journal of Contemporary History*, 28 (1993).

The effect of the war upon housing, food and health has been covered in great depth by Jay Winter in a number of works. His findings are synthesized in *The Great War and the British People* (London, 1986). While it focuses upon Britain, the book does make some illuminating comparisons with other combatant countries. Students should consult his bibliography for more sources on this subject. On the blockade, see M. C. Siney, *The Allied Blockade of Germany* (Ann Arbor, MI, 1957). A. C. Bell's *A History of the Blockade of Germany, Austria-Hungary, Bulgaria and Turkey 1914–1918* (London, 1937) is a handy source of statistics. See also L. Grebler and W. Winkler, *The Cost of the War to Germany and Austria-Hungary* (New Haven, 1940) and S. Kohn and A. Meyendorff, *The Cost of the War to Russia* (New Haven, 1932).

The war's effect upon women is studied in the dense and difficult collection edited by M. Higonnet, et al., entitled *Behind the Lines: Gender and the Two World Wars* (New Haven, 1987). Gail Braybon's *Women Workers in the First World War* (London, 1981), and (with Penny Summerfield) *Out of the Cage: Women's Experiences in Two World Wars* (London, 1987) contain some fascinating material and impressive detail, but Braybon is unreliable when it comes to the political background. The best analysis of the war's effect upon British women can be found in Martin Pugh's *Women and the Women's Movement in Britain* (London, 1992). Susan Kent demonstrates how the war had a conservative effect upon British women in 'The politics of sexual difference: World War I and the demise of British feminism', *Journal of British Studies*, 27 (1988). A complex, but still very helpful study of the war's effect upon labour and class issues in Britain can be found in Bernard Waite's *A Class Society at War* (Leamington Spa, 1988).

Culture and total war are covered in two flawed but still fascinating studies: Paul Fussell's *The Great War and Modern Memory* (New York, 1977) and Modris Ekstein's *Rites of Spring* (New York, 1989). Both tend to over-emphasize high culture, a fault corrected to some extent by Stuart Sillars in *Art and Survival in First World War Britain* (New York, 1987). War losses are discussed in Bernard Harris, 'The demographic impact of the First World War: an anthropometric perspective', *Journal of the Society for the Social History of Medicine*, 6 (1993). For the legacy of the war and the question of mourning, see G. Mosse, *Fallen Soldiers* (Oxford, 1990) and Adrian Gregory, *The Silence of Memory* (Oxford, 1994).

14 Warfare and National Defence

Bond, B., *War and Society in Europe, 1870–1945*, London, 1984. A reliable introduction to the operational conduct of war in this period.

Bucholz, A., *Moltke, Schlieffen and Prussian War Planning*, Oxford, 1993. Bucholz shows how much of German war planning was determined by the technology of the railways.

Corm, J. S., *The Roots of Blitzkrieg: Hans von Seeckt and German Military Reform*, Kansas, 1992. Shows how the German army learned that battles were won by a combination of overwhelming firepower *and* mobility.

Dear, I. C. B. and Foot, M. R. D., *The Oxford Companion to the Second World War*, Oxford, 1995. A useful compendium of brief articles and references on all aspects of the war.

Doughty, R. A., *Seeds of Disaster: The Development of French Army Doctrine 1919–1939*, Hamden, CT, 1985. Argues that the French army concluded that in future battles would be won by the application of overwhelming firepower and neglected the problems of command and control and tactical mobility on the battlefield.

Ferro, M., *The Great War, 1914–1918*, London, 1973. Should be read in conjunction with Liddell Hart.

Howard, M., *War in European History*, Oxford, 1976. An excellent brief introduction to the place of war in European history and to the development of European military institutions.

Kennedy, P. M., *The War Plans of the Great Powers, 1880–1914*, London, 1979. Analyses the extent to which the war plans of the Powers and their alliance commitments made war inevitable in 1914 and examines the failure of politicians to understand the implications of military planning.

Liddell Hart, B., *History of the First World War*, London, 1932/72. The classic account of the war but, with its excessive concentration on military matters to the exclusion of politics and diplomacy, now looking very dated. Should be read in conjunction with Ferro.

Millett, A. R. and Murray, W., *Military Effectiveness*, 3 vols, London, 1988. A multi-authored and generally successful attempt to determine what constituted military effectiveness and why some armed forces enjoyed greater success than others between 1914 and 1945.

Overy, R. J., *The Air War 1939–45*, London, 1980. A critical appraisal on the role of air power in the Second World War which places it in its proper strategic context.

Stone, N., *The Eastern Front 1914–1917*, London, 1975. A controversial interpretation of the war on the Eastern Front which does much to rehabilitate the reputation of the tsarist army in 1916.

Van Creveld, M., *Technology and War from 2000 B.C. to the Present*, New York, 1989. A 'technologically-determinist' account of war from ancient times to the present. The chapters on 1830–1945 repay careful study.

Watt, D. C., *Too Serious a Business: European Armed Forces and the Approach to the Second World War*, London, 1975. Examines the impact of the First World War on the European general staffs in the inter-war period.

Weinberg, G. L., *A World at Arms: A Global History of World War Two*, Cambridge, 1994. Integrates diplomacy, strategy, intelligence with social, economic and political factors and shows how they interacted to determine the outcome of the war.

15 Appeasement

Place of publication is London unless otherwise stated.

Surveys putting appeasement in context

P. M. H. Bell, *The Origins of the Second World War in Europe* (1986); D. C. Watt, *How War Came: The Immediate Origins of the Second World War* (1989); Williamson Murray, *The Change in the European Balance of Power, 1938–1939* (Princeton, NJ, 1984); D. E. Kaiser, *Economic Diplomacy and the Origins of the Second World War* (Princeton, NJ, 1980). John Lukacs, *The Last European War, September 1939–December 1941* (1976) offers a thoughtful analysis. Collections of essays offering guides to recent scholarship may be found in: Robert Boyce and Esmonde M. Robertson (eds), *Paths to War: New Essays on the Origins of the Second World War* (1989); Gordon Martel (ed.), *The Origins of the Second World War Reconsidered: The A. J. P. Taylor Debate after Twenty-five Years*

(1986); W. J. Mommsen and L. Kettenacher (eds), *The Fascist Challenge and the Policy of Appeasement* (1983).

Britain

For coverage of historiographical debate, it is still worthwhile starting with 'Cato' (pseudonym), *Guilty Men* (1940) to catch the flavour of the early assault on appeasement; contrast Quintin Hogg, *The Left was Never Right* (1941). After the war, J. W. Wheeler-Bennett, *Munich: Prologue to Tragedy* (1948) and L. B. Namier, *Diplomatic Prelude* (1948) continued the attack in a more scholarly, though still committed, manner. Even in the early 1960s, Martin Gilbert and Richard Gott, *The Appeasers* (1963) showed that the fire still burned in young historians who had not been involved in the events of the 1930s; though shortly afterwards Martin Gilbert, *The Roots of Appeasement* (1966) reviewed the subject in a more detached style. Keith Robbins, *Munich 1938* (1968) marked the thirtieth anniversary of the Munich agreement with a volume which used newly available records, but not those of the Cabinet or Foreign Office; it remains a landmark of scholarship. Roger Parkinson, *Peace for Our Time: Munich to Dunkirk – The Inside Story* (1971) used the newly-opened Cabinet papers as the basis for a narrative of British policy, which is still a useful work of reference. Keith Middlemas, *Diplomacy of Illusion: The British Government and Germany, 1937–39* (1972) used Neville Chamberlain's personal papers as well as government records, and opened a new phase in historical writing on appeasement.

Memoirs of participants in events formed part of the debate, as well as being sources in their own right. Winston Churchill, *The Second World War*, vol. 1, *The Gathering Storm* (1948) included an indictment of appeasement which carried immense weight. Samuel Hoare (Lord Templewood), *Nine Troubled Years* (1954) was a systematic defence. Anthony Eden (Lord Avon), *The Eden Memoirs: Facing the Dictators* (1962) and *The Reckoning* (1965) contain valuable detail without fully explaining the author's resignation, which forms the dividing line between the two volumes. Duff Cooper (Lord Norwich), *Old Men Forget* (1953) includes chapters on the author's opposition to the Munich agreement and his resignation as First Lord of the Admiralty.

There are now several good **biographies** of all the main figures. K. Middlemas and J. Barnes, *Baldwin: A Biography* (1969) has much detail on the early 1930s. Keith Feiling, *The Life of Neville Chamberlain* (1946), though dated, is still worth reading as a sympathetic account. There are more recent discussions in John Charmley, *Chamberlain and the Lost Peace* (1989), which makes an interesting case for Chamberlain's policy; and R. A. C. Parker, *Chamberlain and Appeasement* (1993), which is firmly based on much primary material – balanced and indispensable for the whole subject. J. A. Cross, *Samuel Hoare* (1977); David Dutton, *Simon: A Political Biography of Sir John Simon* (1992); and Andrew Roberts, *The Holy Fox: A Biography of Lord Halifax* (1991) offer valuable studies of Foreign Secretaries connected with appeasement. The ambiguous figure of Eden is considered in David Carlton, *Anthony Eden* (1981) and Robert Rhodes James, *Anthony Eden* (1986) – the first hostile, the second sympathetic. David Dutton, *Anthony Eden: A Life and Reputation* (1997) provides a balanced study. Martin Gilbert, *Winston S. Churchill*, vol. 5, *1922–1939* (1976) is immensely detailed. Norman Rose, *Vansittart: Study of a Diplomat* (1978) deals with a prominent Foreign Office official, who wielded as much influence as many ministers.

Diaries provide some fascinating (and entertaining) detail, and help to convey the atmosphere of the time. David Dilks (ed.), *The Diaries of Sir Alexander Cadogan, 1938–1945* (1971) publishes the journal of the senior official in the Foreign Office – indispensable; to be supplemented by John Harvey (ed.), *The Diplomatic Diaries of Oliver Harvey,*

1937–1940 (1970), which gives a view from the Embassy in Paris. Harold Nicolson, *Diaries and Letters, 1930–1939* (1967), and Robert Rhodes James, ed., *Chips: The Diaries of Sir Henry Channon* (1967) are lighter in tone, but provide some of the gossip of the time – not to be despised.

Studies of the events may be introduced by reading William R. Rock, *British Appeasement in the 1930s* (Hamden, CT, 1966), which provides a brief and balanced synthesis which is still helpful. Principal events, in chronological order, are dealt with in: J. T. Emmerson, *The Rhineland Crisis, 7 March 1936* (1977); J. Edwards, *The British Government and the Spanish Civil War* (1979); Telford Taylor, *Munich: The Price of Peace* (1979) – see also Keith Robbins, *Munich 1938*, above; Steven Newman, *March 1939: The British Guarantee to Poland* (1976); Anita Prazmowska, *Britain, Poland and the Eastern Front* (1987).

Aspects of appeasement Economic appeasement is analysed in Gustav Schmidt, *The Politics and Economics of Appeasement* (Leamington Spa, 1986). G. F. Peden, *British Rearmament and the Treasury, 1932–1939* (1979) is lucid and enlightening. Brian Bond, *British Military Policy between the Two World Wars* (1980); Malcolm Smith, *British Air Strategy between the Wars* (1984); and Stephen Roskill, *Naval Policy between the Wars*, vol. 2 (1976) deal with the three armed forces. Uri Bialer, *The Shadow of the Bomber: The Fear of Air Attack and British Politics, 1932–1939* (1980) discusses a vital subject. Wesley K. Wark, *The Ultimate Enemy: British Intelligence and Nazi Germany, 1933–1939* (1985) illuminates what was for a long time a hidden aspect of policy. A. J. Crozier, *Appeasement and Germany's Last Bid for Colonies* (1988) is a full account of attempts at colonial appeasement. Ritchie Ovendale, *Appeasement and the English-Speaking World* (Cardiff, 1975) analyses the influence of the Dominions on British policy. Maurice Cowling, *The Impact of Hitler: British Politics and British Policy 1933–1940* (1975) examines the effects of domestic politics on foreign policy. F. R. Gannon, *The British Press and Nazi Germany, 1936–1939* (1971), and R. Cockett, *Twilight of Truth: Chamberlain, Appeasement and the Manipulation of the Press* (1989) deal with different aspects of the role of the newspaper press. Martin Ceadel, *Pacifism in Britain, 1914–1945* (1980) is excellent. Richard Griffiths, *Fellow Travellers of the Right: Enthusiasts for Nazi Germany, 1933–1939* (1980) is balanced and enlightening on a difficult subject. N. Thompson, *The Anti-Appeasers: Conservative Opposition to Appeasement in the 1930s* (1971) is dated but still useful.

France

A selection, mostly in English; but a few vital works in French are included. The best survey of French policy is A. P. Adamthwaite, *France and the Coming of the Second World War* (1977); Jacques Néré, *The Foreign Policy of France from 1914 to 1945* (1975) is rather thin. J. B. Duroselle, *La décadence, 1932–1939* (Paris, 1979) and *L'abîme, 1939–1945* (Paris, 1982); and Jean Doise et Maurice Vaïsse, *Diplomatie et outil militaire, 1871–1991* (Paris, 1991) are volumes in the massive series on *Politique étrangère de la France* – for those with the French to tackle them, absolutely indispensable. Jean-Louis Crémieux-Brilhac, *Les Français de l'an 40*, vol. 1, *La guerre oui ou non?*, vol. 2, *Ouvriers et soldats* (Paris, 1990), though mainly a study of the defeat of 1940, contains valuable material on Daladier, Bonnet and the economic and military position of France. Geoffrey Warner, *Pierre Laval and the Eclipse of France* (1968) is still illuminating, though of necessity it was written mainly from British and German sources. Elisabeth du Réau, *Edouard Daladier* (Paris, 1993) uses the full range of French material now available, including Daladier's papers and those of the French government. On military policy, see: Robert J. Young, *In Command of France: French Foreign Policy and Military Planning, 1933–1940*

(Cambridge, MA, 1978); Jeffrey A. Gunsburg, *Divided and Conquered: The French High Command and the Defeat of the West, 1940* (Westport, CT, 1980); P. C. F. Bankwitz, *Maxime Weygand and Civil-Military Relations in Modern France* (1967); Martin Alexander, *The Republic in Danger: General Maurice Gamelin and the Politics of French Defence, 1933–1940* (Cambridge, 1992).

16   The Second World War

Addison, P., *The Road to 1945: British Politics and the Second World War*, London, 1975. Examines the impact of the war upon British politics and argues for the emergence of a new political consensus.

Bond, B., *France and Belgium, 1939–40*, London, 1975.

Charmley, J., *Churchill's Grand Alliance: The Anglo-American Special Relationship 1940–57*, London, 1995. A critical and controversial assessment of Churchill's policies.

Deakin, F. W., *The Brutal Friendship: Mussolini, Hitler and the Fall of Italian Fascism*, New York, 1962.

Erikson, J., *The Road to Stalingrad*, London, 1975.

Erikson, J., *Stalin's War with Germany*, 2 vols, London, 1975 and 1983.

Fest, J., *Hitler*, London, 1974.

Gilbert, M., *Second World War*, London, 1989. An account of the war by Churchill's biographer which gives a far more sympathetic treatment of Churchill and his relations with Roosevelt than Charmley's book.

Flemming, G., *Hitler and the Final Solution*, London, 1985.

Howard, M., 'Total war in the twentieth century', in *War and Society: A Yearbook of Military History*, ed. B. Bond and I. Roy, London, 1976.

Howard, M., 'A Thirty Years War? The two World Wars in historical perspective', in *Royal Historical Society Transactions*, 6th series, vol. 3 (1993).

Hoyt E. P., *Japan's War: The Great Pacific Conflict*, London, 1987.

Jones F. C., *Japan's New Order in East Asia: Its Rise and Fall, 1937–1945*, London, 1954.

Keegan, J., *The Second World War*, London, 1989.

Keegan, J., *The Times Atlas of the Second World War*, London, 1989.

Mack Smith, D., *Mussolini*, London, 1981.

Man, J., *The Penguin Atlas of D-Day and the Normandy Campaign*, London, 1994.

Marwick, A., ed., *Total War and Social Change*, London, 1988. A collection of essays which consider the social effects of both the First and Second World War.

Overy, R., *The Air War 1939–45*, London, 1980.

Overy, R., with Andrew Wheatcroft, *The Road to War*, London, 1989. A stimulating study of how and why the seven major combatant Powers became involved in the war, by one of the leading authorities on the Nazi military economy.

Parker, R. A. C., *Struggle for Survival: The History of the Second World War*, Oxford, 1989. The best short history of the war.

Smith, Harold L., ed., *War and Social Change: British Society in the Second World War*, Manchester, 1986.

Smurthwaite, D., *The Pacific War Atlas 1941–1945*, London, 1995.

Weinberg, G. L., *A World at Arms: A Global History of World War II*, New York, 1994. A comprehensive one-volume history.

Wright, G., *The Ordeal of Total War*, New York, 1968. Concentrates on social and economic effects of the war.

Index

Flora's Lot

Katie Fforde lives in Gloucestershire with her husband and some of her three children. Her hobbies are ironing and housework but, unfortunately, she has almost no time for them as she feels it her duty to keep a close eye on the afternoon chat shows. *Flora's Lot* is her eleventh novel.

Praise for *Katie Fforde*

'Delicious – gorgeous humour and the lightest of touches' *Sunday Times*

'A witty and generous romance . . . Katie Fforde is on sparkling form . . . Jilly Cooper for the grown-ups' *Independent*

'A heart-warming tale of female friendship, fizzing with Fforde's distinctive brand of humour' *Sunday Express*

'Fforde's light touch succeeds in making this a sweet and breezy read – the ideal accompaniment to a long summer's evening' *Daily Mail*

'Old-fashioned romance of the best sort . . . funny, comforting' *Elle*

Further praise for *Katie Fforde*

'A fairytale-like, gently witty read . . . Heart-warming – made for sunny days in the park' *Cosmopolitan*

'The romance fizzes along with good humour and is a good, fat, summery read' *Sunday Mirror*

'Joanna Trollope crossed with Tom Sharpe' *Mail on Sunday*

'A spirited summer read that's got to be Fforde's best yet' *Woman & Home*

'Acute and funny observations of the social scene' *The Times*

'Can be scoffed in one sitting . . . Tasty' *Cosmopolitan*

'Perfect holiday reading. Pack it with the swimsuit and suntan lotion' *Irish Independent*

'Fforde is blessed with a lightness of touch, careful observation and a sure sense of the funny side of life' *Ideal Home*

Also by Katie Fforde

Katie Fforde
Flora's Lot

arrow books

Published by Arrow Books in 2006

3 5 7 9 10 8 6 4 2

Copyright © Katie Fforde 2005

Katie Fforde has asserted her right under the Copyright,
Designs and Patents Act, 1988 to be identified as the author of this work

First published in the United Kingdom in 2005 by Century

Arrow Books
The Random House Group Limited
20 Vauxhall Bridge Road, London, SW1V 2SA

Random House Australia (Pty) Limited
20 Alfred Street, Milsons Point, Sydney,
New South Wales 2061, Australia

Random House New Zealand Limited
18 Poland Road, Glenfield,
Auckland 10, New Zealand

Random House (Pty) Limited
Isle of Houghton, Corner of Boundary Road & Carse O'Gowrie,
Houghton 2198, South Africa

Random House Group Limited Reg. No. 954009

www.randomhouse.co.uk

A CIP catalogue record for this book
is available from the British Library

Papers used by Random House
are natural, recyclable products made from wood grown in
sustainable forests. The manufacturing processes conform to
the environmental regulations of the country of origin

ISBN 978 0 09 950285 2 (from Jan 2007)
ISBN 0 09 950285 2

Typeset in Palatino by Palimpsest Book Production Limited,
Polmont, Stirlingshire
Printed and bound in the United Kingdom by
Bookmarque Ltd, Croydon, Surrey

To The Thameshead Singers,
especially the subversive second sopranos.
Thank you for letting me be a member.

Acknowledgments

None of this would have been possible without the following people. You know what you've done and I thank you.

Chris and Jean Arnison, Lindsey Braune, Elizabeth Poole, Paul Wakeman, Catriona Aspray, and all the staff at The Cotswold Auction Company. Elizabeth Lindsay and Cheryl Gibson for car boot sale help.

From Random House, in no particular order, Kate Elton, Georgina Hawtrey-Woore, Charlotte Bush, Justine Taylor, the wonderful sales team, Mike Morgan and everyone else who makes being published by Random House so much fun.

To Richenda Todd, as always a meticulous and sensitive copy editor and worth her weight in rubies.

To Sarah Molloy, Sara Fisher and the rest of the A. M. Heath team, who are kind, supportive and money grubbing in a good way!

And lastly, my family, who inspire me, support me and keep me on the straight and narrow (sometimes).

Chapter One

❦

A yowl from the plastic box at her feet made Flora look down anxiously. Was Imelda actually having kittens, or was she still just complaining about being shut up in a pet carrier on a hot summer day?

'Not now, sweetie, please!' Flora implored through gritted teeth. 'Just hang on until I've got this meeting over. Then I'll find you a nice bed and breakfast where they like cats.'

Aware that her pleadings were really a displacement activity, Flora picked up the yowling Imelda, hooked her handbag over her shoulder, hitched her overnight bag over her arm and went up the steps. She was slightly regretting her new shoes. They were divinely pretty with a heavenly fake peony between the toes, but not worn in and therefore killingly uncomfortable. Not one to sacrifice prettiness for comfort, Flora ignored the incipient blisters and pressed the bell. Seeing her own surname on the brass plate above it gave her a strange thrill. The family firm, and she was joining it.

The door was opened by a tall woman wearing a lot of navy blue. She was a little older than Flora, and had a no-nonsense look about her which inevitably made Flora think of Girl Guides. My shoes may be not quite suitable, thought Flora, to give herself confidence, but

1

nor is that colour in this heat. In other circumstances, Flora realised, she would yearn to do a Trinny and Susannah on her.

'Hello,' said the woman, smiling professionally, 'you must be Flora. Do come in. We're so looking forward to meeting you. Especially Charles.'

Flora smiled too. 'I hope you won't mind, but I've got my cat with me. I can't leave her in the car in this heat. Apart from anything else, she's very pregnant.'

A little frown appeared between the woman's eyebrows as she looked down at the box. 'Oh, well, no, I'm sure it will be fine for a short time. Although I'm terribly allergic, I'm afraid.'

'Oh dear. I suppose I could leave her outside the door . . .' Flora bit her lip to indicate that in fact she couldn't leave Imelda anywhere except at her feet. 'But she might have her kittens at any moment.'

'You'd better come in,' said the woman, her professional manner beginning to fray. 'We're in here.' She opened the door of a room which was mostly filled with a table, around which were several empty chairs.

The room's sole occupant, a tall, conventionally handsome man wearing a dark suit and a very conservative tie, got up. Obviously Charles, her cousin fifteen million times removed.

Not promising. Flora depended on her charm to ease her way through life and had learnt to spot the few with whom this wouldn't work. He was a classic example, she could tell; he didn't like girls with pretty shoes, strappy dresses and amusing jewellery. He liked sensible girls who wore driving shoes, or plain leather courts with medium heels. His idea of good taste was a single

2

row of real pearls with matching earrings, and possibly a bangle on special occasions.

When the woman who had brought her in (displaying all these signs of proper dress sense) touched his arm and said, 'Darling, this is Flora,' Flora wasn't at all surprised to see the sapphire and diamond engagement ring on her left hand. They made the perfect County couple.

'Flora,' said Charles, holding out his hand. 'How nice to meet you after all these years.' He didn't sound all that pleased.

'Mm.' Flora shook the hand, smiled and nodded; she wasn't that pleased, either. She had totally reorganised her life to take a part in the family business with, she realised now, desperately inadequate research. Charles and his worthy, conventionally dressed fiancée didn't want her, wouldn't make her welcome, and her spell in the country could turn out to be horribly dull. Still, she'd made her bed, and she'd have to lie in it – at least until the sub-let on her London flat expired. 'It's very nice to meet you, too. I can't think why we haven't met before.'

'You spent quite a lot of your early life out of the country,' he said soberly, as if she might have forgotten.

'I suppose that explains it. We did miss out on quite a lot of family weddings.' She smiled. 'Though perhaps I won't miss out on the next one?'

'Oh yes, haven't you two introduced yourselves? This is Annabelle, Annabelle Stapleton. My fiancée and possible future partner in the business.' His smile, though conventional, did at least prove he brushed his teeth, which was something.

3

'How nice,' said Flora, wishing she'd made more enquiries about the business before telling that nice man of course he could have her flat for at least six months, she wouldn't be needing it.

'Yes,' agreed Charles. 'Now, let's sit down and discuss your part in Stanza and Stanza.'

'Would anyone like a glass of water first?' suggested Annabelle.

'Oh, yes please,' said Flora. 'And could I post a little to Imelda? In the box? I need to check on her anyway.' Flora delivered one of her most appealing smiles to her distant cousin, a last-ditch attempt to get him on her side. 'I wouldn't have brought her if there'd been any alternative, I assure you.'

'That's fine,' said Charles smoothly, almost, but not quite, concealing his impatience. Then, when the water had been dispensed and the cat seen to, he said, 'Tell me, Flora, I hope this isn't a rude question, but how much do you actually know about antiques and the auction business?'

Flora took another sip of water. 'Ah well, you pick up things like that as you go along, don't you?'

'Do you?' asked Charles, who had, she now noticed, rather strange grey-blue eyes which, beneath his sceptical eyebrows, had the look of the North Sea in winter.

'Well, yes.' Flora tried to think of a suitable phrase, to indicate she knew more than what she had gleaned from a lot of recent, frantic watching of various after-noon television programmes on the subject. 'Cheap as chips' didn't seem to apply. 'Of course,' she said airily, 'having spent so much of my youth in Europe, I'm not so up on English furniture.'

4

'But you must be au fait with all those glorious ceramics,' said Annabelle. 'I adore ceramics.'

Just for a moment, Flora felt unsure what ceramics were. 'Oh, you mean china and stuff? Yes, I love it too. I collect teapots, funny ones, you know?'

Charles winced visibly. 'I think we'd better get on.'

'Well, yes, we'd better,' said Flora rashly. 'But I do wonder if we will.'

'What on earth are you talking about?' said Charles. 'Now . . .' He opened a file and drew out a sheaf of papers. He was not a man who would get behind with his paperwork. He had that look about him. He was a filer and a putter-into-alphabetical-order-er. It was painfully clear.

'Now,' he began, 'our mutual great-uncle left things slightly awkwardly.'

'Did he?' asked Flora. 'I thought it was all quite straightforward. You'd already inherited forty-nine per cent from your father, and I got fifty-one per cent when Uncle Clodio died. Clear as sixteenth-century window glass, or something. Although I realise I wouldn't normally have been expected to inherit,' she added as consolation.

'Yes,' explained Charles, openly irritable now. 'But it is awkward. You own more than me. And you know nothing about the business and I've been running this auction house all my life, more or less.'

'Well, obviously I'm not going to sweep in here and make huge changes!' Flora made an extravagant gesture with her arms, observing at the same time that a good sweep, on the floor at least, would be a good idea. 'I want to learn about the business I'm going to be part of.'

5

Charles and Annabelle exchanged questioning glances. 'That's encouraging,' said Charles warily, 'but it still doesn't quite settle the matter. I can't have you having more shares than I have. It doesn't make sense, on any level.'

The cat yowled, possibly showing solidarity with Charles.

'Sorry, I must have a peek. In case this is it.'

'It?'

'The moment when she really is going to give birth. It's her first litter, you see, and the kittens can come in about thirty minutes from when she starts. I've read all about it.'

While Flora fussed with the cat she thought about her own situation. She was obviously totally unwelcome and Charles was horrible. Which was a shame – she hardly ever disliked people. She'd probably better make an alternative plan. Staying in the depths of the country with a couple who deeply resented her presence was not going to be a lot of fun. 'If it wasn't for you, Imelda,' she breathed inaudibly, 'I'd hightail it out of town right now.'

'Tell me,' said Charles, when Flora was again upright, sitting back in her uncomfortable chair. 'What exactly do you hope to get out of your trip down here?' The grey-blue eyes were penetrating and cold – they really were just like the North Sea. Flora felt she was being interviewed for a job for which she had no qualifica-tions – which, in a way, she was. She struggled to remind herself that, technically at least, she was more powerful than Charles.

She took a breath and didn't let herself be distracted

6

by Imelda's yowl. 'I haven't been brought up in the business like you have, but I have known about it. I didn't expect to inherit, as I said. It was such a shock to everyone when Niccolò was killed in that car accident and even then, I never thought Uncle Clodio – did you know him, by the way? He was lovely – would leave it to me.'

'No. I didn't know him.'

'It broke his heart when Nicki died, obviously.'

'It must have been terrible,' murmured Annabelle.

'But really, we – my parents and I – were totally surprised when we heard about how he'd left things.'

'Then I absolve you of forcing him to change his will on his death-bed,' said Charles dryly. 'But it still leaves us in a difficult position. In theory you could come in here and upset everything.'

Flora smiled. 'Yes I could, couldn't I?'

'Of course you won't,' Charles informed her firmly. 'But it would be much better if we could arrange things differently.'

'And how would you do that?' asked Flora, sensing they had the perfect plan all worked out.

'Annabelle could buy three per cent of your shares, so I would have one per cent more than you. Which, considering I am the senior partner, is only right and proper.'

'And Annabelle would have three per cent?'

'Yes.'

'And you're going to get married, so between you, you could do what you liked?'

'Yes, but you'd still have forty-eight per cent which

7

would bring you in a nice amount of money, when we make a profit.'

'Which you're not doing now?' Actually, Flora knew they weren't doing that well. She and her father had discussed it at length, but Charles was so prim and bossy that she wanted to make him say it.

'Not at the moment, no,' Charles admitted, 'but we do have plans to improve things.'

'Oh good. And now you've got me! I don't know all that much about the business, obviously, but I can learn. And two heads are better than one – or should that be three heads are better than two?' She glanced at Annabelle, who did not seem to be enjoying herself.

Charles frowned. '*Have* we got you, Flora? I was under the impression' – he glanced questioningly at Annabelle again – 'that you were only down here for a visit.'

'Well, yes, but I was planning to stay for quite a long time. Six months, at least. To see if I can stand – like – country life.'

'Six months!' said Annabelle. 'But where are you going to stay?'

Flora had been faintly hoping for an offer of someone's spare room, for at least a couple of days. As this was obviously not going to be forthcoming, she said, 'I thought a nice little bed and breakfast? Where they like cats?'

'Flora, before we get into the ins and outs of where you can stay, and I'm sure we can put you up for a short time—'

'No, Charles!' interrupted Annabelle. 'I'm terribly allergic to cats. You must have forgotten.'

'Sorry, yes I had.' He looked pained for a moment.

'But anyway, putting all that aside for one moment, I think I should make myself perfectly clear. There's really nothing for you to do in this business. It'll be better for us – I mean Stanza and Stanza – and ultimately you, if you just sell three per cent of your shares—' Imelda yowled again. 'Have a short holiday if you must, and then take yourself and your cat back to London.'

'Ah – well,' began Flora, not willing to admit to being temporarily homeless.

'Your parents still own that nice little flat in Lancaster Gate?'

'Yes.'

'And you live there?'

'When I'm in London, yes.' And I'm not in London now, you prig, and I've sub-let it for slightly more than I pay in rent to my parents so I can pay off my credit cards, she added silently, knowing not even thumb-screws would make her admit any of that to Charles.

'So you could go back?' asked Annabelle.

'I thought I was coming down here to live. For the time being, anyway. Downsizing!' she added glibly, not feeling remotely glib. 'It's terribly fashionable!'

'But if you sold me the shares, you'd have quite a lot of money. You could rent another flat, pay off your over-draft,' said Annabelle, who also had grey-blue eyes and an irritatingly patient tone of voice.

Bitch! thought Flora, she knows I'm short of money. She and Charles deserve each other. 'Well, put like that, your offer does sound quite tempting. Of course I will have to consult my father. Although I'm over twenty-one – obviously—'

'Not that obviously, actually,' murmured Charles, and

9

earned himself a flicker of a frown from Annabelle.

'I do usually discuss things like this with him. My parents aren't in the country right now, but we talk on the phone and email all the time.'

'Good,' said Charles. 'I'm sure he'd advise you to accept Annabelle's offer.'

'He might if he knew how much that was,' said Flora and smiled. 'Have you got a figure in mind?'

'Ten thousand pounds,' said Charles. 'Quite a lot more than three per cent is worth, of course, but we want to be generous.'

'That does sound generous,' said Flora, who had no idea if it was or wasn't. 'Do you mind if I think about it?'

'How long do you need? To get in touch with your father, discuss it, etc.?' asked Charles.

'A trip to the loo would be a good start.' Flora not only needed the loo, but to rinse her wrists in cold water, to clear her head a little. It was hot and she was tired. She didn't want to find herself bullied into something against her wishes by this *Country Life* couple with colour-coordinated eyes.

'Of course,' said Annabelle. 'Sorry, I should have offered when you first arrived. Stupid of me.'

'No, that's fine,' Flora replied graciously.

'Follow me,' said Annabelle.

'If you could just keep an eye on the cat?' Flora smiled endearingly at Charles, knowing it would annoy him.

Flora dried her hands on the roller towel in the dingy lavatory. Horrid soap, bad light and cheap loo paper, all things she would have changed if she'd been allowed.

10

But although she was very disappointed at the thought that all her plans for country living had been thwarted, ten thousand pounds would sort out her remaining credit-card bills, put a deposit down, and pay quite a few weeks' rent on a new flat. Or she could pay off the tenant in her parents' flat.

She should have felt excited about these new options, but somehow, as she emerged from the converted corridor that was now the Ladies', she felt flat and deflated. Her skills might not have been directly relevant to an auction house, but she did have them.

An elderly man in a brown warehouse coat stopped her before she'd turned into the main passage. 'Excuse me, are you Miss Stanza?'

'Yes.' He was silver-haired and well spoken and yet the shirt and tie, visible beneath the long coat, looked rather worn.

'I'm Geoffrey Whiteread. I knew your great-uncle, years ago. I'm the head porter.'

Flora struggled for a moment. 'The man who holds things up at the sales?'

The man smiled. 'Well, yes, but there is a bit more to it than that.' He looked about him, strangely furtive. 'Things are a bit difficult. I wanted to speak to you.'

Never one to refuse to share a trouble, Flora smiled, even if it did all seem a bit Gothic. 'Speak away.' The man looked kindly and a little troubled.

Just then they heard the office door open and both jumped. The Gothicness was obviously getting to them.

'This will improve the air circulation, at least,' they heard Charles say.

The old man frowned. 'We obviously can't talk here,'

11

he whispered. 'But perhaps we could arrange to meet later? It's very important you don't let that Annabelle woman get her hands on this business.'

'Why not?' Flora whispered back.

He made a gesture to indicate he couldn't go into it just then. 'Because she's a . . .' He paused, clearly on the verge of saying something very rude about Annabelle and then changed his mind. 'We can't talk here,' he repeated.

With the door open, Imelda's next protest was clearly audible. 'I'd better go back.' Flora nodded. 'Isn't there anything you can tell me now?'

The man shook his head. 'Not now. Just don't let her take control of the business. She's a holy terror.'

Scared lest her words be heard, Flora nodded again and set off slowly towards the door. She had obviously strayed into some sort of mystery novel, and she, Flora, would have to rescue this poor old man from the exploitative fiancée.

'She's a complete airhead,' she heard the exploitative fiancée say. 'But I expect she'll take the money. A fashion victim like her will jump at it.'

Fashion victim? Flora exchanged outraged glances with Geoffrey, who was listening with equal horror. She liked clothes, but fashion victim? Huh!

A chuckle, presumably from Charles, greeted this. 'Yes, she's obviously a natural blonde.'

Flora narrowed her eyes. 'Not as natural as all that,' she mouthed to Geoffrey.

'I never dreamt she'd want to stay,' said Annabelle.

Flora was confused. She knew she'd sent an email stating firmly she was going to take some time to learn

12

what was what. She thought she'd been perfectly clear about it.

'I must say I would have thought even someone like her would have mentioned it. It's rude, not to mention inconvenient.'

'Actually' – it was Annabelle speaking – 'I think she may have said something about it in an email. I just assumed she'd take one look and run back to London.'

There was a small silence while Flora held her breath, terrified in case she made a noise and they discovered she was eavesdropping. 'Oh.' This was Charles. 'We'll just have to hope you're right.'

'No need to go on about it, Charles,' said his fiancée.

Even Flora, who wasn't exactly warming to Charles, thought this was a little unfair. He'd only said 'oh'.

'We'll have to try and convince her that staying is a bad idea and hope she takes the hint,' he said.

And before Annabelle could say anything more about her, Flora pulled back her shoulders and marched back into the room. Up until the 'natural blonde' comment she'd been in two minds, but that did it. No way was she going to let herself be chased back to London with a cheque for ten thousand pounds! Even without that sweet old man's Ancient Mariner-type mutterings, she was going to give this a go.

'Well,' she said, having made sure both Charles and Annabelle were looking at her. 'I've had a little think, and at the moment, I don't feel I want to take up your generous offer, Annabelle.'

'What? Why not?' said Charles, indignant and surprised.

'Because I really want to find out about my family

13

business, to work here, to learn about furniture and things.' She was aware that the 'and things' rather detracted from her grand statement, but she hadn't had long to prepare and hoped they wouldn't notice.

'My dear Flora,' said Charles, unwittingly using a phrase calculated to turn his cousin into a bra-burning shrew, 'you know nothing about the business. You have absolutely nothing to offer us. There's no room for you. There would be nothing for you to do.'

'Is that so?' Flora replied tartly. 'Then why are you advertising for a "general assistant" in the local paper?'

'When did you see the local paper?' demanded Charles, as if her buying it had been somehow illegal.

'Before I arrived. I was looking for bed and breakfast accommodation.' She was actually looking for somewhere she might rent, for when the kittens were born.

'The local paper is not the best place to look for that,' said Annabelle. 'And I'm afraid there's absolutely none available at the moment.'

'What do you mean? There must be. This is a very pretty little town. Someone must do bed and breakfast.'

'Lots of people do,' said Charles. 'But there's the music festival on at the moment. The town is seething with violinists.'

'Oh. I wonder what the collective noun for those is,' said Flora. A sound emerged from Imelda's box. 'Perhaps that about covers it.'

A tiny crinkle at the corner of his eyes told Flora that Charles found this quite funny but was not going to allow himself to laugh. Well, at least he had a sense of humour, even if he didn't ever use it.

14

'I had thought of renting, eventually.' In spite of her brave resolutions she was aware that her voice betrayed her misgivings.

Charles sighed impatiently, as if dealing with a toddler he wanted to smack but had to placate. 'We seem to have got off on the wrong foot somehow. We're not trying to stop you being part of the business, it just never occurred to us you'd *want* to.'

This was sufficiently annoying to give Flora another shot of courage. 'No?' Her brown eyes were limpid with disbelief as they met his cold, blue ones. 'But I sent an email. I thought I was quite clear about my intentions. Or didn't you get it?'

Annabelle cleared her throat. 'It, er, it only half downloaded, so we didn't, quite. But I'm sure you can understand that Charles doesn't want you coming in here and messing about with things you don't understand,' she went on more briskly. 'Of course you will want to talk things over with your father, but I'm sure he'll advise you to be sensible and accept my offer.'

'Possibly,' said Flora. 'But I should point out that although he does advise me, I am old enough to make my own decisions.' Aware she was in a position of power, Flora's tones became low and gentle. Let them rant and rave if they felt like it.

'It will take a couple of days to get the legal stuff sorted,' said Charles. 'Perhaps if you had a few days' holiday down here, you might realise that a small market town really isn't the place for a metropolitan girl like you.'

'But where's she going to stay?' demanded Annabelle. 'I can't have her – she's got a cat!'

15

'And because I've got a cat, who might have kittens at any minute, I can't just go back to London. I might cause an accident. Imagine the News! "Ambulance called to help deliver kittens after pile-up on the M4. The RSPCA investigate".'

'Let's not get too worked up about this,' said Charles, not finding Flora's melodrama remotely amusing.

'No, let's not,' agreed Flora, disappointed that he couldn't crack a smile, even to be polite.

'Flora can stay in the holiday cottage,' he went on.

'Don't be ridiculous!' Annabelle dismissed this immediately. 'It's not fit for habitation. Otherwise we would have let it.'

'It's perfectly fit for habitation,' Charles contradicted. 'It's just not quite up to the standard required by the agency.'

'It's in the middle of nowhere!' protested Annabelle.

Charles didn't see this as a problem, in fact it was probably an advantage. 'Flora has a car.'

'Yes, I have.' Flora smiled, not wanting this lovers' tiff to continue in her presence. 'The holiday cottage sounds wonderful.'

'Honestly, you won't want to stay there,' said Annabelle. 'It's right out in the country, near some woods. You'll be terrified of the owls.'

'You think?'

'I don't want you ringing Charles at all hours of the night because you're frightened of the dark,' Annabelle explained.

'Of course not,' agreed Flora pleasantly. 'Just as well I'm not frightened of it. And owls don't bother me, either.'

'Sorry!' said Annabelle. 'It's just that most people

16

from London seem quite incapable of coping with country sounds: mating foxes, owls, cat fights, stuff like that.'

'When you've heard lions roar and elephants trumpet and there's only a thin bit of canvas between you and them, you don't worry about anything that can't eat you,' said Flora, believing this statement to be true, even if she had no experience of anything like that herself.

'Oh. Right,' said Annabelle, wrong-footed. 'I suppose not.'

'Does the holiday cottage have sheets? Saucepans, a corkscrew?' Flora enquired tentatively, not wanting to cause more annoyance than necessary.

'I'll pop home and fetch some things. I've got plenty of bed linen,' said Annabelle. She unhitched a serviceable leather bag from a chair and extracted a large bunch of keys. 'All right if I take the Landy, sweetie?'

'Of course,' said Sweetie.

When she was alone with her cousin, Flora said, 'I think I should warn you, I do want to work here. I'll apply for the job as a general assistant, if you want.'

'I really don't think you'd like it.'

'You can't possibly know me well enough to say what I'd like and what I wouldn't! We've only just met.'

'I know but . . .'

'But what?'

'Did you used to go out with someone called Justin Mateland?'

Flora became wary. 'Yes. Do you know him?'

'We were at school together.'

'Oh, right.'

17

'Yes.' Charles's hard blue eyes drilled into Flora long enough to inform her that he considered she had behaved very badly to Justin. He didn't say it out loud, so Flora could defend herself, he just let her know that that was his opinion of the matter.

'Now we've discussed our mutual acquaintance perhaps we could go back to the matter in hand?' she said sharply.

'Which was?'

'The job? I was about to apply for it. If you could just give me a form I could fill it in.'

Charles sighed deeply. 'Oh, it's all right, you don't have to do that.'

'But if you've got other candidates to see . . .'

'No. There are no other candidates. We've been advertising for the post for weeks, and no one remotely suitable has applied.'

'Why not?' This was a bit worrying. Had Charles got a reputation locally for being mean-minded with no sense of humour and a horrible employer? It seemed perfectly possible.

'Because no one with anything about them wants to work here.'

'But why not?' She wasn't expecting him necessarily to admit to the reason, but she might get some clue.

'The wages, dear cousin, are crap.'

Flora bit her lip. Not good news, but not as bad as it could have been. 'I see.'

When he was quite sure that Flora was sufficiently subdued by the prospect of working for practically nothing, in a firm who didn't want her, while living in a remote cottage in the woods, Charles said, 'I must ring

18

the solicitor. Will you be all right here for a few moments? There are a few magazines . . .'

'I'll be fine. You go and do your thing.' She smiled again, from habit, but he didn't notice.

Chapter Two

While Flora was flicking through ancient copies of *Antiques Trade Gazette* and stroking Imelda's head through the box, wondering if she should just cave in and accept the ten grand, there was a knock on the door and someone's head appeared. It was the sweet old man. Geoffrey someone.

'Are you alone?'

Flora put down what felt like homework with relief. 'Yes. Charles is getting in touch with solicitors and Annabelle's gone to get things for the holiday cottage, where I'm going to stay.' Sensing a sympathetic ear, Flora took the opportunity to get her grievances off her chest. 'Do you know, she had the nerve to make out she didn't know I wanted to stay! I sent her an email making it quite clear. And apparently every b. and b. in the town is full of musicians for a festival.'

'That's right. Bishopsbridge has quite a reputation for music. Our choir opened the festival last week.'

Flora smiled admiringly while Geoffrey Whiteread came into the room. 'So you're not running off back to London then?'

'Not immediately, no.' Flora sighed. She was hot and tired and a bit despondent, and wasn't quite sure how long she'd be able to cope with being so unwanted.

'Good. You hang in there. This place needs someone to shake it up.'

'What makes you think I'm the one? I know nothing about the business.' All her early confidence had been dissipated by Charles's frigid attitude and the reality of her situation.

'You're young. And you're family. Not like that Annabelle.'

'When she marries Charles she'll be family.'

Geoffrey shuddered. 'Just because they've known each other for ever doesn't mean those two should marry! She doesn't even like the auctioneering business!'

'Then why marry into it? Buy into it?' she added, remembering the ten-thousand-pound offer.

'She likes control and if she marries Charles, she'll have control.' He perched on the edge of the table. 'She's already got some disastrous ideas for cost-cutting.'

'What do they involve?' asked Flora.

'Sacking me, number one,' said Geoffrey. 'She's right, I am old, but I've got more knowledge and experience of this business in my little finger than she'll have in a lifetime. She says we don't need a full-time porter, that we can depend on self-employed staff. But all their sorting has to be checked. Charles doesn't have time to do it.'

Flora sighed. 'The thing is, I know nothing about antiques and collectables, or whatever they're called. I can make them let me stay, but I could just make everything worse.'

'Or you could be the breath of fresh air this place needs.'

Flora shook her head. 'You make me sound like an

advertisement for a room fragrance, and I only know what I've picked up from afternoon telly programmes. A few editions of the *Antiques Roadshow* and that one where they have to buy things at an antiques fair and then sell them at auction. That isn't going to be enough.'

'I'll teach you,' said Geoffrey. 'I've forgotten more than you'll ever need to know. I was a dealer for years, before I came back here.'

Flora smiled at him. 'That's a wonderful offer, but it isn't only that. There's the whole living-in-the-country thing. Would I be able to cope with that? Charles and Annabelle obviously think I'm a waste of space already, and will fall apart if not exposed to a shoe shop and a wine bar at least twice a week. And that's before I've even made any awful blunders.' She regarded him seriously. 'I do like shoes, but I did want to give this thing a go.'

'If you really mean that, I might be able to help you fit into the way of life, too.' He smiled, his eyes crinkling at the corners in a friendly way. 'I can't point you to a wine bar within thirty miles, but there are other ways of keeping yourself amused.' He paused. 'Ever done any singing?'

'Apart from in the shower, you mean? I always sing in the shower. And I liked it at school. I was always asked to do the descants for the carols, and I sang a solo at the school concert once.' She frowned. 'It was a long time ago, though. Why do you ask? Are you offering to take me to a karaoke night?'

He chuckled. 'Not exactly. I was going to ask you if you'd like to join my choir.'

Flora almost laughed at the absurdity of the idea. 'What, the one that opened the festival?'

He nodded. 'It's a good way to get to know people, and although we've got high standards, we're a tolerant bunch. We need some higher voices. You'd be welcome.'

'But I couldn't possibly! I haven't sung for years and my sight-reading was never very good.' She couldn't imagine what her friends in London would say if she announced she'd joined a choir.

'Your sight-reading will really improve when you get back to doing it, and we'll all help you along.'

Flora considered. Geoffrey was the first person to make her feel remotely approved of since she'd arrived and she was touched. 'Are you sure? They won't think I'm an awful townie, and resent me?'

He chuckled. 'A pretty girl like you would cheer us all up. Not that we're all old, I don't want to imply that, but there's been no one young, single and female in the choir for years. You are single, aren't you?'

'Currently. A bit of a first for me, actually.'

He laughed again; he seemed to find her very amusing, but in a fond way, not because he found her ridiculous, unlike Charles and Annabelle.

'Then come along with me tonight, and see how you like it.'

It was tempting, particularly when the alternative was staying at home alone in a holiday cottage. And guessing at Charles and Annabelle's standards of what a holiday cottage required, she probably wouldn't even have a television to distract her from Imelda's yelling. Thinking of Imelda, she said, 'There's my cat. She might have kittens at any moment.'

'I'm sure she'll be fine – cats have been doing this for quite a while now. In fact, while there's no one here,

23

why don't you let her out of her box for a bit? It may only be being shut up that's making her so vocal.'

Flora felt a rush of affection for this man; he'd said 'vocal' not 'noisy'.

'Then would you mind watching her while I go and fetch her litter tray from the car? I'm sure she would never do anything she shouldn't, but can you imagine how much Annabelle would hate me if my cat peed on the carpet?'

'About as much as she hates me, I should think.' He smiled. 'You go and get the litter tray and we'll let Imelda out for a bit.'

'You obviously like cats.'

'And so does my wife. I'm fairly sure that she'll be wanting one of the kittens when they're ready. This firm isn't the only thing which needs some young life.' He grinned broadly.

It was such a relief to be with someone who responded to her, who saw her as a person, not just a strappy dress, a pair of unsuitable shoes and expensive highlights, that Flora smiled fondly back. If this man wanted her to stay, she would stay, for his sake as much as her own. 'I'll go and get the litter tray.'

While Imelda was prowling round the office, after Geoffrey had gone back to work, Flora decided to give her best friend a call and got out her mobile.

'Hi! It's me! Good time?'

'Yes,' said Emma. 'I'm at home. How is it?'

'Well, not all that promising, to be honest, but I'm determined to stick it out. For a while, anyway.'

'What's the cousin like?'

'Absolutely dire.'

'Oh. That's a bit disappointing. I was hoping he would provide a bit of entertainment for you while you're out in the sticks. Is he married?'

'Engaged. And so stuffy he could do at-a-glance taxidermy.'

'And hideous? Or just spoken-for?'

'Well, I suppose his features are more or less in the right place, but he has minus amounts of charm and zero sense of humour. I think,' she added.

'So they're not exactly welcoming the new member of the family business?'

'You could say that,' Flora said grimly. 'They've already tried to buy me off. Annabelle lied to Charles about me wanting to stay, implying she had no idea I wanted to.'

'Oh no.'

'And I've got to live in a cottage out in the wilds. It might be a bit spooky.'

'But one of the advantages of being in the diplomatic service is surely that you've lived in all sorts of scary places with your parents, haven't you?'

'Yes, but the "with my parents" part is the thing. It's easy to be relaxed about cockroaches if you have staff.' She sighed. 'I am a bit of a poor little rich girl, Em.'

'Nonsense! You're a tough cookie. You'll be fine.' Emma knew what sort of reassurance Flora was seeking, and was quite happy to provide it.

Flora responded. 'I will, of course, and there's a sweet old man who's been really kind and asked me to join his choir.'

'Oh yes?' Emma sounded sceptical.

25

'No, really, he's terribly nice. Older than Dad, Ems. His wife might want one of the kittens.'

'She's had them already? My God! That must have been awful! Imelda having kittens on the boardroom floor with your cousin stuffing them with his evil gaze as they came out, one by one. You'll have to make some hideous installation with them, and enter it for the Turner Prize.'

'No!' screamed Flora, when she stopped laughing. 'She hasn't had them yet. You're right, it would have been awful. But Geoffrey's wife might have one when they are born. Annabelle's allergic to cats, of course.'

'Of course. Which is not remotely her fault.'

'No. Not at all. She's gone to get stuff for this holiday cottage. I hope she remembers a corkscrew. I might go and get some supplies. You'll have to come down for the weekend sometime. Quite soon, please!'

'I'm a bit tied up for the next couple of weekends, but I promise I'll come and see you as soon as I can.' Emma paused. 'And while I know you'll be absolutely fine, you and Imelda could always come and stay with me if you need to come back.'

Being given a get-out clause stiffened Flora's resolve to stick it out and give country life a proper try. 'That's really sweet of you, Ems, but how would Dave feel about that? Me, a cat and possibly six kittens?'

'I'm sure he'd be happy to have you.'

Something in her friend's voice alerted Flora. 'Everything all right between you two?'

'Oh yes, we're fine,' Emma sighed. 'In fact, I must call him.'

'I'll let you go. Oh my God! I can hear Annabelle and Imelda's loose!'

'Which no one would ever say about you, sweetie.'

'Oh shut up!' said Flora and disconnected.

Flora had just managed to scoop Imelda back into her box when Annabelle came in, her arms full of a plastic container.

'Right, I've got some basics. Sheets, pillow cases, a duvet, a couple of covers. How much do you cook?' she demanded briskly. 'Or are you a takeaway person?'

'Um – do I have much choice? Are there many take-aways in Bishopsbridge?'

'A couple of fish and chip shops, a Chinese and a Balti, which is very good, incidentally.'

'But no sushi bars?'

Annabelle raised her eyes to heaven just for a second, which told Flora her wind-up had worked.

'No.'

'Then I cook. Though not much,' she added, feeling sorry for Annabelle suddenly. It wasn't her fault she looked like a horse, and if she only dressed differently, she might be very handsome.

'But I don't think you'll need a Le Creuset casserole. It's unlikely you'll be making stews in this weather, even if you do cook.' Unaware she was the object of Flora's sympathy, Annabelle pressed on with the matter in hand. 'There are a couple of reasonable pans. Big enough to fit a boil-in-the-bag into, anyway.'

Flora decided to call a mental truce with Annabelle. She might be the nearest thing she had to female company, both literally and figuratively, and it would be much better if they were friends. Besides, Flora was itching to make a Trinny-and-Susannah-type raid on Annabelle's wardrobe, and Flora would have to be

27

on quite good terms with her in order to get near it. She was willing to bet there were pie-crust collars, jumpers with sheep and trousers with stirrups in it.

'I'm sure whatever you've got is fine. Although a non-stick frying pan would be useful. You know how it is when you're tired, you just yearn for an omelette?'

'You've got one of those, but really, you'll need a proper pan for omelettes.'

Flora shook her head. 'A non-stick one is fine. I don't want to put you out more than I have to.'

Annabelle smiled back and Flora felt she should do it more often. It softened her considerably and she had very good teeth. A bit on the large side, possibly, but white and even. 'It's no trouble, really. We should have got the holiday cottage sorted out ages ago. You can tell me if there's anything hugely wrong with it, or missing.'

'I will.'

'There's a dear little garden. I don't suppose you like gardening? It would really help if you had time to clear a couple of the front beds.'

'I'm sure I could do that for you. If there's something to do it with, of course.'

'Oh yes, I was forgetting about tools. I'll see what I can organise. After all, you won't have much to do here, will you?'

Flora smiled. Charles probably hadn't had the opportunity to tell her that she'd applied for, and got, the job advertised in the paper. 'Not just yet, anyway,' she said. 'And it's such super weather at the moment. It would nice to be out in the fresh air.'

'Hmm.' Annabelle crossed the room and opened the

window Flora had closed so Imelda couldn't escape out of it. 'Talking of which – have you noticed? – there's a terrible smell of cat in here.'

'Ah. That might be Imelda's litter tray. I had to let her use it.'

'Oh.' She looked disconcerted. 'You know I can't have anything to do with it, I'm afraid.'

'Oh,' said Flora, forgetting her truce. 'Are you pregnant?'

'Certainly not! We're not married yet. I thought you knew that.'

'I did, but you know how it is in the country.' Flora couldn't resist. 'Very often men don't marry women until they've proved that they're fertile and can carry on the blood line.'

'You were joking, weren't you?' asked Annabelle after a few tortured moments.

'Yes,' Flora sighed. 'I was,' but I won't bother again, she added silently. 'Now, if you could point me in the direction of the nearest supermarket, I can go and get some supplies. Geoffrey will keep an eye on Imelda for me.'

'Geoffrey? Whiteread? You've met him?'

'Yes. We were chatting earlier.'

'Dreadful man,' Annabelle muttered. Louder she said, 'But he'll look after your cat?'

'I think so. If you could just show me where to find him, I'll ask.'

Thanks to Annabelle's remarkably precise directions, Flora found the supermarket easily. It was small, but seemed to have everything anyone could want. She was just hunting for some vegetable stock powder in among

29

the gravy granules when a trolley wheel banged into her toe.

'Ow!'

'Oh my God, I'm so sorry!'

Flora looked up at the owner of a very nice voice. He had sun-streaked hair and a craggy, well-used face. His eyes were very blue against his tan. His shirt was open at the neck and had obviously once been expensive but was now faded and worn to the sort of dilapidation that was highly desirable. His trousers were similarly distressed. He was smiling down at her apologetically.

'I'm so sorry,' he said again. 'I've got a trolley that doesn't steer. Are you all right?'

Flora smiled back. 'I'm fine. It just gave me a bit of a shock, that's all.'

'And your toe isn't broken, or anything?'

They both looked down at her toe, the nail painted bright pink, matching the peony on her shoe. 'It seems fine,' she said.

'I would never have forgiven myself if anything had happened to such a pretty foot,' he said, a definite twinkle in his eye.

'I wouldn't have forgiven you, either,' Flora twinkled back.

He laughed. 'Are you new to the area? Or have I just missed you?'

'I'm new, but I'm glad to hear you don't hit everyone with your trolley, all the time.'

'I only hit people if my trolley's got a wonky wheel. I promise.'

'I'll take your word for it,' said Flora and began to move on. Much as she enjoyed flirting, Charles would

30

be waiting to guide her to the cottage soon, and she didn't want to keep him waiting. He was bad-tempered enough already.

'Maybe we'll run into one another again?' said the man, grimacing at his inadvertent pun.

'Maybe,' Flora called over her shoulder with a grin.

Rather to her surprise, Charles wasn't bad-tempered when she turned up five minutes after the appointed time, he was apologetic.

'I'm most terribly sorry but something's happened to your car.'

'What do you mean?' Flora asked, confused. 'What can have happened to it? It hasn't been anywhere, has it?'

'No. It got run into.'

'But how could it? And who ran into it?'

He looked extremely embarrassed. 'It was Annabelle. She's terribly upset about it.'

'Too upset to tell me about it herself?' Flora snapped.

'Yes,' he said firmly. 'Although she's very sorry. Now let's put all this stuff into the Land-Rover and I'll take you to the cottage. Your car will be sorted out very soon. There's a very efficient garage that we use. Your cat's already in and making a hell of a noise.

'Annabelle's mortified about what happened to your car,' Charles repeated a few minutes later as they drove along in the Land-Rover, Imelda still yelling from her box.

'I know. She told me. It's all right.'

Once Annabelle had ascertained that Flora had not gone ballistic about the car, she had come out to apologise in person. Flora, trying vainly to ingratiate herself with these difficult people, had been very nice about it.

31

'Perhaps if you hadn't parked it quite so near the corner . . .' Charles said now.

Flora sighed. She was a little tired of people trying to make this small incident her fault. As she'd been in the supermarket when it happened, they were never going to convince her. 'She said that, too.'

'She's terribly upset. Nothing like that has ever happened to her before.'

'Oh well. I expect she's got PMS.'

'What?' Charles was horrified.

'Have you never heard of it? It affects women—'

'I know perfectly well what it is, thank you. Annabelle does not suffer from it!'

'Oh well, I expect she was distracted. By a cat or something. Perfectly understandable.'

'Anyway, the damage is very slight. You'll have your car back in days.'

'I know. We've been through all this.'

'You seem very calm about it, I must say.' He glanced at her, puzzled.

Privately, Flora felt she was only being calm in contrast to everyone else, but she said, 'Well, it's not my car. Why should I worry?'

'It's not your car!' Charles reverted to storm mode. 'Whose car is it?'

'My parents'. It's all right,' she said for the tenth time. 'They're not over-sensitive about cars, either.'

'Nor am I, but repairs cost money!'

'I do hope you didn't shout at Annabelle about it.'

'I never shout!' he said very loudly.

'No, of course you don't,' Flora replied, looking out of the window.

32

'Maybe, sometimes, when really pushed.'

'Rest assured, I will never push you, Charles,' she said, wondering how on earth they were going to get along. 'It is very kind of you to drive me,' she added meekly, to put things back on the level of boring politeness. 'And to lend me the holiday cottage in the first place.'

'It's Annabelle's cottage. I just see to the things that involve ladders and heavy lifting for her.'

Flora wondered which of these categories she came into. On balance, she preferred to be a ladder.

'She would have taken you now,' he went on, 'but she hates the Land-Rover. She's gone home for a cup of tea.'

'Good idea,' said Flora, suddenly desperate for a cup herself.

'It is quite basic in the cottage, but if you do stay, you'd probably be better off with something with four-wheel drive.'

'I'm sure I'll manage. I wouldn't want to buy another car.'

'The firm might have something it could lend you. In fact, that's what we'll do if your car takes too long to fix. You wouldn't want to drive this.'

'Wouldn't I?'

'It's very heavy.'

Flora sighed. Would she have to rescue someone from a burning building to convince Charles that she was not an airhead?

Possibly in solidarity, Imelda yowled.

'She's persistent,' said Charles, with a glance over his shoulder at the pet carrier. 'You have to give her that.'

'She's been cooped up for hours, poor little thing,' said Flora. 'If there'd been any alternative to bringing her with me, I would have taken it, I promise.'

'It would have been better if she hadn't been pregnant,' Charles observed.

'Yes. Unfortunately she was pregnant when I got her.'

'And couldn't whoever you got her from take her back? In the circumstances . . .'

'Not really. It was the Grand Union Canal. I found her floating in a carrier bag.'

'Ah.' He paused. 'I'm sorry. I didn't realise. You don't look like the sort of person . . .' He paused again, as if wary of causing offence.

'Who rescues cats in carrier bags?'

'Oh no.' He frowned. 'You look *exactly* like the sort of person who'd do that, sentimental and terribly soft-hearted. I meant you don't look like the sort of person who'd ever been near a canal.'

Amused, in spite of his insulting manner, she hurried to reassure him. 'Oh, it wasn't a real canal. It was in Little Venice. It's terribly smart just there. I was visiting a friend on a narrow boat.'

'That's all right then.'

Just for a moment she thought she spotted a glimmer of humour, but then it vanished.

'I do think you've possibly been a bit unfair to me,' she suggested mildly.

'Oh?'

'Mm. You're assuming things about me because of the way I look, instead of finding out what I'm like under my clothes.' A second too late she realised what she'd said. 'I mean, although I'm not wearing a lot, because

34

it's such a hot day, I am quite sensible and useful, really.'

'I realise you're a very attractive woman, Flora.' She had to be grateful he hadn't said 'girl'. 'But you'll find that you can't rely on your charm and your looks all the time.'

'No.' Flora felt almost as bad as if he'd slapped her.

'I'm sure you do have valuable skills,' he said, obviously not believing a word of it. 'It's just I doubt they're relevant to our business. You have absolutely no experience, after all.'

'I have worked in an art gallery,' she began. 'I was there for two years – up until last month. And I'm good with people,' she went on, knowing it was the sort of thing said about people who had absolutely no other talents whatsoever. 'And I worked at a management consultants' once.' She'd been a receptionist, and very good she'd been too.

'As I said' – his manner made Flora wonder if she could get through the journey without actually killing him – 'I'm sure you're a very accomplished girl—'

'Woman,' she snapped.

'Woman,' he corrected himself after a quick glance at her expression. 'But I don't think your particular – very valuable – skills are suited to an old-established family business.'

'And in what way are old-established family businesses different from new ones? Don't they need to get new business? Be efficient? Make a profit? Or don't they have bills to pay like every other business in the world?'

He sighed. 'Obviously we have expenses, although of course we own the building. We employ several people, have vehicles to maintain—'

'In other words,' she interrupted, 'you're the same as every other business: you need to operate at a profit. Do you operate at a profit? I do have the right to ask,' she added, when he didn't reply.

'No. But Annabelle has some ideas on how to change that.'

'Which are?'

'It's none of your—'

'It is my business, you know. Slightly more mine than yours, actually.'

Thunderclouds gathered in his dark, thick eyebrows. 'I don't think I can discuss these things without Annabelle being present.'

'Oh? I didn't realise she was a shareholder already,' Flora said innocently.

'She's not! But she's – she's been involved in the business for a little while now and it wouldn't be right for me to discuss things with you behind her back,' he said tightly.

'OK, seems fair enough. Tell me,' she went on, 'has Geoffrey . . . what is it?'

'Whiteread.'

'Oh yes. Has he worked for you long?'

'Not that long. But his father used to be a partner in my grandfather's time.'

'But he isn't now? I mean, Geoffrey didn't inherit from his father?'

'No. Geoffrey's father lost his share playing cards, but out of kindness, the family gave Geoffrey a job when he came back to the area.'

'And you'll keep him on until he retires?'

'If he ever does retire it would be a miracle. Here we

are,' he said, which didn't answer her question. He turned down a track. 'As you'll see, if the weather changes, you'd find the road almost impossible to negotiate. You'll regret ever coming here.'

If this was a barely veiled invitation to go back home, she wasn't going to accept it. 'If I'm not happy here, I'm sure I can find somewhere else to stay.'

'Not that easy with a pregnant cat.'

'But not impossible, either. Anyway, my little car is very solid, when it's not being banged into. And it was not that close to the corner,' she reiterated, to avoid a repeat of their earlier argument.

'Yes, but it's also quite low to the ground. It might bottom on some of the rocks in the road.'

'Is that one of the reasons you haven't let the cottage this year?' she asked, when they had bumped their way down a few yards.

'Yup. It needs money spending on it.'

'You might be better to sell it, perhaps?'

'It's not mine to sell.'

'I'd forgotten.' She hadn't, actually, but she was aware of an undercurrent that she didn't understand. Charles obviously disliked her, and not just because she was butting into his family business.

He sighed, possibly aware that his hostility was visible. 'There are a lot of things you will need to know if you stay around, but I don't want to explain everything if you're just a fly-by-night. It's complicated.'

'It always is. Oh, is that it? It's delightful!'

Isolated, the cottage was set against woodland and faced rolling hills. The late afternoon sun shone on to it, making the windows golden. It had a front door, a

37

window on either side, and three windows on the storey above. A small shed leant against the side of the house, and a rambling rose scrambled up the porch and on to the roof.

'It is very charming to look at, yes,' said Charles, pulling on the handbrake. 'Not quite so easy to live in, as you'll no doubt discover. It was a gamekeeper's cottage. You'll find it very lonely.'

Determined not to rise to the bait, Flora took a deep breath, got out of the car, and walked towards her new home.

Chapter Three

When he had let them both in, and gone back to the Land-Rover to start unloading, Flora allowed herself a few moments to settle Imelda in the kitchen and have a look around before helping him.

The door opened straight into the only living room, which contained a fireplace, a staircase and a lingering smell of wood smoke. That could mean two things, she thought, either the fire smokes unbearably and the whole place is impregnated with it, or someone's had a fire quite recently.

She checked the kitchen, a lean-to at the back of the original cottage, was secure for Imelda, let her out of her box, and then went to get her litter tray.

'It's a dear little cottage,' she said to Charles, who was carrying a box of saucepans, a toaster, an electric kettle, and other things Annabelle thought necessary. 'Don't let Imelda out. She's in the kitchen.'

'I'm sure she'll be safe there. I hope you will be too.'

As Flora couldn't decide if this remark was meant kindly, sarcastically or threateningly, she ignored it, and dragged a suitcase out of the back of the vehicle. It was impossibly heavy, but she wasn't going to let Charles see it defeat her.

'Well, I'm here now,' she declared, perspiring freely

and hardly able to speak, dumping the suitcase in the sitting room. 'And you're just going to have to get used to me.'

He turned and stared down at her in a way calculated to make her aware of the sweat between her breasts, her wildly curling hair, the smear of mascara beneath her lashes. She stared back serenely. It would take more than being hot and smudged to put her out.

'I'm sure we'll find that a pleasure,' he said in a way that told her he felt there wasn't a cat in hell's chance he'd do anything of the kind.

Flora sighed. What was wrong with the man? Why couldn't he be more human and friendly? 'I'm not a brainless bimbo, whatever I look like,' she told him. 'Once you've accepted that, we'll get on much better.'

'My dear Flora . . .' His patronising tone affected her like nails down a blackboard. 'Flora,' he began again, possibly seeing her reaction to his first effort. 'I'm sure you're not brainless, and I don't know why you should assume I thought you were.' Lying so-and-so, she thought. 'But I do think it will be difficult for you to find a meaningful place as part of Stanza and Stanza.'

She regarded him, her head on one side. 'You know, if you hadn't said the name, my name, I might have been convinced. But you did. Stanza is my name as much as yours, and for that reason, even if it was the only reason, I feel I have to do what I can for the business.'

Charles sighed and Flora could see he was reining in his temper. 'The best you could do for the business is to go back to London and let Annabelle and me get on with running it. But as you're obviously not that keen

40

on the company's welfare,' he continued sharply, 'we'd better get the rest of your gear unpacked.'

Flora made her way up the twisting staircase with handfuls of carrier bags. Charles seemed to have some other problem. It wasn't only his dippy cousin coming to mess with his favourite toy he was bothered about. But what on earth that problem could be, she couldn't think. She decided to ignore it, dumped her carrier bags on the bed and looked around at the bedroom. It was nearly filled by a large four-poster bed. It was an extremely pretty bed, but it meant that the chest of drawers had to go on the landing, as did the cupboard which did duty as a wardrobe.

The bathroom, when she went to inspect it, was a reasonable size, possibly because it had clearly once been a bedroom. It definitely needed brightening up: some plants, bright towels, or something, but it was fine. The second bedroom had two single beds in it, which meant that if Emma and Dave came to stay, Flora would have to give them her bed.

But it was very pretty, in a quaint, cottagey way. There was a fine layer of dust over everything, but basically it was clean and Flora felt she could be very comfortable there, once she'd got used to it being the only house for miles. And downstairs, there was a corkscrew. Flora checked this while Charles was lugging her case up the stairs. And later, when everything was unpacked, Charles said, 'Oh. There's something I've forgotten.'

He stalked back to the car stiff with irritation and came back with a bottle wearing a plastic sleeve, to chill it. 'Annabelle sent this. She feels guilty about your car, I suppose.'

'That's really kind of her!' And so unexpected, she added silently. 'Shall we open it?'

He shrugged. 'If you like. I can only have one glass, though.'

'I'll find some glasses,' said Flora, thinking that perhaps this was her last chance to get him to lighten up a little. She could have another glass on her own, later, and really relax.

The glasses were very dusty and didn't match. Hastily she washed them and dried them on one of Annabelle's clean tea towels.

'Shall I open it for you?'

'No, thank you,' said Flora, seeing him twitch with the desire to snatch the bottle of fizz out of her hand and open it himself.

'What will you do with the rest of the bottle?' Even watching her pour seemed to be agony for him, and she concentrated very hard on not over-filling the glasses.

'Put a spoon in the neck and drink it over the next few days.' She didn't think it would take her more than two days, actually, but didn't want him to get the impression she had a drink problem as well as everything else that was wrong with her. 'Here's to us, all like us, gae few and we're all dead,' she said.

Charles frowned and picked up his glass and sipped.

Casting desperately around for something for them to talk about, Flora said, 'So, you and Justin were at school together?'

'Yes.'

'And you've kept in touch all these years?'

'Well, no. He found out where I lived through Friends Reunited, and we met up.'

'Oh.' Flora nearly found herself asking, 'And what did you talk about?' just to keep the conversation going, but it really was none of her business. 'OK, here's another toast,' she said instead. 'To you and Annabelle getting the most out of my visit that you possibly can.'

Charles frowned at her. 'I think I've made it clear that we'd get on far better without you, Flora.'

'And I think I've made it clear that you're not chasing me back to London just yet.' She smiled brightly. 'You must come round for dinner as soon as I'm settled. Oh.' She lowered her glass. 'There's no table.'

They both regarded the four chairs, which sat, as if placed, round a table-sized space.

'Damn,' said Charles. 'I'd forgotten. We sold it.'

Flora laughed, and Charles looked at her, confused. Not having a dining table was not something to be taken lightly, obviously.

'It'll have to be a barbecue then, when you come for dinner with Annabelle,' said Flora, hating the idea. Barbecues were very informal things, not suited to the likes of Charles and Annabelle. Paraffin-flavoured sausages and burnt lamb chops were only fun with people you could relax with.

Charles possibly hated the idea of a barbecue too. 'It's all right, I'll bring you another table. Now, is there anything else you're likely to need?'

Flora was tempted to ask for champagne flutes, an ice bucket and a silver salver, but knew he'd just frown and not realise she was joking. 'I don't suppose there's a telephone?' she said instead.

'It's a holiday cottage,' he said, for what seemed the fifteenth time. 'And you've got a mobile.'

'I'll just see if I've got reception.' Flora's insouciance about living in a cottage miles from anywhere all on her own faded suddenly. If you can't ring the police, or your mate, in the middle of the night when you hear something go bump, things are all a lot more scary.

'On the other hand, it would be a good idea to have one,' Charles conceded, as Flora burrowed about in her bag. 'I'll see to it.'

'That would be kind.' Flora's words were more heartfelt than they sounded, so she smiled, to emphasise that she meant them. She found her phone, switched it on and peered at it. 'Not much of a signal. It'll probably be better outside.' She moved out of the front door, still studying her phone.

'No good if it's raining, or you're in bed,' said Charles.

The signal was a little better out of the house but it was still hardly functional. 'Annabelle won't want you to put a phone in here. It's a lot of hassle for a short-term thing.'

'I thought you were determined to stay.'

Flora frowned. 'I am. I was just thinking about it from Annabelle's point of view.'

'I'm sure Annabelle would like you to be as comfortable as possible for the duration of your stay,' he said evenly.

Flora grinned. 'Gosh. I didn't know people really used expressions like the "the duration of your stay" in real life.'

He raised his eyebrows. 'And I didn't know people still said "gosh".'

Flora bit her lip to moderate her smile. 'I bet Annabelle does.'

44

'She doesn't come from London.'

Flora wanted to say that she didn't either, but as she didn't really know where she did come from, she decided not to.

'I'd better go,' said Charles. 'Let me know what's missing – you'll probably find out as you go along.'

'Will you collect me tomorrow?'

'Why?'

'To take me to work?'

'Oh, don't worry about that. You don't have to start until Monday, and your car should be fixed by then.'

Flora opened her mouth to say, 'But you can't just abandon me here in the middle of nowhere with nothing to do,' but didn't, in case Charles suggested she take up gardening, like Annabelle had. 'Fine. I'll amuse myself until Monday then.'

Charles frowned, and Flora realised just what a nuisance her presence was for him. His sense of cousinly duty, a powerful force, was fighting with his extreme irritation at her presence. 'I could come and see how you're getting on, tomorrow,' he said reluctantly. 'And give you an update on your car.'

'It's all right. There's no need. I'll be fine.'

'Annabelle was devastated about the car, you know.'

'Yes, I know. I could see that she was. Even if you hadn't told me about fifteen times.'

'But you had parked it in quite a stupid place.'

Flora sighed. 'You can't make it my fault that Annabelle ran into me, however hard you try. But I admire you for trying. It's very loyal of you.'

He seemed to be confused. 'What do you mean?'

'You know what I mean. It wasn't my fault, it was

45

Annabelle's, but it's nice of you to stick up for your fiancée like that.'

'Oh.'

Flora suppressed another sigh. 'Could you please ring Geoffrey and explain I won't be able to come to choir tonight. I don't want to let him down.'

'Choir? You? Do you sing?'

'Of course. Doesn't everyone?'

'Yes, but Geoffrey's choir is very good. It has a reputation – oh, sorry, that must have sounded very rude.'

'Don't apologise. I'm quite used to it by now.'

'I'm sure I don't know what you mean.'

'I don't see why. I do speak English, most of the time.'

He shook his head. 'I must go. But you think you'll be all right?'

'Yes. I'll be fine.' She opened the door. 'Thank you very much for driving me here.'

'It really was the least I could do.' He regarded her for a few moments and then said, 'Goodbye,' and stalked out of the door.

Flora watched through the window as he drove away. Emma had once declared there wasn't a man in the world Flora couldn't charm if she really set her mind to it. Emma hadn't met Charles. Her mind went to the man who had run over her foot in the supermarket. If only Charles was a bit more like him, even a tiny bit, it would make life so much easier.

As she closed the front door and went to the kitchen to let Imelda out, Flora felt suddenly daunted. If she and Charles, and presumably Annabelle, were going to get on as business partners, it would be easier if they liked her. Charles would obviously turn into granite

46

before he did any such thing, so she'd have to try and get Annabelle on her side. Otherwise she'd die of loneliness and despair.

If only Charles was remotely normal, she could have won him over with a little judicious flirting. Flirting worked with almost everyone and Flora did it almost as she breathed. Once, when faced with a particularly tedious job application form, she put it down as one of her hobbies. She got the job.

When Imelda was settled, Flora unearthed her radio from her overnight bag and switched it on. When her breathing and mutterings to Imelda were no longer the only sounds, she felt better. She would make this little house her home. And ask Charles for a television. A television was a perfectly normal thing to have in a holiday cottage, after all.

She had just begun to get bored with unpacking and sorting out her things and was wondering if putting butter on cats' paws to stop them roaming was really a good idea, or just an old wives' tale which would end up getting greasy marks everywhere, when she heard a car.

It was Geoffrey, and Flora met him at the front door. He was carrying something covered with a cloth.

'Edie's sent a cottage pie over for your supper, and when you've eaten it, I'm taking you to choir.'

'This is so kind!' said Flora, opening the door wider, forgetting about Imelda for a moment. Imelda, seeing the countryside in all its summer glory, shot out.

'Oh no!' Flora shrieked. 'What if she doesn't come back?'

'She will.' Geoffrey came into the house and set the dish down on a small table. 'Where is she going to go?

She won't spend the night outside, not if she's not used to it.' Geoffrey was very soothing. Flora found herself believing what he was saying, as if for Geoffrey to say something automatically made it true. 'You eat your supper, let her have a run around, and then we'll call her.'

They left the door open while Flora ate the still warm combination of tasty mince and mashed potato straight out of the Pyrex dish. Imelda could be seen, picking her way through the grasses, sniffing occasionally. When Flora was full, she put her plate down on the floor and called her cat.

Imelda, possibly hearing the sound of the dish landing on the floor, looked up and ambled back towards the house, her pregnant body almost triangular.

'That must seem awfully rude, but she always comes if she thinks I've put something down for her.'

He chuckled. 'That's all right. She might as well have what's left now. She's expecting, after all.'

'Are you sure it's all right to leave her?'

'I'm sure she'll be fine. Cats mostly like to get on and have their kittens on their own, anyway. Have you made a nice bed for her? They like cupboards, dark places. What about under the stairs?'

Together they made a space for Imelda, having first moved aside a pair of wellington boots. Then Flora fetched a pillow from the spare bed, checking first that it wasn't full of goose-down and therefore expensive to replace. A cardigan, that until that moment Flora hadn't considered old, went on top to make it smell familiar. And when Flora considered it comfortable enough for her cat she called her.

Obligingly, Imelda came to inspect her maternity suite, sniffing and then stepping on to it, her paws still dainty and discriminating in spite of her swollen body. After she'd circled, kneaded, settled and resettled for a while, Flora closed the door a little, to see if Imelda wanted it dark. She looked up at Flora and Geoffrey as if to say, 'That's fine, now run away and play.'

Feeling dismissed, Flora said, 'I expect the boots made her feel at home. She loved my shoe cupboard when I first brought her home, which was why I called her Imelda.'

Geoffrey chuckled in a fatherly way, and Flora realised that it was a while since she'd seen her own father, whom she loved dearly. Perhaps that was why she was drawn to Geoffrey.

'Now you go and get something warm to put on,' he said. 'It's quite chilly in the church, winter or summer.'

Flora bit her lip. It had been so hot in London everyone flopped about, sweating. It seemed even the weather was different in the country. 'The choir seems to start awfully early,' said Flora. Was going a huge mistake? Perhaps she should light a fire to keep the wolves away.

'Well, by the time we've got back to town, and you've popped in and said hello to Edie, it'll be time. We start at seven-thirty.'

'Right,' said Flora, wondering what on earth she'd let herself in for.

Edie, Geoffrey's wife, insisted on lending Flora a fleece, not considering her divinely pretty cardigan sufficient protection against the cold of St Stephen's.

'You could freeze to death in that church, even in high

summer. Don't worry about what you look like. It won't matter in there.' Edie smiled and patted Flora in a way that made Flora wonder if they had grandchildren. They'd be perfect grandparents: indulgent, wise, caring. 'Is your little cat all right?'

Flora nodded. 'We made her a place under the stairs. She probably won't have her kittens for days, but she's so enormous, and you can feel the babies moving about.'

'Well, you let me know as soon as they're born and I'll get Geoffrey to bring me along to see them. And now you two had better get along to choir. It would be nice if Flora could meet one or two of the others before you start.'

Fending off her ministrations and injunctions with fond good humour, Geoffrey ushered Flora back into the car.

'Why doesn't Edie come to choir?' Flora asked.

'Tone deaf. Besides, she usually goes to the pub with her friend on choir nights. Now belt up.' He glanced at his watch. 'We've got time to have a little tour round the town before we go. I can show you what's what.'

The town was a mixture of the stately old and the garish new. There was a row of town houses, one of which was occupied by Stanza and Stanza. Opposite was an ancient stone building which consisted of pillars that supported a small building above.

'That's the old butter market. Been in use since the thirteenth century. There's a very good fish stall here on Fridays.'

On the other side of the butter market was another row of shops, which were made up of two charity shops, an off licence, an Indian take-away – which must have been the Balti house Annabelle had referred to – and an ironmonger's.

'Fred, he's one of the basses, owns that shop. He's very helpful if you need anything for the house. He sells everything but he won't let you go home with the wrong thing, if you know what I mean. Down there's the abbey.'

Flora squinted down the road and caught sight of a pale stone building and a couple of flying buttresses. 'I'd love to see it properly.'

'We'll take you. We're all very proud of our abbey. It has a very nice tea shop, too.'

There was a much smaller church at the end of the street. 'Is that where we practise?'

'No. We sing there sometimes, and several of the choir worship there. There's a cleaning rota several of them are on, but I think it's just an excuse to go to the pub afterwards.

'That's the pretty bit over, but there are some useful shops down there.' He indicated a side street. 'A chemist, newsagent, optician, things like that. There's everything you need here,' he finished proudly.

Flora hadn't spotted anywhere you might possibly buy clothes apart from the charity shops, of which there seemed to be several more dotted about, but she didn't say anything. She didn't actually need clothes, after all, she just liked buying them. It was a pretty town if very quiet-seeming to city-bred Flora.

'Now, if you've seen enough we'll get on. St Stephen's isn't far but I like to be there early to get a parking space.'

Flora couldn't help feeling extremely nervous as Geoffrey ushered her up the aisle to the group of people standing by the piano. She was perfectly happy to go to parties by herself, to meet people in wine bars or pubs, but this little country church was daunting.

Geoffrey led her to a tall man with a commanding presence and a surprisingly shy smile. 'This is Flora, James. I hope you don't mind me bringing her along. She's new to the area, and likes singing.'

A thought gripped Flora like a pall of ice: she might have to do an audition. She could barely smile back at James. Why hadn't she asked Geoffrey about auditions? It was perfectly normal, after all, to check that someone could sing before allowing them into your choir, which had a very good reputation. Charles's words about the standard of the choir, which she suddenly remembered, added tenfold to her anxiety.

'Nice to see you, Flora.' James shook her hand. 'Soprano?'

Flora nodded. 'You probably don't need any more sopranos. I don't have to join the choir . . .'

James, possibly seeing how nervous she was, ignored this. 'You go and sit down over there. Moira will look after you.'

Moira, a tall woman wearing several layers of cardigans and sweaters, smiled and patted the seat beside her. 'Come and sit here, by me. This is Freda, and Jenny. We're the top sopranos. The seconds are the naughty ones, in the back.' She turned round and indicated three women who seemed to Flora to be models of respectability.

One of them said, 'We cherish our subversive natures,' so dryly that Flora couldn't decide if she was joking or not.

But even a joke that might not have been was something, and Flora began to relax a little. Other people drifted in and took their seats, which were arranged in two semi-circles near the piano. They all smiled at her in a friendly way which gave Flora courage to ask Moira, 'Will I have to audition?'

'Oh no,' she said. 'James will soon sniff you out if you can't sing.'

'And then what happens?'

'You get sent a letter with a black spot on it,' said Moira. Then she nudged Flora firmly in the ribs. 'I don't know! It's never happened! Just don't sing too loudly to begin with.'

Certain that no noise would be audible from her lips, however hard she tried, Flora nodded.

'Right.' James called the choir to order, and after a bit more chatting and catching up, he gained their attention. 'Welcome to Flora, who's come to give us a try. Let's do a few scales to warm up. On Ah!'

Flora found, after a few minutes, that she was really enjoying herself. At first, she had wondered why on earth she had elected to be in a freezing cold church, wearing someone else's fleece, on a beautiful summer evening, but as her voice remembered what it had done so easily when she was at school, the joy of singing in a group came back to her.

She was glad of the fleece. She would have appreciated fleecy track-suit bottoms to go with it. Her bare legs and peony sandals were soaking up the cold like water. But she still loved it. Looking over Moira's shoulder trying to sight-read, with Moira's strong, confident voice in her ear, she was sure she made no sound at all, but that was fine, she wanted to be quiet, not to make any mistakes. She badly wanted to be allowed to stay in the choir.

Flora was surprisingly tired when James finally finished with them. She mentioned it to Moira who said, 'It's probably because you haven't breathed deeply for years. You'll get used to it.'

'How was that?' asked James, when Flora went to say goodbye and thank you.

'Fine. I loved it. I'm a bit worried about the sight-reading though. I'm very rusty.'

'That will improve very quickly. I'm glad you enjoyed it. See you next week?'

'Definitely.' Flora felt a sense of achievement. It wasn't really anything to be proud of, stumbling her way through a choir rehearsal, but she felt she'd dipped a successful toe in the water of country life.

As Geoffrey drove her back through the countryside, some of Flora's optimism left her. Would she be able to cope without the comforts she was used to? Out here there would only be the sounds of wild creatures to disturb the night. Even the motorway was too far to hear unless you really listened. There wouldn't be the reassuring tick of taxis delivering people home from parties, the knowledge that a few streets away there was an all-night shop, willing to sell her anything her heart desired. There wasn't a cinema locally, and even the station was a half-hour's drive away. (Charles had informed her of the lack of facilities with dry relish.)

Then the thought of Annabelle, her undisclosed plans for cost-cutting, sacking Geoffrey, taking over the family firm, *her* family firm, stiffened her sinews. She could cope, would cope, admirably, and when she went back to London (which just now seemed something to be longed for, like Christmas was for small children), she would be a stronger, better-qualified woman.

It was a beautiful area, she admitted, observing the trees, the hedgerows, the hills beyond. Perhaps nature would sustain her in the way taxis and shoe shops had in the past.

Geoffrey offered to come in with her, to check everything was all right. She accepted gratefully.

Together they walked up the path. 'Well, the lights still work,' said Flora. 'I can see that.'

'Everything will still work. It's a good little house. I used to come and see to things when they let it last year. I know it's in good order.'

Flora opened the front door. 'I wonder how Imelda is.'

They went to the nest they had made for her so carefully. She wasn't there.

'Oh my God!' Flora's hands flew to her face. 'Where can she be?' Instantly she imagined Imelda escaping through an undiscovered hole and being set upon by foxes.

'Don't panic. She can't have got out of the house. Let's have a look around.'

It was somehow no surprise to Flora when they discovered Imelda, and four little multi-coloured shapes, in among the shoes she'd dumped out of their carrier bag into the bottom of her wardrobe. 'Oh Imelda! How could you? It must have been so uncomfortable!'

'I'll run down and get the bedding,' said Geoffrey,

'while you rescue your shoes. She might not like being interfered with but they need something more than just a heap of spikes to sleep on.'

Forgiving Geoffrey's dismissal of some of her favourite possessions, Flora stroked Imelda's head. 'You're very clever and I'm very proud of you, but do you have any idea how much those shoes cost?' Flora had lived on soup for weeks to buy some of them.

Imelda, who was very proud of herself and her kittens, didn't greatly care, but to Flora and Geoffrey's relief, she seemed to take quite kindly to being gently transferred from the jumble of Manolo Blahniks and Jimmy Choos to the bed Geoffrey brought up from downstairs.

Flora brought up a dish of cat food, which Imelda fell on as if starving, and another of water.

'Should I get some milk for her, do you think?'

'I wouldn't have thought so. Adult animals don't usually drink milk, you know.'

'No, and it does upset her, rather. Oh, I'll fetch the litter tray.'

When at last Imelda and her family were settled, Geoffrey said, 'I'd better be going.'

'Wouldn't you like a cup of tea or something?' Flora's social responsibilities came flooding back to her. 'You've been so kind.'

'I think I'll be getting back, but you have some hot chocolate or something before you go to bed. Help you sleep.'

Flora resisted the temptation to hug Geoffrey. He might not be used to being embraced by young women who were missing their dads.

Tired, but not sleepy, Flora ran a bath. At least the

cottage seemed to have an efficient immersion heater, which was something. She found some scented candles in one of her carrier bags and arranged them in the bathroom. Then she poured herself a glass of wine from the bottle that Charles had brought, switched on her radio, and got undressed. Country life was going to be all right.

Chapter Four

The following morning, Flora slept late. She'd been woken up three times by animals she hoped were foxes but sounded like the ghouls made of latex that were extras in the film *The Lord of the Rings*. The little suckings and breathings from Imelda and her brood had been soothing. Imelda was an extremely competent mother, even if in human terms she should be wearing a gym-slip.

After she'd fed Imelda and let her out for a few moments she went into the bathroom. Once she'd wrestled with the shower and the shower curtain and emerged more or less victorious, she went downstairs for breakfast.

That all done, she felt at a loose end. Of course, Imelda needed quite a lot of stroking, feeding and letting out, but apart from that, not all of which was truly welcome, there was nothing much for Flora to do. So she decided to clean the cottage and make it more homely. Then if Annabelle came to do a spot check, she would be ready for her.

Once she'd got into it, she quite enjoyed it; even if the hoover was heavy, inefficient and heaved out asthmatic sighs of dust with every pass, she felt pleasantly domestic, nudging the furniture out of the way and cleaning underneath it. She found polish and a duster and did quite a lot of spraying and wiping, but the smell of wood smoke still persisted. She didn't really object to it, she just wondered why the smell lingered so. Once everywhere shone as much as it could shine, given its nature, she rearranged the furniture. When she'd had a sandwich for her lunch and gone for a short walk, she moved it again, until she realised she'd put it back exactly as it had been when she'd arrived.

Rather than slump into a huge depression, which, she was aware, would have been only too easy to do, she went into the garden and hacked off some quite large branches of rambling roses, which she put in a chipped but attractive stone storage jar she found in the back of a cupboard. This she set in the fireplace.

'So I can make some sort of impression, a few changes,' she explained to Imelda later. 'Even if they are just cosmetic, they do have impact.'

She went to bed wondering if she would ever convince Charles and Annabelle that she could be remotely useful. Now that the kittens were born, it would be even harder to move back to London. She'd have to stay until they were a bit older, at least. As she lay awake in the moonlight, she came to the uncomfortable realisation that she was trapped.

The following morning, Geoffrey and Edie were on her doorstep before she'd cleared away her toast and Marmite.

'I couldn't keep her away, I'm sorry,' said Geoffrey, as Edie came in and went up the stairs, hardly pausing to say hello or ask the way.

Flora was delighted to have company, especially when the cottage was looking pretty.

'I won't disturb her,' said Edie, tweaking open the door to Imelda's cupboard.

Imelda, purring mightily, allowed Edie to inspect her brood, who were all well attached, pumping their little paws into their mother's body.

'I reckon they've grown already,' said Geoffrey.

'They definitely have,' Flora agreed. 'They were quite tubular yesterday. Today they're rounder, more like balloons.'

'We wondered if you needed to go shopping or anything,' said Edie. 'It's hard for you, stuck out here without a car. That Annabelle should be ashamed of herself.'

'Oh she is, very,' Flora assured her. 'And although I don't need much in the way of shopping – I stocked up the other day – I'd love to go out. Imelda's getting quite fed up with me asking how she is all the time.'

'We'll give you a little tour of the town, and you can see the abbey,' said Geoffrey.

'That would be lovely! I love old churches.'

'We're very proud of our abbey in Bishopsbridge,' said Edie, pleased with Flora's enthusiasm.

'Oh, and is there somewhere I could buy a book? I've nearly finished my current one, and there's nothing much to read in the cottage.'

'We have everything you need in Bishopsbridge,' said Edie proudly. 'Even a bookshop.'

The abbey was beautiful, and sited as it was, nearly in the middle of town, it seemed part of Bishopsbridge, rather than separate. Edie and Geoffrey showed her the tombs, the massive pillars, and the carved woodwork. Then she agreed to meet them in the shop and wandered round on her own, soaking up the mystery of being in a place where people had come to worship for nearly two thousand years.

She had just found the shop and had spotted Edie over by the cards when someone knocked into her. She moved out of the way with a murmured, 'Sorry,' when she saw it was the man who had run over her foot in the supermarket.

'Oh my goodness,' he said. 'I seem to be making a habit of this. Are you all right?'

'Of course.' Flora smiled back at him, pleased to see a familiar, handsome face. 'Unlike most of the contents of this shop, I'm not breakable.'

'"Lovely to look at, delightful to hold, but if you break me, consider me sold"?' he quoted, his head on one side.

Flora found herself blushing. 'I'm not like that,' she reiterated.

'Oh, I'm sure you're some of those things, but before we get that far, perhaps I should introduce myself. Henry Burnet.' He took her hand.

'Flora Stanza.'

'Oh – are you anything to do with . . .?'

'Yes. I'm a partner in the auction house. Although I'm very junior. An apprentice, really.'

'Ah. I know Charles Stanza a little bit.'

'I should think that's about the amount most people know him,' said Flora, wondering if she was being disloyal.

Henry Burnet laughed. 'He is rather reserved. So how long are you down here? Would you like a coffee? They do marvellous cakes in the café, all home-made.'

'Actually I'm with those people over there.' She indicated Geoffrey and Edie, who were now looking at her rather anxiously. It was a shame, it would have been pleasant to be with a man who wasn't a surrogate grandfather, or her stuffy cousin. She could do with some attractive male company.

'They might like coffee too,' suggested Henry, greatly to his credit, she thought.

'It would have been fun, but I don't think now is quite the time.'

Edie and Geoffrey had taken on the closed, solid appearance of parents in the presence of an unsuitable boyfriend met in the street, and moved round Flora protectively.

'Another time, perhaps?' said Henry.

'Perhaps,' said Flora. 'If you bump into me again.'

He laughed. 'I'm almost sure to. I'm terribly clumsy. I only came in to buy a birthday card for my sister.'

'And I'm being a tourist. The abbey is beautiful.'

'We are all very proud of it.'

'Are you ready to go now, Flora?' asked Geoffrey, pointedly.

She smiled at Henry, silently explaining why they had to part. He smiled his reply and Flora couldn't help thinking what fun it was to be able to communicate so easily with someone. Every single word was hard work with Charles.

'That's Henry Burnet,' said Geoffrey. 'He's got a bit of a reputation.'

'Oh. What for?'

'Womanising,' Geoffrey went on darkly. 'He's a philanderer.'

Flora sighed. 'Philanderer' was a very appealing sounding word.

'He's got a very nice house, though,' said Edie. 'But he's probably a bad lot. His wife left him.'

Well, at least he was single, she thought as she followed Geoffrey and Edie out of the abbey and they made their way to the pub to have lunch.

After she had been delivered home, and Edie had had another long goo over the kittens, Flora collapsed on the sofa with her new book. It would have been nice if she and Henry had been able to exchange numbers, but Bishopsbridge was quite a small place. They were bound to run into each other sometime. He did know her name, after all, and could contact her via the office, if all else failed.

She was going to have Sunday lunch with Geoffrey and Edie and felt quite content, but she was very glad when Monday morning came.

'We're going directly to the salerooms,' said Charles as he and Flora travelled down the track. 'We're having a sale the day after tomorrow and we're still getting stuff in.'

'Right. Good.' It was hard to know what she was expected to say.

'I'm sorry I didn't come and see you over the weekend. I know you were all right because Geoffrey told me.'

'I was fine.' Flora decided to be silent on the subject of whether it was right that Geoffrey, not after all a blood relation, should have been left with the responsibility of her welfare.

'We had to go to Annabelle's parents.'

'For the entire weekend?'

'Yes.' Charles's jaw took on the stubborn aspect of one who knows he is in the wrong. 'It was unavoidable. They're not as young as they used to be and they were very good to me when my own parents died.'

She refrained from comment and just said, 'Well, I was fine. Geoffrey and Edie were very kind.'

'I knew they would be.'

'Did you ask Geoffrey to look after me?'

'No, but he mentioned he was going to.'

'So that absolved your conscience?'

'No! I mean, I didn't have a conscience – why should I have? You're an adult, you're not helpless.'

'I would have been slightly less helpless if I'd had a car.'

Charles exhaled deeply. 'I know. I'm really sorry about that.'

'It wasn't you who smashed it.'

'No, but—'

'The cottage is a long way from the nearest shop.'

'Not if you're wearing the right shoes it isn't.'

Flora was not buying this one. 'When did you last walk from the cottage to the town?'

Charles gritted his teeth. 'I've never walked it.'

'It's a long way.' Thanks to Geoffrey and Edie she hadn't actually had to walk the distance herself, but she felt that Charles was being unacceptably blasé about abandoning her miles from anywhere.

'Well, don't tell me you had to buy cat food. You had mountains of the stuff the other day.'

'Imelda had her kittens.'

64

Charles frowned. 'Oh. I suppose that makes her eat more.'

'Yes. She had four,' she went on, furious with his blatant lack of interest. 'There's a ginger one, a tabby, a very pretty one with ginger and black patches on white, and a plain black one. Apparently cats can have kittens by different fathers in the same litter.'

'Oh.'

'Yes. I'm afraid Imelda must have been a bit of a slapper, although she's taking her responsibilities very seriously now.'

'Well, that's something,' he said absently.

'Can I have a cat flap in the cottage?'

'It's hardly worth installing one, is it?'

'What do you mean?'

'You might not stay long enough for the kittens to be able to use it.'

'Oh, I will. The kittens are far too small to move. I'll have to stay at least until they're bigger. Possibly for eight weeks, when they'll be ready to leave their mother. Anyway, Imelda will still need one.' She frowned, suffering a pang of sadness at the thought of the kittens living anywhere but with her.

'Well, if you insist and really think it's worthwhile.'

'I do. To both.'

'Very well.' He frowned again. 'How will Imelda manage until we get a cat flap organised?'

'She has a litter tray and—' She suddenly realised what she was about to confess.

'What?'

'I left the back door ajar. Only a tiny bit and I'm sure there are no opportunist thieves within miles.'

Charles sighed heavily – she was obviously living down to his expectations. 'Well, it's mostly your stuff they'd steal if they did break in, but don't for God's sake tell Annabelle you've left the door open. She'll have a fit! She's very hot on security. All her parents' cottages have burglar alarms and she was very cross with me when I didn't put one in there. I pointed out that there was no point in having something that shrieked like a banshee if no one would be able to hear it.'

'Thank you, dear cousin Charles. It's very nice to be reminded that if I'm attacked no one will be disturbed by my screams.'

He winced. 'I'll get on to the phone people straightaway. And you can certainly have an alarm if it would make you feel safer.'

'What would really make me feel safer is a car. Is there any news on mine?'

'I rang this morning. They're waiting for a part. They have to send away for it. I'd told them they'd better hurry, or there's no point in doing it.'

'I know what you're implying, but I'm not buying it. I'm staying, at least for the time being, and you might as well get used to the idea.'

'You realise you'll just be working as an office junior, the lowest of the low?'

'Yes. I don't mind learning from the bottom up. It's the best way.'

'And you'll stick it out for a while even though the cottage is very isolated?'

'Yes!' Too late she realised that she'd been tricked into revealing her feelings that the cottage was, indeed, very isolated. Still, she couldn't say anything now.

Charles didn't respond immediately. 'I'm sure Annabelle would offer to lend you her car if she knew how isolated you feel.'

'I don't want to borrow Annabelle's car . . . Though it's kind of you to offer,' she added, moments too late.

Charles's firm mouth twitched. 'Well, that's a good thing because I'm not sure she would have offered, actually. I really need an estate car or I'd offer you mine.'

'What about this Land-Rover? Is this needed for anything special?'

He laughed. 'I can't see you driving this behemoth.' It shuddered noisily to confirm its reputation. 'Even Annabelle finds it quite difficult to handle.'

Flora suppressed a sigh and tried very hard to keep all the sarcasm out of her voice. 'I think you might find I'm a better driver than Annabelle.'

'You think?' Charles pulled up at the side of the road. 'Then put your money where your mouth is and prove it.'

Biting her lip to conceal her grin of pleasure, Flora slid down from the vehicle and ran round to the driver's side. This was something she knew she could do. He'd have to lend it to her now.

Charles made the swap with slightly less alacrity. 'It'll probably be all right on the country roads but you might find driving through town a bit more difficult.'

The engine shuddered as Flora turned the key. She turned to him and said seriously, 'I think now is the time to confess that I haven't been a natural blonde since I was about ten years old. I think I'll be all right.'

Flora had to give Charles huge credit for letting a smile force its way from the corners of his eyes and one corner of his mouth. It turned a conventionally good-

67

looking man into an extremely attractive one. Interesting. If she was Annabelle, she'd make strings of jokes so he'd smile more often.

Henry, on the other hand, going on what little she'd seen of him, smiled quite a lot. She did hope he'd manage to get in touch.

After Flora had negotiated the crowded High Street, got through a very narrow lane with cars on both sides and parked in an awkward spot in the yard behind the auction house, circumnavigating two removal vans as she did so, Charles said, 'I'd like to see you do all that with a trailer.'

'I'm sure you would.' Flora smiled sweetly. 'But unless you lend me the Land-Rover, you're not going to get the opportunity.'

'For that reason alone you can consider it yours until your car is ready.'

Flora got out, mentally thanking her father for letting her back his Land-Rover, with a trailer and boat attached, on to a crowded car ferry. It wasn't that Flora was over-confident, she just loved to see strong men with their mouths open.

'Thank you, Charles,' she said, coolly. She made to hand him the keys.

'No, they're yours now.'

She dropped them into her bag with a little skip of glee. They were her independence. She would no longer be marooned on her own, miles from anywhere.

The salerooms were seething with people and furniture and Flora followed Charles through the wardrobes, sofas, tables, chairs and rugs, all of which seemed to be on the move in contrary directions, to where low tables were set up to make an office area. Two women sat at computers and Annabelle stood between them, a clipboard in her hand, dealing out instructions.

'Oh, hi,' she said coolly to Flora, ignoring Charles. 'Good weekend? Lovely,' she went on without waiting to hear Flora's reply. 'I'm afraid, as you see, I'm far too busy to deal with you. Would you like to hang out with the porters? You may be able to help them shift furniture or something.'

Charles frowned. 'Couldn't she go through some of the boxes? Or there are the pictures – she could divide them into prints and paintings, watercolours and oils.'

'I did work in an art gallery once,' put in Flora. 'I could do that easily.'

'No! Looking decorative in an art gallery is not sufficient qualification for this job. I'd just have to do it all again. She'd be better out of the way with the boys.'

Flora suppressed a sigh, but it was her first day. Annabelle might trust her a bit more when she'd had a chance to prove herself. 'Hanging out with the boys sounds fun,' said Flora, glad that Geoffrey had told her to wear old clothes and bring gloves. He'd warned her that Annabelle wouldn't let her do anything except the most menial manual work.

'Annabelle is in charge of the saleroom on sale days,' said Charles.

'That's fine. I want to learn all about the family business, and, as I said, bottom up is best.' Flora delivered Annabelle a dazzling smile designed to disconcert her. 'I'll go and find Geoffrey, shall I?'

Annabelle frowned. 'He's not really the best person. He thinks he knows everything.'

'He was very kind to me over the weekend,' said Flora.

'Oh. Yes, I'm sorry we couldn't get over.' Annabelle didn't look as sorry as all that. 'Family commitments, you know.'

The insincerity in Flora's smile matched Annabelle's. 'That's OK. After all, I'm not very *close* family, am I?' She held back from suggesting that owning half the business strengthened the tie somewhat.

A few wrinkles appeared in Annabelle's otherwise smooth brow, fully exposed by the Alice band she used to keep her hair back. 'Well, go and see if you can help Geoffrey then. I'm certainly too busy to supervise you.'

'I'll take you to him,' said Charles.

'No, no, I'm sure you've got lots to do. I'll find him myself.' Flora smiled and waggled her fingers in a way guaranteed to make Annabelle want to shoot her. Unable to do this, Annabelle turned her irritation on one of the two women beside her, who produced the required piece of paper with admirable calm.

As she made her way through the furniture she wondered if it was worth trying to get on with Annabelle. Would she ever be able to drink instant coffee at a kitchen table with her, or share a bottle of wine in an overgrown garden and talk until it was too cold to stay outside any more? It seemed terribly unlikely, but she did so want to get her hands on Annabelle's wardrobe. Today she was wearing a shirt-waister that was just the wrong length, and not quite on her waist, with a Puritan collar. And in spite of the heat she was wearing quite thick navy blue tights. As for the navy blue velvet Alice band – was the woman stuck in a time warp? Perhaps that was it, Bishopsbridge was in a time warp where people

70

still made 'good marriages' to people chosen by their parents, and fashion never dared encroach in case it frightened the horses.

Flora tracked Geoffrey down in a kitchen off a side hall. He was making tea for, it appeared, about twenty. With him were several people she vaguely recognised.

'Hello, Flora,' one woman said warmly. 'Do you take sugar?'

'Hello. Sorry, I don't think I know your name.'

'We're in the choir,' the woman explained. 'Several of us work as porters, part time. Not like Geoffrey, who's full time.'

'I thought porters were men, on the whole, so they could shift things.' Flora then blushed, worried in case she'd said something enormously politically incorrect.

'There's lots more to portering than moving furniture,' said another familiar face. 'We spend hours sorting the boxes, sticking on labels, making lists. You don't need brute strength for that.'

'While we're on the subject,' said a woman wearing a badge with 'Jenny' printed on it, 'don't forget that Dennis likes the bag left in his tea.'

'Come and help us up on the stage,' suggested the woman from choir who Flora was fairly sure was one of the subversive second sopranos. 'That's where the smaller stuff is: valuables, collectables, things like that. There's a mountain of things which need labelling. If you get confused about which vendor sent what, you're in real trouble.'

'Annabelle said I should be with Geoffrey—'

'Don't take any notice of her. She doesn't know what she's talking about.' Jenny leant in confidentially. 'She's not qualified, you know, or even working for her exams.'

'Oh?'

'She just thinks she knows everything because she did a bit of china mending at a course she went on once, when she was a girl.'

'She's still quite young,' protested Flora. Annabelle was almost certainly a bitch but she was probably still in her twenties, early thirties at most.

'And because she's got Charles twisted round her little finger. My name's Virginia, by the way,' the woman from the choir added. 'I was standing behind you in choir. I don't know what Charles sees in that woman.' She sighed.

'Oh, you know it's because their parents were such friends,' said Jenny helpfully, 'and then Charles's parents died – were they related to you, Flora?'

'Oh yes. Can't quite remember how,' said Flora. 'It was awful when they died. I was very young, but my mother was really upset.'

'So they've known each other all their lives.'

'Ah,' said Flora, trying to imply she thought this was sweet, when actually she thought it was a shame to miss the fun of the chase. Of course one often went chasing off down blind alleys, but it was fun all the same.

'We'll take our teas now, Geoffrey, save you carrying them up the stairs,' said Virginia. 'Flora, grab that packet of biscuits, will you?'

Flora exchanged glances with Geoffrey, to check with him that this plan was appropriate, and he nodded. 'The girls will look after you,' he said.

'Geoffrey!' they chorused. 'That should be "pre-women"!'

'Away with you,' said Geoffrey, unchastened. 'Or I won't make you tea again.'

Virginia flapped her hand, obviously not remotely concerned by political correctness from Geoffrey. '"Girls" is OK among friends.'

'Are you lot going to do any work today?' Geoffrey demanded.

Up on the stage, amid piles of boxes, crumpled newspaper and more extraordinary items than Flora could have imagined existed, she was given a sheet of stickers. Virginia, who seemed to be loosely in charge of the others, said, 'All these items need a sticker with "KGC" on it. Make sure nothing gets left out. Charles will come along later and do the lotting, and we can put things together in boxes, but until we know which of this rubbish is valuable and which isn't, we mark everything.'

'But can't you tell what's worth selling?' Flora regarded a box with a stuffed and mounted Jacob's sheep's head in it. The horns had fallen off and were lying next to the glassy-eyed face.

'We have a fair idea but there's often a jewel among the junk and we can't take chances. Imagine if you're the vendor, wanting every penny from the sale. It would be awful if something really valuable got missed and sold in a miscellaneous box.'

'I see.'

'And of course we have to make sure there's something tasty in every box, not just rubbish, or no one will buy it.'

'I see.'

'And you can't mix up the vendors, even if there is the missing jug from the tea set from another lot. The

73

buyer just has to buy both lots and make up the set himself.'

'Do you ever buy anything yourselves?' Flora asked, putting a sticker on to a plastic cuckoo clock.

'Oh yes. My husband says I get paid in antiques. You develop an eye, and if you wait long enough you'll get your bargain. Then you can do it up and sell it, if you don't want it for yourself.'

'I can see the attraction,' said Flora, spotting a very pretty little tea set with only five cups. 'Are you allowed to bid?'

'You tell Charles if you're interested in a lot and then he'll know to look up here when it comes up. Annabelle won't though. She's just awkward.'

'No one seems to like her, poor woman,' said Flora.

'Poor woman indeed! She comes from a very wealthy family and runs Charles into the ground.'

'Silly Charles for putting up with it!'

Virginia shook her head knowingly. 'She had her eye on him since she was nine years old. The poor man didn't have a chance.'

'He must have done,' said Flora briskly. 'He's free, white and over twenty-one!'

Virginia shrugged.

Flora forgot Charles and his marriage plans when she spotted a small leather case. 'Ooh! Can I play with this jewellery? It looks like a treasure chest, with it all spilling out.'

'You can just put a sticker on it. Annabelle's been through it already. It's all junk – or "costume" as we say in the trade.'

'Oh, let me play, just for a second,' pleaded Flora. 'I

74

just want to look at that brooch of a cat. My cat had kittens at the weekend.'

Virginia allowed herself to be distracted by this news. While describing the little bundles, with their flat ears and slits instead of eyes, Flora tipped out the box of jewellery on to a table and sorted through it.

'Of course you can come and see them when they're a bit bigger,' she said. 'Geoffrey's Edie is having one, and I might want to keep one myself, but there's still two more.'

'And they were born on top of your shoes?'

'Yes! And we'd made her such a nice bed. She's on it now, of course, and seems perfectly happy. I've used all the towels, though, and have to keep washing them by hand. Just as well the weather's fine. My shoes needed a bit of cleaning, too.'

'You should get a washing machine. Pick one up here for a song.'

'I'll speak to Charles about it. Oh look, these pearls are real.'

'They can't be. Annabelle would have spotted them.'

'They are.' Flora pulled out the long string of small, uneven pearls. 'They're gritty when you bite them. That's the only thing I know about anything.'

'Tell Annabelle when she comes round. She'll be cross that she missed it.'

Annabelle took some convincing. 'They can't possibly be real. They're far too long a string.'

'I really do think they are,' Flora said, agonised by the thought that she might not be believed.

'It's terribly unlikely. If anyone had a string that long they'd keep them separate and they were just jumbled together in all that diamanté and glass.'

'Well, you test them, then,' said Flora, beginning to doubt herself.

Annabelle shook her head. 'I can't do that thing with the teeth. So unhygienic.'

'Let's ask Charles,' suggested Virginia, as he appeared on the stage. She waved at him to come over.

'Are these pearls real or not?' she asked.

Charles raised them to his mouth. 'Yup. Freshwater pearls. Well spotted, Annie-bee. They should definitely go on their own.'

Virginia opened her mouth to say it wasn't 'Annie-bee' who spotted them, but Flora. Flora frowned and shook her head. Annabelle had enough problems with her without being shown up by the downsizing bimbo.

'You should have said something,' said Virginia when Charles and Annabelle had gone.

'There's no point in antagonising her any more. She already hates me.'

'She hates everyone she thinks stands in the way of her grand plan.'

'Oh? What's her grand plan?' Flora carefully put a label on each of three broken pieces that had once been a Toby jug.

Virginia regarded the pieces and frowned. 'She wants to close the place down.'

'But why would she do that? It's a good business, isn't it?'

'Could be better, and this building alone is fantastically valuable. There's a nursery school round the back, the rent from that is quite high, and it's used by the locals – drama groups, WI, Cubs and Brownies, Guides

76

– between sales. It would be a real loss to the community if it was sold.'

'So what does Annabelle want to do with it?'

'Divide it up into executive flats and sell them individually for a fortune.'

'Oh my goodness.'

'And then there's the house next door. At the moment there's a flat there that Charles uses sometimes, and the offices. But it would raise a lot of money if it were divided and sold off.'

'I can see it is quite extravagant keeping it, if it's not all being used. But this place is different. It's like a public space.'

'Exactly!' Virginia frowned suddenly and said, 'Who are you again? Apart from being Charles's cousin?'

Flora wondered if she should keep her exact identity secret, but decided that secrets were a luxury no one had round here. 'I've inherited a bit of the company. Annabelle wants to buy some shares from me.' It wasn't the entire truth, but it should be enough to satisfy Virginia. It wasn't fair to Charles that the whole town should know all his private financial affairs, even if they did know most of them already.

'Well, don't you let her, if you can avoid it. So you're learning a bit about the business?'

'That's the idea. Annabelle and Charles think I'll be a liability, but I'd like to prove them wrong.'

'They're not so good at it themselves. Oh, Charles is a good man, knows everything about anything that's likely to come through the doors and beyond, but he's too old-fashioned in many ways. Marketing is not his bag.' Virginia spotted Geoffrey coming up the stairs with a box. 'Over here, Geoffrey. Is that all the same vendor?'

While they discussed who owned what and what list it should be on, Flora resisted the temptation to go through the other boxes of costume jewellery, and hoped, very hard, that Virginia wouldn't have forgotten what she was telling her by the time she and Geoffrey had reached a conclusion.

'No,' Virginia said when they were alone again. 'My daughter offered to do them a website, for nothing, for practice, and Annabelle wouldn't hear of it. Said it was quite unnecessary. They put the better items on the Internet, which does get people down here, but they haven't got a website as such.'

'So how do they advertise?'

'The *Yellow Pages*, and of course the sales are listed in the local papers, but that's not going to get them much new business. All auction houses have websites these days. It's essential. My daughter could do them one very reasonably.'

'Hmm. I'll have to look into that,' said Flora. 'Do you want to do that box or shall I?'

'There's some jewellery and I can see you're keen. You go ahead.'

Chapter Five

While Flora was more than competent to drive the Land-Rover, she was a little less sure of the way. However, after finding herself in a village that was definitely not the one with the village shop and the pub which were currently her nearest civilisation, she managed to find her way back to what she now regarded as her cottage.

It was a heavenly summer evening, and Flora longed to have someone to share it with other than Imelda and her four little kittens. She parked the Land-Rover and got out, enjoying the sudden quiet after the noise of the engine.

'It would be different in winter,' she told herself. 'You wouldn't want to live here then.'

As she unlocked the front door she realised how tired she was. She'd been on her feet all day and done more physical work than she'd ever done in her life. But she'd loved it. The people were what made it, she decided. Apart from Annabelle, who'd been relentlessly unfriendly and dismissive, and Charles, whom she'd hardly seen, everyone had been so kind and helpful. And more than that, they'd made her feel one of the gang, not like an irritating outsider.

After she'd dumped her bag on the table she went upstairs to see Imelda and the kitts, who seemed to have grown since the morning.

Imelda was very pleased to see her, obviously thrilled to have some adult company after a long day alone with the kids. She purred and purred as Flora stroked her, and then went hungrily to her empty food saucer.

'All right, darling, I'll be right up with a sachet of cat food. I got you some new flavours today!'

Flora ran downstairs, all her tiredness forgotten in her delight with her cat and kittens. Perhaps she should become celibate and just live with animals from now on. Animals didn't do stupid things like marry people because it was assumed they would. Although, as she ran Imelda's saucer under the tap to wash it, cats in particular did seem to pick owners who'd spoil them. So perhaps men weren't as different from cats as all that.

She squeezed the food out of its pouch, thinking about her cousin. He was dyed-in-the-wool stuffy and she didn't like him, but unless Annabelle stopped being so controlling about the business, she didn't think he should marry her. What Virginia had told her about Annabelle's plans for Stanza and Stanza had really got to her, and as Flora didn't feel she knew Charles anything like well enough to tell whether he would let Annabelle bully him, she wasn't going to take the chance. She was staying, at least until the old family firm – if not the whole of Bishopsbridge – had joined the twenty-first century.

Imelda joined her in the kitchen, rubbing against her legs in an attempt to make the food come quicker. Flora sighed, recalling Annabelle's bossiness at the saleroom. With or without control, it would take something cataclysmic to turn Annabelle into a nice person. And she wasn't entirely sure Charles deserved the effort –

although everyone else around her probably did.

Flora opened a bottle of wine and a packet of nuts and then went upstairs to run a bath. Aware it was probably hugely extravagant, she had left the immersion heater on all day rather than risk there being no hot water when she got home. She'd been warned she'd be filthy.

She found herself nodding off in the bath and decided to abandon supper. She brushed her teeth in a cursory manner and tumbled into bed, the damp towel still around her. And, very quickly, she slept.

In fact, she overslept. When she woke, still tangled in the towel, she realised it was past eight o'clock and Charles was expecting her at the saleroom at eight-thirty.

She hurled herself out and started dragging clothes out of the wardrobe. She put on her knickers but clutched her bra and her dress to her, planning to put them on while the kettle was boiling. She was halfway down the stairs when she screamed. There was a man standing in the sitting room, looking at her.

'Please don't be frightened,' he said, a startled look on his face. The speaker was extremely tall and lean and was wearing clothes so faded it was hard to tell what colour they'd started life as. He had long curly hair and the bluest eyes Flora had seen for a long time. His nose was aquiline and his mouth beautifully curved. And his voice was low and melodic with no discernible regional accent.

Flora screamed again briefly and fled back into her bedroom to put on her dress. She abandoned the bra. She could run out to the Land-Rover without that. She went back to the top of the stairs.

'I won't do anything to hurt you, I promise. I've been here all night,' he said anxiously.

Flora was tempted to scream retrospectively. All night she'd been sleeping, naked, on her bed with the door half open, while this completely strange, although she had to admit not particularly threatening, man slept on her sofa. It was an outrage.

Imelda came to rub against her legs, probably wondering what the delay with breakfast was.

'Hello, puss,' said the man, and Imelda, the traitress, tripped down the stairs towards him. She allowed him to rub her ears for a moment and then looked up as if to say, 'Perhaps you'll give me breakfast?'

'Look,' said Flora, 'you can't sleep here. I live here. This is my home. You must leave! Immediately!'

'I've been sleeping here on and off all year,' he said apologetically. 'The window in the kitchen is very easy to open and I spent most of the winter here.'

'Oh God!'

'And I've boiled the kettle. Would you like some tea?'

'No! I mean, you can't offer me tea in my own house!'

'I realise it's not quite usual, especially when we haven't met, officially, but it seems the least I can do in the circumstances.'

Flora came down the stairs. She was dying for tea. She was desperate to feed Imelda so she could go to work, but there was this man. 'The least you can do – in fact the most you can do – in the circumstances is to leave. Now. So I can get ready to go to work. And feed my cat.'

'I could do that for you.'

'But I don't want you to! I want you to go!' The whole

82

situation was ridiculous and Flora just wanted it to be over.

'I will go, if you're sure, but wouldn't you like tea first?'

Flora came further into the room and could see through the kitchen door two steaming mugs. She remembered that she'd had two glasses of wine and no water the night before. No wonder her mouth felt stuck together with glue.

He saw that she was tempted and went to fetch one of the mugs. 'Do you want breakfast? I could rustle you up a couple of scrambled eggs in no time.'

'No!' She sipped the tea. It was heaven, but it was an impossible situation. And she *had* to get to work or Charles would think he'd been right about her all along. She just didn't have time for this.

Imelda, having given up on Flora's ability to move, miaowed at the man, making her needs clear.

'Hello, you. Oh, you've had kittens,' he said. 'You must be hungry.'

'She is. I usually give her something last thing at night, but I fell asleep and she's only had a few cat biscuits to keep her going.'

'Are the kittens here?'

Flora nodded. 'Upstairs. Not that it's anything to do with you, of course.'

He smiled. 'I'm William.'

'Flora. Listen, William,' she said firmly, 'you must realise how impossible this is.'

'I do see that it's difficult, but not impossible. After all, I haven't murdered you, have I? Shall I feed the young mother? What's her name?'

'Imelda. Yes please, do feed her. But . . .' She hesitated. She was so late. 'William? I've got to rush now, but could you please leave by the time I get home? About half past six or seven? This isn't my house and if the owners found out you'd been using it, they'd die of shock and have you put in prison for ever.' She took another sip of tea.

'You should eat. You obviously didn't eat last night.'

'Obviously?'

'No dishes, no sign of cooking.'

'Well, I haven't time now,' she almost snapped, horribly reminded of how she'd been with her mother sometimes when she'd tried to press breakfast on her before school. She sighed. 'I must find some shoes. And then I must go. And then you must go. But do, please, feed Imelda first.'

She ran back upstairs and found her sandals. She took a deep breath and reminded herself that he'd had all night to murder her in her sleep if that was his intention, and then ran back down again. Imelda and William were in the kitchen. He was putting food into a bowl and she was tucking into it before he'd even finished.

'I like feeding people, too,' he said.

Flora found herself smiling and tried to stop. She ran out of the door, scrabbling for her keys as she did so, and shouted, 'Go!'

It was only when she was in the Land-Rover and had started the engine that she remembered she wasn't wearing a bra. 'I'll have to buy a cardigan, or a T-shirt or something. Charles would die of shock if he caught the outline of a nipple through my dress.'

As she drove, she thought about William and his silent

84

invasion. It was awful, of course, but somehow not as terrifying as it might have been if she'd been living in London. There the thought of finding a strange man in the sitting room when she woke up was so horrifying, she shivered just thinking about it. Here, it was decidedly odd, but didn't have the same stomach-churning effect, even if she had been frightened at the time.

Thinking about the differences between town and country life made her realise that if she survived her stint in the country she could set up the very course she was looking for herself. 'Living without Sushi! How to survive Country Life.' Or she could get sponsorship from magazines. 'The *Country Living* guide to Country Life.' Or the other way round: 'The *Country Life* guide to Country Living.' Honestly, she was wasted on an old-fashioned, family-run auctioneers!

She didn't feel wasted when she got there, however; she felt needed. Now people had got used to her, had begun to trust her a little, she was sent all over the place on errands. Stickers to put on here, a piece of jewellery that had been mislaid to be hunted for there, vast numbers of cups of tea to be made and distributed, and learning, all the time.

She loved it. There was no other word for it. She found it interesting, exciting and hugely companionable. Charles and Annabelle might not have run the most cutting-edge auction house in the country, but it could be the most friendly one.

Virginia took her to buy sandwiches at about half past one, when there was a slight lull in proceedings. They found a bench in the park opposite the saleroom and ate them, and Flora commented on the family atmosphere.

'We do it for Charles,' said Virginia through a mouthful of chicken and mango wrap. 'Most of us knew his father and it was he who made the business like it is. Before they got engaged and Annabelle came, Charles was running it along the same lines. Then Miss Green-wellies-and-pearls decided to smarten us all up. She wanted us to wear nylon uniforms! Aprons are sensible, they keep the dirt off your clothes. But uniforms! We refused, of course.'

'Of course. Nylon! Yuck!'

'The firm does need updating, of course, but not how she's planning to do it, which, basically, is to maximise the property: turn all the buildings into executive homes.'

'I'll talk to Charles about the website. We should have one. Does your daughter still do them?'

'Oh yes, but she'll want paying now. It's her business.'

'Of course she'll want paying. I'll get on to Charles straightaway. There are a few other things I need to see him about, too. Where's he been all morning?'

'Doing a valuation, I expect.' Virginia leant in confidentially. 'The story is that when Annabelle did them, apart from not knowing very much about how much things were worth, she used to offend the customers. They're often recently bereaved, you see. A certain amount of tact is required.'

'And they get that from Charles?'

'Oh yes. He's wonderful with people.'

'Are we talking about the same Charles? My cousin?'

Virginia laughed. 'He may seem quite reserved, but he's very good at what he does.'

'I'll take your word for it.'

'It's Annabelle you want to watch.'

'If you don't mind my asking, how do you know so much about it all?'

Virginia laughed. 'Well, I keep my ear to the ground – in self-defence really. We all do. And Annabelle doesn't exactly make a secret about what she wants.' Virginia took another bite and chewed thoughtfully. Flora wanted to hurry her but knew she couldn't. 'I don't suppose this business makes very much money,' she said eventually, 'even though we get paid by the buyers and the sellers, but it would be a shame for it all to disappear.'

'Yes, it would. I'll have to see what I can do. After all, I'm the one with the stake in the business, not Annabelle.' Now it was obvious why Geoffrey didn't want Annabelle to have even a small share of it financially.

Driving home at the end of a long day, very tired and filthy dirty, Flora had time to consider how much money she stood to make herself if the buildings were all turned into flats and sold. She was too weary to make a very accurate guess but it was surely a great deal of money. What would she do with over a million pounds? Maybe it was the fatigue, but at that moment she couldn't think of anything she wanted except a hot bath, a packet of crisps and a glass of wine.

She had turned the key in the lock and opened the door before she remembered William. A wonderful savoury smell wafted out from the kitchen, and the cottage looked very cosy. There was a fresh bunch of wild roses on the mantelpiece that she hadn't put there, and a fire laid in the fireplace. Not that you'd need one in this weather, but it looked nice to have it there.

There was no sign of William, however – he'd clearly

seen that Flora was serious about her instructions to leave – so when she had dumped her bag she ran upstairs to see Imelda and the kittens. They were fine, and Imelda's litter tray had obviously been changed. The joke about the gay burglars who tidied the house and left a quiche in the oven came into her mind and made her smile. It must be William – who else could it be? But was he gay? She couldn't possibly tell.

She dragged herself away from the little furry bundles, which were making little swimming movements to get about, and went back downstairs, aware how hungry she was, thrilled that there was something in the oven.

She had just taken it out when there was a knock on the door. 'William,' she said, smiling in spite of her resolutions not to, 'you'd better come in.'

'I just came to check you'd come home roughly when you said you'd come, and that your supper wasn't burning.'

'It was very kind of you to make me supper.'

'It was very kind of you not to call the police and make an awful fuss.'

'Would you like a glass of wine?' She was desperate for one herself and realised that she would enjoy it more in company. And he had cooked for her, after all.

'That would be very nice. Shall I check on the pie?'

'If you like. You might as well share it with me. What is it?'

'Cheese and onion and tomato pie. I'm not a vegetarian, but you didn't have any meat. A bit of bacon goes well with it.'

'I'll get some tomorrow, if I have time to slip out to the shops.'

'I'll find some knives and forks.'

'William,' she said once they'd settled down with steaming plates on their knees, 'how much time do you spend here usually?'

'It varies, but I spent most of the winter here.'

'Is that why it smells of wood smoke?'

'Probably. The fire did smoke a bit when the chimney was cold.'

Flora swallowed a mouthful of pie. It was delicious and, she thought prudently, probably very cheap. 'Do Charles and Annabelle have any idea that you exist?' Then she realised that of course they didn't know, they'd be apoplectic at the thought.

'Who are Charles and Annabelle?'

'They own this cottage. Or at least, Annabelle does. Charles is my cousin.'

He shrugged. 'I don't care much about that sort of thing. If a house is empty, I don't see why I shouldn't use it. I didn't do any damage, after all.'

'I only have your word for that!' declared Flora, laughing. 'It could have been a palace before I moved in.'

William regarded her seriously. 'It was a cottage, it is still a cottage and will be a cottage until some Philistine puts a huge extension on it.'

'You're a fine one to talk about Philistines! Taking over houses without a by-your-leave. What are you doing around here, anyway? Are you a poacher or something?'

'I'm a poet and a portrait painter, but I do take the odd rabbit or pheasant if I need it.'

'And you squat in empty buildings?'

'Do you know why Marxists drink herb tea?' William took a sip of his wine.

'No.' She took a sip of hers.

'Because all proper tea is theft,' announced William. 'Only, of course, it wasn't Marx who said that.'

Flora laughed. 'Can I tell you what joke I thought of when I went upstairs and found you'd changed the cat litter?'

'That was to ingratiate myself with you.'

'I'm sure it was, but it made me think of the joke about the gay burglars, who tidy the house and leave a quiche in the oven.'

He laughed and shook his head. 'I'm afraid I'm not gay, but I'm completely trustworthy and, if it makes you feel any better, although I think you're very pretty, I don't fancy you.'

'That's all right then.' Curiously it did make her feel better. 'Is there any more of this pie?'

She was at the saleroom again at eight-thirty in the morning, and so was nearly everyone else. The sale started at ten. There was another chance to view from nine o'clock, and Virginia had told her that they allowed people to go on viewing on the stage, where the smaller, more stealable items were, until half an hour before the sale got to their lot numbers.

As always, she found a huddle of people in the kitchen, dunking tea bags in and out of mugs. 'Hi, Flora,' said Geoffrey. 'Ready for your first sale?'

'I hope so. I'm really looking forward to it. After you've spent days handling and looking at all this, you almost feel like it's yours.'

He chuckled. 'Well, if you want to bid on anything, let Charles know, and get a card from the office. It's a good way to furnish a house cheaply.'

Flora took a moment to consider how much fun it would be buying things for the cottage and then remembered it wasn't her cottage and that the London flat didn't really need anything extra – it was cramped enough already. 'Not at the moment, Geoffrey.'

'It's how Edie and me got most of the stuff for our daughters. If you work here long enough you'll see everything you could ever want or need pass by. I bought most of the furniture for our place when I was a dealer.'

'That's why you never made a mint when you were a dealer, Geoff,' said another porter. 'You couldn't resist hanging on to the best stuff.'

Flora remembered that Geoffrey and Edie's house had some very nice pieces in it. He laughed. 'You may well be right there, lad. Now, are we going to do any work, or are we just here for decoration?'

Flora was in the yard, helping Geoffrey make a collection of garden gnomes look attractive, when he looked at his watch. 'Five minutes to kick-off. I expect Charles will start but Annabelle should do out here really, get these small lots out of the way.'

'Why won't she then?' Flora felt it might be quite fun persuading people to part with hard cash for these cute little gentlemen who seemed to have fallen on hard times, judging by the state of their pointy hats.

'Because it's beneath her. She only likes doing the posh stuff. Not that she's any good at it, mind.'

'Poor Annabelle! No one has a good word to say for her.'

Geoffrey snorted. 'She's a rubbish auctioneer. She can't get the crowd on her side for one thing. You'll have to learn how to do it. You wouldn't have that trouble.'

Flora sighed. She acknowledged that she might very well be able to get the people on her side, but even her short time at Stanza and Stanza had told her that there was a little more to it than that. And it involved sums. 'I don't think I'd fancy it. When you watch it on television it seems terribly complicated.'

'Once you've learnt the steps you go up in – you know, five, eight, ten, or three, five, eight, ten, whatever is appropriate – you'd be fine.'

'Geoffrey, I have difficulty with my two times table, I don't quite see myself with a gavel in my hand. Do you do it ever?'

He shook his head. 'Very rarely. Only if Annabelle doesn't want to. She doesn't like me doing it because she thinks I'm only a porter, although I reckon I could get more for this lot than she could. Not that she'll try, of course.' He paused. 'Are you going to leave them like that?' He was referring to the gnomes.

'I thought they looked rather sweet standing in a circle,' said Flora. 'Ah, here comes the boss.'

Everything happened extremely quickly. The stuffy Charles Flora had come to know disappeared and turned into the star of the show.

'Good morning, ladies and gentlemen,' he said with a smile, 'and a very lovely morning it is. Now, lot number one, a very appealing collection of garden gnomes who appear to be peeing into a pond. Who'll start me then, twenty pounds? No? Ten? Five? Think how charming they'd look on your patio. Five, thank you, eight? Ten, twelve, fifteen . . . thank you. Sold! And the next . . .'

Flora looked on in awe, aware that she was due to go and guard the small stuff on the stage but unable to tear herself away. It went incredibly quickly, lot after lot was knocked down and yet Charles never appeared to hurry. He had his audience enthralled, twitching their cards, eager to buy what he was selling. He seemed even taller than usual and infinitely more charming. She began to get an inkling of why all the porters seemed so fond of him: apart from the business side, he was good at his job.

But there was no time for Flora to stand and stare at her cousin. At last she stopped watching and hurried through the crowd and the furniture to the stage, where she stood by a table full of tea sets – some beautiful, some mismatched, some frankly bizarre – and apologised to Virginia for being late.

'We've managed fine. Annabelle wanted to tell one of us regulars to go home because of you being here, but Charles wouldn't let her.'

'Virginia! You can't possibly know all that. You're making it up because you hate Annabelle.'

'Nonsense! She was asking me which porter to lay off when Charles overheard. Honestly.'

Flora grinned. She really liked Virginia but felt she was wasted as an auctioneer's porter and a subversive second soprano. She should have been in espionage.

When all the lots on the floor had been sold and many of them removed by quietly working porters with trolleys, the attention of the room turned to the stage.

'We've got some quite valuable lots up here today,' said Virginia. 'I expect Annabelle will sell it. I think Charles lets her in the hope that she'll get to like it, or at least get a bit better.'

Virginia was proved right and Annabelle took over from Charles. She settled herself at the desk, cleared her throat and then took a sip of water. The room waited for her to be ready. Flora could hear Virginia, clutching a huge Staffordshire ornament, tutting at the waste of time.

Even Flora's very limited experience of auction sales was enough to tell her that Annabelle was not good at it. Her voice was high and shrill and she behaved less like someone encouraging people to buy things and more like an irritable headmistress demanding answers to questions. It was little wonder that few people put their hands up.

At first Flora felt self-conscious, standing at the front of the stage holding strange items above her head, but that didn't last long and she spent the time, while Annabelle laboriously sent items under the hammer, looking at the crowd.

There were quite a lot of them. Virginia, next to her, ready to show the lot after Flora's, indicated the people she knew, talking out of the corner of her mouth.

'The man in the hat is a dealer. He buys loads of glass and sells lots of it on. We see the same stuff time after time. He puts quite high reserves on sometimes so it often doesn't sell. But he makes a good living so it must be worth it.'

Flora spotted the private buyers for herself. There were a couple of women who were having a day out together

94

and had obviously had a glass of wine at lunch. They were thoroughly enjoying themselves. The porters enjoyed themselves too, and kept going on sweets and chocolates. Although they urged each other to take proper breaks no one liked to leave the action.

Charles took over from Annabelle quite soon. Flora had seen him at the desk, dealing with customers, and hoped he'd had time for a sandwich, at least.

'They need another auctioneer,' said Virginia to Flora, who was trying not to drop a very valuable lead crystal decanter that was attracting a lot of interest. 'You should train.'

'Not on your life,' said Flora through her smile.

Before the sale was over people came up to collect their purchases. One woman took charge of the pink slips that stated the items had been paid for and found the items, while the others carried on ferrying glass, crystal, and silver from the back to the front of the stage.

With Charles back in charge the lots whistled by and before Flora had seen it coming, the sale was over. The crowd of people wanting to collect their treasures built up. Now the selling was over everyone dealt with customers, helping them pack and finding newspaper for wrapping.

Flora really liked this part. Now the bidding was over the hardest-bitten dealer could appear pleased with what they'd bought, although they always muttered that they'd paid too much for it.

The pair of women were now extremely giggly, thinking up extravagant stories for their husbands as to why they felt they needed so much when they'd only come to buy a wedding present for a niece.

Virginia and the others knew many of the people and laughed and joked with them. Flora, as a new face, received a few curious glances. After a hurried consultation, Virginia introduced her as a new porter. Flora didn't want everyone knowing she was a family member, until it was either impossible to keep secret or politic to announce it.

She could have gone home; the others encouraged her to do so as it was her first sale. But Flora wasn't going to go until Charles and Annabelle did and she felt fairly certain Charles wouldn't leave until the floor had been swept and every last cup washed. She didn't want him accusing her of slacking.

'Is there anything else for me to do?' she asked Charles when it was only him, Annabelle and Louisa, the secretary, left. It was the first time she'd had an opportunity to speak to him and she wanted to congratulate him on being so good at his job.

'I don't think so.' Charles regarded her with his usual, barely-concealed contempt, all remnants of the charming auctioneer vanished. 'How did you enjoy your first sale? It's not quite like it is on television, is it?'

Hurt that he should still be so stuffy when she had seen him be so different, she said, 'Oh no. It's much better in real life than it is on television.'

'Oh!'

She had the satisfaction of knowing she had surprised him.

'It's not so bloody tiring on television,' said Annabelle. 'Or as dirty. I'm filthy. I'm going straight home for a bath, Charles. You don't need me?'

'I just want to let Louisa know what's going on. We're

doing a valuation over at a house in Churchfields tomorrow, Lou.'

'Oh, Charles!' Annabelle broke in. 'Do I have to? Can't you do it on your own?'

'I could, but it will take me ages. The tape recorder's broken. I need a note-taker.'

'Take Flora, then.'

Charles regarded his cousin, obviously debating who was preferable, a reluctant Annabelle or a completely inexperienced Flora. He pursed his lips.

'Really, darling, I can't.' Annabelle decided to help him in his decision. 'I need to go over to the cottage and take a proper inventory. You don't mind, Flora, do you?'

Flora did mind, for lots of reasons, principally William. 'But, Annabelle, Imelda and the kittens! You're allergic to cats.'

'Oh, I'd be all right for a bit. As long as I don't touch them or anything.'

'But do you really need an inventory? I'm hardly going to steal the furniture. And you can get Paris goblets at the local supermarket if I break any.'

'Yes,' Annabelle replied, 'but I'd like to list what I've lent you. When you go in a couple of months, I might have forgotten what we'd taken out when we decided not to rent this year.' She smiled. 'It would be awful if I blamed you for losing something that had never been there, wouldn't it?'

Not quite as awful as Annabelle discovering William in the cottage, Flora thought, but of course couldn't say.

'Do you know what time you'll be there?'

'No, but you'll be out with Charles, anyway. It won't make any difference.'

97

'Annabelle! I really don't want to take Flora. She's only just got here. She knows nothing.'

'I learnt a lot today, Charles,' said Flora in a way she hoped would both convince him and warn him that he couldn't treat her like an ignorant townie for ever.

'Flora! I don't mean to be insulting—'

'Then don't be.'

'But you are as much use to me as a chocolate teapot. Or the novelty ones that you collect.'

'But they are useful. You can make tea in them. And I can take notes, or do whatever it is you need me to do. You shouldn't believe all those blonde jokes you know. Blondes are no stupider than anyone else.'

'Oh, all right then! You can come with me. But for goodness' sake put some more clothes on!'

It was only then that Flora remembered she was not wearing a bra.

'You won't be wearing an apron tomorrow,' Charles reminded her.

Flora slipped away feeling surprisingly chastened. And she'd have to warn William to stay out all day. Poor Imelda would have to survive on fly-blown Kittikins and her litter tray. Life was never simple.

Chapter Six

❧❧❧

Not having to be at work until half past nine seemed like a lie-in to Flora – although she would have enjoyed it more if she wasn't worried about William turning up at the cottage while Annabelle was there.

The previous evening when she'd got home there had been a note from him saying that he'd seen to Imelda and pointing out the salad he had made. He seemed to have used some lettuce and tomatoes that she had in the fridge and a lot of very strange bits of plant which he must have gathered from less orthodox sources. She recognised tips of hawthorn and what might have been some sort of wild sorrel but nothing else. After she'd spent a time-wasting half-hour with Imelda and the kittens, she had eaten it. Either the bits of plant tasted very good, or the vinaigrette, which he'd also made, disguised any unpleasant taste.

Grateful though she was to come home to a delicious meal, she would rather have actually seen William so she could have warned him about Annabelle. She could hardly leave him a note telling him to keep out of the way – Annabelle was far more likely to find it than he was.

Still, at least she had a television now. Charles had bought one for her from the sale the previous day. He'd put it in the back of the Land-Rover for her and said, 'I suppose you might as well have this. No one else seemed to want it.'

She had thanked him in a manner appropriate to such a grudging gift but a tiny part of her wondered if he was actually being quite kind, but didn't want her to know. The porters all seemed to like him well enough, but then they would, wouldn't they? He was good-looking in a conventional sort of way and if they'd known and liked his father, they were bound to feel motherly towards him. And, of course, he wasn't trying to force any of them to leave.

After she had got the TV to work, she settled down in front of it. But instead of concentrating on six young women from very sheltered homes struggling through the desert carrying Kalashnikovs and backpacks the size of small cars, which appeared to be the latest in reality television, she found herself thinking about the business and Charles.

Yesterday she had noticed that he had been constantly following on Annabelle's heels. Was he soothing ruffled feathers, or checking she'd done things right? If she'd been Annabelle and Charles had done that, she'd have killed him. Annabelle seemed oblivious. Did she not know? Or not care? It was hard to believe that Annabelle was really as bad at the job as she appeared to be, but going on what the porters said, she was worse, and bossy with it.

Flora yawned, aware that if she didn't go to bed soon, she'd wake up in the middle of the night on the sofa, cold and stiff. As she sleepily locked doors and windows, brought up more food and water for Imelda, and unplugged the slightly dodgy electric kettle, she decided that Charles and Annabelle were nothing to do with her and went to bed. They had certainly gone way past the 'in love' stage of their relationship.

So was their relationship purely for practical reasons? It was none of Flora's business of course, she told herself firmly, but she was a compulsive people-watcher and couldn't help but be fascinated by this oddly distant couple set on marrying. Why on earth were they together? If Annabelle wanted control of a business, why didn't she use her money to start one she liked, instead of muddling about with furniture and knick-knacks that gave her no pleasure at all?

Unless, of course, it wasn't that way round. Maybe she wanted to be financially involved in Stanza and Stanza so that when she persuaded or bullied or convinced Charles to sell the buildings, she would get her cut. Or even just be married to Charles to share his bit.

Charles was possibly hoping that Annabelle would invest some of her money in the business so he could improve things, do a little marketing, some proper advertising. But that seemed terribly cold. Maybe Flora was barking up the wrong tree completely. The trouble was, their private life could be a sea of endless passion but they were both so buttoned up and conventional the rest of the world would never know. And if they'd known each other from childhood, perhaps they'd never shared the white heat of a new relationship.

Thinking of new relationships reminded Flora of Henry. She liked Henry; he looked as if he could be fun. The twinkle in his eye was such a relief after Charles's

101

disapproval, and in a town this small she was sure she'd run into him again. She was rather looking forward to it.

'I might just have to get one of those stickers saying "I Love My Landy",' declared Flora as she and Charles got out of their vehicles at roughly the same time. 'It's such fun being able to see into the gardens. And being so high up makes me feel empowered, sort of. Strong,' she added, in case the word 'empowered' was too frighteningly feminist for him.

Charles raised an eyebrow, possibly a little surprised at being greeted in this light-hearted way. 'Well, there's no reason why you shouldn't carry on driving it. It's a firm car – they're still waiting for that part for yours, by the way.' He frowned, and carried on. 'As long as you don't mind us using it to collect odd bits of furniture from time to time.'

'I would have thought a big old Volvo would be better for things like that?'

Charles held the door open for her. 'It would, actually, but Annabelle had her heart set on a Land-Rover.'

Flora had told herself she was going to see the positive in Annabelle at every opportunity. 'I expect she likes being able to see into the gardens, too.'

'No. She said it made her feel safe.'

'I can understand that. The roads round here must get quite icy in winter.'

Charles looked down his nose at her – probably by accident, he was so much taller. 'Not really. It's very mild here.'

Flora really wanted to go to the Ladies' but felt that

this conversation should be finished first so she followed him into the office. 'But I thought you said she found it difficult to drive. Where is she, by the way?'

'Going to your house, later. She does find the Land-Rover awkward to park.'

'Then why are you keeping it? It's quite new.'

'I think we need to have this conversation sometime, but not now,' said Charles. 'Can you pick up a notebook and a reliable pen and we'll be off? I don't want to keep these people waiting. They've travelled a long way to get their uncle's estate settled.'

It was very frustrating. Flora couldn't exactly accuse him of being secretive, but he simply wasn't telling her anything.

They were both silent as they set off in his old but roomy Citroën. Flora was wondering why the firm bought a Land-Rover it didn't really need when Charles was driving such an old car. Surely it couldn't just be Annabelle's whim?

Eventually Charles said, 'We mostly use tape recorders to do valuations these days, but ours has broken and it'll be good training for you. In the old days they were always written out by hand and typed up later. You had to have two of you doing it.'

'Doesn't Annabelle like doing them?' Annabelle had said as much herself, but Flora wanted to prod a little deeper.

'Not really. We don't do all that much fine furniture these days and she's not really into everyday household effects, which are the bread and butter of our business.'

Flora filed away the snippet about the fine furniture and stuck to her questions about Annabelle. 'Tell me to mind my own business – I'm sure you will – but does Annabelle really like working for – in – an auction house?'

He was silent, as if thinking about his answer.

'If she doesn't,' went on Flora, trying not to show her impatience, 'why does she want to buy the shares so you have the majority shareholding?'

'She likes to be in control,' he said slowly. 'She's very organised.'

'But she wouldn't be in control,' said Flora. 'You would.'

'Annabelle and I are going to be married. It's more or less the same thing.'

'Charles! It's not the same thing! Marriage doesn't bind you at the hip!' She thought of how her mother would react if anyone suggested that getting married gave either partner 'control'. And remembered, rather uncomfortably, Virginia's comments about Annabelle's plans.

'I really don't want to discuss my private life with you, Flora,' Charles said coolly, at his very stuffiest.

'You brought it up! I just wanted to know why Annabelle wanted to get involved with a business she didn't like. After all, she could run her own business. She doesn't have to be linked to yours.'

'She could but she feels . . .' He paused, drumming his fingers on the steering wheel, apparently going through a mental thesaurus for the right words.

Flora gave up trying to hide her frustration with his reserve. 'She feels that it's a failing business and that you'd be better to sell it?' This was probably far too far too fast but she was fed up with gossip and wanted to know the facts, straight from the stuffed-horse's mouth.

'Who told you that?' the horse demanded.

'All the porters know, Charles, and they are not at all happy. I don't know if you were trying to keep it a secret, but you've failed.'

Charles sighed deeply. 'I suppose it's inevitable that it should get out. The thing is, we may not be able to stay in business even if Annabelle did want to. We haven't made a profit for a couple of years.' Flora bit her lip, knowing what he was going to say. 'If we liquidated our property, we – you included – could make an absolute fortune.'

Flora thought about the enormous house, only partly used, the huge hall next door where the day before she'd experienced her first auction, and where the local community put on plays and flower shows and held discos, that also housed a nursery and a playgroup. With the amount of executive housing they would provide, the fortune probably amounted to millions.

'I can see why you're tempted,' she said.

'I'm not tempted!' Charles sounded really angry. 'I love the business. But if it doesn't make money, we can't keep it on like a family retainer or an aged pet!'

'If you feel like that about it,' said Flora quietly, 'don't sell.'

'Aren't you tempted by the money yourself?' He glanced across at her, genuinely curious.

She had had time to think about this already, but she considered the matter again, to check her feelings. 'Not really,' she said after a while. 'I haven't any dreams unfulfilled because of lack of funds. Besides . . .' She paused. What she was about to say sounded so sentimental, but then she said it anyway. 'I'd prefer to see Stanza and Stanza succeed. I haven't been here long, but I see why you love it. I think if you gave me a chance I could come to love it too. So, what we have to do,' she went on quickly, before Charles could possibly comment, 'is to make the business work, make it make money, then Annabelle won't put you under pressure to sell.'

Charles sighed. 'We could never make as much money as the property would raise.'

'I know, but if it was more profitable, very profitable, possibly, she'd feel happier about it. And as I said before, she doesn't have to work in it if she doesn't want to. You've got me now.'

He frowned. 'You're just here for the summer. The moment the lanes get muddy and it gets a bit chilly you'll be back off to London before you can say Jack—'

'I never, ever say Jack Robinson,' Flora interrupted. 'It's an absolute rule of mine. Come to think of it, I've never heard anyone else say it, either.'

He pursed his lips, possibly suppressing a smile – but, thought Flora, more likely suppressing irritation.

'Tell you what,' she said, 'as your far-off cousin and your partner in this firm, I will undertake to get this business on a better footing. Of course I can't promise to put it into profit, but before the lanes get muddy and I'm even tempted by the thought of bright lights and sushi bars, we'll be doing better. I give you my word.'

'That's very kind of you, Flora,' he said quietly, 'but how on earth are you going to do that when you hardly know more about it than you can have picked up on the *Antiques Roadshow*?'

'I know a lot more about it now,' she said confidently.

'I've been at my first sale, don't forget.' She became thoughtful. 'The *Antiques Roadshow*,' she murmured. 'Hmm.'

The house where they were to do their valuation was on what had once been a council estate. It was a very tidy, well-ordered estate where many of the houses were now privately owned, but as it wasn't a gated community, full of large, detached properties with professionally mown lawns and indoor swimming pools, Flora thought she knew why Annabelle hadn't wanted to come.

'It's unlikely that there'll be anything of huge value here,' Charles said, 'but it's important to remember that these are the effects of a much-loved relative. You must be tactful. In fact, it would be better if you didn't say much at all.'

As Charles had no reason to think she'd be anything other than the soul of tact, Flora realised he'd probably suffered from being with a less-than-sensitive Annabelle. 'Of course,' she said. 'And there might very well be a Steiff teddy about to be thrown out.'

Charles frowned at her. 'Very unlikely.'

The door was opened by a well-dressed woman in her fifties. 'Oh, hello. Was it difficult to find?'

'No, not at all,' said Charles, smiling at the woman with a mixture of kindness and charm which Flora couldn't have imagined directed at her. He didn't have to be so stuffy, Flora noticed. He could unbend if he wanted to.

'It's my uncle's house,' the woman went on, still holding the door open, but not letting them in. 'It's in

107

a bit of a state, I'm afraid. He didn't like to throw anything away.'

'Don't worry about that, Mrs Jenkins. I'm Charles Stanza and this is my colleague Flora – Stanza.'

'Oh, are you married?' asked Mrs Jenkins.

'Heaven forbid!' said Flora, laughing. 'We're distant cousins. Very distant. I'm just helping Charles out today.'

'Oh, sorry,' said Mrs Jenkins, slightly embarrassed to have jumped to the wrong conclusion.

Charles and Flora hovered on the doorstep, waiting to be allowed across the threshold.

'I was expecting a Spanish or Italian gentleman,' said Mrs Jenkins, not asking them in, possibly for a reason.

'It's an Italian name but our branch of the family has lived in England for generations.'

By now Mrs Jenkins had stepped back sufficiently for them to get into the little hallway. Charles and Flora did so, then waited patiently.

'It's the most awful mess, I'm afraid. I've done what I can, but . . .' She put out a hand and opened the door to the living room, deliberately not looking inside. 'I suppose you'd better know the worst.'

The smell was appalling and at first Flora couldn't tell where it was coming from, it was so dark. Thick curtains covered the windows and there was so much furniture piled up in front of them what little light penetrated the curtains was blocked off. Then she saw the mountain of take-away food cartons littering the floor and a row of half-empty milk bottles.

'We had to stay in a bed and breakfast last night,' said Mrs Jenkins, obviously greatly distressed. 'I was going to try and make a start on it this morning but my husband told me it was better not to, not without proper equipment.'

'Quite right,' said Charles. 'This is a job for professionals.'

'My uncle got a bit eccentric towards the end. He was always a hoarder, and towards the end he wouldn't even throw away rubbish.'

'I can recommend a very good firm who'll deal with all this for you, Mrs Jenkins.' He smiled again. 'But don't worry, I've seen much worse than this.'

'So have I,' said Flora, 'when I lived in student accommodation.' It wasn't true, and she suspected that Charles was lying, too, but it was in a good cause.

'Some rubber gloves might be a good idea,' said Charles.

'I'll pop out and get some,' offered Flora. 'I spotted a shop on the corner. Is there anything you need, Mrs Jenkins? Air freshener? Milk? Chocolate biscuits?'

Mrs Jenkins laughed. 'Some chocolate digestives might make it seem less awful. I'll fetch my purse—'

'I'll pay for them,' said Flora. 'It's all part of the service. And don't worry about all this, we're here now.' Flora gave Mrs Jenkins an encouraging smile and went.

Aware that Charles couldn't do much without her, she was as quick as possible. When she got back, Charles, Mrs Jenkins and a man who was presumably Mr Jenkins were in the kitchen. It was a little less like the town dump than the first room they had seen and Mrs Jenkins had made a pot of tea.

'He never ate in here,' she explained, 'and the hot water's going, so I could wash a few cups and things. But it's so dreadfully sordid. It's like one of those television programmes I can't bear to watch.'

'You would come down here,' said Mr Jenkins. 'I said you'd be better just getting someone in to clear the house.'

'But there might be valuable antiques in among this filth!' This was obviously a well-worn argument. 'We can't afford just to pay someone to take it all away.'

'I'm sure there'll be enough in this room alone to pay for that,' said Charles.

'Really?' A spark of hope brightened Mrs Jenkins's anxious expression.

'I can see there is without even moving,' Charles reassured her. 'All that enamelware, it's very collectable.'

'I would so hate to have wasted your time.'

'You won't be doing that, I assure you,' said Charles. 'Got your notebook, Flora?'

'Let the poor girl have her tea first.' Mrs Jenkins smiled at Flora and offered her a biscuit, obviously relaxing a little.

'The village is very pretty,' said Flora, blowing crumbs.

'It is,' agreed Mrs Jenkins. 'It would be nice to have a little walk, but I don't suppose there'll be time.'

'There's no reason at all why you can't just leave us to it,' said Charles. 'At least to begin with. Why don't you two go and have a stroll and enjoy summer while we've got it.'

'Good idea,' said Mr Jenkins. 'This place gives me the creeps.'

When their clients were safely out of the way, Flora looked at Charles.

'I'm sorry,' he said. 'I had no idea it would be as bad as this . . . but on the other hand,' he went on after a pause, 'it's as well to know how bad the job can be.'

'Yes,' agreed Flora, aware that her reaction was a sort of test. One little wrinkle of her nose and she'd be castigated for being squeamish.

'I'm glad Annabelle didn't come. She'd be retching and heaving and having a fit.'

'It is a bit gag-making,' said Flora, who was breathing through her mouth so as not to have to endure the smell. 'Have you really seen much worse than this?'

Charles shook his head. 'I don't suppose so, although you do get used to some pretty dire situations.' He sighed. 'It was nice of you to buy the biscuits.'

'It was nice of you to tell them to go for a walk.'

'We'll get on much quicker without them.' He shrugged off her compliment as if it were a cobweb.

'Shall we make a start, then?' said Flora, a little hurt, but determined not to show it. She had just started to warm to him, because he'd been so nice to the people, then he went cold on her again. 'Here are your rubber gloves.'

'Right,' said Charles, when he had pulled them on. 'A collection of enamelware. Twenty to fifty pounds. A nineteen-thirties kitchen cupboard, it's in fairly good condition under the grime, possibly fifty to seventy.'

Flora started writing, hoping she'd be able to read it later.

Charles took Mr and Mrs Jenkins to the pub for lunch, an expense Flora was quite sure would never be claimed from petty cash.

'We're going to need to go back in there this afternoon,' he explained, 'but I suggest you stay out of the way. When we've done our valuation and you've

111

decided what to keep, I'll contact the removal firm, the house-clearance people and the cleaners.'

'I'm sure we don't want anything from there.' Mr Jenkins put his glass down with a shudder. 'It would never feel clean.'

'There are some quite valuable pieces,' said Charles and Flora remembered removing half a dozen bottles of sour milk so he could inspect a sofa table. She had retched but Charles had carried on with the work.

'It would be wonderful if you could arrange all that,' said Mrs Jenkins. 'My husband's right. I'm sure we don't want anything and I just can't cope with the mess. It's so squalid, I feel ashamed.'

'We all have eccentric relations,' said Charles, casting a quick glance in Flora's direction so she was in no doubt about whom he was referring to. 'They often have eccentric wills, too.'

'We're spared that,' said Mrs Jenkins. 'I'm his only surviving relative. Really, Mr Stanza, you've been very kind. I don't know how we're going to repay you.'

'Well, there's a seller's premium and a small lotting fee,' said Charles with another of his charming smiles. 'So I'll be making lots of money out of you.'

Seeing the way he was with this upset, embarrassed woman made Flora warm to him. He had a stuffy and conventional veneer but not far beneath it was a man who could be very kind and very tactful. He would just never be like that with her.

They were on the way home, both exhausted and in need of steam cleaning and sterilisation (or at least, that was how Flora felt), when Flora's phone went.

'Is that you, Flora?'

'Annabelle? Do you want Charles? I'll just wait till he's pulled over and pass him the phone.'

'No! It's not him I want, it's you! But not when Charles is there, I want to speak to you alone.'

She sounded rather odd and Flora's stomach churned. What could be the matter? Had Imelda taken a fit and ruined the cottage? Or worse, and much more likely, had she discovered William? But if so, why would she want to talk to her on her own about it? Surely Annabelle could rant and rave on that subject in Charles's hearing. 'Of course, Annabelle,' said Flora meekly. 'When would be convenient?'

'What does Annabelle want?' asked Charles. 'Hang on, I'll pull over.'

'No, it's me she wants.'

But it was too late. A handy lay-by had appeared and Charles had swung into it before Flora had finished speaking. He took the phone from her. 'Darling? What is it? Ghastly valuation. I'm so glad you weren't there.'

Flora harrumphed in her seat. He wouldn't want Annabelle having to deal with sour milk and filth, rat droppings and cockroaches, but for her it was considered good training.

Charles handed back the phone. 'She wants to discuss the inventory with you. She'll meet you in the Coach and Horses. It opens at six. I'll drop you off and she can take you to the office to pick up the Land-Rover.'

'Hang on! Annabelle?' But Annabelle had disconnected. 'I'm filthy, Charles! Besides, it's choir night.'

He frowned. 'Is that so important to you? You've only

113

just joined, after all. You can't be making such a huge contribution yet.'

This hurt, but she ignored it. 'Maybe not, but they welcomed me in. I can't just not turn up.'

'And you can't leave Annabelle at the Coach and Horses. I do think you should make some effort to get on with her, Flora.'

'But I'm filthy! I probably stink! Wouldn't Annabelle understand if I told her I needed to go home and change?'

'I'm sure she'd understand but I'm not sure she'd appreciate it. Give her a call and say you can't be long. Shall I find the number for you?' He made to take her phone from her.

'No, it's OK,' she snapped, 'I've got it. Annabelle? I won't be able to stay long because I'm really grubby and must check on my cat. It's choir tonight or I'd do that all first and meet you later.'

'In my experience you always get dirty doing valuations,' Annabelle said loftily. 'It's one of the reasons I hate doing them. OK. We'll sit in the snug. There won't be anyone we know in there.'

If Flora hadn't been suffering from a guilty conscience about allowing William to stay, she would never have agreed to meet Annabelle.

'It looks like it's my turn to cook tonight again,' said Charles a few moments later, making what would qualify for anyone else as polite conversation.

'Oh.' In spite of herself, Flora was surprised. 'Do you cook often?'

'Oh yes. Annabelle always cooks if we entertain, but the humdrum stuff gets left for me, mostly.'

Flora felt an unexpected pang of sympathy. He'd had

114

a very long day. He probably didn't want to start cooking the moment he got home. 'If I were you, I'd get a take-away, or go out.'

Charles sighed. 'I probably will. I've got a lot of phoning to do when I get in and I won't have time to do much in the way of cooking.'

'You went the extra mile for those people today, didn't you? You could have just given them the names of the house-clearance people, and the removal firm. You didn't have to say you'd arrange it all.'

He shrugged. 'I felt sorry for them, that's all.' He brightened up. 'Although there's quite a valuable estate underneath the squalor.'

Flora did the best she could in the pub's Ladies', but apart from getting the streaks of dust off her face, there wasn't much she could do. Already her standards had slipped, she thought, turning up at a pub wearing clothes she'd been doing a mucky job in all day.

Annabelle had already ordered two glasses of mineral water and was looking quite untidy too. She was fiddling with her hairband, trying to put it back in, but not doing very well, for some reason.

'Here,' said Flora, taking it from her. 'Let me help.' She put the Alice band on the table. 'Much better.'

'Oh, but . . .' began Annabelle, and then said, 'Perhaps you're right.'

'What did you want to see me about?' asked Flora.

Annabelle sat forward in her seat. 'Well, when I was at the cottage, taking the inventory, I saw a man.'

'Oh no,' said Flora nervously, unable to decide if she should admit to knowing William or not.

'He was in the garden, doing some sort of exercises. He was stark naked.'

'Oh my God!' Flora was genuinely shocked this time. 'Did you call the police?' Really, William was the giddy limit! He had the whole damn forest to prance about naked in, why did he choose to do it in her garden?

'No!' said Annabelle, leaning closer. 'He looked – I mean, he didn't look like a criminal, or anything. He wasn't doing any harm. It was just very odd.'

'Oh,' said Flora again, surprised. She hadn't expected Annabelle to discriminate – any naked man in the garden was trespassing, surely?

'Flora' – Annabelle gave her a hard look – 'do you know him?'

Flora took a long sip of her mineral water, wishing for a minute that it was something stronger, like a magic potion that would spirit her away. 'I may do,' she said cautiously. 'Of course, I don't know for sure.'

'Flora! How could you?' Annabelle looked furious. 'I lend you my cottage, and within a week you've got strange men moving in!'

Flora flushed angrily. 'Well, that's not exactly—'

'I'm honestly shocked, Flora, I really am.' Annabelle was clearly determined not to let her get a word in. 'And I can't imagine what Charles will say!'

'Oh, for God's sake, Annabelle. Stop over-reacting,' Flora snapped, and then took a breath to regain her temper. She couldn't quite imagine what Charles would say either – and didn't particularly fancy finding out. 'I think,' she said in a calmer tone of voice, 'that he may be . . . er . . . a friend of a friend,' she improvised. 'Perfectly harmless,' she added in what she hoped was a reassuring way.

'Well, I don't know, Flora.' Annabelle didn't look re-assured. 'Will he be back?'

'It's possible,' Flora admitted. 'But I'm not at all sure Charles needs to be bothered with something like this. I know he's terribly busy, and . . .' Her voice trailed away as Annabelle gave her a long stare which made it perfectly clear that she knew full well that Flora wasn't thinking about Charles's best interests.

'OK then,' Annabelle said after a moment's thought. 'But if you're going to have a strange naked man hanging around my cottage I need to meet him. I'll have to check him out.'

Flora frowned. 'Check him out how, exactly?'

Registering Flora's confusion, Annabelle erupted into a peal of nervous laughter. 'Oh, don't be ridiculous! I don't want to check him out like that! Just check he's not a burglar.'

Flora was very tired. She wanted to go home, see her cat, have a proper drink and something to eat before she had to rush out for choir. 'I'll see what I can do, Annabelle, as long as you promise never to wear that Alice band again.'

'Don't you think it suits me?'

'I think it makes you look like a horse.'

Chapter Seven

'You don't really think I look like a horse, do you?'

Annabelle's expression of horror filled Flora with compassion and guilt. She shouldn't have been so outspoken, and if Annabelle hadn't been so annoying about William, she wouldn't have let her mouth get away with her like that. But the truth was out now and nothing Flora could do could put it back in again whole. She'd just have to backtrack as best she could.

'Well . . . not really. No, of course not, Annabelle, I'm just awfully tired. I spoke without thinking.'

'Oh.' Annabelle still sounded despondent; it was strangely pathetic.

'And I was a bit – surprised – by you telling me there was a man in my garden,' she added.

'A naked man,' said Annabelle.

'That's it. A naked man. Very shocking. I'll do my best to—'

'Although he was rather beautiful, in an aesthetic way.'

'Was he?' Flora squeaked. She would not have put Annabelle down as someone who saw men's bodies as aesthetic.

'Mm. The thing is, what am I going to say to Charles about him?'

'Well, I definitely wouldn't mention you thought he

was beautiful,' said Flora, knowing this was not the right answer.

'You know what I mean, Flora. Charles is already very unhappy about you being here. If I tell him I saw a naked man in your garden, he'll pack you off to London before you have time to put on your lip-gloss.'

Flora took a deep breath, then a sip of mineral water. She needed time to think. 'Charles could hardly blame me if – the man – is nothing to do with me. Just a friend of a friend.'

'Charles could blame you if there was a cyclone and the crops were ruined.'

This was the plain truth, there was no denying it. 'Unless you didn't tell him,' suggested Flora, not at all happy to find herself at Annabelle's mercy.

'Exactly.'

Flora frowned. 'But why wouldn't you tell him? You don't want me here either, do you?'

Annabelle flapped a hand. 'Look, shall we get proper drinks?'

'I shouldn't.' Flora got to her feet. If she really hurried, she should have time to get back home to feed Imelda and throw another layer of clothes on top of her dirt. 'It's choir night.'

'Sit down, Flora.'

Flora sat.

'I won't say anything to Charles because relations are already bad enough between you, but you must arrange for me to meet this man so I can check him out. If he's a bad lot, I'll have to report him to the police.'

'But supposing when I get back I find out he's not this friend's friend. Suppose he's nothing to do with me?'

Annabelle looked her firmly in the eye. 'I think what would be a good idea would be for you to arrange a little dinner party, so Charles and I can meet this man under civilised circumstances.' She paused, to make sure Flora knew that any stories she might come up with of finding no trace of anyone when she got home would not wash with her, then she said, 'I'm going to get us both a glass of wine now.'

She certainly went in for straight talking, thought Flora, while she waited. You had to hand it to her.

When Annabelle came back with the wine and sat down again she said, 'Now, there's something else I'd like your help with.'

Although her words were her usual 'order-poorly-disguised-as-a-request' type, there was something a bit more tentative in her manner than usual. Flora sipped her wine.

Annabelle sipped hers, too. 'I wouldn't usually ask you about anything as you're obviously much younger and completely . . . I mean, well . . . Anyway, you are quite pretty.'

'Yes?' Flora wasn't going to waste time arguing about her looks.

'I've been invited to a school reunion.'

'Oh.'

'And' – Annabelle looked momentarily embarrassed – 'and I really want to look my best. I wonder if you could give me some tips on how to improve my appearance?'

Flora translated this as: 'You're a complete nit-wit but men seem to fancy you – tell me your secrets.' She sighed. She was often dismissed as being pretty and blonde as if these two things combined precluded any ability in any sphere except shopping.

'Well . . .'

'I was just wondering if it's a bad thing that I always go shopping with Mummy?'

Flora thought how best to phrase her reply. 'I don't think it's a bad idea in principle. I quite often go shopping with my mother when we're in the same country, but the difference may be that she always takes my fashion advice, not the other way around.'

Annabelle sighed. 'I've never much cared about fashion. I just want to look tidy and reasonably smart. But . . .'

There was a horrible pause while Flora waited for what she knew would follow.

'I think men may like women to be pretty, don't you?'

'There won't be any men at your school reunion, will there?' If Annabelle had gone anywhere that wasn't a clone of Benenden or Roedean, Flora would eat her filthy dress.

'Well, no, but women are more critical, don't you think?'

'Well, yes, but Charles obviously likes you the way you are. You don't need to change anything for him.'

'I know that!' Reassuringly, Annabelle reverted to type. 'I just don't want to turn up at the school reunion looking . . . like a horse.'

Flora resigned herself to missing choir. She would go and ring Geoffrey in a minute. 'I only said that—'

'I know, but many a true word spoken in jest, or something. I have become aware, since you've been here, that perhaps I dress a little . . .' She paused again.

121

Flora waited, not daring to fill the word in for her. 'In a rather old-fashioned way and if you could see your way to helping me, I would be very grateful.'

'Of course, I'd be happy to help.' Particularly, Flora added to herself, if that stops you telling Charles about my houseguest.

'Would you?'

Mischievously, Flora was suddenly struck by a vision of Charles's face, confronted with an Annabelle decked out in strappy dress and kitten heels. 'But you don't think Charles would mind if you looked completely different?'

'Well, I won't look completely different and even if I did, our relationship is very solid, you know. It's not likely to be affected by mere clothes.'

That was clothes put in their place! 'Oh?'

'Our relationship is based on all we have in common: companionship, a business we share. Well, nearly share,' Annabelle added.

'What about love?' asked Flora rashly. Possibly love was too frivolous an emotion for the likes of Charles and Annabelle.

'Of course I love Charles,' said Annabelle. 'And I know he loves me, very much.' She paused for a moment. 'Look, Flora. I know you think Charles is stuffy and old-fashioned, and I know you think I'm far too uptight.'

Flora started to protest, but Annabelle was on a roll.

'I can see it in your eyes every time we talk, and it's fine. Really. I can't imagine being you, and you can't imagine being me. You can't appreciate what Charles sees in me or what I see in him. But I have to tell you, Charles and I are completely committed to each other. We've been friends for ever – I can't remember a time I didn't plan to marry him – and knowing that we're going to be together for the rest of our lives makes us both very happy.'

Flora didn't think they looked very happy, but Annabelle's little speech was the most passionate thing Flora had ever heard come out of her mouth. She felt rather guilty over her musings about whether their engagement was almost a business arrangement.

'And so I don't think a few new clothes and a haircut are going to change any of that, do you? Charles has been in love with me his whole life.'

Flora finished her wine. She hadn't the heart to go to choir now, even if she would just make it if she ran.

'So shall we make a date to go shopping sometime, then?' went on Annabelle, unaware of Flora's low spirits.

'If you really want me to, of course I will.' She could hardly refuse a few fashion tips. Charles might well appreciate a less horse-like Annabelle. Those pie-crust collars must irritate any sensible man.

'In that case, I'll press on. I think I might cook Charles something rather delicious for supper. Oh, and you won't forget about the dinner, will you?'

William was making a stir-fry when Flora got in. She didn't know if she was delighted to see him because he'd cooked and taken care of Imelda and was a friend, or furious with him for letting himself be seen by Annabelle.

'I have had such a day!' she told him, gratefully accepting the chilled glass he handed her.

'You're back late,' he said mildly, looking into his glass as if for portents of the future.

'I had to go and have a drink with someone after work and miss choir.' She frowned at him. 'It's all your fault.'

'My fault? Why?'

Flora sank on to the sofa and pulled a cushion into the small of her back. Considering how many sofas must go through their hands, she thought, you would have thought they'd have provided their holiday cottage with a more comfortable one. 'Because Annabelle, who's sort of my boss, engaged to my cousin, saw you here today.'

'But I didn't come into the house. I heard a car and kept out of the way.'

'You were doing exercises in the garden, naked.'

'T'ai chi. And I was not in the garden. I was only just out of the woodland. I really didn't know anyone could see me. I am so sorry.'

Flora sighed. She knew she should be angry, but just didn't have the energy. 'I think you're the one who may be sorry. Annabelle wants to meet you. Just to check you're not a sinister person she should report to the police. And I warn you, she's terrifying.' Annabelle on the prowl would daunt anyone, even laid-back William.

'Is she really? Why is that?'

'She just is. She's very businesslike and efficient.'

'Is she pretty?'

Flora felt very tired indeed. 'Not yet.'

'How do you mean?'

'She wants a few tips on style and stuff. She's asked me to help her. She's got a school reunion coming up and wants to look her best.'

'Well, I'm sure you're just the girl.' His gaze flicked

over her, with, she noted, a certain amount of approval, but no real desire.

It was odd, Flora realised, but she didn't fancy him, either. It was probably why they had become so relaxed with each other so quickly – sex hadn't reared its ugly head between them.

'I'm sure I am. Once I've got her underwear sorted out we can get somewhere.'

'Underwear's important, is it?'

Flora nodded. 'If you've got substantial breasts, definitely. Annabelle's currently wearing what is known in the trade as sheepdogs. They round them up and point them in the right direction, but they do nothing for shape.'

William was starting to look more interested and Flora wondered idly if perhaps she shouldn't have mentioned Annabelle's breasts. Partly to change the subject, she said, 'And now I've got to think up who you should be.'

'What on earth are you talking about?'

'I mean, I'm supposed to try and find out about you and invite you to dinner, so she can give you the once-over.'

'Couldn't you just tell her there was no trace of anyone when you got home?'

Flora shook her head. 'She didn't put it in so many words, but she made it pretty clear that she'd tell Charles about you if I didn't let her check you're not a psychopath.' She bit her lip for a moment. 'I suppose I could say I found a note from you, that you're a friend of a friend come to call, who obviously just took the opportunity to do a bit of t'ai chi in the buff when he was in

125

an isolated spot.' She paused. 'I'm really surprised Annabelle didn't call the police.'

'Why should she? I wasn't doing any harm.'

'Annabelle would consider trespassing harm, and I would have thought she'd have considered nakedness a police matter, too.'

'But she didn't.'

'No, but we still have to explain your presence without them finding out you've been living here all winter. I'll say you're a friend of a friend who lived near and came to look me up. That suit you?'

'I have been living on my own for a while, but do you think someone looking up the friend of a friend would be likely to take off all their clothes and do a spot of t'ai chi while they're waiting?'

'Well . . . yes, if that's your bag. After all, there can't be many opportunities for doing stuff like that.'

William nodded, conceding this point.

'Let's eat, William. I'm starving.'

When supper was disposed of, the kittens had been marvelled over, and William had decided to go to his shack in the forest, Flora found a spot in the garden that had reasonable reception and called Emma.

'Is this a good moment?' she pleaded, when Emma picked up the phone.

'Yes. Dave's out. I'm just watching a movie and it's not very good. It's a perfect time to ring.'

'Thank goodness. I need advice, Em!'

'Really? Well, on the whole green is considered the best colour for wellies but you could get away with blue at a pinch.'

'What are you talking about? Now listen, Annabelle, who's engaged to my cousin Charles, and wants to buy me out of the business, well, not completely, but a bit . . .'

'Go on.' Emma was obviously on the move. 'I'm just going into the kitchen to make a cup of tea.'

'Anyway, she saw this man William, who's been living here in the holiday cottage all winter, and is still around.'

'Nice?'

'Very.'

'Fit?'

'Well, I suppose so but definitely not my type. Although Annabelle tells me that upside down and naked he is – what did she say? – aesthetically beautiful.'

'He sounds extraordinary. If you want him, I'd take him.' Emma sighed a little wistfully.

'I don't want him. I want you to listen to me. You see the thing is, Emma, Annabelle has more or less ordered me to have a dinner party so she can meet him.'

'And?'

'Well, should I introduce Annabelle to William?'

Emma thought for a moment. 'Sorry, Flora, I don't see the problem. I really don't see why you shouldn't have a little dinner party and introduce this Annabelle to the naked man.'

Flora sighed. 'That sounds so easy in theory, but you don't know Charles! Having him, Annabelle and William round for dinner would be torture. No one would have anything in common, it would be ghastly!'

'Well, invite some other people then! That way you won't notice Charles so much.'

Flora felt that however many people she asked she was bound to notice Charles. He took up quite a lot of space. But it would certainly dilute him. 'That is a good idea. I could invite Henry.'

'Who's Henry?'

'Oh, someone I met in the supermarket when I first arrived. We haven't actually been out yet, but he's very nice.'

'You met him in the supermarket? You're so jammy! The only people I meet in the supermarket are other wild-eyed singletons looking for low-fat Chardonnay. We bond over the fromage frais.'

'I may not be jammy, he may not turn out to be any good at all, but it's nice to have someone to think about. The trouble is, I haven't got his number. But with luck, I'll run into him soon. Annabelle didn't give me a date for this dinner party, after all.'

'I should check him over for you,' said Emma. 'Make sure he's not another Justin.'

'You can't tell just by looking. And do you know, Justin was at school with Charles! But I've just had a brilliant idea! If you came down for a weekend, you could come to the dinner party. That would make it much more fun.'

Emma laughed. 'A dinner party with your stuffy cousin and his ghastly fiancée does sound tempting, but on the other hand, we could wait for you to come back to London and have a really nice time.'

'I'm not doing that! I've only been here five minutes and I'm beginning to love it. The whole auction house thing is so exciting, even though I spent all day today in a filthy house looking at furniture. It's terribly hard work but so fascinating.'

Emma spoke in tones she normally used when confronted by a psychopath on the tube. 'Well, honey, if that's the way you feel about it, I don't think I can help you. You need a professional.'

Flora ignored this slight on her sanity. 'I've just had a thought.'

'Go on.'

'If you came down for the weekend, I could say that William is a friend of yours.'

'I don't think I'd have a friend who took off their clothes in other people's gardens.'

'Well, no, but you wouldn't necessarily have known about his passion for naked yoga, or whatever. I think that's a very good idea. Now, when can you come?'

Emma sighed. 'I'd quite like to come down. I don't suppose Dave would be able to get away.'

'That's perfect! I mean, it's a shame, but it's perfect from my point of view. You and William could be a couple.'

'I don't quite understand what your thinking is on this one, Flo.'

'I don't either, but come down, one weekend some-time soon, and we can make a plan when you get here.'

'I'll see what I can do. It's not easy at the moment.'

'Oh darling!'

'But don't worry, I'll try to sort something out.'

'Annabelle tells me she saw a man at your house yesterday.'

The wretch! Annabelle had definitely said she wouldn't tell Charles if Flora agreed to have a dinner party! Determined to keep her cool for as long as possible, she said, 'Hi, Charles, I'm fine. Yes, it is a lovely day, but it looks like rain later. Though we do need it.' Bloody Annabelle! And bloody Charles! He might have said hello before he confronted her about William.

'Who is he?'

'Well, when Annabelle first told me about him, I hadn't a clue, but when I got back I found a note. He's a friend of a friend in London. He lives quite near here. Not sure where,' she went on quickly, before he could ask her awkward questions. 'The friend thought I might be lonely and asked him to look me up.'

This sounded feasible as long as Annabelle hadn't mentioned the naked t'ai chi.

'Oh. Right. So you didn't meet him yourself?'

To lie or not to lie? 'No. He might be calling again tonight. He's going to give me a ring on my mobile. Talking of which, any chance of that land line? The reception's not good there.'

He frowned. 'Sorry, yes. I'll get on to it. And would you mind making a start on typing up that valuation we did yesterday? Louisa is off and I want to get it done as soon as possible. I realise it's not what you do, but I would really appreciate it. Louisa can do it properly next week, but it would save her some time.'

'No probs, Charles,' said Flora, keen to be helpful. 'I'll get started just as soon as I've hung up my jacket. Is the computer on? There is a computer, isn't there? Not just an ancient Underwood typewriter that didn't sell in an auction?'

Charles almost smiled. 'No, there is a computer. Just

do as much as you can. Annabelle said something about you wanting to go shopping.'

Trust Annabelle to make her out to be the one in need of retail therapy. 'I don't want to sound patronising, but to me shopping means London, Paris, New York, Milan if you're in Italy, not some jumped-up market town. It's Annabelle who wants to go, for her school reunion, but if I've got work to do, she can go on her own. Or with her mother.'

'Keep your hair on. You're perfectly entitled to take time off whenever you like, you don't work for us.'

'Oh yes I do, Charles,' she replied, somewhat disconcerted that he seemed to have forgotten. 'Now point me in the direction of the computer and I'll get on.'

By the time Annabelle arrived to take her shopping at about two o'clock, Flora had not only typed the valuation, but she'd taken advantage of being entirely alone to have a good prowl round the building.

Annabelle came in looking prettier already, partly because her hair was loose and clean. It still needed a good cut, though. 'Charles told me I'd find you typing. I expect you hunt and peck?'

'I don't hunt, Annabelle. I think it's cruel.'

'I didn't mean that sort of hunting. I meant typing, but never mind, you can leave it now. Louisa will do it later. There's no great hurry, after all.'

Flora picked up her jacket, not disclosing that she was in fact a very fast touch typist. Her mother had once told her, 'Learn to type, it's useful, but don't tell anyone or you may not get to do anything else.'

'Where are we going shopping, then? Bristol?'

Annabelle looked shocked. 'Do we need to go so far?'

'I think we do. Now, shall we lock up?'

'I'll do it.'

'And, Annabelle,' said Flora as she watched her set the burglar alarm and memorised the numbers, just in case, 'you said you wouldn't tell Charles about . . . the man, and you did.'

'I know,' said Annabelle breezily, making the building ring with the sound of the alarm. 'I changed my mind. He was surprisingly cool about it,' she went on, as they came out into the street, all safe and quiet behind them. 'I think he's coming round to the idea of you.'

Chapter Eight

'Yes, you do have to be fitted. It's the most important thing. Get measured properly. My mother taught me that.' This last accompanied a shove in the back which finally got Annabelle into the changing room.

The kindly sales assistant added, 'I'll check your size and then go and find some bras I think might suit you.'

'And I'll be back when you're in one of them,' said Flora. 'Now I'm going to buy knickers.'

In fact, having forced Annabelle to be measured, Flora picked up a few bras that were in the sale and didn't even think of trying them on. Her mother had indeed given her that sound advice and Flora believed it wholeheartedly. She just didn't think her size 34 B needed quite as much attention as Annabelle's double D cup.

She was queuing up to pay for them when she became aware of a man behind her. It was Henry. She laughed.

'I know, I know, what's a man doing in the lingerie department?' he said.

'Obviously shopping.' Flora indicated the pile of cotton in his hand. 'For you?'

'No! My sister. It's her birthday tomorrow. I was buying a card the other day but I didn't find anything in the abbey shop that she would want that I could post.'

'So, what have you bought her?'

'A nightie – it's what she said she wanted. Do you think she'll like it?' He held up a rather mumsy white nightie which would certainly leave everything to the imagination.

'It's . . . er . . . lovely. I'm sure she'll be thrilled.'

'Oh good. I'm just not sure of her size.'

'Oh my goodness! Don't tell me you're buying her clothes and you don't know her size!'

'Is that very bad?'

'It's a disaster! Have you any idea at all?'

'Well.' He regarded Flora for rather a long time. 'She's probably about the same as you are.'

Flora took hold of the offending item and checked the size. 'This is a sixteen. If she's my size it'll be much too big.'

'I'll go and get a couple of sizes down then,' he said meekly.

'Sorry, Henry, but just think how horrible your sister would feel if she thought you thought she looked two sizes bigger then she is.'

He shrugged. 'It seemed sort of roomy, but I thought it'd be OK.'

'No. OK is not good enough. Off you go.'

'I will if you give me your telephone number,' he said with the twinkle she remembered from the abbey card shop.

Flora smiled and let the lady standing behind Henry, who'd been enjoying their exchanges, go in front of her. 'Only if you give me yours.'

'It's a deal.'

* * *

'I still don't see the point of spending so much money on something that won't ever be seen!' said Annabelle a little later.

'Charles will see them, and the rest of the world will see the effect,' insisted Flora. 'Feel good on the inside and you'll look good on the outside.'

'Is that something else your mother told you?'

'No, but it's just the sort of thing she would say. Look, I've bought you the matching knickers for the black and the red bra.'

'Oh! That's very kind. They were a horrendous price.'

'I know, but it would be a shame to spoil the shop for a ha'p'orth of knickers. Now, let's make a move on to Ladies' Fashion. It's much better to go to the little shops, really, but I don't know where they are.'

Forcing Annabelle, even in one of her new bras, into a V-necked top was almost beyond Flora's powers of persuasion. She had to get a sales assistant on her side and between them they eventually convinced Annabelle that showing a bit of chest was not slutty, but was, in fact, very attractive.

'Oh, Annabelle! You look lovely! You've got great boobs now we can see you haven't got four of them. Let's find a skirt to go with that top. Does it come in other colours?'

'Yes. White, black and scarlet.'

'Let's see the scarlet. It may not be your colour, but definitely the black and white.' Flora frowned. 'We should probably get your colours done, only you may not want to bother.'

'My colours done? What are you talking about?' Annabelle, who'd begun to like the image of herself with a cleavage, now regarded Flora with alarm.

'It's great fun,' said the assistant. 'You find out which colours suit you and which don't.'

Annabelle became thoughtful. 'I mostly stick with navy blue.'

'You may want to be a bit more adventurous than that,' suggested the assistant tactfully. 'Let's find you some skirts. I've got a lovely fuchsia linen.'

'I don't wear fuchsia.'

'Why not?'

'I just don't.'

Flora hissed with irritation. 'Get back in that changing room,' she ordered, 'and do as you're told for once.'

Then she wondered if the power had gone to her head.

Later, any regrets about bullying Annabelle disappeared. Sartorially, Annabelle was vastly improved.

'Charles is going to be absolutely thrilled,' Flora said, wondering if she was mad for going to so much trouble to make a woman she barely liked look so gorgeous. 'Now I want to go through your wardrobe and get rid of all the things you shouldn't wear.'

'I can't get rid of perfectly good clothes! I always buy the best quality.' Annabelle was clinging on manfully to the remnants of her bad taste.

'But, sweetie, if the clothes make you look like a dog you shouldn't wear them. It's bad for you to feel un-attractive, and now you know how gorgeous you can look, you won't be happy looking ungorgeous.'

'I don't think that's a word,' said Annabelle, petulant but compliant.

136

Flora softened. Annabelle really was being very good. 'If you think it's wasteful to have a clear-out we could have one of those parties where everyone prices up their old clothes and then buys them from each other. Most of the money goes to charity, but you can take a cut if you like. You have wine and nibbles. It's a great evening out, usually. One person's expensive mistake may well become another woman's favourite outfit. Someone's mother is bound to like pie-crust collars and navy blue.' Flora frowned. 'The trouble is I don't know anyone round here, really, and I don't suppose your friends . . .?'

'No.' Annabelle was very firm. 'My friends would not enjoy buying second-hand clothes.'

'Even from each other? For charity?'

'I don't think the Conservative Party needs us to go to quite those lengths yet.'

Flora laughed. 'OK, no need to sound quite so head-mistressy. It was only an idea. But I do want those pussy-cat bows out of your wardrobe. They can go to the charity shop.'

Flora would really have preferred to go home, but she stuck with Annabelle not only to continue with the revamping process, but because she wanted to find out what really excited Annabelle, something that would take all her time and attention. Annabelle needed a hobby of her own, something to replace the auction house that she would enjoy and be good at, so that Flora could get on with dragging Stanza and Stanza into the real world, and from there, with luck, into profit. And she also wanted to see the look on Charles's face when he saw his new fiancée.

It was the first time Flora had been into Charles and Annabelle's house. Having parked the Land-Rover in the little street next door, she followed Annabelle up the front steps with strangely mixed feelings.

What she saw was partly a relief and partly a disappointment, it was so predictable. She should have been able to predict the pale, safe colours, the polished wood floors, the textbook good taste that had no individuality. Everything was smooth and immaculate, and although some of the things were obviously old – the fire basket and the chimney-pot-turned-vase – they were all restored to within an inch of their lives. She scanned the walls for something, a picture, a photograph, which indicated the personalities of the inhabitants, but found nothing. A few old maps of the county, an enormously fat pig, which on inspection proved a modern reproduction, and a portrait of a lady in pearls, was all there was. Flora, depressed, felt she already knew the answer to her first question. 'Do you and Charles own this house together? It's lovely.'

'No, it's mine.' Annabelle kicked off her low-heeled loafers. 'I'm glad you like it. Would you like something to drink before we go upstairs? Come on, let's open a bottle of wine. I'll get Charles to run you home later.'

'Or I could take a taxi. Charles could pick me up for work tomorrow.'

'No! Don't be silly. Charles won't mind.'

'He might want a drink himself when he gets in.'

'Well, he can wait.'

Flora wished she had the strength of character to stick to mineral water herself and so be able to drive home, but the thought of a glass of wine was far too tempting.

After the day she'd had, she felt she deserved it. Annabelle was very hard work, and might be less so if both their senses were a little dulled by a nice, crisp Chardonnay.

When Annabelle, showing a generosity Flora hadn't suspected, had filled two huge glasses to the brim with wine, she said, 'Come on then. Let's go upstairs and carry on with this.'

Flora, following her, aware that if she drank even half that amount of wine driving herself home was out of the question, decided that abandoning the Land-Rover was the only answer.

Annabelle led the way into a thickly carpeted bedroom that was as bland and tasteful as the sitting room. She pulled open the door of a row of mirror-fronted cupboards.

'Oh Annabelle! What a fantastic wardrobe!' Flora, who had taken a hefty sip of wine on her way up the stairs, sank on to the bed and stared at the masterpiece of space-saving, categorising and colour co-ordinating before her.

'I thought you'd come to trash my wardrobe,' commented Annabelle, taking a deep drink from her own glass.

'The contents, not the thing itself. It's completely fab. I want one.'

'Not in the holiday cottage you don't.'

'No, but where I end up eventually.'

'I got a firm in to do it for me. Charles was all for getting a little local man to do it, but I felt I wanted a professional. It's an investment, really. It will add value to the house.'

'Quite right,' said Flora, not sure she agreed with herself. 'Now, let's get started.' If they hung around too long they would both fall asleep and Charles would find them on the bed together, possibly snoring lightly, which would worry him in all sorts of ways. Besides, she was beginning to miss her kittens. 'All round-necked jumpers, out.'

'But—'

'They make your boobs look like bolsters, even with the new bras. You can try one if you don't believe me. Oh, and polo-necks.'

'But it gets so cold in winter!'

'OK, keep the polo-necks, but just remember they won't flatter you.'

The super-de luxe wardrobe system meant a pile of unsuitable sweaters were soon placed neatly on the floor.

Flora now got off the bed and started going through the rail designated for shirts and blouses. 'Pie-crust, pie-crust, pussy-cat bows.' A pile of Liberty prints hit the floor. 'And any of these that go straight down should go really unless you promise to tuck them in. They should be a bit fitted, or you get too much bulk in your waistband. Those have to go anyway. Those flowers are too busy.'

'I always wear that under a jumper, so you only see the collar.'

'Would that be a jumper with a round neck?'

Annabelle nodded ruefully.

'Then you won't be needing it any more, will you?'

'But it's smart and comfortable. I like it.'

'It looks like a school uniform, only not in a sexy way.'

Flora fixed her with a steely eye as she added the shirt to the discard pile. 'I'm not sure the flowers are quite right with your skin. We really should get your colours done.'

'No, that's fine,' said Annabelle, obviously reluctant to submit to more tyranny. 'I trust you, Flora.'

'Good! Now, skirts. Oh, this is wonderful! They're all neatly together. This is so easy. Knee length box-pleats haven't come back yet, Annabelle, and I don't see it happening soon. Out! A kilt?' She looked at Annabelle who was looking a little pathetic as all her favourite outfits were cast aside. 'OK, you can keep the kilt, but promise me you'll only wear it in Scotland. Anywhere else it will make your hips look enormous.'

'But not enormous in Scotland?'

Flora chuckled. Perhaps Annabelle did have a sense of humour in there somewhere. 'In Scotland, they're allowed.'

In celebration of this dispensation, Annabelle went downstairs for the rest of the bottle.

'Shall I make some pasta and salad? I've got one of those fresh sauces we could have with it?' Annabelle tore open a packet of nuts with her teeth.

'It's sweet of you, Annabelle, but I'd like to get back. My cat and kittens, you know. But the nuts are lovely. Oh, look, a whole section for ball gowns. You are a party girl.'

'Hunt balls, mostly. Things like that. Oh, can't I keep that?'

'Royal blue is quite a difficult colour, Annabelle, and look how high cut it is. It won't show off your boobs and will cling to your stomach. You want something

141

low cut, but with sleeves. No frills, though,' she said, extracting something reminiscent of Princess Diana's wedding dress. 'When you're over thirty it's better to stick with something simple and sexy.'

'OK.' Glum but obedient, Annabelle put a handful of peanuts into her mouth.

'Now, shoes.'

'I have to be comfortable, Flora. It's no good trying to make me teeter about on high heels. I can't do it.'

Flora was merciful in defeat. 'Well, just promise me you'll buy one pair of black court shoes—'

'I have three pairs of black court shoes.'

'With heels. Even small heels. Just something. And remember, the more you pay for shoes the more comfortable they are.'

'Your mother's advice again?'

Flora tried to remember. 'I think it was more something she told my father after she'd spent a lot of money on some shoes. But it is true.'

They sank back on the bed and both dived into the nuts at the same time.

'This has been quite fun,' said Annabelle. 'I didn't expect it to be, but it has.'

'I think you'll enjoy the new you. I should take you up to London to get your hair cut, really, but I expect there's someone down here who's quite good.'

'You're positive I must have it a bit shorter?'

Flora nodded. 'And a few layers. It looks lovely now, for instance, when it's all mussed up from you trying on jumpers. And I was right about the bolster, wasn't I?'

'I suppose so. Now I want to go out and show off my

new look. When can you arrange that little dinner party? The one you're giving so I can check out the naked man in your garden.'

Flora giggled. 'You make it sound like there's always one there.'

'I suppose they do mostly come in bronze.' She sighed, and it occurred to Flora that she was probably very tired.

'I thought I'd do it when my friend from London, Emma, comes down for the weekend. She was at university with William.' The wine had gone to Flora's head a little and she couldn't remember if she was supposed to know William's name or not. She blundered on. 'It's more fun if there are several people there, don't you think?'

'Yes . . .' Like cats, they both became alert as they heard a key in the door. 'There's Charles.'

Flora shifted to the edge of the bed and got up. 'I'll run down and see him, tell him not to have a drink until he's driven me home, while you make sure you're looking completely fab.'

Annabelle got up off the bed and smoothed her top down over her skirt. 'OK, but there's no need for you to hurry down. We're up here, darling,' she called, hitching up her breasts. 'In the bedroom. Can you drive Flora home?'

Charles came up the stairs and stood in the doorway, half embarrassed, like a father at a teenage sleepover. He didn't know quite where to look. 'Oh my God!'

Flora felt a bit like a cross between a Fairy Godmother and a gooseberry. Annabelle was looking surprisingly sexy, and any normal man would want to do something about it. But not, apparently, Charles, who just stood and stared at her.

'Well, doesn't your fiancée look stunning in her new clothes?'

'She certainly looks different.'

'In a good way,' said Flora, determined to force him into the right reaction. 'Do a twirl, Annabelle.'

Annabelle twirled and Flora felt her hard work had paid off.

'The girls at the reunion will be very impressed,' said Flora. 'Fancy frumpy old Annabelle turning out to be so sexy.'

'The reunion?' said Annabelle. 'Oh, I'd forgotten about that for a moment.'

Charles was frowning. 'I think I liked you better the way you were before, pumpkin.'

'Oh, for goodness' sake!' said Flora, exasperated. 'She hasn't changed her whole personality! Just her clothes! And she looks gorgeous! Admit it.'

'Well, yes. I suppose she does.' Charles came further into the room and kissed Annabelle on the cheek and then on the lips. 'But beauty is only skin deep. It's what's inside that counts.'

Flora rolled her eyes. 'We all know that, we've been hearing it since we came out of the egg, but the point is, the inside is still the same! Annabelle is still Annabelle, she just looks younger and prettier and sexier.' It was certainly uphill work teaching Charles not to judge by appearances.

'Flora's right, you know,' said Annabelle. 'It's only my clothes and the way I wear them that's different. I'm still your little pumpkin inside.' Flora shuddered. 'By the way,' Annabelle went on, getting into the role that went with her new look. 'Flora needs a lift home, sweet-heart.'

'Oh.'

Flora didn't bother to check Charles's expression. He was bound to be looking like there was a poker fused to his spine. 'No, really. I'll order a taxi. I don't want you love-birds to be kept apart for another minute, and it's a good half-hour to the cottage, and then another back. Annabelle, cook Charles something delicious, and Charles, order me a cab. Please?'

Charles moved away from Annabelle and came to look sternly at Flora. 'I'm perfectly happy to drive you.'

This was a bit of a surprise. 'No, honestly. I'd much rather take a taxi.'

'Are you sure?'

'Of course she's sure,' said Annabelle. 'She's not a child, even if she does look rather young. And do you know, sweetie? Flora's going to invite us for dinner when her friend comes to stay. Such fun.'

Oh God! She'd have to do it now Charles knew about it. Why did she drink all that wine? Look at the trouble it was getting her into. Perhaps Emma was right, and living in the country had got to her, and not in a good way.

'You will have to get me a dining table first, though. I couldn't have you eating on your laps.'

'I can certainly arrange that,' said Charles. 'Come down and we'll phone for a taxi. Are you coming, darling?'

'I just want to tidy myself a little,' said Annabelle. 'My hair's a mess.'

'Annabelle,' said Flora warningly. 'You're not to put that headband back on!'

'You see, Charles?' she said to him as they walked down the stairs. 'She may have changed on the outside, but she's still tidy Annabelle underneath.'

'I'm very relieved to hear it. I wouldn't like that aspect of my life being turned upside down, too.'

'What do you mean?' She turned to him as they reached the hallway.

'You've caused quite enough upset in my life without messing about with my perfectly satisfactory fiancée.'

Flora took a breath and then saw that Charles was almost smiling. 'Oh. You're teasing. I wish you'd warn me when you're going to. It's so unexpected, coming from you.'

'You could make me a little sign that I could hold up when I'm going to do it, like the bidders.'

Flora chuckled. 'It's a good idea, but it's unlikely to happen enough to make it worth my while.'

'Oh, I don't know about that. So, you girls have done some shopping?' He flicked through the *Yellow Pages*.

'Some. We've also done a lot of sorting out. But I want you to tell me if Annabelle doesn't make a trip to a charity shop very soon.'

'You're not telling me you've been shopping in charity shops?'

Flora couldn't tell if Charles's horror was his own, or on behalf of Annabelle. 'No,' she said coolly. 'We haven't. But a lot of Annabelle's current wardrobe is quite wrong for her and she should get rid of it. It's all in a pile. Well, a heap, really.'

146

'Oh.' Charles found a number and started pressing buttons.

'Do we advertise in the *Yellow Pages*?' she asked him while he was waiting to be connected.

'Just a small entry. Large ads are very expensive.'

'I really think you ought to have a proper advertisement, you know.'

'Most of our business comes from local people, who know about us.'

'But think of that valuation we did the other day. They weren't local, even if their uncle was. How did they know to ring you?'

'A friend of the uncle's recommended us.'

'But if he hadn't, and they came down here and wanted an auctioneer, what would they do?' As Charles seemed to be being rather slow, she answered for him. 'They'd look in the *Yellow Pages*.'

'Ah, yes. Can you take someone out to Fiddler's Wood, please?'

When the taxi was arranged, Flora continued, 'I want to have a talk about the business, Charles. I've had some ideas.'

'Have you?'

He was obviously very tired. His usually immaculate shirt and tie was looking a little rumpled. A strand of hair had fallen away from the rest. Flora had a sudden, almost irresistible urge to smooth it away. Only the fact that she couldn't have reached it unless he had bent down a little stopped her.

'I have. But we won't talk about them now, you look tired.'

'Oh, I'm all right. It's been a bit of a long day, that's

all. You won't want to come into the office tomorrow as it's Saturday, but I'll drop the Land-Rover off. Annabelle can follow me in her car and give me a lift back.'

'Are you working tomorrow then?'

'I have got a few bits and pieces to tie up, yes.'

'Then I'll come in too, at least for the morning. Apart from anything else, it'll save Annabelle having to come.' She frowned as she realised that she'd only achieved half her goals regarding Annabelle – she still hadn't found out what sort of business she would really like to go into. Though probably not anything connected with fashion.

'Are you sure?'

Something in Charles's tone made Flora vehement. 'Yes! It's my business too! Besides, I haven't got anything else on, much.'

'You wouldn't like a day to relax?'

'I'll do that on Sunday.'

'That's showing great dedication to duty, Flora.'

'Did you expect anything less?' She couldn't help teasing him just a little.

'If I did before, I certainly wouldn't dare now. Oh, and your car is ready, by the way. I'd collect you in it tomorrow, only there's something I want to deliver for the cottage that you might find useful.'

'That sounds exciting. It's not a dining table?'

'Alas, no.'

'And it's good about my car. I hope it wasn't horribly expensive.'

'Don't worry about that. And you can go on using the Land-Rover if you like.'

'I do like it.'

148

At last they heard someone coming up the front steps and ring the doorbell.

'I'll say goodbye, then,' said Flora.

'Goodnight, Flora.'

The following morning, she saw Charles's car come slowly down the lane and went out to meet him. She was feeling oddly jittery, although she didn't know why. He got out of the car and stood there while Flora came up to him.

'Hi, Charles, how are you?'

'Fine.'

'Did Annabelle give you a fashion show? She got some lovely things.'

'I think you've finally proved to me that it's not a good idea to try and judge a book by its cover, yes,' he said, with a twinkle oddly reminiscent of Henry's.

Flora smiled and bit her lip. 'Good!'

'Come and see what I've brought you. Not a dining table, but something a bit similar.'

It was a white painted metal table and two chairs for the garden.

'Oh, that's lovely! It will be perfect in the corner by the roses. I can just see myself sitting there with a glass of wine.' She frowned a little. 'Wasn't this, or something very like it, at the last sale? I seem to remember it went for a reasonable sum.'

'Yes, it did. I bought it. Geoffrey bid for me. I thought it was just what you needed here.'

'Is that legal? Buying stuff when you're the auctioneer?'

'As long as your bid is the highest, yes.'

'That's really kind, Charles, thank you.'

'I will make sure there's also something to eat off before . . . when is it?' It was his turn to look thoughtful. 'I hope Annabelle hasn't railroaded you into having a dinner party. She seemed very keen to come for some reason. I was very pleased, though,' he went on, 'I would really like Annabelle and you to become friends. She doesn't have many close women friends.'

'No?'

'It would be good for her to get some young company.'

'She's not that much older than me, Charles.'

'No, but currently her best friend is her mother, which is all very well, but I think you need friends your own age, don't you?'

'Absolutely!'

'So we can come for dinner?'

Flora found herself nodding. 'Of course! It'll be fun.'

'I'll just put these things where you want them and we'll be off. How's Imelda?' He carried the table to the corner of the garden where some rambling roses made a natural arbour.

Flora picked up a chair. It was unexpectedly heavy. 'I didn't think you cared about Imelda, or her kittens.'

Charles looked surprised. 'I did, but I didn't want to ask if I could come and see them in case she ate them, or something.'

'Oh. Well, you could come and see them now, if you're interested.' Perhaps she'd misjudged him a little.

He glanced at his watch. 'I'm meeting some people at eleven. I shouldn't really.'

Flora was disappointed. 'Perhaps you could come and see them another time.'

'I'd love to.' He put the second chair down by the table.

'It looks wonderful,' said Flora. 'Like something out of a magazine. It only needs a bottle of wine, a loaf of bread, some olives and a book.'

'*A book of verses underneath the bough, A jug of wine, a loaf of bread – and Thou,*' he quoted softly.

'What's that?'

'Oh, just a bit of poetry. Now, have you got everything? We should be off.'

When they got to the office, Charles said, 'What are you going to do?'

'I'd like to get on with sorting out those old filing cabinets. There's stuff in there no one's looked at for years. I'm not going to destroy any of it, just put it into document boxes and label it, so you can throw it away later.' She was quite looking forward to a day of getting on with things together in companionable silence. And perhaps they might even have a proper chat about the business without everyone else around.

He smiled. 'That doesn't seem a very nice way to spend a sunny Saturday.'

'Well, you're working, so I should be, too. And once those filing cabinets are empty, we can put them somewhere else and have much more room in the office.'

'Um, I'm only working until eleven. The people I'm meeting, with Annabelle, are friends.'

'Oh.' Flora felt suddenly put out. 'Well, I'll only work till twelve then.' Then, worrying she sounded a bit dependent, she hurried on, 'I've got a friend I've been trying to meet for lunch for ages.'

'Oh?'

This was obviously an invitation to tell him who the friend was. Flora decided to refuse it. It was none of his business, after all. 'We'd better get on, then, if we're only working for a couple of hours.'

When Charles was out of the room, doing whatever he had to do, Flora decided to ring Henry. She didn't usually ring men until the relationship was fairly well established, but this was an emergency. She couldn't be seen as Flora-No-Mates when Charles and Annabelle were going to be all couply and have lunch with friends.

'Henry? It's Flora Stanza.' For all her confidence, Flora always felt a little shy telephoning people she didn't really know.

'Flora! How very nice to hear from you!'

His enthusiasm was a great relief. 'I'm working this morning, but as I'm in town, I wondered if we could meet for lunch, or a drink, or something.'

'That would be delightful. Shall I pick you up from the office? I know a very nice little pub we could go to.'

'That would be lovely. About twelve?'

'Great. See you soon. Cheers.'

Charles was standing in the doorway when she put the phone down. 'So you're going out for lunch too?'

'Yup. Something to look forward to after all this sorting out.' She smiled at him, sensing that for some reason he was dying to know whom she was going out with.

'I heard you say the name Henry. Would that be Henry Burnet?'

Flora had to think for a moment. 'Yes, I think that would be him.'

Charles frowned. 'I should tell you, Flora, that he's

not someone I would wish any relative of mine to go out with.'

'Isn't he? Well, never mind, we're not that closely related.'

Charles pursed his lips and strode off.

Chapter Nine

They left Flora's Land-Rover in town and drove to a charming pub with a sloping garden that was full of people with their dogs and children.

'I was so glad you rang me,' said Henry as he delivered a glass of Pimm's to her. 'I was going to ring later, but I never thought you'd be free for lunch today.'

Flora felt rather guilty, aware that she'd arranged a date with Henry almost as much for Charles's benefit as for the pleasure of his company.

'I was really lucky you were free, but I was in town already, and it's such a lovely afternoon, I wanted to take the chance.'

'Well, here's to you,' said Henry, picking up his own Pimm's and looking down into her eyes.

Flora met his eyes for only a second, but then inspected the fruit salad floating in her drink. She didn't want Henry to get too keen until she'd decided how much she liked him. If he did get too eager for her company, she'd go off him immediately. In fact, she rather hoped Geoffrey was right about him being a philanderer – the last thing she wanted right now was a complicated relationship.

Fortunately, he seemed to take the hint. 'Now, what do you fancy for lunch? They do excellent home-cooked ham and a particularly good salad dressing.'

Flora chuckled. 'And I thought I'd left all the gourmet flesh-pots behind in London.'

'Seriously, the ham is outstanding.' Henry was laughing too. 'You should definitely try it.'

'I will then. And the particularly good salad dressing.'

While Henry was away, placing their food order, Flora thought about him. He was good looking, and laughed at her jokes, which was a definite plus – she'd had enough of people not getting her jokes all day. He would definitely do for the time being.

Later they went for a walk along the canal tow-path and Flora kept asking Henry about the various wild flowers growing along the path.

'I'm afraid I know nothing about any of them. Flowers have never interested me that much.'

Flora was disappointed. 'I think, because of my name, I should know more about them. I'll get a book.'

'So do you think you'll stay around for a while?'

It was the first remotely serious question he had asked her and Flora considered how best to reply. For some reason she didn't want to reveal her passion for her family business too early in their friendship.

'Oh yes, for a bit, anyway. I'll probably go back to London when the weather gets horrible, but I'm definitely here for the summer.'

'Oh good,' said Henry, 'then so am I.'

Henry kissed Flora's cheek when he dropped her back at her car. It was very pleasant. She liked Henry and she could tell he liked her, but not in an oppressive way. He seemed very relaxed and laid back about things, and that was just what she needed.

* * *

Flora was in the garden pulling up the goose-grass that covered everything with a sort of green mist. She had taken her breakfast out and eaten it at the little table and then felt inspired to do what she could to make the garden look better. She was surprised at her enthusiasm but even more surprised when she heard a car, looked up and saw that it was Charles.

'Good morning,' she called. 'I didn't expect to see you again so soon.'

'I've got some garden tools for you. Annabelle wanted you to have them,' he said through the window. 'But I see you've started without them.'

'Just this green stuff. It comes out easily, although it's given me a bit of a rash.'

Charles got out of the car. 'You need long gloves.' He went round to the back of the car and opened the boot. 'I've got a fork, a trowel, some fairly ancient gardening gloves and a bucket with a hole in it. To put the weeds in.'

By this time Flora had joined Charles at the boot. 'Where did these come from? Another sale?'

'No, I think these are throw-outs from Annabelle's parents. They're great gardeners. Annabelle's keen, too, although of course there isn't much garden with her house in town.'

'She didn't want me to have an idle Sunday, obviously,' Flora said wryly.

'Actually, I offered to bring them over. Not because I want you to get stuck into clearing out the bindweed . . .' He paused.

'What?'

'I couldn't just have a peep at the kittens, could I?

156

I've been dying to ever since they were born.' He appeared a little embarrassed by this request. 'As I said, I didn't like to earlier, in case it upset Imelda.'

Flora was strangely touched. And since William had left a note saying he was off for the day and wouldn't be back until suppertime, she didn't have to worry about him suddenly appearing.

'Come on then.'

As Flora led Charles through the house she worried briefly in case William had left some trace of his presence, but if he had, Charles didn't notice. And she had at least made her bed, so if her room was a bit untidy, it didn't look too slutty.

Charles knelt down on the floor in front of where Imelda was ensconced, feeding her babies, purring loudly. Seeing his large form hovering over the tiny bodies, who were pumping their mother for all they were worth, was surprisingly touching.

'Can I pick one up?'

'Take that one who's stopped feeding for a minute. Aren't they heavenly?'

He put the kitten next to his neck and stroked it with a long finger. 'Mm. I do wish we could have one, but . . .'

'It's all right. I know. Annabelle's allergic to cats.'

'And she doesn't like them, either.'

'I suppose if they make you sneeze, or itch, it would put you off them a bit.' Flora was trying to be generous. How could anyone not like cats?

He shook his head. 'Her mother's the same. She's not allergic, she just doesn't like them.'

'Is Annabelle like her mother in other ways? You know

157

what they say,' she went on playfully, wishing she could shut up, 'you should always check out the girl's mother before you commit yourself, because that's who you'll end up married to.'

'She's a very fine woman.' He frowned slightly. 'I think I remember meeting your mother once.'

'Oh?'

'Yes. She looked very like you, Flora. Very pretty.'

Usually Flora would have accepted this compliment with grace and aplomb. Now she felt embarrassed. It was probably because Charles didn't usually say things like that: it made her feel awkward. 'Well, it's a shame neither of them like cats. But some people like dogs better.'

'What about you, Flora?'

'Oh, I like both. They're like men and women – although not actually like men and women. I don't think dogs are like men and cats are like women, or anything like that. I just think they offer you different things.'

'Yes?' Charles had helped himself to another kitten and put it in the same place as the first one.

'Dogs build you up, make you feel better. Cats keep you in your place. They love you but they don't need you. Dogs are needy.'

'When we get married we might get a dog. A nice black Labrador.'

'Mm. I can see Annabelle with a Labrador.'

'They are very sensible dogs.'

Flora didn't comment. For her Labradors were on a par with flat shoes, knee-length skirts and Hermès headscarves: pleasant enough in their place, but not very exciting.

Charles went on. 'Now *you* I can see with something

much more frivolous and decorative, like a poodle or a Cavalier King Charles spaniel.'

Flora, content with his choice of breed for her, replied, 'You, on the other hand, should have something stately and enormous, like an Irish wolfhound.'

He turned away from the kittens for a moment. 'Is that how you see me? Stately and enormous?'

Flora nodded. 'And kind. You can be quite kind when you're not being bossy. Wolfhounds are very gentle. I used to know one when I was a child.'

Charles detached the kitten and sighed. 'I can't see Annabelle putting up with anything that size.'

'Well, I suppose if you're both working, it would be difficult. Just the same for any dog, though.' She found Charles being in her bedroom, within touching distance, too intimate, somehow.

'Do you worry about leaving Imelda during the day?'

She was just about to say that William came in and checked on her at lunchtime when she remembered that Charles didn't know about William. 'I leave lots of food and the kitchen window open. She's fine.'

He got to his feet, putting himself safely out of reach again. 'I must get that cat flap organised. Annabelle would not be happy if she knew about you leaving the window open.'

Flora glanced at herself in her dressing-table mirror but resisted the temptation to pick up her lip-gloss and add a layer. As a reward for this restraint she allowed herself to dig about Annabelle a little. 'Annabelle doesn't seem that happy about working in an auction house either,' she said.

'No,' said Charles as he followed her down the stairs, making Flora feel like a midget pursued by a giant. 'She prefers proper antiques to the house-clearance stuff we mostly get. Poor girl. I don't think she realised how much of the things we handle would be so run-of-the-mill.'

'Would you like a cup of coffee?'

'I should be getting back, really. Lunch with the in-laws.'

'Are they coming to you, or are you going to them?'

'We're going to them.' As he showed no signs of leaving she went through to the kitchen. He followed her and watched while she put the kettle on.

'Um.' He cleared his throat. 'How was your lunch with – Henry Burnet yesterday?'

'Oh, lovely! He took me to a really nice pub and we ate ham and salad. He's great fun.' Flora displayed a little more enthusiasm than she felt, although she had enjoyed herself. Something about Charles's cosy lunch with his in-laws made her want to seem a bit attached too.

'Good. But I do think I should warn you, as your cousin, that he hasn't got a very good reputation with women.'

'Hasn't he?'

'No.'

'I'll watch my step, then,' said Flora.

'I hope you don't mind me saying.'

'Not at all!' She smiled. 'So you will have coffee?'

'Oh, go on, then.'

'No need to be so gracious, Charles. I had an idea.' She opened a jar of coffee and found a teaspoon.

'About what?'

'About the business. How to improve the quality of the lots.'

'Yes?'

'I got it when you mentioned the *Antiques Roadshow* the other day. Why don't you do them?'

'What on earth are you talking about?'

'Put on a roadshow. You'd have to advertise, of course, but you could ask people to bring in their antiques, stuff they have lying around and don't really want or need, and then, if they're valuable, they might want to sell them.'

'Well—'

'You could do it in all the small towns nearby. Hire a room, or something. People would love it, I'm sure. And it would be a good advertisement for you anyway.'

'It would be terribly expensive. And if people didn't want to sell their stuff, it would all be for nothing. There's no slack in this business for mistakes, Flora.'

'You need some capital.'

'I know that.'

She bit back her question about Annabelle's capital. She'd been happy to use it to buy Flora out, so why wasn't she happy to use it to invest in the business in other ways? Annabelle by herself had been quite fun on their shopping trip, but as far as Stanza and Stanza went she was a disaster.

Instead she said, 'You have a huge house which you only use a very small part of as your offices. If you sold it you'd have plenty of capital. You wouldn't have to sell the hall.'

'You mean I could buy you out?'

Flora smiled weakly. 'You could, if I was willing to sell, of course, but that's not the point. What I'm saying is, if you sold that building, dividing it up into flats first

161

if you like, you could afford to do lots to make Stanza and Stanza work.'

'I don't know what Annabelle would think about that.'

Flora got the impression that this was just an excuse. 'Annabelle is not your partner! I am! And if she's not really interested in the business, why should she worry about what you do with the house?'

'It's not that she'd worry about selling the house. In fact, I think she's had some idea of doing that, too. It's what we did with the money that would worry her. And Flora, she's been involved for a while. She does have a right to her opinions.'

'Oh.' Crossly, Flora poured boiling water on to the coffee. 'I could do with a coffee grinder if I'm going to have a dinner party. Or a cafetière, or something.'

'I'll see what I can do. I'm sure Annabelle's got a spare one.'

Neither of them were really thinking about coffee or how to make it. 'Shall we use the table and chairs and take it out into the garden?' suggested Flora.

'I really mustn't be long. Annabelle will be expecting me.'

'We'll stay in the kitchen then.' Flora sat down and picked up her cup. It must be hard for Annabelle, being engaged to a man whose life was so taken up with a business she was part of but didn't enjoy.

'That house has been in the family a very long time,' said Charles.

'I know,' Flora replied, although she hadn't known, really, but only guessed.

'But we can't afford to be sentimental, I suppose. If Annabelle is . . .'

'Is what?'

'Unwilling to put capital into the business—'

'She was willing enough when she wanted to buy shares from me.' Flora felt a rush of indignation.

'That was different.'

'Why?'

'Because Annabelle would get something tangible for her money. She's helped a bit in the past but just putting money into the business generally wouldn't be the same at all.'

Flora sighed and sipped her coffee, which wasn't very nice. It wasn't that she wanted Annabelle investing in her family business – she might have to become a director or something. But if Annabelle could invest enough to make Stanza and Stanza profitable without selling the house, she should be encouraged to do so.

'Why don't you tell her about the *Antiques Roadshow* idea? If she could see that having a bit more capital, to advertise further afield, would make better stuff come in, it would be more interesting for her.'

'But if we sold the house or raised money from it, we could buy up a couple of auction houses owned by people who want to retire. Someone asked me only the other day if I'd be interested in buying them out. I had to refuse, but it would be a good way of getting more business.'

'Talk to Annabelle about it. And while you're on the subject, let's get a proper website. It's ridiculous not having one in the twenty-first century. And don't forget the proper ad in the *Yellow Pages*.'

Charles looked exhaustedly at Flora. 'We'll have a meeting soon. You, me and Annabelle.'

'Fine.' It wasn't fine, really. Annabelle wasn't a partner and had no real right to be there. But if Charles wanted his fiancée present, she could hardly complain.

'Changing the subject . . .'

'Yes? This coffee's disgusting, isn't it?'

'Yes, but I wasn't going to say that. I was going to ask if I could bring an old friend to your dinner party.'

'A male or a female friend?'

'Male. It wasn't my idea, I have to say.'

'Annabelle's?'

'Yes. She thought it would be nice for you to have someone to show you about the place.'

'It's a kind thought. And of course he can come, but I do have Henry.'

Charles stiffened. 'Oh yes. So you do. But Jeremy would be far better than Henry.'

'Really?' She was longing to tell her mother about this. Her mother knew that this sort of statement was destined to send Flora catapulting away from Jeremy into Henry's arms.

'Yes. He's a good, steady chap.' He frowned, as if he wanted to say something else, but then thought better of it.

'Yes?'

'Nothing.' He got to his feet. 'I should be getting along. Annabelle will be waiting.'

Flora smiled. 'Thank you for bringing the gardening tools.'

'That's all right. Have a pleasant Sunday, Flora.'

Later, she rang Emma and told her with satisfaction that things were going much better with Charles.

*   *   *

164

Monday morning found Flora awake early and full of energy, if a little stiff after her gardening. William had not appeared the night before so she had had a bath and gone to bed early with her book.

'I must have early nights more often,' she told Imelda, as she gave her a last cuddle before leaving for work. 'I feel great!'

It was only when she reached town and realised there was very little traffic about, that she looked at her watch. 'It's only seven o'clock!' she squeaked to herself, horrified. 'I must have got up at about half past five! I'm such a dilly – how could I not have realised? Still' – she swooped the Land-Rover round in a generous curve – 'it gives me the whole yard to park in!' Thank God she had a key and didn't have to sit on the doorstep waiting for someone to let her in.

By the time she had got into the building, unset the alarm, and put the kettle on, she decided it was time to stop talking to herself and do some work. There was no point in turning up hours early if there wasn't anything dramatic to show for it.

Sipping her tea, she went back to the files she was sorting out, but after she'd consigned several years' worth of garage bills to a file, she decided it was too lovely a day to spend among ancient dust. She went into the main office and looked around.

The first day she had arrived she'd thought the place looked dingy. And while there was no spare money for major refurbishment, surely a little decorating was not out of the question? There was a piece of peeling paper on the ceiling that had been driving her mad since she got here.

Determined to be safety conscious, she carefully cleared the computer off one of the desks and put a chair on it, so she could easily reach the paper. She was glad she'd put on a pair of loose linen trousers today. She couldn't have done this if she'd been wearing a little strappy dress and frivolous shoes.

The first piece came away beautifully and Flora started to think about colours. A subtle yellow, to bring sunshine into the room? A pale straw, stylish and light? Or a fresh green? She dug her fingernail under the next strip and found that too was easy to remove.

She was making good progress and tugging away merrily when suddenly there was a crash followed by what felt like a minor landslip. Dust, plaster, paper and quite large chunks of stone showered down. It felt as if someone had emptied a rather lumpy bag of flour over Flora's head. Coughing, she stood still until everything stopped. 'Oh my God,' she said aloud. 'The paper must have been holding everything else up.' She looked around her as the dust slowly settled, and took in the chaos. What on earth had she done? A large chunk of ceiling had come down and a substantial part of the wall was bare. And a thickish layer of dust covered everything – including the computers. Oh no, the computers! Please let them be OK.

She glanced at her watch. Half past eight. Her heart sank. Charles could appear any time from now. She had to do something. She felt a rising panic, and tried to swallow it.

First, she clambered down and ran to get a dustpan and brush, then she swept up as much as she could easily. The place had to stop looking like there had been an earthquake before anyone else arrived. She dumped the debris in the bin, then she regarded the paper, hanging from the ceiling in a way that no one could possibly avoid seeing – or indeed bumping into. However much she swept and dusted, that paper would betray her. What a disaster.

Drawing pins? Could she pin it up out of the way? No, they would never hold in all the crumbling plaster. Then she remembered seeing a tub of Copydex in a drawer. That would be perfect! She could stick the paper back up, stuff what she'd already pulled down in the bin, and then wipe and polish away all traces of her abortive attempts at decorating. Fingers crossed Charles wasn't in too early.

She was just standing on the chair, teetering a little as she reached up, holding the glue in one hand, the brush in the other when the door behind her opened.

'What the blazes are you doing?' Charles demanded loudly, making Flora jump and dislodge the chair.

He caught her before she fell but before she could thank him he took a deep breath and started. 'What the bloody hell do you think you're doing? You could have broken something if you'd fallen!' Thinking he was concerned for her, she was about to reassure him, but he thundered on. 'The place is covered in rubble! Is that you thinking you'd move on from *Bargain Hunt* and play at *Changing Rooms* or something?'

'Charles! Calm down! I—'

'For God's sake, Flora. Those computers aren't paid for yet! If anything happens to them, we're stuck, we can't buy new ones.'

'I was just trying to help!'

'Trying to help? Trying to sabotage the whole caboodle more like! Honestly, Flora, I've had enough. The sooner you go back to London and leave us to get on with our work, the better!'

As she'd slithered through Charles's arms on to the floor, Flora had felt guilty. She had been foolish, she could have damaged the computers with falling dust and detritus and she had been quite willing to apologise. But not now.

'Leave you to rot in your own failure more like! There are breweries round here that haven't had piss-ups for years because you couldn't organise them! This business is going from bad to worse because you have less business sense than my cat!'

'Less business sense than your cat! Grow up, Flora. You're being infantile. You—'

'Infantile!' Now Flora was really furious. 'How dare you? From the moment I walked in here, you've behaved appallingly. You took one look at me and decided I was just young and silly and pointless.'

'Well, if the cap fits—'

'And you were determined not to listen to a word I said. You're so stuck in your ways that you can't even imagine that a fresh pair of eyes can see something you can't. Yes, I'm younger than you, but I'm not a child! And I do have something to contribute.'

'Don't be ridiculous. You're playing at country life and country living. You're just a spoilt little princess used to getting her own way and as soon as you get bored you'll run off back to London.'

Spoilt little princess? Flora couldn't believe it. 'What on earth makes you think you know me so well? You know nothing about me – because you and your bloody fiancée can't think further than getting rid of me. But you're destroying Stanza and Stanza in the process!'

'You have absolutely no right to say that!'

'Oh yes I have, because in case you've forgotten, I'm the senior partner here!'

A look of shock passed across Charles's face and Flora herself felt rather shocked that she'd been so blunt. She hadn't meant to say that. 'You're nothing of the kind!' he shouted. 'You just happen to own more than me owing to the blundering of a poor old man who must have been suffering from senile dementia when he left anything to you, let alone half a business!'

'He had not got senile dementia, he was perfectly lucid and perhaps he left it to me because he knew what a crap job you were making of it!'

'I doubt that! I expect he was just seduced by your big brown eyes and pretty ways. He was just manipulated by you, same as every other sucker you get your claws into!'

'What the hell are you talking about?'

'You know perfectly well what I'm talking about. Don't try and play the innocent with me, because unlike most of the people round here, I'm not fooled!'

'And nor am I! Just because you're your father's son, the women round here seem to think you're God Almighty. Well, not me! I know what a hopeless businessman you are.'

They confronted each other, both breathing hard. Flora felt a little dizzy, possibly because she'd used up so much breath shouting at Charles. Charles was flushed; his usually ordered hair was falling over his forehead.

'I may not be Richard Branson but at least I never pulled the building down about our ears! Now could you try and get this lot cleared up before Annabelle gets here.' And he stormed past her out of the door.

Flora shook her head to clear it. Anger lent her wings and very quickly she got the office looking more or less as it had been. She turned on both computers and, much to her relief, they both worked. But once the adrenaline faded, she felt exhausted and horribly near tears. She went into the Ladies', to wash, and then slipped out to the shop to buy a bar of chocolate. There was something in chocolate that made it good for you, she told herself.

She met Charles in the passage. He looked down at her, as frosty and far away as Everest. 'I apologise if I said anything inappropriate,' he said formally.

If? 'I accept your apology, if that is what it is,' she replied, thinking that 'I apologise' is what you say if you're not remotely sorry. 'I probably said things I shouldn't have, too.'

He nodded, and then stalked out of the back entrance to the car. Flora suddenly longed to go home to bed.

Chapter Ten

Flora spent most of the rest of the day in a mild state of shock, with her files, where she could do no damage. She left promptly, while Charles was out, and said goodbye to people briefly. She was fairly sure she'd hidden the fact that anything was wrong, but when she got home, she saw that there was still quite a lot of plaster in her hair. 'This job can turn you white overnight,' she said to her reflection, in an attempt to cheer herself up. It didn't work, she still felt rotten.

The following day she crept in, but was pleased to see Louisa, who didn't work on Mondays. At least she could be normal with her.

'Hi, Louisa. Nice weekend?'

'Lovely, thanks. My husband takes my children swimming and to the library on Saturday mornings so I got a lot done in the garden. You were in on Saturday?'

'Only in the morning. I went out for lunch with a friend in the afternoon.'

'Well, you did a very good job on that valuation. Are you a typist, then? No one told me.'

Flora checked to see if anyone else was in earshot. 'Well, I can type. It's useful, but I wouldn't want to do it for a living. I temp from time to time if I can't get anything more interesting to do.'

'So what did you do, actually?' Louisa settled herself at her desk. 'Before you came here, I mean.'

Flora shrugged. 'Nothing specific. I just had jobs, really, not a career. The longest I've ever stayed in a job was two years in an art gallery. This is the only thing so far that I've really enjoyed. It's hard work but it's so varied. You're doing a valuation one day, being a porter the next, and typing up stuff the day after.'

Louisa smiled enthusiastically at her. 'You can help me type the next catalogue. They were supposed to be getting me an assistant but nothing ever happened.'

Flora bit her lip guiltily. 'Oh, I think I'm supposed to be doing that. When I first came, Charles didn't want me to be here at all, so I applied for the job as assistant so he couldn't send me back to London. And I haven't really assisted you at all.'

'Well, be around for the next catalogue and I'll forgive you. And you did do the valuation.' Louisa got up out of her seat and peered out of the window. 'Here's Annabelle. Goodness, she's looking very . . . different.'

Flora rushed to see what Annabelle was wearing. It was the long, slim-line fuchsia skirt and the black V-neck top. Her hair was held back by a black velvet band, which was against the rules, but on the whole she didn't look at all bad. 'We went shopping the other day,' said Flora. 'I was doing a Trinny and Susannah on her.'

'My God! That was brave! Did she kick up a lot of fuss? And why on earth did she agree to let you?' Annabelle disappeared through the front door at that moment and they knew she would be with them in seconds. 'Oh, here she is.'

'Annabelle, what is that thing on your head?' asked Flora, on the attack.

'My hair kept flopping all over the place, it distracted me.'

'What's wrong with her hair?' asked Charles, who came into the room a few steps behind, looking daggers at Flora. He obviously hadn't forgiven her.

'It's lovely hair,' said Flora, realising that she was not going to win this one. 'It's just that Alice bands aren't usually a good idea for anyone older than Alice in Wonderland was.'

'I'm sorry, Flora,' said Annabelle briskly. 'I've got to be able to see.'

Flora sighed, 'OK. It does look quite sweet, I suppose,' reluctantly relinquishing her position as the style Nazi.

'Charles says you want a meeting?'

What else had Charles said, she wondered? And how much of it would have been repeatable? 'Well, I have got some ideas I'd like to discuss.' Although she'd much rather discuss them when Charles was actually speaking to her.

'Oh God,' said Annabelle with an exasperated sigh. 'Your ideas are so expensive. I spent a fortune the other day.'

Flora gave a tense little smile. Annabelle had asked Flora to help her with her clothes, and she herself had donated two very expensive pairs of knickers to the cause. 'You have to speculate in order to accumulate,' she said, more breezily than she felt. 'So, when can we have our talk?'

Charles glanced at his watch. 'I have to go over to a farm a bit later. If we're quick, we can do it now.' The heat in his expression made it very clear to Flora that if she said anything he didn't agree with, he'd be down on her more heavily than the office ceiling had been.

Annabelle smoothed down her new top, revealing a well-defined waist. 'I wish you wouldn't do those farm sales! They're so dreary! All that plastic binder twine and fertiliser sacks, and there's never anything remotely valuable in the house.'

'Annabelle, you're going to love my idea.' Flora took hold of Annabelle's arm, prepared to bully her even more thoroughly than she'd bullied her before. If Charles was more set against her than ever, Annabelle was her last hope.

'Let's talk about it in the boardroom,' said Charles, sounding impatient, and led the way to the room where Flora had been interviewed what seemed like a lifetime ago.

'I thought,' said Flora, anxious to cut to the chase and wondering if Charles would let on that she'd told him her plans already, 'that if we had our own antiques road-shows, got people to bring in their forgotten treasures for a valuation, they might be willing to sell them some-times. It would get a better class of item to the auctions.'

'Flora, that's such a romantic idea!' For 'romantic' Annabelle really meant 'ridiculous'. 'What you'd really get is hundreds of people with car-boot finds and Barbie dolls without their boxes, wondering if they're collec-tors' items yet.'

Flora had watched enough afternoon television shows to know this was true. 'Well, yes, there would be a bit of that, of course, but it would raise our profile.'

'But if we got any amount of people, they'd be queuing

for hours,' went on Annabelle. 'Charles is the only one who can do valuations. I'm not qualified.' She managed to say this with the air of someone who declares they don't smoke, or drink, or anything else dubious but fun.

'On the other hand,' said Charles, carefully addressing Annabelle rather than Flora, 'I suppose I could ask Bob Butler – he's been an auctioneer for years – if he'd help.'

'Why would he do that?' demanded Annabelle. 'He hasn't retired yet has he? Although he's about a hundred. We're in direct competition.'

Charles hesitated before answering. 'There's something else we need to talk about, darling. Flora and I had a discussion.'

If he was calling it that, he couldn't be referring to their row, thought Flora with some relief.

'As I said, if Flora's involved it'll be expensive,' repeated Annabelle, as if to make quite sure Charles saw her as an extravagant dilettante who was bound to cost the firm money.

'Or, a much cheaper idea, we could ask Geoffrey to help with the valuations,' suggested Flora, biting her lip.

'But he's just a porter!' protested Annabelle.

'Not "just a porter",' Flora contradicted her. 'He used to be a dealer and is extremely knowledgeable.'

Charles pursed his lips, clearly reluctant to agree with anything Flora said. 'If we used Geoffrey, we could get going on the roadshows right away,' he conceded reluctantly.

'Well, if you insist on employing him full time, he might as well do something for his money,' said Annabelle.

'So you think the roadshows are a good idea?' If she

hadn't still been reeling from her row with Charles she might have clapped her hands with glee.

'How would they work, exactly?' asked Annabelle, oozing scepticism.

'Well,' said Flora, 'we'd rent a room somewhere, if we weren't in Bishopsbridge, advertise, and people would flock to us with their valuables, which we would then sell.'

'I think "flock" might be putting it a bit strongly, Flora,' said Charles.

'Oh. Well, yes. I suppose it's the television that brings all those people.' She fell silent, but the word 'television' had lodged itself in her brain. No idea concerning it had come to her immediately, but she was prepared to be patient.

'It's not a bad idea, I suppose,' said Annabelle.

'Flora also wanted to discuss rethinking the buildings,' said Charles, apparently leaping in to prevent Annabelle thinking any good of Flora.

'What do you mean?' Annabelle suddenly sat up very straight.

'Flora thinks we should sell the house and use the money to put some capital into the business.'

Annabelle was silent for a few moments. 'Of course, I can see that having this whole house for just the office does seem a bit wasteful, but there is Charles's flat at the top.'

'Or we could divide it up into flats and he could keep it. Anyway, why does he need a flat? You live together.'

'That's Annabelle's house,' said Charles firmly. 'I like to have somewhere that's mine.'

'If we did that,' said Annabelle, who hadn't noticed

176

Charles's statement, 'we could buy another house and do the same thing. Bishopsbridge is such an up and coming town – practically commuting distance from London, the music festival—'

'I thought we should invest the money in the business, the auction business,' snapped Flora.

Annabelle took a sharp breath. 'Which would just be throwing good money after bad. It's about time you faced that. There's no money in auctioneering.'

'There isn't a lot of money, I admit,' said Charles, forced to come over to Flora's side. 'But we employ a lot of people and the hall is used by all of the local community, in one way or another.'

'Oh, wake up and smell the coffee, Charles! You can't really keep a failing business going just because a few old-age pensioners and children use the hall! That building would be worth an absolute fortune if it was divided up and sold off! It would raise even more money than this house would.'

Flora opened her mouth to wonder how many flats in large houses a town like Bishopsbridge really needed, but closed it again. This was between Charles and Annabelle.

'Stanza and Stanza is a very old, established business, and while I'm prepared to consider selling this house, or dividing it into flats to raise capital, I am not even going to think about selling the hall and converting that to flats.'

'Well, I think you're mad. You're letting sentiment rule you,' said Annabelle.

'I'm sorry you think that, but I'm not budging on this one.'

The two confronted each other. Flora felt she should have left the room a few minutes before, but was far too interested to do anything of the kind. Now she let them stare at each other for a few moments before clearing her throat.

'Well,' she said. 'We could have the first roadshow without having to sell anything. An ad in the paper isn't going to break the bank, is it?'

'I suppose not,' said Annabelle.

'And nor would getting a website,' Flora added, while the going was good.

Annabelle turned to Flora. 'Haven't you got any money you could invest in the business? After all, it's half yours.'

'I'm afraid not.' She didn't think now was the time to remind Annabelle that she owned slightly more than half.

'What about your father, couldn't you ask him for some?'

Flora was outraged. 'No, I could not! I've just become an heiress, for goodness' sake! I'm not going to ask Dad if he could put money into a business which should jolly well be able to afford to pay to market itself!'

'Oh,' said Annabelle. 'I know for a fact that if I asked my father for a bit of capital he'd be only too keen to let me have it.'

'Well, I'm thrilled for you, Annabelle,' said Flora, still furious. 'But I'm still not going to ask him.'

'So we'll go ahead with the roadshow idea,' said Charles, attempting to smooth things over. 'Flora, you write the advertisement and I'll speak to Geoffrey about helping with the valuations.'

'And Bob Butler?' asked Flora. 'In case he was willing to help, too?'

'I hardly think that will be necessary, Flora,' said Annabelle nastily. 'It'll only be two damaged Staffordshire figurines and a fake Steiff bear.'

Flora pulled back her lips in a fake grin. She would get people there in their hundreds, if she had to sell her body to do it!

'Well,' said Charles tensely, looking at his watch. 'I must go.'

When the two women were left alone, Annabelle said, 'I'm really looking forward to your dinner party. Have you got a date yet?'

Flora couldn't believe the way Annabelle changed track so fast. 'I need to check when Emma can come down,' she said cautiously.

'And have you found out anything else about that man? Why he was in your garden?'

'Actually, I have! Well, I was right – he's a friend of Emma's from university. She told him where I was and he came to look me up, only of course I wasn't in.'

'But he didn't leave a note or anything. I checked.'

'No. Emma explained he couldn't find anything to write with, or something.' Flora regarded Annabelle firmly. 'It wasn't as if he was in the house, or anything.'

'No,' Annabelle admitted. 'Have you seen him again?'

'He's gone away, but he should be back for the dinner party.'

'Oh good.'

'But I must get a dining table before then.'

'I'll see to it,' said Annabelle. 'And did Charles ask if he could invite Jeremy?'

'Yes, but I'm not sure—'

'Good.' She smiled, suddenly refreshingly girlish. 'I must think what to wear for it.'

'What? The reunion?'

Annabelle's forehead wrinkled a little. 'Oh yes! I must think what to wear for that. But the dinner party comes first.'

Flora nodded vaguely. Either she or Annabelle seemed to be losing the plot a bit, and she had a horrid suspicion it was her.

The next fortnight flew by. The kittens seemed to grow daily and would be killing their own prey and dragging it back to the lair any day now. And Flora'd been for drinks with Henry twice after work. The more she saw of him the more she liked him, although in spite of his obvious attractions – and he was a very attractive man – Flora wasn't convinced there was sufficient spark between them for it ever to be much more than a bit of fun. And she was pretty sure he felt the same. He was always wildly flirtatious and certainly quite persistent, flatteringly persistent in fact, but she thought it more than likely that he was like that with a lot of women, which was a relief, in a way. But she'd played it safe by always keeping things low-key: she'd refused all his dinner invitations, sticking to casual drinks and suppers in the pub where she could pay for herself and it didn't feel too much like a date. The last thing she needed was him misreading her signals. Plus, if she was really honest with herself, the degree to which her appearing to date Henry annoyed Charles was part of the pleasure of seeing him.

Charles, unfortunately, had still not forgiven Flora. The little glimpses of a nicer, more human Charles she'd seen at the auction and at the valuation had completely disappeared. Or they disappeared the moment Flora walked into the room, anyway. He only spoke to her when absolutely forced to either by extreme necessity or politeness – he was always icily, meticulously polite – and so Flora, inexperienced as she was, was reduced to trying to organise the roadshow pretty much single-handed. If they'd actually been on speaking terms she might have been able to persuade herself that his leaving her to it was a gesture of faith, but as things were it was quite clear that he wanted her – expected her – to fail. Worst of all, Flora was feeling horribly guilty about everything she'd said in their row. How could she have thrown the fact of her owning more shares at him? It was a terrible, childish thing to have said and Flora felt desperately ashamed of herself.

And now the dinner party loomed. The date was set, although Emma was still not definitely coming.

Flora was writing Emma another begging email from the office computer when Annabelle who, self-involved as she was, had remained blissfully unaware of the tension between her fiancé and his cousin, came into the room.

'You type awfully fast! No one told me you could do that.'

'No I don't! I'm not typing! I'm just exercising my fingers. It's good for the nails.' Flora checked her nails to see if in fact they'd survived her flurry on the keyboard.

'Oh, Flora! You're so vain!' said Annabelle, pleasingly

gullible. 'I just came to remind you to write the advert for the paper about the roadshow. They have to have it in by today, or it won't make this week's paper. Charles and I decided that Wednesday the week after next would be good. Almost two weeks' notice should be enough, don't you think? Do you think we'll need the big hall? Or just the small one at the back, where the playgroup is? If so, we need to tell them.'

'Don't they meet on Wednesdays then?'

'Oh yes, every day, unless there's a sale on. This would count as a sale. It's in their lease that they can't use that room if we need it.'

Flora thought of all the mothers and children who would be inconvenienced if they couldn't go to play-group and said, more grandly than she felt, 'Oh, we'll definitely need the big hall. No one uses that on a Wednesday, do they?'

'Not during the day, no. But that shouldn't make any difference. We own the hall. We should use the space we need.'

'You seem quite keen on the idea, anyway,' said Flora, pleased that her idea had proved popular even if it was unacknowledged as hers.

'Quite keen' wasn't part of Annabelle's vocabulary when connected to the auction house but she shrugged. 'Well, you never know. Doesn't hurt to try. Don't suppose many people will come.'

'I'd better get on to it,' said Flora. She turned away from Annabelle and laboriously started a new document. When she was alone again she thought guiltily about the advertisement she had already written and dispatched to every local newspaper in the county. She had also made posters which she had gone round the town begging shops to display. She was determined to fill that hall with people desperate to sell their family heirlooms.

Her phone rang as she drove back home. She knew it was Emma without even looking, and pulled into a convenient lay-by to answer it. The reception was better there, anyway. Emma was initially full of reasons why it was out of the question for her to come and stay the weekend after next, but eventually she said, 'Sounds quite fun, anyway. Dave won't like it when I tell him he's not invited.'

'It'll do him good for you to do something on your own for a change,' suggested Flora hopefully.

'Mm,' said Emma. 'I wonder what I should wear.'

'I wonder what I should cook!'

'Oh, don't worry about that yet. It's a fortnight away. But clothes – they take thinking about.'

It occurred to Flora, as she made the rest of the journey home, that country life had already changed her. Not long ago she'd have shared Emma's priorities. But not long ago she had shared Emma's access to wonderful little shops that sold food it was easy to pass off as home-made. Down here, 'entertaining-lite' was not an option. Here it would have to be hard-core cooking.

When she got home, she rang Henry. He'd left two messages on her phone and she wanted to ask him to the dinner party. He'd be jolly, open the wine, see everyone was happy and if Charles didn't like it, well, too bad.

'Hello, you,' he said when he heard her voice.

'Hello, you, too,' she said, smiling. He had a nice voice and was soothingly non-confrontational.

183

'Do you fancy coming out for a drink?'

'I'd love a drink. I need some cheerful company. It's been so hectic at work lately.'

'Well, why not make it dinner, then?'

'Oh, I'm glad you mentioned dinner,' Flora replied, gaily side-stepping the invitation. 'I want to invite you to come to a dinner party at mine. The weekend after next.' She crossed her fingers.

'Oh Flora, I'm going to be away.'

Flora's heart sank. 'How can you be away? Can't you change it?'

Henry chuckled. 'I'm afraid not, but I could take you out to dinner tonight, instead.'

'That is not at all the same thing!' Flora said grumpily, knowing she was being unreasonable.

'No. It's better from my point of view.'

Flora suddenly felt very tired. 'Are you sure you can't come to my dinner party?'

'Quite sure. Big meeting in Switzerland; I can't possibly miss it, or change it. I am sorry.' He paused. 'But I could take you out for a very nice steak and hand-cut chips.'

'It sounds very tempting, but I'm just too tired to go out tonight.'

'You weren't too tired a moment ago.'

'I know, but I am now. Can we do it tomorrow?'

'What, steak and hand-cut chips? Certainly.'

'I meant the drink. I'm better at going out if I haven't gone home first. It's like the gym.'

'What?'

'Oh, never mind. Shall I meet you in the Fox and Grapes at six?'

'Great. And I'll try and talk you into dinner, too.'

'We'll see, shall we?'

When Flora had put the phone down she wondered if her reluctance to have dinner with Henry was her subconsciously punishing him for not coming to her dinner party. But then she decided she didn't have enough emotional energy for a deeper relationship just now. He was good company, though, and it was lovely to spend time with someone who didn't disapprove of her all the time.

Flora hadn't envisaged life in the country being quite so busy, but now she was wondering how she was going to get everything done, what with choir rehearsals, Henry, and everything that needed doing at work – which included a little light decorating. She did it after work one evening, very carefully.

Charles caught her yawning, the morning after she'd stayed on into the evening to redecorate, and said sourly, 'Henry keeping you up late, is he?'

Flora delivered a very sarcastic smile but said nothing, perversely pleased that he hadn't noticed either the repaired ceiling or the paint on her nails.

Choir had suddenly sprung voice tests on everyone, too. Geoffrey had to physically drag Flora to the rehearsal they were taking place in.

'Every choir has to do this from time to time,' he insisted. 'It's only sensible. It'll be very low key. James won't make you do anything terrifying, honestly.'

Although she wasn't asked to leave (in fact her small but tuneful voice received a grave compliment from James), Flora's palms sweated for days afterwards, just thinking about it.

If it hadn't been for William, who had come back to his place on the sofa, Imelda and the kittens would have almost been neglected. The following Friday Flora went home, planning to have a very quiet weekend – organising the roadshow all by herself on top of everything else had left her exhausted – refusing even a Sunday lunchtime drink with Henry. She would do a little light gardening if the weather held, lots of reading and have plenty of little naps.

Geoffrey had other ideas. He rang her up on Saturday night.

'There's a good car-boot sale on tomorrow.'

'Is there?' Flora said without much enthusiasm.

'Edie and I are going and we're planning to take you.'

'Are you?' Flora was still a novice at country life but even she knew that car-boot sales started very early and that Geoffrey would probably want to be one of the first people there.

'Can you get here by seven? We'll go in my car.'

Flora felt even more exhausted just thinking about it. 'Geoffrey, I'm awfully tired. I was hoping to have a lie-in. Sleep a little,' she added, in case the concept of staying in bed was so foreign to him that he didn't know the jargon.

'It's a valuable part of your training, young woman. There'll never be time for me to teach you much when there's a sale on. A car boot, a good one, is a very good place for you to get your eye in. We might even buy some things for the next auction. Make a bit of money.'

Flora sighed deeply. 'OK. At your house, at seven. Tomorrow. Sunday morning. When every sensible person is asleep.'

Flora went to bed extremely early, leaving William washing up downstairs – as the weather was still fine he planned to go and sleep in the woods later. Flora no longer cared what he did. Although mostly she was grateful for his company and more so for his cooking, part of her felt he had unwittingly caused her a lot of work. If Annabelle hadn't spotted his naked antics, Flora might not be contemplating a dinner with a lot of people she didn't know, without a dining table.

Chapter Eleven

On Sunday morning Flora dragged herself out of bed at six o'clock and saw that the weather had changed. Instead of the misty dawns that had lit her little garden, the fields and woods beyond with the promise of gold, it was cloudy and looked as if it would rain. She decided to wear jeans and a pair of loafers. Car-boot sales were bound to involve a lot of walking.

'How are the kittens?' asked Edie, the moment she saw Flora. 'Have they opened their eyes yet?'

'Yes. They're quite wide open now, but to begin with they were just little black slits. The book said it would happen at about twelve days and I was terribly worried they wouldn't open them on time' – Flora, listening to herself, had a sudden flash of how neurotic mothers felt – 'but then I woke up one morning and there they were, squinting at me. They're very sweet. You must come and see them.'

'It must be a worry for you, having to leave them alone all day.'

'Mm. It is a bit. But Imelda's a very good mother. She goes straight back to them the moment one of them squeaks.' While she wasn't lying to Edie, really, she felt dishonest, and hoped, once the dinner party was over, that she could be more honest about William's presence and role as co-carer for Imelda.

'Stop gossiping, you two, and get in the car,' said Geoffrey.

'Flora was telling me about the kittens,' said Edie.

'But if you want real gossip, have you heard about the roadshow?' Flora clambered into the back of the car.

'No. What's a roadshow?' asked Geoffrey.

'I can't believe Charles hasn't told you!' she said, when she'd explained. 'You're going to be one of the valuers! Charles said so.'

'Really! I bet that didn't please her ladyship,' said Edie.

'Well, no,' Flora admitted. 'But she did say it would make Geoffrey better value for money and that we probably wouldn't get many people. I think we might, though. I've already got Virginia's daughter to put an ad on the web somehow, as well as to make us a website of our own.'

'Hm. I expect that's a good idea,' said Geoffrey, sounding dubious.

'Oh, it is. Trust me. And can you stop at a cashpoint machine? I need some money if I'm going to buy anything.'

Flora tapped in her pin number and waited for a balance, trying to remember which day of the month her tenants paid their rent. She had deliberately made it a few days before her standing order to her parents went out. When her balance came up on the screen she frowned and decided she needed to have it printed. Apparently she was within a whisker of exceeding her overdraft limit. How had that happened when she had hardly had a moment to breathe, let alone spend money?

Aware of Geoffrey and Edie waiting for her in the car, she couldn't make major financial decisions immediately, and just took out the thirty pounds that she had left before incurring massive charges. When the ATM obligingly gave Flora her card back, she murmured a heartfelt 'Thank you' under her breath. Only when she was confronted by the news in print did she remember how near her limit she had been when she first came down here. That little spending spree with Annabelle had taken her dangerously near the edge of poverty.

She got back in the car with a sunny smile to cover her dismay. Then she started making frantic plans and rejecting them all, equally frantically. The first, to find something wonderful for nothing at the car-boot sale and put it into the next auction was fine, except there wasn't a sale for some time. It was a long-term plan. Putting up the rent on her flat didn't seem like an option, either. Emptying the contents of the holiday cottage and taking it along to the car-boot sale to see how much she could get for it wouldn't work because she couldn't fit it all in the Land-Rover and the stuff was mostly Annabelle's anyway. Her last idea, which seemed the most impossible, the most unacceptable, was apparently her only option. She would have to ask Charles for the wages she would have earned had she really been an office assistant. He'd said himself that they were crap, but they would have to do.

If it wasn't for the dinner party, she wouldn't have been so worried. Flora bit her lip. 'I wonder if Mum's got a recipe for rabbit she could give me?' she wondered aloud.

'What's that, dear?' asked Edie from the front of the car. 'Did you say something?'

'No, nothing really. I was just wondering how far away we were.'

'Not long now. You don't feel sick, do you?'

Flora did, a bit, but she didn't think it was anything to do with the motion of the car. 'I'm fine,' she said breezily, feeling anything but.

'It's obviously a popular boot sale,' said Geoffrey as they glided to a halt behind the last car in a long string of traffic. 'The change in the weather hasn't put people off.'

'It's not actually raining,' said Edie. 'That does deter them a bit.'

'Well, I hope it's not all just housewives clearing out their bits and pieces,' said Geoffrey.

'What's wrong with that?' asked Flora.

'Nothing wrong with it in itself,' Geoffrey amended, sensing Flora's defence of people wanting to declutter. 'But they tend to have modern stuff, not anything with any antique value. You want the small-time dealers for that, people who pick stuff up at jumble sales for a few pennies and are happy to sell it on for a couple of pounds.'

Edie sighed. 'Geoffrey says all these programmes about antiques are spoiling it for the professionals. Everyone knows to look on the bottom of things to check for hallmarks and makers' names.'

As those very programmes were the source of what little knowledge Flora had, she didn't reply.

191

The airfield was already bustling with activity by the time they had finally parked the car and walked the long distance to where the action was. 'We have to be methodical,' said Geoffrey. 'Make sure we visit every stall.'

'Good thing I put on comfortable shoes,' muttered Flora, suddenly wishing she could go back to bed.

The first stall they reached was a burger van selling coffee and tea as well as hot food.

'Let's have a cup of tea now,' said Edie. 'We can drink it while we look.'

Geoffrey shook his head. 'You can't have a good root through a box if you're holding a cup of coffee.'

'Well, Flora and I will have a cup and you can do what you think best. I know I need a cup of something.'

Geoffrey made a growling noise, but when Edie got to the front of the queue and looked enquiringly at him, he nodded. Flora was very grateful for her cup of tea. Her anxiety about money was colouring her enjoyment of the day out, and she hoped the tea might help.

'Now come along, Flora,' said Geoffrey, halfway down his cup of tea. 'You're here for your education.'

Flora wandered over to where a cheerful-looking woman stood behind a table selling, among other things, a climbing frame and a skateboard. Reluctantly, Geoffrey followed.

'Those ramekin dishes look useful,' she said to him.

'Ten pence each,' said the woman quickly. 'There are six.'

'Sixty pence for six ramekin dishes!' said Flora, fishing for her purse. 'That's a bargain!'

'What do you want those for?' asked Geoffrey. 'You can't sell them on at the auction.'

'I know, but I've got people coming to dinner. Almost anything looks better in a little dish, doesn't it, Edie?'

Edie was inspecting an electric grilling machine advertised by a boxer and didn't answer.

'Well, I like food in proper dishes,' grumbled Geoffrey, and moved on.

Flora paid for the dishes, put them in her bag and hurried to catch Geoffrey up. Already she was feeling better as her first little hit of retail therapy took effect.

Then she spotted the most wonderful teapot. She'd almost forgotten about her collection of novelty teapots, which she'd started when she was twelve, and now rarely added to. But this was perfect! It was supposed to be a ball of wool. A coil of it was used to form a base for the pot, the handle was the sleeve of a half-knitted jumper, and the spout was the other half. It was studded with kittens, clawing their way over the wool in a way that was so delightfully vulgar Flora knew that money shortage, or no money shortage, she had to have it.

'Look!' she called to Geoffrey as Edie, who would have appreciated it more, had gone off in search of plants.

Reluctantly, he came back and saw what she was exclaiming over with such pleasure. 'Hm, not bad. There's a market for kitsch. How much?' he asked the vendor, a businesslike young woman who was mostly selling children's toys.

'That's ten pounds. It's a genuine Carter.'

Geoffrey sucked his teeth. 'Ooh, I doubt that it is. Doesn't have the quality. I'll give you three for it.'

'Sorry. Can't do that.'

'Four pounds?'

She shook her head again. Geoffrey sighed and pulled

a five-pound note out of his pocket. 'Here you are then. Call it a deal.' He handed the note to the woman in such a way that she had to accept it.

She sighed, picked up the teapot and started wrapping it in newspaper. 'You've robbed me, but it's not to everyone's taste, I don't suppose.'

Geoffrey handed Flora the teapot as they walked away. 'Here you are.'

'Hang on, I've got a five-pound note here,' she began.

'Nonsense. It's a present. On a good day it could fetch fifteen quid at auction.'

'Oh, I want to keep it! I collect teapots. Thank you so much.' Privately the thought of how much Charles would hate it made her quite skippy inside.

'It's a pleasure. But I do think you should consider selling it next time we have a sale.'

Flora stood by Geoffrey as he went through boxes of old tools. She was watching the groups of people as they inspected the bottoms of pots, no doubt still hoping to find an undiscovered Clarice Cliff. Clothes fluttered on rails and she wondered if her own clothes would fetch enough to make any difference to her financial state. While Geoffrey's attention was elsewhere, she took the opportunity to inspect the nearest rail. She found a dark brown suede skirt.

'How much for this?' she asked the stallholder, a young woman who had two small children with her and was obviously not entirely focused.

'Oh, I don't know. Make me an offer.' She looked longingly at the skirt in Flora's hand. 'I loved that skirt. I just don't think I'll ever fit into it again.'

'Of course you will!' said Flora, who instantly rejected

the idea of buying it now she knew it was so precious to its owner.

'Give you a couple of quid for it,' said another woman, who obviously lacked not only Flora's sensitive nature, but also her figure.

The young woman started to take the skirt off its hanger. 'No!' Flora interrupted quickly. 'I'll give you a fiver.'

The young mother looked hopefully at the woman who had offered two pounds.

'No way,' she said disgustedly and moved away.

'She wouldn't have got into it,' muttered Flora, watching her move through the crowd.

'She'd sell it on,' said the skirt's owner. 'Do you really want it for a fiver? I'd like you to have it. I wouldn't feel so bad about selling it if I knew it was going to a good home.'

Flora found her purse again, cursing her sentimental nature. The ramekins she could justify, but spending five pounds on a skirt she didn't really need, when she was so broke, was just silly. Perhaps she would have to put her teapot into the next sale.

'I don't think I'll bother to sell my clothes,' said Flora as she caught up with Geoffrey, forgetting he was unaware of her financial straits. 'I wouldn't get much for them.'

'Why would you want to?' he asked.

'Oh, I was just wondering, you know, what I might get for them.'

'I think you'd be better off buying than selling, if it's clothes you're interested in. What have you got there?' He indicated the plastic bag containing the skirt.

'Oh, a dear little skirt. It was only a fiver.'

'A fiver! You were robbed, my dear. Did you haggle?'

'Er . . . not really,' Flora admitted. 'I thought it was a good price.'

'You should always haggle. I could have got that for you for no more than a couple of quid.'

'Oh.' Flora smiled, feeling foolish. It wasn't that the skirt wasn't worth what she'd paid for it, it was just that she was unlikely to want to wear it before the autumn and it had cost a sixth of all the money she had in the world at that particular moment. 'I felt sorry for the woman,' she said quietly.

'You're daft, you are,' said Geoffrey. 'Now come along and I'll show you how it's done. There's a tool stall up there. Some of them sell very well at auction, and the sellers aren't always so aware of what's valuable. Ceramics, collectables, people know can be worth a bit. There won't be the margin in it.'

Geoffrey and Flora walked slowly along the tables. Although Geoffrey was looking for tools he allowed Flora to pick up things and examine them. Some things seemed to be wildly overpriced to Flora, but she had learnt her lesson and didn't let herself get involved with the sellers. 'Who wants an old Tressy doll with no hair?' she asked Geoffrey when they were out of earshot of her owner.

'Some little girl with a few pennies to spend. But if she was in good condition, with her box, she'd be worth money.'

'And what about those ghastly china ornaments?'

'The little ones probably aren't worth a lot, but some of those big heavy horses will fetch quite a bit. They

196

have to be undamaged, though. Ah, here we are.'

Finding herself quite unable to be interested in a jumble of carpenters' tools, old planes, files, chisels and saws, Flora had a little wander on her own. Her mind was not on the job. She was supposed to be learning her craft but she was too concerned with her financial situation at the moment. Her parents wouldn't let her or Imelda starve, but ever since she'd left home Flora had been extremely independent and wouldn't take subsidies, except in the form of the fare to whatever country her parents were residing in and, of course, free board and lodging while she was there.

Determined to snap out of her despondent and unhelpful mood she went over to yet another stall run by a young woman who looked vaguely familiar and also rather despondent. She was selling children's toys and clothes, some handbags and a few bags of cakes. She was perched on the tailgate of her car and perked up a little when Flora approached.

'It's Flora, isn't it? I'm Amy, from the choir. Alto.'

'Hello! I thought you looked familiar,' said Flora. 'Do you do this often?'

'Never by myself before. I'm hopeless at it and I forgot to bring anything to eat or drink.'

'Well, I could go and get you something, if you liked.'

'No, it's all right. I'll manage. It's really the chance to have a wander round that I'm missing.'

Flora glanced up and down the aisle of tables and spotted Geoffrey, deep in conversation with someone. Edie, miles away, appeared to have bought a tree. 'Well, if you like, I could mind your stall while you have a look. My friends – oh, it's Geoffrey and Edie – they seem occupied and wouldn't mind if I was here for a little while. Of course, you don't really know me. You might not trust me.'

'Of course I trust you!' The young woman became enthusiastic. 'Would you mind? I find selling terribly difficult. I'm only here because there are a few things we must make space for, and if my friend had come with me, we'd have made a bit of money. Enough to buy a bit more stuff with, anyway.'

'I thought the idea was to make space, not fill it.'

'It is. It's just different space. Would you really mind my stall for a bit?'

'Sure.' The saleswoman in Flora awoke. Amy would never sell anything as things were, she needed a bit more enthusiasm for the task. 'Would you mind if I played with the things? I'd quite like to test my selling ability. I want to know if I could ever have a stall at a car-boot sale myself.'

Amy shrugged. 'Help yourself. I've hardly sold anything so far.'

'You go off then and I'll see if I can sell anything for you. What about prices?'

'Oh, just get what you can for it. I'm hopeless about prices.' Amy hitched her bag over her shoulder and, looking far more cheerful, set off into the crowd.

Flora set to work, using skills developed during a holiday job in Bond Street when she'd worked for a friend of her mother's.

She took the toys out of their plastic bags and grouped them together in a way that made them look as if they were already being played with. She forced the Barbies to sit around under a toy umbrella, with outsize cans of lemonade in their hands. A teddy bear she made read a book, miniature to a child, enormous for the teddy. A tea set was set out with plastic cakes and hot dogs and a toy cart was filled with two plastic apples. Everything was the wrong scale, but Flora still enjoyed herself.

Once the toys were dealt with, she turned her attention to the handbags. Under the dust, she discovered that a couple of them were very good makes. She found the napkin she'd been given with her cup of tea and wiped them down. Then she plumped them up and made a little display of them. Everything that was for sale was regrouped, rearranged and made to look more appealing.

Her first customer was Geoffrey. 'What are you doing here? I only left you alone for a minute.'

'This is Amy's stall. From choir? She asked me to mind it while she had a cup of coffee and a look round. I thought it would be good practice for me, selling stuff.'

'I have no doubts about your selling abilities, dear. It's whether you know tat from quality that I'm concerned with.'

'Oh, don't worry about that now. I've got plenty of time to learn all that stuff. You go and see if you can pick up some bargains while I look after the stall.'

She didn't want any witnesses to her barrow-boy antics, that's if she had the nerve to perform them.

Flora decided to target the buyers rather than depend on what she was selling to attract them. She spotted a father with two little girls. He was obviously entertaining them while his wife got on with things at home.

Flora came out from behind her stall and said hello to the little girls. 'Do you like Barbies?'

'We have a million Barbie dolls at home,' said the father, looking weary.

'But have you got these Barbies?' Flora decided that flirting was allowed when she was doing it to help someone, and smiled. 'They're extra special and an absolute bargain. Look, they're having a picnic,' she turned her attention to the girls again. 'Fifty pence each. The food is extra,' she added, glancing up at the father with a sideways grin.

'Oh, Daddy! Can we?'

'It's up to you. You've got your own money to spend.'

Flora handed over three Barbie dolls for one pound fifty pence, hoping she hadn't sold them far too cheaply. 'And do you need the food as well? Look, you get all this too.' She shook the plastic bag that contained the more battered toy boxes and tins of groceries. 'Twenty pence. Now, what about the picnic set? Then you could have a big party, with all your dolls.'

Having screwed every penny out of the two little girls, but given them, in her opinion, very good value for their money, she turned her attention to their dad.

'What about a nice bag for your wife? This one is a very good name. Not quite Prada, but getting there. You have heard of Prada, have you? No? Obviously a serious-minded person, but let me assure you, your wife has heard of Prada, and a bag like this, while obviously not Prada, or it would be worth about a million pounds . . . '

The words poured out of her. She smiled, she flirted, she made him laugh, and by the time he'd gone away he was laden with plastic carriers of toys, a handbag, and a set of Mr Men books. Although fairly satisfied,

Flora was disappointed that she hadn't managed to convince him that a rabbit hutch was a pleasing garden ornament, even if you hadn't got, and didn't want, a rabbit.

She was just counting the money she'd made, hoping Amy wouldn't be furious with her for selling so much so cheaply, when a man came up and asked about the rabbit hutch. 'How much for the hutch, love?'

'Twenty pounds.'

'I'll give you five.'

'Five pounds! Are you trying to rob me? Do you know how much they are new?' As Flora didn't know this herself, she was rather hoping he'd tell her.

'I don't want a new rabbit hutch. It's only for my ferrets. Five pounds. All it's worth to me.'

'Fifteen then. I'm practically giving it away.'

'Six pounds, that's my absolute top offer.'

'Twelve. Cheap at twice the price.'

'Ten. And I'm being robbed. I could keep them in an old crate for nothing.'

'But then they'd escape. Ten pounds is fine. Thank you very much.'

'I've had a brilliant time,' said Flora, when Amy came back. 'But I expect I've sold everything far too cheaply.'

'You've sold it, that's the main thing. And that looks like loads of money.'

'A fiver of it is mine, I'm afraid. I sold a very nice suede skirt I'd bought by mistake.' She frowned slightly. 'I hope the man was right, and his wife was a size ten.'

Once back at the cottage, when she'd seen to her brood and shown them the teapot, which now had pride of place on the mantelpiece, Flora lay on the sofa, contemplating the prospect of a dinner party with no money. Having too little money to buy posh ready meals was bad enough, but barely having enough to buy basic ingredients was worse. The rain was pouring down outside and, she reflected, a less buoyant personality than her own could get pretty miserable.

William came in through the back door, shaking his hair, sending water flying off him. 'I'll sleep here tonight if you don't mind, Flora.'

'Don't blame you. The kittens are so adorable! I could hardly bear to leave them. Go up and look.'

'I will in a minute. Tea?'

'I'm already on the wine, I'm afraid. What am I going to feed these people on, William? I've hardly any money.'

'Vegetarian then. Far cheaper.'

'But I don't know how to cook any vegetarian dishes. Isn't it all goats' cheese and aubergines and that bean curd stuff?'

'Tofu? Not necessarily, but aubergines are good.'

Flora winced at the thought. She felt too tired to think about big shiny vegetables she never knew what to do with. Didn't they require something complicated to do with salt? 'I'll see if I can get some recipes off the computer.'

'I could cook for you,' William offered amiably.

Flora opened her eyes. 'Could you?'

'I've worked as a chef and I used to cook in the Buddhist centre where I lived for a while. Vegetarian dishes are my speciality.'

'That would be fantastic! But wouldn't it look a little

odd, you doing the cooking? Did I tell you that you have to pretend to be Emma's partner?'

'No! Why do I have to do that? Why can't I just be another friend?'

'Because where would you sleep?'

'On the sofa, where I always sleep.'

'Yes, but no one's supposed to know that! And although I could put a guest up, I suppose, you're meant to be Emma's partner, calling on me, while I'm down here!'

William frowned. 'This is all far too complicated.'

'I've got to explain your presence somehow, for your sake as much as anything.'

'It would be much better if I were just Emma's friend. Far less complicated.'

Flora thought about this. Having a handsome, heterosexual male as a regular caller was not going to do her any good in the eyes of Charles and Annabelle. 'You wouldn't pretend to be gay?'

'No.'

'There's no stigma—'

'No, Flora. I'll be pretend to be Emma – is it Emma? – Emma's old friend from university, who she got back in touch with, and told that you were living down here and didn't know anybody.'

Flora nodded slowly. 'That could work. That could explain why you were doing t'ai chi naked on the lawn. Emma doesn't know you very well and you've changed over the years.'

'That part at least is true,' he said with a grin. 'I'll have a think about what to cook and give you a shopping list.'

'And I'll make chocolate mousse for pudding. I can use my new ramekin dishes. Oh, and I must ring Henry. I'm still hoping he'll cancel his conference in Switzerland and come.'

But Henry resisted all blandishments.

Chapter Twelve

'I can't believe you've joined a choir!' said Emma as Flora drove her back from the station on Friday evening. 'It's such a – well – you know . . .'

'What?' asked Flora defensively.

'"Old person" thing to do.'

'Nonsense! I love it! It's very soothing, singing. You have to concentrate, really hard, all the time – or at least I do because I'm not very good – and that means you can't think about work. We're going to do a concert. You must come down for it. Now, how are you?'

Emma knew that this meant 'how are you and Dave?' 'Well, OK. He's just lost interest in me, I think. All the little things I do that he used to think were sweet now just irritate him.'

'Oh, I do understand! That happens to me all the time!'

'What?'

Realising that she was about to say how she got irritated by the little habits that used to enchant her, Flora hurriedly inverted her statement. 'About how they sigh when you do things wrong when they used to do them for you, in a really sweet way.'

'Exactly.'

'Well, what you need is a new man, sweetie. And I've got just the one.'

'You mean William, the naked tae kwon do expert?'

'T'ai chi. It's quite different. And he mostly wears clothes.'

'Still don't fancy it, Flo.'

'It's him you have to fancy. You probably will, no problem. He's gorgeous.'

'So why don't *you* fancy him, then?'

Flora had thought about this, and presumably so had William. 'Don't know. The chemistry's not right, I suppose. But he's really nice, funny, cooks, everything a girl wants, really.'

'Perhaps you fancy someone else. Henry?'

Flora wrinkled her nose and then remembered it would give her lines and stopped. 'Yes, I do fancy him, sort of, but not in a gut-wrenching way.'

'It doesn't always have to be gut-wrenching. It can creep up on you slowly, from behind.'

'Well, if it does, it does, but it hasn't yet, and quite honestly I have no emotional energy left to spare for a relationship, just at the moment. The business is my obsession.'

'So do you fancy your business partner, then?'

'Charles! What? No way!'

'Why not?'

'Apart from the fact that we had a blazing row, he can't wait to get rid of me and I hate his guts, you mean?'

'Never stopped anyone fancying anyone before.'

Flora laughed. 'True, but not in this case. He's too stuffy to live. I mean, when I'm not hating him, I do admire him, for the way he does his job, but definitely not the way he runs his business.' She thought for a moment. 'And he is good-looking, and I suppose his sternness could be sexy, but no!'

'Why not?'

'Come on, Em, he's spoken for, for one thing, and even if he wasn't, it would take years to get him to unbend.'

'You've always liked projects before. A challenge, someone who doesn't just fall in love with you immediately they see you. Treat her mean and keep her keen was always the way to get you interested.'

'No, it wasn't,' Flora denied, wondering if what Emma said had any truth in it. 'Anyway, Charles would be more than a project, he'd be like climbing Everest without any training. Or oxygen.'

'Hm.'

'Anyway, even if I did fancy him, which I *so* don't, he loves Annabelle. I couldn't disturb that.'

'Are you sure he's happy with Annabelle?'

Flora thought about this. 'I think so. I don't know he's not. They're very well suited and they've known each other for a long time.' Before her huge falling-out with Charles she'd probably have said that Annabelle didn't deserve him. The Charles she'd seen when Annabelle wasn't around, the Charles who was passionate and knowledgeable about his business and great with the people he employed, deserved better than a woman who wanted nothing more than to sell up and get out. And although Flora had warmed to Annabelle a bit when they went shopping together, she was still incredibly self-centred and utterly self-obsessed, which couldn't be fun to live with. But since the collapse of the ceiling, Flora rather thought they were perfect for each other:

the strict, austere Charles she saw when Annabelle was in the room was clearly the real one, and Annabelle was welcome to him!

'Sounds terribly boring,' said Emma, and Flora realised she hadn't been listening properly, off in her own little world. She laughed.

'It does, doesn't it? But I don't suppose it is really. So, let's talk about Dave or your work or something metropolitan.'

'Oh no, don't let's. I'd like to forget about Dave just for a weekend.'

Flora glanced at her friend, worried, but the look on Emma's face told her now wasn't the time. 'Fair enough. Shall we call in for some chips?'

'Haven't you prepared a gourmet meal for me on my first night with you?'

'No.'

Emma laughed. 'Chips it is then. I do miss you, Flo. I'm really looking forward to you coming back to London.'

'You'll have to ring him,' Emma insisted the next day, putting down her tea towel. 'He's your landlord and you need a dining table. Now.'

Flora smoothed on some hand-cream. She and Emma had just done the washing up after lunch and William was scooping the insides out of aubergines.

'It's Annabelle's cottage. She's responsible,' Flora pointed out.

'Ring her then! I'm sure she'd understand about having people to dinner and not having a table.'

'OK. But it'll have to be quite a big table. It'll take up all the space in the cottage.'

208

'Not if it folds down or has leaves or something. I don't know why you didn't get it sorted out earlier.'

'I told you, Charles and I had this awful row, and although we did both apologise, it was in that way when you know you have to say sorry, but you're not.' It had been nearly two weeks since they'd had a civil conversation.

'I do understand but we still need a table.'

'I was busy, Em! I'll do it now,' Flora snapped, feeling more harassed by the minute.

'We'd have much more room it we ate outside,' offered William. 'The rain's cleared up and it could be a really nice evening.'

'Weather wise, you mean,' said Flora, who didn't think it could possibly be nice in any other way.

'Yes. Why don't you ask your cousin—'

'His name is Charles,' said Emma, who wasn't getting on with William quite as well as Flora would have liked.

'If he's got a large picnic table we could put a bit of board on,' William went on.

'How many people are we going to be?' asked Emma.

'Only six,' said Flora. 'It's not a huge number. An ordinary table would be fine.'

'As long as it doesn't come on to rain and we have to rush indoors with it,' William explained.

'Oh no, you're right. Annabelle would freak if inside furniture got wet or anything. I'll suggest something like that,' said Flora. 'But I'll go and get it. We want to get the table set in plenty of time. If we're going to eat out it would be nice to decorate it with wild flowers and things.'

'Aren't you getting just a little too rural, Flo?' suggested Emma.

'Not at all. It's just nice to appreciate nature's bounty.'

'Pick up the phone,' ordered Emma, not impressed.

'There isn't a phone. I'll have to take my mobile outside, for the reception.'

Flora went into the front garden, glad to be on her own for a minute, but not relishing having to ring Charles. At least if she got Annabelle, she knew she'd understand the problem.

Charles answered. Although she knew he was perfectly likely to pick up the phone, hearing his voice panicked her. 'Er hello, it's me.' Flora always forgot her name when she was nervous.

'Flora,' he said.

'Yes, sorry. I'm just ringing about the table. For tonight?'

'Oh. Yes. You'll be needing one.' Flora heard Annabelle's voice in the background. Then she snatched the phone.

'Flora? What's the matter? You're not cancelling, are you?'

'No. I'm just asking if there's a table we could use. We don't want to eat on our laps.'

'Oh God, I forgot we'd sold the table. I'll organise Charles to do something about it immediately. When do you want it?'

'Well, I would like to have time to set it before you all come, but I suppose—'

'Of course you must have it sooner than that. Don't worry. Um, did your friend arrive all right?'

'Oh yes. I picked her up from the station last night.'

'And – um – the man I saw . . . ?'

In her slightly frazzled state, Flora couldn't remember

quite what she'd said to Annabelle about William, but decided to stick to William's suggestion that he was an old friend of Emma's. 'Oh yes, he's here too. He's doing the cooking.'

'OK. I'll send Charles over with the table, then.'

Now they'd convinced Flora that they couldn't possibly pass as a couple, William and Emma began to get on much better. They'd gone off to the woods together quite happily. Whether they were intending to gather the makings of a starter, Flora wasn't entirely sure. She was making chocolate mousse when Charles arrived.

She saw him drive up and went out, wiping her chocolatey hands on the tea towel she had tucked into her belt as an apron. She was in some ways relieved to see him – it would have been such a bore if they'd had no time to set the table nicely – but she wished Emma and William were here to diffuse things if it got heated.

'Hi, Charles,' she greeted him neutrally. 'This is very kind of you.'

'Not all that kind. You should have had a table all along. I'll bring it in. I've got some wine, too. Save bringing it later.'

'Lovely. Emma and William have brought some too.' A thought occurred to her. 'It's not a very precious table, is it? We thought we'd eat outside. It would be a bit cramped in the cottage for six.'

'No. It's an army surplus one. But it would have been for the officer class,' he added.

Flora was taken aback. That was definitely a joke. 'That's all right then. I wouldn't want my guests sitting at anything that wasn't worthy.' Flora smiled, deciding

211

that as Charles was obviously making an effort at being more civil, she should too.

'Have you enough chairs? I brought a couple of plastic stacking ones, in case.'

'Chairs.' Flora mentally trawled the two bedrooms and the bathroom. 'Actually, a couple of chairs would be very useful, thank you,' she added, making proper eye contact for the first time since the fight.

'Where are your other guests?'

'In the woods. Picking something, probably. I hope you like nettles.'

'Oh, absolutely. My favourite.'

'You think I'm joking, but I'm not,' she said solemnly.

He nodded, equally serious. 'Flora . . .' He looked oddly embarrassed for a moment. 'I've also got a cheque here for your back wages. If you give me your bank details we can do it by standing order in future.'

Flora regarded him quizzically. That was definitely the last thing she'd expected, but maybe he was as daunted as her by the idea of a hideously uncomfortable evening, and was trying to engineer some kind of truce. 'You've forgiven me for pulling the ceiling down, then?'

Again, he looked a little shame-faced. 'You did put it up again, very neatly. And while I do think you're a liability, you're quite a hard-working liability, and deserve to be paid something, even the pathetic wages we're offering. And . . .' He paused again, clearly feeling awkward. 'And Geoffrey said something to me.'

Flora flushed. She wasn't entirely sure she wanted to be the subject of discussions between Geoffrey and Charles.

212

'He said there were relatively few people who'd give up a job in London to come and work for the minimum wage in a small business in a small town, and we were lucky to have you – and to be honest it was only then that I realised that actually you've been working very hard for us for several weeks for free. Which, even though you're a shareholder, obviously isn't on.'

'Oh.' Flora felt inordinately pleased at this grudging approval.

'I'll get the paperwork.'

While he was gone she did a quick check on her feelings for him. Perhaps he wasn't the most horrible man on the planet. Perhaps he was almost human. It took a bit of work to make the mental adjustment, but hell, she was flexible, she could do that.

When he came back he had a stern, businesslike expression and he gave her a look which seemed to draw attention to the amount of chocolate smeared over her. She reverted to disliking him. Life was simpler that way.

He produced a cheque. 'Is there somewhere I can put this where you won't lose it?'

'I won't lose it! But if you're worried, you can put it on the mantelpiece.'

He crossed the room and then caught sight of the teapot. 'Oh my God!'

'It's lovely, isn't it? Geoffrey gave it to me. We found it at a car-boot sale.'

'It's the most revolting piece of kitsch I've seen in a long time. I'm surprised Geoffrey let you have anything to do with it.'

Flora grinned. 'Well, to be honest, he wouldn't have,

only he could see I had my heart set on it and thought I'd pay too much if he didn't do the deal for me.'

'So how much did he pay for it?'

'A fiver.'

'Hmm. That's not bad, actually. I should sell it, if I were you.'

'But, Charles, it'll fit in so well with the rest of my collection!'

He rolled his eyes. 'Sell all of it. On a good day you'd get quite a lot of money.'

'I may be a bit hard up, but I'm not ready to sell my precious teapots, yet.' Although it was a good idea, she acknowledged silently. She could do it on the Internet, and get her mother to pack them off to eager buyers.

'You're hard up?'

'Did I say that? No! I'm fine, now you've paid my wages.'

He frowned. 'I'm sorry that our rather sticky relationship meant you couldn't tell me something like that.'

She shrugged.

'On the other hand, our sticky relationship is entirely your fault.' He smiled, and for a second Flora caught a flash of the charm which all other women seemed to get all the time. 'I don't suppose I could have another peep at the kittens? I wouldn't like to ask in front of everyone else or they'll all want to see them too and it might be a bit much for them.'

'That's very considerate of you, and of course you can see them. They've opened their eyes since you last saw them, I think.'

As he followed her upstairs she felt suddenly anxious at the thought of him being in her bedroom, it was so untidy. Still, it was too late now. She could hardly bring the whole caboodle downstairs, Imelda would hate it.

'You'll have to excuse the mess,' she said as they reached the landing, getting more anxious by the second.

Her bedroom did indeed have that 'just burgled' look and he glanced around it, trying and failing to disguise his horror at the clutter of make-up and beauty preparations on the dressing table, and the heap of clothes on the bed.

'I'm a bit short of clothes storage and I'd put a lot of my things in Emma's room,' Flora explained hurriedly. 'I had to bring it all back here when she came.'

'I see.'

Then, because in spite of everything she was annoyed by his silent disapproval, she added, 'And some of them are waiting to be washed. I can't decide if I should just wash them all by hand or take them to the launderette.'

This little dig went home. 'I did promise you a washing machine, didn't I? I promise I'll get on to it. Now I've seen how great your need is . . .' He paused. '. . . I'm less likely to forget. Now, are the kittens still where they were before?'

Flora nodded. 'In the cupboard with my shoes. Imelda and I are almost psychically in tune, you know.'

He chuckled and knelt down.

'This little black one is my favourite,' he said, plucking it up from the others.

'He's very shy. He usually squeaks like mad if you pick him up.'

But the little bundle didn't squeak, it purred, snuggling into Charles's neck.

Flora felt a pang of irritation at the sight of her kitten

215

taking so well to someone else. 'He likes you.'

'Is it a boy?'

'I think so. It's quite hard to tell. No, don't look! He's happy where he is.'

She stood up too quickly and, swaying slightly, put her hand on his shoulder to steady herself. 'I'll leave you to it. I must get on.'

'Yes, sorry, I must get back.' Charles put the kitten back in its box and got up. 'Things to do. Jeremy's really looking forward to it.'

'Is he? I don't know if he should. I think we're having nettle quiche to start.'

'It wasn't the food I was thinking about when I was giving him details.'

'Oh?'

'It was the company.'

Charles started downstairs, Flora behind him, suffering from mild shock. He was being nice. Or polite, at least.

'Are you going to wear that dress?' Charles asked.

Flora glanced down at the little slip dress covered with a tea towel. 'No. It's got chocolate on it.'

'Oh, so it has.'

Flora became thoughtful. She was sure she'd seen him looking at the chocolate smears with distaste. Perhaps she'd got it wrong.

When he'd gone she went back to the kitchen and started whipping egg whites, wishing there was an electric beater in the cottage. Charles really was a law unto himself – talk about inscrutable! He made the sphinx seem like easy reading.

*　　*　　*

216

William, the cook, in charge of it all, was the calmest during an afternoon of preparation. He just stayed in the kitchen, doing his thing, while Flora and Emma cleaned and tidied and panicked. Flora was nervous for so many reasons that they'd merged into a single mass of anxiety. Loyally, Emma picked up on her feelings and did her best with the downstairs, which wasn't too bad, while Flora attacked her bedroom.

The disadvantage of having kittens in your bedroom, she realised, was that people were likely to go in there and look at them. Thus it had to be tidy. She was still blushing with embarrassment about how it had been when Charles came, although they did seem better friends now than before, which was definitely a good thing.

Now her bedroom was a picture of ordered simplicity. Her bed was made so perfectly it looked as if no one had slept on it, ever. The clothes and shoes, which had been strewn everywhere earlier, were packed into suit-cases and hidden in the Land-Rover. The fact that even the clean ones would now have to be ironed again, possibly even washed, had not deterred her. She had a travel iron, after all, and she was aiming for the nun's cell look.

To this end, all the detritus of womanhood had been swept from sight, put into shoe boxes and hidden under the bed, and a simple bouquet of wild flowers adorned her dressing table in their stead. If she could have persuaded Imelda and the kittens to stay in their current, artistically arranged positions, she would have been completely satisfied, but as they'd look beautiful what-ever they did, she wasn't too bothered. Annabelle wouldn't go up to see them anyway. That Jeremy might, though, and now she wanted Charles to admire them again, so he could see she wasn't always a slut. She could do minimalism, she just didn't, often.

They had spent hours decorating the dining table. Emma, after scoffing at Flora's ideas initially, had become particularly enthusiastic.

'I want it to be very French,' Emma said, 'like a picture out of a posh cookbook. You know, when they have really pretty children in white dresses with garlands of flowers in their hair, and the mums are all really thin and gorgeous, even the cook.'

She had gathered tiny bouquets of wild flowers and pinned up the corners of Annabelle's double sheets that were doing service as tablecloths.

'You don't think it looks a bit – bridal?' said Flora when Emma had finished. 'It just needs a big white cake in the middle and a priest.'

'It's totally how I want my wedding to be,' said Emma. 'Only with champagne, of course.'

'Sorry about that,' said Flora. 'Have some frascati instead.'

Emma took the glass without thinking. 'I wonder if Dave would like a wedding like this?'

'Darling,' said Flora seriously. 'Don't think about the wedding, think about the man. It's not worth going through all the hassle of getting married to end up with . . .' She paused.

'Dave?' suggested Emma.

'Well, yes. Sorry, Em. I just don't think he's good enough for you.'

'He doesn't want me, anyway.'

Flora glanced at her watch. Sympathetic as she was to Emma's feelings, and usually very willing to let people talk about their problems, she just felt there wasn't quite time for it all now. 'He probably does, but you have to think really carefully about whether you want him. Now I want you to take time this evening, when we're all chatting and laughing – please God we do all chat and laugh – and think about whether he makes you happy. Not necessarily all the time,' she went on, reasonably, 'no one can expect that, but most of the time. Now, I'm just going to get a cloth and polish the cutlery. It still looks smeary. And the glasses.'

'Let's have another glass of wine first,' said Emma. 'Then I'm going to change.'

Both women were in the kitchen, getting in William's way, when they heard a car drive up. They both rushed into the sitting room so they could see who it was before Flora went to the door.

'Do you think they'll all come together?' she asked Emma.

'How on earth would I know?'

As the doors of Charles's car opened and a large man emerged, they exchanged glances. 'Don't fancy yours much,' murmured Flora to Emma.

'Oh I don't know,' said Emma. 'I think he's OK. Now let's have a look at this Charles.'

Fortunately for Flora, her hostessly duties meant she had to go out and greet her guests and not listen to her friend's opinion of her cousin and business-partner, who she had recently discovered was not quite as loathsome as she'd once thought.

Jeremy, whom Flora would have paired with Annabelle, had she been playing Happy Couples, a card game she had yet to patent, was pleasantly tall, with slightly sparse curly hair, and wore a striped shirt and the sort of corduroys that look good in the country.

He was also the kind of man who kissed everyone, even on a first meeting. This set the tone for everyone else, otherwise Charles would never have kissed her, possibly fearing that such an action might turn him to stone. Not that you'd've noticed before, she added, with a secret chuckle. But he had loosened up a bit that afternoon.

After the initial introductions were over, and they had moved inside to the sitting room (William was still in the kitchen), Flora murmured to Annabelle, 'Just come upstairs a minute.'

'Going to see the kittens, sweetheart?' said Charles.

'No,' said Flora briskly. 'Emma, can you and William do drinks?'

'Why have you dragged me up here?' demanded Annabelle. 'I must say, it looks very sweet. Oh, there are the kittens.'

'Never mind the kittens, it's your hair! What's with the hairband?'

Annabelle crouched down and regarded herself in Flora's dressing-table mirror. 'I used to get house points at school for having tidy hair.'

Flora tugged off the hairband and ruffled Annabelle's glossy locks. 'Why not go for some life points and muss it up a little?'

Annabelle, surveying her newly tousled hair and accepting its attractiveness, turned to Flora. 'It's very kind of you to do this.'

'Yes, isn't it?' Flora said wryly. 'I hope Charles has noticed the improvement.'

'Charles loves me no matter how I look,' Annabelle announced rather smugly. 'This – er – change, is just for me.'

'And the school reunion?'

'Yes, and that. Now let's get back down and join the others.'

Imelda yowled suddenly from her space in the bottom of the wardrobe. Flora stayed to comfort her so she could have a few moments alone.

Chapter Thirteen

Downstairs, Flora found that Jeremy, Charles and Emma were still standing round drinkless. William had just emerged from the kitchen and introductions were being got through. She took over in time to say, 'Right, well, Emma, this is Annabelle, and Annabelle, this is William, an old friend of Emma's.'

William took Annabelle's hand. 'I believe you saw me the other day. I'd come over to look up Flora, on Madam's instructions' – he glanced at Emma – 'and as she was out, I thought I'd do some t'ai chi.'

Jeremy regarded William with suspicion. 'Is that one of those martial art things?'

'Sort of.'

'I don't think he's remotely dangerous,' said Flora, and Jeremy smiled.

'I hope not,' said William. 'I'm a pacifist – and a portrait painter, and a bit of a poet, too.'

'All the p's,' murmured Emma.

'I'm ex-Army, myself,' said Jeremy.

Seeing what could become a problem, Flora rushed to save the situation. '"Ex", you say? What a shame. I do love a man in uniform.'

'I prefer men who don't need clothes to give them status,' said Annabelle, horribly against type.

Flora, rather thrown, rushed on, 'Shall we all have a drink? What would everyone like? Wine, red or white, elderflower pressé, apple juice . . .'

'I've got a glass of wine in the kitchen,' said William, 'and if you'll excuse me, I'll go back to the cooking.'

'Can I help?' asked Annabelle, quick as a knife. 'Did you say you were a portrait painter?'

'Among other things, and thank you,' said William, 'I could do with a hand.'

Flora knew perfectly well that if it had been she cooking, Annabelle wouldn't have dreamt of offering help, but she seemed peculiarly intrigued by William. Then again, the whole point of the evening was for her to make sure William was safe to trust around her cottage. 'Better take a drink then, Annabelle. White wine?'

'Marvellous, thank you.'

'What about the rest of you?' asked Flora, hoping that William needed Annabelle to tear up raw nettles.

'White wine for me, too, please,' said Emma.

'Right.' Flora tipped the bottle up to pour the wine and realised it was empty.

'Here, let me,' said Charles, and took the corkscrew from Flora's hand.

Usually she would have protested and opened the bottle herself, but the corkscrew was the kind that required you to put the bottle between your feet and pull like mad, nearly cutting off your fingers in the process. She surrendered the bottle and the corkscrew.

'I'll have red,' said Jeremy. 'If that's open already.'

Flora smiled at him as she handed him his glass and saw his response. Oh, don't do that, she thought. This dinner party is complicated enough already.

'Let's go outside,' she said instead, leading the way out of the front door. 'It's such a lovely evening and we're eating out there. Besides, you might have noticed, there's nowhere to sit here. All the furniture's in the garden.'

'It looks very pretty,' said Jeremy, who had followed. 'Did you decorate the table, Flora?'

'No, Emma did, actually. She's very artistic. She's got a real flair for design.'

Emma, following him out, looked appropriately modest.

'So, are you in that sort of business, Emma?' asked Jeremy. 'You're obviously really gifted.'

Flora watched with satisfaction as Emma drew Jeremy away to where the wrought-iron table and chairs that Charles had brought had been pulled into a little area by the hedge. There was a cloth on the table and, on that, a vase with a single sprig of honeysuckle and a small dish of pistachios. The garden, untidy as it was, was still extremely pretty with rambling roses scrambling over the hedge, honeysuckle scenting the air and poppies spilling their petals shamelessly on to the grass.

'What are you having, Flora?' asked Charles from behind her. She turned, unnerved, to see him with his hands full of bottles.

'Oh, I think I'll just have elderflower. Emma and I had a glass of wine earlier.'

'Well, it's not stopping me,' called Emma, hearing this. 'I'm surprised it's stopping you, Flo. It's not as if we've got to drive anywhere.'

'I have to drive,' said Charles. 'I'll have elderflower, too.'

224

'So, tell me all about what you do now you're no longer in the army,' said Emma to Jeremy, turning back to the matter in hand. 'I've learnt far more than I want to know about auction houses from Flora. She's totally hooked.'

'Is that true?' asked Charles quietly, following Flora, who'd gone to perch on the arm of the sofa.

'Well, I probably have chewed her ear off a bit,' she admitted.

'I mean that you're hooked on auction houses.'

'I wouldn't put it in the plural, but I am hooked on our auction house, yes.' She looked him in the eye. 'But you did know that, Charles. I have told you. On more than one occasion.'

'I suppose you have.'

Flora took a breath, thinking about their row and how it still hung between them. She badly wanted to just sit in silence, enjoying the beautiful summer evening and not say anything about anything, but she couldn't.

Did he mind about Annabelle disappearing into the kitchen leaving him to make polite conversation? Was he fighting the urge to go storming in there, demanding that Annabelle rip off her rubber gloves and come back to the party? Would there be a fight? The thought made her smile slightly – it was so unlikely.

'What's making you smile?' asked Charles.

'Oh, nothing really!' She, who could chat for Britain, was totally at a loss. It might be that she was tired, but she feared it was because that she knew she had to apologise properly for the terrible things she had said to him during their row. She took another sip of her drink, wishing she hadn't been so abstemious and had allowed herself another glass of wine. She couldn't apologise when anyone was likely to overhear her – she didn't want the whole thing common knowledge.

'Do you think Annabelle's all right in the kitchen?' she said awkwardly. 'Perhaps I should go and see?'

Charles was standing in her way, and would have to move if she did want to escape back inside the house. 'Annabelle's perfectly capable of leaving it if she's not enjoying herself, I assure you,' he said.

Was there something a little cold in Charles's voice when he said this? Perhaps they'd quarrelled on the way over. Except they'd had Jeremy with them in the car. That would cramp Charles's style, if not Annabelle's. 'I'll try not to worry about it then.'

She wasn't really worried, just a bit uncomfortable. She racked her brain for a neutral topic of conversation.

'Just relax, Flora,' said Charles, putting a hand on the small of her back for just a second as he came round to sit on the sofa next to her. 'I know entertaining is stressful, but I'm sure William's got it all under control. And if not, Annabelle's very capable.'

Flora sighed again. If only it was William, Annabelle and nature's bounty that was worrying her. Fortunately, William and Annabelle both appeared just then, carrying plates.

'A few little nettle quiches to keep you going,' said William.

'He's so clever!' said Annabelle enthusiastically. 'He's created the whole meal out of things he'd gathered from the hedgerows. Oh, and some aubergines.'

Flora, who knew this, had been hoping to keep the information from her guests and had sworn Emma to

226

secrecy. Still, the cat was out of the bag now.

'I hope that doesn't mean we're having hedgehog,' said Jeremy, guffawing in a way Flora feared would put Emma off for ever.

'Oh no. It's strictly vegetarian,' said William. Flora had vetoed rabbit pie, although William had said he had a wonderful recipe for it. The thought of the skinning and disembowelling was all too disgusting.

'Oh!' said Jeremy.

'But not vegan,' added William, by way of reassurance. He and Flora had agreed that while they were keeping costs down, as Emma had brought a hunk of very nice Parmesan cheese with her, it would be a shame not to use it.

'It's nice to try something different,' said Emma, who'd had a sample quiche earlier and knew they were nice. 'Mm! These are gorgeous.'

'Here goes, then,' said Jeremy, putting one into his mouth whole. 'Actually,' he said a moment or two later, blowing crumbs. 'These are excellent.'

'Don't sound so surprised, Jeremy,' snapped Annabelle. 'William's a brilliant cook.'

'The secret with nettles,' said William, 'is to only pick the top two leaves, like you do with tea.'

'Have another quiche, Jeremy,' said Emma, seeing his slightly horrified expression. 'And don't worry about the food. I happen to know that the pudding's quite normal.'

'I'm sure it will be delicious,' said Jeremy, looking at Emma. Emma looked back.

Observing this, Flora felt pleased. It would do Emma's ego so much good to be admired and it would do Dave good if he discovered that Emma wasn't above a little extra-relationship flirting. Maybe he'd start to appreciate her.

'So, what are we having?' asked Charles.

'I think it should be a surprise,' said Annabelle. 'Then we can all guess!'

'As long as none of it's poisonous,' said Jeremy.

'Of course it's not poisonous!' said Annabelle, who obviously found Jeremy irritating, in the way that women often found their partner's male friends irritating. 'William's been doing this for ages!'

'And I think I should go back and check on it all,' said William. 'I'm not used to having to leave my cooking and make polite conversation.'

'I'll come with you!' declared Annabelle and dashed after him.

Flora looked up at Charles. He didn't seem remotely bothered. 'Don't you mind Annabelle spending all her time in the kitchen?'

'No. It'll make a nice change for her.'

And so, with Emma and Jeremy deep in the exchange of information that goes on when people meet and fancy each other, Flora was left to entertain Charles. She still couldn't think of a word to say to him. Her guilt loomed between them and she couldn't get past it. She'd have to find an opportunity to do it. This was too painful. She put her glass down on the coffee table, which was a bit wobbly on the grass, and sank back into the sofa, wishing she could go to sleep, then wake up and find that everyone had gone home.

'So, what are we having to eat?' Charles asked. He was sitting on the arm now.

'Do you really want to know?' Flora wasn't quite sure of the details, having blanked out a lot of what William had said about the rules of picking from the countryside and what you could eat when. He could get a bit obsessive.

'No. I was just making conversation.'

Flora chuckled. 'We could talk about work.'

'We could, but I don't think we should.' But he did smile as he spoke.

'No. And I can't show you the kittens because really, they haven't changed at all since you last saw them.'

'They were very sweet. I wouldn't mind seeing them again.'

'Well, you could pop up and have a look. You could see how tidy my bedroom is now. But I won't come with you. I must stay down here and see to things.'

'What things?'

'Oh, you know, just unspecified "things".'

'Then I won't bother with the kittens again.'

Flora wondered briefly if this was a good moment to get her apology out of the way. She and he could nip up, she could say sorry, and they could nip down again. But Emma would notice and perhaps say something embarrassing.

'I think I need another drink,' she said. 'And I'll make it wine, this time.'

He took her glass. 'Red or white?'

'White, please.'

He was back with it in an instant. If Flora hadn't known better she'd think that Charles was being gallant. It couldn't be, it was impossible. Charles couldn't be gallant with her any more than she could hang-glide, but he was doing quite a good impression of it.

'Here's to us, then,' she said, taking a gulp, realising too late it was probably quite the wrong thing to say. 'To Stanza and Stanza, I mean.'

'To Stanza and Stanza.' Charles raised his glass and looked down into her eyes. 'Which is comprised of "us".'

Fortunately, before Flora succumbed to her desire to scream and go running out into the woods, William and Annabelle emerged bearing between them a basket of bread rolls and a pile of soup plates.

'It's ready,' said Annabelle. 'People should sit down. Have you a *placement*, Flora, or would you like me to do one?'

'No, I've worked out where everyone should sit,' said Flora, grateful for her mother insisting that this was an essential part of entertaining. 'Now, as William did the cooking, he should sit at the end, as host.' She sent him a smile she hoped conveyed her gratitude for this. 'I'll go the other end, of course. Emma and Annabelle, you go next to William, and Jeremy and Charles sit next to me.'

'As long as I don't sit next to Charles, that's fine by me,' said Annabelle.

Jeremy managed to hide any disappointment he felt in not sitting next to Emma and everyone sat down except William and Annabelle.

'Shall I see to the wine?' asked Charles.

'Yes, that would be lovely. I should go and help William bring stuff out, really.'

'I think Annabelle's doing that,' said Charles.

Flora subsided, deprived of her duties as a hostess. She fiddled with her cutlery. 'The little garlands round the napkins look very pretty, Emma,' she said.

'It must have taken you hours,' said Jeremy.

'I really enjoyed myself.' Emma looked across the table at Jeremy, obviously still enjoying herself.

'I hope it won't get chilly later,' said Flora, more anxious about the food than the weather, but unable to express that. 'I've got a couple of pashminas upstairs if it does.'

'Are you cold now, Flora?' asked Charles, putting his hand on her upper arm, as if to check.

'No, I'm fine! It's just later it may—'

Before she could blunder on with more boring prognostications about the temperature of the glorious summer evening, William appeared with a tureen that Flora and Emma had bought that morning from a junk shop. Annabelle was holding a butter dish.

'Right,' he said. 'We're having cold watercress soup to start with, and some rolls I made earlier.'

'Wow,' said Emma. 'Home-made bread! You are good!'

'Then what are we having?' asked Jeremy, still a little anxious. 'After the soup?'

Annabelle glowered at him, but William said, 'It's a sort of pudding made with—'

'I thought you weren't going to say until they'd tried it, William,' said Flora briskly, glad the meal was actually going to start at last. 'William, you serve the soup. How's everyone's wine?'

Charles got up and refilled glasses, including Flora's. She knew perfectly well she should have put her hand over her glass, but she didn't.

'This is fantastic!' said Jeremy, when everyone had been served and were taking their first tentative sips.

231

'It is, William,' said Flora. 'Thank you so much for doing it all.'

Her anxieties about the meal subsided a little. A good bowl of soup, which was full of cream and therefore filling, with bread and butter, should keep people going until the chocolate mousse, if the main course was disgusting.

'William was telling me he's been hearing nightingales in the wood,' said Annabelle excitedly.

'But not recently. They've pretty much stopped singing now.'

'But I thought you said you heard one last week,' said Annabelle.

'How long have you been down here?' asked Charles. 'I thought you came with Emma for the weekend.'

'Oh I did,' said William smoothly, 'but I live quite near. I know this wood well.'

'No need to stay the night then, really,' muttered Jeremy, looking at Emma possessively.

'So, where do you live, exactly?' asked Charles.

Flora got up. 'Excuse me, I've just forgotten something really important.' She almost ran into the house.

Once there, she went upstairs to her bedroom. What on earth would William say? If it was the wrong thing, it would be worse for him than for her, but she still didn't want to witness his lies. She glanced out of the window. Everyone seemed to be chatting, and just as she peeked out further, laughter broke out among her guests. A moment later, she rejoined them.

'Sorry,' she said, as everyone regarded her questioningly. 'I realised I hadn't put any lip-gloss on for hours. More soup, anyone? Jeremy, you'd like some. And another roll.'

As Flora took the soup plates into the kitchen and put them down on the floor, the only surface available to her, she consoled herself with the fact that everyone was almost full already. She met William coming in with the empty tureen followed by Annabelle with the empty bread basket.

'Annabelle! You shouldn't be helping still. Go and sit down and enjoy yourself. William and I can manage fine, now.'

'Oh no, I insist. I find this whole "food for free" thing fascinating.' Annabelle giggled, positively girlish.

Flora went out to join her guests.

'So, Jeremy, what do you do now you're not in the Army?' she asked.

'Computer consultant,' he replied.

'Oh! Emma's in computers, too. What a coincidence.'

Jeremy leant forward a little. 'What does William do again? I'm sure someone's told me, but I seem to have forgotten.'

Flora swallowed. 'He's a poet and a portrait painter. Did he do art at university, Emma?'

Emma opened her mouth as if seeking extra oxygen. 'No. Something to do with the environment, I think,' she said eventually. 'You'll have to ask him yourself, Jeremy.'

'I was just wondering what sort of a living you could make painting people's pictures.'

Both women hoped passionately that Jeremy wouldn't ask William this as he'd probably just tell the naked truth, which in his case could be very naked.

'Ta da!' carolled Annabelle as William put a plate on the table. On the plate was something resembling a cloche hat swathed in green material.

'Now will you tell us what it is!' Jeremy was half pleading half impatient.

'Dock pudding,' said William.

'And salad, all picked from the hedgerows,' announced Annabelle proudly.

'I'll just go and get the potatoes,' said Flora, who'd insisted on a nice substantial dish of them, cooked in the oven with cream and onions. It may have been mostly 'food for free' in a financial sense, but certainly not in a calorific one. There was also a tomato salad, that Emma had made, which added a little colour to the table.

'More wine, anyone?' said Charles.

'Well, that was super!' said Annabelle, sitting back in her chair and looking extremely relaxed. 'Now I want to hear the nightingales.'

'It's really very unlikely you'll hear any. They stop singing at the end of May.'

'But you said there might be a rogue one. Oh, do take me, William. It's such a heavenly evening.'

Annabelle, Flora thought sourly, had clearly decided William wasn't a criminal.

'What about you?' Jeremy asked Emma. 'Would you like a walk in the woods?'

Emma obviously would like one, judging by the look she gave Flora.

Flora felt like the head girl. Was she to forbid the expedition? Or condone it? Personally she didn't care what anyone did, but she found she didn't want Charles to be upset.

Although he was the only member of the party who was not now on the drunk side of tipsy, he seemed quite

234

relaxed. As the driver, he could have announced it was time to go home.

'I really don't feel like a walk myself,' said Flora. 'But I'll pop up and get a couple of shawls for you two. It is getting chilly. What about you, Charles?'

'I don't need a shawl, thank you. But I'll help you clear up if the others want to go.'

'Thank you.'

When the others had set off into the trees Flora started to clear plates. Charles put his hand on her arm and stopped her. 'Why don't you just sit down and look at the stars while I clear up?'

'I couldn't possibly do that. Besides, I can't recognise any of the constellations.' In spite of her protest she sank on to the sofa and stared up into the heavens. 'Why don't you sit down too, or I'll worry about you washing up without me.'

He remained standing. 'I don't mind doing it.'

Flora shifted herself to the edge of the sofa so she could confront him. 'No, don't. I really want to talk to you.'

'Oh? I didn't realise I was your favourite agony aunt.'

'This is no time to develop a sense of humour,' she said sternly. 'I want to apologise.'

'What for? You didn't step on my foot, did you?'

'Charles, please! You've never been funny before, please don't start now. I want to say how sorry I am for saying those dreadful things. The other week, in the office, when I pulled the ceiling down.'

'I thought you knew that I'd forgiven you for your attempts at decorating.'

'Yes, but that wasn't what I wanted to apologise for.

235

It was for saying you couldn't run a piss-up in a brewery and that you were hopeless, and that I was the senior partner, things like that. I do think we should work hard to advertise and all that stuff, but I don't think you're bad at your job. At all. I was just angry and said the most hurtful things I could think of.'

'I was angry too,' Charles said quietly. 'I probably said unforgivable things.'

'Well, not totally unforgivable, but I was a bit upset that you thought I was heartless and manipulative.'

'I don't think that now. And I must say, I'm glad not to see Henry here. He's not the sort of man you should be spending time with.'

'Oh.' Flora was a bit thrown by that. 'Well, I did invite him, but he couldn't come.'

'Oh.'

Flora wondered if she should have admitted this as Charles reverted to his normal state of buttoned-up inaccessibility. She sighed. 'So why did you think I was a heartless bitch?'

'I didn't say that.'

'Not in so many words but it's what you meant.'

It was his turn to sigh. 'It was Justin.'

'Justin?'

'Justin Mateland. You broke his heart, you know. Or at least, that was what he told me.'

'I don't think Justin's heart was remotely involved,' Flora said crossly. 'He just got annoyed because . . .'

'Why?'

'Because he obviously expected me to . . . Well, he'd bought me dinner and assumed . . . I really don't want to go into details.' Flora shuddered at the memory; it

236

had been so sordid. She'd had to fight him off and she'd been extremely frightened.

'Oh.' Charles blanched as he suddenly realised what she meant. 'I didn't realise. I had no idea. When he got in touch with me he was very upset. Now I realise he was angry.'

'He was certainly angry when he left my flat.' And bleeding, she remembered.

'God, I'm sorry, Flora. I shouldn't have made the assumption that he was right without getting to know you first.' Charles did, to his credit, look genuinely abashed. 'What Justin had told me about you, that you were a . . .' He coughed, unable to think of a polite way to put it. 'Well, anyway, what he told me about you meant that I'd made up my mind before you even arrived. I suppose I didn't want anyone new arriving and sticking their nose into what, I'm afraid, I do still think of as my business, and particularly not a spoilt little girl who would come in and mess everything up and then disappear off as soon as she got bored.' He shook his head. 'Annabelle and I didn't exactly give you a warm welcome, did we?'

Flora smiled. 'No, not exactly. But you're not the only one guilty of going on first impressions. I should have seen beyond the "at-a-glance taxidermy".'

'The what?'

'I thought you were so stuffy that one look from you and any living creature would become glassy-eyed and full of sawdust.'

'Good God! I hope it's not how you see me now.'

'I can't see you at all, Charles. It's too dark.' She opened her mouth to ask him again to come and sit down on the sofa next to her, but shut it again. The summer night was having a strangely sensual effect on her and it wouldn't be a good idea to have him sitting next to her, in the near-dark, when she'd had too many glasses of wine.

He came and perched on the arm of the sofa. 'Perhaps we should clear up. Or at least, perhaps I should.'

'No, don't. There's nowhere to put anything.'

'The kitchen's not really designed for entertaining.'

'No. Would you like some more coffee or anything?'

'No, thank you.'

The silence hung between them for a moment. Flora struggled to think of something to say. 'They must have gone for quite a long walk. I wouldn't have thought Annabelle was the sort to go trudging through the woods in the dark.'

'She has hidden depths.'

'And have you and she been engaged for long?' She didn't really want to know, but it gave them something safe to talk about.

'We've been engaged officially for about a year, but it was always understood that we would marry. We've known each other from the cradle.' He paused. 'I did fall in love with another woman, briefly, while I was travelling. But it didn't last. I was very glad to come back to Annabelle.'

With anyone else, Flora would probably have asked if this woman had broken his heart, but not with Charles.

'Will you let me wash up, now?'

'No—'

'I just don't think it's a very good idea to go on sitting here in the dark with you.'

238

'I'm not a vampire, Charles,' said Flora, strangely pleased.

'You're a lot more dangerous than that. Come on.'

Charles and Flora were still drying up when the others came back. They all seemed a little more dishevelled than when they went out and Emma had goose-grass draped over her shoes.

Flora put down her tea towel and picked it off. 'My mother calls this "wild sellotape". Did you hear any nightingales?'

Annabelle sighed. 'No, but it was so beautiful. We should all walk at night more often, it's a forgotten pleasure.'

'Well, I think I'm going to take you home now,' said Charles. 'Flora, thank you for a lovely evening.' And he kissed her cheek, disturbingly near her ear.

'Yes, it's been great,' said Jeremy. 'A really splendid meal.' His kiss was quite hearty. 'Emma? I'll be in touch.'

'Yes, do,' said Emma, with a smile that was only just short of a smirk.

'Flora!' Annabelle took hold of Flora's shoulders and kissed her. 'Fabulous meal and everything.'

'I didn't cook it, Annabelle.'

'I know, but you did set it up and it was all super.'

'I'm so glad you enjoyed yourself.'

Annabelle turned to William. 'What can I say? That walk was magical.'

'I'm glad you enjoyed it.'

'You know so much about the countryside and everything.'

'Well, I spend a lot of time in it.'

'Come on,' said Charles. 'It's late.'

Charles at last got Annabelle and Jeremy into the car and Emma, William and Flora watched them drive away from the doorstep.

'I think that went really well,' said Flora. 'What did you two think?'

'Jeremy was very nice,' said Emma. 'Annabelle was a bit scary, though.'

'Did you think so?' said William. 'I thought she was very friendly and she has really interesting features, in that strong, Pre-Raphaelite way. I'd really like to paint her.'

Flora took this in for a moment, wondering if her make-over could possibly take any credit for Annabelle's strong features, and deciding that it couldn't. 'Well, anyway, you were a star! And so economical!'

William shrugged. 'Why pay for food when you can get it for nothing?'

Later, while Flora was brushing her teeth, she reflected that she and Charles seemed to have moved on. Now she knew why he was so wary of her, assuming she was a bitch because of Justin, things should go much better. She was surprised to realise quite how relieved she was that the atmosphere between her and Charles had been cleared. It had obviously been getting to her more than she'd known, and if she was back in his good books then they could both stop treading on eggshells and get on with getting Stanza and Stanza back on track.

Yes, things had definitely changed between them tonight, but it wasn't just that they'd gone back to how they were before the row – it felt more as if they were actually becoming friends, rather than polite partners, and she was surprised again to register how much that meant to her. Perhaps if the roadshow went really well, he might stop thinking of her as a dumb blonde and see her as a really useful person.

Chapter Fourteen

❦

'Thank you so much for dinner,' said Charles on Monday morning.

He and Annabelle were getting out of their car. Flora had just parked the Land-Rover and waited when she saw them arrive. She felt strangely excited to see Charles again and put it down to their new, improved relationship.

'Yes, it was wonderful! Imagine! All that lovely food for free!' said Annabelle.

'Well, add a couple of pints of double cream and some parmesan,' said Flora. 'Any old weed tastes nice if you know what to do with it.' She smiled, hoping she hadn't sounded churlish.

'The chocolate mousse was delicious,' said Charles.

Flora suddenly remembered him looking at the smears of chocolate on her and found herself blushing. She cleared her throat. 'Well, I'm really glad you both enjoyed yourselves.'

'So did Jeremy,' said Annabelle. 'He seems very taken by your girlfriend. You must tell me all about her sometime.'

By now, the three of them had reached the back entrance to the office, so Flora was spared having to respond to Annabelle's request for information about

Emma. It was Monday morning and she wanted to focus on the week ahead. She was feeling much more optimistic about everything now things were better between her and Charles. It would surely be easier to get Stanza and Stanza profitable now Charles realised she was on the same team. And she was rather hoping for some help with the roadshow.

'Where's Louisa?' asked Annabelle as they all arrived in the office. 'I'm desperate for a coffee. Oh, of course, it's Monday!'

'I'll make it,' said Flora. 'How do you like it?'

'Black, two sugars.'

'Charles?'

'The same, please.'

She brought a tray of coffee through to Charles's office where Annabelle and he were ensconced.

'Have you brought coffee for yourself?' asked Charles. 'We need to discuss this roadshow on Wednesday.'

'Ah yes. So we do,' said Flora, thanking God he'd decided to get involved. 'I'll run and make myself a cup of tea.'

She was putting off the moment, she knew. By now someone, probably Charles, would have read the various advertisements she'd placed and found out what she'd done. Or at least, some of what she'd done. She hadn't paid for all her sins by the word – some of them would come to light later.

'Right,' said Charles, when Flora had pulled up another chair to the desk. 'I've spoken to Geoffrey. He's on side. And I've got Bob Butler and another couple of retired auctioneers to come along.'

'Darling, we won't need all those people,' said

Annabelle. 'What on earth were you thinking of?'

'I think it's good to have plenty of people there to help,' Charles went on smoothly. 'We don't want to keep people waiting too long.'

'For goodness' sake! We'll be lucky if anyone comes at all. No way will there be enough people to form a queue.'

'You never know,' said Flora brightly, realising that Charles had seen the advertisements but that Annabelle hadn't and he hadn't told her about them. It seemed to give them a sort of solidarity. 'Do you think we should have somewhere where people can get drinks and snacks?'

'Excellent idea,' said Charles. 'The porters will organise that if I ask them.'

'They'll need to be paid, don't forget,' said Annabelle, 'and this is all very speculative. It's probably far too short notice for them to organise anything, anyhow.'

'Actually, I spoke to one or two of them at choir,' said Flora.

'What?' Annabelle frowned.

'Because I see them at choir, I took the opportunity to ask them if they could do something at short notice, should it be necessary.' This wasn't quite how she'd put it to the Subversive Second Sopranos, but the general effect was the same.

'Good idea,' said Charles.

'I know, why don't you ask William if he'll come along and help with the refreshments?' suggested Annabelle who, Flora had noticed, was wearing her hair in a pleasantly untidy way.

244

Flora felt a bit confused. Why on earth did Annabelle think William might like to help? 'I don't think it would be quite his thing, Annabelle. I know he's a fabulous cook, but selling chocolate bars and ham rolls isn't really what he's into.'

'Besides, I expect he's gone home by now, hasn't he, Flora?' asked Charles, rather stern.

'But he lives quite near,' said Annabelle. 'He said. It's why he knows the wood so well.'

'I haven't got his address,' said Flora firmly and, at last, truthfully.

'Oh,' said Annabelle. 'But you could get in touch with him via Emma?'

'Possibly, but Emma's away for a few days,' she improvised, and rapidly changed the subject. 'Now, what other preparations do we need to make?' Really, she was far too busy to think about William and his availability. Annabelle must have approved him by now, or why did she go wandering around a wood with him at night? 'What else do we need to organise?'

'There's only so much we can do before the day, but we'll get the tables set up and the chairs put out. Please remember there might not be thousands of people, Flora. I don't want you to be disappointed.'

'Definitely not!' said Annabelle. 'I don't know why you two are making all these preparations. It's not the *Antiques Roadshow*, after all!'

Flora and Charles exchanged glances. 'No,' said Flora. 'It's not.'

'Well, if you two don't mind, I want to go and get some things for Mummy. You don't need me for anything, do you, Charles?'

'Not at the moment, no,' said Charles.

Did he really love her? Flora wondered as she and Charles watched Annabelle leave the room. Surely some sort of endearment would have been appropriate just then? But there was nothing, not even a 'darling'. They both professed to be in love, but from where Flora was sitting there was something strangely cold about the whole relationship.

'So,' said Charles when he and Flora were alone, 'how many people do you think will turn up?'

'Well, thanks to Geoffrey, almost everyone at choir will bring something. Edie's got the WI and various other local groups interested.'

'And then there's the advertisements,' Charles said levelly.

Flora nodded and confessed. 'Which I put in every local paper for miles around.'

'So I noticed.' Flora couldn't tell if he was pleased at her initiative, horrified, or just accepting.

'And there's one more thing I should tell you,' she said.

'Yes?'

'You know all those antiques programmes on telly have really lovely young male presenters?'

'Flora, I don't have time to watch daytime—'

'Of course, sorry. Well, they do. And one of the tenors in the choir looks really like one of them. He's going to wear the right clothes and hang around.'

'Are you saying you've hired a television presenter look-alike, when the genuine article probably doesn't know anything about antiques, let alone the fake version, so people think they might be on television?'

246

Charles didn't seem nearly as annoyed about this as he would have been last week, Flora realised. 'Those presenters have all been in the antiques trade for years,' she protested.

'That's not the point I'm making, Flora.'

Emma had hinted there was something sexy about a man being stern and Flora now had to agree with her. 'It's just a bit of set-dressing. I'm not really deceiving anyone.'

The sternness continued just long enough to make Flora genuinely anxious, and then he said, 'Actually, there's something I ought to confess to you, although why I should when you didn't tell me any of what you've been getting up to . . .'

'What, Charles? God, you're so maddening sometimes!'

'I know one of the experts those programmes use. He's coming down to help. And he might bring a small television crew with him. It depends on what else is on.'

Flora got past the furniture and into his arms without knowing how she'd done it. 'Charles! You are such a star! I love you!' She kissed him hard on the cheek and then stepped away. 'Only in a cousinly, co-director sort of way, of course,' she added.

'Of course,' he said after a second or two. 'I would never imagine you meant it in any other way, ever.'

'Oh, I don't know, Charles,' said Flora, made reckless by his news and her recent encounter with his smooth cheek and subtle aftershave. 'If you weren't already spoken for . . . No, only joking,' she added hurriedly, not sure which of them she was teasing, Charles, or

247

herself. 'Now, given what you've just told me – have you told Annabelle, by the way?'

He shook his head. 'She's still expecting a man, his dog and a rickety kitchen table the dog will probably fall in love with.'

Flora smiled delightedly. 'You have got a sense of humour – that's so nice!' She frowned suddenly. 'How do you think she'll react?'

'I think,' he said carefully, 'we might find she does some dressage on Wednesday, so she need only find out about it when the Sheraton chairs come flooding in.'

'But you don't think they will.'

'Actually, I know they will because Bob Butler's got a very nice set he's bringing, just in case the film crew turn up and the whole thing becomes real.'

'Is he the one who asked if you wanted to buy him out?'

'Actually, there are two of them. They've both been in business for ever, but can't quite bring themselves to retire if no one will take on the business.'

Flora sighed. Bearing in mind they hadn't been speaking for most of the last two weeks, she couldn't believe he'd done so much to help make sure her roadshow was a success. Perhaps he didn't think it was such a silly idea after all. 'This is fantastic! I do hope the caterers can cope. I only asked a few of them to come.'

'Don't worry. The WI will spring into action if the need arises.'

'They're more into making sexy calendars than sandwiches these days, aren't they?'

'I promise you, most rural women have been making tea out of urns and buttering baps since they were in

248

short socks. With a blunt knife, and at speed. Trust me on this one.'

'I trust you on everything, Charles.' She bit her lip. 'We'll need loads more fliers. Shall I do them on the computer, or get them printed? I could buy some coloured paper, so they look a bit more interesting.'

'Fine. It will save time just to print them off, and then we can do more if we run out.'

'I'll organise that then. Anything else?'

'It might be as well to contact the local paper. They might like to send someone along. It is a first, after all.'

She skipped out of the room, inexplicably happy. Her mock *Antiques Roadshow* was going to be a stunning success thanks to Charles. And to her, of course, but mostly Charles. A real 'television' expert would mean more to the punters than any number of people who just knew everything there was to know about antiques. It was a cynical thought, she realised, but true.

The days before the sale merged into a blur of activity, and Flora had never felt so happy and fulfilled. Annabelle didn't seem to be around much, but Flora and Charles became a team. They were not quite equals, thought Flora, but she was no longer the idiot child.

'Thank God it's not raining!' said Flora as she looked out of her window very early on Wednesday morning. 'We don't have to worry about people not turning out because of the weather.'

Now all she had to worry about was what to wear. It was important, what she looked like. Should she be businesslike in a suit? Practical in jeans? Or pretty in the dress that Charles had complimented? No contest, really. She plugged in her travel iron and found the dress, hand-washed the previous Sunday and now a crumpled mess. She arrived at the hall an hour later, a little chilly, but confident that the sun would soon warm her.

Charles appeared shortly after she'd let herself into the building and had started putting white sheets on the trestle tables that had been put up the day before.

'Good morning,' he said.

'Hi,' she said, suddenly feeling incredibly shy and wishing she'd worn jeans.

'You'll get your dress dirty. Why don't you put on an apron? There's a drawer full of them in the back room.'

'Good idea.' She left Charles with the tablecloths and found herself an apron. Someone had once told her that there was something very sexy about a woman in an apron over a pretty dress.

When she came back Charles was talking with two men in tweed jackets and flannel trousers. They were both elderly and distinguished-looking.

'This is Flora Stanza. Flora, this is Bob Butler, and this is George Woodman. They've both been in the business since Noah was a boy, but they're rivals, not friends.'

They both laughed. 'And we've neither of us been going quite that long, but long enough.' Bob Butler took Flora's outstretched hand. 'You look far too young to be a co-director of an old established business, if you don't mind my saying so.'

'I am quite young, but I like to think I'm picking it up. What do you think, Charles?' Although she was only making conversation, she found she was pathetically eager to hear his answer.

250

'Oh yes. Flora's doing very well. This was all her doing, you know.'

George Woodman looked around sagely. 'Well, there's no saying how many people will turn up, but it's a good idea.'

'I must get on,' said Flora. 'I'm going to put the kettle on when I've done the cloths. Tea, coffee?'

The men told her what they wanted. 'Nice to have a pretty girl to make you tea, Charles,' one of them said as Flora left.

'We all make tea from time to time at Stanza and Stanza, even the directors,' said Charles. Flora felt very pleased: Charles had referred to her as a director – yes!

At five to nine Flora peered out of the window to see if anyone she knew had turned up, terrified she'd be greeted by an entirely empty street. 'Argh!' she shouted.

'What?' Charles came running.

'About a million people! All queuing up outside, clutching things.'

'You'd better let them in then,' he said with a broad grin. 'They're all there because of you, you know. It's a good thing I told the local television news team about it. This'll be very good advertising for us. Do you need a hand with those doors?'

'It's just like it is on television,' said Virginia a couple of hours later. She was now in charge of the snack bar.

Flora, just back from the supermarket, put two four-litre containers of milk down on the counter. 'Here you are. That should keep you going for a bit, anyway. It's amazing! We'll have made a fortune on the snacks alone.'

'A man was telling me that he and his wife had driven

251

all the way over from Trowbridge. They were so excited to have their pot examined by Eric Someone.'

'Oh, you mean the expert? He's awfully nice, isn't he. A real charmer.'

'They were certainly very happy. Now, have you had anything to eat, Flora? You've been running about since the moment you got here, probably at sparrow's fart, looking after everyone else. Let me make you a nice ham roll.'

Flora had been dreaming of ham rolls since about ten a.m. when she'd remembered she hadn't had breakfast. Now she hadn't had lunch, either. 'That would be lovely. I keep seeing people coming away from here with their trays and I've had to stop myself mugging them. I'd love a cup of tea, too.'

'I'll make you a fresh one. Oh my goodness, look who's just come in.'

Flora turned round. 'Annabelle!' She instantly felt guilty, convinced Annabelle was going to tell her off, although it was obvious the whole event was a stunning success.

'It's all right, she's not coming over,' said Virginia. 'She's seen Eric Someone and has gone over to him.'

'Phew. I'm sure I should still be writing down people's names and addresses and getting them to sign up to sell their treasures, or something more director-like.'

'Keeping us supplied is very important, and Louisa's doing a great job, now her mother's come to take her little boy home. Don't you worry about Annabelle.'

Flora didn't know her mixed feelings about Annabelle were quite so apparent. 'It was really kind of Louisa to come in on one of her days off.'

'It's all hands to the pump at Stanza and Stanza – or it is now you've joined us.'

'Virginia! That's the nicest thing anyone's ever said to me!'

'It's only the truth. Annabelle, on the other hand, doesn't show anything like your commitment.'

'But it's different for her.' Flora tried to be fair. 'It's only her fiancé's business, not hers.'

'She knew what she was taking on when they got engaged, though.'

'When you're in love, you don't always take practical things into consideration.'

Virginia frowned. Flora was aware that all around them people were busy and felt guilty for wasting time, but she really wanted to know what Virginia had to say about Charles and Annabelle – because, personally, she found them rather mystifying. 'I don't think Charles and Annabelle were ever in love, really,' said Virginia after a moment's thought. 'Or if they were, it never showed when they were in the office together.'

'I would think they're both quite private people, really. They wouldn't canoodle in public.'

Virginia giggled. 'Canoodle! That's a nice old-fashioned word. But I didn't mean that, really. On the other hand, how can you tell what goes on in anyone else's relationship? It's hard enough to keep track of your own, sometimes. But with Charles and Annabelle it always seemed more like a sort of business relationship than anything else.'

'Oh.' This tied in with what Charles had told her at the dinner party – not in so many words, but it gave the same impression.

'Well now,' said Virginia, 'if you've had your tea, you'd better take some over to Eric Expert. He's about due for another cup.'

Flora nodded. 'I'll find Charles first, and check on his name.'

'Oh, he's got a huge queue. Take him some tea, too.'

Flora set the cup and saucer at his elbow and Charles glanced up from the cow-creamer he had just described as 'having a nice touch of antiquity about it' and smiled. She felt inordinately pleased for a moment and then realised it should have been Annabelle who was supporting him, not her.

Flora hadn't realised she knew so many people in Bishopsbridge, or that they knew her. So many people came up and said hello, all thoroughly enjoying themselves. 'That man off the telly told me my old pot's worth thirty pounds! Can you believe it! It was the dog's water bowl. Better buy him a plastic one instead.'

'Well, my aunt died a couple of months back. I was going to get one of those house-clearance people in, but I reckon I'll get one of your lot over to value the furniture.'

'That's the best thing to do,' said Flora. 'There's bound to be a few valuable things there.' Flora wasn't sure if she knew this woman or not, but as she seemed to know her, she carried on as if she did. 'Have a leaflet.'

She'd gone back to the office to print off more fliers twice already, and had nearly run out again.

Flora saw that Charles had handed his queue over to Geoffrey. The crowds were thinning now and he came over, carrying his cup and saucer.

'I've asked Annabelle to open up the office to use as

254

a temporary store. There are people who don't want to come back with stuff they've agreed to put in the next sale.' He looked at Flora, particularly at her dirty face and feet. 'We'll have to put on an extra one. We didn't have anything scheduled until the autumn.'

'You must be thrilled, Charles,' said Virginia. 'This was a brilliant idea of Flora's.'

Annabelle joined them. 'Yes, it was an amazing success. Who'd have thought it? How did everyone know they were going to be on television? Eric only agreed to come at the last minute. And then the local TV news turned up. It must have been pure fluke.'

'Not quite a fluke, Annabelle,' said Charles. 'I did contact the news office.'

'Yes, but why did all those people come?'

'Flora put a very attractive advertisement in all the local papers,' said Charles.

Flora looked down at her feet, which were now very grubby. She should have worn jeans, or a suit, not a skimpy summer dress and sandals.

'I must say, Flora,' said Annabelle. 'You've turned out to be surprisingly useful.' She put her hand on Flora's shoulder. 'Come and have a little word. There's something I want to ask you.'

'Don't keep her too long, Annabelle,' said Charles. 'She's been here since before dawn and must be exhausted.'

'Not before dawn,' said Flora. 'I think Dawn and I arrived at about the same time.'

He laughed, showing his teeth, which were very straight and white, either the product of good genes or good orthodontics.

255

'I won't keep her long, you don't have to worry. There's just a little question I want to ask her about clothes. School reunion?'

Trust Annabelle, thought Flora, to have ducked out of all the work involved in the roadshow and then just expect Flora to put her mind to what she should wear to her school reunion.

Annabelle checked that the little room they had squashed themselves into, full of child-sized chairs and tables, plastic ride-on toys and space hoppers, was far enough away from the main hall to be safe from anyone listening. 'First of all, it's lovely that you and Charles are getting on better. He was so annoyed with you at first.'

'I know.'

'And I was thinking of wearing a navy suit, but' – she raised a hand in mock reproof – 'I knew you'd tell me off if I didn't add a scarf or something. What colour, do you think?'

Aware that outside everyone was clearing up and sharing in the aftermath of their success, Flora tucked a strand of hair behind her ear. 'I really wouldn't wear a suit, Annabelle. Terribly matronly, unless you wear it with nothing underneath and show a lot of cleavage.'

'Oh.'

'And navy? It sounds more suitable for a Conservative Party meeting than a girlie night out.'

'The Conservative colour is royal blue, you know.'

Flora slumped in her tiny chair. 'So it is.'

'So I won't wear the suit then, but there was something else I wanted to ask you.'

'Yes?' Virginia and some of the others were going to

256

the pub afterwards. Flora was hoping that Charles was going too. If Annabelle kept her too long, they might all go off without her.

'Can you give me William's mobile number?'

'He hasn't got a mobile.'

'He hasn't! How on earth does he manage?'

Flora shrugged, as mystified as Annabelle. 'Why do you want it, anyway?'

'I've had an idea. It's a bit of a secret.'

'What?' Annabelle didn't seem a 'secret' sort of person, really.

'I want him to paint my portrait. As a wedding present, for Charles! Do you think he could do it by November?'

It seemed terribly soon, somehow. 'Is that when the wedding is? What a funny time of year.'

'Yes, it is, rather, but the abbey gets terribly booked up in spring and summer. It's also when Daddy's insurance policy matures, to pay for it.'

'You're all practicality, Annabelle.'

'I know, and a jolly good thing too. But I do think a portrait of me would be something Charles would really like. Don't you?'

Flora thought. Her father had had a pastel done of her mother when they were first married, and it *was* a lovely thing to have. 'Yes, I do. And William did say . . .' Should she tell Annabelle what William had said? She decided that she should. 'He said he'd really like to paint you.'

'Did he? Oh, that's so cool.'

Flora laughed. It was nice to hear Annabelle using contemporary language. 'Mm.'

Annabelle appeared inordinately pleased, but then, thought Flora, it was a nice thing to hear about oneself.

'But how can I get in touch with him if he hasn't got a mobile?' said Annabelle, all practicality again.

'I'll try and see if I can get a message to him.' She didn't want to say she could just ask William to ring her, as she didn't think Annabelle knew that William was more or less living with her.

'Could you do that? He could ring me. But it would have to be on my mobile as I really wouldn't want Charles to find out. It would spoil the surprise,' she added.

'I'll see what I can do.'

'Do please try quite hard, Flora.'

'I will!' Honestly, once Annabelle decided she wanted something, she wanted it immediately. Flora got to her feet, longing to go back to the others.

Annabelle got up too. 'Tell me, Flora, rumour had it that you were going out with Henry Burnet?'

'Oh, well, sort of.'

'I just wondered why you didn't invite him to your dinner party, or was that because of Charles?'

'I did invite him but he couldn't come. But why would Charles care? Don't he and Henry get on?'

'No, not really, and I don't think he'd like it if he knew you two were going out.'

'Why not?'

'Henry's a bit of a bad lot, actually. Charles knew his ex-wife Natasha a little, and I think Henry treated her quite badly – I know Charles ran into her shortly after she'd found out about the affair and she was utterly distraught. He was horrified. And he feels quite protective towards his baby cousin.' She smiled, in case Flora was in any danger of misinterpreting the word 'protective'. 'Come on. Let's get out of this hell-hole. By the way, Flora, do you really think that dress is suitable for an event like today?'

Chapter Fifteen

✦

The hall was nearly empty when they got back to it. Charles was there, looking impatient, and all the euphoria seemed to have evaporated. They were just in a dusty hall, waiting to go home.

'The others have all gone to the pub, Flora,' he said. 'They wanted you to join them, but I thought perhaps we three might go out for a meal.'

'That's a lovely idea,' said Flora, keen to celebrate their success. 'I'm starving.'

'Oh good.' He seemed very pleased. 'Then let's think where to go.'

'But, Charles,' said Annabelle sharply, 'have you forgotten? We're having dinner with Clarissa and Benjamin.'

'Oh. I'd completely forgotten.' He looked at Flora, who instantly felt like a remnant from a jumble sale that no one wanted. 'Could we bring Flora with us?'

'Don't be silly! They don't know her. And she wouldn't want to be dragged along and make things difficult for them!'

'No, I wouldn't,' Flora agreed, suddenly feeling near to tears.

'You go to the pub with the porters,' said Annabelle. 'Have a nice drink with them.'

Flora knew she had to get out of Charles and Annabelle's presence very quickly or make the most awful fool of herself. 'Actually, I'm quite tired. I might just go home. Goodbye, both of you!'

'Flora?' Charles called after her, but she didn't stop.

Once in the car park, Flora took some deep breaths and thought about what she wanted to do. She could ring Henry. He'd already rung her during the sale and asked her out, but she'd hoped – assumed, possibly – that she'd be going out with the people she'd been working so hard with for the past few days.

But if she went out with Henry now, while she was feeling so anti-climactic, she might drink too much and get maudlin and depressed. So, should she join Virginia and the others?

No. She'd go home, have a glass of wine, and tell William that Annabelle wanted her portrait painted. Then she remembered she hadn't actually got Annabelle's mobile number. Oh well, she could always get it tomorrow.

As she drove home, summer seemed to gather its skirts, and prepare to leave. Thunder began to rumble and in the distance, sheet lightning lit the darkening sky. It had not yet started to rain, but the air smelt of it, and even London-bred Flora, who wasn't so aware of the signs, knew that when it came it would be torrential.

The first spots of rain hit the windscreen as Flora turned the Land-Rover into the lane that led to the cottage. They were the size of pound coins and after the first few seconds, they became a waterfall. She slowed right down and swore mildly. As she negotiated the car through the rain the events of the day ran through her head. It would have been so nice to have gone out for a cosy meal with Charles and the others, and that hadn't happened, but otherwise it had been a huge success. People had come in droves and, according to Geoffrey, who was the only person she'd been able to ask, the quality of the items had on the whole been reasonably high.

And there was Henry. She hadn't accepted his invitation for that evening, but when she'd said no, he hadn't sounded too fed up: he'd ask her again.

It was only when she thought about Charles her spirits got low, which was silly. They were getting on much better and had really worked together well. That's all she wanted, after all. She was inordinately pleased to see William.

After she'd had a hot bath and come down again in her dressing gown, he handed her a glass of wine.

'I expect you deserve that,' he said.

'Oh, I definitely do!'

'How did it go?'

'Wonderfully. We had loads of people, the local paper sent someone and we might even be on the local news on telly.'

'So, what's bothering you?' He handed her a bowl of sunflower seeds and cashew nuts that he had roasted in the oven and sprinkled with soy sauce.

'Nothing. Why do you ask?'

'You're just not your cheery little self, that's all. And if something you've organised has gone really well, you should be on cloud nine.'

Flora took a sip of wine. She'd been trying hard to convince herself that she was perfectly fine, but she wasn't, really. 'I expect I'm just tired. And I did think we might all go out for a meal together, afterwards. But Charles and Annabelle had plans. Oh! Annabelle! I nearly forgot. She asked me about you.'

'I thought she'd done all the checking out and I came out with top marks.'

'You did! That's the point. She wants you to paint her portrait.'

'Oh? A commission? That's nice. We were talking about it a bit the other night, but I didn't realise it was a portrait she had in mind.'

Flora frowned. 'What did you think, then? Beautiful as it is, I don't think she can be after you for your body. She's engaged to my cousin.'

'The estimable Charles. Well, if you say so.'

'I do say so! Annabelle is just not the type to cheat, it would all be far too messy for her. She wants a portrait as a wedding present for Charles, which I think is a very nice idea.'

'It is.'

'The only problem is, I forgot to get her mobile number to give you, but I can get it tomorrow.'

'Hmm. I wonder what sort of portrait she had in mind.'

'Oh, very conventional, I should imagine. Possibly like the old photos they used to put in *Country Life*, when they looked naked but for their pearls.'

'That would be a good choice for Annabelle. She has lovely arms and shoulders.'

Personally, Flora thought Annabelle's arms were on the large side, but she didn't comment. 'You'd be happy to do it, then?'

'Oh yes. Definitely. The only thing is, I was thinking of moving on tomorrow.'

'You're abandoning me?' Flora hadn't expected that.

'Flora, if you remember, you weren't at all keen on my being here when we first met.'

'But since then I've got used to your little ways. And your cooking.'

He laughed. 'I've got some things I need to attend to over the other side of the wood. A friend is building a house from straw bales and wants my advice. I'll probably be back in a week or two. If you'll let me come back.'

'Of course I'll let you. Especially if I can smell some wonderful smell coming out of the oven.'

'More quiche. And I've made soup and a salad. That suit you?'

'Oh, fab! Thank you so much.' And she gave the most enormous yawn. Later, she only just got up the stairs and into bed before she fell asleep, Imelda purring in the crook of her knees before her family needed her again.

It was still raining hard the following morning. The lane resembled a small river and Flora got soaked just running out to the Land-Rover for her wellingtons.

'You won't go off today, will you, William? You'll drown.'

'It will ease off a bit later. Bound to. I'll be gone by the time you get home tonight.'

Flora felt bereft. 'You don't really have to go, do you, William? If Annabelle wants her portrait painting, she'll want you to do it soon. They're getting married in November.'

'You don't need to worry about that, Flora.'

'I'm not worried, but Annabelle will be. She likes to get ahead with her life!'

'Really, it's time I was moving on. I'll be back soon.' He smiled. He had a very kind smile. 'I've been getting awfully soft, living here with hot running water and electricity.'

'And me,' added Flora.

'Of course,' he said, 'but so far it's been me pampering you, not the other way round.'

Flora chuckled. 'I must say, I could not have managed that dinner party without you, even cooking normal food.' Flora picked up a slice of toast that he had made, and buttered it.

'Well, don't have any more dinner parties until I'm back, then.'

'No way! Far too much stress. Although I did enjoy it.' The memory of sitting on the sofa under the stars flickered into her mind. Then she snapped herself back to the present. 'I'd better go.' She looked at William who was crunching into a piece of toast. 'So will you really not be here when I get back?'

'That's it. I really won't be here when you get back. Not even a ghost of me.'

Flora laughed and came round the table. 'I'll kiss you goodbye then. I'm really going to miss you.'

'It'll do you good to cook your own meals for a bit. Make you a bit more independent.'

'It's not as if I can't cook my own meals! It's just that you've been here and simply done it.'

William put his arm round her and gave her a hug and then kissed her cheek. 'Go to work, Flora.'

* * *

265

At the office, everyone was very buoyant about the previous day's activities, especially Geoffrey. 'Charles is talking about me doing a bit of selling. I've done it before, of course, years ago, but it's been a while.'

'And Virginia's daughter is going to put the better items up on the website,' said Louisa. 'When she's created it, of course. But she says it won't take too long because she'd done a bit of work on it before.'

'I can't think why you haven't had a website long since, Charles,' said Flora, feeling a bit flat in the face of everyone else's optimism.

'It's hardly been worth it up till now. We're just a small country auction house, after all,' said Annabelle, deputing herself to speak for her fiancé. 'But we got some good stuff in yesterday, didn't we, Charles?' She paused.

'Yes. One old lady had about a dozen carrier bags of silver. All completely black, but Georgian, some of it.'

'And there was that wonderful Art Deco tea set with triangular handles that Eric valued. He was really enthusiastic. Are you OK, Flora?'

Flora hadn't been aware that she'd been less than sparky. Honestly, first William and now Annabelle thinking she was miserable – she must remember to smile more. 'I'm fine!'

'You just seem a little . . . flat. Doesn't she, Charles?'

Flora did not want to have to listen to Charles speculate on the state of her spirits. 'I'm fine, really, it's just that William – you know, from the dinner party?'

Charles nodded. Flora didn't look at Annabelle. 'Well, he's been staying with me and he's going today.'

She laughed, hoping she didn't sound shrill. 'I'll be fine on my own, of course, but he's company and a great cook.'

'Oh,' said Annabelle.

Flora regarded her and wondered if her low spirits had instantly affected Annabelle.

'Can I have a word, Flora?' Annabelle asked.

Flora suddenly remembered about Annabelle's mobile phone number not being in William's possession and why. Luckily she knew of a portrait painter in London she could offer as a substitute for William, if one was required. She followed Annabelle out of the room, taking her handbag with her.

'So? Did you – um – manage to give William my number?' Annabelle asked, sounding anxious.

'No. Unfortunately, I didn't have it. I suppose we both thought I already had it. But I hadn't.'

Annabelle tutted with irritation. 'You'd better put it in your mobile now.'

Flora produced her phone and Annabelle recited the numbers. When Flora had them stored she said, 'I'm not quite sure when I'm going to be able to give it to him, but don't worry, I know a portrait painter in London, who's really good and not expensive.'

Annabelle considered. 'I would feel happier sitting for someone I knew, even if only a little.'

'He's only gone for about a week.' William had been slightly less specific, but Flora thought a week's delay might be considered bearable.

'You don't understand! Portraits take ages. He'll have to start very soon if he's to get it done.'

'I did tell him about you wanting a portrait.'

'Oh? What did he say?'

'He was keen. He said you had lovely arms and shoulders.'

'Really?' Annabelle's expression became almost dreamy. 'That's so nice. So, he hadn't left yet?'

'No. He was going to wait for it to stop raining.'

'Right. OK, then.' Annabelle swallowed. 'Um . . . I wonder if you could give me the keys to the Land-Rover? I've got to go and deliver something to a farm and will need it. My car isn't awfully good in mud.'

Flora clutched her handbag to her. She thought of the Land-Rover as hers. 'Are you likely to be long? It's choir tonight. I want to get away on time.'

'Take your car then. It's fixed and it's just sitting in the yard waiting for you.'

'But the lane! I won't be able to get my car up and down it. It isn't awfully good in mud, either.'

'Oh, Flora, I'll bring it back in plenty of time. I'm only going to be a couple of hours.'

Reluctantly, Flora burrowed about in her bag and handed over the keys. 'You will be careful, won't you, Annabelle?'

Charles opened the door. 'What are you two gossiping about?'

'We're not gossiping!' Annabelle was very indignant. 'I'm just getting the Landy keys from Flora. I'm going up to Stringers Farm, and then I might pop in on Mummy.'

'Oh. I was going to do that. They've got a pair of rather fierce collies, don't forget.'

'I'll be fine! I'm not frightened of dogs. Bye, you two!'

Flora felt all this was a bit odd, but as Charles seemed

to think it was perfectly normal, she supposed it must be.

At five o'clock there was still no sign of Annabelle.

'I'm so sorry, Flora,' said Charles. 'I'll run you home now, and pick you up in the morning.'

'That's not necessary, really. It's choir tonight. I'll pop across the road and get a sandwich, and work until it's time for choir. If you could leave the Land-Rover keys somewhere obvious, I'll just pick them up and drive home.' She smiled brightly. Ever since the roadshow, when he'd tried to drag her along to the dinner party he was going to with Annabelle, Flora had decided that now he no longer hated her, he felt a bit sorry for her.

'That doesn't sound much fun.'

'Or I might give Henry a ring! We could have a drink,' she said before remembering how Charles felt about Henry. But honestly, she was perfectly capable of looking after herself – and Charles should realise that.

'Oh. Very well,' he said stiffly. 'I'll put the keys under the dustbin by the back steps.'

'Fine.' Flora smiled more genuinely. Ringing Henry was a very good idea. It would do her good to see him.

When Geoffrey heard that Flora was stuck in town and was planning to go for a drink with Henry, he shook his head, very disapproving. 'You could have had some tea with me and Edie, Flora. It would have been no trouble.'

'You're very kind. Do you think it will matter if I turn up without my music? I had actually put it in the car, but Annabelle's got it.'

'No one will mind sharing. I'm just not all that happy about this Henry Burnet.' Geoffrey obviously considered himself *in loco parentis*.

Because it was Geoffrey, whom she loved, rather than Charles being bossy, Flora found this rather sweet. 'This way I can finally keep a date with him, but not spend a whole evening, or have to get him to drive me home or anything. And really, you don't need to worry.'

Not entirely pacified, Geoffrey went home and Flora made her way to the pub.

'It's good to actually see you, Henry,' she said, kissing his cheek. 'I've been so busy lately, and then you couldn't come to my dinner party.'

'I'm flattered you could find the time to see me now.' He raised a slightly cynical eyebrow that tweaked at Flora's conscience.

She patted his hand. 'And I'm really flattered you still want to bother with me. I know I'm far too busy to be any fun.'

Mollified, Henry smiled. 'Better the occasional drink together than none at all. Now, what would you like?'

'These drinks are definitely on me. And do have a bar snack with me. I've got to be at choir in a couple of hours.'

Henry sighed. 'I'm lucky you could fit me in.'

'You are! But now the roadshow's over things shouldn't be quite so frantic. I'll make it up to you, I promise.'

As she carried the drinks over to where Henry was sitting she reflected that she had treated him very badly and that she must do something nice for him soon. As long as he didn't expect anything she wasn't prepared

270

to give, he was good company. And good for her slightly bruised ego.

Flora arrived at choir slightly late, having had one and a half glasses of wine. She apologised profusely, but luckily Moira had brought in a very nice station clock the day before, which had been valued for five hundred pounds; Flora was definitely in her good books.

Afterwards, she was surprised to see lights on at Stanza and Stanza as she approached. Geoffrey, who had insisted on walking with her, hurrying through the pouring rain, was too.

'Charles does keep very late hours, sometimes,' he commented, 'but half past nine is later than usual.'

Charles greeted them at the top of the steps. 'I'm afraid Annabelle didn't get back.'

Flora felt suddenly sick. 'My God, how awful! What could have happened?'

'She's all right. She rang, but I'm afraid she put the Land-Rover in the ditch. She's spending the night with her parents.'

Relief mingled with a Cassandra-like feeling that all would have been well if she hadn't given Annabelle her car keys. 'As long as she's all right. What about the Land-Rover?'

'It's all right, too. We'll get it pulled out in the morning. In the meantime, I'm going to drive you home.'

'As I see you're in good hands now, I'll be off,' said Geoffrey. ''Night, Flora, 'night, Charles.'

When he had gone, Flora said, 'There's no earthly need for you to take me home. I'll drive myself. My car's just in the yard.'

'It'll never get down the lane in this.'

'Then I'll call a taxi. You've been here hours. You must be longing to get back.'

'I'm fine, and I'm not having you waiting hours for a cab that will probably get stuck, too. We'll be fine in my car.'

Flora realised that Charles was annoyed and could sympathise, but she didn't really want him driving her home in that sort of mood.

'I'll call a cab. It's miles out of your way and you'd have to come and pick me up in the morning. It's silly for you to drive me. Logistically.'

'Don't use words you don't understand. Now come on.'

Flora opened her mouth wide with indignation.

'Only joking. Have you got everything?'

Chapter Sixteen

'It's still raining,' she said, aware that she was stating the blooming obvious for about the eighteenth time, but finding it necessary to break the silence. They were driving very slowly, the windscreen wipers going at double speed. 'Was Annabelle with her parents all day?'

'I don't know. Her mobile was switched off for most of it.'

'Well, there's not much point in wasting the battery when there's not much coverage.' Flora did her best to sound nonchalant, but she couldn't help wondering if William might have had something to do with her absence. But he hadn't had any painting materials with him, so they couldn't have actually made a start on the portrait, could they?

'No.'

'I haven't seen rain like this for a long time,' said Flora, a little later. 'The last time I did, I was in the Caribbean.'

'And it's been dry for so long, the water's all staying on the surface and the drains can't cope. Still, don't worry, I'll get you home all right.'

'I'm sure you will. And I can always get a taxi in tomorrow morning. You really won't want to drag yourself all the way out there to collect me.'

Charles gave her the briefest smile. 'There's always the kittens, Flora. They make any journey worthwhile.'

'But won't you have Annabelle with you? She doesn't like kittens, remember.'

'She can drive herself in, like she did today. It suits us better sometimes. She likes to come in a bit later and I'm not always ready to finish at five.'

Annabelle did not deserve such a hard-working fiancé. No wonder she was set on marrying him. In Annabelle's eyes, if she could only get Charles to give as much dedication and energy as he did to the auction house to something more lucrative, he would become the perfect husband.

'I know. I'm so sorry about you having to drive me back. You've been working so hard today, you must want to go home and pour yourself a large drink.'

'It's not your fault you can't drive yourself, Flora, and you've been working just as hard. The roadshow has put a huge extra load on everyone, although they're all really pleased about it,' he added, possibly aware that Flora might feel this was a criticism. 'But I must admit, at home there's a very nice single malt that's got my name on it.'

'Has it? That's very grand, Charles. I know you can have—'

'Not literally.' He took his eyes off the road for just a second. 'It actually has the name of an unpronounceable Scottish island on it.'

'I must say I might well change my name to Svetlana, or something. Emma brought some vodka with her. There's a bit left.'

'It won't be long now before you can get at it.'

274

Flora frowned. 'Not at this rate. We're only going about five miles an hour. How many miles is it?'

'I don't know. It's not far, really. It's such a nuisance about the Land-Rover. I probably wouldn't have let you drive alone, but I could have got you home safely.'

'You're not implying you can't get me home, are you?' The thought of spending the night with Charles in a roadside inn set up a feeling of panic she couldn't quite explain.

'Not at all. It would have been easier in the Land-Rover, that's all.'

'At least Annabelle is OK. That's the important thing.'

'Yes. And I don't expect the Land-Rover will have anything wrong with it either, once it's out of the ditch. I don't know what's got into her. She isn't usually so careless.'

'The road conditions are awful. She probably wasn't careless at all.'

Charles didn't answer and they sat in silence. The road was getting worse and, like Charles, she was concentrating on it, trying to see through the rain that the wipers couldn't quite keep up with, watching for flooding or obstructions.

'How was choir tonight?'

'A lot of people didn't make it. I probably wouldn't have come out in this if I'd gone home.'

'And what did you do beforehand?'

'I had a drink and a snack with Henry.'

'Oh yes.' Charles cleared his throat, fiercely focusing on the road ahead. 'So are you and he "an item"?'

Flora stifled a laugh. The words sounded so strange coming out of Charles's mouth. The inverted commas were almost audible. She was about to deny there was anything serious going on between her and Henry, but then remembered his original opinion of her. She didn't want him to think she was a hussy just when her hard work and dedication to duty had convinced him she wasn't. 'We're not an item yet, but who knows? He's very good company.'

'That rather depends on your definition of "good company". I don't know if I'd describe him like that myself. He's divorced, after all.'

'So are lots of people! It doesn't necessarily make you a bad lot! Besides, I define "good company" as someone who makes me laugh.'

'That rules me out, then.'

Flora allowed her chuckle to escape. 'You do make me laugh sometimes, Charles. But sometimes – like now, for instance – you can be awfully stuffy.'

'I think you've told me that before.'

'Well then. Stop being stuffy!'

'I'll do my best.' He took his eyes off the road again and smiled at her. 'But it's hard to go against nature.'

'It's not nature! It's habit. Anyway, did I tell you? We've got a concert coming up. The choir, I mean, not you and me.' Flora was aware that she'd suddenly become flippant, but couldn't decide if it was a good or a bad thing.

Charles ignored the flippancy. 'A concert? How nice. Annabelle and I should come.'

'I'm thinking of asking Mum if she'd like to come over for it. She hasn't been to England for a while and she really wants to see the cottage. She can't quite believe how I've taken to country life.'

Charles laughed. 'Well, I must say, you've surprised us all.'

'I don't see why!'

He laughed again. 'I know now that I was quite wrong, but when you first appeared you didn't look like such a hard worker.'

'I've told you before, you shouldn't judge by appearances. It's a great mistake.'

'It's not a mistake I'll make again. Not with you, anyway. So, how are the kittens?' he asked, as the road improved a little.

'Fine. They haven't changed much since the weekend.'

'I don't suppose they have. I was just making conversation.'

'Well, please don't on my account. I'm your work colleague and your cousin, not someone you need to charm.'

'Oh, I don't know about that.'

'Charles?'

'I sometimes wish I had your social skills, that's all.'

'But I'm always putting my foot in it!'

'You make people feel relaxed and good about themselves. It's a great gift. One I don't share.'

'Yes, you do!' Flora was indignant. 'Think how lovely you were with those people in that grisly house. You made out it was all perfectly normal and they believed you. Hell, I believed you! I was really worried that I'd be facing squalor like that every week!'

'That's different. That's work.'

'Well, as you work most of the time, that's OK. You probably don't have much time for a social life anyway. Talking of which, how's Jeremy?'

277

'He's fine. Very keen on your chum Emma, by the way. Is she available?'

'Yes and no. She's with someone but I don't think he's anything like good enough for her.'

'And what does Emma feel?'

'I don't think she knows, really. But she liked Jeremy, too. It would be good for her to be with someone who's kind to her.'

'I really brought him along for your benefit, Flora. I thought it would be nice for you to have someone to take you out while you're down here.' He scowled through the rain-drenched windscreen. 'But you didn't need my help in finding someone to squire you around.'

'That is a lovely, old-fashioned expression,' she said, refusing to be drawn on Henry. 'Only you would use it.'

'Don't change the subject.'

'I'm not, I'm just not willing to talk about Henry.'

'It's not my place to comment, but—'

'Then please don't comment. As you said yourself, it's not your place. And it's only been a couple of drinks and perhaps a lunch.' Just at that moment, Flora couldn't think how many times she'd been out with Henry. 'Like you, I'm far too busy to go out much.'

'Forgive me if I doubt that it's always like that for you, Flora.'

'Of course I'll forgive you, and no, it isn't always like that for me. It's just that this time it's half my business. It does make it a whole lot more interesting.' She frowned. 'Although actually, I think if I was just working for Stanza and Stanza I'd feel the same. It's so fascinating.

I'm seriously considering training, although I know it takes a long time.'

He glanced at her briefly before turning his gaze back to the road. They were still travelling very slowly. 'You could do it part time, while you work. Lots of people do.'

'Well, isn't that nice? That's the first time you've behaved as if I'm going to be here for longer than the summer!'

He chuckled. 'I must be beginning to believe your propaganda.'

'Propaganda, indeed.'

'You wouldn't think there could be so much rain in the sky, would you?' he said a little later.

'No. I expect the land needs it though, doesn't it?'

'Mm, if it doesn't all run off. Slow, steady rain that sinks in is what farmers like.'

'So Annabelle's father will be happy?'

'He's not really a farmer in a way most people would recognise. More an "agri-businessman". He makes most of his money from investments. Property, by and large.' He paused, as if debating whether or not he should pursue this conversation. 'I owe him a great deal, and he'd like me to join him.'

'Oh.' Flora stopped herself from saying more. It explained why Annabelle only liked Stanza and Stanza for the property it owned.

'But I can't really see myself getting interested in renting office blocks in London.'

'You could get interested in starter homes, though?'

'Annabelle's father doesn't do starter homes. He's not interested in anything other than the top end of the market.'

'Oh,' said Flora again.

'Besides, I have a business I love.'

'And I love it too.'

His sigh was audible over the sound of the engine. 'Annabelle and her parents think I should sell out to you. Let you take it over.'

Flora realised that for him it must be like them suggesting to a mother that they put their child up for adoption. They had probably tried to convince him that it would all be for the best.

'I'd never buy you out, Charles. Apart from the fact that I'd never have the money, I couldn't run Stanza and Stanza without you – even if I trained and had a bit more experience. It would take me years and years before I had even a tiny fraction of your knowledge.' She frowned. 'What on earth must they have been thinking to suggest something like that?'

'That you're very enthusiastic, you already own slightly over half of it, and could employ Geoffrey to help you.'

'They really have discussed it, haven't they?'

He nodded.

'They're talking absolute gibberish, aren't they?'

He nodded again.

'You wouldn't sell out to me if I offered you a million pounds, would you?'

He shook his head. 'Not to you, and not to anyone, unless I absolutely had to.'

'Well, you won't have to. Not if I have anything to do with it,' said Flora briskly.

Charles looked at her a little oddly, and she wondered why. Yet she didn't feel able to ask him.

'I won't be able to give you alcohol,' she said, 'but I can offer you a nice cup of tea when we get home,' she said. 'Possibly a biscuit.'

'I'd really appreciate that,' said Charles. 'Especially the biscuit. It's taking longer than I expected.'

'And we're not there yet. I'll ring Annabelle and tell her how slow we're being. We don't want her to worry.'

'Oh, I'm sure she's not doing that.'

'I think I'll stop here,' said Charles a little later. 'Before it gets too narrow. Will you be all right on foot?'

'Of course. But how will you turn round?'

'I should manage to turn here OK. But I won't take you up on your kind offer of tea.'

Flora couldn't decide if she was relieved or sorry. 'I'll stay with you in case you need a push.'

'There's no need—'

'Oh, shut up and do your three-point turn.'

He did. Perfectly. Flora was forced to get out into the mud. 'Thank you so much!' she said through the car window.

'I should have just taken you home with me.'

The words tugged at her heart in a strange way. 'I couldn't have gone. The kittens.'

'Oh yes. Well, goodnight, Flora. Don't stand there in the rain. Go home. And I suggest you take your shoes off and go barefoot.'

She grinned, already soaked down to her knickers.

It seemed a very long time since she'd left home that morning. She was completely drenched. She padded to the kitchen to wash the mud off her feet before going upstairs to feel the hot tank and check on Imelda and her brood. The tank was hot and Imelda and the kittens were all fine, and Flora began to relax. She turned on the taps and began to run herself a bath. While the water was running, she climbed out of the skirt that was sticking to her, and pulled off her top and then her underwear. She was chilly without her clothes and pulled on her dressing gown. What she needed was a hot cup of tea. She turned off the taps and went back downstairs.

The kettle had just boiled when she heard the knock on the door. It was either William or Charles, she decided, and went to answer it. It was Charles.

'I got stuck a bit further along the lane,' he said, dripping on the doorstep. 'Can I come in?'

Flora opened the door wide, finding a smile forcing its way past her embarrassment at being caught in her dressing gown when she wasn't expecting visitors. She found herself very pleased to see him. 'Oh dear. But never mind, I've just run a bath and the kettle will have boiled by now. Which would you like first, a bath or a cup of tea?'

'You must have run the bath for yourself. I couldn't take it from you.'

The thought that they could share it floated into Flora's mind from nowhere, like a wicked butterfly. She mentally brushed it off. 'Tea then? Or coffee? Will you ring the AA or someone?'

'No. I've rung Annabelle and told her I won't be home.'

'Oh! And she didn't mind?'

'She said you had a very comfortable sofa and it would be better to sort it all out in the morning, when the rain will have stopped.'

'Oh.' Almost too generous, Annabelle.

'I realise you probably don't want guests tonight, when you must be so tired.'

'You're tired too. And you don't need to sleep on the sofa. There's a perfectly good guest room. I'll make some tea.' Suddenly feeling very naked under her dressing gown, Flora retired to the kitchen and then turned in the doorway. 'Or there's the vodka?'

'Let's have the vodka and the tea.'

She found a glass and some tonic and made him a drink. 'I tell you what, I'll get in the bath, just quickly, and then you can have it after me. You must be chilly and it would take ages for the water to heat up again.'

'That sounds fine. In the meantime, I'll make a fire. Or is it too late to be worth it?'

Flora glanced at her watch. It was past eleven. On the other hand, the thought of a fire was so cosy.

'That sounds a lovely idea. I'll go and hop in the bath.' She almost ran upstairs. Supposing William had used all the logs Charles was expecting to find? She'd just have to hope he couldn't remember how many had been there. She slipped off her robe and got in the bath.

The hot water against her cold limbs was heaven. She closed her eyes. Strangely, she found herself thinking about Charles downstairs, lighting a fire. It was such a domestic thing to do. If they were a couple, he'd come up when it had got going and hurry her out of the bath so that he could get in it. She would go down and make a snack, which they would eat together, with the sofa pulled up to the fire.

'Flora?'

She stifled a scream as she heard Charles's voice.

283

When she opened her eyes she realised he was outside the door, not in the bathroom with her. 'Yes?'

'I thought you might have gone to sleep in the bath. The fire's going quite well now. There was more wood than I thought and lots of kindling.'

'Oh good. Yes, I think I had drifted off for a minute. I'll get out now and you can get in. If we boil a kettle we can make it a bit hotter. I think I used all the hot water.'

'I'll go and boil the kettle.'

When Flora joined him downstairs in the kitchen, her robe was so tightly belted it would have taken Houdini to release it. She hadn't gone so far as to get dressed, or even put on her nightie, but she had put on a pair of knickers, and was covered from neck to ankle in white towelling. She trusted Charles not to jump on her more than she trusted Imelda not to break into song, but she couldn't spend the evening with him without knickers.

'I've put a clean towel in the bathroom, and I found one of my father's old sweaters I stole from him once. It's a bit holey, but cashmere, and wonderfully soft.'

'It sounds perfect.'

'So you take the kettle up and I'll make some supper. Did you get something earlier?'

'Not very much, and it seems a long time ago. I'd love something, but don't go to any trouble.'

She ignored this. 'Can you put the kettle outside the door when you've finished with it? We might have to have Cup-a-Soup.'

He laughed. The vodka seemed to have relaxed him. 'Is that all you can offer me? I would have thought you'd done a cordon bleu cookery course at some time in your career.'

'I did, but for that you need ingredients. Now run along.'

On her mettle, Flora was determined to produce something half decent, but what? It was quite late to eat a big meal but, on the other hand, she was starving, and Charles was too. She had spaghetti and a jar of pasta sauce, but somehow she had to make it more special.

She'd learnt a lot from William, subliminally. First, she toasted seeds and nuts and splashed tahini on them. Then she cut up a crust of sliced bread, rubbed it with garlic, cut it into cubes and fried it in olive oil, glad that William had insisted that she bought a good quality one. With something to nibble ready, she started on the sauce. She ran out into the rain and found marjoram, then dug out some salami that Emma had brought and chopped it up. It would still be spaghetti and sauce, but it would be a bit better than just that. There was parmesan left from the weekend that Emma had stayed. Her greatest coup of all was a bottle of red wine that had somehow not been drunk at the dinner party.

She put another log on the fire, lit candles and turned off the lights, and, for a final touch of cosiness, she brought down the box of kittens and settled them by the fire. She fiddled with her hair but didn't put scent or make-up on. There was still a little smudge of something round her eyes. That would do. She wanted the room to be cosy and comfortable, but she did not want it to look as if she was setting out to seduce him. Because she definitely wasn't.

'Oh,' said Charles as he came down the stairs into the room. 'It looks – very cosy.'

'Good. Now come and sit down. Supper's nearly ready. Glass of wine?'

'Flora, I'm only staying over because I can't get home. You don't have to provide a romantic dinner for two.'

'I have to provide something to eat, and you lit the fire.' She suddenly felt slightly embarrassed. 'We might as well sit in front of it. And I've brought the kittens down for you to play with, so just stop being grouchy. And here, have a nibble.'

He laughed and the sound of it affected Flora somewhere in her breastbone. The timbre of his voice was one of the most attractive things about him, she realised, wondering how or why she hadn't noticed before.

Everything took a little longer than she had anticipated and when she finally went into the sitting room, with two plates of spaghetti and sauce, Charles had fallen asleep. A kitten, the little black one who was far shyer than the others, was nestled into his neck.

As quietly as she could, she set the two plates down on the low table that was in front of the fire. She went back to get her glass, the parmesan, and a jug of water. By the time she'd come back for the last time, he'd woken.

'I must say, this looks delicious,' he said.

'It's just spaghetti and sauce out of a bottle, you don't have to go overboard with the compliments,' she said. 'Tuck in.'

'I'm sorry. That remark obviously stung. What I meant to say was that you didn't need to go to a lot of trouble. A Cup-a-Soup and a bit of toast would have been fine.'

286

'That's what you'd've got if I'd had any bread,' she laughed. 'Not sure what I'll give you for breakfast. Nettle soup, possibly.'

He raised his glass to her. '*Slainte.*'

'What?'

'It's what they say on Scottish islands with unpronounceable names.'

'Oh. All right then.' She raised her own glass and then took a sip. The look in his eyes when he'd lifted his glass in her direction had done something strange to her.

'Oh, napkins,' she said, and hurried out to the kitchen. What was going on with her? Just because it was late, and the cottage was cosy, there was no need for her to go all girly. It was Charles she was with, not Mr Darcy.

Chapter Seventeen

❦

'This is extremely nice!' said Charles, having taken a few mouthfuls.

'No need to sound so surprised. I did do the course. It wasn't cordon bleu, but it taught me a few basics.'

'But I thought you needed ingredients.'

'I had ingredients – well, a jar of sauce and some spaghetti. The rest is just . . . my special magic.' She laughed. She was glad it had turned out so well, but she knew the special magic was pretty much fluke.

'I'm surprised you're not married, Flora.'

'Oh?'

'You're lovely and you can cook. What more can a man ask for?'

Flora frowned, hoping he was at least in part joking. 'It's not what more a man can ask for, Charles, but what a girl can ask for. These days women are not prepared to settle for mediocre. There has to be a good reason to give up your freedom and independence.'

'That's me put in my place then.'

'Yes.' Flora didn't dare look at him. She knew he was laughing. She was trying not to laugh herself.

'Has this little chap got a name?' he asked. He had put his plate down and started stroking the little black kitten again.

'No. He's terribly shy, usually.'

'I think I'll call him Macheath.'

'Oh? Why?'

'Because I like the name, and because this is the one I want to keep.'

'But, Charles, you can't have a kitten. Annabelle is—'

'Allergic. I know. But I thought we could have an office cat. Everyone would love it.'

Flora coiled up her last forkful of spaghetti thoughtfully. Charles poured out the last of the wine.

'I was going to offer you tea,' said Flora, suddenly very drowsy.

'I'll make it. It's your turn to have a nap on the sofa.'

'I'll be fine with just the wine, I expect.'

Charles scooped up another kitten. 'This is so cosy.'

'Mm.' Flora closed her eyes. She wanted to ask if Charles had cosiness like this with Annabelle, but realised she didn't want to hear the answer.

She was aware of clattering in the kitchen but she allowed herself to doze through it. Eventually she was forced to open her eyes again. Charles was standing in front of her. He put out a hand and pulled her upright. Then he wrapped his arms around her and hugged her, very, very tightly, and rested his cheek against the top of her head.

She was buried in cashmere that confusingly smelt of both her perfume and of Charles. His arms about her were crushing, making it difficult to breathe, but she would quite happily have stayed there, quietly suffocating, for ever.

At last he released her. 'Goodnight, little one,' he whispered. 'Now go upstairs quickly. Please.'

She flew up the stairs and into bed, aware that the kittens were still downstairs, but so confused about how the evening had progressed that she didn't want to go downstairs and fetch them – because it would mean facing Charles again. And not the Charles she'd seen at work for the last few weeks, but a rather different man: softer, warmer and infinitely more sexy. A Charles who, as long as he was engaged, she was much better off not seeing.

She suddenly felt a rush of jealousy of Annabelle. No wonder she was so determined to marry him! Although somehow, she wasn't convinced that the man she'd just seen a glimpse of was the man who got into bed with Annabelle every night – he just didn't seem Annabelle's type.

How had things changed so fast? It must be the drama of the storm, the lateness of the hour and the vodka, she decided. In the morning, everything would be back to normal – and the strange man downstairs would have reverted to type and she'd be faced once more with the old Charles, who was definitely no threat to her sleep patterns. Although, frustratingly, there was a nagging part of her which hoped she was wrong. Complicated as it made things, the new Charles was certainly interesting.

Before sleep claimed her, which, in spite of her frustration, it was threatening to do, Flora wondered what she'd do if Charles and Annabelle broke up. She was asleep before she'd decided on an answer.

Flora got up early, and went downstairs to check on the kittens. They weren't there. The washing-up was all done, but she'd been vaguely aware of Charles doing that the night before. The kittens were a mystery. She realised as she went back upstairs that Charles must have taken them, and Imelda, into his bedroom, for safe-keeping. If she hadn't recently seen a side to him that was nowhere near as unfeeling as he'd appeared at first, that gesture alone would have brought her round. Although she was determined not to like him too much; she had felt rather too drawn to him for comfort last night. Luckily, she was sure it was only the circum-stances. The fire, the food, the wine, the kittens, and the fact that they were both very tired, made them think of bed when normally it wouldn't have crossed either of their minds. Still, it might add a certain frisson to their working day!

She met him coming out of the bathroom. 'Good morning!' she said brightly.

'Are you a morning person, Flora?' Charles asked with a smile.

'I think so. Are you?'

'Not specially. I took the kittens and Imelda into my bedroom. I thought they would probably have been all right downstairs, but I knew they were used to human company and I didn't want them to get lonely.'

'That was very sweet of you. They would have been fine, but they are used to being with me. Or is it that I'm used to them?'

'Whichever. Shall I go downstairs and see what I can find for breakfast?'

'That's a good idea. I think it's stopped raining, but everything is still pretty soggy.'

'I expect it is. See you in a minute.'

Flora dressed with all her normal care, although now he'd seen her first thing without her make-up, and last thing when what make-up she had left on was all under her eyes, so it was a little late to impress him. She smiled at her reflection. To her relief, things seemed back to normal this morning. The cold light of day had brought back a rather less sexy, rather more cousinly Charles, which, bearing in mind the situation they were all in, had to be a good thing. She and Emma had once confessed to each other that wherever they worked, they tried to find someone they sort of fancied. They didn't do anything about it, or at least, only if everything else was right, but it sort of cheered up the working day.

This situation, however, was rather more tricky. If things worked out as Flora increasingly hoped they would, she and Charles would be involved in running Stanza and Stanza together for a long time. A crush, though entertaining, would be disastrous if unrequited – and she had no illusions about either Charles or Annabelle breaking off the wedding. It was only a few months away now, and Charles was hardly going to risk a ten-year relationship for the sake of someone he'd only known a few weeks. As Annabelle had pointed out, he'd been in love with her all his life.

Yes, Flora decided briskly, it was infinitely better that things returned to a businesslike, friendly but not too friendly footing.

She went into the spare room to retrieve the kittens and to feed Imelda. Everyone seemed fine after their night with Charles. Flora felt quite envious, and then chided herself. If anything had happened between them they would have hated themselves and each other now.

292

Charles had found some of the real coffee left over from the weekend with Emma and was making it. He had also found some bits of ciabatta, which he was toasting.

'Why is everything worth eating in this kitchen Italian?'

'Emma works near a really good Italian deli and brought a lot of stuff down,' Flora explained. 'I stuffed that ciabatta in the top of the fridge. It must be quite stale.'

'It'll be fine toasted.'

Flora suddenly longed for a corner shop where she could buy fresh bread and orange juice. 'I don't have much time for shopping, myself.'

'Nor you do.' He smiled at her, and for a moment Flora wondered if this having a slight crush was actually going to make things quite difficult. It couldn't, she decided. The business was far too important to jeopardise with random hormones.

She pulled up a chair and sat down at the little table. If he was happy making breakfast, she didn't want to interfere.

'You've made this cottage very homely, Flora. Even if you don't have much time to spend in it.'

'I made an effort before the weekend, when Emma and you all came. But it is very sweet. I could happily live here for ever.'

'I'm so glad. I would have thought you'd have got lonely.'

Flora shook her head and sipped the coffee he placed in front of her. She didn't like to tell him she usually had tea, first thing. Or that she'd had very little experience of living in the cottage alone.

293

'I hope Annabelle's all right,' she said, after a moment's mastication.

'Why shouldn't she be?'

'No reason. Some women might be a bit miffed if their fiancé spent the night with another woman.'

'Annabelle and I have far too good an understanding of each other for her to worry about things like that.'

Flora frowned. This sounded just a bit too complacent, in her opinion. It wasn't as if there hadn't been an undercurrent of something not quite platonic between them the previous evening. 'Oh. Very modern of her.'

'She knows she can depend on my sense of responsibility, in all things. Some things are too important to endanger.' He took a sip of coffee and looked across the table at her, as if making a point. 'Sometimes the grass appears a bit greener, but it never is if you do climb over the fence.'

'I can't imagine you ever scrumped apples, Charles!' said Flora, to lighten the atmosphere, but in spite of all her best intentions, Flora couldn't help feeling rather crestfallen. There was absolutely no ambiguity in what he'd said – he was clearly slightly embarrassed about the atmosphere the night before and wanted her to know she shouldn't read anything into it.

'You don't actually have to go into the lion's den to realise it isn't a very good idea,' he continued.

'Do you talk in riddles to Annabelle every morning?' Flora asked slightly irritably.

'I have to confess that Annabelle and I don't talk much in the mornings any more. We've reached that contented stage when you don't have to make an effort all the time.'

'But to begin with, you did? All women like to be romanced, Charles!' She couldn't help it – she was intrigued.

'One of the things that attracted me to Annabelle – when I was an adult, I mean—'

'I know you've known each other for ever.'

He nodded. 'Was that she was so practical.'

'A safe pair of hands,' said Flora. Of course she didn't know for sure but she was convinced that his heart had been broken by the woman he had met when he was travelling.

'What do you mean?'

'You saw Annabelle as someone reliable and steadfast.'

He laughed. 'You make her sound very boring.'

Flora laughed too. 'Of course not.'

'I'm a man who sticks to things.'

'Like chewing gum on the bottom of your shoe, you mean,' said Flora, not feeling nearly as flippant as she sounded.

'We'd better get going,' he replied. 'I'll just wash these few things.'

'Don't bother, I can easily do them when I come home, and you did all the washing-up last night.'

While Charles was brushing his teeth with Flora's spare toothbrush, Flora stacked the plates. The intimacy, the happy closeness of the previous evening had been spoilt, and she made a decision to put it entirely out of her mind. She and Emma had been wrong to think it was fun to have a crush on someone you work with. Sometimes it was a really bad idea. Just as well she had Henry to think about.

*   *   *

295

'At least we've got boots on this time,' said Flora as they walked back to the car through the mud.

'Yes. It was lucky for me that William left his behind.'

Flora wondered idly how William was managing without them, and why on earth he forgot them when it was raining so hard.

'Do you think the car will be all right?'

'If it isn't, I'll ring Annabelle's father and ask him if a tractor can come and get us.'

'I have got some Sunday papers, if we could do anything clever with them.'

'What we'd need would be old carpet, or something with some grip. I think it'll be the tractor or nothing.'

'Oh God! Supposing the tractor can't come?'

'We'll walk to the end of the lane and get a taxi or Annabelle to pick us up.'

Flora didn't think Annabelle would like that suggestion very much, but didn't say so. After all, she was his chosen one. It wasn't for her to comment.

'This may not be a good time to discuss it,' said Charles, 'but after the roadshow, Bob and George were both really keen that I – we – should buy them out. They're both well past retirement age.'

'And we could afford it if we sold the house?'

'We haven't talked money yet, but I should imagine so.'

'Well, let's do that then,' Flora said excitedly. 'We don't need a huge great building. We just need a little office somewhere.'

'And I would like a flat. It's useful and when Annabelle and I get married we might move further away.'

'Right.'

'And we should buy somewhere for you to live, too. We could buy the holiday cottage from Annabelle if you liked.'

'I'd have to think about it,' said Flora, wondering why the thought of living down here after Charles and Annabelle had got married was so depressing. 'Maybe somewhere a little nearer town might be more sensible.'

'Whatever.'

'On the other hand, how much is the building likely to raise? Buying out a couple of auctioneers, an office, a flat for you, a cottage for me – it's asking quite a lot of one building.'

'If we do what Annabelle suggests, and convert it into flats first, we should manage it. But I agree, it might be stretching our resources too far.'

'And it all takes time,' said Flora. If she did feel she had to leave, she wouldn't want to do it before Stanza and Stanza was on the way to profit, but she couldn't ask Charles and Annabelle to postpone their wedding. 'Although I'm quite happy in the cottage. Perhaps I should pay Annabelle rent.'

'Actually, you are. Or rather I am, on behalf of Stanza and Stanza.'

'Oh?'

'I have a tiny private income. I can't get at the capital, but the interest is useful. Annabelle likes to keep her books in order,' he went on, 'but that's something else we must sort out.'

'What is?'

'The financial situation. We should know what money is the company's, and therefore yours too, and what is mine.'

'I'm beginning to feel bad for not having a private income,' said Flora. 'It would make life so much easier.'

'On the contrary, it's much better you not having one. If I hadn't had any other money to keep me afloat, I might have gone on and got the business on a proper footing before now. Having you here, you needing to earn a living from it, has galvanised me, not before time.'

'But you love the business! And you work so hard!'

'Hard, but not smart,' he said thoughtfully. 'I've just kept doing it the way we always did it, making a loss year on year and taking no notice. That will all have to change now you're here.'

'Well, I'm glad I have my uses.'

'Oh, you do. Now, let's see if we can get this car to go.'

It took quite a bit of backing and filling and mud churning, but eventually the car was on the track and slowly they progressed along it. Once they reached the main road, Flora said, 'We're both quite muddy, actually. I expect you want to go home and get some clean clothes.'

'I'd better. Now, would you like to come back with me and drink coffee while I sort myself out? Or would you rather go back to the office? I'm afraid going home and getting a change of clothes isn't really an option for you.'

'Oh, take me to the office, please. I've got lots to do.' She didn't want to sit in Annabelle's drawing room sipping coffee, knowing Charles was showering on the floor above.

Flora did have quite a list of things to do, but before

she had done more than wash the flecks of mud off her face, Geoffrey came and found her.

'There's a bit of an emergency with choir,' he said. 'James rang me, quite late last night. It turns out that there's a problem at the house we were supposed to be doing our concert at.'

'Oh dear.'

'Yes. The valley guttering in the roof collapsed when it first started raining heavily. It so happened that James was on the phone to the woman who owns it shortly afterwards. She was in a terrible state.'

'And so is her valley guttering, apparently,' said Flora, wondering what valley guttering was.

'Yes. And it won't be fixed in time for the concert. We need a new venue.'

'Couldn't we just cancel?' This option was very attractive for Flora as she didn't know any of the work very well. She'd welcome an opportunity to learn everything more thoroughly before performing it in public.

'No!' Geoffrey was horrified. 'We've got an audience, practically ready made, and it's for a very good cause. We really can't cancel unless it's absolutely vital. Besides, the choir is getting paid and we need the money.'

'Well, let's ask Charles if we can have the hall. We could get chairs from somewhere, it would be fine, I'm sure.'

Geoffrey shook his head. 'No, Flora.'

Flora had sensed that no simple solution would do for Geoffrey and that what he had in mind involved her, somehow. 'What then? It seems a good idea to me. We wouldn't have to pay to rent it, I'll see to that. It's local, there's parking, sort of. What's wrong with it?'

'The concert has been advertised as "A Stately Summer: Music for a Summer Evening". The hall won't do. We need a wonderful house to have it in.'

'I'm awfully sorry, Geoffrey, I'm fresh out of wonderful houses. Now, had you asked me last week . . .'

Geoffrey ignored Flora's flippancy. 'We know which house we want. We just need you to go and ask if we can use it.'

'Why me?'

'Because apart from the fact that you weren't at the meeting to say you wouldn't, you know the owner of the house.'

'Do I?' She didn't think she knew anyone with a stately home.

'Yes. It's Henry Burnet.'

'Oh. Oh, Geoffrey, I'd much rather not.' It felt terribly awkward.

'Why?'

'You can't just bowl up somewhere and demand the use of a house to have a concert in! I would hate to make him think I was just using him.' She cast around for more reasons. 'He may not have a suitable room, for one thing.'

'James knows the house. He says there's an orangery which would be perfect and has lovely acoustics.'

'Then why doesn't he ask about it, then?' Flora asked tartly.

'He's far too busy. He's got so much on at the moment. He'll go and check it out if we get permission to go there, but you have to make the first approach.'

'But I'm busy! I've got a lot on, too! Why me? I'm not the only female member of the choir, you know.'

300

'Of course, I know that, but you work for yourself, Flora. You can take time off when you want to. And you know the owner.'

As things turned out, however, Flora couldn't quite take time off whenever she wanted. In the aftermath of the roadshow Stanza and Stanza was receiving an unprecedented number of enquiries, and before Flora knew it it was six o'clock and she hadn't had a minute to think about going to view Burnet House and charm Henry into lending her his orangery.

So it wasn't until the next morning, after a couple of hours of catching up with all the admin she hadn't had time to do the day before, that she got round to Geoffrey's mission. Annabelle had delivered the Land-Rover back to Flora the morning after the storm – once out of the ditch it had turned out to be fine – so Flora wasn't expecting to see her in the office on a Saturday. But just as Flora was about to leave, she materialised.

'Are you free for lunch, Flora? I feel I ought to take you out as an apology for putting the Landy in the ditch. Charles was furious.'

'Oh dear, there was no need for that. But I'm afraid I can't make lunch today, Annabelle. I've got to go somewhere. Tomorrow, perhaps?' It seemed a good idea to put a bit more distance between her cosy evening with Annabelle's fiancé and a girly lunch.

Annabelle seemed genuinely disappointed. 'Where have you got to go?'

'Somewhere Geoffrey told me about. It's a large country house, and I need to visit it personally.'

'Oh? That's interesting! Are they thinking of having a sale? Nothing could be better for us than a proper country-house sale. Hen's teeth these days, of course, but it would be a brilliant feather in our cap. Shall I come with you?'

The thought gave Flora goosebumps. 'Better not. It's Henry's house.' Frantically she tried to think of a good reason why she should see it on her own. 'I haven't seen him lately,' she lied. 'Things might be a bit tricky.'

'Then better to have me with you, surely? I'd love a snoop round Burnet House. I hear it's lovely. Is it?'

'I don't know! I haven't been there before, but I should go if I'm going. Thank you for rescuing the Land-Rover.'

'It's all right. I was the one who put it in the ditch, after all. Was it all right having Charles to stay the other night?' Annabelle went on. She looked at Flora slightly questioningly. Was she asking if anything had 'gone on'?

Flora wasn't going to respond to unspoken questions. Besides, Annabelle might scratch her eyes out if she got the answer wrong.

'Oh yes. He did the washing-up and everything. You've got him very well trained, Annabelle.'

'Oh yes. He's very good. A perfect husband.'

Flora smiled. 'Now, I must fly.'

'We'll do lunch soon, Flora.'

Flora smiled and nodded absent-mindedly.

Sitting in the Land-Rover half an hour later, Flora had a road map borrowed from the office, she had a map drawn by Geoffrey, and she had a description of the house, but she still didn't know exactly where she was going. She rang Henry, to warn him she was coming, but there was no answer. He'd be surprised to see her turn up at his front door but, she hoped, not displeased. She couldn't quite decide how much Henry cared about

302

her. Was he just after some fun and company, like she was? Or was his heart engaged? Either way, he was her only possible love interest, and should therefore be cherished.

She eventually found Burnet House. It was at the end of a long avenue of beech trees, and even in the aftermath of so much rain, looked beautiful. She turned the Land-Rover in between the open gates and made her stately way up the drive, which was heavily potholed. Before she'd even decided if she should park in front of the house, or try and find somewhere at the back, she'd become aware that the house was in desperate need of repair. She parked, got out, and then knocked on the door. The bell didn't work. She turned and regarded what had once been a lawn and was now a paddock. There seemed to be a ha-ha, but there was no stock to keep away from the house. If there was going to be a concert there, someone would have to do something about the grass. Perhaps a member of the choir had a ride-on mower.

Eventually, she heard footsteps approaching and braced herself, hoping it wasn't a stranger. 'Hello, Henry,' she said when the door opened.

Chapter Eighteen

'Flora! How lovely to see you! This is an unexpected pleasure!'

'Don't be too pleased, I'm on the cadge.' Flora felt hideously embarrassed.

His expression became quizzical. 'It's rather a long way to come to borrow a cup of sugar.'

'Don't joke. It's not sugar I'm after, it's your house.'

'My house?' Henry looked confused.

'Not all of it. Look, may I come in? I could explain better if I'm not on the doorstep.'

'Of course, but I should warn you, I don't usually do favours.'

His smile was mocking and very sexy. Flora smiled back. It was much more fun flirting with someone who wasn't engaged. 'Do something you don't usually do every day,' she said. 'That way life doesn't get stale.'

'Oh? Have you become a life coach, or something since Thursday?'

Flora frowned. 'No. I'm still an apprentice auctioneer, but that's not why I'm here.'

'Good. There's very little here of any value. Of anything at all, actually.'

'That's fine,' said Flora. 'You have got an orangery, haven't you?'

'Well, yes, but it's not for sale.'

'I know!' She smiled again. 'I – we – only want it for one night. Not too much to ask, is it?' Flora was beginning to get the feeling that visiting Henry in his house might turn out to have been a mistake. Still, she'd promised the choir she'd ask about the orangery, and they'd been so supportive of her with the antiques roadshow and things, she had to give it a go.

'We'd better go through to the kitchen.'

Flora didn't want to waste time being given coffee and biscuits. 'Could we cut to the chase and go to the orangery?'

'Flora! I thought you'd come to see me, as at least part of your errand.'

'I'm working today, actually, Henry. I can't be too long.'

He shrugged, possibly not used to having his hospitality dismissed so summarily. 'OK, but I warn you, it's in about the same condition as the rest of the house.'

The auctioneer and valuer in her (as yet a small, undeveloped part) still noted, as they strode through the house, that there were no antiques, no rooms stuffed with old toys, paintings or other apparent rubbish that would turn out to be worth a fortune when discovered by the cognoscenti. That meant Annabelle's country-house sale was a non-starter and Flora could concentrate on the challenge Geoffrey had set her.

'You may remember, I'm a member of a choir.'

'I do, but I don't think you look old enough.' He smiled. 'Or, for that matter, young enough.'

'You don't have to be old, or a choirboy, to enjoy making music,' she replied primly.

Henry shrugged and opened the door to the orangery. By now Flora was fully prepared to find it completely unusable, and then it would have to be the hall. At least she would be able to go back to Geoffrey and tell him she'd done her best.

'Ah,' she said. There was a puddle the size of a small lake on the floor. 'Why is that water there?' she asked.

'Possibly because there's a hole in the roof.'

Flora looked up. One of the rooflights was broken, but she could only see one damaged pane, not a whole slew of them. 'Is it fixable?'

'Sure. If you've got enough money. Unfortunately, I haven't. You need scaffolding, you see, and it's more than just a broken pane. The woodwork is rotten so the whole frame needs replacing. It makes it all prohibitively expensive.'

'I see.'

'So, what was the favour?' He regarded her with the faint, not unattractive, arrogance of a man who is confident with women.

Flora pulled her shoulders back and returned his gaze. Her confidence wasn't quite equal to his, but she wasn't going to let him know that. 'Oh, didn't I say? I'm a member of a choir—'

'You said that.'

'And we would like to do a concert in your orangery. If you don't mind. And if it's suitable.'

'Well, obviously it's not suitable. There's a hole in the roof and a puddle on the floor.'

'There is that, but I expect we could mop up the water and pray for a fine night.'

He raised an unconvinced eyebrow. 'Supposing your prayers aren't answered? It was like Niagara here last night.'

306

'I can imagine.'

'Although, to be fair, considering how hard it rained and how long for, it's not too bad.'

Flora regarded the village-pond-sized pool and didn't comment.

'I expect you're wondering what I'm doing, living here in a house that's a candidate for a television appeal. Why I haven't mentioned it.'

Flora raised her eyebrows. She had more than her fair share of human curiosity and now he had brought the subject up, she did want to know.

'I had been thinking about going abroad,' he said, 'but I can't sell the house in this condition, or at least, for only a fraction of what it would be worth if it was properly restored. I want to earn the money, do it up, and make a killing.'

'Thank you for sharing,' said Flora, realising that she was unaffected by the news that he might be leaving the country.

'You are unusual. Most women go gooey at the thought of a beautiful house in need of restoration, especially if it comes attached to a . . .' He paused.

Flora raised her eyebrows, unable to resist a chuckle. 'You've shot yourself in the foot there, Henry! You can't possible say what you're thinking without appearing to be unbearably conceited.'

He laughed back at her.

'You obviously are fairly conceited,' she continued. 'But possibly not unbearably so.'

He smiled apologetically. 'Sorry, but you can see why I don't invite women back. They're either horrified and run away, or get pound signs in their eyes and prowl.'

She chuckled. Annabelle would have prowled. 'I won't do that, I promise.'

'I don't think I'd mind too much if you did.' They exchanged glances. Flora knew he was interested in her, and was making an effort to summon up more interest in him. He was available, after all.

'Can I make you a cup of coffee?' he offered. 'To make up for being such a prat? Although now I think about it, it'll have to be instant which probably won't make up for anything.'

Flora had previously decided to refuse coffee as she was so busy, but she didn't want to be churlish. She'd be furious with any woman of her acquaintance who didn't maximise her opportunities.

'I'd appreciate a cup of something. Instant coffee would be fine.'

Flora followed him into a seventies-style ginger-pine kitchen which she yearned to take an axe to. 'So why did you get divorced, Henry? It's the one fact about you that everyone knows and talks about.'

He sighed. 'Very much as you'd expect, I'm afraid.'

'Philandering?'

He frowned. 'You could call it that, I suppose, but there was only one woman.'

'And you are properly divorced, not just separated?'

'Divorced. She took me for every penny.'

'Good for her.'

'What do you mean, "good for her"? I was a good husband.'

'Who cheated.'

'OK. I was a good husband who cheated. That doesn't make me all bad, you know.'

308

'But not all good either. I don't suppose you have a tea bag instead, do you? Or did your wife take those, too?'

'I managed to hide a box from her. You can have tea. I even have biscuits, of a sort.'

Flora helped herself to a seat and watched as he filled the kettle, found biscuits and was generally hospitable. She understood, now, why she had been sent. Henry was a bit touchy about his house and if someone else had gone, even a young and female member of the choir, they might not have got the right result. Indeed, thought Flora, there was no guarantee that she would be successful, but at least she was in with a chance.

'Here's your tea. Only dried milk, I'm afraid.'

'That's OK.'

He pulled round the bench that was on the other side of the table where Flora was sitting.

'So, where abroad might you go?' she asked. 'If you went, I mean?'

'The States. Or maybe Switzerland.'

'Oh. They both sound quite exciting.'

'Mm. Well, to be honest,' he said with a glint in his eye that left Flora in no doubt at all that he was about to be far from honest, 'I'm only planning to sell up and leave because I'm broken-hearted. I mean, I'm getting nowhere with you and—'

Flora blushed, even though she knew he was joking. 'But you're not getting nowhere! We had dinner—'

'Bar snacks. Not the same.'

'And it wasn't my fault you couldn't come to my dinner party.'

'Probably just as well. Charles Stanza doesn't approve of me.'

309

'Oh? What makes you say that?'

'I met him in town the other day. He was perfectly polite and all that, but I got the impression he didn't really like me going out with his baby cousin.'

'I'm not his baby cousin! I'm his business partner.'

Henry shrugged. 'So, you want my orangery for some sort of concert.'

'Yes. My choir needs an appropriate venue for a concert called' – what was it Geoffrey had said? – '"A Stately Summer – Music for a Summer Evening".'

'And you want to use the orangery?'

'Yes. We'd be terribly tactful about it. We would hardly annoy you at all.'

'But what about the lake in the middle of it? Anyway, why on earth would I let a whole lot of strangers use my house?' He seemed to be joking, but Flora couldn't be sure.

'Well . . .' She took a breath. 'It's perfectly possible that among the choir members there are people who could fix the hole in the roof. That would be a good pay off, wouldn't it?' She knew one of the basses was a partner in a firm that made fitted kitchens. It wasn't quite the same as one who repaired glass roofs, but he probably had connections.

Henry looked thoughtfully at her for a moment. 'Well, yes. It would. But what about the other stuff? I really don't like people in my house, snooping round, and there'd be cars parked all over the lawn.'

'Your grass hasn't been a lawn for some time,' said Flora bluntly. 'And you could go away for the weekend. Then you'd come back to a manicured lawn and an orangery without a swimming pool. And you'd have

310

that much less to do up before selling it.'

'And of course I may change my mind about selling. I may do it up and live in it. If I get over my broken heart.'

'I'm sure you'll recover, but you'd have to earn lots of money to sort this place out. What do you do, again?' She knew she should have known this, but her mind just hadn't been engaged when they first exchanged all this information.

'IT.'

'Oh. That's all right then. You can earn lots of money.'

'But sadly, not enough. Not right now, anyway. This house would swallow up a hundred grand and still have room for seconds.'

The thought that Burnet House might be perfect for Annabelle and Charles had flickered through Flora's mind quite early. The thought of them living there made her uncomfortable for some reason and the fact that it would be so fabulously expensive to renovate was perversely cheering. She decided to be helpful.

'I bet there's something here, something that's valuable, that your wife didn't know about.'

'It wasn't my wife who was the problem. It was her solicitor.'

'Sorry. Solicitor. I bet though, if I had a look around, I could find something worth selling. I'm an auctioneer, after all.'

'Apprentice, you said.'

Flora laughed. 'Well, OK, but I'm not a complete idiot, and if I found anything even half interesting, I could get Char— someone to come along to give you a proper valuation.'

'Well, there's a library, but I think I'd have known if there were any first edition Dickenses in it.'

'Or James Bond. He's valuable too.'

'Only if the dust-jackets aren't torn and therefore in pristine condition.'

She laughed. 'We obviously both watch the same television programmes.'

He regarded her. 'Why don't you finish your tea and come and look,' he said.

She hesitated for a moment.

'I assure you there are no etchings involved. Although I might ask you out to dinner, later. We still haven't done dinner, have we?'

She inclined her head politely.

'Would you come?'

'I was brought up to wait until I was asked,' she sidestepped. 'Shall we inspect the library?'

'The solicitor did send someone to look at everything,' Henry explained as they reached a room lined with bookshelves, obviously a custom-made library. 'But he admitted he wasn't all that up on old books. He searched for anything that was obviously a first edition, but didn't find any. He put a blanket value of five hundred pounds on the lot, and then went home. I think he was tired by then.'

'Are these books precious to you? If you sold them, would you miss them?'

'No, not really. This is a family house, but I didn't inherit it from my parents, but from an uncle. Sounds a bit unlikely, I know, but it's true.'

'Oh, I believe you. I'm involved in the auction business because of an uncle who died, too.'

'You never told me that before.'

'Didn't I?' Flora was not willing to be distracted. 'There are a lot of books here. Even if there are no very precious ones, the value in each one would mount up, don't you think?'

He shrugged. 'I don't know. You're the apprentice auctioneer.'

'You'd have to get rid of them, anyway, if you were going to do up the house. Unless you stored them. That might be quite expensive.'

'I certainly wouldn't want to do that. Tell you what, if you get your cousin, or whoever, to come and have a look, and if they agree there's enough here to have an auction that will make a bit of money, I'll let your choir use the orangery.'

'I see.'

'But I'd want to pay a lower commission. I know auction houses, they take money from the buyer, money from the seller and add in a lotting fee as well.'

'I don't think you quite understand how many expenses are involved in arranging an auction,' Flora started.

'No, I don't. But you want a favour. Can you offer me a deal in exchange?'

Flora thought for a moment. 'No. Not off my own bat. I don't know if there's anything here worth a damn.'

'I want the books gone.'

'We could arrange a house clearance, that wouldn't be difficult, but if you want one of our experts' – Henry wasn't to know there weren't loads of them kicking their heels in the office – 'to come and give a valuation, to look at everything, we'd need all the commission we're likely to earn.'

'In which case, I'm not sure, Flora. I could get any auction house to do that for me. I want a bit more, in exchange for the favour.'

'I didn't realise that favours were exchanged. I thought people just did them out of the kindness of their hearts.'

'Not this people,' he said with a grin that contradicted his words. 'The kindness of my heart is all run out.'

'Well, that's a shame. But no matter. The choir can easily have their concert in our hall in town.' She batted her eyelashes just once and then looked at her watch, but didn't actually take in what it said. 'I'd better be going. Thank you so much for your time. I'm sorry to have wasted so much of it.'

'Hang on! Don't walk off in a huff! There's still room for negotiation.'

Flora had hoped this was the case. 'Oh?'

'Will you come out to dinner with me?'

She enjoyed flirting with Henry. He, like her, seemed to be a natural flirt – he flirted as naturally as he breathed – and that reassured her that he didn't have any particularly serious intentions towards her. It did seem to be delightfully free of complications, though as she was pretty sure she didn't want the relationship to develop beyond a few casual evenings she rather felt she should make her feelings clear. 'Well,' she answered, 'it rather depends. Would I be doing you a favour in going to dinner with you? In which case you're more in my debt than I am in yours. Or are you doing me a favour by feeding me, when I'm obviously so near starvation? Because I could only come to dinner if I was the one doing you the favour.'

He had a very sexy laugh, she decided. 'Don't worry,

Flora. I won't read anything into dinner. So shall we sort out the favours at a later date?'

'Could do,' she agreed.

'And in the meantime, could you ask one of your experts to give the library the once-over?'

'I could do that, too. But I can't make any deals about commission or anything. That would be up to my cousin.'

'Well, I could talk to him when he comes to look at the books.'

'No,' she said hurriedly. 'It won't be him, and our book expert isn't a company director. He won't have the authority to make that sort of decision either. But when we know if there's much of value here, we can sort it out.'

'I suppose I'll have to be satisfied with that.'

She put her head on one side. 'And with the pleasure of taking me out to dinner.'

'That is some compensation.'

'Also, the pleasure that the choir will repair your roof and cut your grass and very much enjoy singing in your orangery.'

'Did I agree to let the choir come? When did that happen?'

'When I said I'd go out with you.' She gave him her most provocative smile.

'I know taking you to dinner will be a pleasure, but I'm still not sure about the choir.' He did genuinely look a bit worried.

'Trust me. It will be a very positive experience. I'll get Geoffrey to come and give your library a thorough going-over.'

'Will you come too?'

'I might.'

'I'll walk you to your car.'

Dear Henry, he was a sweetie. And quite sexy too. She wished she could develop a crush on him. It would be much more convenient.

As Flora opened the door of the Land-Rover, he said, 'I might see if they've got a table at Grantly Manor. It's very good. They've got a chef down from London going for his third Michelin star.'

'Sounds horrifically expensive.'

'Oh, it is, but far less than it would be in London.'

'That would be lovely,' she said, and kissed his cheek.

'Well?' demanded Geoffrey, when Flora had tracked him down in the cellar of the house, sticking labels on the furniture that had come in via the roadshow. 'How did you get on?'

'Not bad, but not perfect, I'm afraid. The orangery has got a hole in the roof, and therefore there's a small lake in it. I suggested we could mop up the water and pray for a dry night but Henry Burnet wasn't too keen on that idea. I don't think he believes in the power of prayer.'

'I feel a bit bad sending you, Flora. It's why I thought I'd better come in and do some work.'

'It was fine! Henry's a friend, after all.'

'Just a friend, Flora?' asked Geoffrey, *in loco parentis* again.

'Well, maybe a bit more than that. He's going to take me to Grantly Manor.'

'Oh. Very grand.'

Flora was tired of talking about Henry. 'I did say the choir would fix the hole in the roof. One of the basses is a builder, isn't he?'

'One of them is a cabinetmaker, if that's what you mean.'

Flora made a gesture with her hands that asked Geoffrey to be a little more helpful. 'For the choir, do you think he'd go down a few grades and fix a hole in the roof? He must know people with scaffolding and stuff.'

'Now you're talking big money.'

'Well, if it's impossible, there's always the hall. But although I wasn't too keen on having to beg Henry to let us use it, I do think the orangery would be lovely to sing in.'

'I'm sorry, my dear. I wasn't thinking. I'll ask about fixing the roof.'

'He also wants you to go and value his library. He doesn't think there's much there, but you never know. Someone did give them a cursory glance before, when they valued everything when he got divorced, but they didn't look thoroughly.'

'I expect I can do that. If I'm not needed here. It'll be a real pleasure to use my knowledge and experience for once, instead of pretending I haven't any.' He regarded Flora seriously. 'Annabelle won't like it if she finds out. She's always been dead set against me doing anything except moving things from one place to another.'

Flora inwardly protested the waste of his talent. 'I'll square it with Charles. It'll be all right.'

Geoffrey smiled. 'Well, that's all looking very promising, Flora. You've done well.' Geoffrey was obviously

317

very pleased at the notion of being a valuer again, instead of just a porter. 'If there's enough to give us a basis, we could do a specialist book auction. Put all the stuff up on the Internet.'

'Right. I'm glad you're pleased. I just hope it's not all just book club editions and Sunday school prizes.'

'Very collectable those, you know, especially if they've got good book plates in the front.'

'Yes, well, I'd better go and see if anyone's missed me upstairs.'

She met Annabelle in the hallway. 'How did you get on at Burnet House?' she asked.

'OK. He has some books that might be quite valuable.'

'That's good. But I have to warn you, Charles was livid! I told him it was very unlikely there was a house sale in the offing, but he was really cross about you going there alone.'

'But he knows I know Henry, that we've been out a couple of times.' Charles's over-protectiveness could be exasperating sometimes.

'It's the going to his house thing that so upset him.'

'Oh. Well, there isn't enough furniture for a house sale, but Geoffrey's going to look at the books.'

'Is he now. Well, do check with Charles first. He can be so bloody difficult at times.'

'I'd better go and find him, then. Do you know where he is?'

'He's out. Why don't we pop across to the pub and see if they'll make us a sandwich? I know it's late but we need to eat. You certainly do.' Annabelle eyed Flora's slim figure with envy. 'It is Saturday, after all.'

Flora thought about it. An angry Charles was possibly better not faced on an empty stomach.

'Oh, OK. Just quickly. I ought to stay and work, really, as I've been out all morning.'

'You don't want to get like Charles, and do nothing but work, work, work. Besides, I want to hear all about Burnet House.'

They sat in the pub garden. It was a bit chilly, the air having not yet warmed up after the rain, but it was rather smoky inside and neither of them wanted to advertise the fact that they'd been to the pub when they got back.

Annabelle had bought two white wine spritzers and ordered a couple of egg salad sandwiches. She took a sip.

'Now, tell me about Burnet House?'

'It's in awful condition. Henry says—'

'There you are!' Charles's voice suddenly declared behind them. 'Flora, I was worried about you!'

Chapter Nineteen

'Why were you worried about Flora, darling?' asked Annabelle.

'I just heard she went chasing off to Burnet House. There's no earthly point. There's nothing there to sell.' Charles pulled out a chair, the metal grating horribly on the flagged courtyard.

'Can I get you a drink?' Flora got up. 'A pint? A spritzer?'

'Oh, just something soft,' said Charles, obviously not quite happy with a woman buying him a drink and still distinctly grumpy.

'A sandwich? Crisps?'

'Um . . .'

Flora retreated to the bar. She didn't know why Charles was in such an awful mood but she would have to tell him why she'd been to Burnet House. Learning that her visit wasn't even work-related might make him even crosser. On the other hand, he might prefer her asking to use the house for a concert to her having some mad idea about getting Henry to have a country-house sale when he knew there was nothing worth selling.

She came back with an elderflower pressé and two packets of crisps, having ordered another sandwich. He was possibly more bad-tempered than necessary because he was hungry. Her mother had always commented that her father was impossible to deal with if remotely peckish.

'I think I should tell you,' she declared, setting down her booty, 'that I went to Burnet House to see if the choir could use their orangery. I know we're frantic and I was going to work, but it was an emergency.'

'And now you're in the pub?'

'Charles! It's Saturday! And the girl's got to eat!' Annabelle said.

'Was Henry Burnet there?' Charles tore into the crisp packet.

'He was. He showed me the orangery. There's a huge puddle on the floor. I don't suppose you know of a good builder who could fix that?' She looked at Annabelle and Charles hopefully. This was really the choir's responsibility, but it would be useful to have a fall-back position, especially as it might divert Charles's mind from Henry Burnet.

'Oh God yes, I'm sure we do,' said Annabelle, helping herself to crisps. 'I'm starving.'

'He didn't . . . make a nuisance of himself, did he?'

'Who?' asked Flora, being deliberately obtuse, annoyed with Charles for being so old-fashioned, but oddly charmed by it as well. 'The builder?'

'Henry Burnet! He's got a bit of a reputation. I know you've been out with him a couple of times, but it's different you being at his house. You're my cousin and I feel responsible for you.'

'For goodness' sake, Charles! Flora is an adult, and I'm sure she's been round the block a few times. There's no need to be so stuffy.'

'Well?' demanded Charles.

Flora suddenly decided she liked Charles being so indignant about Henry, even if it was just in a cousinly way. 'He did say he'd try to get a table for Grantly Manor. I don't know if that counts as making a nuisance of himself.'

'Grantly Manor! Flora! How super! It's wonderful. We had a family party there for Mummy and Daddy's wedding anniversary. Henry must be really keen.'

Charles scowled.

'I think Henry's rather attractive,' Annabelle went on, either not noticing, or ignoring, Charles's reaction. 'And his wife made such a fuss. It was only one affair, after all. You could do a lot worse than him, Flora.'

'You think it's acceptable for a man to cheat on his wife, do you, Annabelle?' said Charles.

'Not if he made a habit of it,' Annabelle replied. 'I just think a marriage should be worked at, and there are worse things a man can do than have a little fling.' She smiled and put her hand on Charles's. 'Don't think I'm giving you permission to get up to anything, Charlie, I'm just saying I wouldn't break up a relationship for one misdemeanour. What do you think, Flora?'

'I don't know, really. I've never been in a relationship for more than a couple of years, but I suppose if you've got children, a home, all that stuff, it would be a shame not to make an effort to try again.'

'Well, don't think I'm so relaxed about extra-marital affairs,' said Charles, glancing at Flora, trying hard to relax.

Annabelle laughed and for a second Flora wondered if there was an edge of hysteria in it. 'Darling, I'd never cheat on you when we're married! As if I would!'

At that moment, the sandwiches arrived. As cutlery, napkins and seasonings were distributed, Flora hoped it would mean Charles would have to stop being grumpy. If I was his partner, she thought, I'd have fun charming him out of his bad mood.

'Oh, jolly nice sandwich,' said Flora, when the waitress had finally gone, managing to ooze quite a lot of the filling out as she took a bite. 'How is yours, Charles?' she mumbled.

'Excellent, thank you.'

'So tell us about the house,' said Annabelle, her mouthful not quite finished either. 'I'm dying to hear all about it.'

Flora chewed hard and swallowed. 'Well, as I said, it's in a terrible state. He – Henry – told me that it needed about a hundred grand spending on it.'

'As much as that?' Annabelle was shocked. 'Shame. I thought it might do for us, Charles.'

'It's enormous!' said Flora. 'You'd have to have about seven children to justify living in it.'

'Or you could just entertain a lot. And a yoga studio would be nice,' said Annabelle, becoming a little dreamy. 'Or t'ai chi.'

'A yoga studio?' said Charles. 'What would you want that for?'

'Oh, I just thought I could take it up. It's very calming and a good way of getting rid of negative karma.'

Flora glanced at Annabelle, momentarily distracted. 'And the kitchen is vile, it's that very orange pine, with too many small cupboards,' she said. 'You'd have to rip that out and start again.'

323

'Well, I said his wife was a stupid woman. No taste,' said Annabelle.

'No taste but a lot of furniture,' said Flora. 'She left Henry hardly any.'

'I suppose if he wanted to keep the house he had to sell off a lot of it to pay her off,' said Annabelle. 'I wonder who did the sale?'

'Not us, obviously,' said Charles. 'So did he say if he was likely to sell the house itself?'

'He said he wanted to earn some money to do it up, then sell it. Or he might keep it. I don't think he quite knows what he wants to do.' She took another bite of sandwich, for protection.

'Well, you could do a lot worse than him,' Annabelle repeated.

'Don't be ridiculous!' said Charles. 'Why on earth do you think Flora should go out with Henry Burnet, of all people?'

Annabelle shrugged. 'No need to get all worked up, Charles. He's quite good-looking and Flora needs someone to take her around, doesn't she? You told me she was a girl who liked to have lots of boyfriends.'

Flora blushed at being referred to in such terms. 'I've really been too busy for much of a social life since I've been down here, but it is nice to have a friend.' She looked at her handbag as it moved slightly and played 'Jingle Bells'. 'Oh, so sorry,' she said, embarrassed. 'That's my phone. Do you mind if I take the call?'

'Of course not,' said Annabelle.

Flora moved away from the table. It was Henry.

'I've got a table. Grantly Manor. Are you interested?'

324

'Yes. When for?'

'Tonight. Terribly short notice, I'm afraid.'

Flora considered. She'd lent her copy of *The Rules* to a girlfriend, but she was fairly sure you weren't allowed to accept an invitation for Saturday made later than Wednesday. There had to be three clear days in between the invitation and the date. No way were you allowed to accept a date for the same day.

'It's extremely short notice.'

'Sorry. I thought I should strike while the iron was hot. You're always so busy.'

'Next week would be better.'

'No tables available for next week. It's now or about three weeks away.'

'I was going to wash my hair . . .'

Henry laughed. 'That takes about five minutes. You can't use that old excuse any more.'

Flora considered. *The Rules* were made to be broken and she didn't want to marry this man, after all. 'I'll wash it anyway. Shall I meet you in town?'

'No, I'll pick you up.'

Flora hesitated for a second. 'OK. I'd better give you directions. Or do you have a fax?'

'I do.'

'I'll send a map from the office.' She didn't necessarily want Charles and Annabelle to hear her giving Henry directions to the cottage.

When she came back to the table she couldn't help a little smile of satisfaction tugging at her mouth. 'That was Henry. He's got the table at Grantly Manor.'

'Oh?' asked Charles, frowning. 'When for?'

325

Flora wished he hadn't asked that. It took the gilt off the gingerbread, somewhat. 'Tonight.'

'They must have had a cancellation,' said Annabelle, who obviously hadn't read *The Rules*.

'Well, it'll be fun, whatever. And now I must fly, I've got loads to do because I was out half the morning.'

Flora went back to the office in a buoyant mood. She was excited about the thought of going out with Henry, she told herself. If Charles was cross about it, then too bad. He was a silly old stick-in-the-mud. She reflected that usually when men were grumpy she just wanted to tip a bucket of water over them and tell them to snap out of it, but Charles's grumpiness was quite sexy in a Mr Darcy kind of way. And she was uncomfortably aware that at the back of her mind there was a small voice asking whether perhaps Charles was annoyed at her going out with Henry just because it was Henry, or whether he'd have objected to anyone she went out to dinner with. But no, mentally she gave herself a little shake, he'd made his position quite clear on Thursday night.

'Hi, Geoffrey,' she called when she got back. 'What are you up to?'

'Oh, Flora, I'm glad to see you. Virginia's daughter was on the phone. She wants photos of all the good pieces for the website. I wouldn't know where to start.'

'No probs. I'll borrow the digital camera. I'm sure there's somewhere in the cellar we could rig up an area with a white cloth to set the pieces off. Shall we go and look?' They went downstairs together. 'I've done this sort of thing heaps of times. When I worked in an art gallery.'

'Charles has put stickers on the ones to be on the

website,' said Geoffrey, opening a door. 'What about in here? Not too crowded. You're very cheerful.'

'Just back from the pub. Charles and Annabelle are still there. Charles was in a grump, but I expect Annabelle knows how to make him feel better. They're very well suited, after all. I think this would be fine.'

'Well suited, are they?'

'Oh yes. Both stiff as pokers, although at least Annabelle tried to stop him going on at me about visiting Burnet House. I'll borrow that cloth over there. It looks big enough.'

'Should be, it was a double sheet, once.'

Flora found a nail to hang it on. 'Henry wants a reduction in commission. I said I couldn't give him one, that I'd have to ask Charles. I wish I had the authority to do it myself. After all, I'm an equal partner, technically speaking, anyway. But not in any other sense. Anyway, what are you doing working on a Saturday?'

'I told you. And you know there's a lot on at the moment, and Edie's gone off to a plant sale with a friend.'

'Ah.'

'And you don't see Charles and Annabelle working on Saturday unless there's something very special on.'

'Charles does work very hard. He was at a farm valuation until late last night.' She knew this because she had seen the note he'd left for Louisa when she came in. She'd been tempted to type it up herself and might have done if she hadn't gone out. In a bizarre way the thought of sitting with ear plugs, listening to Charles, was quite pleasant.

'Shall we start with the chest-on-chest?' said Geoffrey. 'As it's in here already?'

'Good idea. Thank heavens there's two of us, Geoffrey,' she went on as they heaved the heavy furniture around. 'It's too much for anyone on their own. Do you think we can get it in front of the sheet, or shall I try to think of something else?'

'We'll manage it all right between us.'

Flora was breathing hard by the time they had eased it out from between a couple of commodes and got it in position. 'Now I'm going to have to practically climb out of the window to get it all in. Perhaps if I stand on this chair . . . It's all right, I'll put this bit of cloth on it – it's not an antique camel rug, is it? OK. You couldn't just pull out the corner of the white sheet. It looks a bit . . . That's better. Now smile, please. Look natural.'

Geoffrey chuckled.

'Well, it's important it looks its best. I think this is the piece Charles's genuine television expert was so enthusiastic about.'

'Television expert! Honestly, what do they know?' said Geoffrey.

'But it is a nice piece. It might go for three grand if it's properly advertised and the buyers turn up. George the Third, he thought.'

'Well, I'm not saying he's got the date wrong, but those are London prices, if you ask me.'

The chest-on-chest duly recorded, Geoffrey and Flora edged it back to its nook in the corner. 'So why is there such a hurry to get all this photographed?' he asked again, wiping his brow with a tartan handkerchief.

'It's partly so there's plenty of time for dealers to realise that Stanza and Stanza have decent stuff to sell. Because we've been a bit down-market in recent years, with few real antiques, we've got to build up our reputation. If the stuff is on the website, and all the links are right, the dealers will find out we're here, so to speak.'

'You're not going to be working all day, are you?' said Geoffrey, lifting a table with the skill that revealed his years of experience.

'Oh no. I've got a date tonight, with Henry. Grantly Manor. Charles was not pleased to hear about it. He seems to think Henry's some sort of Lothario and I won't be safe.'

'He's only looking out for you, as he should,' said Geoffrey, taking on the appearance of someone about to give a lecture.

'Don't you start, Geoffrey!' said Flora. 'A girl's got to have a bit of fun. Now, what's next? And don't let me forget to fax Henry a map.'

'It's always cheering, getting ready for a date,' said Flora to Imelda and the kittens. 'I'm determined to have a good time tonight. I deserve one! I've worked very hard lately, and Henry is fun.' She thought briefly of someone she would not describe as fun and then pushed him out of her mind. Henry liked her, he was very attractive and most of all he was available, so she was determined to give herself one more shot at developing a crush on him.

She put on her prettiest dress, did her hair and her make-up carefully, and put the shoes with the peony on them into a bag. Her mother, who was a fount of slightly dubious advice, had always told her to have running-away shoes to hand, in case. She'd also told her to keep enough money for a taxi home in her bra, in case she got separated from her handbag.

'So?' she asked Imelda, lacking anyone with more sartorial sense. 'Do I look OK?'

Imelda purred obligingly, and turned her attention to Charles's favourite kitten, who obviously needed a very thorough wash.

'I'll take that as a yes,' said Flora and sprayed herself liberally with scent, realising too late it was rather sexy, and was best applied sparingly. She shrugged and went downstairs to wait for Henry. She'd faxed him a map which Geoffrey, obliging but reluctant, had drawn for her.

She had barely had time to plump up the cushions and throw the dead flowers into the fireplace before she heard Henry's car drive up.

'The map worked OK, then?'

'Very well.' He kissed her cheek. 'Mm. You smell gorgeous.'

'You smell quite nice yourself. Shall we go?' She picked up her pashmina and her house keys, called 'Goodbye' to Imelda and they left the house. Henry's car was an old Jaguar XK120. 'Mm. Nice car,' she murmured, thinking that it was exactly the sort of car she'd thought Henry would own.

'A bit of a cliché, I'm afraid. I bought it in a fit of rebellion after Natasha left, taking most of my worldly goods with her. This represents most of what was left. Fifteenth-hand, of course.' He opened the passenger door and Flora slid in.

Grantly Manor was everything its name and reputation promised – a venerable old house set back from the road and arrived at via a carriage sweep. A good-looking young man arrived to park the car. Flora was impressed.

Henry was investing quite a lot of what he didn't spend on the car to show her a good time. Good for Henry!

'It would be better if they drove you home again afterwards,' he said, relinquishing his keys, 'but I suppose that would be rather expensive.'

'I could drive, if you like. That's a very nice car.'

'Not that I don't trust you, Flora, but it's only insured for me to drive.' His grin became rakish. 'Besides, this way, I can ply you with alcohol and stay perfectly sober myself.'

'Not that I don't trust you, Henry, but I won't drink too much, I don't think.'

He laughed, and ushered her into a panelled bar furnished with comfortable-looking sofas and small tables. Although it was summer, and not cold, a small log fire smouldered in the huge grate.

'This is gorgeous!' said Flora. 'I love having fires in summer. It's so decadent, somehow.'

'They do pay attention to detail. I think that's the secret of a really good hotel or restaurant. So, what can I get you? A glass of champagne?'

'Mm, that would be lovely.' Flora smiled and settled back into the cushions.

Henry brought menus with the drinks. Flora took hers.

'Why don't you have the oysters?' suggested Henry.

She looked at him over the top of her menu. 'I don't think I want an aphrodisiac.'

He laughed. 'I thought they only affected men.'

'I think I'll have the smoked salmon, as I don't want to leave room for pudding.' She regarded him. 'My mother has an old recipe book that says "Never trust a man who refuses apple dumplings".'

'I never do. Are they on the menu?'

'No, so I can't test you. I heard someone else say, "Never trust a man who owns a picnic set". Do you?'

'I don't think so.' Henry feigned anxiety. 'There may be one in the attic. I'm not sure.'

'Oh, if there is, put it in a sale. They sometimes go quite well if they've got all their fittings. My colleague Geoffrey was telling me the other day.'

'I didn't bring you here to talk about work, Flora. Think what you want to eat.'

'Guinea fowl sound interesting.'

'They don't, actually, they just make a quite boring clucking sound.'

'I meant to eat! Now don't get distracted. The girl will be back in a minute. It's such a bore when guests don't make up their minds because they're chatting. I've been a waitress,' she added, 'so I know.'

When they had eventually chosen, the waitress, who looked as if she was moonlighting from her day job as a model, so long were her legs and so short was her skirt, asked them if they'd like to sit outside. 'We've set a few tables at the end of the garden. It's very pretty.'

'It sounds lovely,' said Flora. 'What do you think, Henry?'

'If you'd like that, we'll eat there.'

They were led to a table by the French doors that opened on to the lawn that led down to the river. It was a glorious summer evening. The air was scented with jasmine and philadelphus, and peacocks strutted about, adding their raucous cry to the murmurings of people enjoying themselves.

Henry had ordered more champagne. 'I only want

332

one glass, so it might as well be the best. Here's to you.'

His eyes glittered down into hers as Flora raised her glass to his. He really was very attractive, in a rakish, obvious way, and, still determined to make an effort, she flicked back her hair with a slanting smile.

They were halfway through their starters when Charles and Annabelle drew to a halt just by them. Flora had her elbows on the table and was explaining to Henry how exciting working for an auction house was. She was very animated and slightly flushed, and the strap of her dress had slipped off her shoulder.

'Oh,' said Charles. 'Hello, Flora.'

Annabelle, slightly behind Charles, said, 'Surprise! We were so jealous to think of you both here, on this lovely summer evening, that we thought we'd treat ourselves. It was Charles's idea.'

'Oh really,' said Flora dryly, not at all pleased to see them. 'You just had a sudden urge to come here, Charles?'

'That's right,' he said rather woodenly.

'Tonight?'

'Yes, tonight.' He had the grace to look slightly self-conscious; he clearly knew she knew that he was there to keep an eye on his cousin and the philanderer he thought she needed protection from. Really, thought Flora, irritated, what century did he think he was living in?

Henry had already got to his feet and Flora leapt to hers, losing a shoe in the process. 'Fine. What a . . . er . . . surprise. Let me introduce you to Henry. Henry Burnet, Charles Stanza.'

333

'Actually, we have met,' said Charles, crushing Henry's hand in a trial of strength.

'Henry, this is Annabelle, Charles's fiancée,' said Flora, trusting that Annabelle would be more friendly.

'We know each other too, Henry.' Annabelle had followed Flora's instructions as to her appearance and was looking almost glamorous. 'We met at the Williams-Ellises – remember?'

'How could I forget?' Henry bowed over Annabelle's hand. Then he looked at Flora. 'Didn't you trust me?'

'Of course!' How embarrassing! 'Annabelle, I didn't ask you to come, did I?'

'Dear me, no! As I said, we just thought it was a perfect night for this place, and when we phoned on the off-chance they had a table.' She addressed Henry. 'I expect they had a large cancellation.'

'I expect so,' Henry agreed resignedly.

'Do you mind if we join you?' suggested Charles. 'You've only got as far as your starters.'

'Ooh, that would be fun!' said Annabelle, either oblivious to Flora's dirty looks or choosing to ignore them. 'It's quite dull going out when it's just the two of you, isn't it?' She pulled up a chair.

'Yes,' said Charles. 'After all, we know it's not a first date, so you won't mind.'

'Won't we?' said Henry.

Flora shrugged.

Seeing that he couldn't save the situation now, Henry said, 'You can join us on the firm understanding that next time Flora and I dine, it'll be on our own.' He smiled. 'She's a very difficult girl to get to go out with.'

'Is she?' said Charles blandly. 'That's reassuring.'

334

The waitress appeared. 'We could order another bottle of champagne,' said Henry, 'or would you rather not?'

'I don't want to drink too much,' murmured Flora.

'Oh, go on,' said Annabelle. 'Relax! Have another glass of champagne.' She leant in and whispered, 'If these two are going to be like dogs about to fight, we might as well get drunk and enjoy ourselves.'

Flora couldn't decide if having Charles to annoy would enhance the evening or not, but she silently agreed that a second glass of champagne might help things along a bit. 'Oh, OK. It's Sunday tomorrow. As long as Geoffrey doesn't make me go to a car-boot sale.'

'What?' asked the others in unison.

'Never mind. Here's to us all!'

335

Chapter Twenty

As she lowered her glass, Flora remembered her resolution to enjoy herself, and smiled warmly at Henry. His evening had been thoroughly mucked up – and her resolution to develop a crush on him wasn't exactly helped by Charles and Annabelle's presence.

'Well, Charles, are you the director of the firm where Flora works?' asked Henry, good-naturedly.

'The firm that Flora half owns, yes,' said Charles.

Henry frowned at Flora. 'You half own it? Why didn't you tell me? And why on earth couldn't you agree a lower percentage with me?' He turned to Charles. 'I wanted her to give me a special rate – a lower commission – and she said she couldn't.'

'I did say I was an apprentice,' Flora pointed out. 'That sort of decision is entirely up to Charles. And as it isn't his choir who wants to go and sing at Burnet House, he probably isn't open to offers.'

'Well?' demanded Henry, in a way that made Flora like him a little less.

'Oh, let's not talk about business,' said Annabelle, smiling at Henry. 'We're here to have a break from work. I'm part of Stanza and Stanza, too,' she added.

'Quite right,' said Flora. 'It's Saturday night. We're all in this lovely place – the food is wonderful, by the way

– we shouldn't sully the occasion with mere commerce.'
She took rather a large gulp of champagne.

'That's fine by me,' said Charles.

'So, Henry,' said Flora, touching his hand with her finger. 'How was your day?'

Flora found herself tuning out while Henry regaled the company with horror stories about viruses and worms and other IT disasters. She noticed quite a lot of it involved Henry saving various companies millions, but quite how he did it passed her by.

'Jolly interesting,' said Annabelle gamely. 'Now tell us about your car?'

That filled the conversational gap until Annabelle and Charles's food came, but as the evening went on, Flora began to wonder how much in common she actually had with Henry. He was very amusing, he told quite good, if slightly off-colour, jokes, but she couldn't help feeling that his conversation was rather vapid. Not that philosophy was exactly flowing out of her, it had to be said. Charles, on the other hand, was much more interesting. He'd travelled, to quite unusual places, and was widely read. Henry was a man who didn't read much unless he was on a plane.

The alcohol flowed, mostly between Flora and Annabelle, and there was never a ghastly silence, but Flora found herself faintly bored. She had really wanted to hear about Charles's experiences in Mongolia, but Henry seemed keener on telling stories about spotting stars at Cap Ferrat.

Eventually, it was time for pudding.

'Now, what would you girls like to drink with it?' said Henry.

Unusually for her, Flora found herself objecting to being referred to as a girl. She didn't say anything, though. 'I think I've probably had quite enough to drink, thank you.'

'Oh, go on, don't be a wuss. I'm sure Annabelle will have a glass of Monbazillac or something.'

'Oh, OK,' said Annabelle. 'I've drunk loads of water, after all. It's why I've kept going to the Ladies'.'

Flora had noticed that she'd popped out rather a lot. 'I still won't have any more to drink, thank you. Although I'd love some peppermint tea.'

'Peppermint tea it is,' said Henry, looking at her in a way which told her he was looking forward to the next part of the evening.

'Yes. I've got a bit of a headache,' she replied, suddenly deciding, rather recklessly, in view of the latest bank statement that she was definitely going to split the bill with Henry rather than let him pay for her. 'It's frightfully good for that.'

Henry behaved very well, considering, thought Flora, as she let herself into the cottage. He'd been expecting a dinner à deux, and possibly a little light lovemaking afterwards, and he got Charles and Annabelle and only the briefest kiss in the car afterwards. It was not unreasonable of him to expect to be asked in for coffee, she had led him on a bit even though her insistence on paying her half of the bill had made her caution clear, but the headache was now real, and she didn't want any more wet kisses.

She rang him the next morning feeling a bit guilty, and asked him if he wanted to go for a walk that afternoon.

'I'm sorry Flora, I'd love to, but I'm afraid I'm going out to lunch with some friends.' He did sound sorry, and Flora realised she really had to make her feelings clear to him. She liked him, he was good company most of the time, but hard as she'd tried to fancy him last night, the spark clearly wasn't there.

'Well, I'm glad I caught you,' she started. 'I wanted to . . .' God, this was awkward. How to put it? 'I just wanted to say how much I enjoyed last night, the place and everything, and that I value our friendship.' Oh dear, that sounded horribly formal. 'But—'

'But you don't want anything more than that?' Henry interrupted.

'No, I'm sorry. I just . . .' She paused to collect her thoughts, 'I'm just not in the right frame of mind, really. I don't know how long I'll be in Bishopsbridge anyway, and I'm so involved with Stanza and Stanza and learning about the business that I'm not sure I've got the energy for a proper relationship.'

'Yes,' he said dryly. 'I had noticed that you were . . . how should I put it? Distracted?'

'I'm sorry, Henry. I do want to be friends.'

'Me too.' He softened. 'But don't worry, I always knew your mind at least was elsewhere. It's been ridiculously hard even to organise a drink in the pub, so I was under no illusions about your priorities.'

'I really am sorry.'

'There's no harm done,' he said lightly. 'I do like you, Flora, but I'm not falling in love with you if that's what you're worried about.' It was, rather. 'So if you want to be friends, then we'll be friends. I might not give up trying to persuade you,' he added flirtatiously, 'but you

339

know I might well be selling up and leaving the area as well, so it doesn't make sense for either of us to get involved in anything terribly serious.'

'Thank you, Henry. It's good of you to be so nice about it.'

'I'm a nice man,' he replied with a smile in his voice, and then dashed off to his lunch.

Instead of a walk with Henry, Flora made rock cakes in a fit of domesticity and ate most of them herself, talking to Imelda, wondering why the little black kitten allowed Charles to pick him up, but still shied away from her.

Just under two weeks later, Flora was making up the spare room for her mother. She was so excited, and longing to see her. In many ways her life was perfect, but something was missing. She was fine when she was at work. She still found it all fascinating, and absorbed every scrap about the job that either Charles or Geoffrey let slip, but at home, she found she missed William. Or something. She still went out with Henry from time to time, but although she tried very hard, she didn't find him quite as fascinating as he seemed to find himself.

Her mother would know what was wrong. She was an excellent agony aunt – and also an excellent cook. Flora was looking forward to being looked after and cosseted, something her mother did particularly well.

Almost every hour had been accounted for since the bizarre evening at Grantly Manor. They had at last got the website going, and the date for the next sale was booked for early September. It was going to take one and a half days, and Henry's books, declared by Geoffrey to be sufficiently interesting to get a few collectors along, were going to start the sale. At work, everyone was buzzing with excitement and busyness, and even Annabelle had become more enthusiastic about life – not necessarily about work, but she was generally more skippy and happy.

The concert, the excuse for Flora's mother's visit, was tomorrow. Flora was beside herself with nerves, in spite of having had several private practice sessions with Moira, the unofficial head girl of the choir.

'If I mess up,' she explained to Moira, who had patiently bashed out the tunes of all the music on the piano until Flora knew them backwards, 'I'll ruin it for everyone.'

'You won't mess up,' Moira had said, sounding a little bored with having to repeat herself. 'You know the music, just concentrate, keep looking at James – he's the conductor, you know – and you'll be fine.'

'I think I just about know who James is.'

'Then you'll be fine! Enough panicking!'

Now Flora went into the garden to pick flowers for her mother's bedroom. She was driving down from London that evening and Flora wanted everything to be perfect for her. She had already found roses, lady's-mantle and mauve geraniums for the sitting room and bathroom. Now she wanted something extra sweet and tiny for the little mantelpiece in the bedroom.

'You're jolly lucky I'm not making you all wear bows round your necks,' she said to the kittens, who had grown up enormously and were tearing round the house like motorbikes out of control. Flora wasn't looking

341

forward to explaining to Annabelle about the curtains. They were definitely taking on a hooked appearance from being swarmed up and down so often. Could she convince Annabelle that the curtains had always had that uncut-moquette look? The sofa she had protected with throws – a little too late, but she could leave the throws and Annabelle might never take them off.

She waded through the kittens to get to the garden. 'I'll have to find homes for you soon, those two of you who aren't going to live with Uncle Geoffrey and Auntie Edie. I might keep one.' She sighed. Charles had said he wanted the little black one, but he hadn't said anything about it recently.

As she climbed over the barricade she had erected to stop them getting outside, she wondered if talking aloud to kittens was on a par with talking to oneself on the guide-to-madness scale. Definitely not, she decided, kittens were animate. Mind you, so was she.

Having constructed the most perfect tiny posy, using forget-me-nots, tiny branches of yellow lady's-mantle and white ground elder, borage flowers, and a couple of spires of purple linaria, she came back inside. She had been tempted to add the little white flowers of the goose-grass which was currently weaving a net over the garden like something out of a sci-fi movie, but had decided she hated the weed too much. Early that morning, Flora had attacked it with a fork, winding it round and round the tines like spaghetti, but in parts of the garden it was still threatening to pin everything to the ground.

Now, she put the posy in the milk jug from a doll's tea set. She had bought the set from a recent car-boot jaunt. It wasn't complete, but it had only cost a couple of pounds; it was perfect for this purpose. Her mother would love it; she had a passion for tiny things.

In the kitchen, Flora had all the makings of a wonderful supper. Two bottles of Sauvignon Blanc from New Zealand, as recommended by the nice man in the off-licence, were in the fridge. To have with it, she had made lacy parmesan wafers, which had involved a lot of testing, they were so delicious. Smoked salmon on blinis with sour cream and pancetta were laid out on a very pretty platter, another car-boot find, and she had even sprinkled a few beads of lumpfish roe, in lieu of caviar, on the top, for decorative effect. As a main course they were going to have a William-inspired salad, enhanced with bits and pieces from the garden, chicken breasts poached in white vermouth with a lemon sauce, and accompanying it, in case it looked too much like diet food, was potato salad with home-made mayonnaise sprinkled with chives. For pudding she had made a raspberry pavlova, using the egg whites from the mayonnaise and raspberries given to her by Geoffrey and Edie when they heard her mother was coming. Everyone was looking forward to meeting her.

Restraining the kittens with difficulty, Flora climbed back out into the garden. It was such a beautiful evening she thought it would be nice to eat at the little table and chairs Charles had brought her, when she first moved here. It seemed a lifetime ago, and in a way it was – her life had changed so irrevocably since.

At last Flora saw a car appearing along the lane and rushed out so she was there the moment her mother got her first foot out of the car.

343

'Sorry, darling, I got a bit lost,' said her mother and crushed her daughter so tightly she couldn't breathe.

'Mummy!' said Flora, reverting to a form of address she hadn't used for years. 'It's so lovely to see you!' Flora hung on to her mother a little longer than she would have normally because she found herself weeping a little, and didn't want her mother to see. She wanted to be the adult daughter one hundred per cent.

'Let me take your bag. Oh, it's so nice having you here!'

Hermione Stanza looked about her. 'Isn't this pretty! Darling, no wonder you're so happy here.' She gave her daughter a quick glance and frowned a little.

Flora hoped her mother couldn't tell she hadn't been sleeping properly. She'd made such an effort to sound totally enthusiastic about everything in her emails and phone calls, she didn't want to reveal anything untoward when face to face. After all, her vague, underlying unhappiness was totally illogical. It wasn't fair to worry her mother with it when she couldn't do anything to help.

'Come on in. I've got a bottle of wine in the fridge. Goodness, this bag is heavy! What have you got in it?'

'A bottle of vodka, some gin and sweet Martini so we can cobble together some Pimm's and some lemonade, in case you didn't think to buy any. Oh and a dessert wine – Muscat and Flora, because it had your name on it.'

'Oh Mum, you're a star!'

Hermione needed a guided tour. She loved her bedroom, which Flora had made very pretty, and she adored the posy. She approved of the various unguents Flora had put in the bathroom, as well as the huge jug of cow-parsley that Flora put at the end of the bath.

'And this is my bedroom. And that's the cupboard where Imelda had her kittens.'

'But, darling! It's full of shoes!'

'I know. Imelda likes shoes. I had to clean out each one afterwards.' Her mother made an uncomfortable noise. 'Let's go downstairs and have a drink.'

They were both quite tipsy and had eaten the parmesan wafers and the smoked-salmon blinis when they saw a vehicle come down the lane. It was Charles.

'I'm so sorry to interrupt,' he said as he got out and saw them sitting in the garden, surrounded by plates and bottles, 'but I wanted to come and say hello to Hermione. It's been a while since we met.'

Flora's mother got to her feet in order to embrace Charles, who leant down and hugged her.

'It's been years, Charles,' said Hermione, 'but I'm going to resist the temptation to tell you that you've grown. Have you eaten? Come and join us. There seems to be masses of food.'

Flora smiled, feeling suddenly very shy. 'The trouble is, I can only do recipes for four people or over. I've never got the hang of half measures. There is loads.'

Charles looked at his watch. 'Well, I haven't eaten. I'll just give Annabelle a ring and see if she's cooked. If she hasn't, I'm sure she'll be glad not to have to.'

'I'll get some things,' said Flora. 'Will you have a glass of wine, or a home-made Pimm's?'

'The Pimm's is a bit strong, I'm afraid,' said Hermione.

'I couldn't quite remember how my husband makes it. And we've run out of lemonade.'

'A glass of wine would be lovely. Are you sure this isn't all too much trouble?'

'No,' said Flora. 'It's all too much food. You'll be helping us out.'

Charles came into the house to help. 'There's a chair there you could take,' said Flora, when he asked.

Charles wasn't showing much interest in chairs. 'I haven't seen the kittens for ages. They've grown up so much!' He picked up the little black one and inspected it while it chewed his finger.

'I thought you'd come to see my mother,' said Flora, feigning indignation. Her heart was warmed by the sight of him with the tiny creatures, although she was still a bit miffed about the black kitten cowering away from her, and yet going to him.

'I did, but the kittens were second on the list.'

Flora sighed, suddenly wishing she had a place on the list herself. If she had, it was probably about number seven, somewhere after the cottage, the garden and the state of the sitting-room carpet.

Once they had got back over the barricade with extra things, Flora piled Charles's plate with chicken and potato salad. 'There's another plate there you can put your green salad on if you like,' she said.

'It's wonderful,' mumbled Charles, his mouth full. 'You really can cook, Flora. Or did you do this, Hermione?'

'No, no. It's all Flora.'

'And has Henry sampled your cooking yet?' he asked Flora, once his mouth was empty.

Flora shook her heard. 'Not yet. We've both been

busy. I've been doing a lot of extra rehearsals with choir and with Moira. She's sort of head girl,' she explained. 'Although soon, maybe.' She added this for Charles's benefit as much as anything. Although neither of them had ever referred to it, she was still faintly embarrassed at the thought of the night he'd stayed in the cottage after the storm, and the thought of the long, close hug he'd given her as he'd sent her off to bed made her feel a bit peculiar. All of which meant that, inconvenient as his particular dislike of Henry was, it was far better that he thought she was occupied and in a sort of a relationship than that she was pining for him. Which obviously she wasn't.

'Have some salad, Charles,' said Hermione. 'It's really delicious. Full of all sorts of weeds.'

Charles heaped some on to his side plate. 'I've experienced Flora's salad before. She gave a dinner party soon after she first arrived.'

'Except William made that salad. I just copied his ideas this time.' She looked at her mother. 'Have you met William? Friend of Emma's?' she asked, wondering whether if you told a lie often enough, it would eventually become the truth, or only for the originator of the lie.

'I don't think so,' said Hermione.

'Oh, well, he's an excellent cook.' Flora went on, 'He's great on cooking food from the wild.' She regarded Charles's side plate. 'You don't have to eat all that if you don't want to.'

'Flora and I will eat the rest of the salad tomorrow. Possibly for lunch, before Flora goes to her concert rehearsal,' said Hermione. 'Are you coming, Charles?'

'Um . . . I'm not sure I knew about it.'

'Well, you should,' said Flora, suddenly indignant. 'Geoffrey and all your porters, or at least nearly all of them, are in the choir. And there's a huge poster in the window of the office. Anyway I did tell you, ages ago.'

'I've just never had it put in front of my nose, I suppose. And the poster would have its back to me.'

'I think you should go,' declared Hermione. 'Support your workers. And Flora.'

'Unfortunately, Annabelle and I have been invited out for dinner tomorrow night,' said Charles.

'Oh, OK,' said Flora, disappointed yet relieved. She wasn't really sure she wanted Charles watching her as she stood in the front row, trying to look as if she knew what she was doing.

'Next time, perhaps?' suggested Hermione.

'Definitely next time. You must give me plenty of notice, Flora.'

Flora indicated she would, knowing it was unlikely she would still be around to be in another concert. This was the choir's last event for a while and by the time the Christmas fixtures started, she would probably have gone back to London. The choir was one of the many things that she would miss terribly.

'Shall we move inside for pudding? I'm getting a bit chilly,' suggested Hermione.

'Good idea,' said Flora. 'I'll get it organised. Bring your chairs and your glasses. We can probably leave the rest.'

Hermione decided to rescue the salad and a few other bits and pieces as well. By the time they were all back in the house, most of the table outside had been cleared.

Hermione sat down on the sofa and picked up the nearest kitten. 'Aren't these just adorable?'

Charles found the black one. 'They are.'

'I haven't managed to stroke that one yet. He's very shy, but he seems OK with you.' Hermione frowned. She was good with cats.

Charles continued to stroke his kitten. 'It's very unfortunate that Annabelle, my fiancée, has an allergy to them. But I'm still hoping we can have one in the office.'

'You couldn't leave it alone at night while it's still young,' said Flora protectively, clearing a space on a little table.

'Oh, that's all right. I could stay in the flat for a while, until it's a bit older.'

'There's a flat in the office building?' asked Hermione.

'Yes. It's an old town house. We're thinking of putting it on the market, to realise some capital. Or possibly part of it, converted into flats. It was Flora's idea,' said Charles. 'She's been really innovative since she's joined us.'

'Flora always was an ideas person,' said Hermione, glancing at her daughter with pride.

'We were expecting a ditsy blonde,' explained Charles. 'Who knew nothing about auctions and antiques.'

Flora laughed, and handed him a plate of meringue, raspberries and cream. 'Well, you were right. I am blonde and I did know nothing about antiques or auction houses. I know a bit more now, though. And you hate my teapot.'

Everyone inspected the ball-of-wool-shaped pot, covered in ceramic kittens.

'Oh, darling, I'd thought you'd given up collecting

those,' said Hermione, obviously wishing that Flora had.

'I have to confess I prefer the real thing to the china variety of kitten, but those teapots do have a certain market,' said Charles.

Flora chuckled softly at this display of tact. He glanced at her and carried on, 'But generally you picked it up very quickly, and you have a great gift with people.'

'There!' said Hermione triumphantly. 'I told you that personal skills were more important than academic qualifications!'

'Thank you, Mother' – Flora handed her mother a loaded plate – 'for more or less telling Charles I didn't do too well in my exams.'

'Exams aren't everything and I'm sure Charles knows that.' Hermione smiled and Flora could almost see Charles softening under the warmth of it.

'Well, I do now,' he said.

Flora perched on the arm of the sofa where her mother sat. 'These are Geoffrey's raspberries. Dig in.'

'Delicious!' Hermione got to her feet after a short time when the scraping of plates replaced conversation. 'Can I get you some more, Charles?' She took his plate. 'Are you sure? I'll just tidy up the edges and start my diet tomorrow. Have you heard about it? You don't measure calories, just G. I.s or something.' She frowned. 'I haven't finished reading the book, but it's really good! Not that you need to think about anything like that, Flora. I'll go and put the kettle on.'

'Your mother is very like you,' said Charles.

Flora was used to hearing this. 'Is that good or bad?'

'Very good. She's delightful.'

Flora smiled. 'She's a fun mother to have, I must say.'

She fell silent, suddenly shy. Then she spotted the kitten, curled up on his neck, fast asleep. 'He really likes you. You must have him.'

'Annabelle might become accustomed to him. I've heard of people who are allergic to cats but are all right with their own.'

Flora sighed. 'But she wouldn't like the process of getting used to him.' She wondered if part of her sub-clinical misery was worry about how well Annabelle and Charles were suited. The thought of Charles spending the rest of his life with the wrong woman was deeply depressing. He deserved to be happy. He worked so hard.

As if agreeing with her, Charles sighed. 'No, I suppose not. I'll work something out.'

Flora slid off the arm and on to the sofa. She felt very tired. What she wanted more than anything else in the world was just to fall asleep, next to Charles. She let her eyes close.

Hermione came in with coffee and peppermint tea. Flora opened her eyes and accepted a mug. Her mother arranged the little table and put Charles's coffee near him.

'I need a shot of caffeine to wake me up,' he said. 'I was getting really drowsy just now. This is really good.'

'I brought the coffee with me. Flora said it isn't always easy to get good coffee down here.'

'Oh, you can't know the proper shops!' said Charles. 'There's a wonderful coffee shop. I must take you there.'

'That would be nice,' said Flora, in a small voice. Why did this casual, almost meaningless invitation mean so much to her? It was ridiculous. After all, Henry would take her to the coffee shop if she asked him.

Conversation ceased. They sat sipping their drinks, sleeping kittens on their laps, all perfectly content with the silence.

Eventually Charles got to his feet, detached the kitten and placed it where he had been sitting so it wouldn't feel cold. 'I must go. I've had a lovely evening. Thank you both, so much.'

He kissed Hermione on the cheek. Flora, he just waved at. For a moment, she experienced a horrid pang of jealousy and hated herself.

When he was gone, Flora's mother said, 'He's gorgeous! I can quite understand why you're in love with him.'

Flora burst into tears.

'I'm not in love with him!' she hiccuped. 'He's engaged to Annabelle.'

'I know, darling,' said Hermione sympathetically as she put her arms round her daughter, 'but it's not enough to stop you falling in love with him, is it? It should be, I know, but it doesn't work like that.'

'But really – I mean, he's so stuffy and—'

'He's not stuffy with the kittens,' Hermione pointed out sadly, 'and you told me he's really good at his job. There's something about him, Flo, and I can't blame you for responding to it.'

'Is that what's wrong with me, then? I've been feeling so odd, so discontented, when everything is going so well! I love it down here, and yet I know I can't stay here once Charles and Annabelle are married. Is that because I'm in love with Charles? How awful!' Ever since the storm Flora had done such a good job of persuading herself that she felt nothing more than cousinly affection for Charles that suddenly facing up to the fact that she'd accidentally gone and fallen in love with him was quite a shock. Although she realised it had been true for quite a while now.

Hermione led her daughter back to the sofa and sat down next to her. 'Tell me everything. Things may not be as bad as they seem.'

Sadly for Flora, once she'd told Hermione the whole story, her mother agreed with her that things were just as bad as they seemed.

'You could seduce him away from Annabelle,' Hermione suggested tentatively.

'No I can't! He might be perfectly happy with her, and even if he isn't, it would have to be his decision or he'd blame me if anything went wrong. No, I'll just have to go away when the business is going really well, and forget him. I can't stay for the wedding, in November. It would kill me.'

Hermione sighed. 'It seems a shame.'

'It's a tragedy! But there it is.' She blew her nose on a by now much-used tissue. 'Although if I thought he was happy, I suppose I'd be OK about it. Sad for me but happy for him. Perhaps I could just go away for a bit, and come back.'

'Well, I'm bound to meet Annabelle while I'm here. I'll tell you if I think she's right for Charles, ultimately.'

'But even if she isn't, it's up to him to discover that. I can't do anything about it.' She thought back to what Charles had said the morning after the storm, about the grass only appearing to be greener on the other side and about being a man who stuck to his promises, and

353

realised that even if he did have doubts about his relationship with Annabelle, he'd feel obliged to do the honourable thing and at least give the marriage a very good chance.

Hermione sighed. 'That is a very grown-up way of looking at it. I think if it were me I might just go all out and seduce him. He obviously likes you.'

'No he doesn't, apart from in a cousinly way. He likes the kittens and feels protective of me, like a big brother might. Which is why he doesn't like me going out with Henry.'

'Tell me about Henry.'

'Oh, he's fine. Very good-looking. And free! Which is quite a major plus. I keep trying to fancy him, but somehow I just don't. Now I know why.'

'I think we should both go to bed. Things won't look so bleak in the morning.'

What Flora didn't tell her mother was that things always looked bleaker in the morning when, after a night of broken sleep, she awoke, and all her depression – now identified as heartbreak – came flooding back to hit her.

That night, however, whether because of the alcohol or her mother's comforting presence, Flora slept like a baby or, as her mother put it, a teenager. 'Babies don't sleep all that much,' she explained when they saw each other the next day.

They found themselves invited to have lunch with Edie and Geoffrey. 'It's only a salad and quiche,' explained Edie as she ushered them into the garden at the back of the house where there were chairs to sit on. 'Geoffrey wouldn't let me cook you a proper meal. He doesn't like to eat anything heavy before a concert.' Her glance at her husband implied she thought this was a bit prima donna-ish.

'You can't sing on a full stomach and we've got to be there for the rehearsal at five. Now, glass of sherry, Mrs Stanza?'

'Hermione, please, and sherry would be lovely.'

'Flora?'

'Yes, please, but could I possibly have a lump of ice in mine?'

'Of course you can, my dear. And there's only rasp-berries and cream for pudding,' said Edie, opening a packet of crisps and putting them in a bowl. 'Do you need a hand, Geoffrey?'

'Certainly not. You show Hermione the garden.'

While this was happening, Flora went into the house to find Geoffrey. 'Could I just check I've got my music in order?'

Together they went through their folders until at last Flora was convinced there was nothing missing and she wouldn't suddenly turn a page and find she was singing the wrong arrangement.

When Edie and Hermione had finished their patrol of the garden, Hermione had several plastic bags full of plants. 'We'll leave them here until after the concert,' she said, rather apologetically. 'And I'll put them in the garden tomorrow morning. Charles and Annabelle won't mind, will they?'

It was nice for Flora to go to Burnet House with Geoffrey. Apart from anything else, it meant that she would arrive at the right place at the right time. Edie had ironed her scarf for her and Hermione had Geoffrey's clear written directions how to get to the venue.

'I'm so nervous I feel sick,' Flora said as she settled herself on the seat next to Geoffrey.

'There's no need for all that. A few nerves are good, because it means you'll concentrate, but you don't need to go overboard with them. You're not singing a solo, after all.'

'I know! But I'm afraid I'll mess it up for everyone else.'

'You won't. Not if you focus and look at James, all the time.'

'What about the words?'

'You'll know them by heart, almost, by now.'

Flora sighed. 'I haven't been in the choir as long as you, Geoffrey.'

Chapter Twenty-One

Flora was so focused on the choir and her nerves about singing in it that she had almost forgotten about Henry. He had not forgotten about her, however. He was in the field designated as a car park, theoretically telling people where to park, but in fact waiting for Flora.

She did not feel at her best in her long black skirt and black blouse, but she smiled brightly at him as he helped her out of Geoffrey's car.

'Hello, Henry. I do hope you don't regret this.'

He kissed her cheek and nodded to Geoffrey. 'I've had no reason to regret it so far. The hole in the orangery roof is fixed, the grass has been cut and I get to see you looking like . . .' He paused for the perfect metaphor. '. . . a nun without the wimple.' Something about him implied he did not find this look unattractive.

'You remember Geoffrey?' Flora found his slightly lecherous glance both unexpected and extremely unsettling. She grabbed Geoffrey's arm so he couldn't abandon her.

'Of course,' said Henry. 'We did spend an entire afternoon together. I was surprised there was so much value in that library.'

Geoffrey unhooked himself from Flora so he could lock the door of the car. 'There are a few nice early editions, and although I don't think there's anything there that's worth a huge amount of money on its own, put together, we should make you a tidy sum.'

'Oh, look, there's Euan! He's one of the tenors,' she told Henry. 'He breeds Cavalier King Charles spaniels and is a bit eccentric,' she explained. 'He seems to be going in the wrong direction. Perhaps you'd better chase after him, Henry, before he gets lost.'

'Euan never gets lost,' said Geoffrey after Henry had reluctantly gone to round him up.

'Doesn't he? Well, never mind. I can't chat just now, I need to focus. I'm so nervous.'

'You'll be fine,' said Geoffrey.

Flora thought she might very well vomit from terror, while those oft-repeated words were still echoing about her.

Carloads of choir members arrived in dribs and drabs. Almost everyone exclaimed at the beauty of the building and the pleasantness of the weather. They were all reluctant to leave the pleasantly cool summer evening to go inside to the orangery, which they knew was going to be on the warm side.

'These black clothes get awfully hot sometimes,' explained Virginia. 'We keep thinking we should have a different summer uniform, but we can never agree on what to have. We don't want anyone fainting. Have you got your scarf, Flora?'

'Yes, Moira gave me one. It's folded carefully in my bag. Edie ironed it for me. I don't think she trusted me not to burn it.'

'Well, you do have to be careful. And is your mother coming?'

'With Edie. They'll be along later. It's been lovely having her.'

'It must have been a bit lonely for you here, not knowing many people. Now, how do we get in?'

'This I do know. Follow me,' said Flora.

Henry came into the orangery just as they were going to start the rehearsal. He waved at Flora but she ignored him. It was hard enough to remember how they were walking in, where they were to stand so they could all see James, where the basses were going to be positioned so they could be heard by but not drown out the second sopranos. She fixed her gaze on James, waiting for the signal to start. How could people chat just before a dress rehearsal? Her palms were sweating and she still felt slightly sick.

But she couldn't ignore Henry in the break before the performance. Wine, soft drinks, tea, sandwiches and cake were laid on in a room off the kitchen. A woman in a black dress and white apron ushered them to it, saying Henry had arranged it.

The choir were thrilled and as they all wanted to thank Henry personally, it was some time before Flora could get to him. 'This is very kind of you, Henry,' she said. 'A few soft drinks would have been perfectly adequate.'

'I wanted to do something a bit better than that.' He looked down at her with a look that indicated he was hoping for some kind of reward.

'It's for the choir,' she said firmly, making it clear that no reward would be forthcoming. 'But it is nice of you.'

He appeared to accept this and shrugged. 'It seemed only fair to do something after they did all those repairs.'

359

'Roof OK now?' asked one of the basses who had access to ladders and window-repairing skills.

'Fine, thanks, David. Are you really sure I can't pay you?'

David shook his head. 'Nah. The materials didn't cost much and my boss gave me the time off work to do it.'

David had a wonderful voice and Flora loved it when they were arranged so she could hear it thrumming through her at the end of John Tavener's 'The Lamb', her favourite, but the most challenging piece they sang.

'It's a lovely venue,' said one of the other choir members. 'You should rent it out for functions. You could charge quite a lot, I should think.'

'Or get it registered so you could have weddings in here,' agreed another.

Henry became thoughtful. 'So I could. With the hole in the roof I never thought of it as being somewhere that could earn its keep.' He paused. 'So why am I doing it for you for nothing?' he asked, smiling at Flora.

'Because before we came along there was a field instead of a lawn and a puddle the size of Lake Windermere on the floor,' she said. When she had last seen Henry, this reply would have sufficed. Now, he seemed different. Or was it just Flora's nerves making her over-sensitive?

'That's a bit unfair. The puddle wasn't much bigger than the Serpentine.'

She laughed, to oblige him. 'You're doing it for the sake of charity and the good of your soul, which could probably do with improvement.'

'You're probably right.' This time his smile was less calculating and Flora recognised how attractive he was.

360

Come on, heart, she said to herself. He's nice, he's single! Be attracted to him! Why aren't you?

But she knew the answer and nothing she could tell herself could stop her wanting a rather stuffy man whose own heart belonged to another. Must try harder, she told herself firmly, and if you can't fall in love with Henry, find another romantic distraction.

Henry put his hand on Flora's shoulder and was about to speak when James said, 'The audience are beginning to come in. Could we get ourselves together, please? And can I tell you once more? Don't forget to smile! Flora?'

Flora found it very difficult to smile when she was so nervous. She tried a smile now, but her cheek muscles seemed to be made of plaster of Paris, and wouldn't let her. She found Moira, whom she was following in, and stood behind her. Moira adjusted her scarf for her and gave her shoulders a little hug of encouragement. 'You'll be fine! Got your music? In your left hand? That's right.'

Moira turned away and, a moment later, they processed in, the women in black with blue scarves, the men in dinner jackets with matching bow ties. Flora hadn't liked putting on black clothes and black tights on a lovely warm evening, but she admitted to herself that they were smart when they were all together.

The orangery looked magnificent. Although too nervous to look around much, Flora couldn't help recollecting how it had been when she'd first seen it: empty and dank, with a puddle on the floor. Now there were chairs arranged in rows in one half. Some huge plants, one of them a genuine orange tree in a huge pot, stood in the corners; someone had done something clever with the lighting and all the floor-to-ceiling windows were open, so the breeze wafted in. They had been rehearsing there not long before, but the addition of the audience, bright in their summer silks, added colour and excitement.

'Angela, in the altos, lent the plants,' Moira breathed to Flora out of the side of her mouth as they reached their places. There was no platform, but they had practised carefully where they were to stand so everyone had a good view of James, and could be seen by the audience.

Flora, terrifyingly, was on the end, in full view of everyone. 'Good luck!' whispered Moira as they settled in their positions.

Flora didn't reply. She could see her mother and Edie out of the corner of her eye. They were smiling encouragingly, but Flora realised she'd have felt happier if she hadn't known any of the audience. She wanted her humiliation to be kept private. There was Henry, of course. He was sitting at the back. She had no trouble forgetting about him.

James came into the room, turned to the audience and gave a short, witty introductory speech. The audience laughed. The choir laughed. Then he turned to his singers, regarded them all, then held up a sheet with a picture of a grinning face on it. Flora did her best to oblige him but didn't think it was a very good effort.

The accompanist played the opening bars of 'The Entrance of the Queen of Sheba'. The choir took a collective breath and opened their throats. 'Rejoice! Rejoice!' The orangery had lovely acoustics. Flora forgot her nerves and began to sing with joy.

* * *

'It's going awfully well,' said someone during the interval.

The choir were back in their room where a fresh lot of sandwiches and drinks had been laid on. Flora was sipping a glass of elderflower, not allowing herself wine until it was all over.

'And there's a very good crowd,' said Geoffrey. 'Someone's done really well with the ticket sales.'

'It's the venue, I'm sure,' said Moira. 'People are so curious. They'd listen to anything just to get the chance to get a look at a house like this.'

'And there's been a fair amount of scandal, hasn't there? Does anyone know any details?'

'Flora's going out with Henry,' said Geoffrey, to save Flora more embarrassment. 'It's how we've been allowed to be here.'

'It's just coincidence. We've only been out a few times.' Flora, aware that everyone was looking at her, found herself blushing. 'I don't know any scandal, I'm afraid, except that his wife left him and got most of the money.'

'Well, however we come to be here, we're very grateful,' said one of the altos whom Flora hadn't really got to speak to before. 'A "Stately Summer" from a church hall wouldn't have been the same.'

'The sandwiches are jolly good too,' said Euan with his mouth full. 'Egg and cress, my favourite.'

Eventually everyone stopped eating and drinking, James gathered his flock, and they filed back into the orangery. Flora felt much more relaxed now and felt she could get into the rather complicated version of 'The Lord's My Shepherd' with her mind totally on the matter in hand. Then she foolishly looked up to see if her mother was happy and saw Charles. He was sitting at the end of one of the rows. She felt herself go pink and looked hard at James, trying to concentrate. James caught everyone's eyes, saw Flora, and held up his picture of the grin again.

Just forget about him, she told herself and forced her lips to smile.

Like a tongue constantly seeking out a sore tooth, Flora found her eye go to Charles often. Dragging her eyes away she saw something that caused her to miss a couple of bars and, very nearly, her place in the music. Sitting next to each other, a couple of rows behind Charles, were William and Annabelle.

What on earth were they doing here? Together? Flora sincerely hoped that some sort of sense of performance meant that her shock was kept private. She didn't dare look at the audience again, and smiled in between songs with a vacancy she feared might be the fast track to the Asylum for the Bewildered. What was going on? Could she possibly avoid seeing any of them afterwards? No, she realised. After all, if William and Annabelle were there with Charles, in full view of everyone, she had nothing to worry about.

While they sang an English folk song with words so suggestive Flora was almost embarrassed, she concluded that guilt was like attraction, you couldn't just turn it on and off. If there was something going on between Annabelle and William, she was convinced it was all her fault. And no matter how much she tried to make herself fancy Henry, who had so much going for him, principally his lack of a partner, she couldn't. 'Riddle fol di ree!' she carolled, with feeling.

As the audience clapped enthusiastically, Flora tried to make a plan. James would say something, and then they'd do the encore. Then they'd file out, back to their room where they'd left their handbags and bottles of water and music cases. Could she dash out of the side door, steal a car and escape? No, she couldn't. Even if she delved into the handbags for a car key, it would take her ages to find out which car the key she stole belonged to. It was no good. She took a breath and prepared to sing 'Bobby Shaftoe', in parts, with complicated extras. Then after more clapping, she followed Moira out of the orangery, accepting her fate.

'Thank you, everyone,' said James. 'That went very well, I thought. Lovely venue, Flora. Thank you very much for getting it for us.'

'That's fine,' she said, hoping that the choir didn't all think she had had to sleep with Henry to get him to agree to let them use it.

'Oh, but if you hadn't asked so effectively we wouldn't have got it,' said James, confirming, in Flora's view, that he definitely thought she had slept with Henry. 'And the evening wouldn't have been quite so "Stately", would it?'

'I know Henry's very grateful for the repairs David did for him. He's done well out of it,' said Flora.

'Oh yes, it's been good for him, too,' agreed James. 'I gather he might rent it out for functions.'

Flora nodded, not knowing what to say. Geoffrey came up. 'Are you coming out to meet our audience, young Flora?'

'I suppose so.'

'Come on! You were fine. They'll have loved it. I

thought the Stanforth had never gone better, James.'

James nodded. 'I knew you could do it, if you all just concentrated.'

'Come on, Flora. Come and meet the crowd.'

Flora summoned up a smile and followed Geoffrey out of the room, clutching her music bag like a security blanket.

Long before they reached her mother and Edie, Flora spotted that they were chatting with Annabelle, William and Charles so there was no chance of avoiding them.

'Darling! It was wonderful!' Her mother gave Flora a huge hug as she reached them. 'Were you terrified? You looked a bit scared at the beginning, but I thought the standard was so high! It's a super choir!'

'The quodlibet went well, Geoffrey,' said Edie. 'You got it right at last.'

'Is that the one when the men sang one melody and the women another?' asked Hermione. 'The conductor explained it?'

'That's right,' confirmed Geoffrey. 'It's always a crowd pleaser.'

'You must have wondered why the audience suddenly got bigger after half-time!' Annabelle laughed. 'Charles said he'd promised he'd come along, and so William, Beatty and I thought it would be rather fun to come too. We were at dinner at her house. Beatty's gone home now.'

'To do the washing-up?' suggested Flora.

'No. She has staff!' Annabelle regarded Flora as if she'd gone mad. 'And Hugo. He's her husband.'

Flora nodded. The Asylum for the Bewildered seemed both nearer and more attractive than ever.

'You were awfully good,' said William, whom Flora hadn't seen for ages.

Flora smiled at him. He was very good-looking and seemed to have become very civilised since his days of living in the woods. And when had he become part of Annabelle's social circle?

'Have you met my mother?' she asked him. 'Mum, this is Emma's friend, William.'

'Who's Emma?' said Annabelle.

'You met her at my dinner party,' said Flora firmly. 'The dinner party where you and Charles met William.'

'Oh yes, I remember, the one Jeremy fancied.' Emma satisfactorily dismissed, Annabelle went on, 'Is there any chance we could get a look round the house, do you think? We did have that very jolly dinner with him. We're hardly strangers, after all.'

Henry was talking to James and a couple of other choir members, Flora could see. 'He's very touchy about letting anyone in. I was only allowed across the threshold myself because I knew him already.'

'He knows me already, too. We all had that dinner together,' she repeated. 'I'll go and ask him. Are you coming, Charles?'

'I want a quick word with Flora and if she says we wouldn't be welcome in the house, I'm not going to press the point,' said Charles.

'Then you come with me, William.' Annabelle took hold of William's arm and marched off.

Hermione drew Geoffrey and Edie to one side. 'I gather we can't see the house, but shall we go and get a breath of fresh air before we leave? I want to see if that's jasmine I can smell or someone's perfume.'

As they went off together, embarrassment, which had been ebbing and flowing over Flora all evening, suddenly flooded. She had no idea what to say to Charles.

'You were wonderful,' he said. 'I mean, the choir was wonderful. I had no idea my porters were all so talented.'

'It was nice of you to come. Oh, here's Virginia.'

'Charles! I don't think you've ever come to one of our concerts before,' said the ruler of Charles's saleroom, not unreproachfully. 'It must be Flora's influence.'

'I've seen the error of my ways, Virginia. I'll come to all of them now. I was very impressed.'

'So I should think. I'm not sure "The Lamb" was quite right, was it, Flora? I thought the tenors were a bit off.'

Flora shook her head. 'I'm afraid I was just concentrating so hard on my own bit, I couldn't pick out the other voices, really. My ear is just not good enough.'

'Never mind. You got us a lovely venue. Are you coming for a drink?'

Flora needed a drink, and certainly wanted one, but she wanted it in the privacy of her own home, where it went with a bath, and bed immediately afterwards. 'I've got my mother with me.'

'Oh, she's up for it! I've just been talking to Geoffrey and Edie.'

'I'll take you home if you're tired, Flora,' said Charles.

'That's settled then,' said Virginia. 'Your mother can drive your car home from Geoffrey's, can't she?'

Flora nodded. She ferreted out her car keys and handed them to Virginia.

'And Charles will take you home, so I'll just run and confirm which pub we're going to. You're sure you don't want to come?'

'Quite sure.'

Just as Virginia left and Charles turned to talk to someone he knew, Henry appeared. 'I thought I'd never get away from that lot. Come on, Flo.' He drew her away from the crowd a little. 'Let's go in for a nightcap. I'll drive you home later. I've got some very nice brandy. You certainly deserve some reward for all that hard work.'

'Actually . . .' Henry had never called her Flo before, and Flora wasn't at all sure she liked it. She only put up with it from close friends and family. '. . . I am quite tired.'

'Nonsense. You need something to help you wind down. And then, whenever you're ready, I'll take you back and tuck you up in bed. I'll even make you hot chocolate.'

As he came near her, Flora realised that he had been drinking, which was unusual for him. 'Really, Henry, I'd rather not. I'm exhausted.'

Henry was beginning to get belligerent. 'Oh, come on! I put my house at the disposal of your bloody choir and you won't even have a glass of brandy with me?'

Flora drew breath, not certain how to deal with the situation, and then suddenly Charles joined them. 'Actually, I'm taking Flora back,' he said smoothly.

'No need,' said Henry. 'You've got your fiancée – what's her name? Annabelle – to look after. Flora and I have things to attend to.'

By now there was no doubt about what things he had in mind and Flora started to feel very uncomfortable. She'd made it plain she didn't want to be anything more than friends, and had been careful not even to flirt with him since Grantly Manor.

369

'Flora's coming with me,' said Charles, ratcheting up his determination several notches.

Flora looked at the two men squaring up to each other and said nothing. She didn't know what to say.

'She's my girlfriend,' claimed Henry, beginning to get cross.

'She's my cousin and I'm taking her home.'

Flora began to feel anxious. This was by no means the first time men had competed for the privilege of taking her home, but they didn't usually get quite so tense.

'I think the relationship between us takes precedence over some distant blood link, don't you, Flora?'

'I—' began Flora.

'I don't think—' began Henry.

'Oh shut up,' said Charles, and punched Henry in the nose.

Flora's first thought was relief that no one was about to witness Henry clutching at his now bloody nose. Her second was a mixture of thrill and horror as Charles took hold of her elbow and marched her away from the scene of the crime.

'I'm so sorry, Flora,' he said when they were back at the car.

'Don't apologise to me! You didn't punch my nose.'

'I couldn't let him take you back. He'd been drinking and after what happened between you and Justin – well, I could see it happening all over again.'

'Me and Justin?' For a moment, Flora had forgotten all about Justin.

'Yes, when he – hit on you, I think the expression is, because he'd taken you out to dinner. Henry obviously felt you owed him something.'

Flora felt she owed him something, too, but not a free pass to her body. 'But what about Annabelle and William?'

'Oh Christ! I'd forgotten about them – I mean William – for a moment.' A thought passed across Charles's face that Flora couldn't identify.

'Well, you can't go back and look for them now,' said Flora, managing to conceal the nervous laughter that was beginning to erupt. 'But I can easily get a lift . . .'

'Hardly.' The corner of Charles's mouth began to twitch. 'I'll ring Annabelle on my mobile.'

As he pulled it out, Flora said, 'But what can you say?'

'Hi,' he said briskly. 'Flora's exhausted and I'm taking her home. Will you get home on your own? Or will you wait at the pub until I can come and collect you? Good girl. Fine. 'Night, 'night, sweetie.'

He disconnected. 'She and William will get a lift. Now we'd better get off the premises before Henry comes after me with a shotgun.'

Chapter Twenty-Two

❧

'This is silly,' said Flora, getting into Charles's car.

'I know, I'm sorry. I'll apologise in the morning. I don't know what came over me. I don't usually get into fights.'

'It wasn't a fight. Henry didn't hit you back.'

'Thank goodness. He probably could have pulverised me.'

Flora didn't respond. She doubted Henry cared enough about her to risk more damage – and at the moment Charles punched him Flora had been certain that Charles would have followed it up with more had there been an excuse.

'I'll send him a bottle of wine, or something, to apologise.'

'You realise he'll probably never want to go out with me again.'

'I can't say I'm sorry about that. I never did like you having anything to do with him.'

'In his defence, up till now, he never laid an unwelcome finger on me.'

'But he did just then?' Charles looked as if he was considering going back and punching him again.

'No! No, but he might have – I mean – oh, you know what I mean.'

'I know he fully intended to seduce you.'

'That's such a sweet, old-fashioned word.'

'There's nothing sweet about it, I assure you. You could have got into serious trouble if you'd stayed with Henry.'

'I am a grown-up, Charles,' she said quietly. 'Technically, at least.'

'I couldn't permit it. Sorry.'

Flora began to smile. 'I don't actually have to ask your permission.' She bit her lip to stop herself chuckling.

'I know that perfectly well.' Charles changed gear, driving rather fast. He sighed deeply, obviously making an effort to calm down. 'I admit I was in the wrong. I shouldn't have hit him. Violence is never the answer but I acted instinctively, as I would have done if you were my sister.'

'You haven't got any sisters.'

'That's beside the point! And really, there are plenty of good men out there. You don't have to scrape the barrel.'

'Well, thank you for that,' she said humbly. 'I'm so glad you don't think I'm so unattractive I have to go looking in seedy bars and gutters to find a companion.'

Charles bit his lip. 'You know perfectly well what I mean.'

'Are you suggesting I get you to vet any man who asks me out, then?'

'It wouldn't be a bad idea. After all, you're new to the area.'

Flora was giggling openly now. 'Perhaps I should tell you that my father didn't have much luck doing that when I was fifteen.'

Charles was forced to laugh, too, but Flora could tell he wasn't really amused.

'My father used to try and substitute suitable boyfriends for the unsuitable ones.'

'I did introduce you to Jeremy.'

'That didn't work, either. He fancied Emma.'

'I have other friends. Good men, who won't mess you around.'

'Not so long ago you were accusing me of messing your friends around.'

'I know you better now, Flora. I know you wouldn't do anything to hurt anyone, voluntarily.'

'Unlike you.'

'Unlike me.' He chuckled. 'Poor Henry. He just didn't see it coming.'

'Well, you're lucky I wasn't madly in love with him or I'd never speak to you again.'

'If you'd been madly in love with him you wouldn't have hesitated when he asked you in for a brandy. You'd have just gone.'

'I suppose so.' Flora tried to sound non-committal but she knew it was nothing but the truth. If Charles had invited her to drink brandy with him, however tired she'd been, she'd have just gone, too. But it wouldn't have worked the other way round. If Flora had invited him to drink brandy he'd have told her off, said she was far too young to drink spirits, and that she should go home and get an early night. 'I'm quite glad you haven't got sisters, younger ones at least.'

'Oh? Why?'

'Because you would have been a terribly bossy older brother.'

He laughed. 'I was Head of House at school. I probably learnt to look out for the younger ones then.'

That was her put in her place, then. He saw her as a sort of Smith Minor, in danger of getting into the wrong crowd, needing a steady, older boy to keep an eye on him.

He glanced at her. 'Do sleep if you feel like it.'

'It's all right. I don't feel so tired now.' She did actually, but was determined not to waste a second of this odd yet surprisingly enjoyable journey. 'So have you and Annabelle and William been socialising?' she asked.

'Yes. Annabelle needed a spare man for something and thought of him.' He frowned. 'I thought you knew that. I thought Annabelle said you'd given him her number.'

'Oh' – she hadn't, had she? Flora thought rapidly – 'yes, but I thought Annabelle just wanted some hurdles made or something.' Hurdles, that sounded suitably rustic and *Far From the Madding Crowd*. 'I didn't realise it was for social reasons.'

'We must have you and Hermione to dinner.'

Flora felt she'd rather sing a solo in a cathedral than endure an evening of watching Charles and Annabelle play Happy Couples. 'She's not here for long. Next time she comes, perhaps?'

'Do you know when she's coming back?'

'I'm not sure. Sometime before Christmas, I hope.'

'Annabelle and I might well be married, by then.' He stared ahead at the road.

'You might,' agreed Flora, discovering tears forming at the corners of her eyes. She wiped them away and yawned.

He saw her. 'You're shattered.'

'Yes.' People seemed to have been telling her that all evening.

'Nearly there, now.'

'Good.' The tears were falling faster now. In a few moments he was going to leave her at her door and then drive back to Annabelle, and probably (she forced herself to confront this thought) have passionate sex with her.

They turned into her lane. 'It's still quite muddy, isn't it?'

She cleared her throat. 'It's OK as long as you take it slowly.'

'Your voice sounds a little strange. Perhaps you've strained it, singing.'

She wanted to say, 'Actually, it's my heart. It's breaking and now the tear has reached up into my throat.' But she didn't, she just said, 'Mm,' in agreement. It was all she could manage.

At last he pulled up outside the cottage. 'If I came in and saw you were all right, made you a hot drink, would you think I was trying to seduce you?'

'No, Charles,' she said, in control at last. 'That is the absolutely last thing I would think.'

'I wouldn't ever do anything to hurt you, Flora.'

Not on purpose, no, she thought.

'Then make us some hot chocolate, if there's enough milk, while I get into my nightie.' She opened the door of the cottage.

'Actually, don't get into your nightie.'

'Why not? These black clothes are awfully hot.'

'I'm not a bloody saint, Flora!' He strode off into the kitchen and her spirits lifted, just a tiny bit.

*　　*　　*

Flora slept surprisingly well. The hot chocolate and the memory of Charles's chaste kiss on her cheek were very soothing. She heard her mother come in but didn't move. She needed her sleep.

Next morning, Hermione was full of praise once more. 'Well, darling, I have to say, I was very impressed. Very impressed indeed. And the choir are such a nice bunch. I had a lovely time at the pub last night.'

'I am glad. They are fun, aren't they?'

'So, did you find out what William and Annabelle were doing together?'

'Apparently William became part of their social life when Annabelle needed an extra man for something. He scrubbed up very well, I must say. I was shocked to see him with Annabelle, though. But Charles was cool about it.'

Hermione glanced at her daughter, who was crunching into toast and marmalade with enthusiasm. 'And Charles, he didn't tell you that he and Annabelle were a terrible mistake and he was going to break off the engagement immediately?'

'No. Though he did hit Henry! It was awful and yet really funny, at the same time.'

'Why did Charles hit Henry? It sounds very out of character.'

'It is, totally out of character. But he explained to me on the way home that he was Head of House at school and so he's programmed to look out for the younger boys.'

Hermione seemed confused. 'Are you telling me Charles looks on you as someone he has responsibility for?'

'Yup.'

'Oh, darling!'

'I'd be kidding myself if I thought any different, Mum. He does care about me, but only as a sort of older, terribly bossy brother.'

Hermione sighed. 'It's a pity. He'd make such a lovely dad. Think how sweet he is with the kittens?'

Flora laughed, as she was supposed to. They both knew that if they went any deeper into this conversation, Flora might get upset. Neither of them wanted that when she was just going off to work.

As Hermione was leaving a couple of days later she hugged her daughter. 'You will be all right, won't you?'

'Oh yes. The sale is coming up and we're really busy.'

'And will you see Henry again?'

Flora wasn't too sure. Henry had phoned, mortified, the day after the concert to apologise for his behaviour. It had been so completely out of character for him that Flora, once she got over her anger about the position he had put her in, was almost concerned for him – and it turned out she had reason to be. He'd apparently received a rather unpleasant phone call from his ex-wife earlier in the day to break the news, none too gently, that she was remarrying. That had come at about three in the afternoon and he'd stiffened his sinews with a shot of brandy, and never really stopped after that. By the time Flora arrived on the scene, his hurt pride at Natasha moving on and building a new family while he remained alone had swelled to such a point that he was determined to prove he had someone special in his life – and Flora had got in his way.

He was clearly horrified at his own behaviour, and Flora didn't think there was any reason to worry he'd do it again, but the incident still left a nasty taste in her mouth. And she rather thought their friendship had been soured by it.

'I'm not sure, Mum,' she said carefully. 'I'm not too sure Henry will want to see me, to be honest.'

'It's a pity in some ways. You need a distraction.'

'I'm working far too hard for distractions.'

Hermione shook her head. 'Working with Charles will not help! What about that nice William?'

'William and I don't fancy each other. We decided that ages ago.'

'What a shame!' Her mother hugged her again. 'Love can be such hell.'

Flora had expected to find meeting Charles after the concert at Burnet House embarrassing – he had behaved so extraordinarily, punching Henry – but he was completely blasé about it.

'I didn't mention the matter to Annabelle, but I did send some rather good claret to his house, and he was decent enough to thank me,' he said. 'But I do apologise again to you for involving you in a rather sordid incident.'

'Oh, Charles, you are so stuffy! Sordid incident, indeed! You punched him! Drew blood! But I'm glad you've made it up with Henry. It means I could see him again if I wanted to.'

He frowned. 'I don't think so.'

Flora sighed. 'No, I don't think so, either. Oh well. Now, do you want me to start putting numbers on?'

* * *

Everyone was keyed up on the first morning of the sale. It was one of those golden mornings in early September that make the passing of summer so poignant. As Flora drove through the countryside before the rest of the world was awake, she was struck by its beauty, and wondered if she had accidentally become a rural person when, by rights, she should be a City slicker. She got to the auction rooms by seven. Charles was there by half past, and even Annabelle turned up by eight-thirty. This was the sale of furniture and effects resulting from the roadshow. The sale that would prove if Flora was remotely useful to Stanza and Stanza or not – or that was how it seemed to Flora. But everyone felt it was a new start, a step forward.

Unusually for her, Annabelle helped Flora arrange the chairs. It amused Flora that all the chairs in any sale were put out for people to sit on. The logical conclusion to this would be to sell cups of tea in the Mason's Ironstone tea sets and seat the punters at the Sheraton tables, but she kept this thought to herself. Annabelle was unlikely to understand.

'These are pretty chairs,' said Annabelle. 'I might put in an offer myself. We've got some nice ones, but they're rather large, you can't fit many round the table.'

'And you could always put the ones you've got now in the next sale.'

'Of course. I don't know why I didn't think of that.'

Flora didn't know either, after all she'd worked in an auction house much longer than Flora had.

'It's exciting, having a half-decent sale for once,' Annabelle went on. 'There's been loads of interest. And I think that little item we had on the local news probably helped quite a lot. Several local antique shops have put in stuff that's been hanging around too long. You just need one or two items to attract a lot of attention, and people realise there's going to be extra interest and put their own stuff in. Charles has roped Bob Butler in to help as he can't do it all.'

'Well, I'm glad you see it my way at last,' said Flora evenly.

Annabelle was inspecting the underside of a Windsor chair. 'It's a bit wormy – still, caveat emptor and all that.'

Flora didn't speak Latin. 'As long as we don't imply it's perfect in the catalogue. Oh, I never asked you about the school reunion.' Flora had lost track completely of when it was and felt it must have happened by now.

'The school reunion?' Annabelle looked blank for a moment. 'Oh, that! It was fine, thank you. Caught up with some old chums I must invite to the wedding.'

'How are the preparations going? And the portrait?'

Annabelle smiled, looking a little dreamy, which was perfectly understandable. 'Fine for both. And by the way, I was going to ask you – it's a bit short notice I know, because dresses take ages to be made, but I wondered if you'd help me choose mine? I was originally going for something very traditional, but since you took me in hand, I thought I might have something a bit simpler. I've got the dressmaker all lined up, but she tells me I've got a week or so before she really gets going so there's time to make a few changes.'

'I'd be thrilled to help!' Manfully, Flora summoned up enthusiasm for a wedding that was going to end her chance of happiness for ever. 'I see you in something

381

quite slim-fitting, oyster satin, something like that. Elegant and simple.'

'Great. We'll have a look at some mags together soon, but we'd better get this sale over first. I'm going to be on the phones most of the day. Will you and Louisa share the book for Charles? You know, make sure he doesn't overlook any commissioned bids? God! I hope I wasn't being patronising! I've had a lot on my mind lately.'

She strode off, leaving an amazed Flora dumbstruck. Annabelle apologising for being patronising! It was like the sea apologising for going in and out all the time, apparently never able to make up its mind. Annabelle had definitely improved lately, and not just because she'd had her hair cut shorter, and was emphasising her physical assets to the full. She had more enthusiasm for life. Flora decided it was because Stanza and Stanza was looking up at last, becoming more the sort of business Annabelle would like to be concerned with. And she was going to help Annabelle decide on a wedding dress . . . Flora sighed. Usually, she liked irony, but now, it felt like a poisoned dart.

There wasn't much time for further philosophical speculation as ten o'clock came and the public were let in for half an hour's viewing before the sale started at ten-thirty.

The sale had been going fantastically well, but now, at nearly four o'clock, it was almost over. Flora had been deputed earlier to apologise to the landlord of the local pub, whose car park had become full of buyers. Fortunately Flora had managed to convince him that the extra business would make up for some loss of local trade. It was something to think about. If they were going to become much bigger, parking space had to be considered.

Although the room was still quite full, earlier it had been positively heaving with people. A lot of bids had been left 'on the book' by people who had put in a bid but were unable actually to be present, and most of the day, Flora had sat next to Charles (or whoever was on the podium), just in case a bid got overlooked. It never was overlooked when Charles was there, but he had said it was good training for her.

Having been sent off for a break, Flora had taken her cup of tea to the back of the room, not wanting to leave the excitement of the saleroom. Or at least that was what she'd told Virginia when they'd met at the tea counter. Flora knew it was so she could watch Charles in action.

I'm sure it's not just that I'm in love with him, she decided, watching him hold the attention of the room with such skill and mastery. He's simply a fantastic auctioneer. And having the room so full and so busy was making him even better. It was brilliant! She found herself smiling with joy because he must be happy.

She shifted her position so she was standing in front of a complete set of Georgette Heyers, early editions and potentially very valuable. Charles and Geoffrey had been a little dismissive about them when they were discovered in Burnet House, but Flora knew they were special and her instinct was borne out by the interest in them shown on the website.

Her attention was distracted by a woman's striking, obviously home-made cardigan for a moment, but when she looked up again, she saw Louisa hand Charles a cup of tea and a home-made rock cake. He didn't usually drink tea while he was at the podium, but he'd been there a long time. Louisa probably felt he needed some sustenance. He acknowledged the tea, took a sip and a bite of the rock cake and then winced sharply, as if in pain. Louisa, having taken her seat beside the podium, stood up again and put her hand on Charles's arm. Her face as she looked up at him was worried, and he leant down and whispered something in her ear, at which she looked even more worried, and urgently whispered something back. Charles shook his head.

'I'm awfully sorry, ladies and gentlemen,' he said awkwardly, 'but I seem to have done something to my tooth. I hope you can hear me all right.'

He leant back to Louisa and spoke again, and she whispered to Virginia, who was on hand near the front. Then he carried on, appearing nearly normal, but Flora longed to get to him. She edged her way to the front. Then Bob Butler appeared. 'I'll now hand you over to Bob Butler for the last few lots,' he said, smiling through his obvious agony. 'I'll be back with you tomorrow.'

'Charles! Are you all right?' said Flora. She followed him into the little side room they used as an office on sale days.

'Broken a tooth. Bloody rock cakes.'

'Oh, I'm so sorry!' said Virginia. 'It was my fault! My sister made them.'

'Nonsense,' said Annabelle, 'he should have had that tooth sorted out ages ago! We'll make an appointment. They always keep a slot for emergencies.'

'I can't go to the dentist when there's a sale on,' Charles said with a panicked look in his eyes.

'If you're in pain, you must!' said Flora.

'I can't! This is the biggest sale we've done. I must be here.'

'That's just silly,' said Flora, aware she was being bossy, but too worried about him to help herself. 'Bob and George will do it for you. I'll catch Bob when he's finished and ring George at home. He's in the book under Woodman, isn't he? Bob's here tomorrow anyway, to finish off the furniture.'

Charles shook his head. 'No, that won't do. Bob doesn't usually do books and he's nearly eighty, his wife will never speak to me again if I make him do even more. He's got a bad heart, he shouldn't work when he's tired, and he'll be exhausted after today.'

'He loved it today. He'll be fine,' said Louisa.

'He won't,' said Charles forcefully. 'Look, I can't just abandon ship because I've got toothache! I'll just have to keep going.'

'You wouldn't be abandoning anything. It's called delegating, and it's a very good thing to do. You go to the dentist. We'll manage here until you get back.'

'I can't.'

'You can. No one is indispensable, Charles.' Still he remained looking at her. Flora decided it was time to pull rank. 'I am your partner. And I'm telling you to go to the dentist!'

He laughed, in spite of his pain. 'You're getting to be a very bossy woman, Flora.'

'I know. Good, isn't it?'

'God, Charles! You would never have agreed to that for me,' said Annabelle. 'It must be because Flora's the senior partner.'

385

Flora felt herself go white. She would never be the senior partner, even if she owned every share in the business and Charles owned nothing. She looked at him, aghast that he might think she valued herself so highly. 'Um, not really,' she murmured.

'Well, until Charles has got his tooth fixed anyway,' said Louisa, to Flora's enormous relief.

'Come on. I'll take you home and then make an appointment,' said Annabelle.

Watching them leave the building together forced Flora to confront the idea of them as a couple, to imagine them, years down the line, a happy, married twosome. Even with Annabelle's arm round Charles, she couldn't quite picture it.

Flora went to find Geoffrey, her prop and source of advice. Everyone had obviously heard the news and knew that, for the time being, Flora was in charge. She looked for Geoffrey everywhere except the Gents'. And then went back to ask Virginia.

'Have you seen Geoffrey, Virginia?' she enquired. 'I've looked for him in every logical place and several illogical ones.'

'I saw him go out the back with a huge armoire. I expect he was taking it to someone's van and will be back in a minute. Give us a hand while you're waiting.' Virginia at least was not treating Flora any differently. 'We'll spot him when he comes back in.'

Flora joined Virginia on the raised stage where Virginia was matching slips of paper to items stacked on and under the trestle tables.

Flora took a slip from a middle-aged man who looked like a successful dealer and saw he'd bought some glasses at a very good price. 'Would you like me to wrap them for you?'

'No, thank you, dear. Newspaper damages them. I'll do it myself with the proper stuff. If you just bring them over to me, a few at a time, I'll be fine.'

Flora, worried in case she missed Geoffrey while she was doing this, got the glasses to him almost too quickly for safety.

There was still no sign of Geoffrey, so she took another slip. She stared at it for a while and then said, 'I have no idea what a companion set is!'

Virginia pointed to a corner. 'Poker, tongs and shovel, over there.' Then she picked up a blue and white printed meat dish, which would have been worth a small fortune if it hadn't been damaged, and carried it carefully to its new owner.

'Oh, there's Geoffrey,' Flora said to the owner of the fire irons. 'You don't need me, do you, Virginia?'

'No, it's all right, Anne and I can manage. We know where stuff is.'

Dismissed, Flora followed Geoffrey into the kitchen, where he was eating one of the rock cakes that had caused Charles to break his tooth. He too had already heard about it.

Flora had decided that Charles was right about Bob: it wasn't fair to ask him to do more work tomorrow when they'd stretched his capacity to the limit already today.

'Geoffrey, I don't think we can ask Bob to stand in for Charles, but I'm sure George will, until Charles gets back after the dentist. And you could stand in too, if necessary, couldn't you?'

387

'Well, the thing is . . . Oh, you ring George. See what he says.'

'Flora!' George Woodman declared delightedly when he heard her voice on the phone. 'You can be the first to congratulate me! Our daughter's had a little girl! It was a difficult pregnancy and she's been in hospital for the past week, but now the baby's born and she's fine.'

'Oh, congratulations! You must be so thrilled!'

'We are. My wife's just throwing a few things together and we're off to see her. They've got a little boy already and her parents-in-law have been there, helping to look after him. Now they've got to go and we're taking over. Was there anything you wanted?'

'Nothing that won't wait until you get back,' said Flora. 'And congratulations again.'

She found Geoffrey again. 'He's just had a new grand-child and they were off to look after his daughter, so I didn't ask him.'

'Oh.'

'Bob's going to finish the furniture though. It's only the books. You can do books. They're your subject.'

'I can do them up to a point, Flora.'

'What do you mean?'

'Quite a lot of books towards the end of the catalogue are mine. I can't auction those. It wouldn't be ethical.'

Flora gulped. 'It's quite likely Charles will be back by then.'

'Quite likely.'

'And if he wasn't, you could do them. No one would know they were yours.'

'I would know,' he said firmly. 'If it got out it would damage the reputation of the firm irrevocably.'

'Oh.' For once, Flora was lost for ideas. 'So we'll just hope it won't come to that. I wonder what they'll have to do to Charles's tooth?'

'I couldn't say, but, Flora . . .'

'What?'

'If Charles isn't here, you'll have to do it.'

'Do what?'

'Auction the books.'

A fine film of sweat covered Flora as she realised what Geoffrey meant. 'Oh no. I couldn't do that.'

'Everyone's got to start sometime.'

'But . . . I wouldn't get the best price for you! This must be your pension, after all. You need to get the very best price for your books. So you don't want someone who's never done it before selling your life savings.'

'Flora, they're not my life savings, and you're just as likely to get a good price for them as I am. If Charles isn't back, you've got to bite the bullet and get up there and sell. I'll give you a bit of coaching tonight.'

Flora exhaled as slowly as she could. 'But, Geoffrey, I couldn't possibly! Think how nervous I was just singing in a choir with twenty other people! I couldn't stand up in front of all those people and sell things when I don't know what I'm doing!'

'Yes, you could,' he said in a broken-record voice.

'I couldn't!'

He sighed. 'Tell you what, you're tired and this idea has been sprung on you. You go and see to Imelda and the kittens, and then come back to me and Edie. Stay the night with us, and I'll give you a crash course in auctioneering. It's only counting in threes, fives and tens, that's not hard.'

'I can't count in ones! How am I ever going to be able to do that?'

'I'll train you. Now go home and sort out the cats and come straight back to me.'

'I can't go now, there's so much to do here.' She was aware that inside there was a mountain of paperwork and tidying and sweeping to be done. No one else would leave for a couple of hours, at least.

'They'll manage without you. They did before you joined the firm, didn't they?'

'And Charles, and Annabelle? They're usually here, aren't they?'

'I've told you, we'll manage. I'll explain what's going on. Now, shoo!'

Chapter Twenty-Three

Guilty, because she knew she should have stayed and finished the day's work with everyone else, but glad to escape, Flora climbed into the Land-Rover and set off for the cottage. The thought of a hot bath lured her like a siren; after it, she knew she'd feel much bolder about the prospect of standing up in front of a lot of strangers. It might not happen anyway. How long could any dentist appointment be?

But she was worried about Charles. Not just the dentist, he was probably one of those hardy types who could tolerate his teeth being filled without vast numbers of painkilling injections, but generally.

Was Annabelle really the right woman for him? Previously when she'd been in love (if you could call those girlish crushes love) her feelings had been very self-centred. She had wanted to go to Paris with him, she had wanted to share bubble baths with him, she had wanted to kick up dead leaves in autumn while they walked hand in hand through Richmond Park (or similar).

But this time, while she would have sacrificed anything to be the one with him while he experienced those pleasures, simple or otherwise, she wanted him to have them with a woman he truly loved and who truly loved him more than she wanted the happiness she would have gained herself.

She didn't consider herself to be a selfish person. She was kind to animals (Imelda was proof of that), to people (sometimes too kind, indeed), and she wanted to do good in the world. But never before had she wanted another person's happiness more than she wanted her own.

She kept on thinking like this until she turned into the lane that led to her cottage. Then she allowed herself to admit that if Charles wanted her, she would go to him, to hell with her pride. As long as he was honest with her, of course.

The kittens were a wonderful distraction for a little while. They were everywhere in the cottage now. Annabelle would probably never be able to go inside there again, because of her allergy, but then, she probably didn't want to anyway. Would she let Charles have a kitten? Would she cramp his style for the rest of his life? And, most likely, would marriage to her allow him to become set in his stuffiness? What he needed was someone a bit younger, a bit more frivolous, as committed to the business as he was, who really liked cats, to be with. He needed her, in other words. But, being a man, and sadly lacking in intuition, he might not ever realise that.

When she had fed the cats and made a cup of tea, about her tenth that day, Flora put on the television and curled up on the sofa so Imelda could have a proper cuddle. Watching Richard and Judy sitting on the sofa, bantering with each other and their guests, was very soothing. Imelda, who now had no time for her kittens, was very grateful for an opportunity to curl up on Flora's lap, hissing at any kitten that came near her. Flora closed her eyes. In a few minutes she would make sure there was enough food left to keep them going tomorrow, sort out the litter tray, pack a bag, and go to Geoffrey and Edie's house. While she was here, in her little cottage, she could pretend her life was both normal and happy. Once she arrived at Geoffrey's, she'd have to concentrate on learning to be a stand-in auctioneer. And all night she would pray she wouldn't have to perform.

'If only I'd practised when I first arrived. That first sale we had was quite little, with hardly any people, I could have coped with that! Oh, why did I meddle and make everything so busy?'

Imelda purred consolingly. Although she'd lost a little condition after having her kittens, she was turning into a very elegant cat. Flora had never seen her unpregnant and was pleased to see her filling out.

When Richard and Judy said goodbye, Flora got up and started her chores.

Flora wished she'd taken the opportunity to have a little nap while she'd been at home. 'I'm going to coach you until you're word perfect,' Geoffrey announced as she got through the door.

'But not until you've eaten, love,' said Edie. 'I've got a nice cottage pie waiting for you.'

'I love your cottage pie! You gave me one when I first arrived, do you remember?'

'Certainly. I know some people don't eat food like that in summer, but I think it's comforting. I've done

393

peas and carrots with it. I'm afraid we've had ours. Cup of tea, Flora?'

'Give the girl a glass of wine,' said Geoffrey, pulling up the chair opposite Flora's.

'And how are my kittens?' asked Edie as she poured the wine. 'I can't wait to have them. Just let us get our fence sorted out so that next door's dog can't get in and menace them.'

'Edie, could you find us some paper and a pen? Flora might like to take notes.'

Edie went over to a drawer and produced a pad and pen. 'You should think about getting Imelda done, dear. You don't want her getting pregnant again, do you?'

'Certainly not, she's only young. Too young to be a mother, really,' said Flora. 'Although she's managed brilliantly.'

'Flora, we really should get on,' said Geoffrey.

'Let the girl eat her supper first, Geoffrey.' Edie set Flora's supper down in front of her. 'She's got enough on her plate without you giving her indigestion.'

Flora, confused as to whether Edie was referring to the food or the fact that she might have to conduct her first auction tomorrow, stuck her fork into a pile of mashed potato that had been browned in the oven.

'This is delicious, Edie. Comfort food – you're quite right. Just what I fancied.'

'Now, don't you worry about tomorrow,' said Edie, ignoring Geoffrey's frown and pulling up a chair so she could talk to Flora. 'It'll go swimmingly. Geoff'll be on hand to see nothing goes wrong.'

'I probably won't have to do it anyway. Charles will rush back from the dentist,' said Flora.

394

'And I keep telling you, Edie, that if it's my books going under the hammer, I can't have anything to do with it.' Geoffrey pulled the top off a pen and started fiddling with it.

'I hope they go for a good price,' said Flora. 'What do you hope to do with the money? Or shouldn't I ask?'

'It's a bit of a secret,' said Geoffrey. 'I'll tell you if I get what I need.'

'It won't be me—'

'It's not for a cruise,' broke in Edie, but Flora couldn't tell if this was a bit of a disappointment for her.

'You'd have to tell me if you were going away,' said Flora, 'so I could keep – what have you decided to call them?'

'Flora and Fauna, after you, and, well – Fauna sort of goes, doesn't it?'

Suddenly overcome with emotion, Flora hid behind another forkful of pie. 'That's so sweet!' she squeaked, as soon as she decently could.

'We really should be getting on,' said Geoffrey. 'We haven't got all night.'

'Flora is staying over,' Edie reminded him. 'Although I think she should have an early night. She looks all in. Have some more veg?'

Flora nodded. As long as she was eating, Geoffrey couldn't teach her to count in twos, fives and tens. Or threes and eights, or any other complicated way there might be that she had never heard of.

'And you've got homes for all of the kittens?' Edie spooned carrots and peas on to Flora's plate.

'Well, Charles was going to have one, to live in the office, but I don't know . . .'

'That Annabelle! She always was selfish,' said Edie.

'But if he loves her . . .' said Flora.

'Well, I hope he does, but they never seem very lovey-dovey, do they?' She turned to her husband.

'No one knows what goes on in anyone else's marriage, Edie.'

'But they're not married yet, are they? More pie?'

'No, thank you. I can hardly move as it is. It was so delicious.'

'You could do with feeding up a bit. Nothing but skin and bone, you are.'

'Stop fussing, Edie. Flora and I have got work to do.'

'There's apple and rhubarb crumble for pudding.'

Even her desire to put off Geoffrey's crash course in auctioneering didn't make it possible for Flora to accept this offer. 'I'd love some later, but I need to have a bit of time to digest this.'

'And we must get on!' insisted Geoffrey.

'I'll just make a cup of tea for you both, and then leave you in peace.'

'The thing you have to remember is that you only deal with two bidders at a time. There may be other people waving their numbers in the air who think you haven't seen them, but until one of the other two drop out, you just ignore them.'

'Right,' said Flora, writing this down.

'And you know about the book?'

Of course Flora knew about the book, but Geoffrey obviously felt it was his duty to explain everything. 'The place where the bids that people have placed are written down?' she said, to indulge him.

'Yes. And you have to make sure that the person in the room is not at the same place in the bidding as the amount on the book.'

Flora thought she understood this, but did feel a bit blank. 'Don't you just pretend that they're a person and that they drop out when their bid's been overtaken?'

Geoffrey had to think about this. 'I think so. Anyway, Louisa will keep you straight on that. She's very good.'

'I don't know why Louisa couldn't do the selling.'

'She could if your voice gives out completely, but this is your opportunity to take your proper place in Stanza and Stanza. It's all very well you having all these good ideas, but until you've been on that podium you won't be seen by the world as a proper partner in the business. You'll just be the pretty blonde.'

Flora had spent quite a lot of her life being seen as the pretty blonde, and while it did have a lot going for it, it wasn't her preferred sobriquet. 'OK, I'll do it, but only if Charles doesn't get back from the dentist.'

'Of course. Now,' said Geoffrey, 'you know about the counting? When you get someone to open, you go up in fives. If that won't wash you do threes, but then jump to the ten.'

Flora realised she had a long evening in front of her.

'Tell you what,' said Geoffrey. 'Me and Edie will pretend to be punters. You run the auction. I'll help you.'

Eventually Edie sent Flora to bed, having run her a bath and put Lily of the Valley perfumed bubbles in it. She was very glad to go. Her brain had turned to soup and she felt more confused about the whole process than she had done before Geoffrey started. She climbed into the little narrow bed in Edie's spare bedroom and fell asleep almost instantly, knowing her hair would be a sight in the morning and that she'd left her hair straighteners in the cottage.

'Annabelle phoned,' said Louisa, as soon as Flora and Geoffrey arrived. 'Charles's appointment is at twelve. He wanted to come in this morning, but I told him not to. We don't need him and he's in a lot of pain.'

'Poor Charles,' said Flora, weakly. 'Louisa, what time do you think Bob will finish? I mean, um – how likely is it that I'll actually have to do some selling?'

'Flora! Why don't you want to do it? You'll be great! And it's such good experience for you. After all, you are the senior partner.'

'No I'm not! Not really, the thing with the will was just a sort of fluke.' She frowned. 'Anyway, I didn't think anyone knew about that.'

'Oh, nothing's a secret in this place.'

'So tell me what time we'll get to the books that Geoffrey can't do?'

'Well, Bob's very fast, so we'll get through his really quickly. Then Geoffrey. He hasn't done it for a while so he'll probably be a bit slower.'

'And if he's truly my friend, he'll spin it out until Charles gets here,' put in Flora.

'Which means we should get to the books at about two.'

'Plenty of time for Charles to get back from an appointment at twelve!' said Flora, relief flooding over her.

'I suppose so,' said Louisa.

'I do wonder why he didn't make the appointment for earlier, though,' said Flora.

Louisa shook her head. 'Have you any idea how difficult it is to get a dentist appointment in this town? They always keep one at about midday for real emergencies, otherwise you have to wait weeks.'

'Oh.' Chastened, Flora went to check what else needed doing, grateful that she would be too busy to worry too much about having to conduct an auction. For once the words 'cheer up, it may never happen' seemed appropriate.

She was doing a stint in the little café area, selling rolls and cups of tea in between washing up. She liked it in there. You got to see all the punters, you could overhear their opinions of the sale, but the work wasn't too stressful and was almost completely free of any decision-making. She'd just coped with a little flurry of customers when she checked her watch. It was half past one! Where was Charles?

The almost-octogenarian Bob was getting through the remaining furniture in record time. He'd once sold cattle at auction and hadn't lost the rapid delivery required, in spite of his bad heart.

'Slow down!' Flora urged him from the back of the room when she'd abandoned the café, leaving any other customers to make their own tea. She'd sold all the rolls already.

Virginia loomed up beside her. 'Geoffrey's on next, then you.'

'But where the hell is Charles?' Flora whispered. 'His appointment was at twelve, and it's half past one. He should be back by now!'

'Stop fussing about where Charles is and just focus on what you've got to do. I'm willing to bet that when you come down from the podium you'll be aching to go back up there again.'

Geoffrey apparently had only a few lots to sell, either that or the time it took him to sell them whistled past so quickly that Flora blinked and missed it. Virginia took her elbow and marched Flora to the front of the building, just as he was finishing.

'You're going to be fine,' said Louisa, as Flora, her legs shaking, climbed up beside her at the desk.

Geoffrey winked. 'You'll need this,' he said, and put a gavel into her hand. 'It's Charles's. He told me to make sure you had it.'

Flora clutched it tightly, willing the years of experience it had gained with Charles to flash into her like a bolt of electricity. At the same moment she realised that Charles had never intended to be there, either because of the dentist, or because he thought it was good experience for her. She loved him and hated him in the same heartbeat.

She thought about the time at school when she'd been the compère for the end-of-term show, how she'd held the audience's attention, in spite of being terrified. She thought of her drama classes, how she'd been taught to think herself into the role. She thought of Charles, how she wanted to do well for his sake, and for Geoffrey and Edie and everyone else who'd been so kind and welcoming to her. She glanced down at the ledger in front of her, checked to see where the porter was standing, holding the book up, and took a deep breath. She looked at everyone and waited until they were all looking at her. Then she smiled – as brave a smile as she could manage – and began.

'A fine example of *The Caine Mutiny* by Herman Wouk, nice edition, good condition, who'll start me off? A hundred pounds? No? Fifty then, yes! Fifty pounds I'm bid. Fifty-five? Yes? You, madam . . .'

She soon got into the swing of things. She found she had taken in Geoffrey's coaching with regard to counting in threes, fives and tens, and with Louisa at her side keeping her on track with the book, and both phones in use, she found she was exhilarated. It was like spinning plates, trying to keep all the balls in the air at the same time. She was surprised how quickly she learned to identify the bidders, to keep their attention. Virginia was manning one of the phones and having her calm presence was an added support.

Halfway through she noticed Charles, standing at the back. But she hadn't got time to decide how she felt about this, she was too preoccupied with what was going on.

Sips of water kept her throat lubricated when she thought her voice would fail and eventually, when Geoffrey came to relieve her, she realised she was exhausted.

'I thought you couldn't do it because it wasn't ethical,' she said to him as he waited for her to give up her seat.

'My books are all sold. Do you know you raised over twenty thousand pounds for me?'

'Did I? I realised we were getting some good prices, way above the estimates, but I didn't know which, or how many of the books were yours, of course.'

'Go and get a cup of tea. You deserve one.'

Flora's knees nearly gave way as she climbed down and the audience, most of whom had learnt that it was her first time, gave her a round of applause.

Virginia was there and hugged her tightly. 'Well done, Flora! You were fantastic! You did so well. We all knew you would.'

Suddenly, everyone was congratulating her on her success.

'That's thousands of pounds' worth you've sold – and for far more than it's worth, going by the guide prices,' said Louisa.

'But you know the guide prices are always fairly low to encourage people to come,' said Flora, embarrassed.

'Those last two bidders just competed with each other for your attention! They must have known they were paying over the odds.'

'Well, as long as everyone is happy. I think I did make a couple of mistakes with the book.'

'Yes, but you put it right by inventing an imaginary bidder,' said Louisa. 'Did Geoffrey tell you to do that?'

'He certainly did. He was coaching me for hours last night.'

'Well worth it! You've made him thousands!'

'I'm glad about that, but we can't stand around here feeling smug, we've got loads to do before we can go home.'

Then she was caught from behind and turned round. Almost before she registered who it was, Charles had his arms round her and was crushing her half to death. 'Well done, Flora,' he breathed into her ear. 'I knew you could do it.'

Then he kissed her, full on the lips.

For a moment, it was just a kiss between friends, a congratulatory kiss, that she might have exchanged with anyone, but then, for the briefest moment, it took on a quality of passion that made her catch her breath.

They broke apart, both astounded and horrified. They stared at each other, neither knowing what to say. A lifetime passed before Flora licked her lips. 'Um . . .'

'So,' said Annabelle in a flat voice. '*Flora Pulls It Off!* Or something. How does it feel to be the title of a girls' school adventure novel?'

Flora tried to laugh. 'Er – fine.' She looked at Charles's white face and knew it was a reflection of her own. 'I, er . . . excuse me. I think I'll just pop to the Ladies'.'

She was washing her hands when Annabelle came into the room and stood with her back to the door, so they couldn't be interrupted. Flora felt shaky, a mixture of shock, guilt and a nervous reaction to her performance as an auctioneer.

'What the hell do you think you're doing?' Annabelle looked hot and bothered, but her gaze as she stared at Flora was icy.

'I . . . I don't know what you mean,' Flora stammered. How much had Annabelle seen?

'Don't give me that. I saw you. You and Charles.'

'Oh,' said Flora weakly. 'You mean when he kissed me just now? It was just over-excitement, Annabelle, really, don't read anything into it. He was just—'

'I'm not talking about the kiss, Flora,' Annabelle said furiously. 'That was a bit of meaningless sentimentality. I mean the look.'

'Look?' echoed Flora weakly. 'What look?'

'Oh, grow up, Flora,' snapped Annabelle. 'You're in love with him, aren't you?'

'No—' said Flora hotly.

'Don't try to deny it! It was plain as a pikestaff.'

Flora shook her head. Everything suddenly seemed to be happening so fast that she didn't know what to think. Charles's kiss had been unnerving enough, but Annabelle was right. It was the way he had suddenly pulled back, the way they had looked at each other, that gave everything away.

She felt an inappropriate little rush of pleasure. Charles didn't just think of her as his little cousin, he thought of her as a woman. And clearly found her attractive. But what about Annabelle?

'Look, I'm sorry, Annabelle, really, I—'

'Honestly, Flora, I don't want to hear it. I can't imagine there's anything you could say that I'd want to hear. But there's one thing you should know. Even if Charles did think you were more than just a minor irritation in his life, he'd never leave me for you.'

'Why not?' Flora was surprised to find she'd spoken out loud.

'Because without me, he'd lose everything.'

'Everything? What do you mean, everything?'

'I mean he'd lose the company. He'd lose Stanza and Stanza.'

'That can't be true.' Flora didn't understand. 'I'd know about it, if that was the case.'

'Not necessarily. He doesn't tell you everything, you know,' Annabelle said nastily. 'In fact, he doesn't tell you much at all.'

'So *you* tell me then. How would he lose the company if he left you?'

'The office building needed completely rewiring. My

father paid for it, with Charles's half of the business as collateral.'

'You mean, your father lent Charles the money?'

'Sort of, but the arrangement is that the debt will be written off when we get married. So however much he loved you – even if he does, which I sincerely doubt – he'd still never leave me. His precious company will always be more important to him than any woman.'

'I see. Well, thank you for making things clear to me. And I hope you'll be happy knowing that Charles is only marrying you for your father's money!'

'Not "only", darling, but he has got an awful lot of it.' She looked pityingly at Flora. 'I did try to tell you. I thought I'd made it quite clear how things are. Charles and I are going to get married, we've always been going to get married, and that's that.'

Flora's mouth filled with salt water and she knew that, unless she was very lucky, she was about to be very sick. She also knew she couldn't retreat to a cubicle and throw up where Annabelle could hear her. With a huge effort of will, she swallowed hard and pushed past Annabelle.

'Excuse me. I've got to go.'

She stood in the corridor for a few moments, feeling sweat prickle along her hairline, wishing she could just die of humiliation and not have to endure the process of going back into the saleroom, where everybody would want to talk to her. She opened the door to a storeroom, obviously used by the playgroup, and full of tricycles and scooters, space hoppers and lorries. There was hardly space for her, too, but she squeezed in and stayed

405

there until she heard Annabelle leave the Ladies'; then, when her nausea had passed, she emerged, feeling her life was as much of a road smash as the pile-up of plastic vehicles behind her.

She had to go to the little room they used as an office to get her bag. She didn't know if it was good or bad that only Charles was in there.

'Flora! Are you all right? Where have you been? You look awful!'

'I just feel a bit shell-shocked,' she said, trying to brush it off. 'The excitement, I suppose. How's your tooth?'

'Oh fine, now. Shall I drive you home?' He stared at her with what was unmistakably an echo of the look in his eyes after they kissed. 'We need to talk, Flora. I want to—'

'No.' She stopped him before he could get any further. She had to sort things out in her mind before everything got any more confused, and the last person she could talk it all over with now was Charles. 'No, Charles, sorry.' Good, she was sounding more composed. 'I would like to go home, but I don't want you to drive me. Really. I'll be fine. Could you just pass my bag? It's in the bottom drawer of that filing cabinet.'

He looked hurt and confused. 'But, Flora, I don't want you going home on your own when you look so ill. And we have to—'

'I really will be fine on my own.'

Looking into her eyes, he could see her determination and backed off gracefully. 'You were a star today, Flora. I saw it all. And we can talk tomorrow, can't we?'

Flora regarded him, feeling she didn't know whom she was looking at. 'I'm glad I didn't let you down, Charles.'

And then she left, too miserable to weep.

Chapter Twenty-Four

Flora felt overcome with loneliness and despair once she got back to the cottage. She put the kettle on and then realised she didn't want tea, so she opened a bottle of wine, poured a glass, and didn't want that either. She knew that a really good cry would release some of her tension and be healthy, but tears wouldn't come. She collapsed on to the sofa and let Imelda and the kittens comfort her. The kittens weren't interested in her for long, but Imelda was satisfyingly soothing. She sat on Flora's lap and purred loudly, dribbling as she kneaded Flora's knee with her paws. Flora sat there with her eyes closed, stroking Imelda on automatic pilot.

'This is ridiculous!' she said aloud. 'You came to the country to learn about your family business and you've done it! You've learnt about it and improved it and today you made thousands of pounds for Geoffrey. You should feel ecstatic! The whole thing with Charles is neither here nor there, really. He was engaged to Annabelle, and he's still engaged to Annabelle. Nothing's changed.'

But something had changed. That kiss, that look, and Annabelle witnessing both. Even if she'd wanted to, she felt she couldn't pretend nothing had happened – Annabelle wouldn't let her. And Annabelle held the whip hand – over her, over Charles and, currently, over Stanza and Stanza. A lot of things now made sense.

She went into the garden to ring her mother. She wasn't ready to talk about Charles yet. When she'd got her thoughts together, she would, but not now. But her mother knew she might have had to do some selling today and would be longing to hear how it went.

At first the call went to plan. Her mother was even more excited that Flora expected.

'Oh, darling, I knew you'd find out what you were really good at eventually!'

'What do you mean?' Flora was indignant. 'I'm good at lots of things. People always want to give me jobs and hate it when I leave.'

'I know, I know, but an awful lot of that's because you're blonde and pretty. And they were just jobs. This is a career, and you're good at it in spite of being blonde and pretty.'

Flora didn't want to pass on what Louisa had said about the last lot, when she thought the two bidders just kept bidding so they could watch Flora. 'I've never thought that not being a dog to look at was a disadvantage. People have been very kind to me. Do you think that's why? That's a dreadful thought.'

'Well, maybe, initially, but if you're just a pretty face they won't go on indulging you. That's what I mean, really. This is a job where looks don't count. I'm so proud of you, darling.'

'Thanks, Mum.'

'Your dad's here. Do you want a word?'

Flora really wanted a hug, but a word would have to do. After a long chat with her father, who wanted to know exactly how it all worked, Hermione came back on.

'So, what about you and Charles?'

'We're not – a "we", I mean. He's with Annabelle and will be for ever.' She sniffed. The tears she had tried to force away earlier threatened now.

'Are you sure?'

'Yes! He kissed me after I got down off the podium and Annabelle saw.'

'But everyone would have kissed you, surely?'

'Not like that. And we looked at each other. That was the worst, the most revealing part. Then she followed me to the Ladies' and told me that if Charles . . .' She gulped back a sob. 'That even if Charles wanted to leave her for me he couldn't because . . .' Another hiccup. '. . . he owes her father loads of money and he put up his half of the business as security.'

'Why does he owe Annabelle's father money? Was it gambling debts or something?'

'No! He had to have the office building rewired.'

'Oh, good. I mean, I'm glad it wasn't anything dreadful.'

'Quite dreadful enough. Mum, I've got to leave. I can't stay around and watch him marry Annabelle. And I couldn't ask him to do anything that would risk him the business.' This realisation had been filtering through to her slowly, but now it had arrived it was perfectly clear.

'But are you sure it's true? This story? Before you do anything irrevocable, check that Annabelle's telling the truth. She might easily have made it up. Phone Geoffrey. He'll know.'

'There's still the kiss thing. She knows I'm in love with Charles—'

'And is he in love with you?'

Flora was silent for a long moment. 'I think so. I mean, that's what it felt like. When he kissed me, and then when he looked at me afterwards. But—'

'Don't turn your back on the business you love and have put so much into without making sure there's absolutely no choice. Ring Geoffrey. And then ring me back.'

Geoffrey answered the phone, sounding very cheerful. 'Hello, dear! How nice to hear you. I didn't see you to say goodbye, are you all right?'

'I'm fine, Geoffrey,' she said, realising she sounded anything but. 'Tired, of course, but otherwise fine. I was just wondering if you could tell me something. I was thinking about the wiring in the office building.' She hoped Geoffrey didn't think it a strange thought, but she had to know if Annabelle was telling the truth.

Fortunately, Geoffrey didn't seem to think her thoughts were all that strange. Or if he did, he didn't mention it. 'What about the wiring?'

'Does it need redoing?'

'Oh, I shouldn't think so. They had it all redone about a year ago. Annabelle's father paid for it all.'

'How on earth do you know that?'

'I had to check the bills. He wouldn't write any cheques until I'd reported that the work was done. Annabelle was very cross that her father had asked me to do it. You know she never had any time for me.'

Good manners forced Flora to continue the conversation for a bit longer, then she rang her mother and reported the news.

'Oh, love! My heart bleeds for you! My friend said that the hardest part of motherhood was watching them break their hearts and being able to do nothing about it. Now I know what she means.'

'I'll be fine, Mum. I'm strong. I've just got to decide what I'm going to do now.'

There was another long pause.

'Well, darling' – Hermione stepped into the silence – 'you know we're always thrilled to have you. If you'd like to come and stay—'

'No, Mum,' Flora said tiredly. 'It's a lovely thought, but I need to be practical, and you're not exactly round the corner, are you? I think I do have to leave though – I can't face Charles.' A memory of his face looking worriedly at her after her confrontation with Annabelle came back to her. He'd been very keen to talk – presumably about their kiss – but whatever it was he wanted to say, she couldn't bear to hear it. If he wanted to tell her it was a mistake, and he was in love with Annabelle and Annabelle alone, it would break her heart. But if he told her he was in love with her but tied to Annabelle by Stanza and Stanza, that wasn't any better. She couldn't ask him to give up the business he cared so passionately about – and to be honest she didn't really want to know what choice he would make were he forced to make that decision. No, there was nothing for it. She couldn't stay in Bishopsbridge.

'I might go and see Emma for a bit,' she said slowly, thinking it out. 'But you must promise not to tell Charles where I've gone. He might want to follow me to make sure I'm all right, but I don't want him to. Do you understand? Leaving is going to be quite hard enough, but

412

it'll be even worse if I have to talk it all through with him. I couldn't bear that.'

Reluctantly, her mother agreed.

When she disconnected she burst into tears and drank the glass of wine.

After that, and some bread and Marmite, she felt robust enough to ring Emma. She might not be in, but Flora thought she could leave a message, warning her that she might be getting a visit very soon. But, luckily, Emma was there.

'Sweetie!' she shrieked. 'How are you?'

Flora felt utterly exhausted, suddenly. 'Well. I've just conducted my first auction. It was brilliant. Very exhilarating.'

'So are you celebrating with a glass of wine?'

'Mm.'

'So why don't you sound happy?'

Flora bit her lip. Crying was healthy, but it did interrupt conversation rather. 'Because the rest of my life has gone pear-shaped.'

'Is it Henry?'

'Henry? No! Charles! I'm in love with him, Ems, and he'll never leave Annabelle.'

'The one that William wanted to paint? She did have a sort of heavy, pre-Raphaelite sort of beauty. Well, just get him away from her. Should be easy, pretty girl like you,' Emma said briskly.

'It's not that simple. Even if I could, if they don't get married he'll lose his half of the business. Oh, my God. Can you imagine sharing a business with Annabelle's dad! How scary!'

'But it would be OK, because you'd have Charles.

413

Then you could do anything.' Emma paused. 'Is he still as stuffy as ever?'

'Pretty much. I'm just so in love with him I don't mind any more.'

'He is extremely attractive, in that Mr-Darcy-in-need-of-an-enema kind of way.'

'Emma! That's very unkind. You should see how kind he can be—'

'He's not being very kind if he's breaking your heart,' she retorted acidly.

'He's not doing it on purpose!'

'I know, I know, I'm sorry. I'm just a bit off men at the moment.'

'Oh, Emma, I'm so sorry! I've been so wrapped up in my own problems – are you and Dave OK?'

'Yes, because he doesn't live here any more.'

'What?'

'Life is so much easier without him. Man-free and proud, that's me. Jeremy rings me from time to time but we haven't met up yet.'

'Does that mean . . .'

'What?'

'That I could come and stay for a bit? I've got to get away from here.' Then she told Emma everything. When she'd finished, Emma said, 'Get in the car as soon as that glass of wine has gone away, and get your arse up here!'

Flora rang Geoffrey, although it was quite late, and arranged to leave Imelda and the kittens with him, early in the morning. Then she cleaned. She knew she wouldn't sleep and so didn't even attempt to go to bed until the cottage was as gleaming as it could be. Every

414

plate, cup and knife was washed and stacked in a freshly wiped cupboard. The future Mrs Stanza would not be able to criticise her housekeeping.

When the physical exercise of sweeping and wiping and dusting had finally exhausted her, she had a bath in what was left of the hot water and fell into bed, Imelda on top of her.

She awoke at dawn and packed her clothes. Downstairs she saw the teapot on the mantelpiece. Should she leave it? Or take it as a souvenir? Or would her heart break all over again whenever she saw it? Without consciously making a decision, she wrapped it in the cashmere sweater of her father's that she had once lent to Charles and put it in her little flowery shopper, along with her make-up.

Loading Imelda and the kittens into the Land-Rover, which she was now going to steal, made her cry again. The little cottage had been the kittens' only home. They'd been so happy here. Flora had been so happy here, in a way. She sniffed hard and wiped her nose on a tissue she found in her jacket pocket. It was one her mother had given her, and it had shoes printed on it. The sight of it made her cry even more.

Flora had forgotten how awful London traffic could be, even on a Saturday, and realised that while the Land-Rover was perfect for country roads, it was a bit hefty for the back streets of Clapham. But someone was on her side because she found a parking spot right outside Emma's house.

Emma must have been looking out for her, because as soon as Flora opened the car door she came running down the steps. She hugged Flora for some minutes. Then she said, 'That's an awfully big car.'

'I know. And it's not even mine. Mine's still parked in the yard behind the office.'

Although she'd been away for less than a day, and wouldn't normally have gone into work on a Saturday, she felt a terrible pang of homesickness. 'It's great to be here. I've missed London.'

Emma frowned. 'Let me help you in with your stuff.' Then she looked at Flora's bags. 'Is that all you've got?'

'I didn't take all my clothes down with me. I'll have to get them out of the loft in the flat.' Usually the thought of delightful, but forgotten, little outfits to rediscover would have given Flora quite a thrill. Now they just seemed like clothes that belonged to a former life.

'Well, come in, do. I've put a bottle in the fridge, or is it too early?'

As Flora gathered up carrier bags and cases she decided that getting drunk was the only option. 'I don't think it's too early at all. It's nearly lunchtime.'

The wine set Flora properly weeping. She curled up with her feet on the sofa and alternately sobbed and drank and told Emma her woes, until Emma got up and made cheese on toast.

'Sorry, Ems, I am being the most complete pain, I know. Do you want to talk about Dave?'

'No. Not being in love with Dave any more, if I ever was, I don't want to talk about him.'

'Fair enough. Is there a corner shop that might be open?'

'Just off the main drag. Why, what do you want?'

'More wine and chocolate. At times like these a girl

needs her props and so does her friend. We need a few good DVDs, too.'

They spent the rest of the afternoon and evening eating chocolate and watching their favourite films. When Bridget Jones said, 'I choose vodka,' they both cheered.

Eventually it was bedtime, and Flora staggered into the spare bed feeling drunk and slightly sick. 'I'll feel fine tomorrow,' she said. 'I'll be strong again tomorrow. I just needed today off.'

But she didn't feel fine the next day. She pulled on the cashmere sweater over her pyjamas, having put the teapot on the windowsill in her room. It was stupid, she knew, but she felt the sweater was her last link with Charles, the nearest thing she would ever have to having his arms round her. She didn't tell Emma this. She knew how tiresome broken-hearted girlfriends could be but she couldn't snap out of it, no matter how sternly she ordered herself to.

When Emma came home from spending the day with friends Flora was still in her pyjamas. She had made a cursory attempt to clear up the dirty tissues and chocolate wrappers from the day before, but she hadn't washed her hair or put on make-up. Even brushing her teeth seemed like a waste of time, though she did at least force herself to do that.

Emma didn't comment, and cooked them both some pasta. She was being such a good friend, Flora realised. I must pull myself together soon or she'll go off me, and then where will I be?

The next day, Flora was immersed in a programme about couples buying property abroad when her mother rang.

'Darling,' she said carefully, 'I don't want to make you feel even worse, but there's something I think you should know.'

'What? Nothing's wrong with Dad, is it?'

'No, no. Nothing like that. It's just that we've had a wedding invitation. From Annabelle's parents. To Charles and Annabelle's wedding,' she went on as Flora still hadn't reacted.

'Oh.' They'd obviously been sent out a couple of days before Flora had left. Annabelle wouldn't call it off now, and Flora's last faint hope evaporated. 'That's it, then.'

'It does rather look like it.'

'Well, it's only what I knew already.'

'I know. But I'm really, really sorry, darling.'

Flora ate a packet of custard creams even though she didn't like custard creams, possibly hoping that the nausea would be a distraction from her utter misery.

When she heard Emma's key in the lock, she flew to the kitchen and began to peel some onions to chop. She had to have some excuse for her newly red eyes and nose.

'Oh, Flo, what now?' Emma demanded, not convinced that pulling the brown skin off an onion could have had that effect so quickly.

'Mum rang. She's had a wedding invitation. They're definitely going to get married. My life is over.'

'No it's not! You knew they were going to get married. You're no worse off than you were before.' Emma was obviously trying to ward off another Niagara-sized weeping session.

'I know, but I suppose that deep down I'd been hoping that they'd had a huge row after I left. I suppose I hoped that kissing me might have made Charles think twice, that he might have decided to cancel – or at least postpone – the wedding, but I shouldn't have let myself hope really.'

'Well, you're not to let it make you slump into despair. I know it's hard but lounging around all day in a sweater that's far too big for you isn't helping.'

'It's a lovely sweater,' said Flora, clutching its softness.

'It is, but it's making you soft. You'll have to get out – do something about getting a job. You can stay as long as you want, but I can't manage the rent here on my own. If you don't pay me rent, I'll have to find someone else.'

'Emma!'

'Tough love, sweetie. And you'd be so much happier if you were doing something.'

'I'll need a job before I can pay you.'

'Haven't you got savings? Didn't they pay you at the auction house?'

'Not really, not in a way that would count as being paid in London. I didn't have to pay rent, you see.'

'Well, I'm sure you'll pick something up, if you're not too fussy. I'm not sure if Sotheby's will take you on just like that, though.'

Flora smiled obligingly. 'No, but when I've sorted myself out a bit, I will think about working for an auction house. It's so exciting.'

Emma wasn't very enthusiastic. 'But I've a feeling if you want to work for one of those places and live in London, it helps if you've got a private income.'

'You're probably right. Maybe I should find a country

419

auction house who wants to take on an apprentice. I can always do bar work in the evenings.'

'Or you could get better-paid work. You've had loads of quite high-earning jobs in the past.'

'They were just jobs, not careers,' said Flora. 'I don't know if I'd be satisfied with that now.'

'Well, don't be too fussy. And why don't you go and have a shower and wash your hair? I fancy going out tonight. Some people from work are meeting up at a new wine bar. You can come and meet them.'

'Oh, Emma, do I have to?'

'Yes! I don't want to leave you here on your own, and besides, I said I'd be bringing my pretty friend.'

'I'm not pretty now,' said Flora glumly.

'But you would be if you did something about yourself! Get in that shower!'

An hour and a half later Flora was in the sort of bar that had been her natural habitat before she went to the country and ruined herself for civilised life. She tried really hard to be bright and amusing and live up to the reputation Emma had created for her. If her heart had not been broken, it would have been as easy as breathing. As it was, every smile, every flickered eyelash, every little hand gesture felt forced. Fortunately, it seemed to have the right effect.

'So, Flora, what do you do?' came the inevitable question from Emma's boss, who was called Tim.

'I'm between jobs at the moment, but I've just finished helping run an auction house.' She smiled and sipped her spritzer, wishing she could go home and put her sweater back on. 'What about you?'

Flora ran the conversation on auto-pilot until Tim said,

'We're sponsoring an art exhibition. I know nothing about art, don't even know what I like, but apparently it's a good marketing tool.'

Flora began paying attention, wondering what William would have to say about the word 'art' being included in the same sentence as 'marketing tool'. 'You don't need any extra help, do you? That's just the sort of thing I'm good at.' It would be easy, and it would get her out of Emma's hair.

'What? What are you good at?'

She shrugged, smiling, trying to blag herself a job. 'Talking to people, handing out leaflets, showing people artworks. I can do it all.'

Tim frowned. 'Well, I suppose we could do with some extra help. Do you know anything about merchant banking?'

'No, but I'm very good at learning things by heart, and acting, and believe me, I can sell ice to Eskimos.' She delivered him a full-on smile that didn't often fail her. Charles was the only man who had seemed immune to its wattage.

Tim smiled. 'I think you've talked yourself into a job, Flora.'

'You see! I'm just the girl you need.'

'I'll need you to wear business clothes.'

'I know just what you mean! Darling little suits, crisp shirts and heels.' Or perhaps no shirt, just a hint of cleavage. She would have to raid Emma's wardrobe. Her own darling little suits were currently suffocating in black plastic bags in the Lancaster Gate flat. She didn't have a key and wouldn't be able to arrange to retrieve them in time.

'You seem very keen.'

'I am! It's just the sort of job I love. You can leave me in total charge, and I'll cope. I'm good at responsibility.'

Tim's scepticism was gradually worn away until he was convinced that Flora was just what he needed. The pay was quite good, too.

In the taxi home, Emma was just as enthusiastic. 'I knew it wouldn't take you long to get a job. I said you always fall on your feet. And while it might not be the most demanding job in the world, it'll get you out there. You'll have loads of fun.'

Flora sighed. 'I know you're right about me needing to get out into the world, but I think "loads of fun" is a bit beyond me at the moment.'

Flora, wearing one of Emma's suits, the button of which came a little far down even for Flora's liberal attitudes, was sipping water from a bottle. The gallery was full of people screaming at each other. No one seemed to be looking at the art, but a lot of people had come up to chat to her about merchant banking. To a man – and they were all men – they knew more about it than she did but they all stayed to hear her patter and offer to get her another drink. Several had slipped their business cards into her pocket. It was quite good for the ego, she decided, and promising when it came to looking for more permanent work. One of those City types would have a vacancy for her, doing something. She had many more skills now than she had when she'd lived in London before.

There was a small lull in proceedings and Flora was resting her voice, rehydrating, waiting for the next man bored with art to come up and be told things he knew by a girl who didn't know them, when she saw what seemed to be a familiar head bobbing through the crowd. She dismissed it as her crazed mind seeing Charles where Charles could not possibly be, and then he appeared.

Her mouth went numb and she broke out into a sweat. She tried hard to form her mouth into a semblance of a smile but it wasn't a very convincing attempt. Speaking was beyond her.

'God, it's taken me a long time to track you down!' he said crossly. 'Why the hell didn't you leave a forwarding address?'

Flora tried to work some saliva into her mouth so she could speak. 'Hello.' Her voice was husky and she cleared her throat. 'What are you doing here?'

'I've been looking for you!' Charles seemed irritated, as if they'd had an assignation and she'd failed to turn up.

'Why?'

'Oh, for God's sake, Flora! Have you got a coat? No? Good, then come on.'

'Just a minute!' Flora's backbone re-formed itself. 'Who are you to tell me to "come on"?'

Charles frowned down at her, confused. 'Flora, I've come to take you home. Now come on.'

'I can't leave here, I happen to be working, in case you didn't notice!'

'Standing round handing out leaflets is not what I call work!'

'Well, sorry about that! It's the best I could do in the time! I've only been in London a short while—'

'And it's time you came home again.'

'No it's not! I'm working. Now please go away and let me do my job.' She smiled over his shoulder, to make out there was someone waiting for her attention.

Charles clicked his teeth and took her bottle of water out of her hand. He looked for somewhere to put it and, failing to find anywhere, dropped it on the floor. 'No one's that bloody indispensable,' he misquoted back at her, as she had when he hadn't wanted to take time off for the dentist. 'Come on.'

Chapter Twenty-Five

Flora found herself being grabbed by the wrist and pulled. As digging her high heels into the parquet floor would have been both difficult and embarrassing, she allowed her body to follow her wrist. 'I can't go anywhere with you, Charles,' she said when they got outside. 'And if I leave early, I won't get paid and I need the money.'

'What do you need money for?'

'To pay my rent. And I've got a flat to look at when I've finished here.' That wasn't true, but it sounded good.

'Look, Flora, it took me a long time to track you down—'

'How *did* you track me down? Don't tell me my mother told you where I was?'

Charles pushed his hair out of his eyes. 'Can we have this discussion somewhere other than in Cork Street?'

'Where do you suggest? Shall we ring up Rent-a-Boardroom and hope they've got one available?'

Charles smiled. 'A restaurant would be good. I'm starving.'

Excitement, adrenaline, and sheer pleasure at being with Charles again, even if they were fighting, made Flora's heart give a little skip. 'OK.' She struggled to sound non-committal. She didn't want to give Charles the impression she would just go meekly home with him.

'There must be one somewhere round here.' Still holding on to her, they walked past several places that were closed.

'A lot of restaurants are closed on Monday nights,' explained Flora. 'It's something to do with the fish. Or that may just be chip shops.'

Charles scowled down at her, as if despairing of ever understanding her.

They turned into a little side street down which could be seen an awning and fairy lights. Sounds of a busy restaurant emerged. They got to the door; the maître d' regarded them sadly and shook his head, 'I'm sorry—'

'Listen,' said Charles, polite but very firm, 'we're hungry, we need a small table for two. We don't mind if we have to sit by the kitchen, we don't mind if there's a bit of a draught, we just want somewhere we can eat.'

'Certainly, m'sieur. If you would just wait here, I'll see what I can do.'

While they were waiting, Flora looked around her. It seemed as if there wasn't a spare square inch to sit down in the entire place. However, not many minutes after their arrival, the maître d' came back to them.

'We have found a little corner for you.'

They squeezed past other diners and Swiss cheese plants until they came to the corner described. Even with the table pulled out, Flora could hardly get behind it. She collapsed on her seat with a giggle, which she partly put down to nerves. Charles took the menu from the waiter, who had followed their progress with difficulty.

426

'Steak frites, salad, and – can I see the wine list? That all right for you, Flora?'

'Are you ordering my food for me, Charles?'

'Yes. Have you got a problem with that?'

Flora sighed. 'Not on this occasion.'

Charles scanned the list that was on the other side of the menu. 'We'll have the Barolo, please, and some water. Sparkling or still, Flora?'

'Sparkling,' she said meekly.

She didn't approve of men ordering food for their companions as a rule, but in this instance it was quite nice. After all, if he'd ordered something she hated, or just didn't fancy, she'd have said something. And she was too intrigued by Charles's presence to fuss about it.

The wine came with satisfying alacrity. 'I don't need to taste it,' said Charles. 'I'm sure it's not corked.'

The waiter tried not to show he was offended and poured them each a glass of wine and then retreated. He was obviously experienced enough to know when customers wanted to have a good row in peace.

'Now, Flora. Oh, bread. Thank you.'

Flora took a bit of bread and nibbled it. She realised she was hungry, too. She hadn't eaten anything except nibbles since breakfast.

'As I was saying. Why did you run away? You must come home!'

'I didn't run away! I went away for the weekend and decided to stay on for a few days. It's not at all the same.' She didn't want to explain why she'd gone, it was too humiliating, too painful.

'You may have told Geoffrey that, but it didn't fool

427

me. And if you only went for the weekend why did you get a job? And you said you were looking at a flat!'

Flora checked her watch. 'Thank you for reminding me. I'm due there at nine. It was the only time they could see me. I mustn't miss the appointment.' Her pride made her keep up this pretence. It made her feel more in control, somehow.

'You're not going to look at any flat! What is going on with you? You come down to Bishopsbridge, cause havoc at every turn—'

'I did not cause havoc! I caused . . . prosperity, publicity, a lot of good things. And we made loads for Geoffrey's books.'

'I know. I was there. We must let you have another go sometime, when you're more experienced.'

Flora was on her feet before he'd finished speaking. He grabbed her wrist. 'Only joking, honestly. You were a star, and everyone has gone on and on about it ever since.'

Flora regarded him suspiciously. 'Tell me, Charles, honestly, did you deliberately stay away so I'd have to do the sale?'

Charles raised a comical eyebrow. 'If I tell you, will you promise not to throw anything?'

'No. I won't promise,' she snarled, 'and you've betrayed yourself by asking that question.'

'Think how disappointed you'd have been – Geoffrey would have been – if you'd done all that coaching and studying and then didn't get to go on stage. It would have been like the star turning up at the theatre at the last moment when the understudy has been told she's going to go on.'

428

Flora allowed herself to subside. 'I suppose so. Did you see it all?'

'Yes, I did and I was genuinely impressed. Geoffrey did a really good job of coaching you.'

'Don't I get any credit?'

'You know perfectly well you're a natural. And people love you.'

Flora felt a smug little smile start at the corner of her mouth and bit it back, glad she didn't have to go rushing off into the night in a huff without having had her steak frites. 'I'm not a natural at all. Geoffrey spent hours coaching me.'

'Well, it was worth it. I didn't dream we'd get anything like that for them.' He frowned. 'Geoffrey was of the opinion that people kept bidding just so they could get your attention.'

'It's not true. People aren't idiots. It was the website that did it. People heard the books were on sale and turned up to buy them. Nothing more than that.'

'I'm not jealous of the punters.'

'Good.'

'So why did you go?'

Flora exhaled, fiddled with her napkin and ate some more bread. It was lovely that Charles had come after her, but it didn't actually change anything. He'd still lose the business if he chose Flora over Annabelle – assuming he wanted to, that is. He wasn't behaving terribly like a heartbroken lover right now; instead he'd reverted to his bossy older cousin persona. Nothing had really changed, and so Flora didn't feel she could be honest with him about what had happened. She decided instead to be a bit economical with the truth.

She fixed her gaze on a flaw in the tablecloth. 'Annabelle saw us kiss. She got the wrong end of the stick and' – she forced herself into an attempt of careless laughter – 'thought there was something going on between us.' Charles's expression changed, but she found she was unable to read it. She carried on regardless. 'So she told me that if you and she didn't get married, you'd lose your half of the company.'

Charles shook his head. 'But why did that make you leave?'

'What do you mean? I couldn't ask you to—' She checked herself. She couldn't say she couldn't ask him to choose as that rather presupposed that he wanted her, and she wasn't sure if he did or not. 'I couldn't ask you to jeopardise the company. It's your life.'

'I thought it was your life too, Flora.'

'It was – is' – God, this was difficult – 'but it has been yours for longer.'

'I see.'

'So what are you doing here?' she asked. 'You and Annabelle are going to get married. Don't try to deny it! My mother got the invitation.'

'Oh God, I'm sorry. I expect Annabelle's mother sent them out before she knew we'd broken up—'

'Broken up?' Flora couldn't believe what she was hearing. 'You mean you and Annabelle have broken up?'

'Yes, Flora. I rang you on Sunday, and got no answer. I asked Annabelle if she knew where you might be and she told me that she'd sent you packing.'

Flora's head was spinning. 'But if you don't marry Annabelle, how will you pay back her father for the rewiring?'

'I haven't a clue about that, either. I expect I'll think of something.'

'Charles, this is so unlike you!'

'I know. I think I got bored with being like me. I'd rather be more like you. I'm living in the office flat. I'm going to pick up my kitten as soon as we get back.'

'Is that the royal "we"?' she asked cautiously, not wanting to misinterpret.

'No! It means both of us. You've learnt a lot, you've become really useful.'

'You said I caused havoc.'

'It means the same.'

Flora backtracked. There was too much to take in all at once. 'You still haven't told me why you came to find me. Or how, for that matter.'

'I'll take the fifth on that last bit.'

As Flora had a strong suspicion her mother was involved, she let that pass. 'What about the first part of the question?'

'We need you, Flora! And you can't expect Geoffrey to look after your cats for ever.'

'There's only Imelda, and two of the kittens are his anyway.' She frowned. 'Do you want to go on living in the flat? Because if we sold it, we could raise enough to buy Bob and possibly George out. Perhaps there'd be enough to pay off Annabelle's father, too. If not, there's still my half of the company. We could raise a loan on that. The wiring couldn't have cost that much.'

'You'd be prepared to do that?'

'Uh-huh.' Flora was suddenly aware how much she had exposed her feelings.

'For me, or the company?'

431

She swallowed. 'The company, of course.' This was a lie, but she felt too vulnerable to tell him the truth.

'So you do care about Stanza and Stanza?' he asked softly.

'Of course I care!' said Flora and, a second later, she realised she'd been tricked in a way she'd tricked Charles in the past.

'So why did you run away?'

'I told you. I thought you'd lose the company if I stayed. Why did you come after me?'

'Do you really need to ask me that?'

Flora's vehement affirmative was interrupted by the appearance of their food. She was grateful. It gave her time to think. What reason could she possibly give for running away that didn't involve her feelings for Charles? And Annabelle. She cut herself quite a large bit of steak so she couldn't possibly be expected to answer difficult questions for some time.

'It was quite hard to track you down,' said Charles who, having taken a smaller mouthful, was able to speak quite soon.

Flora nodded, chewing.

'I had to get in touch with Henry in the end.'

Flora frowned. 'How did he know where I was?'

'It was he who suggested we got in touch with Emma.' He frowned. 'And strangely, although they were supposed to be friends, William didn't have Emma's number.'

'Oh?'

'No. Fortunately your mother had it. She told me where you were working.'

Flora made a note to either kill or hug Emma and her

mother later, depending on how things worked out.

'So were Emma and William old friends?'

Flora shrugged. 'Maybe not.'

'Still, he paints a very good portrait.'

'Oh, did Annabelle get it done? What's it like?' She picked up her glass.

'It's very fetching. She's naked.'

Flora sprayed red wine all over her plate, the surrounding table and even, a bit, on Charles. The waiter rushed up, to see if she needed patting on the back. He was sent away by Charles's frown.

'Didn't you know?' asked Charles. 'I thought you were in her confidence.'

Flora shook her head and sipped some water. 'She never told me she was going to have herself painted naked! It seems so unlike her!'

'I don't know about that. Since you did your Trinny and Susannah act on her, she's been a changed woman.'

Flora suddenly became very hot. If she hadn't meddled with Annabelle's wardrobe, thrown out the pie-crust collars, got her to stop doing her shirts up to the neck, she and Annabelle might not have been any happier, but at least Charles might have been. He must have liked the pie-crust collars.

'I'm so sorry,' she whispered as guilt flooded over her.

'I don't think you're aware of your powers, Flora,' he answered, looking maddeningly inscrutable.

Flora got hold of herself. 'Oh, come on, you can't blame it all on me! She's a strong-minded woman, Annabelle.'

Braced by his unreasonableness, she attacked another section of steak. She didn't bother with the chips, deli-

433

cious though they were, she needed iron, a few red corpuscles, to keep her emotional flag flying.

'So you don't take responsibility for Annabelle behaving out of character?'

'No!' She concentrated on deepening her voice so she didn't sound too mouse-like. 'No. You can't take responsibility for the actions of adults in their right minds. It's just neurotic, blaming yourself for everything.'

'A moment ago you were blaming yourself for Annabelle's improved dress sense making her skittish, now you won't accept any culpability for her having her portrait painted naked.'

Flora suddenly wondered if that was all that was going on between Annabelle and William. Despite her threats to Flora, it seemed Annabelle had ended up relinquishing Charles quite quickly – maybe William had been a factor. After all, taking your clothes off in front of a man was a very intimate thing to do, even if only in the capacity of artist's model. She didn't mention this rogue thought.

'Only you would use a word like "culpability" in conversation, Charles.' She took another sip of wine. She had been about to say that it was one of the things she loved about him. Not because it was in any way lovable, but because it was so characteristic of him.

'Are you going to eat your chips?'

'No. Do have them.' She watched as he piled his plate with frites. 'Honestly, how you can eat so much . . .'

'What?' Charles chewed stolidly.

'At a time like this,' she managed, deliberately being unspecific.

He put down his knife and fork and glanced at his watch. 'Half past eight?'

434

Flora folded her lip behind her teeth to stop herself smiling. 'I said a time like this, not this specific time.' Then she remembered her fake appointment to visit a flat. She thought it was about time she referred to it again. 'And if it's half past eight, I must go. I've got to get to Islington, and I have no idea how long that'll take me.'

'Too long. And why go to Islington anyway?'

'I told you, to look at a flat.'

'But I told you I've come to take you home.'

'Well, I can't possibly go. For one thing, the Land-Rover's in a residential parking space outside Emma's house.'

'I must remember to report the fact that you stole it to the police.'

'It's half mine, anyway. And apart from Imelda, who I am sure is perfectly happy being fed sardines by Edie, give me one good reason why I should go back to Stanza and Stanza?' She took a breath and carried on, in case he didn't give her the answer he wanted. 'The business is picking up no end, you can buy out Bob and George and get all their business, the website works brilliantly. You can really become profitable.'

'Did Geoffrey tell you he wants to buy into the business?'

'No, really? How fantastic!' That must be the plan for the money the books had raised that Geoffrey was being so mysterious about. 'He knows so much about everything and the extra cash would come in very useful.' In fact, Flora realised, it would be more than useful – it would enable Charles to repay Annabelle's father's loan. And Annabelle's hold over Charles would disappear.

'Extra cash is always useful.' Charles smiled ruefully. 'But it would go to you, not to the business.'

'What?'

'You'd get the cash, not the business, because it would be your shares he'd be buying, wouldn't it?'

Flora shook her head. 'Not necessarily, they could be some of yours. But if he wants to buy some of mine, that's fine by me. In fact, if he wanted to buy me out entirely, that would be great.'

Charles frowned, rattled for the first time. 'But, Flora, I thought you loved the auctioneering business.'

'I do,' she agreed in a small voice. 'But it doesn't have to be Stanza and Stanza, does it?'

'No other business has your name on the letterhead, Flora. Doesn't that mean anything to you?'

'Yes, it does, but . . .' Tears clogged the back of her throat. She felt very tired, and very despondent. Charles had travelled all the way up to London to ask her to come back, but it now seemed very clear it was only for business reasons.

'But what?'

'It might be better if I became an auctioneer with another auction house, somewhere else.'

'Why?'

'Because . . .' What could she possibly say that would make any sense?

'There's no reason at all, is there?'

She gave a little shrug and looked into the middle distance which happened to be the specials board. There was a reason, a very good reason, but not one she could possibly give Charles.

'Would you like pudding?'

'No, thank you.' She regarded him. 'But don't let me stop you. Why not have the profiteroles?'

'There's something I want more than chocolate-covered pastries.'

'What?' Flora scanned the blackboard again. 'Tarte au citron? Tarte tatin?'

'No, you silly creature, I want you. Come on.'

He tossed a large sheaf of ten-pound notes on to the table and got to his feet.

Rather than face the embarrassment of his high-handed behaviour with the matter of the bill, Flora allowed him to take her arm and rush her out of the restaurant and on to the pavement, which had suddenly become quite busy.

'Now where?' demanded Flora, trying to remember she was a twenty-first-century woman and therefore not to be hauled about willy-nilly.

'A hotel, I think. Taxi!'

A taxi pulled up and Flora got into it. Charles collapsed on to the seat next to her.

'Where to?' asked the taxi driver over his shoulder.

'A decent hotel,' said Charles. 'Can you recommend anywhere?'

Flora hid her face in her hands, trying not to die from mortification. 'What will he think?'

Charles looked down at her and chuckled. 'Frankly, my dear, I don't give a damn.'

Behind her hands, Flora laughed.

Chapter Twenty-Six

❧❧❧

Flora was still hiding behind her hands when the taxi drew up, several minutes later. It wasn't surprising, really: they were in the centre of London; it was stuffed to the gills with hotels.

'This should do you. Small and discreet, just what you need, sir,' said the taxi driver.

Flora clambered out of the taxi and stood next to Charles, blushing, while he paid. She followed at a safe distance as he strode up the steps to the hotel. What could he possibly say at the desk that wouldn't make the whole situation look incredibly sordid? She hung around in the foyer, studying the modern art which surrounded her, indifferent to her state of acute nervousness. It wasn't that she didn't want to rush up to a bedroom with Charles, it was just that the process of getting there was toe-curling, to say the least.

'Come here and sign this,' said Charles. His words were commanding, but his tone was gentle. Flora signed obediently, hardly glancing at the nice-looking young woman behind the desk.

'As you see, we haven't got any luggage so could you kindly send up toothbrushes, toothpaste and – do you need anything, darling?'

The 'darling' made them seem married but as it was

the first time he'd used that endearment it made her blush even more.

'Some sort of moisturiser would be good,' she mumbled, still not looking up.

A horrid thought occurred to her. What about contraception? But if she reminded him about it now, he'd ask this nice woman for some condoms to be sent up with the toothbrushes and then she really would die of mortification. Such a death might be a medical first, but she was quite sure it was possible.

It wasn't the sort of hotel that told you which floor your room was on and expected you to find it. Although there was a conspicuous lack of bags to carry, a young man – gorgeous, Flora noted, and therefore even more embarrassing – took them along carpeted corridors and down a little flight of stairs to their room.

Once inside the room, after showing them the wardrobe, the mini-bar and how to work the television, he left them to it.

Flora went straight to the bathroom to inspect the shampoos and shower gels and found them to be Molton Brown – very satisfactory. When she went back, she found that Charles was inspecting the mini-bar.

It wasn't so much a bar as a cupboard with a fridge in it. Inside the fridge was gin, vodka, champagne, white wine, and the usual jelly beans and mixers. Outside was whisky, red wine, a disposable camera, snacks and something called a Comfort Pack.

Flora seized it and pulled off the top. 'Oh look! It's full of useful things! Sticking plaster, painkillers, a sewing kit and—' A packet of three condoms fell out on to the bed.

'Only three,' said Charles after a moment. 'That's a bit of a disappointment. But I expect they'll send up more if we ask.'

Flora allowed her gaze to meet Charles's head on for the first time since they left the restaurant. 'I can't believe we're doing this when we haven't even kissed properly.'

He smiled at her and opened his arms. 'Then let's kiss – properly.'

His arms folded round her and his mouth locked on to hers as if drawn by a magnet. He tasted minty, and she realised that he must have eaten a breath-cleansing sweet at some point. She wished she'd done the same – there was something in her bag – but she hadn't thought of it. Then she stopped worrying, stopped thinking, even, and just gave herself up to the sensation.

At first it was clumsy, too passionate for technique, and it took a few seconds before his lips took control and Flora felt her body melt into his. Her knees gave way and they subsided on to the bed, first sitting, and then lying on all the bits and pieces from the Comfort Pack. Then he really applied himself to what he was doing and Flora began to catch fire.

He was just battling with the safety pin that was holding Emma's jacket together at the top of her breasts, when there was a knock on the door, so discreet that Flora was sure the knocker knew what was going on inside the room.

Charles got up to open it, and Flora fled to the bathroom so her flushed cheeks, rumpled hair and general dishevelment weren't exposed to whoever it was came with the toothbrushes. Where did Charles learn to kiss like that? she wondered. Surely not from Annabelle!

Banishing Annabelle firmly from her mind, she undid the safety pin while she was waiting for Charles to deal with room service. It seemed to take a long time to deliver a couple of toothbrushes and some moisturiser.

When she came out Charles was opening a bottle of champagne.

'That didn't come out of the mini-bar. It wouldn't fit,' she said.

'It's complimentary. For honeymoon couples.'

Flora opened her eyes wide. 'But we're not on our honeymoon! And it can't possibly look as if we are.'

He shrugged. 'Maybe they mean honeymoon in a more metaphorical sense.'

Flora bit her lip and blushed.

'I must have a shower before – we get too carried away,' he said. 'I've been on the road all day and must stink.'

Flora hadn't thought he stank. He had a pleasant, metallic, masculine odour, of course, but she'd liked the way he smelt. Now he'd mentioned it, she began to feel self-conscious about how long it had been since she had had a shower herself.

'I might have a bath. I must stink, too.'

'I'll go first, then I'll bring you a glass of champagne while you're in there.'

At least the first time he saw her naked she'd be covered in bubbles – Molton Brown bubbles. Flora found the thought surprisingly erotic. But she realised any thought connected with Charles was surprisingly erotic. She picked up the small pot of moisturiser that had come with the champagne. It smelt divine. This was a very expensive hotel. The taxi driver must have thought

441

Charles looked affluent and she supposed he did. His suit was well cut, his shoulders were broad and his shoes were shiny. Very Alpha Male. She giggled.

The Alpha Male marched back into the bedroom wearing only a towel round his waist. Flora had never seen his naked back before, or indeed his naked anything. His muscles were surprisingly impressive for someone who, as far as she knew, didn't work out. She looked away. The sight of him made her catch her breath. She shot him a quick, provocative glance as she moved behind him to get to the bathroom.

Hotel baths fill very quickly and it was only moments before Flora was in hers, the bubbles forming a protective layer. She wasn't usually self-conscious about her body, but it had never mattered as much before. She'd yearned to be with Charles for so long and had never thought it would happen. Now it was happening, she wanted it to be as good as possible. She realised she hadn't had a hot bath since she'd left the cottage and the feeling of the water around her was both shocking and relaxing. She closed her eyes, thinking of what lay ahead.

She heard him come into the room and opened her eyes as he sat on the edge of the bath and handed her a glass. Putting out her hand to take it revealed, she knew, her naked breast, partially concealed by foam. She saw his eyes go to it, and bit her lip. Her initial shyness and embarrassment were rapidly turning to lust. It must be the combination of hot water and cold champagne.

'You're very beautiful, you know, Flora.'

'I'm not beautiful. Quite pretty when I'm done up, but not beautiful.'

'To me you're beautiful, and have been from almost the moment I first saw you.'

Flora sipped her champagne and tried to think what she'd been wearing. Not quite enough, she remembered, and very unbusinesslike shoes. 'I thought you were terribly stuffy.'

'I was. Still am in some ways, but better than before, I hope.'

'You're OK,' she said into her glass. 'I quite like you.'

'I do a great deal more than like you, Flora. I love you, very much indeed.'

'That's all right then.' This time she looked at him over the glass.

'Are you ever going to get out of there? Or do I have to come in and get you?'

'I don't usually get out until I've turned into a prune. A pink prune.'

'I can't wait that long.' He took her glass and set it down.

'Pass me a towel, then.'

'No. You can share mine.' He pulled her up out of the bath and into his arms. For a moment she just stood against him, the tips of her breasts just below his pectorals, but not touching. He looked down at her speculatively, then, without touching any other part of her, he ran one finger lightly down her spine. She caught her breath and he drew her towards him, and his hands slid all over her body. Then he put his hands on the back of her waist and held her close. They kissed for a long, dizzying time before he pulled away and she heard him swallow. 'Come on.'

Still welded together they got from the bathroom to

the bed, where they collapsed, kissing, only moving when Flora realised she was lying on top of a packet of safety pins.

Charles stripped the covers off the bed, scattering the Comfort Pack. He had lost his towel by now and as he scooped her up and tossed her on to the bed, Flora giggled breathlessly until his mouth came down on hers.

'You can't ring for more condoms,' said Flora. 'I won't let you.'

'Well, what do you suggest we do, then?'

Flora thought about it and then glanced at the clock radio. 'It's five to midnight. There's probably something open still. You could ask at the desk.'

'Then I might as well save myself the bother of going out. They'll know what I'm going for. Besides, I'm hungry again.'

'Order some sandwiches, then – or something.'

Somehow she wasn't surprised when, emerging from the bathroom a little later, she found not only club sandwiches, chips and two huge portions of profiteroles, covered with chocolate sauce and cream, but two packets of condoms.

'Charles, you didn't ask for them? From room service? How could you? And I thought you were respectable!'

'I was until I met you, then I realised that it wasn't a lot of fun. Have some chips. I suddenly wanted to eat all the things we didn't eat at the restaurant. And there are a lot of good things you can do with a profiterole.'

Flora looked at her lover with admiration. Not so stuffy, after all.

Previously unaware how hungry she was, she picked

444

up a sandwich and wondered how to get it into her mouth. Then she pulled out the cocktail stick that was holding it together and, somehow, took a bite. After a couple of mouthfuls she suddenly had a thought.

'I must ring Emma,' she said, horrified that it hadn't occurred to her before. 'She'll be worried if I don't come home!'

'Surely not. You're a grown-up, after all.'

'I can be home late, but I can't not come home at all without telling her. Where's my phone?'

'Use the hotel phone.'

She shook her head. 'Can't remember her number. Pass me my bag, could you?'

She watched as he reached over for it and saw the muscles in his back ripple. If they moved to a really warm country, she decided, they need never put clothes on again. But perhaps having all that male beauty covered most of the time was in a way actually more exciting.

She took the phone and got back on to the bed before pressing the relevant buttons. She pulled the sheet up a little to partially cover herself. It would be more enticing if he couldn't look at her completely naked. After all, if he'd gone to the trouble and embarrassment of ordering the condoms, it would be an awful waste not to use them.

Emma had begun to worry. 'Did you meet someone nice at the gallery and go out for drinks?' The optimism in her voice was almost painful.

'No. I'm in a hotel.'

'Darling! Why? Check out immediately and come home.'

'I haven't got any clothes on.'

'What! Then get dressed! Have you just had a bath? I expect they'll make you pay if you've messed things up.'

'I have messed things up.' Flora looked at the chaos about her. Clothes, bedcovers, and now plates of food, all over the place. The box of safety pins had come open and was now scattered on the carpet. 'And I've no intention of getting dressed.' She shot Charles a look which caused him to come and sit on the bed. He took her breast in his hand and caressed her nipple with a knowing finger. 'Don't do that! Emma? Sorry. You may have gathered I'm not alone.' She giggled, in spite of trying not to.

There was an audible silence from the other end of the phone. 'Darling, I know you're hurting just now, but do you think a one-night stand is going to make you feel any better? How will you look yourself in the mirror in the morning?'

Flora felt it was time to put her friend out of her misery. 'It's all right, I'm with Charles.' Then she held the phone away from her ear while Emma screeched.

'Oh my God! That's so romantic!'

'It is, rather. But, obviously, I can't talk much now . . .'

'I want all the details, just as soon as you can tell me. Oh, that's so sweet! I'll let you go now.' She was still cooing as she disconnected.

Charles held a hot thick-cut chip out towards her. Flora opened her mouth and closed her eyes. It was delicious. He went on feeding her chips until she opened her eyes again. 'Can I have pudding now?'

* * *

446

Flora had made an effort with her appearance. She had washed all her underwear the night before and used her emergency make-up kit to good effect. She hadn't bothered with the safety pin to keep her décolletage to a discreet minimum and her hair was a little wild. It had been washed (by mistake, while they were in the shower) and conditioned, courtesy of the hotel, but she hadn't had her frizz-controller and mousse and the other things she used to tame it with. But she felt her attempts at respectability weren't too despicable.

Charles, wearing yesterday's shirt and a very satisfied expression, stood at the desk with complete lack of embarrassment.

'There you are, Mr Stanza,' said the girl on reception, handing him the bill. 'We do hope you enjoyed your stay.'

'Oh, we did, very much,' said Charles. He signed the credit-card slip and then opened his wallet. 'Do you have a staff box?'

The girl indicated a discreet brass-bound opening in the wooden desk. Charles posted a couple of notes in it. 'The room service was really excellent,' he said.

'Good. That's very kind.' The girl caught Flora's eye and smiled. 'I do hope you enjoy the rest of your honeymoon, Mrs Stanza.'

Flora opened her mouth and shut it again as she realised what had happened. Because they had the same surname, the hotel had assumed they were married. There were advantages to keeping things in the family.

When they reached the pavement she allowed her giggle to emerge. 'They really did think we were on our honeymoon, because of our names being the same!'

447

Charles frowned. 'Yes.'

'I expect you've got used to being engaged now. You were for such a long time.'

'I'm thoroughly fed up with it, actually. I think I'd definitely prefer to be married. What do you think?'

'I might quite like to get married, one day, when I've had plenty of time to decide what my dress should be like, but I'm not taking your slot at Bishopsbridge Abbey,' she said firmly.

'So you probably don't want me hanging the picture of Annabelle naked above our bed?'

'No,' she said patiently, 'I wouldn't like that. Although I must say I am quite curious to see it.'

He kissed her nose. 'I might ask William to do one of you.'

She squeaked and hit him.

Their journey back to Bishopsbridge took longer than their separate journeys to London had taken. This was because Charles flatly refused to allow them to drive their own cars home. He insisted on Flora parking the Land-Rover at the house of a friend of his who lived in Richmond.

'If I got home without you, I'd be lynched by practically the whole town,' he explained as he handed her into his car. 'Now I've got you, I'm hanging on to you.'

As they fought their way through the traffic and on to the motorway, Flora was contemplative. She was ecstatically happy but she wanted to make sure that Charles was, too. 'Were you upset when you and Annabelle broke up? You'd been together for ages. Your heart's not broken?'

'What do you think?' He looked at her so lustfully his feelings on the matter were fairly clear.

'It's your heart I'm talking about, not – you know.'

'Annabelle and I were just a habit, really. We'd both become so accustomed to the idea that we were together that we'd stopped thinking about it. And once we thought about it, I think we both realised that we'd changed and moved on since we got engaged. I was – am – very fond of her in a way. You never saw her at her best, but—'

'I made her "her best"!' Flora was indignant. 'Without me she'd still be wearing pussy-cat bows and skirts just the wrong length.'

'Well, anyway, she's out of our way now.'

'Charles, you don't just want to marry me for the sake of the business, do you?'

Risking both their lives, he leant over and kissed her nose. 'When I knew how much in love I was with you, all my feelings for the company felt pretty pathetic in comparison. If you wanted us to sell up, I'd do it in a heartbeat, for you.'

'Oh,' said Flora in a very small voice, trying not to cry.

There was a garland of flowers round the architrave of the house. Everyone, all the porters, were gathered in the doorway. Geoffrey had a tray of champagne. As they got out of the car, Flora said, 'How did they know when we were coming?'

'I rang from the last service station, when we got petrol.'

'But you're not supposed to have your phone on in service stations!'

449

'I know, I'm such a rebel,' he said dryly, and then laughed.

They walked up the steps arm in arm. 'It's like getting married,' murmured Flora before she found herself being embraced by Virginia.

'Welcome back! We've missed you!'

'I was only away for – oh!'

Geoffrey gave a note and acted as conductor and then what there was of the choir, mostly sopranos, but with Geoffrey, Fred from the ironmonger's across the road, and a couple of other men and some altos obviously roped in for the occasion, broke into 'Brightly Dawns Our Wedding Day'.

Flora laughed and cried at the same time. 'That's so lovely!'

'Here,' said Edie, at her elbow. 'This person might cheer you up.' She put Imelda into her arms, who instantly started purring and putting cat hairs on Emma's black suit.

'Imelda, how lovely to see you!'

When Flora looked up again, she saw that Edie had the kittens with her as well. She was led into what was once the boardroom but was now set for a party. Louisa, grinning like mad, was protecting the plates of food.

Having put Imelda down, Flora hugged everybody, even people she realised she'd never met before, and Geoffrey opened more champagne. Everyone congratulated Charles, who was holding his kitten. They were kissing him, patting him on the back, and generally behaving in a way that they never would have done before.

'We're not actually married, you know,' said Flora, taking a glass of champagne from Geoffrey.

450

'Just as well. The whole choir is looking forward to singing at your wedding. By the way, can you ring your mother? She's a bit worried.'

Flora stifled a scream, found her phone and the cupboard under the stairs, and rang her. 'It's all fine! I'm so happy. Charles came and found me in London and took me to a hotel and – well, you can guess the rest.'

'And are you engaged?'

'Not officially, but we have discussed it.'

'For one dreadful moment I thought you were going to say you were married.'

'No, no. The choir want to sing at the wedding.'

When her mother had enough details to be going on with, Flora reappeared from the cupboard to find everyone assembled for toasts.

'To Flora,' said Charles, 'who's not only put the sunshine in my life but has had some jolly good ideas for the business as well.'

Everyone laughed.

'To Stanza and Stanza,' said Geoffrey, 'which I suppose could either mean Charles and Flora, or the auction house. But whatever, may it go from strength to strength.'

'I'll drink to that,' said Charles.

'Oh no, Imelda's stolen a sandwich,' said Flora.

'No, she didn't,' said Edie. 'I gave it to her. No reason why she shouldn't join in the celebrations, is there?'

'By the way, Virginia,' said Flora later, 'do we know what happened to Annabelle?'

'Well, about half an hour after Charles left, Annabelle stormed about, clearing her desk, slamming cupboards and generally being very upset. But then, a couple of days later I saw her in the ironmongers, looking so different I almost didn't recognise her.'

'I did give her a make-over,' murmured Flora.

'But it was her whole body language that was different. She seemed all dreamy and disorganised and was carrying a wicker basket.'

'Oh my God,' muttered Charles.

'Well,' broke in Louisa, thrilled to be the bearer of good gossip. 'I've got more recent news!'

'What?' chorused everyone.

'My mother met hers at a fête. She was furious! Annabelle's mother, I mean. Apparently Annabelle's run off with an artist and is living in a gipsy caravan in the woods!'

'William!' said Flora, looking aghast at Charles who had started to laugh.

'Good for Annabelle,' said Charles. 'Who said she was inflexible?'

'Not me, darling,' said Flora, trying to scoop up the black kitten and failing.

Charles picked it up without difficulty and presented it to Flora. It sat on her chest, between them, looking bemused.

'Will you, Flora, take this black kitten as a symbol of my undying love?'

'No!' said Flora, trying not to become sentimental, 'I gave you the kitten.'

'Have this instead then.' He rummaged in his pocket and produced a twist of tissue paper.

Inside was a tiny diamond and jet brooch in the form of a cat. It had emerald eyes and a distinct look of Imelda.

Flora looked at the brooch and then up at Charles.

452

She nodded. She couldn't speak. He kissed her nose.

'You think he'd have got her a proper ring,' someone murmured in the background.

'They'll need to choose that together,' said Geoffrey and then, a moment later, 'If this kissing's going to go on much longer, I think I'll get back to work.'

If you enjoyed Flora's Lot, *why not
try Katie Fforde's irresistible new novel . . .*

Practically Perfect

Anna, a newly qualified interior designer, has decided
it's time to put her money and her expertise where her
mouth is. She's risked everything on buying a tiny but
adorable cottage so she can renovate it, sell it on, and
prove to her family that she can earn her own living.

Outside, the chocolate-box cottage is perfect, but inside
all is chaos: with a ladder for a staircase, no downstairs
flooring, candles the only form of lighting and a sleeping
bag and camping mat for a bed, Anna's soon wondering
whether she's bitten off more than she can chew.

Her neighbour Chloe comes to the rescue, providing tea,
wine and sympathy – and a recently rescued greyhound,
Caroline. But just as Anna's starting to believe she's
found the perfect idyll, the good-looking yet impossible
Rob Hunter arrives on the scene, putting up more
obstacles than the Grand National. Can Anna get over
all of life's hurdles?

Read on for an extract . . .

CENTURY

Chapter One

The candle at her side flickered, and Anna shifted her position on the pair of steps where she was perched. She was beginning to regret having the telephone connected so promptly. There was very little mobile reception and without a conventional phone she'd have been almost unreachable. As it was, her ear was getting hot and her hand was getting cold, but her sister was still interrogating her. Anna didn't bother to cut her short – it would only involve another telephone call later – she tucked her free hand into her sleeve and listened politely. The bib-and-braces dungarees she was wearing were fairly warm when she was moving around, but now she was getting chilly.

'So why was it you moved there again?' asked Laura for what felt like the hundredth time. 'You know, property's much cheaper up here in Yorkshire. We could have done the project together. Much more fun.'

Anna embarked on her explanation again – rather patiently, she thought. 'I didn't want to be so far from London, and Amberford is a much more desirable area. Commutable from London, just. We've been through this.'

Laura sighed. 'I just don't like you doing it all on your own, so far from us. And I really wish you hadn't rushed into buying it, without me having a chance to see it first.'

In fact Anna did feel a bit guilty about this. 'I'm sorry, but I had to decide very quickly. There were lots of other people after it. It was such a bargain.'

'You were a cash buyer,' Laura pointed out rather snappily.

Anna sighed. 'I know, and that's partly thanks to you. But so was the other guy. It would have gone to him if I hadn't been a position to write a cheque for a deposit on the spot.' She paused. 'I'm eternally grateful, Lo. Without that loan I couldn't have done it.'

'You know I was happy to lend you the money, and you're paying me more interest than I'd have got from anywhere else, I just don't trust you to buy—'

'I know you don't,' said Anna, quite gently considering her frustration. 'But it's time you did. I know you're my older sister, but I am an adult, you know.'

'Twenty-seven is not—'

'Yes it is.'

'I don't mean that, of course you're an adult, but this is all your capital and a bit of mine. It's your inheritance.'

'I know the money didn't come from the tooth fairy.'

Anna wished she'd supplied herself with pencil and paper and a space to sketch – she could have got on with some drawings while all this was going on, not that it would have been possible in this light. She just hated wasting time.

'What I'm saying is,' Laura continued, 'you won't get that money from Granny again. And you could lose everything, you know.'

Anna shifted uncomfortably on the step. 'I watch all the same television programmes you do. I'm just as aware that the property market goes down as well as up, all that stuff. I haven't lived the last five years with my head in a sack.'

Laura sighed again. 'I expect I'm just jealous. It was such fun doing up the flat in Spitalfields together.'

'It *was* fun,' Anna agreed, 'but I'm a big girl now. I'm a qualified interior designer. It's time for me to go it alone.'

There was a silence. Laura was obviously still not convinced. 'So how much money have you got left to live on?' she asked, setting off on a new tack. 'You won't be able to do everything yourself, however handy you are with your Black and Decker and your Workmate – and I admit you are quite handy. And you still need to pay the mortgage.'

'I took out a slightly larger mortgage so I can use some of it to pay it—'

'That doesn't sound sensible—'

'But I thought I might get a part-time job anyway,' Anna said soothingly before Laura could get any further, 'just to get to know people.'

'Ah! So you're already worried about being lonely and you haven't even spent a night in the house! Sell it quickly, and do the same thing up here, where I can keep an eye on you. You might still make a bit of a profit. You could get in touch with the other man who was interested—'

'No, Laura! I love this house! I'm not going to sell it.'

Laura pounced like a cat on a daydreaming mouse.

'Ah! I knew it! You've fallen in love with an investment project. Fatal mistake.'

Anna cursed herself for letting slip this sign of weakness. 'I didn't say "in love",' she said, knowing she sounded pathetic. '"In love" is quite different from loving it.' She bit her lip while she waited to see if her sister bought this rather specious argument.

'OK.' Laura seemed resigned at last. 'Just promise me you'll sell it when it's done. Falling in love is always a mistake.'

'I know.'

'With men or with property,' she continued menacingly.

'Come on, Laura! You and Will are ecstatically happy. You and the boys could rent yourself to cornflakes ads as the perfect family!'

Laura laughed, trapped by her own argument. 'I know, but—'

'You've all got good teeth and shiny hair. You eat the right food—'

'This conversation is not about Will and the boys,' said Laura firmly.

'I know,' Anna admitted, 'but I was hoping I could steer it in that direction. How is Edward's spelling coming on?'

'Anna!'

'OK, but I really want to know if Jacob has got off that vile reading book.'

'Oh yes.' Her sister was momentarily diverted from sorting out Anna. 'At last. But getting back to you, and falling in love—'

Anna accepted the inevitable. 'You don't trust me to

fall in love as sensibly as you did?' Will was the perfect husband – not only loving, good-looking and a good provider, he also did DIY.

Laura was silent for a moment, possibly realising that falling in love with the right person was about luck as much as anything else. Anna enjoyed the respite.

'You make me sound terribly bossy.'

At the other end of the phone, Anna nodded agreement.

'But I'm just looking out for you,' persisted Laura. 'Mum's a bit taken up with Peter these days and doesn't pay attention to what you're getting up to.'

'Mum's entitled to be obsessed with her new husband. I am an adult.' Although Anna was beginning to wonder if this was true, her sister seemed so unable to accept it.

'And of course you're just as capable of falling in love with the right man as I am. As long as I've checked him over first.' But at least there was a smile in her voice now.

'Fine. I promise I won't marry anyone without consulting you. Oh, I can hear the boys. You're needed, Laura.' Never had her nephews' shrieks sounded so endearing.

'Oh yes, better go. Speak soon!'

'Right.' Anna uncrossed her fingers, and then replaced the receiver on the handset and tucked it back into the little niche in the wall. It was only a white lie, she told herself as she stepped down to the floor. And you have to fall in love with a project a little bit, to really throw your heart into it. As for falling in love with the right man, that ship had sailed, too. She'd fallen in love with the wrong one years ago, and even knowing he was the wrong one didn't affect her feelings. One of the reasons she had come to look at the house in the first place was because she remembered Max saying that his mother lived near here. It had seemed like a good omen.

Anna blew out the candle and then reversed carefully down the ladder that was currently her staircase. Sometimes she let herself fantasise about meeting his mother, or running into Max while he was visiting her. She always chuckled at this dream in spite of herself. If he did run into her, she'd more than likely be wearing dungarees and builder's boots, and while she had always been a jeans and sweater girl, her clothes were even more utilitarian now than they had been when she was a student.

Still, she'd carried the torch for a very long time and it still burned as brightly as when Max had been the guest lecturer at college.

He'd been the hot young architect, coming in to talk to them, and she'd just been one of the students, taking notes. She was willing to bet she wasn't the only one who'd fallen in love with him, either. He'd been so dynamic and vital. Not really handsome, but with such a massive personality that his looks didn't matter. But she'd never talked about him to anyone else and, thank God, this included her sister. She hadn't wanted to find out that he'd slept his way through half the class but passed over her. Then, at their Graduation Ball, he had picked her out and danced with her. It was right at the end, and Anna had had to leave because there was a whole group of them sharing a minicab home. There'd just been time for Max to write his number on a menu. 'Call me,' he'd said, his voice a husky whisper.

Anna had fully intended to call him, even though the

thought was more scary than finals had been, but some hideous bug had laid her low for days. The first day she felt well enough to go out she had been on her way to the chemist when she saw him – with a woman. She had rushed home and torn up the menu and then burnt the pieces. It was only a couple of days later, when the last remnants of the bug had left her and she felt less wobbly, that she realised she'd been incredibly stupid. The woman could have been anyone: his sister, a colleague, anyone. She'd regretted her folly ever since.

Anna went to the place where the electric kettle and the toaster were plugged into the only part of the house where they could be. There was also a small wash-hand basin there, so it counted as a kitchen. To satisfy the demands of the building-society-turned-bank, she had left the slightly rusty cooker and cracked sink in place until after she'd been given a mortgage. Luckily for her, the address, and the relatively small amount she needed to borrow, meant the valuer didn't actually need to go into the property. She had secured her money on a 'walk by' – which normally would have been a drive by – and so the cottage was hers.

Of course the mortgage didn't seem small to her, it seemed enormous, but from the building society's point of view, it was fairly insignificant.

While she made herself a cup of tea, using the last of the milk, she forced herself to stop thinking about the man she hadn't seen for three years and calculated how long it would be before Laura could stay away no longer and would descend, handyman husband in tow, to 'sort her out'.

Anna loved her sister dearly, and when they'd lived

together they'd got on fine. But since Laura was no longer able to supervise her dates, steer her wardrobe in the right direction, and generally mother her, the word 'bossy' was becoming more and more appropriate. If she'd known where Anna intended to spend her first night in her very own home – investment project, she corrected herself hurriedly – she'd have had a blue fit. She would not consider a sleeping bag and a camping mat a suitable resting place, even if Anna did have a couple of blankets she could pull over herself. But without Laura adding her capital to hers, her mortgage would have been much larger.

And surely Laura wouldn't blame Anna for falling in love with the cottage, at least a little bit. It was heavenly! Or it would be when it had floors, a staircase, a proper kitchen and a bathroom. The previous owners had ripped all these things out and then either run out of money or interest. The estate agent was rather cagey about it.

Anna had tossed and turned her way through a week of sleepless nights while she waited for the surveyor's report. She was certain he'd discover some major problem: the reason why the previous owners had abandoned something with 'such terrific letting potential' as the estate agent put it. When no such reasons were revealed, Anna felt it was probably because there was so little left in which to discover death-watch beetle, dry rot or perished timbers. The ground floor had been stripped of almost everything, including most of the floorboards. There was no staircase, so the only way to the first floor was via a ladder. Here there was at least a floor to walk about on, but there was no bathroom.

And the very top floor, the attic, which in Anna's mind's eye was already the most wonderful bedroom-bathroom-dressing-room suite, was very much as it had been hundreds of years ago. Anna planned to sleep up there when things were straighter downstairs, but at the moment she felt she needed to be nearer things. Up in the attic, the rest of the house could burst into flames and she would be unaware of it until it was too late. She'd bought and installed a smoke alarm, even without her sister's prompting.

Its lack of amenities had made the house very cheap, considering its position, both in the country as a whole and in Amberford in particular.

It was part of a row of cottages which stood behind long gardens and overlooked the village. Laura would say that having the garden open plan would detract from the value. But there was a smaller, enclosed garden at the back, and if your children needed lots of playing space (and Laura's two boys definitely did) there was an attractive bit of common land not far away. A church, a school and a pub, and an easy journey to a mainline station, made it a very desirable spot. There was even a shop and a post office and, not too far away, a Chinese takeaway.

Of course it only had two bedrooms, and Laura would say that cut Anna's target market down considerably. Anna had already prepared her speech saying it made it an ideal second home, although she didn't like the idea of second homes making once-thriving villages barren and empty during the week.

She had yet to meet her neighbours, and because it was beginning to get dark and people would be putting their lights on, a walk along the row would tell her which cottages were occupied permanently, and which were not. She needed a few things from the shop anyway; now would be a good a time to investigate discreetly.

It seemed strange walking so close to people's windows and although she couldn't quite resist looking inside, she made her glances oblique and fleeting. She was grateful that she was the end cottage (she would tell her sister that 'end of terrace' was better than 'mid') so no one could look in at the building site she currently called home.

Her immediate neighbour was definitely a permanent resident. Anna could hear children and there were lights on everywhere. A sideways glance through the kitchen window as she passed showed a reassuring amount of mess. Anna's sister was terribly organised and it was what they argued about more than anything else. Anna didn't want to find herself living next door to another neatnik.

The next house was either a holiday home or belonged to someone not yet home from work: a commuter, possibly. The curtains were open but no light showed. Anna could see hints of a very stylish, modern kitchen, full of expensive appliances.

The house next to that was clearly occupied by an elderly lady. Her windowsill was covered with china ornaments, visible in front of the curtain that was already drawn. A cat sat on the porch, evidently dismissing Anna as a blow-in, and refusing her offers of friendship.

The first cottage in the row, and the last one Anna

passed before she reached the main road, was definitely a holiday cottage. The Christmas decorations were still up, even though it was mid-March. Going by the quality of the decorations, which were of the tasteful corn-dolly and red-ribbon type, she judged the house was not owned by disorganised people who just didn't get round to taking them down. More likely they were spending the winter somewhere warm.

Out of the five cottages, three – possibly four – including her own, seemed occupied which, considering how small they were, was not a bad ratio.

The shop bell jangled in a friendly way. It was a small supermarket, with a couple of short rows of goods and a counter for bacon and cheese. The man who stood at the counter, doing the crossword, looked up when she entered and smiled. 'Evening.'

'Evening.'

'Can I help you?'

'I think I can probably manage,' said Anna, feeling a little shy. She was used to the anonymity of London shops, where only the proprietors of shops you used very frequently ever spoke to you.

'Well, let me know if there's anything you can't find. Just moved in, have you?' he added later, when Anna had put a few things into her basket.

'That's it. I just need some basic provisions.'

'So you've moved into Brick Row?'

'Yes. How did you know?' This omniscience took some getting used to.

The shopkeeper smiled. 'It didn't take much detective work. We knew the house had been bought by a young woman; you're obviously dressed for work; and who else would come in here just before closing, at this time of year, whom I don't know?'

Anna smiled. 'I suppose it does make sense.'

'Don't worry, we're not all nosy round here, and those of us that are are well meaning on the whole.'

Anna placed her basket of goods on to the counter so he could ring them up. 'I'm sure you are.'

She walked home feeling very satisfied. The shop didn't sell fresh meat or fish but otherwise it seemed to have everything else Anna might need and the town was only a short bike ride away. Amberford was perfect, well worthy of being fallen in love with, and if being there without a car caused a few problems, well, she'd deal with them as they came up.

As Anna walked back along the lane she saw a young woman standing by the front door next to hers, looking anxious. Anna was pleased to see her as she'd been intrigued by the row of three small pairs of Wellington boots, arranged in size order, on the windowsill of the cottage. She overcame her shyness and smiled. The young woman smiled back, still preoccupied.

'Hello,' she said. 'You've moved into number five? You're very brave! It hasn't even got floors, has it? I was going to invite you round for a bath, but just now we can't even have one ourselves. I'm waiting for a plumber. He promised he'd be here before two, but I don't suppose he'll come now.'

'Oh dear, what's the problem with it?' Anna asked.

Presumably hearing her voice, three small boys abandoned their toys of mass destruction and clustered round their mother, eager to see whom she was talking to.

'Blocked drain,' the woman said with a grimace. 'I've

pulled out the plug and nothing happens. It's full of cold soapy water. If these three don't have a bath at night, they take ages to settle. And it's beginning to smell.'

'Well, I might be able to help,' said Anna.

The woman's face lit up. 'Really? How?'

'I have a few building skills, which is just as well given the state of my house, but, more to the point, I have a tool that unblocks drains. I'll just pop home and get it,' Anna offered, 'if you'd like me to.'

'I'd love you to! I'll put the kettle on. Or open some wine?'

Anna grinned back at her. 'I'll be back in a minute.'

It took Anna a little longer than that to find the tool that she and her sister had had cause to use so often in the Spitalfields flat. When she knocked on the door of her neighbour's house and was let in, she found an agreeable amount of chaos.

'I'm Chloe,' said the woman.

'Anna.'

'And these are Bruno, Tom and Harry. Two, four and six, only in reverse order.'

'Hello,' said Anna, suddenly shy in front of three pairs of inquisitive eyes. 'I've got my gadget, if you'd like to show me upstairs.'

They all went up the steep and very winding staircase to the second floor, where the bathroom and the boys' bedroom were. The boys grabbed hold of her and towed her towards it.

'We haven't had a bath for two days!' said the eldest, who was probably Bruno, but might have been Harry.

'My husband's away,' said his mother. 'He would be, just when there's an emergency.'

Anna didn't think a blocked bath plug quite qualified as an emergency, but accepted that some people might well do, and Chloe obviously did. She rolled up her sleeve as far as it would go, which was not far enough.

'I don't suppose you'd all like to go downstairs while I do this?' she suggested. 'I want to take my jumpers off.'

'We want to watch,' announced one of the boys.

'Yes, we do,' said another.

Anna sighed. 'OK.' She undid her bib and peeled off the two jumpers that covered a long-sleeved T-shirt. Fortunately that sleeve rolled up obligingly high, and she plunged her arm into the cold, scummy water. 'Right, pass me my plunger, would you?'

'This is so cool,' murmured Bruno.

'You're right there,' said Anna, shivering. 'Very cool indeed.'